# Hitler's Luftwaffe

# Hitler's Luftwaffe

**A pictorial history
and technical encyclopedia
of Hitler's air power in World War II**

Tony Wood/Bill Gunston

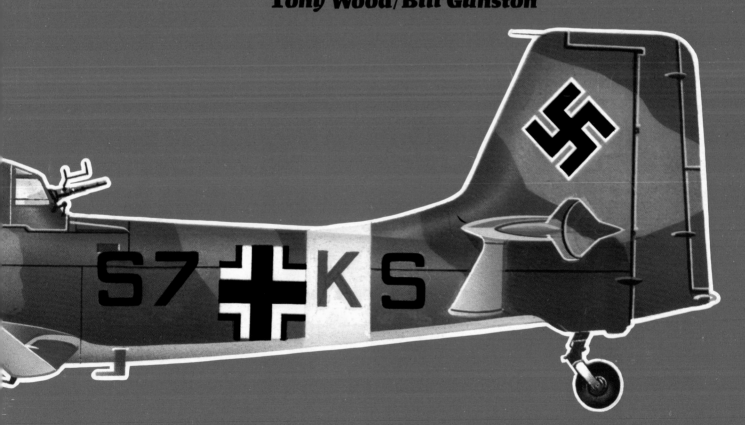

Salamander Books

Published by

**CRESCENT BOOKS**
New York

# A Salamander Book

Library of Congress Catalog Card Number: 77–89611
All rights reserved
This edition is published by Crescent Books, a division of Crown Publishers, Inc. by arrangement with Salamander Books Ltd.
abcdefgh

Crescent Books, a division of Crown Publishers, Inc. One Park Avenue, New York, N.Y. 10016

**ISBN 0-517-22477-1**

© Salamander Books Ltd 1977
27 Old Gloucester Street, London WC1N 3AF

Third impression 1979

All correspondence concerning the content of this volume should be addressed to Salamander Books Ltd.

This book may not be sold outside the United States and Canada

# Credits

**Editor:** Philip de Ste. Croix

**Designer:** Chris Steer

**Color, cutaway and line drawings of aircraft:** © Pilot Press Ltd

**Filmset** by SX Composing, England

**Color** reproduction by Metric Reproduction Ltd, England, Paramount Litho Co, England and Autographic Lithoplates Ltd, England

**Printed** in Belgium by Henri Proost et Cie, Turnhout

# Introduction

From the very start, the Luftwaffe was an exceptional force. Whereas in the 1930s most air forces were little more than adjuncts on the fringes of society, that consumed part of meagre defence budgets and occasionally gave public displays that seemed unrelated to everyday life, Hitler's Luftwaffe was, with the Wehrmacht, the very foundation on which the international aspirations of the Führer rested. Unlike other air forces, which ostensibly existed for defence, the true pupose of the Luftwaffe was to attack. At first it did not need to attack; its very presence, grossly and successfully magnified by propaganda when in reality its power was small, served to deter all opposition by much stronger nations as Hitler marched his goose-stepping legions into the Saar, the Rhineland, Austria, the Sudetenland and finally the whole of Czechoslovakia.

The crunch came in August 1939. Having failed to act when Germany was relatively weak, France and Britain finally pledged their support for Poland. By this time the Luftwaffe was strong, and Hitler

went ahead anyway. In a famed Order of the Day, Goering — architect of the Luftwaffe — said "Born of the spirit of the German airmen in the First World War, inspired by its faith in our Führer and Commander in Chief — thus stands the German air force today, ready to carry out every command of the Führer with lightning speed and undreamed-of might." A year later the Luftwaffe had swarmed over the whole of Western Europe, and save for the stubborn British had conquered everywhere.

History knew nothing like it. Germany's conquests were resumed in 1941, with smashing blows to the south-east through the Balkans, Crete and into North Africa. On 22 June the might of the Luftwaffe thundered to the east, deep into the Soviet Union. Work proceeded apace on jet engines, rockets, guided missiles, new guns, and many new aircraft which ranged across Asia to the Japanese and on test flights as far as New York. Yet in fact these were mainly side issues that did not affect the course of the war. As early as the Battle of Britain the Luftwaffe had been defeated in a major objective. In the bitter winter of 1942-43 at Stalingrad it failed again in an equally impossible task, and what was left of Von Paulus's 6th Army surrendered. At home, city after city was laid waste by RAF night bombers, while the USAAF 8th Bomber Command mounted increasingly damaging attacks by day.

Before the war Goering had said "If any enemy bomber penetrates to Germany, my name is no longer Hermann Goering. You can call me Meier". On 21 April 1945 the leader of the Luftwaffe drove out of Berlin for the last time, heading south without plans and with little left to command. On the way he had to take cover in an air-raid shelter. "Let me introduce myself," he said, "my name is Meier".

There have been many books about the Luftwaffe, and their appeal has never been stronger than today. Never, we venture to suggest, has there been a book quite so attractive as this. There have been scholarly accounts of the history of the Luftwaffe, some outstanding works on the Luftwaffe's aircraft, and numerous first-hand stories of the Luftwaffe in action, many of them autobiographies or biographies of famous men. There have also been a few books and magazine articles containing colour photographs and drawings, but now for the first time a package is presented which, for most students of the Luftwaffe, will be near-total coverage between one pair of covers. The cutaway drawings of selected important aircraft are outstanding, and the quality of the colour profile drawings will be evident even to those who do not know a 109 from a 190.

It is especially worth noting that this book is not just an account of Hitler's Luftwaffe in World War II. It traces the genesis, formation and growth of the Luftwaffe in pre-war years, and the Technical Section includes descriptions of not only all the aircraft that served with the embryonic Luftwaffe before 1939 but also all the military aircraft that failed to make the grade. There is not the slightest doubt that this will fast become a best-seller in aviation and military publishing.

*Bill Gunston*

# Contents

**Part One**

**Chapter 1**
**A Phoenix from the Ashes** 8

**Chapter 2**
**The Onslaught** 14

**Chapter 3**
**The Battle of Britain** 20

**Chapter 4**
**The Night Blitz** 28

**Chapter 5**
**The Luftwaffe Strikes South** 32

**Chapter 6**
**From Barbarossa to Stalingrad** 40

**Chapter 7**
**The Struggle in the Mediterranean** 48

**Chapter 8**
**The Holding Campaign in the West** 58

**Chapter 9**
**Maritime Operations of the Luftwaffe 1939-1945** 64

**Chapter 10**
**The Prospect of a Long War** 76

**Chapter 11**
**Russia 1943-1944** 78

**Chapter 12**
# The Mediterranean 1943-1944     **84**

**Chapter 13**
# The Defence of the Reich     **90**

**Chapter 14**
# Horrido!     **96**

**Chapter 15**
# Pauke! Pauke!     **102**

**Chapter 16**
# The Last Battles     **108**

**Part Two**
# Aircraft of Hitler's Luftwaffe     **120**

# Appendix:
## The Luftwaffe Chain of Command     **242**

# Glossary of Terms and Abbreviations     **243**

# Index     **245**

# Picture Credits     **248**

# Chapter 1
# A Phoenix from the Ashes

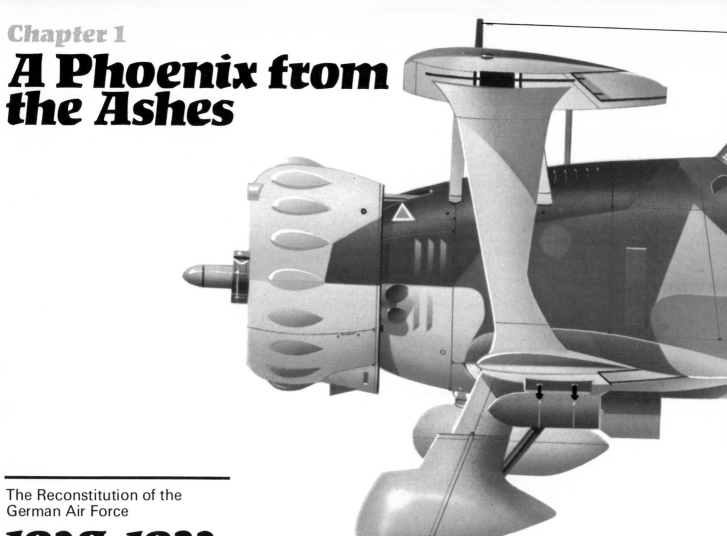

## The Reconstitution of the German Air Force

# 1920-1932

The economic bankruptcy to which the might of Imperial Germany was reduced over four years of bloody fighting forced her to sue for peace and to accept cruel Armistice terms signed in November 1918. Within the borders of Germany, the political and social structures were in ruins; her population subsisted at starvation level, yet the armed might of her Army, Navy and Flying Corps was still considerable, notwithstanding the low morale of her fighting men. The rapidity with which Word War I came to an end was a prime reason for the ineptitude subsequently displayed by the victorious Allies when it came to convening an international body to decide the future of Germany. Born of the spirit of vindictiveness and war-weariness, the Treaty of Versailles, signed in June 1919, was aimed at the total dismemberment of Germany's economic and military powers.

The Treaty of Versailles contained Air Clauses intended to end military aviation in Germany and preclude resurrection of the German Flying Corps. Under the supervision of an Allied Control Commission, Germany was obliged, in 1920, to surrender all aeronautical material to the governments of the Allied and associated powers. At the end of World War I Germany had possessed approximately 20,000 military aircraft, of which some 2,400 were bomber, fighter and reconnaissance aircraft with front-line combat units. In accordance with the Treaty, over 15,000 aircraft and 27,000 aero engines were surrendered. So far the Treaty was effective. The Achilles Heel of the Treaty with regards to aviation matters, however, lay in the exclusion of any long-term clause prohibiting manufacture and mass production of civil aircraft. Such was the state of infancy of civil aviation in 1919 that the Allies overlooked its potential importance. It is true that, by 1922, there were

some limitations on the actual size of civil aircraft that could be built, but the Paris Air Agreement of 1926 withdrew even these restrictions.

The Germans seized upon the opportunity proffered by this lack of restriction for expansion in the civil sphere, and began an unprecedented expansion of commercial aviation; airlines, flying clubs and aviation training establishments. The design and development of new aircraft, and the training of pilots and crews now went ahead virtually unhindered. Under this mantle of pacific respectability the foundations of the new German Air Force were clandestinely laid.

The widespread subsequent belief that Adolf Hitler and Hermann Göring were the founders of the new German Air Force had no basis in fact. As early as 1920 General Hans von Seeckt, then Chief of the Army Command at the Defence Ministry, was convinced that military aviation would some day be revived in Germany. To this end he secreted a small group of regular officers in the sections of his Ministry clandestinely dealing wholly and exclusively with aviation affairs. The fact that some of these officers, notably Felmy, Sperrle, Wever, Kesselring and Stumpff, became high-ranking commanders in the Luftwaffe was to reveal clearly von Seeckt's foresight and the profound mistake on the part of the victors of the 1914–18 war in allowing this military nucleus to be maintained in Germany. Once the statutory six-month standstill expired following the signing of the Treaty of Versailles, German aircraft manufacturers resumed operations. Tempo was slow at first, being dictated by the stagnant economic situation then prevailing, but natural

commercial enterprise rather than leanings of a quasi-militaristic nature soon raised momentum. Germany was not short of brilliant and energetic aircraft designers and engineers.

Early in 1920, Professor Hugo Junkers formed an aircraft company at Dessau producing the Junkers F 13 all-metal transport. Later this concern, named the Junkers Flugzeug und Motorenwerk, was to expand into one of Germany's largest aircraft and aero engine manufacturers, with branches at Aschersleben, Bernburg, Halberstadt and Leopoldshall. In 1922, Ernst Heinkel formed his company at Warnemünde, on the Baltic coast, and in that same year Dr. Ing. Claudius Dornier formed his company from the old Zeppelin-Werke Lindau at Friedrichshafen. Two years later, Heinrich Focke and Georg Wulf founded the Focke-Wulf Flugzeugbau at Bremen and, in 1926, the Bayerische Flugzeugwerke was founded at Augsburg from the remnants of the Udet-Flugzeugbau. This concern, eventually to be led by Professor Willy Messerschmitt, was to change its name to that of Messerschmitt A.G. in 1938.

By 1926, when the Paris Air Agreement loosened the last fetters that bound the German aircraft industry, the firms of Junkers, Heinkel, Focke-Wulf and Messerschmitt, along with several others, were keeping pace with the rest of the world, both in terms of quantitative production and technical development. But, hand in hand with the production of airframes and aero engines, ostensibly for civil application, went training and organisation of manpower; tasks achieved through the medium of civil airline companies and numerous flying and gliding clubs.

Two small air transport companies had been

### Henschel Hs 123
*An Henschel Hs 123A of 7./St.G.165 "Immelmann" at Furstenfeldbruck, October 1937 (see also pages 196-197)*

operating in Germany from 1920 onwards. In 1924, General von Seeckt had made the astute move of securing the appointment of his nominee, a Captain Brandenburg from the old German Flying Corps, as head of the Civil Aviation Department of the Ministry of Transport. Co-operation between this department and von Seeckt's Defence Ministry was thus assured, and thenceforward the development of civil aviation came under clandestine military control. When the State airline, the Deutsche Lufthansa, was formed in 1926, one more stage in the growth of the new German

Air Force had been reached. Lufthansa proceeded to encourage construction of large airfields. It began to exercise considerable influence in the aircraft industry itself, simultaneously experimenting with and improving flying instrumentation and radio aids to navigation. Under its Chairman, Erhard Milch, Lufthansa rapidly became the best equipped and operated airline in Europe, with its experienced pilots, navigators and crews later to provide the nucleus of the training organisation of the embryonic Luftwaffe.

In addition to Lufthansa, Germany could

*Below: Focke-Wulf Fw 56 Stössers (left) and Heinkel He 51s and Arado Ar 65s at a Jagdfliegerschule (circa 1937) when the Luftwaffe pilot training programme was gaining momentum*

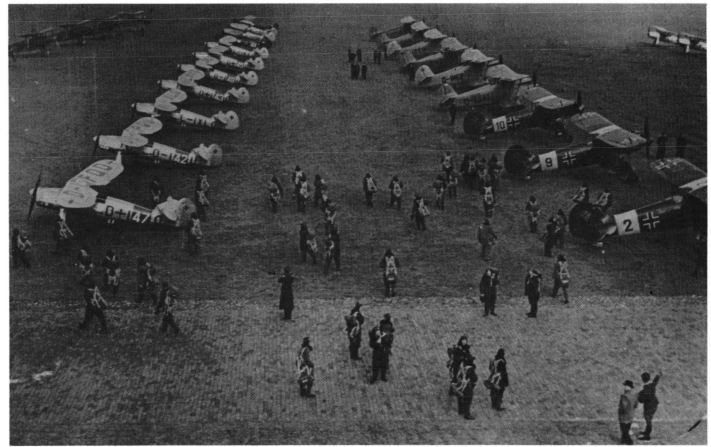

call upon the membership of its main air society, the Deutscher Luftsportverband, for her future aircrews. Within ten years of its foundation in 1920, this society had a membership of over 50,000. The source of this encouragement in gliding and sports flying came from Seeckt's Defence Ministry which saw this as another way to circumvent the strangleholds of the Versailles Treaty. By 1926, the Luftsportverband was already returning rich dividends; while the rest of Europe slept, Germany was becoming the most air-minded nation on earth.

A complication was provided by a clause in the 1926 Paris Air Agreement that severely limited the number of German service personnel allowed to fly. Von Seeckt, however, evaded such restrictions, drawing his nucleus of military aircrews primarily from Lufthansa, wherein they were perforce obliged to operate as ordinary airline crews, but through a clandestine agreement with the Soviet Union he was also able to send service personnel to Lipetz. This was a military flying training centre for German officers which had been established under a blanket of secrecy.

Such were the foundations in men and machines on which the Germans were able to build up their new Air Force. That they were able to do so with such rapidity was due to the short-sightedness of the Versailles Treaty and to the energy and skill of a few regular officers. The advent in power of Adolf Hitler and the Nazi party in 1933 merely provided the political background for which the regular officers had been waiting; they were glad to become fellow-travellers of the Nazis and thus further their aeronautical aspirations.

## From the Creation of the Third Reich to the Outbreak of War

# 1933-1939

The dissillusion and discontent fostered by world economic depression proferred a rich harvest for Adolf Hitler and his Nazi Party (NSDAP); Germany could only survive through renewed vigour in industry and commerce and the Nazis seemed to offer the panacea. In July 1932, a general election in Germany returned the NSDAP as the strongest single party in the Reichstag, so that Hitler became Chancellor on 30 January in the following year. For the armed services the first change occurred in 1934, when conscription was introduced and the title of Defence Minister was changed to Minister of War and Commander-in-Chief of the Armed Forces – perhaps two of the first tangible pieces of evidence of the new aggressive military thinking within Germany.

In August 1934, von Hindenburg, the old Chancellor, died and Hitler thus gained complete control of Germany. Henceforward the oath of allegiance to the law and people of Germany, taken by men entering the new Armed Forces, was to be made to Hitler personally. Hitler still remained in the background in military matters, however, and it was not until February 1938 that he assumed the title and powers of Supreme Commander. His Chief of the High Command (Oberkommando der Wehrmacht – OKW), von Blomberg, was dismissed and his place taken by General Keitel who was to hold the post until the German surrender in May 1945.

The support given to Hitler early in his career stood Hermann Göring in good stead. He had served in World War I as a pilot, finally commanding the prestigious 'Richthofen Jagdgeschwader', although his career had not been outstandingly auspicious. When, in 1933, Hitler came to power, he saw in Göring his perfect collaborator and a man

to whom was attached enough of the glory of the by now almost legendary 'Richthofen days' to appeal to the popular imagination. Honours and high administrative posts were showered upon Göring and, in April 1933, he became the Air Minister. His deputy was Erhard Milch who accepted the post while still retaining his Chairmanship of Lufthansa, and it was Milch, by reason of Göring's preoccupation with politics, who found himself virtually head of the Air Ministry.

Under Milch's able direction, Lufthansa was enlarged while at the same time the aircraft industry underwent expansion. By 1933, the aircraft industry had for long been experimenting with specifically military types, some being built in relatively limited quantities; in 1934 new types began to appear in really substantial numbers, including the Heinkel He 51 biplane fighter with two 7·9-mm machine guns and a top speed of 210mph (338km/h), comparing with the best fighters extant. Reconnaissance types included the Heinkel He 45 and He 46 with speeds of the order of 150mph (242km/h). Main emphasis at this time, however, was upon trainers, such as the Arado Ar 66 and Focke-Wulf Fw 44, and the trimotor Junkers Ju 52/3m, being produced for Lufthansa as a transport, was also being manufactured in bomber form, whilst the Ju 86 and He 111 were in their early experimental stages. These were to be delivered to Lufthansa as airliners, but were, in fact, designed from the outset primarily for the bombing rôle.

In the political sphere, Hitler's foreign policy was beginning to assume progressively more aggressive form, and through Göring, Milch was ordered to make preparations to meet possible consequences of this changing policy. Milch was already busily expanding the existing resources of the aircraft industry: locomotive firms such as Henschel, rolling stock manufacturers such as Gotha and ATG,

and ship-builders such as Blohm und Voss, were instructed to expand into the production of aircraft and aircraft components. By January 1935, Milch was ready to embark upon a new and ambitious plan for the modernisation and expansion of the Luftwaffe, as the new German Air Force had already come to be known to the more perceptive elsewhere in the world, although *officially* it did not yet exist.

In March 1935, Hitler and Göring felt sufficiently secure to proclaim the existence and true nature of the new Luftwaffe – the air arm of Germany's military forces. Hermann Göring was appointed Commander-in-Chief of the new force, which became an independent part of the Armed Forces subordinated to the Chief of OKW (Oberkommando der Wehrmacht, or High Command of the Armed Forces), General Keitel. Milch, as Secretary of State for Air, was still largely in control of the new Luftwaffe; General Wever was appointed as the first Chief of Air Staff. Other staff posts were given by Göring largely to ex-flying officers and particularly those who had served under him in the old 'Richthofen Jagdgeschwader'. Units that had disguised their existence in flying clubs or as SA units were incorporated into the Luftwaffe as regular squadrons. An Air Staff College was set up and the year also saw the development of an anti-aircraft or Flak arm – which was subordinated to the Luftwaffe – and a Signals Service. In its organisation, the Luftwaffe was divided into four main Regional Groups (Gruppenkommandos), centred at Berlin, Konigsberg, Brunswick and Munich. Administration, supply and maintenance, airfield staffing, certain signals functions, recruiting and training, were all controlled by ten Air Districts.

By the time that its existence was publicly revealed, the Luftwaffe's strength stood at 1,888 aircraft of all types with some 20,000

*Above left: Dornier Do 23G bombers of I Gruppe of Kampfgeschwader 253 based at Gotha in summer 1936, this aircraft being a product of the 1934 Luftwaffe expansion programme*

*Above: Junkers Ju 52/3m g3e bombers of the I Gruppe of Kampfgeschwader 152 'Hindenburg' early in 1936, the makeshift trimotor bomber equipping two-thirds of the bombing component*

*Right: The latest Bf 109E fighters were assigned to the Condor Legion during the final phase of the Spanish Civil War and are seen here serving with the Legion's Jagdgruppe*

officers and men. With this considerable nucleus of men and machines, and with the support of between 30 and 40 airframe and engine manufacturers, the new Luftwaffe began to organise itself upon the lines which were to continue up to and after the outbreak of war in 1939. Meanwhile, Milch's long term plans for the expansion and modernisation of the Luftwaffe gained momentum: The first six months of 1935 saw a monthly delivery total of 180–200 aircraft which increased during the latter half of that year to an average of 300 aircraft. The accent on modernisation can be gauged by the fact that the Erprobungsstelle (Test Centre) at Rechlin was completing its service trials of 11 new types in March of 1936. These included the Messerschmitt Bf 109 and Bf 110 fighters, the Junkers Ju 88, Dornier Do 17 and Heinkel He 111 bombers, and the Junkers Ju 87 and Henschel Hs 123 dive-bombers.

Milch had been transferred to the Luftwaffe as a General in 1936, and his undeniable brilliance in the fields of planning and organisation soon aroused Göring's jealousy

and enmity. It was not to be long before Milch was to feel the baleful influence of Göring's efforts to have him replaced in the various posts that he held. In June 1936, Ernst Udet, a World War I fighter ace with 62 'kills' to his credit and the doyen of German inter-war aviation circles, became the Director of the all-important Technisches Amt (Technical Office) at the Air Ministry – a position previously held by Milch. Ernst Udet continued to profit at the expense of Milch's waning influence, and, by February 1939, had become the General-Luftzeugmeister of the Luftwaffe – a position that offered him omnipotent influence in the design and production of all Air Force equip-

ment. And in this capacity, Udet – the popular 'fighter pilot's man' – was to prove to be a disaster. He was not alone in his belief in the concept of a short war, possibly lasting as little as eighteen months in which the Luftwaffe's prime rôle would be support of the Army. Two major results of his policy were to be the abandonment of the relatively orthodox long-range strategic bomber designs, such as the Do 19 and Ju 89, in favour of the much longer-term development of the very much more advanced He 177 and a grossly under-estimated rate of aircraft production.

It was the Luftwaffe's involvement in the Spanish Civil War of 1936–39 that was largely

instrumental in fostering the belief that the prime rôle of the German Air Force in war was the support of ground forces – to the detriment of all other considerations. Hitler was quick to side with the Nationalist forces of General Franco in the fight against the Republicans: In August 1936, six He 51B fighters and 20 Ju 52/3m transports were despatched to Spain, along with 85 volunteer air and groundcrews. This small force was to expand into a powerful, semi-autonomous air component known as the Legion Condor, led at first by Generalmajor Hugo Sperrle and later by General Wolfram von Richthofen.

The Legion Condor achieved little until the early summer of 1937, when it began to receive the latest Messerschmitt Bf 109B fighters, and Heinkel He 111 and Dornier Do 17 bombers. One event which was to shape future German policy of air strategy occurred at the end of March 1937. In an attack on the northern Republican front, He 51s equipped as fighter-bombers, and each carrying six 10-kg bombs were employed in low-level attack on fortified positions with astonishing success. This attack marked the true beginnings of close-support operations which were to contribute substantially to Germany's lightning military successes of 1939 and 1940. The bombs were released by formations of nine He 51s from a height of 500 feet (152m) and up to seven sorties a day were made. Subsequently, three Staffeln of close-support He 51s were organised and were usually to operate with a Staffel of Bf 109s acting as top-cover. Later in 1937, the Junkers Ju 87A and Henschel Hs 123 dive-bombers made their appearance and close-support operations began to increase in efficacy as more experience was gained. These operations were

the work of Wolfram von Richthofen, later to command the formidable Fliegerkorps VIII ground-attack formation, who also developed the close co-operation between ground and air forces by R/T link.

The air fighting over Spain offered front-line combat experience of incalculable value to the Luftwaffe. German pilots and crews received short tours of duty in Spain before returning to Germany where they were immediately posted to schools and conversion units. Fighter tactics, themselves, underwent a revolution. The orderly, set-piece fighter-formation exploded into a medley of individual pilots, each fighting his own battle as soon as combat was joined with enemy forces: this was now replaced by small highly flexible formations with the accent on tactical manoeuvering rather than neat formation flying. The basic format was the Rotte (pair) consisting of two aircraft, with the leader responsible for attack, navigation and fuel surveillance while his wingman covered his tail at all times; the two aircraft flew sufficiently far apart to enable both pilots to give mutual cross-cover while, at the same time, the No 2 man was close enough to his leader to follow his violent turns, barrel-rolls and loops. The process was enlarged to enable two Rotten to fly together, thus producing the Schwarm. Henceforth, German fighter formations of any strength were separated into individual Schwarme and Rotten. To the untrained eye it may have appeared untidy but in the cut-and-thrust of aerial combat the system worked with deadly effect. Other nations ignored this revolution in fighter tactics to their eventual cost.

Far removed from Spain, the year 1938 began as one of great agitation in Europe. Since 1935

*Above: The first Luftwaffe fighter to be built in quantity, the Heinkel He 51 is seen here serving with Jagdgeschwader 132 'Richthofen' during a 1937 inspection by Charles Lindbergh*

*Above right: The Bücker Bü 133 Jungmeister was undoubtedly a classic among single-seat aerobatic trainers, the example illustrated serving with Jagdfliegerschule 2*

Germany had already gained the Saar through a plebiscite and had marched into the Rhineland. Now she was to annexe Austria and occupy the Sudeten borders of Czechoslovakia. The Spanish Civil War was to reach its climax and the postponement of a war in Europe was to be assured by the agreement between Chamberlain and Hitler at Munich on 29 September. Hitler's political successes in the Saar and the Rhineland confirmed his belief in his own infallibility; the pace was beginning to quicken. The Luftwaffe was gaining in strength and deliveries of new types to the combat units were accelerating.

The Munich agreement of September 1938 gave a breathing space to Europe, though by now a major war was viewed by the knowledgeable as inevitable. The Luftwaffe, itself, was no less relieved at this postponement; it was, in fact, in the middle of a period of transition and was not yet ready for a major war. Full production of the latest aircraft types had still to be attained, but it was anticipated that another year would see substantial improvement in the

situation. Indeed one year later, at the end of August 1939, Luftwaffe strength stood at 3,750 aircraft as against 2,928 a year previously. Of this figure 1,270 were twin-engined bombers, mostly He 111s and Do 17s, but with a few of the new Ju 88As which had entered production earlier in the year. Behind this first-line strength there was but a small reserve, varying between 10–25 per cent of the first-line strength according to individual types. Added to this strength and its reserve was the training organisation with between 2,500 and 3,000 training aircraft, as well as some 500 operational types used for conversion training.

German aircraft equipment at this time was in some respects superior to that of potential European opponents. The one and only possible exception, and one which could only be proved by operational usage, was the combat performance of the Messerschmitt Bf 109E vis-a-vis that of the Supermarine Spitfire Mk. I of the Royal Air Force. Both were to prove outstanding; each was to enjoy certain advantages over the other, but the British warplane was in strictly limited supply. The Kampfgruppen (bomber groups) were equipped mainly with the He 111P and Do 17P-1 and Z-2 twin-engined bombers. The Junkers Ju 88A-1 was just entering service with the Staffeln, while the Heinkel units had begun to receive the latest He 111H-1 bomber which was eventually to supplant the P-version. There was still one Gruppe of the obsolescent Ju 86G bomber which was soon to join other variants of this warplane in transport, training and other second-line rôles. The dive-bomber force was by now equipped with the Ju 87B-1 'Stuka'* which could carry up to 1,500lb

*Sturzkampflugzeug

(850kg) of external stores. The advantage of this sturdy dive-bomber lay not so much in its speed or range but in its ability to place its bombs with great accuracy.

The single-engined Jagdgruppen (each equivalent to an RAF wing) were now almost totally equipped with the latest marks of the Messerschmitt Bf 109, the E-1 and E-3 versions which carried two Rheinmetall MG FF 20-mm cannon and two MG 17 7·9-mm machine guns. Of Swiss Oerlikon design, the 20-mm cannon was a formidable weapon and its widespread installation in both the Bf 109 and the Bf 110 twin-engined fighter was a measure of its reliability and efficiency. Whereas the Bf 109 was undoubtedly superior to any fighter produced by the Allies, with the exception of the Spitfire, the heavy Bf 110C-1 fighters of the strategic fighter element, the Zerstörergruppen, were unable to match the single-engined fighter in terms of manoeuvrability, lack of appreciation of the significance of this fact in the initial operation of this strategic fighter later costing the Luftwaffe dear. For reconnaissance and army co-operation the Luftwaffe employed the Henschel 126, while the transportation of troops and supplies was mainly the task of a considerable force of Ju 52/3m aircraft.

If its equipment was for the most part superb, so was the quality of the Luftwaffe's aircrew and groundcrew. In the summer of 1939 manpower had increased to 1½ million men (of which nearly two-thirds were Flak† personnel). Göring had done his utmost to ensure that his Luftwaffe was the élite arm of the Wehrmacht. The career structure in the Luftwaffe was an attractive proposition along

†Fliegerabwehrkanone

with all the kudos of belonging to a new service equipped with the most advanced weapons that science and technology could devise; little wonder that the Luftwaffe attracted the cream of German youth to its battalions.

The slide to war now accelerated. In May 1939, Germany and Italy signed the 'Pact of Steel', ostensibly welding Europe's strongest Fascist dictatorships. The summer was preoccupied by the question of Danzig and the Polish corridor, to which Hitler's eyes had now turned. As early as March 1939, Britain and France had announced a joint guarantee to Poland and Rumania to intercede in the event of aggression from outside and, on 25 August, the Anglo-Polish Mutual Assistance Pact further reinforced this guarantee. Two days prior to signing of this last pact, Ribbentrop and Molotov signed a non-aggression pact between Germany and the Soviet Union – a political bombshell that decided the fate of Poland. Hitler could not believe that the Western Powers would go to war over Poland and pressed his demands for a solution to the Danzig question. But to no avail; the Poles remained adamant in their insistence on Polish administration of Danzig. It was enough for Hitler. In the early hours of 1 September 1939, without declaring war, he ordered his armies across the Polish frontier. The following day Chamberlain sent his ultimatum to Hitler: If Germany did not withdraw her troops immediately she must consider herself at war with Britain. On 3 September, Hitler received and ignored the ultimatum, and at 11.00hrs on that day the ultimatum expired. Britain and France were at war with Germany.

# Chapter 2

# The Onslaught

## Poland

# 1939

At 04.43 hours on 1 September 1939, high above the Vistula River, three Junkers Ju 87B-1 dive-bombers of 3./StG 1 swung into echelon formation on the hand signal of the leader, Oberleutnant Bruno Dilley. The target, the Dirschau bridge, lay 12,000 feet below, half hidden in the early morning mist as each pilot hurriedly completed his vital actions prior to the plummeting dive. First the pitch control set to 2,250rpm, then the supercharger control to 'automatic'; arm the Lärmgerät (screamer siren) and throttle back to 0·8 Ata boost pressure; close the radiator flaps, deploy the dive-brakes and finally open the small ventilation window.

Dilley was already on his way down, an angular pale blue undersurface surmounted by huge black crosses highlighted by the rising sun, and then he was gone. The other pilots half-rolled and aileron-turned into a near vertical dive, eyes alternating between the red lines painted on windscreen, to check the dive-angle, and the bridge – steadily increasing in size beyond the strobing arc of the propeller. At 3,000 feet, still almost vertical, each Stuka released its bombs and pulled out of the dive, its crew crushed into their seats by the acceleration force of over 5 'g' as the horizon swung down from the canopy roof to hover athwart the gunsight.

Dilley's attack occurred eleven minutes before the might of the Wehrmacht, consisting of eleven Panzer divisions and 40 infantry

divisions, poured onto the Polish plains under cover of smoke screens and morning mist, bringing with it a new term, 'Blitzkrieg' (Lightning War), and plunging the world into an agony of chaos that was to last for six years.

The possibility of British and French intervention resulting from the German invasion of Poland forced the Oberkommando der Luftwaffe (OKL) to keep a considerable number of combat units in the West, thus limiting the forces earmarked for the attack; nevertheless the 1,550–1,600 aircraft of Kesselring's Luftflotte 4 and Löhr's Luftflotte 1 were considered sufficient for the task. The Kampfgruppen consisted of KG 2, KG 3, KG 76 and KG 77 with Do 17Z-1, Z-2 and Do 17M-1 types, and LG 1, KG 4, KG 26 and KG 27 with Heinkel He 111P-1 and H-1 types. The Stukagruppen (384 on strength: 300 operational) consisted of IV(Stuka)/LG 1, I/StG 1, II and III/StG 2 and 4.(Stuka)/Trägergruppe 186 under Luftflotte 1, and I/StG 2, III/StG 51, I/StG 76, I and II/StG 77 under Luftflotte 4. The single ground-attack unit, II(Schlacht)/LG 2, operated Henschel Hs 123A biplanes. Escort and support missions were flown by Bf 109B-2s and E-1s of I(Jagd)/LG 2, JGr 101, JGr 102, I/JG 1 and I/JG 21. This list does not include a powerful reconnaissance force.

On the morning of 1 September, fog hampered air operations initially, but after widespread reconnaissance of the main Polish airfields, a massive air strike was mounted with complete surprise against these objectives. At the same time Generaloberst von Bock's Army Group North (III and IV Armies) struck south-east from Pomerania and East Prussia, while von Rundstedt's Army Group South (VIII, X and XIV Armies) thrust eastwards towards Krakow

and Lodz. On the first day of the campaign, the Luftwaffe followed its primary task – the widespread destruction both on the ground and in the air of the Polish Air Force. Kattowitz, Krakow, Lodz, Radom, Lublin, Wilna, Lida Grodno and Warsaw airbases were bombed by He 111s and Do 17s, while strafing attacks were made by the Bf 109s. The destruction was total and the obsolete Polish PZL P.7 and P.11c fighters that took to the air stood no chance against the fast Messerschmitts. Only 67 Bf 109s were lost throughout the campaign, and these succumbed mostly to ground fire; of the Ju 87B units, only 31 aircraft were lost to enemy action. By 3 September, the destruction of the Polish Air Force was considered complete and some diversion in direct support of the army was considered feasible.

The impetus of the German advance had left numerous nests of resistance in the rear, and it was to the reduction of these that the diversion of effort was now turned. In this phase the major part was played by the Stukagruppen of Fliegerkorps VIII and II, commanded by Generalmajor Wolfram Fr. von Richthofen and General Bruno Lörzer respectively. The Ju 87s offered direct support to the army by bombing strong-points, artillery batteries and troop concentrations whenever and wherever the Poles chose to offer resistance. It was here that the legend, however spurious, of the Stuka dive-bomber was born. Operating under conditions of total air superiority the weight and accuracy of its attacks were demoralising and devastating. It was a sturdy close-support dive-bomber, capable of sustaining severe damage and of carrying useful ordnance, and while it operated under fighter cover, it was to be the workhorse of the Blitzkrieg until 1943.

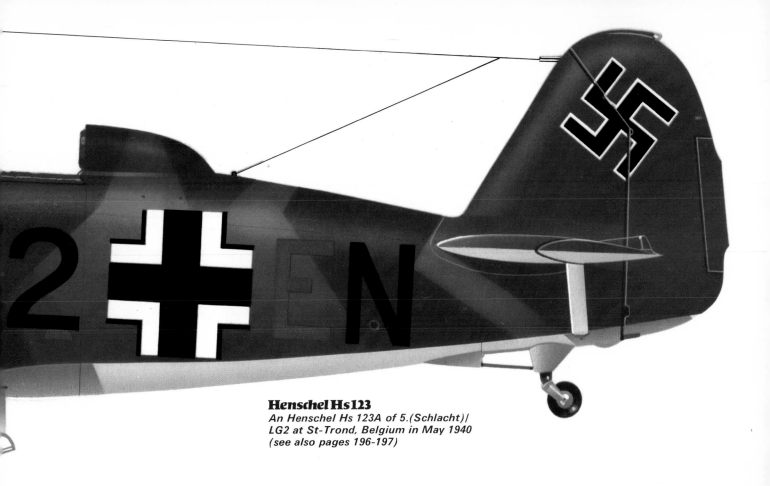

**Henschel Hs 123**
*An Henschel Hs 123A of 5.(Schlacht)/
LG2 at St-Trond, Belgium in May 1940
(see also pages 196-197)*

The rapidity with which the objectives of the Polish campaign were achieved staggered even the Germans. By 9 September, the IV Panzer Division had reached the outskirts of Warsaw and a few days later the last Polish counteroffensive on the Buzra river had been halted and turned to rout. On 17 September, the Russians invaded Poland from the East, capturing Lwow a week later. Warsaw still held out, but, on 25 September, the city came under heavy artillery bombardment accompanied by large-scale bombing by the Kampfgruppen; the final assault on Warsaw started and, by 27 September, the city had surrendered. The lightning campaign was over.

The success of the campaign was overwhelming. The contribution of the Luftwaffe had been outstanding, and credence was given to the wildest claims concerning the potentialities of German air power. Later, Albert Kesselring was to write: 'Beyond all other military arms, the Luftwaffe, by virtue of its mobility in space, accomplished tasks which in former times had been inconceivable . . . The Polish campaign was the touchstone of the potentialities of the Luftwaffe and an apprenticeship of special significance. In this campaign the Luftwaffe learned many lessons . . . and prepared itself for a second, more strenuous and decisive clash of arms.'

*Left: A Heinkel He 111P Staffel en route for a Polish target during the initial phase of the invasion of Poland*

## The Scandinavian Interlude— Denmark and Norway

# 1940

Little operational activity save for reconnaissance took place in the West during the bitterly cold winter of 1939–40, while the Luftwaffe faced the Armée de l'Air and the RAF Advanced Air Striking Force. The air defence of Kriegsmarine naval installations and shipping was efficiently executed by the Jagdgruppen; RAF Bomber Command received an early rebuff to its daylight bombing theories on 18 December 1939, when Bf 109E-1s and Bf 110C-1s of 10.(Nacht)/JG 26, II/JG 77, JGr 101 and I/ZG 76 despatched 12 Wellingtons in the Schillig Roads.

Meanwhile the planning staffs of the Luftwaffengeneralstab were far from idle. The projected campaign for early 1940 called for the invasion of France and an advance to the Channel coast, but first it was essential that Germany's northern flank be secured against possible invasion by the British; the deepwater harbours of Norway were particularly required if an effective offensive was to be mounted against Britain's vital sea communications.

The simultaneous invasion of Denmark and Norway, Operation Weserübung, demanded considerable support from the Luftwaffe. However, in addition to its role of tactical and strategic support, the Luftwaffe was required to provide a large transport force to air-lift paratroops, infantry, supplies and fuel in keeping with the air-sea nature of Weserübung.

Fliegerkorps X, commanded by Generalleutnant Hans Geisler, was earmarked for the Weserübung operations; the prime rôle of this formation was anti-shipping strikes, and its selection for this task was in anticipation of strong intervention by the Royal Navy. The force of 290 He 111H-1s and Ju 88A-1s was drawn from KG 4, KG 26, Kampfgruppe 100 and KG 30, the last-mentioned based at Westerland with 47 Ju 88s. Scant resistance on the ground was anticipated and for this reason only one Gruppe of Ju 87R-1 dive-bombers was assigned, this being the I/StG 1. The fighter force consisted of II/JG 77 with Bf 109E-1s and I/ZG 1 and I/ZG 76 with Bf 110C-1s. The transport force, consisting primarily of 571 Ju 52/3m aircraft, was drawn from KGzbV 1, KGzbV 2, KGzbV 101 to 104, KGzbV 106 and 107, and I, II and III/KGzbV 108(See). In the course of the initial campaign, the Ju 52s were to ferry 29,280 men, 2,376 tons of supplies and 259,300 gallons of aviation and M/T fuel in 3,018 sorties. Reconnaissance was the task of Aufklärungsgruppen 22, 120 and 121, while coastal reconnaissance was provided by Kü.Fl.Gr 106 and 506.

Weserübung demanded the closest possible co-operation between the land, sea and air components, and provided for surprise sea-borne and airborne landings at Oslo, Arendal, Kristiansand, Egersund, Stavanger, Bergen, Trondheim and Narvik. At exactly the same time, the occupation of Denmark was to be accomplished by a border crossing by German troops timed to coincide with seaborne landings.

After extensive reconnaissance of Scapa Flow and other Royal Navy bases for two days prior to Weserübung, at 05.00 hours on 9 April 1940, German forces crossed the Danish frontier without a shot being fired. By 08.30hrs, the Bf 110s of I/ZG 1 and I/ZG 76 had completed the virtual neutralisation of the tiny Norwegian Air Force at Oslo-Fornebu and Stavanger-Sola, and the first paratroops had dropped on their allotted objectives from Ju 52s. By mid-day transport aircraft were disgorging troops and supplies at Fornebu and Oslo-Kjeller, wherein I/StG 1 and I/ZG 76 were shortly installed, II/JG 77 flying to Kristiansand on the following day. Air opposition from the remnants of the Norwegian Air Force and from the RAF was negligible.

The British landings at Narvik on 15 April resulted in its re-capture, but in the isolated campaign that followed the joint British, French and Norwegian force withdrew on 10 June, effectively bringing to an end the fighting in Norway. During this period FlKps X concentrated its effort on Allied landing points at Narvik, Andalasnes and Namsos, while diverting KG 26 and KG 30 against the Royal Navy. At the peak of the fighting the strength of FlKps X rose to 710 combat aircraft, and on 24 April, this command was subordinated to Luftflotte 5 under General-oberst Hans-Jurgen Stumpff, with Head-quarters at Stavanger.

## The Battle For France

# 1940

Three days after Hitler had made a disarming declaration of friendship to Holland and Belgium on 6 October 1939, he issued his secret Directive No. 6 to OKH Generalstabes ordering preparations to begin for an offensive in the West against Holland, Belgium, France and eventually Britain. While stressing that the prerequisite for such an operation would be the securing of the northern flank, i.e., Holland and Belgium, he stated that the primary task of the Wehrmacht would be 'to destroy as many French and Allied forces as possible, to overrun the bases necessary for an aerial and naval assault on Great Britain, and to secure the vital Ruhr area'.

The planning of this ambitious programme, code-named 'Fall Gelbe' (Plan Yellow) was the task of Generaloberst Erich von Manstein and his staff at OKH. After several amendments and alterations, the plan called for the primary offensive in the Sedan-Namur area of the

rugged Ardennes, followed by a rapid exploitation to the north. The armies of the French and Gort's British Expeditionary Force were expected to rush into the northern sector and then be effectively cut off by a strong Panzer advance from the Meuse to the Channel coast at Abbeville. Having isolated and surrounded the Allies in the north, the second phase was to consist of an offensive striking southwards from the Somme, coupled with another offensive against the rear of the Maginot Line.

'Fall Gelbe' possessed a considerable element of risk, but by powerful and direct air support by the most concentrated air forces yet employed in war, acting in close co-operation with swiftly advancing columns of armour, the offensive was believed capable of succeeding. As in Poland, the Luftwaffe was required to offer massive and overwhelming support of the ground forces – but on an unprecedented scale.

Luftflotte 2 (Kesselring), with FlKps I and IV subordinated and including the sea-mining Fliegerdivision 9, supported Army Group B under Generaloberst von Bock to the North. Von Rundstedt's Army Group A, in the Ardennes sector, was supported by Luftflotte 3 (Sperrle) consisting of von Richthofen's FlKps VIII and Lörzer's FlKps II. Against the defences of the Maginot Line, to the south, Army Group C was supported by Ritter von Greim's FlKps V, operating under Loftflotte 3 control.

Luftwaffe units ranged in the West for 'Fall Gelbe' consisted of 1,120 bombers, half of which were He 111s, drawn from KG 1, KG 2, KG 3, KG 4, KG 26, KG 27, KG 51, KG 53, KG 54, KG 55, Kampfgruppe 100 and LG 1, KG 76 and KG 77, and the mine-laying unit KGr 126. The Ju 87B-1 and B-2 dive-bombers were concentrated within Fliegerkorps VIII, and consisted of Stab, I, II, III/StG 2 with I/StG 76, and Stab, I, II/StG 77 with IV (Stuka)/LG 1 numbering some 380 aircraft; also within this command was II(Schlacht)/LG 2 with Hs 123As. The single-engined fighter force was

*Above: Four He 111-equipped bomber Kampfgeschwader participated from the outset in the assault on Poland and were responsible for bombing attacks on all major Polish cities*

*Right: Terrifying in conditions of complete air supremacy, the Ju 87B "Stuka" proved vulnerable to fighters. Here one lets go a 250kg (551lb) bomb during the Polish campaign*

drawn from Gruppen of JG 1, JG 2, JG 3, JG 21, JG 26, JG 27, JG 51, JG 52, JG 53 and JG 54 numbering some 860 Bf 109E-1s and E-3s. The Zerstörer Gruppen were I and II/ZG 2, I/ZG 1, I and II/ZG 26 and I(Zerst)/LG 1 with 355 Bf 110C-1s and C-2s. The long- and short-range Aufklärungsgruppen had a total strength of 640 aircraft. For supply and paratroop operations there were 475 Ju 52/3m transports and 45 DFS 230 gliders subordinated to Fliegerkorps zbV (General Putzier), drawn from four Gruppen of KGzbV 1 and four Gruppen of KGzbV 2, with KGzbV 101, 104 and 106.

At first light on 10 May 1940, this massive force struck without warning. The attacks on airfields proceeded in what was to become a familiar pattern, with strikes by He 111s and Do 17s on Dutch and Belgian air bases, as well as those of the AASF and the Armée de l'Air. At the same time, the Kampfgruppen ranged deep into enemy territory, striking at rail and transportation centres at Metz, Dijon, Romilly-sur-Seine and Lyon. Following the large-scale dawn attacks on airfields in Belgium and Holland, the first of a series of airborne landings took place after 05.00 hours; not all the troop landings and parachute drops at Dordrecht, Moerdijk and Delft, Waalhaven, Valkenburg and Ockenburg were entirely successful, however, due to stiff resistance, and attrition amongst the Ju 52 transport units was as high as 40 per cent. The glider assaults on the key fortress at Eben Emael and the bridges at Kanne, Veldwezelt and Vroenhoven were carried out with dash and efficiency, the men

of Hptm. Koch's I/FJR 1 and Oblt. Witzig's Parachute Engineer Battalion being conveyed to their objectives in DFS 230 gliders of I/Luftlandgeschwader 1 towed by Ju 52s.

By 12 May, Guderian's I and X Panzer Divisionen had pushed their way through the wooded Ardennes country to reach the River Meuse at Sedan, the Army being assisted throughout by day and night reconnaissance by the Luftwaffe that secured a continuous picture of enemy positions, movements and weaknesses. On the following day, the main armoured spearhead of Army Group A debouched across the Meuse, between Charleville and Sedan, and struck West. The Luftwaffe quickly assured air superiority over the entire front, and whenever enemy resistance was encountered Richthofen's FlKps VIII was called in to eliminate opposition. The Stukas inflicted a paralysis on the French and British armies that was a revelation to even the Germans themselves; some Stukagruppen flew up to nine sorties per serviceable aircraft during periods of intensive operations, losing only four Ju 87B-2s on the first four days of the campaign. Once again they were permitted to fly in conditions of total air superiority and thus the legend of the Stuka dive-bomber continued to flourish.

Such was the numerical and technical superiority of the Bf 109E fighter over those of the RAF and the Armée de l'Air that the Allied fighters were never in a position to interfere seriously with the Luftwaffe's tactical operations. By 18 May, the German armoured thrusts in the centre had reached Peronne and Cambrai; two days later Amiens fell and by that evening the leading elements of

II PzDiv had reached Abbeville on the Channel coast, splitting the Allied armies in two.

After an unsuccessful Allied counter-attack at Arras, the Germans swung north, up the Channel coast, taking Boulogne and investing Calais by 24 May. At the same time, von Bock's forces in the north had reached Ghent, setting in motion the final stages of a massive pincer movement that was to make the position of the Allied armies untenable. On the evening of 26 May, the first elements of Lord Gort's British Expeditionary Force were evacuated from the beaches at Dunkirk and De Panne, and over the next ten days of the evacuation the Luftwaffe made a determined effort to sink shipping in the Channel and bomb the beleaguered forces on the beaches. The whole weight of Fliegerkorps I, II, IV and VIII was committed to frustrating the evacuation attempt, and for the first time met more resilient air opposition from Air Chief Marshal H. C. T. Dowding's RAF Fighter Command.

It was over Dunkirk that the Messerschmitts first encountered the Spitfire Mk I, flown by resolute and skilful pilots; in combat with this nimble RAF fighter, the German pilots found that their own aircraft could be outturned and out-climbed, and for the first time were forced to fly their Bf 109Es to the limits of their performance. While the Jagdgruppen were now operating from airfields close to the Dunkirk sector, the RAF fighter squadrons fought at a distinct disadvantage, far from their bases and beyond the range of effective radar control. The German fighters frequently found themselves engaged in dogfights with Spitfires and Hurricanes so that they missed the rendezvous for the escort of their bomber

*Above: The Ju 87B-equipped Stukagruppen moved forward to occupy French airfields as soon as these were taken by the ground forces. The remains of an RAF Hurricane are seen here*

*Above right: The Junkers Ju 86G-1 equipped only one Kampfgruppe, IV/KG 1, when WW II began and this was deactivated at the end of the Polish campaign*

*Right: When Germany went to war in September 1939, the Dornier Do 17P-1 long-range reconnaissance aircraft equipped 22 Staffeln but had been largely phased out by late 1940*

forces. The bombers suffered considerably in consequence, as also did the Stukas, and Luftwaffe losses over Dunkirk were heavy. For the first time the Luftwaffe had met an opponent of equal fighting capabilities in the air and failed to prevent the Dunkirk evacuation in consequence, this operation being completed at 02.23hrs of 4 June 1940.

Freed of its commitment in the north, the Luftwaffe now turned to support the sporadic fighting which culminated in the German occupation of Paris on 14 June, and by 25 June, the campaign in France was over. The Luftwaffe was now withdrawn for rest and re-fit for the next and expected final phase of the war in the West, the invasion of the British Isles. As yet, however, the Luftwaffe had only had a foretaste of effective and determined fighter opposition, but in the flush of victory neither Göring nor his senior commanders had yet recognised its implications.

# Chapter 3

# The Battle of Britain

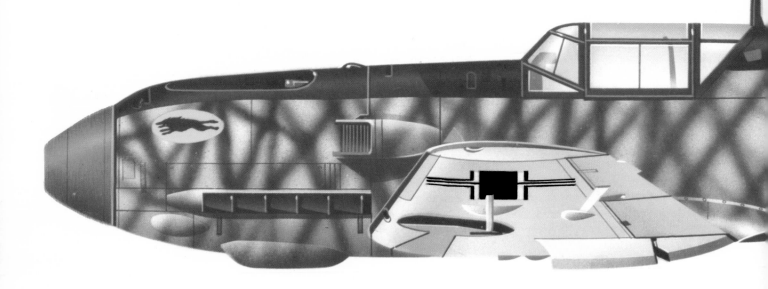

The conclusion of the lightning German campaign in Belgium, the Netherlands and France, on 25 June 1940, left the German General Staff with the enormous task of preparing and executing an invasion of Great Britain within the three months of good weather to be expected before the autumn gales would render such a task impossible. The plan for invasion, code-named 'Seelöwe' (Sealion), had been initiated as early as 1939, but had since suffered serious set-back by disagreement between rival army and naval factions. One aspect, however, was agreed to the effect that it would be better to plan an assault by land forces on the United Kingdom rather than face months, possibly years, in a slow campaign of economic strangulation, with its inevitable attrition, by sea and air forces.

Admiral Raeder, C-in-C of the Kreigsmarine, raised the question of invasion with Hitler on 21 May, but largely because of diplomatic peace moves then being made, it was not until 2 July that the Führer finally ordered preparations for Sealion to be made. The plan appeared simple enough and was a projection of the Blitzkreig theory that had stood the test so well in Poland and France. The assault would be made across the English Channel and would represent little more than a large-scale river crossing, with the RAF and the Royal Navy engaged and destroyed by the Luftwaffe. Firstly, the plan called for the establishment of a bridgehead in Kent and Sussex; this would be followed by other landings in the west culminating in a drive northwards to the line Gloucester-St Albans-Maldon. Subsequent to this no further serious opposition by the British was expected.

The first condition before such a crossing could take place was the defeat of the Royal Air Force so that the essential prerequisite of German air supremacy would be assured. Thus, the German High Command, in regarding the whole undertaking in the same light as a large-scale crossing of a river such as the Meuse, allotted to the Luftwaffe its normal preliminary task – the neutralisation of enemy air opposition and the destruction of its ground installations.

After the cessation of fighting in France, most Luftwaffe units were withdrawn for rest and refit while preparations for the assault were made within the commands. Both Luftflotte 2 and 3 merely extended their bases into France and took over existing airfields. Their common boundary on the Channel coast, at the estuary of the Seine, was extended northwards through the centre of England so that each was allotted its own sphere of operations. Fliegerkorps I, II and IX were subordinated to Kesselring's Luftflotte 2, while FlKps IV, V and VIII were under Sperrle's Luftflotte 3 to the west. During July 1940, the combat units were gradually deployed to airfields between Hamburg and Brest, and by 17 July, when the order for full readiness was given, the striking force had been built up to its intended strength. The actual strength of the forces controlled by Luftflotte 2 and 3 for the assault on southern England and the Midlands comprised:

| | |
|---|---:|
| Bombers (He 111, Do 17 and Ju 88) | 1,200* |
| Dive-bombers (Ju 87B) | 280 |
| Single-engined fighters (Bf 109E) | 760 |
| Twin-engined fighters (Bf 110) | 220 |
| Long-range Recce (Do 17, Bf 110, Ju 88) | 50 |
| Short-range Recce (Hs 126, Do 17, Bf 110) | 90 |
| | 2,600 |

In addition to the above, Luftflotte 5, with FlKps X subordinated, retained a force of 130 He 111s and Ju 88s, 30 Bf 110 long-range fighters, and 30 long-range reconnaissance aircraft. While this force played little part in the subsequent fighting, it offered a valuable diversionary rôle, forcing the RAF to retain fighter defences in the north of England.

While this massive strike force was gathering on the airfields in France and Belgium, the intervening weeks before the start of large-scale operations were used by RAF Fighter Command to restore its depleted squadrons and build up its reserves. After the Dunkirk fighting, the position of the Command had been desperate and its operational strength had sunk to the lowest level of 1940, notwithstanding the subsequent Battle of Britain. During the operations covering the Dunkirk evacuation alone, RAF Fighter Command had lost over 100 fighters and 80 pilots killed or missing. This baleful episode had been the culmination of a month's air fighting in which, during the period 10 May–20 June, RAF combat units based in France and Britain had lost 944 aircraft, including 386 Hurricanes and 67 Spitfires. On the morning of 5 June, there were a mere 331 Hurricanes and Spitfires, with a further 36 on immediate reserve, available *Serviceability on 20 July 1940 stood at 69 per cent of this figure.

for operations in RAF Fighter Command. However, these figures were soon to improve as a result of the growing inflow of fighter aircraft from the production lines. Whereas RAF Fighter Command could rely on a steady replacement rate of its aircraft the same could not be said of aircrew; trained pilots were already in short supply and a critical shortage was to come.

While the Spitfire had already demonstrated that it was the equal of the Messerschmitt Bf 109E, the majority of Fighter Command's squadrons were equipped with the Hurricane I. This type had proved inferior to the Bf 109E but was of rugged construction, highly manoeuvrable and destined to be the mainstay of the RAF's strength in the crucial weeks that were to follow. These prime weapons were of limited use without proper fighter control, but due to enlightened thinking during the pre-war years, the RAF had a Ground Controlled Interception (GCI) system that was without parallel. The radar stations that were positioned around the coasts of Britain were backed by a highly efficient system whereby the information was analysed, passed to the controlling stations and, through the medium of a Fighter Controller, relayed via R/T to airborne squadrons. There was to be no element of surprise to the advantage of the enemy and no fuel-wasting standing patrols for the defender, at this point in time the GCI system was untried. It remained to be seen how it would operate in the face of unrelenting enemy air attack by day and night.

Within the compass of Operation Sealion the task of the Luftwaffe as detailed to the respective Luftflotten in the middle of July, was twofold:

(a) The elimination of the RAF, both as a fighting force and in its ground organisation.

(b) The strangulation of the supply of Great Britain by attacks on its ports and shipping.

The elimination of the RAF was to be accomplished in two stages. In the first place, the fighter defences located to the south of a line between London and Gloucester were to be beaten down and, secondly, the Luftwaffe air offensive was to be covered northwards by stages until RAF bases throughout England were covered by daylight bombing attacks. Meanwhile, as part of the plan, a day and night bombing offensive was to be directed against the British aircraft industry.

The all-out offensive to eliminate the RAF

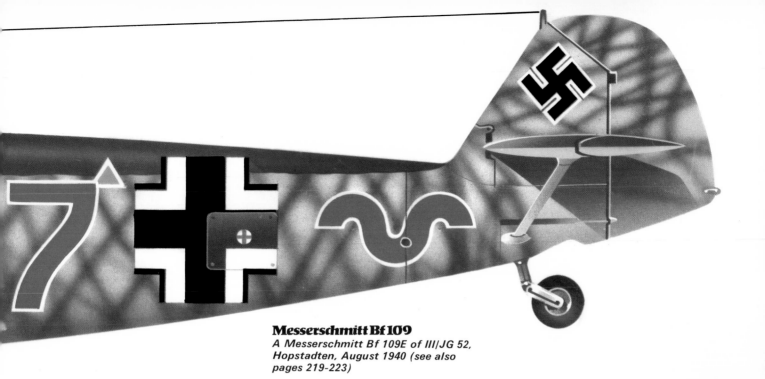

**Messerschmitt Bf 109**
*A Messerschmitt Bf 109E of III/JG 52, Hopstadten, August 1940 (see also pages 219-223)*

and lay waste the British aircraft industry was code-named 'Adlerangriff' (Eagle Attack) and the day of its launching, known as Adler Tag (Eagle Day), was originally fixed for 10 August 1940. German Air Intelligence estimated that four days would be needed to effectively neutralise the RAF fighter defences in the South, with a further four weeks required to eradicate the entire RAF as a fighting entity. With the RAF effectively out of action, it was anticipated that Sealion could go ahead as planned in the first two weeks of September.

After the initial skirmishing over the Channel and South Coast during the first week of July, Luftflotte 2 and 3 were deemed fit to increase the tempo and scale of their operations. Although historically there were no fixed delineations in the various phases of the conflict, it is, however, convenient for reasons of clarity to enumerate the differing objectives to which the Luftwaffe found itself committed in relation to periods in time.

## Phase 1: Testing of Fighter Command
### 10th July–7th August

# 1940

In order to test the mettle of RAF Fighter Command before commencing the assault, it was decided to launch a limited campaign on the periphery of Fighter Command's sphere of influence rather than a direct confrontation over its own bases. Accordingly Fliegerkorps II (Lörzer), based in the Pas de Calais, and Fliegerkorps VIII (von Richthofen), based in Normandy, were assigned the twin tasks of gaining local air superiority over the Channel and closing the same to British convoys. In addition to these formations, a battlegroup consisting of KG 2, II/StG 1, IV(Stuka)/LG 1 and various Jagdgruppen were concentrated into a shipping strike force under Oberst Johannes Fink.

On 10 July, the first large attack came at 13.35hrs when some twenty-six Do 17Z-2s of I/KG 2, escorted by the Bf 110s of I/ZG 26 and Bf 109Es of I/JG 3, attacked the convoy BREAD off North Foreland. The raid was

*Right: A Junkers Ju 88A-1 about to take-off on a bombing sortie*

intercepted by Nos. 32, 74 and 111 Squadrons, and a fierce dogfight involving over a hundred aircraft ensued off Dover. From this day onwards, the German bomber forces began to show themselves in greater strength over the Channel, Straits of Dover and South-East coast areas of England by daylight. Their activities were still, however, mainly confined to the ports and shipping, and occasionally to coastal airfields.

At the same time, large formations of Bf 109Es began to trail their coats at medium and high altitudes over Southern England. These sweeps, or Frei Jagd (Free Chase) missions, were designed to draw RAF fighters into combat. At first, Fighter Command obliged; Spitfires and Hurricanes suffered tactical disadvantage while climbing for altitude, being bounced by the 109s and suffering accordingly. RAF fighter tactics, consisting of rigid 'Fight-

*Above right: A Junkers Ju 88A-1 about to take-off with an SC 250 bomb inboard of each engine nacelle; (below) the navigator/bomb aimer of an He 111 checks the position of his aircraft during a sortie over the United Kingdom*

ing Area Attacks', 'vic' formations in which only the leader could maintain an adequate look-out and line-astern manoeuvering, could not maintain the balance in face of the fluid German fighter formations. But the lessons were quickly learned and digested with pure fighter-versus-fighter confrontations being avoided and by the adoption of the German Rotte and Schwarm.

## Phase 2: The Assault
## 8th August–23rd August

# 1940

The losses sustained by the Luftwaffe during the initial stage had been bearable: 192 combat aircraft were destroyed and a further 77 damaged to varying degrees. But it was clear that the RAF was still an effective force and was not suffering sufficiently heavy casualties in the actions on the coastal fringe. It now became necessary for the Kampfgruppen to penetrate further inland in order that the Messerschmitts could engage and destroy a higher proportion of RAF fighters than hitherto. The initial phase had also highlighted serious shortcomings in both quality and quantity in the German fighter arm. Such was the aggressiveness of RAF fighter pilots that up to three times the number of escorting German fighters over the figure originally estimated were found to be needed to provide adequate support for the bomber formations. In addition, the Bf 110C-4 fighter, vitally required for long-range escorted penetrations,

was found to be completely out-classed by the Spitfire and Hurricane in fighter-versus-fighter combat. When attacked the Bf 110s were forced into defensive circles and, in the more extreme cases, needed the protection of the 109s.

A new and serious phase of the battle opened on 8 August when bombing was intensified. Fierce air fighting developed with higher losses to both sides and a month of attrition began when the RAF was strained to the utmost. On this day there were three major Luftwaffe attacks on convoys with the Stukas of FlKps VIII bearing the brunt of the action. Over the next ten days the Stuka legend was finally destroyed. In the face of determined enemy fighter attack, the Ju 87 was proved a costly liability, and after the slaughter of StG 77 which lost sixteen Ju 87B-1s on 18 August, the type was withdrawn from the battle.

Bad weather dictated postponement of Adler Tag until 13 August, and even then it was not until the afternoon that the Luftwaffe appeared in force to start the sustained offensive on the RAF's air and ground forces. Portland and Southampton were bombed, in addition to the airfields at Eastchurch, Detling and Middle Wallop. The Luftwaffe flew 1,485 sorties for the loss of 46 aircraft, but the general lack of cohesion and poor bombing results provided a dismaying start to the offensive.

If Adler Tag had misfired then a serious effort was made to redress the situation on 15 August when the Luftwaffe put up no fewer than 1,786 sorties – of which 520 were by bombers – during the 24-hour period. It was a decisive day in which no effort was spared in

*Above: This Do 17Z of 8.Staffel of Kampfgeschwader 76 succeeded in regaining France in September 1940 after a sortie of Britain but not its base at Cormeilles-en-Vexin*

*Above right: Despite its poor showing during the Battle of Britain, the Messerschmitt Bf 110C was not an unsuccessful warplane and fought with distinction elsewhere*

*Right: The Ju 87Bs of the IV(Stuka) Gruppe of Lehrgeschwader 1, seen here during a sortie, participated only briefly— and disastrously—in the 'Battle of Britain' under II Fliegerkorps*

the attempt to smother RAF air opposition and wreck airfields and radar stations. At mid-day, after Hawkinge and Lympne airfields had been attacked, Luftflotte 5 attempted raids in the north-east of England. Sixty-five He 111s of I and III/KG 26 escorted by I/ZG 76 attacked Newcastle and Sunderland, while 50 Ju 88s of KG 30 raided Driffield aerodrome. The raids were intercepted and the RAF shot down 16 bombers and seven Bf 110s, and largely on account of its poor showing Luftflotte 5 was to take no further part in the battle. Raids by formations of 100–150 German aircraft continued throughout the day, these suffering the shattering loss of 75 of their number.

During the succeeding week, the scale of attack on airfields of all types in southern England was of the heaviest and great air battles were continuously fought over Kent,

Sussex and Hampshire. Meanwhile, the day and night attacks on shipping continued, and special targets of the aircraft industry were singled out for bombing. Losses of both bombers and fighters increased. By comparison with RAF claims of 755 German aircraft destroyed, the Luftwaffe actually lost 403 with a further 127 damaged throughout this period, and if somewhat less than was claimed, these figures were nevertheless extremely serious. But RAF Fighter Command's casualties were equally grievous with 94 pilots killed or missing and 60 wounded between 8–19 August and the losses in aircraft amounting to 54 Spitfires and 121 Hurricanes.

## Phase 3: The Tactical Revision
## 24th August–6th September

# 1940

In a directive issued by Göring on 20 August, the prime task of the Luftwaffe remained the destruction of the Royal Air Force in the air and on the ground. But time for the establishment of air superiority over England was running out and its achievement now called for the most desperate measures. During this phase, the Luftwaffe's major effort was devoted to the attack on RAF airfields and installations in the extreme south and southeast of England, with emphasis laid on the RAF fighter concentrations deployed around London.

To provide 'overwhelming' escorts of Bf 109s, it was decided to transfer most of the single-engined fighter strength of Luftflotte 3 to Luftflotte 2, and in the following days the bulk of Jafü 3 was transferred to bases in the Pas de Calais. Poor as the combat radius of the Bf 109E was without the much-needed jettisonable fuel tank, operations from the Pas de Calais bases enabled the fighter to penetrate deeper into RAF airspace, but because of mounting bomber losses the German fighter leaders were now ordered to stay close to the bombers – a complete negation of all the design advantages inherent in the Bf 109E.

In addition to the bomber raids aimed at specific targets, this phase of the battle was characterised by extensive employment by Luftflotte 2 and 3 of diversionary feints by bombers and reconnaissance aircraft, and intricate fighter sweeps primarily aimed at catching Fighter Command's squadrons on the ground refuelling.

Perhaps this phase was the most crucial for Fighter Command. By devoting all efforts against the RAF in the south of England to the almost complete dereliction of everything else, the Luftwaffe might have succeeded in its primary aim. On 31 August, Fighter Command's casualties were the highest of the battle – 39 aircraft destroyed in combat and 14 pilots killed. By now the aircrew situation within Fighter Command was approaching crisis level. On paper the numbers appeared sufficient for the task, but in reality it was the loss of experienced Squadron and Flight commanders that was causing intense concern. The major share of the fighting was born by a fast-diminishing band of battle-tried pilots in squadrons that were flying up to 50 hours per day, while fresh units – lacking combat experience – were being decimated by the 109s within one or two weeks.

Throughout this period Fighter Command suffered 295 fighters destroyed and 171 damaged, but far more serious was the loss of 103 pilots killed or missing and a further 128 withdrawn from combat because of injuries. The Luftwaffe's losses amounted to 378 aircraft with a further 115 damaged.

# Luftwaffe Order of Battle in the West

13 August 1940 (Adler Tag): 09.00 hours
LUFTFLOTTE 2
Generalfeldmarschall Albert Kesselring

### Fliegerkorps I: Gen. Oberst Ulrich Grauert : Beauvais

| Unit | Type | Location | Officer Commanding | |
|---|---|---|---|---|
| Stab KG 1 | He 111H | Rosieres-en-Santerre | Obstlt. | Exss |
| I/KG 1 | He 111H | Montdidier | Maj. | Maier |
| II/KG 1 | He 111H | Montdidier | Obstlt. | Kosch |
| III/KG 1 | Ju 88A-1 | Rosieres-en-Santerre | Maj. | Fanelsa |
| Stab KG 76 | Do 17Z | Cormeilles-en-Vexin | Obstlt. | Fröhlich |
| I/KG 76 | Do 17Z | Beauvais-Tille | Hptm. | Lindeiner |
| II/KG 76 | Ju 88A-1 | Creil | Maj. | Möricke |
| III/KG 76 | Do 17Z | Cormeilles-en-Vexin | | |
| 5.(F)/122 | He 111, Ju 88 | Holland | Hptm. | Bohm |
| 4.(F)/123 | He 111, Ju 88 | Belgium | | |

### Fliegerkorps II: General Bruno Lörzer : Ghent

| Unit | Type | Location | Officer Commanding | |
|---|---|---|---|---|
| Stab KG 2 | Do 17Z | Arras | Oberst | Fink |
| I/KG 2 | Do 17Z | Cambrai-Epinoy | Maj. | Gutzmann |
| II/KG 2 | Do 17Z | Arras | Obstlt. | Weitkus |
| III/KG 2 | Do 17Z | Cambrai-Niergnies | Maj. | Kreipe |
| Stab KG 3 | Do 17Z | Le Culot | Oberst. | Chamier-Glisczinski |
| I/KG 3 | Do 17Z | Le Culot | Obstlt. | Gabelmann |
| II/KG 3 | Do 17Z | Antwerp-Duerne | Hptm. | Pilger |
| III/KG 3 | Do 17Z | St Trond | Hptm. | Rathmann |
| Stab KG 53 | He 111H | Lille-Nord | Oberst | Stahl |
| I/KG 53 | He 111H | Lille-Nord | Maj. | Kaufmann |
| II/KG 53 | He 111H | Lille-Nord | Maj. | Winkler |
| III/KG 53 | He 111H | Lille-Nord | Maj. | von Braun |
| II/StG 1 | Ju 87B | Pas de Calais | Hptm. | Keil |
| IV(St)/LG 1 | Ju 87B | Tramecourt | Hptm. | von Brauchitsch |
| Epr.Gr 210 | Bf 109E, Bf 110C | Calais-Marck | Hptm. | Rubensdörffer |
| II/LG 2 | Do 17 | St Omer | Hptm. | Weiss |

### Fliegerdivision IX: Gen.Major Joachim Coeler : Soesterberg·

| Unit | Type | Location | Officer Commanding | |
|---|---|---|---|---|
| Stab KG 4 | He 111H | Soesterberg | Obstlt. | Rath |
| I/KG 4 | He 111H | Soesterberg | Hptm. | Meissner |
| II/KG 4 | He 111H | Eindhoven | Maj.Dr | Wolf |
| III/KG 4 | Ju 88A-1 | Amsterdam-Schiphol | Hptm. | Bloedorn |
| KGr 100 | He 111H | Vannes-Meucon | Hptm. | Aschenbrenner |
| Stab KG 40 | Fw 200C-1 | Brest-Guipavas | Obstlt. | Geisse |
| I/KG 40 | Fw 200C-1 | Brest-Guipavas | | |
| KGr 126 | He 111 | | | |
| Ku.Fl.Gr 106 | He 115, Do 18 | | | |
| 3.(F)/122 | Ju 88, He 111 | | Obstlt. | Koehler |

### Jagdfliegerführer 2: Gen.Maj. Osterkamp : Wissant

| Unit | Type | Location | Officer Commanding | |
|---|---|---|---|---|
| Stab JG 3 | Bf 109E | Samer | Obstlt. | Viek |
| I/JG 3 | Bf 109E | Colombert | Hptm. | von Hahn |
| II/JG 3 | Bf 109E | Samer | Hptm. | von Selle |
| III/JG 3 | Bf 109E | Desvres | Hptm. | Kienitz |
| Stab JG 26 | Bf 109E | Audembert | Maj. | Handrick |
| I/JG 26 | Bf 109E | Audembert | Hptm. | Fischer |
| II/JG 26 | Bf 109E | Marquise | Hptm. | Ebbighausen |
| III/JG 26 | Bf 109E | Caffiers | Maj. | Galland |
| Stab JG 51 | Bf 109E | Wissant | Maj. | Mölders |
| I/JG 51 | Bf 109E | Wissant | Hptm. | Brüstellin |
| II/JG 51 | Bf 109E | Wissant | Hptm. | Matthes |
| III/JG 51 | Bf 109E | St Omer | Maj. | Trautloft |
| Stab JG 52 | Bf 109E | Coquelles | Maj. | von Merhart |
| I/JG 52 | Bf 109E | Coquelles | Hptm. | von Eschwege |
| II/JG 52 | Bf 109E | Peuplingne | Hptm. | von Kornatzki |
| Stab JG 54 | Bf 109E | Campagne | Maj. | Mettig |
| I/JG 54 | Bf 109E | Guines | Hptm. | von Bonin |
| II/JG 54 | Bf 109E | Hermalinghen | Hptm. | Winterer |
| III/JG 54 | Bf 109E | Guines | Hptm. | Ultsch |
| I(J)/LG 2 | Bf 109E | Calais-Marck | Maj. | Trübenbach |
| Stab ZG 26 | Bf 110C | Lille | Obstlt. | Hüth |
| I/ZG 26 | Bf 110C | Yvrench | Hptm. | Macrocki |
| II/ZG 26 | Bf 110C | Crécy-en-Ponthieu | Hptm. | von Rettburg |
| III/ZG 26 | Bf 110C | Barley | Hptm. | Schalk |
| Stab ZG 76 | Bf 110C | Laval | Maj. | Grabmann |
| II/ZG 76 | Bf 110C | Abbeville-Drucat | Hptm. | Groth |
| III/ZG 76 | Bf 110C | Laval | Hptm. | Dickore |

Notes.
1. Aircraft types listed denote the primary type used by the unit. Fighter units with the Bf 109 were operational on the E-1, E-3 and E-4 subtypes; Bf 110 Zerstörer units used the C-2, C-4 and long-range D-0 types. Kampfgruppen used the Ju 88A-1, Do 17Z-2 and the Heinkel He 111P-2, H-1, H-2, H-3 and H-4 subtypes.

## LUFTFLOTTE 3
## HQ: Chantilly
## Generalfeldmarschall Hugo Sperrle

### Fliegerkorps IV: Gen. Kurt Pflugbeil : HQ: Dinard

| Unit | Type | Location | Officer Commanding | |
|---|---|---|---|---|
| Stab LG 1 | Ju 88A-1 | Orléans-Bricy | Obst. | Bülowius |
| I/LG 1 | Ju 88A-1 | Orléans-Bricy | Hptm. | Kern |
| II/LG 1 | Ju 88A-1 | Orléans-Bricy | Maj. | Debratz |
| III/LG 1 | Ju 88A-1 | Chateaudun | Maj. Dr. | Bormann |
| Stab KG 27 | He 111H | Tours | Obst. | Behrendt |
| I/KG 27 | He 111H | Tours | Maj. | Ulbrich |
| II/KG 27 | He 111H | Dinard | Maj. | Schlichting |
| III/KG 27 | He 111H | Rennes-St Jacques | Hptm. | von Sternberg |
| Stab StG 3 | He 111, Do 17 | | | |
| KGr 806 | Ju 88A-1 | Nantes | | |
| 3.(H)/31 | Bf 110, Hs 126 | North France | | |

### Fliegerkorps V: Gen.Lt. Ritter von Greim : HQ: Villacoublay

| Unit | Type | Location | Officer Commanding | |
|---|---|---|---|---|
| Stab KG 51 | Ju 88A-1 | Orly | Obst.Dr. | Fisser |
| I/KG 51 | Ju 88A-1 | Melun | Maj. | Schultz-Hein |
| II/KG 51 | Ju 88A-1 | Orly | Maj. | Winkler |
| III/KG 51 | Ju 88A-1 | Etampes | Maj. | Marienfeld |
| Stab KG 54 | Ju 88A-1 | Evreux-Fauville | Obstlt. | Höhne |
| I/KG 54 | Ju 88A-1 | Evreux-Fauville | Hptm. | Heydebrock |
| II/KG 54 | Ju 88A-1 | St André-de-l'Eure | Ostlt. | Köster |
| Stab KG 55 | He 111H | Villacoublay | Obst. | Stöckl |
| I/KG 55 | He 111H | Dreux | Maj. | Korte |
| II/KG 55 | He 111H | Chartres | Maj. | von Lachemaier |
| III/KG 55 | He 111H | Villacoublay | Maj. | Schlemell |

### Fliegerkorps VIII: GenMaj. von Richthofen : HQ: Deauville

| Unit | Type | Location | Officer Commanding | |
|---|---|---|---|---|
| Stab StG 1 | Do 17Z | Angers | Maj. | Hagen |
| I/StG 1 | Ju 87B-2 | Angers | Maj. | Hözzel |
| III/StG 1 | Ju 87B-2 | Angers | Hptm. | Mahlke |
| Stab StG 2 | Ju 87B-2 | St Malo | Maj. | Dinort |
| I/StG 2 | Ju 87B-2 | St Malo | Maj. | Hitschold |
| II/StG 2 | Ju 87B-2 | Lannion | Maj. | Enneccerus |
| Stab StG 77 | Ju 87B-2 | Caen-Carpiquet | Maj. | von Schönborn |
| I/StG 77 | Ju 87B-2 | Caen-Carpiquet | Hptm. | Lichtenfels |
| II/StG 77 | Ju 87B-2 | Caen-Carpiquet | Hptm. | Pleweg |
| III/StG 77 | Ju 87B-2 | Caen-Carpiquet | Hptm. | Böde |
| V(Zerst)/LG 1 | Bf 110C-2 | Caen-Carpiquet | Hptm. | Liensberger |
| Reconnaissance | | | | |
| II/LG 2 | Do 17 | Böblingen (Germany) | Hptm. | Weiss |
| 2.(H)/11 | Do 17 | Le Bourget | | |
| 2.(F)/123 | Ju 88 | | | |

### Jagdfliegerführer 3: Obst. Werner Junck : HQ: Cherbourg

| Unit | Type | Location | Officer Commanding | |
|---|---|---|---|---|
| Stab JG 2 | Bf 109E | Evreux-Fauville | Obstlt. | von Bülow |
| I/JG 2 | Bf 109E | Beaumont-le-Roger | Maj. | Strümpell |
| II/JG 2 | Bf 109E | Beaumont-le-Roger | Maj. | Schellmann |
| III/JG 2 | Bf 109E | Le Havre-Octeville | Maj. | Mix |
| Stab JG 27 | Bf 109E | Querqueville | Maj. | Ibel |
| I/JG 27 | Bf 109E | Plumetôt | Hptm. | Neumann |
| II/JG 27 | Bf 109E | Crépon | Hptm. | Lippert |
| III/JG 27 | Bf 109E | Carquebut | Hptm. | Schlichting |
| Stab JG 53 | Bf 109E | Cherbourg | Maj. | Cramon |
| I/JG 53 | Bf 109E | Rennes | Hptm. | Blümensaat |
| II/JG 53 | Bf 109E | Dinan | Hptm. | Maltzahn |
| III/JG 53 | Bf 109E | Sempy | Hptm. | Harder |
| Stab ZG 2 | Bf 110C-2 | Toussous | Obstlt. | Vollbracht |
| I/ZG 2 | Bf 110C-2 | Amiens-Glisy | Hptm. | Heinlein |
| II/ZG 2 | Bf 110C-2 | Guyancourt | Maj. | Carl |

## LUFTFLOTTE 5
## HQ: Stavanger-Sola (NORWAY)
## Generaloberst Hans-Jurgen Stumpff

### Fliegerkorps X: Gen.Lt. Hans Geisler

| Unit | Type | Location | Officer Commanding | |
|---|---|---|---|---|
| Stab KG 26 | He 111H | Stavanger-Sola | Obstlt. | Fuchs |
| I/KG 26 | He 111H | Stavanger-Sola | Maj. | Busch |
| III/KG 26 | He 111H | Stavanger-Sola | Maj. | von Lossberg |
| Stab KG 30 | Ju 88A-1 | Aalborg | Obstlt. | Loebel |
| I/KG 30 | Ju 88A-1 | Aalborg | Maj. | Doensch |
| III/KG 30 | Ju 88A-1 | Aalborg | Hptm. | Kellewe |
| I/ZG 76 | Bf 110D-0 | Stavanger-Sola | Hptm. | Restemeyer |
| II/JG 77 | Bf 109E | Stavanger & Vaernes | Hptm. | Hentschel |
| Ku.Fl.Gr 506 | He 115C | Stavanger & Trondheim | | |
| 1.(F)/120 | He 111, Ju 88 | Stavanger-Sola | | |
| 1.(F)/121 | He 111, Ju 88 | Stavanger-Sola | | |
| Aufkl Gr.Ob.d.L | Do 215 | Stavanger-Sola | | |

## Phase 4: The Bombing of London
## 7th September–30th September

# 1940

The conditions necessary for the launching of Sealion had not been attained and possibly could never have been achieved by adherence to the original two-fold plan. On the night of 25 August, RAF Bomber Command launched a retaliatory raid on Berlin, and Hitler, in a speech on 4 September, seized upon this attack as an excuse for announcing his intention of a revenge bombing of London. The bombing of Warsaw and Rotterdam had been partly instrumental in causing the respective governments to sue for peace, and to Hitler there seemed no reason to suppose that a similar tactic could fail against the British. Two days before his speech, Hitler directed that the Luftwaffe should carry out attacks on the populations and defences of large cities, particularly London, by day and night.

This decision was in part an admission of defeat by the Luftwaffe, but at the same time Göring still hoped that the RAF fighter arm might be finally exhausted and that a turn of fortune would produce victory at the last moment. It was a fatal blunder, and from thence onwards RAF Fighter Command was able to operate in the air and on the ground with an impunity that it had not experienced since the start of Adlerangriff.

On the afternoon of 7 September, the Luftwaffe flew 372 bomber and 642 fighter sorties against targets in East London starting large fires and causing considerable damage. That night a further 255 bomber sorties were directed to the same area. During the succeeding days and nights, forces of similar strength – although never exceeding the effort of 7 September – were in operation, but extended their target area to Central London generally. Again Luftwaffe casualties mounted on a scale that far exceeded the results achieved; recrimination within the Luftwaffe bomber and fighter arms followed, each sharply criticising the other for its apparent shortcomings. Even the use of fast Ju 88s escorted by large numbers of Bf 109s failed to stem the attrition and loss of 60 German aircraft on 15 September was further proof that the goal of air superiority was as far away as ever. Two days later, Hitler ordered Seelöwe to be postponed indefinitely, but the invasion fleet was nevertheless to remain on readiness until the second week of October.

## Phase 5: The Fighter Bombers
## 1st October–31st October

# 1940

Three months less ten days had elapsed since the start of the intensive air battles of July, but for all the Luftwaffe effort there was little to set against the loss of 1,653 aircraft. In order to avoid bomber losses by day, Göring resorted to the use of fighter-bombers operating at high-altitude.

Specialist fighter-bomber units (Epr.Gr 210, I and II(Schlacht)/LG 2) were bolstered by the addition of a Staffel from each Jagdgruppe which hastily fitted its Bf 109Es with a bombrack capable of carrying a 550-lb (250kg) bomb. No formal fighter-bomber training was given to the pilots of these units and as a result the accuracy achieved was poor. Nevertheless the speed and altitude (generally above 25,000ft) at which the fighter-bombers operated rendered their interception extremly difficult. Despite widespread use of bomb-carrying Bf 109s and Bf 110s, and single Ju 88s using weather as cover, RAF Fighter Command continued on its course of recovery. The main Luftwaffe effort was directed now to night attacks which the RAF was woefully unable to counter, but to all intents and purposes the threat by day had been neutralised. The crisis was over.

By the end of October, the Luftwaffe was glad to call a halt to daylight operations due to the deterioration in weather. It was Göring himself who took the decision. The Battle of Britain had been a failure for the Luftwaffe, although none overtly admitted the fact, and it was still hoped to wear Britain down to the point of capitulation by massed night attacks on industrial cities, by making seaborne supply impossible through the destruction of the main ports, and by sea-mining and shipping attacks.

Combined losses of Luftflotten 2, 3 and 5, from 10 July until 31 October 1940, amounted to 1,733 aircraft destroyed compared with 915 aircraft lost (415 pilots killed or missing) by the RAF.

*Right: Adolf Galland, considered by many to have been one of Germany's best fighter pilots, resting during the Battle of Britain, possibly at Caffiers*

*Below: The Heinkel He 111H bomber played a major role in the 'Battle of Britain' but was severely mauled by RAF fighters owing to its inadequate defensive armament*

# The Battle Of Britain

**RAF FIGHTER COMMAND**

HURRICANE  SPITFIRE
BLENHEIM  DEFIANT
GLADIATOR  PRINCIPAL TARGETS
COMMAND BOUNDARY

**LUFTWAFFE BASES**

BOMBER  DIVE-BOMBER
HEAVY FIGHTER  FIGHTER
COMMAND BOUNDARY

## THIRTEEN GROUP

Castletown **3**
Sumburgh **232** Drem
Montrose **145** Dyce **145**
Glasgow
Turnhouse **65 141**
**605**
Prestwick **615**

Aldergrove **245**
Belfast

**LUFTFLOTTE FIVE**
(from Norway and Sweden)

Acklington **32 610**
Newcastle
Sunderland Usworth **607**
Middlesbrough
Catterick **54 219**

Cover of
high-level
radar
(15,000 ft)

Cover of
low-level
radar (500 ft)

Church Fenton **64 85 302**
Hull
Kirton in Lindsey **74 264**
Manchester
Sheffield

## TWELVE GROUP

Liverpool
Nottingham
Digby **29 151 611**

**NORTH SEA**

Wittering **23 229 266**
Bircham Newton **229**
Coltishall **242 616 266**
Norwich

Birmingham
Coventry

Duxford **19 310** Ipswich Martlesham **25 257**
Castle Camps **73**
Debden **17**
North Weald **249 257**
Pembrey **92**
Swansea
Cardiff
Bibury **87**
Northolt **1 303 504**
London
Stapleford Abbots **46**
Rochford **41**
Hornchurch **222 603 600**
Bristol
Heathrow **1**
Biggin Hill **79** Gravesend **501**
Bath
Croydon **72 111**
Kenley **66 253**
Canterbury
Middle Wallop **234 604 609**
**ELEVEN GROUP**
Boscombe Down **56**
Tangmere **43 601**

## TEN GROUP

Southampton
Warmwell **152**
Exeter **87 213**
Portsmouth Goodwood **602**

St Eval **238**
Plymouth **247**

*ENGLISH CHANNEL*

Wissant
St Omer Lille
Etaples Tramecourt
Montreuil St Pol
Crecy-en-Ponthieu
Denain
Abbeville Cambrai
Arques
Barley Amiens
Rosieres-en-Santerre
Montdidier Laon
**LUFTFLOTTE TWO**
Beauvais (Tille)
Couvron
Creil

Cherbourg

Le Havre
Deauville
Cormeilles
Beaumont-le-Roger
Caen Evreux
Caudron Guyancourt St Andre de l'Eure
Orly
**LUFTFLOTTE THREE**
Dreux Chartres Villacoublay
St Leger Melun
**FRANCE**
Alencon
Etampes

Brest
Dinard

Rennes Laval
Le Mans
Chateaudun Orleans
Bricy
Vannes Nantes Tours Bourges

27

# Chapter 4

# The Night Blitz

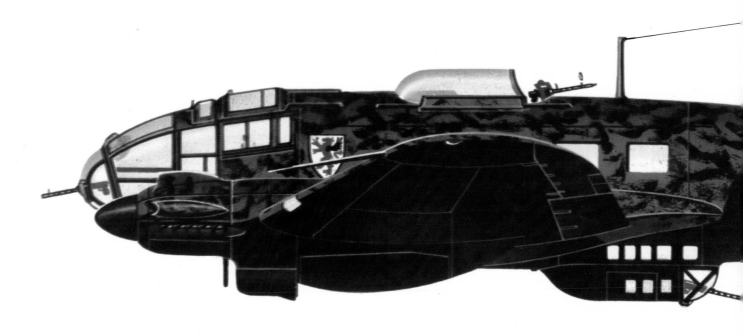

From September 1940 onwards, Göring's daylight offensive against RAF Fighter Command continued on a gradually reducing scale, with heavy bomber attacks giving way to raids by escorted fighter-bombers. During the same period, attempts to reduce the morale of the civilian population and force the British Government to surrender were made through the medium of heavy raids on London followed by a maximum-effort nocturnal assault on the capital. In November, this assault was expanded to other British cities and centres of industry, alternating between deliberate attempts to wreck civil morale and carefully planned attacks on Britain's supply and production centres. These phases of the German night bomber offensive, beginning with the raid on London on 7 September and dragging on through the winter to cease finally in May 1941, became known in Britain as the Blitz.

The main reasons why the Luftwaffe turned to night attacks lay in the alarming rate of attrition suffered by the Kampfgruppen in their attacks by day. Within the RAF at this time, night fighting techniques relying on visual contact assisted by searchlights and the well-proven GCI system achieved few successes. Until the availability of efficient Airborne Interception (AI) radar, the German night bomber was to come and go with little hinderance. The first operational radar set, the AI Mk IV, was about to enter service but only on a very limited scale and was still highly experimental.

The adoption of night bombing also presented problems to the Luftwaffe. There were those of accurate night navigation and bombing, and these were compounded by an overall reduction in efficiency of bomber crews owing to the massive loss of experienced men during the Battle of Britain. The Germans, however, considered that any deficiencies in night operational training would be compensated by the use of radio aids to navigation that were in the hands of a few specialised bomber units. The Germans had been far ahead of any other combatant power in the design and development of such aids, but by using the various types of equipment prematurely they allowed their secrets to be compromised and effective jamming by the enemy to be initiated. To summarise, the three principle aids to

blind-bombing and navigation then in use were as follows:

1. 'Knickebein' (Bent Leg): This relatively unsophisticated equipment could be used by bombers equipped with the Lorenz blind-approach aid. The pilot flew his aircraft along an approach radio beam to the target, the bomb aimer releasing his bombs on receipt of a second radio signal beamed to traverse the approach beam at a particular point. The aid was easily jammed and could even be 'bent', and its only advantage lay in its ability to be used by a considerable number of aircraft.

2. X-Gerät (X-Equipment): Specialised aid to blind-bombing installed only in the He 111H-4s of Kampfgruppe 100 (Maj. Friedrich Aschenbrenner) operating from Vannes and Chartres.

It consisted of one approach beam traversed in the vicinity of the target by three others. When the pilot received the first signal 31 miles (50km) short of the target, he lined up accurately on the approach beam, compensating for drift. The second and third signals occurred at 12 miles (20km) and 3 miles (5km) respectively. A computer calculated the aircraft's groundspeed and utilising this information automatic bomb release followed pressing a button on receipt of the third signal.

*Below: Camouflaged for nocturnal operations, a Heinkel He 111H of Kampfgeschwader 26 is seen here being bombed up at its French base before an attack on Britain in the late autumn of 1940*

**Heinkel He 111**
*An Heinkel He 111P-2 of Kampfgeschwader 55, Dreux, Chartres and Villacoublay, Autumn 1940 (see also pages 180-185)*

X-Gerät was very accurate but could be effectively jammed.

3. Y-Gerät (Y-Equipment): Specialised aid installed only in the He 111H-4s of III/KG 26 (Maj. Victor von Lossberg) based at Poix-Nord. Once again an accurate target approach beam was used, but in this case bomb release was made at an accurately-measured range along the beam. This range was computed automatically by the associated ground radar station. The station sent an interrogator pulse. After a set interval special equipment in the bomber returned an answering pulse. Range was then deduced by the time signal (a matter of milli-seconds). At the correct range, the ground station relayed a bomb release signal. Y-Gerät was another very accurate system but again one that could be jammed effectively.

## The Night Blitz
## 7th September 1940–31st May
# 1941

The Kampfgruppen engaged in the Blitz comprised the same units that had participated in the Battle of Britain under Luftflotten 2, 3 and 5, with the addition of some 90 bombers that had been held in Germany. Some 1,300 bombers were available for operations, but low serviceability kept the maximum effective strength to about 700 of these. After the mass daylight attack on London docks on 7 September, raids by 60 to 260 bombers took place after dusk during every night of the month. The effective jamming of Knickebein by No. 80 Signals Wing of the RAF rendered this equipment useless and throughout October the Luftwaffe had to make use of bright moonlight for navigation and bombing. During the early part of that month, London suffered a nightly assault by an average of 200 bombers. On 9 October, the Luftflotten were ordered to increase the effort, and that night London received 386 tons of HE and some 70,000 1-kg incendiary bombs in the course of 487 bomber sorties; on succeeding nights the attack was repeated by forces mounting 307, 150, 303 and

320 sorties. The Germans anticipated that the civil population would panic and force a surrender, but they, and in turn the Allies, underestimated the resilience of civilian morale in the face of indiscriminate heavy bombing.

Early in November, Göring decided to extend the Luftwaffe effort to a long-term attrition against the whole British industrial effort. Parallel with this new plan came the decision to use KGr 100 and the X-Gerät system as target finders. On locating the target KGr 100 was to drop incendiary bombs as target-markers for the follow-up force of bombers. The new plan as set out for the Luftflotten by Göring was as shown in the accompanying table.

On the night of 14/15 November, the target was Coventry. Using X-Gerät, twelve He 111s of KGr 100 crossed Lyme Bay, in Dorset, at 18.17hrs heading north-east. At 20.15hrs, the Gruppe dropped over 1,000 incendiaries on the city starting numerous conflagrations, and as they droned away into the clear night, three separate bomber streams converged on Coventry from the Wash, Dungeness and Portland. Throughout the night successive waves of KG 1, KG 26, KG 27, KG 55, LG 1 and Kü.Fl.Gr 606 flew in to add to the devastation, and in the course of 469 sorties, the Luftwaffe delivered 394 tons of HE bombs, 56 tons of incendiaries and 127 parachute LMB 5 sea-mines; the latter caused considerable blast damage. Air defences were minimal and most of the bombers returned to base unscathed.

Birmingham came under heavy attack on the night of 19 November. Once again the now-established pattern was followed, with KGr 100 leading KG 26, KG 54, KG 55 and Kü.Fl.Gr 606. This time five bombers were brought down by the defences, one, a Ju 88A-4, was shot down over Dorset by Flt. Lt. J. Cunningham and Sgt. J. Phillipson, flying a Beaufighter IF of No. 604 Squadron and using the new AI Mk IV radar. This was the first radar kill of the war, but many months of experiment and disappointment lay ahead for the RAF night-fighter crews before their airborne radar equipment was to bring consistent results. The onus of night fighting still lay on Hurricanes, Defiants and Blenheims, their crews relying on visual contact to achieve

indifferent success. The Birmingham attack was followed during the remainder of that month and December by a succession of large-scale raids on London, Bristol, Plymouth, Liverpool, Southampton and Sheffield.

The year closed with a sharp attack on London in the evening of 29 December 1940. The raid was abandoned by the Luftwaffe some two hours after its commencement owing to deteriorating weather conditions. Only about 130 bomber sorties were mounted in the event, all aircraft carrying incendiaries, but by the time the weather closed in after 22.00hrs, the City of London was suffering its worst ordeal by fire since the Great Fire of 1666! Contrary to belief, this attack was a routine one and not a deliberate attempt to wreck the City. That evening, the X-Gerät approach beam was actually laid in a SE–NW direction over the Charing Cross and Tottenham Court Roads. A fresh wind was blowing from the south-west and insufficient allowance for this wind was made by KGr 100 whose incendiaries fell about

## Göring's Plan for the Luftflotten

1. LONDON to remain the main target
   a In daylight attacks by escorted fighter-bombers and, according to the availability of cloud cover, by single bombers.
   b In night attacks by equal forces of Luftflotten 2 and 3.

2. Attack industrial targets in Coventry, Liverpool and Birmingham by small forces at night.

3. Mining of the Thames, Bristol Channel, the Mersey and the Manchester shipping canal by Fliegerkorps IX.

4. Destruction of the Rolls-Royce aero engine works at Hillingdon (Glasgow) by III/KG 26 using Y-Gerät.

5. Damaging of RAF fighter arm by day sweeps by the Jagdgruppen.

6. Attacks, with fighter escort, on convoys in the Channel and on assemblies of shipping in the Thames Estuary.

7. Destruction of enemy aircraft industry by special crews of Luftflotten 2 and 3.

8. Attacks on enemy night fighter bases.

9. Preparation for attacks on Coventry, Birmingham and Wolverhampton by KGr 100 using X-Gerät.

one mile to the East and immediately to the North-West of St Paul's Cathedral. The aircraft of the main bomber force, seeing the resultant fires, contributed their loads of HE and incendiaries.

In January 1941, the Luftwaffe still maintained a considerable force of bombers in the West: Fliegerkorps I, IV and V mustered 26 Kampfgruppen based in France and Belgium for attacks on Great Britain. By this time, however, a general lack of confidence in the blind-bombing aids was apparent, owing primarily to British mastery of the X-Gerät and to the widespread use of decoy fires. The Kampfgruppen turned once again to moonlight raids, concentrating on British seaports over which minimum interference to the radio beams could be expected. Accordingly ports such as Plymouth, Bristol, Swansea, Cardiff and Hull came under night attack.

In April, the German campaigns in the Balkans and Greece were already underway. Several fighter, dive-bomber and reconnaissance units had been detached from Luftflotte 3 in Northern France and deployed to the south during the winter and early spring. The anti-shipping force, Fliegerkorps X, had been transferred from Norway to the Mediterranean at the end of 1940. During May 1941, Luftflotte 2 left France for the East, along with KG 1, KG 27, KG 51, KG 54, KG 55, KG 76, KG 77 and I/LG 1. The moves were made under a cloak of secrecy, and as a cover to these movements, bomber raids on Britain were accompanied by false radio traffic to simulate larger forces. To maintain the semblance of a large force in being, the Luftwaffe executed the heaviest raid of the entire Blitz against London on the night of 10 May, crews flying two and even three sorties and 708 tons of HE and 87,000 incendiaries were dropped, causing great damage to greater London in the course of 550 sorties. Three nights later the raid was repeated in similar strength.

By the end of May 1941, Kesselring had moved with the whole of Luftflotte 2, along with the bomber units of FlKps IV and V, to Germany and Eastern Poland in readiness for the attack on the Soviet Union, leaving in the West the anti-shipping units of Fliegerkorps IX and Fliegerführer Atlantik, and a mixed force of bombers and single-engined fighters under Luftflotte 3.

In time, these units were to be whittled away by the more important commitments in the Soviet Union and the Mediterranean, leaving only a small force of mine-laying and anti-shipping units in the West. The Blitz was over. The programme for the subjugation of Britain had overrun its time, and although considerable damage had been wrought to British cities and industries, the time for the hoped-for collapse had passed. The Luftwaffe had had every opportunity to bring Britain to her knees but failed because there had been no firm and continuous policy of attack: a shortcoming compounded by the manifest unsuitability of much of the equipment of the Luftwaffe for the task with which the service had been presented. Lack of coherent policy from OKL had all to frequently allowed hard-pressed cities to recover from large-scale raids where one more raid could have produced complete breakdown. The only solution now lay in the starving of Britain of food and supplies by air and sea attacks on her shipping, and awaiting or forcing surrender after the expected defeat of Russia in the autumn of 1941.

## Bomber Units Based in the West

### 31 May 1941

| | |
|---|---|
| II/KG 2 | Dornier Do 217E-2 |
| Stab, 1. and 3./KG 4, III/KG4 | Heinkel He 111H-6 |
| Stab, I and III/KG 26 | Heinkel He 111H-6 |
| Stab, I Gruppe and 4. and | |
|   5./KG 30 | Junkers Ju 88A-4 |
| KGr 100 | Heinkel He 111H-6 |
| KGr 606 | Dornier Do 17Z-2 |
| KGr 806 | Junkers Ju 88A-4 |
| | |
| Fliegerführer Atlantik | |
| Stab and I/KG 40 | Focke Wulf Fw 200C-2 |
| II/KG 40 | Dornier Do 217E-1 |
| III/KG 40 | Heinkel He 111H-6 |

*Right: The view from the He 111 as it manoeuvred to attack. The glazed nose offered no protection to the machine-gunner/bomb-aimer and casualties were high*

*Below: The Dornier Do 17Z bombers of Kampfgeschwader 2, one of which is seen here, were responsible for some of the first nocturnal attacks on London in September 1940*

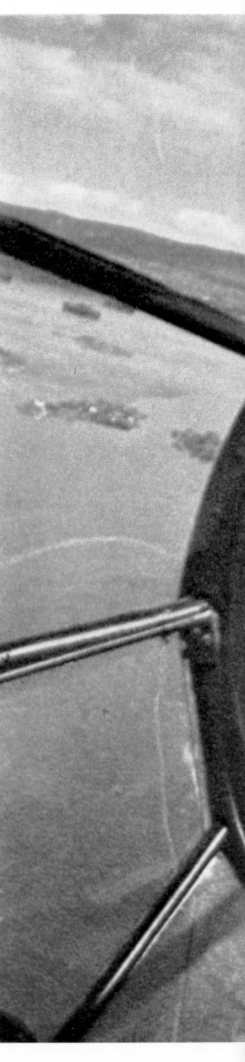

# Chapter 5

# The Luftwaffe Strikes South

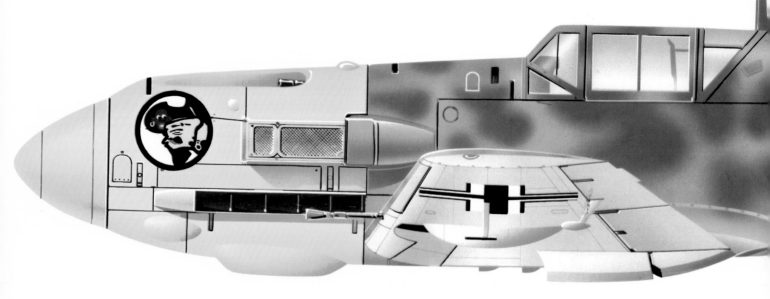

## The Luftwaffe Strikes South
## January–May
# 1941

While the Battle of Britain was being fought German eyes were already turned towards the Soviet Union, the ultimate goal, but Italy's prevarications in North Africa and the Mediterranean forced German commitment in this theatre before any major assault could be made in the East. Although the Luftwaffe was well equipped for additional commitments in the Balkans, the Mediterranean and North Africa throughout the Spring of 1941, and was to achieve brilliant victories in the course of its campaigns, its involvement on two war fronts came at a time when all effort should have been made to conserve its strength. When, finally, the main weight of the Luftwaffe was to be turned against the Soviet Union in June 1941, a considerable proportion of its strength was already diverted elsewhere.

By December 1940, Italian plans in the Mediterranean had begun to go seriously awry. The invasion of Greece had met with stiff resistance, had ground to a halt, and had resulted in Commonwealth forces establishing themselves in Greece and on Crete. In North Africa, Mussolini's forces, after initial successes, had been thrown back to Bardia with massive losses in men and material. In addition, the Regia Aeronautica and the Italian Navy had proved incapable of stopping British convoys supplying Egypt, and their own convoys were losing heavily in the face of joint RN/RAF strikes from Malta.

These reverses promised to complicate the forthcoming assault against the Soviet Union, and Hitler decided to intervene in order to secure his southern flank before committing himself in the East. This intervention was incidentally, against the advice of the Oberkommando der Wehrmacht, and the ensuing commitments which resulted in a widespread diversification of Luftwaffe effort can be summarised as follows:

1. The First Assault on Malta, from January to March 1941, by Fliegerkorps X partly against the island but primarily against British shipping routes from Gibraltar to Egypt.

2. The establishment of Fliegerführer Afrika in Cyrenaica for the support of Generalfeldmarschall Erwin Rommel's Afrika Korps in early February 1941, resulting in the recapture of El Agheila and the subsequent advance to Sollum, on the Egyptian frontier, in April 1941.

3. The commitment of Luftflotte 4 to the Balkans for Operation Marita, the invasion of Yugoslavia and Greece on 6 April 1941, culminating in the campaign in Crete of 20–30 May 1941.

The Luftwaffe presence in Italy was established as early as June 1940, when Mussolini

*Below: Junkers Ju 52/3m transports and two of their Messerschmitt Bf 110 fighter escort during a resupply operation*

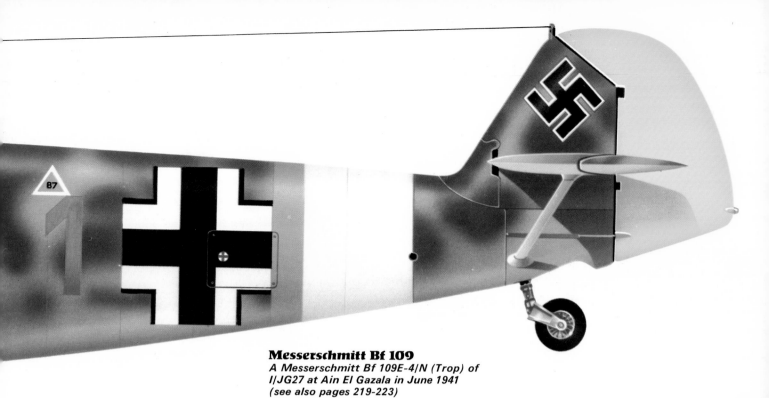

## Messerschmitt Bf 109
*A Messerschmitt Bf 109E-4/N (Trop) of I/JG27 at Ain El Gazala in June 1941 (see also pages 219-223)*

declared war, in the form of 'Italuft', a liaison mission under General Ritter von Pohl. At first the Luftwaffe's effort was restricted to ferrying Italian troops from Foggia to Albania by Junkers 52/3m transports, and the first combat units did not appear until the arrival of Generalmajor Hans Geisler's Fliegerkorps X in Sicily in December 1940. The operational area of FlKps X was extensive and included the Central Mediterranean, Sicily, Southern Italy and parts of Sardinia and North Africa. By mid-January 1941, FlKps X could muster about 330 aircraft and by March this figure had risen to 450, including 200 under the subordinated Fl.Fü. Afrika. Transport aircraft made up the bulk of these numbers, but the combat units available for operations, primarily against Malta and the shipping routes, were as shown in the accompanying table.

The first action came on 7 January, when a British convoy was sighted off Bougie consisting of four merchantmen under strong naval escort, including the aircraft carriers HMS *Ark Royal* and *Illustrious*. Fliegerkorps X attacked with about 40 Ju 88s, Ju 87s and He 111s in company with SM 79s of the Regia Aeronautica. The *Illustrious* suffered heavily from dive-bomber attacks when about 120 miles off Malta on 10 January, Stukas of I/StG 1 and II/StG 2 achieved four direct hits with 1,100-lb (500kg) armour-piercing bombs, leaving the carrier almost sinking. On 15 January, however, Luftwaffe reconnaissance noted that *Illustrious* had docked in Valetta harbour, Malta. The following day the 'Illustrious Blitz' started. After early morning reconnaissance flights by 1.(F)/121, the carrier once again

came under attack from successive waves of Ju 87s of Fliegerkorps X. These concentrated on Valetta harbour in general but the *Illustrious* in particular, with the pilots of I/StG 1 (Hptm. Werner Hözzel) pressing home their attacks with great courage. In fact they achieved only one hit on the carrier, also damaging the supply ship *Essex*, owing to the violent AA fire and continuous opposition from RAF Hurricanes and RN Fulmars. The price was heavy – 2./StG 1 being wiped out with the sole exception of its Staffelkapitän.

Two days later, the airfields at Luqa and Hal Far came under heavy attack, while, on 19 January, Stukas managed to hit the *Illustrious* once again, but makeshift repairs were by now well underway and, on 23 January, the vessel set sail, albeit in parlous condition, for Alexandria. Against almost daily Luftwaffe raids on Malta, the RAF and RN never succeeded in putting more than three Fulmars, six Hurricanes and a single Gladiator into the air to face the onslaught which varied between 40 and 80 sorties per day.

Throughout February and March, Fliegerkorps X hammered at Valetta, and the three Maltese airfields – Luqa, Hal Far and Takali. The raids usually took the form of dive-bombing attacks, low-level fighter-bomber attacks by Bf 110s of III/ZG 26 (Maj. Schülze-Dickow) and medium level raids by Ju 88s and He 111s. Escort was provided by 7./JG 26 (Oblt. Müncheberg), which was joined later in March by I/JG 27 (Hptm. Edu Neumann). Both units flew the Bf 109E-7 capable of carrying a 66-gallon (300-litre) drop-tank. March also saw the arrival of a Gruppe of Ju 88A-6s (III/KG 30)

at Gerbini, and II and III/StG 1 replacing I/StG 1 and II/StG 2, which were transferred to Cyrenaica.

The supply position on Malta fell to a critical level until alleviated by the arrival of a small convoy from Alexandria which reached Valetta on 23 March 1941; a prompt strike by Fliegerkorps X in the form of 30 Ju 87s escorted by 20 Bf 109s damaged two merchantmen at anchor in the harbour. Fourteen RAF Hurricanes sent up to intercept managed to claim seven Stukas, while Valetta's increasingly efficient AA accounted for four. Owing to its commitment in support of the forthcoming Balkan campaign, this attack was to be the last by Fliegerkorps X against Malta for some time, although small-scale harassing raids and anti-shipping strikes continued.

By mid-March 1941, some 400 German aircraft, under General Alois Löhr's Luftflotte 4, were concentrated on the Bulgarian airfields at Sofia, Plovdiv, Krumovo, Krainitzi and Belitza for the proposed invasion of northern Greece in support of the Italians. Neighbouring Yugoslavia was expected to co-operate in this venture but a revolution in Belgrade against the pro-Nazi government of Prince Paul forced Hitler to act quickly. Orders were given on 26 March for the rapid transfer of some 600 combat aircraft from France, Germany and the Mediterranean to bases in Bulgaria and Rumania. These included KG 2, III/KG 3 and II/KG 26 for the establishment of a long-range bomber force. Stukagruppen consisted of I and III/StG 2 'Immelmann', which were joined by II/StG 2 from El Machina in North Africa; one Zerstörergruppe, the II/ZG 26, was posted from Germany to Turnu Sverin, and Messerschmitt Bf 109E-4 and E-7 fighters of I/JG 27,* Stab, I and III/JG 77, I(Jagd)/LG 2 and I (Schlacht)/LG 2 were posted from France and Germany to supplement the already established II and III/JG 27 at airfields in the Deta/Arad sector.

Tactical control of all close-support aircraft was placed under the command of Gen. Wolfram von Richthofen, whose Fliegerkorps VIII was to be enabled once again – after the drubbing in the Battle of Britain – to launch its own pattern of warfare on the classic Blitzkreig style, unmolested by effective fighter opposition.

The simultaneous assaults on Yugoslavia and Greece, code-named Operation 'Marita', started on 6 April 1941 with a massive Stuka

## The Disposition of Fliegerkorps X

**Fliegerkorps X**: Officer Commanding: Gen. Maj. Hans Geisler: OC Operations Ia: Oberst Harlinghausen
HQ: Taormina, Sicily: 12 January 1941

| Unit | Type | Location | Strength (serviceable) |
|---|---|---|---|
| Bombers | | | |
| Stab LG 1 | Ju 88A-4 | Catania | 4 (2) |
| II/LG 1 | Ju 88A-4 | Catania | 38 (38) |
| III/LG 1 | Ju 88A-4 | Catania | 38 (38) |
| 2./KG 4 | He 111H-6 | Comiso | 12 (12) |
| II/KG 26 | He 111H-6 | Comiso | 27 (29) |
| Fighters | | | |
| III/ZG 26 | Bf 110C-4 | Palermo | 34 (16) |
| Dive-Bombers | | | |
| Stab StG 3 | Ju 87R-1* | Trapani | 9 (8) |
| I/StG 1 | Ju 87R-1 | Trapani | 35 (11) |
| II/StG 2 | Ju 87R-1 | Trapani | 36 (23) |
| Reconnaissance | | | |
| 1.(F)/121 | Ju 88D-5 | Catania | 12 (2) |

*In transit to North Africa.

*Left: An Henschel Hs 126B-1 tactical reconnaissance and army co-operation aircraft of one of the Aufklärungsstaffeln (H) engaged in the assault on Greece*

*Above: Messerschmitt Bf 110D-3s of 9.Staffel of Zerstörergeschwader 26 operating in the convoy protection role over the Mediterranean during the summer of 1941.*

attack on Belgrade and heavy bomber raids on the Piraeus. The city of Zagreb fell on 10 April, and seven days later the Yugoslav army capitulated. In the south, resistance by valiant Greek forces, supported by the Imperial Expeditionary Force under General Wilson, was reduced to a withdrawal accompanied by stubborn rearguard actions in the face of List's XII Army. The Greek army surrendered on 20 April, and one week later the fall of Athens brought the campaign to a conclusion. Within the space of less than one year, the British and Commonwealth armies had again been forced to evacuate the Continent in extremis.

# Crete—Operation 'Merkur'
# 1941

The decision to invade Crete was an opportunist one. After the rapid success of the Wehrmacht in Greece, the German General Staff had initially considered no further action in the direction of Crete. It was largely the brainchild of Generaloberst Kurt Student, the commander of Fliegerkorps XI, who conceived the idea of an airborne landing on the island. He ventured to Göring that Crete, besides being a vital operational base, would be a useful stepping-stone for a similar invasion of Cyprus with

the further possibility of linking up with the Axis in North Africa on the Suez Canal. Göring gained Hitler's permission for the undertaking with the proviso that it took place within the shortest possible space of time, and the decision was taken in late April to launch the airborne invasion on 16 May 1941. The whole operation, code-named 'Merkur' (Operation Mercury) was in Luftwaffe hands and the Army General Staff was not consulted.

Student's newly formed Fliegerkorps XI, a specialised paratroop and air-landing organisation, comprised a large force of Ju 52/3m transport units and the Fliegerdivision 7, wherein were concentrated three parachute regiments (Fallschirmjäger Regiment: FJR) with subordinated flak and engineering battalions. For 'Merkur', Fliegerkorps XI mustered 493 Ju 52s and 80 DFS 230 gliders of KGzbV 1, 101, 102, 105, 106, the specially formed KGzbV 40 and 60, and Luftlandgeschwader 1. These units were deployed to Eleusis, Tatoi, Megara and Corinth, while the troops of Flieger-division 7 made their way by road, rail and air from Germany to the Athens area.

Air support for the operation was to be provided by Fliegerkorps VIII. Long-range bombers based at Eleusis, Salonica, Sofia and Plovdiv consisted primarily of I and III/KG 2 and III/KG 3, but were bolstered by the addition of LG 1, II/KG 26 and III/KG 30 under Fliegerkorps X, which flew operations from Foggia, Brindisi and other bases in Apulia. In all, 280 bombers were available. For close support, all three Gruppen of Obstlt. Oscar Dinort's StG 2 'Immelmann' Geschwader were distributed between Molaoi, Melos and the island of Scarpanto. These bases were also

shared by the Bf 109E-7s of Stab, II and III/JG 77 and I(Jagd)/LG 2, and lay within 100–120 miles of the northern coast of Crete. The remainder of the strike force was made up of 40 reconnaissance aircraft and the Bf 110s of II/ZG 26 based at Argos and Corinth.

The plan for 'Merkur' called for the seizure of the three main airfields on Crete – Maleme, Retimo and Heraklion – and the capture of Canea town and the important harbour at Suda Bay. These objectives were to be taken on the first day by airborne assault, followed by the landing of troops by Ju 52 and then by sea. It was proposed that 750 troops be landed from gliders, some 10,000 by parachute, 5,000 from relays of Ju 52s and 7,000 from small ships. German military intelligence, which had marred many an operation by its ineptitude, estimated that not more than 15,000 British and Commonwealth troops were stationed on Crete; the actual figure was double this, and did not include some 11,000 Greek troops. Arms and equipment, however, were in woefully short supply.

In the meantime, the Luftwaffe pursued its campaign of softening up the defences of Crete which suffered attacks by Ju 88s, He 111s and Dorniers, and considerable strafing by Messerschmitts. The original date set for 'Merkur' was postponed due to transportation difficulties. In the event, the attack opened at 07.00hrs on 20 May 1941, in moderate visibility but with heavy ground haze. Very heavy

attacks by bombers, dive-bombers and fighters were launched on British positions at Maleme and Canea, the objective being primarily gun positions and particularly AA batteries. Then there was a short lull before the first airborne attack materialised at 08.00 hours. In the course of the morning and afternoon the assaults were executed as follows:

Maleme Airfield:
Under the command of Gen. Meindl (Group West), 500 troops consisting of part I and elements of III/Sturm FJR landed from DFS 230 gliders at 08.00hrs in the vicinity of Maleme airfield. These consisted of three separate detachments: the task of Major Braun's detachment was to take the bridge over the Tavronitis river; Lt. Plessen's unit was to storm the AA batteries at the mouth of the Tavronitis and then make its way to the airfield, while Major Koch's men were to storm Hill 107 which dominated the airfield to the south. At the same time 1,860 paratroops, the remainder of Sturm FJR, dropped from Ju 52s along the Tavronitis and around the airfield.

Canea and Suda Bay:
Under the command of Oberst Heidrich (Group Centre: 1st Wave), the landings from gliders and by paratroops started shortly after 08.00 hours. Gliders carrying 270 men of the Sturm FJR landed on the Akrotiri peninsula, overlooking Suda Bay, and to the south-west of Canea to neutralise the AA batteries. At the same time paratroops of I and II/FJR 3 dropped astride the Canea-Alikianou road, while III/FJR 3 was dropped to the east of Galatas village. All assaults suffered heavily, and by the evening most units were pinned down in small defensive positions. This force consisted of 2,460 men.

Retimo Airfield:
This was the objective of Oberst Sturm (Group Centre: 2nd Wave) whose force of 1,380 paratroops dropped during the afternoon. Starting at 16.15hrs, the drop lasted almost an hour due the congestion of traffic at the Ju 52 bases. Fallschirmjäger Regt 2 was split into two groups under Hptm. Weidemann and Major Kroh after landing, but met stiff resistance from the defenders.

Heraklion Airfield:
Under the command of General Ringel (Group East), the first paratroops arrive at 14.30hrs, but on account of the havoc wrought to the timing by congestion, the last elements of Oberst Brauer's FJR 1 and a battalion of FJR 2 did not arrive until 19.30hrs. Casualties among the 2,360 men dropped were extremely heavy.

By the evening of 20 May, the position of the German airborne troops was critical. At first the very nature of their attack, its terrifying unfamiliarity, had thrown the defenders off balance. But within minutes of the first landings, successive drops by paratroops were met by a hail of smallarms fire. That night, however, the lynchpin of Maleme's defence – Hill 107 – was abandoned by the defenders owing to confusion and misunderstanding, and from 16.00hrs on the following day, German troops began to land by Ju 52s on the newly-captured airfield. Desperate fighting followed, particularly around Galatas and Canea, but by 27 May, the Germans were in control of Canea and Suda Bay. That day General Freyberg's

*Above: During the assault on Crete, the Ju 87B dive-bombers—a 4.Staffel aircraft being seen here—flew from Molae, Mycenae and Scarpanto with spectacular success*

*Right: The Junkers Ju 87B dive-bomber, the so-called ''Stuka'', seen here on a Greek airfield, played a major role in the Wehrmacht's campaign in Greece and the Balkans*

force was authorised by Wavell to commence a withdrawal to Sfakia in the south for eventual evacuation. A day later Heraklion fell, but 4,000 of its defenders had been evacuated by the Royal Navy. By 31 May, the whole of Crete was in German hands.

Brilliant in its conception and an airborne operation of a scale never before attempted, the German invasion of Crete nevertheless suffered the heaviest of casualties. With airborne forces of Fliegerdivision 7 bearing the heaviest losses, German casualties in Crete amounted to 1,990 men killed, 1,955 missing presumed killed and a further 327 drowned at sea. In addition, the wastage in aircraft, principally Ju 52s, amounted to 220 destroyed and 148 damaged in the course of the campaign. Due to the confused nature of the fighting, the Luftwaffe was unable to take any further part in support of the ground forces after the initial parachute landings. However, its bombers and in particular the Ju 87s of StG 2 achieved considerable success in actions against the Royal Navy, which remained heavily committed in the seas around Crete without having

any effective air cover.

After bombarding Scarpanto airfield, HMS *Juno* was attacked and sunk by StG 2 on the early morning of 21 May. On the following day, StG 2, II/KG 26 and KG 2 sank the cruisers HMS *Gloucester* and HMS *Fiji*, the destroyer HMS *Greyhound* and sustained hits on the battleships *Warspite* and *Valiant*. On 23 May, the 5th Destroyer Flotilla suffered the loss of HMS *Kelly* and HMS *Kashmir*, both being sunk by Dinort's StG 2 dive-bombers. Kampfgeschwader 2 damaged the battleship HMS *Barham* on 27 May, and on the next day high-level attacks and dive-bombing accounted for the destroyers *Hereward* and *Imperial* while damaging the cruisers *Dido* and *Orion*. The Navy's agony was not yet over, for on the final day of the Cretan evacuation, the Luftwaffe attacked and sank HMS *Calcutta* when a mere 100 miles off Alexandria.

# North Africa
# 1941

While the Germans pursued their campaigns in Greece and Crete, Axis fortunes in Cyrenaica and Libya had taken a turn for the better due to the intervention of Rommel's Afrika Korps. When Rommel arrived with the nucleus of his Korps at Tripoli on 12 February 1941, the British headlong advance had reached El Agheila, but its lines of supply and communications were stretched to the limit. Rommel was quick to profit from this weakness and by 24 March had re-taken El Agheila and launched an offensive of his own. Over the succeeding weeks, Wavell's forces were withdrawn in good order to Marsa Brega, Agedabia and Benghazi, and, by 15 April, Rommel had

encircled the Tobruk garrison.

Rommel achieved this advance with little air support. However, as early as March, Fliegerkorps X had detached some reconnaissance aircraft and a strike force consisting of 7. and 8./ZG 26 and I/StG 1 and II/StG 2 to bases in Libya. These units, joined on 20 April by the Bf 109E-7/Trop fighters of I/JG 27 and 7./JG 26 based at Gazala, were to increase the tempo of air operations in attacks on Tobruk and with close-support sorties in the line of the German advance. By 25 April, Rommel had taken Halfaya Pass and pushed the British back to Mersa Matruh on the borders of Egypt.

The arrival of 238 tanks in the Tiger convoy on 12 May, enabled the British 8th Army to launch a counter-offensive, Operation Brevity, three days later. The objective was the reparation of the British position on the Egyptian frontier, but after initial successes, including the re-capture of Halfaya Pass, the British withdrew to Sollum and Capuzzo. A counterattack by Rommel re-captured Halfaya Pass on 27 May. On 14 June, the 8th Army again went over to the offensive in an attempt to relieve the Tobruk garrison (Operation Battle-

axe), but its Crusaders and Valentine tanks were decimated by 88-mm anti-tank fire and, by 17 June, the British had withdrawn to the borders of Egypt to consolidate.

Despite its numerical inferiority, the Luftwaffe was able to gain a measure of air superiority over the battle areas. Hauptmann Eduard Neumann's I/JG 27 was an experienced and battle-tried unit, and the Messerschmitt Bf 109E-7 fighter was vastly superior to the Hurricane Is and Curtiss Tomahawk IIs of the RAF Desert Air Force, whose fighter units composed Nos. 2 SAAF, 3 RAAF, 4 SAAF, 33, 73, 94, 112, 213 and 250 Squadrons. I/JG 27 fought numerous dogfights with these units in the course of daily escort missions for the Stukagruppen and the Ju 88A-4/Trop bombers of III/LG 1. Several of its pilots, notably Oblt. Ludwig Franzisket, Homuth, Wolfgang Redlich, Lt. Stahlschmidt, Lt. Körner, Lt. von Lieres, and Ofw. Espenlaub, were to achieve

*Above: A Messerschmitt Bf 110C reconnaissance aircraft of 2.Staffel of Aufklärungsgruppe 14 operating in North Africa during the summer of 1941*

## The Components of Fliegerführer Afrika

| Unit | Types | Location | Strength (serviceable) |
|---|---|---|---|
| Reconnaissance | | | |
| 2.(H)/14 | Hs 126, Bf 110 | Ain El Gazala | 18 (13) |
| 2.(F)/123 | Ju 88D-5 | Derna | 7 (2) |
| Single-engined Fighters | | | |
| 7./JG 26 | Bf 109E-7/Trop | Ain El Gazala | 17 (13) |
| 1/JG 27 | Bf 109E-7/Trop | Ain El Gazala | 34 (25) |
| Twin-engined Fighters | | | |
| III/ZG 26 | Bf 110E-1 | Derna | 25 (22) |
| Bombers | | | |
| III/LG 1 | Ju 88A-4/Trop | Derna | 27 (11) |
| Dive-bombers | | | |
| I/StG 1 | Ju 87B-2 | Tmimi | 25 (21) |
| II/StG 2 | Ju 87B-2 | Tmimi | 27 (27) |

*Above: A Dornier Do 17Z-2 bomber of Kampfgeschwader 2 seen over the Aegean while participating in the spring of 1941 in the offensive against Greece*

*Left: A Messerschmitt Bf 109E-7/Trop of the 7.Staffel of Jagdgeschwader 26 'Schlageter' operating from Ain El Gazala in June 1941 under Fliegerführer Afrika*

numerous combat 'kills' over Libya during that summer. The most outstanding, however, was to be Oberfahnrich Hans-Joachim Marseille of 3. Staffel. He gained his 11th 'kill' over Acroma on 30 April, after a career that had been marred by instances of indiscipline and clashes with his superiors, but the campaigns in North Africa and the combat successes he was to achieve during them were to make him a legend in his own time.

Following the failure of 'Battleaxe', both opponents in North Africa regrouped to await supplies of men and material, and the situation on the ground remained relatively static. The Luftwaffe command in the Mediterranean, Fliegerkorps X, was compelled to devote most of its effort to the supply and support of the Axis forces in North Africa. By late June 1941, all units were withdrawn from Sicily and distributed to either the newly-constituted Fliegerführer Afrika (Gen. Maj. Fröhlich) or to bases in Greece and Crete. On the eve of Operation 'Barbarossa', Hitler's invasion of the Soviet Union, Fliegerkorps X had 240 combat aircraft based in Southern Greece, Crete and on Rhodes, while a further 150 were in North Africa. The components of Fl.Fü. Afrika on 21 June 1941 were as shown in the accompanying table.

# Chapter 6

# From Barbarossa to Stalingrad

## The Luftwaffe in Russia
# 1941-1943

Shortly after 03.00hrs on Sunday, 22 June 1941, 117 German infantry and armoured Divisions, supported by 14 Divisions of the 3rd and 4th Rumanian Army and the Hungarian Army Corps, rolled forward on a 1,200-mile (1930km) battle-front into the Soviet Union. The greatest clash of arms in the history of mankind had begun. The reasons behind Hitler's decision to attack the Soviet Union lie outside the scope of this chapter, but it is reasonable to assume that all Hitler's peacetime preparations and subsequent war aims were levelled at the eventual conquest of Soviet territory and the acquisition of the Lebensraum (Living space) so dear to Nazi ideology. As early as June 1940, after the fall of France, both OKH and OKL were informed of the plan, and although several senior staff officers voiced misgivings, even Hermann Göring was unable to sway Hitler. To many the prospect of committing Germany to a war on two fronts was appalling and in their view was inevitably to lead to the loss of the war, just as it had done in the Great War of 1914–18. The Führer believed that Britain was beaten, however, and that a massive campaign against the demoralised facade of bolshevist Russia would lead to its collapse in as little as six weeks. In the light of the Wehrmacht's brilliant and precipitate triumphs, few had had the temerity to oppose this view.

For the Luftwaffe, preparations for the war in the East had started as early as October 1940; the 'Ostbauprogramm' (Eastern Construction Programme) was already projected and from then on until the end of the year Luftwaffe works units and construction material were steadily moved into newly-occupied Polish territories. By early spring, the construction of airbases, the establishing of fuel dumps and the deployment of Flak units were well under way, but it was not until April and May 1941 that preparations to receive combat units were started. By mid-June, the Luft-

waffe had moved 2,770 front-line aircraft to the East from France, Germany and the Mediterranean, this force included 775 bombers, 310 Stukas, 830 Bf 109s, 90 Bf 110s and 765 reconnaissance and coastal types, out of a total Luftwaffe first-line inventory of 4,300 aircraft.

Four Luftflotten in all were engaged at the opening of the campaign against the Soviet Union, code-named 'Barbarossa', and these were disposed as the table shows.

In addition to the powerful reconnaissance arm, the long-range bomber units were KG 1, KG 3, KG 4, 6./KG 30, KG 51, KG 53, KG 54, KG 55, III/KG 76 and KGr 806. Now operating the Ju 88A-4 and He 111H-6, these units were mostly concentrated in FlKps II in support of the centre thrust. Zerstörergruppen and fighter-bombers consisted of I and II/ZG 26 and Schnelleskampfgeschwader 210.

While several Jagdgruppen were still using the Bf 109E-4 and E-7 fighter, the majority now based in the East were mounted on the new Messerschmitt Bf 109F-2. Powered by a Daimler-Benz DB 601N-1 engine but relatively lightly armed with two 7·9-mm MG 17 machine guns and a single 15-mm MG 151 cannon, this model added a dazzling high-altitude performance to the already sound attributes of the basic design. With the arrival of the Bf 109F-4 in August 1941, the Luftwaffe could count on a fighter that possessed an overwhelming degree of performance in comparison to anything that the Soviet Air Forces could put into the air. Indeed, if General Josef 'Beppo' Schmidt's Air Intelligence 1C department of the RLM could be believed, Soviet Air technology bordered on the mediaeval, and although quantitively the V-VS was the equal of the Luftwaffe, qualitively its equipment, aircraft and aircrew

## Luftflotte Disposition at the Opening of 'Barbarossa'

**Luftflotte 1**
Commanded by Generaloberst Alfred Keller, with Fliegerkorps I subordinated. Based in East Prussia for the support of Army Group North (XVI and XVII Army, IV Panzergruppe) under von Leeb, on northern flank operating along the Baltic coast, through Lithuania, Latvia and Estonia, with Leningrad as objective.
Jagdgruppen assigned to Fl.Kps I: Stab, I, II, III/JG 54.

**Luftflotte 2**
Commanded by Gen.Feldmarschall Albert Kesselring, with Fliegerkorps II and VIII subordinated. Based in the Suwalki-Lublin sector of Eastern Poland for the support of Army Group Centre (IV and IX Army, II and III Panzergruppe) under von Bock for the main thrust between the Pripet Marshes and the Baltic States to Smolensk.
Jagdgruppen assigned to FlKps II and VIII: Stab, II, III/JG 27; Stab, I,II,III,IV/JG 51; Stab, I,II,III/JG 53.

Stukagruppen under FlKps VIII (von Richthofen): Stab,II,III/StG 1; Stab, I, III/StG 2; Stab, I,II,III/StG 77; IV(Stuka)/LG 1.

**Luftflotte 4**
Commanded by Generaloberst Alois Löhr, with Fliegerkorps IV and V subordinated. Based on Lublin-Przemysl and Jassy (Rumania) sectors in support of Army Group South (VI, XI, XVII Army, I Panzergruppe, 3rd and 4th Rumanian Army) under von Rundstedt for main thrust into western Ukraine and to Kiev.
Jagdgruppen assigned to FlKps IV and V: Stab, I,II,III,IVErg/JG 3; Stab, I,III/JG 52; Stab, II,III/JG 77; I(Jagd)/LG 1.

**Luftflotte 5**
Commanded by Generaloberst Hans-Jurgen Stumpff. This was a small detachment engaged in northern Norway in support of General Dietl's offensive in the Petsamo sector in co-operation with the Finnish Army.

**Junkers Ju 87**
*A Junkers Ju 87G-1 on the Eastern Front, October 1942—probably of 10.(Pz)/SG2 (see also pages 205-207)*

*Above: Although replacement in the ranks of the Aufklärungsstaffeln (H) by the Fw 189 was imminent, the Henschel Hs 126B saw much service on the Eastern Front until spring 1942*

were of very low standard.

During the Spring of 1941, a German Industrial Commission brought back favourable reports concerning Russian productive capacity and in particular, the appearance of new aircraft designs based on sound technology, but all had been largely ignored by the Luftwaffe hierarchy. Schmidt's 1C department dismissed the report as an elaborate bluff and there was much evidence to support this view.

On the morning of 22 June 1941, the Luftwaffe unleashed its forces. Fliegerkorps II and VIII were heavily committed in support of Army Group Centre with Stuka and bomber attacks on Soviet troop concentrations and communications. Due to widespread aerial reconnaissance, principally by Oberst Rowehl's Aufklärungsgruppe Ob.d.L, during the preceding months, every forward V-VS airbase had been pinpointed. These now came under sustained attacks by Ju 88s and He 111s, while low-level strikes were made by Bf 110s and bomb-carrying Bf 109s. The few Soviet fighters that got airborne were mostly despatched with ease. On this day, for the loss of a mere 32

aircraft, the Luftwaffe destroyed 1,811 Soviet aircraft, all but 322 of these being destroyed on the ground.

After a month of scorching advance, Army Group North halted west of Lake Ilmen to regroup its exhausted forces. To add impetus to the drive on Leningrad, Richthofen's FlKps VIII transferred its 400 Stukas from Luftflotte 2 to Luftflotte 1 at the end of July. In the centre, von Bock's armies had encountered stiff Soviet resistance but, on 5 August, completed the encirclement and destruction of the Soviet forces in the Smolensk pocket. In the south, the drive to the Ukraine resulted in the fall of Tarnopol and Zhitomir, the encirclement of the Soviet armies in the Uman pocket, and the capture of Odessa and Nikoleav, and had reached Kiev by 19 September. By the end of that month, Leningrad was under siege, Army Group Centre was within 290 miles of Moscow, Kiev had fallen and the southern groups of the Wehrmacht had advanced to a 300-mile front from Konotop, through Zaporozhe to the Crimea. In the annihilation battles of Uman and Kiev,

665,000 Russian troops were either killed or captured – nearly one-third of the entire strength of the Soviet Armies at the outbreak of 'Barbarossa'.

Throughout these advances the Luftwaffe retained almost total air superiority, although the strong reaction by Il-2s and Pe-2s, covered by MiG-3 and Yak-1 fighters, during the Kiev fighting came as something of a surprise to the Germans. The scale of Soviet losses during the first months of Barbarossa can be shown by the claims of the Luftwaffe: totals of 1,570 and 1,360 Soviet aircraft were destroyed by combat units on the Central and Southern fronts respectively, from 22 June to 28 June, while Luftflotte 1 claimed 1,211 in the air and 487 on the ground from 22 June to 13 July 1941. These claims were undoubtedly exaggerated but

there was no gainsaying that Soviet losses were enormous.

The claims of the Jagdgruppen were colossal. On 30 June alone, they claimed to have destroyed in combat no fewer than 114 Soviet aircraft. Commanded by the brilliant Obstlt. Werner Mölders, JG 51 was the first Luftwaffe fighter unit to achieve 1,000 combat 'kills' in the war; JG 53, under Major Günther Fr. von Maltzahn, was next to achieve the one thousand mark, followed by Major Hannes Trautloft's JG 54, and Obstlt. Günther Lützow's Jagdgeschwader 3. These achievements came within six weeks of the start of the Soviet campaign. Several of these Jagdgeschwader were destined to see action on the Soviet Front throughout the remainder of the war, the principal being JG 51, JG 52 and JG 54, while JG 3, JG 53 and JG 77 all saw extensive action until redeployed to the Reich and the Mediterranean in 1943. Jagdgeschwader 5 also fought a gruelling campaign in northern Norway and on the Soviet-Finnish Front.

That the air fighting over the Soviet Union was 'easy' is a matter of considerable conjecture, particularly when the massive combat scores of individual German fighter pilots, operating in the Soviet Union, are compared with those fighting on the Channel Front, over Germany and in the Mediterranean theatre. There is no doubt, however, that, for the first two years, the German fighter pilots held complete hegemony in Soviet skies, and only after 1943 did they finally meet a foe who fought on relatively equal terms. Their combat claims, large though they were to be, possessed the same measure of credence as was attached to those of Luftwaffe fighter pilots fighting elsewhere. The possible reasons behind the successes of the 'Experten'* in the East are explained in the accompanying table.

Nowhere is the scale and nature of air combat over the Soviet Union revealed more clearly than by the career of Lt. Günther Scheel of 3./JG 54 'Grünherz'. Lt. Scheel joined his unit in the Spring of 1943, and before his death near Orel on 16 July 1943, he had shot down 71 Soviet aircraft in 70 sorties! The first pilot to score 150 victories was Major Gordon M. Gollob, Kommodore of JG 77, in August 1941; Hptm. Hermann Graf of 9./JG 52 was the first with 200 'kills', this score being attained on 2 October 1942; Hptm. Walter Nowotny, Kommandeur of I/JG 54, was first to achieve 250 'kills' on 14 October 1943, but the greatest eastern 'Expert' was Major Erich Hartmann of JG 52 who claimed 352 'kills' between 1943 and 1945.

*Luftwaffe equivalent of 'ace': Lit: Experts.

## Operation Typhoon and the First Russian Offensive

# 1941

Code-named Operation 'Taifun' (Typhoon), the German drive on Moscow started on 1 October 1941, but due to Hitler's pre-occupation with the campaigns in the Ukraine, this assault was too late in being launched. Prior to operations in support of II, IV and IX Armies, the III and IV Panzergruppen and the II Panzer Army of Army Group Centre, a force of 1,320 combat aircraft was concentrated in Luftflotte 2. This was achieved by transferring FlKps VIII along with the entire bomber and fighter force of FlKps I from Luftflotte 1 in the north, in addition to Jagdgruppen transferred from Luftflotte 4. As a result, the strength of Kesselring's Luftflotte 2 rose to almost 50 per cent of the total Luftwaffe strength in the Soviet Union. The close-support forces within Luftflotte 2 were assembled in the Konotop sector and SE of Smolensk, extending towards Roslavl.

The offensive started in ideal weather conditions and, by 7 October, the Panzergruppen had sealed off massive troop concentrations in the Bryansk and Vyasma

## The Reasons for the Success of Luftwaffe Aces in the East

a. The technical superiority of the Bf 109F, Bf 109G and later the Fw 190A over all Soviet aircraft, including those supplied by Lend Lease.

b. The closer proximity of German fighter airfields to the frontline, and therefore the area of operations.

c. The frequency with which combats took place: in good weather German fighter pilots flew as many as eight sorties in one day, possibly seeing combat on the majority of occasions.

d. The German fighter pilots were tactically superior to their Russian opponents, at least up to the Battle of Kursk (July 1943), and psychologically superior to the end of the war.

e. Widespread use of tactical air power by the Soviet Air Forces offered considerable opportunities for combat, generally with height and sun to the advantage of the German fighter pilot.

f. The average Soviet pilot was of a lower standard as compared to those of the RAF and USAAF. The élite "Guards" units were a different matter.

g. Air combat over the battle area usually enabled Luftwaffe "kills" to be quickly confirmed by the army.

*Above: Messerschmitt Bf 109G-2s of II and III Gruppen of Jagdgeschwader 54 on the Northern Sector of the Eastern Front in the summer of 1942*

pockets. On the following day, it rained heavily and in the days that followed roads and airfields were transformed into morasses. By 25 October the impetus of Typhoon had been halted by over-stretched lines of supply and increasing Russian resistance. For a time, the Wehrmacht consolidated its gains, but when the second phase was launched the drive became paralysed in 20° of frost and even stronger resistance. On 27 November, the Panzers were within 19 miles of the suburbs of Moscow, but this was destined to be the limit of the German advance.

For the first time, the Germans realised that their equipment was not capable of withstanding the sub-zero temperatures. By November, airfield conditions had become exceedingly difficult, alternating between mud in which aircraft became bogged and hard frozen surfaces that caused damage to undercarriages. Heating equipment for early morning starts was non-existent, forcing tired groundcrews to run-up engines during the night and even light open fires under the aircraft. On the other hand the Soviet Air Forces showed that they were largely unaffected by the weather, operating as they did from permanent airfields around Moscow.

After days of furious argument between Hitler and his generals in the field, the Moscow offensive was finally abandoned on 5 December, but on the following day the Russians went over to the offensive. To the Germans, it seemed impossible that the Soviet Army and Air Forces could be capable of sustaining a large-scale offensive: German military intelligence estimated that the Russian attrition in men had been 300,000 at Minsk, 650,000 in the Kiev pocket and another 663,000 in the Vyasma-Bryansk debacle, and added to this was the claim by the Luftwaffe of 15,877 Soviet aircraft destroyed from 'Barbarossa' to 20 November (although the Russians later put this number at 6,300). But over the next three months the Soviet Army managed to push the Germans back to Cholm and Smolensk in the centre, while in the south threatened the important centres at Kharkov and Kursk.

*Right: An eighth "kill" on the Soviet Front being painted on the tail of a Messerschmitt Bf 109F by its pilot during the initial phase of the conflict in the East*

The Luftwaffe was already weakened by the transfer, in December 1941, of Kesselring's Luftflotte 2 and Fliegerkorps II which had been redeployed to Sicily. This decision had been taken as early as October, when Axis fortunes in North Africa had worsened. Among the units that left the Soviet Union for the Mediterranean were II/JG 3, III/JG 27 and three Gruppen of JG 53 with Bf 109F-4s, and elements of KG 54, LG 1 and KGr 806 with Ju 88A-4s. While these did not amount to a serious weakening of the Russian Front, the transfer came at a time when several combat units were in Germany re-fitting. Thus, the Luftwaffe in the Soviet Union was reduced to some 1,700 aircraft. In the north, Luftflotte 1 and FlKps I remained, with FlKps VIII alone in the centre engaged on a 400-mile front. In December, Fliegerkorps V, which had been engaged in the assault on Kharkov in the Kursk-Stalino sector under Luftflotte 4, was withdrawn. Later it was to be used, in part at least, as Sonderstab Krim (Special Staff Crimea) in support of Fliegerkorps IV in neutralising the bastions in the Crimea in June 1942.

Throughout the first six months of the Russian campaign, the Luftwaffe had operated perforce in all weather conditions, averaging 1,200 sorties per day, with peaks at 2,000 during high-intensity periods, for its establishment of some 2,500 aircraft. Particularly in winter, the rate of attrition had been high due to operation from poor airfields and the extremely efficient Russian AA fire. The wastage in the Soviet Union caused a reversal in the expansion of Luftwaffe first-line strength, reducing it to about 4,300 aircraft by December 1941, and for the first time it became apparent that the production of aircraft was inadequate to sustain a long period of heavy air operations. It was primarily this, coupled with his failures

elsewhere, that forced the Generalluftzeugmeister, Ernst Udet, to take his life in November 1941. His place passed to the able Erhard Milch.

## The Road to Stalingrad
# 1942

The original Barbarossa plan to knock out the Soviet Union in a gigantic, three-pronged invasion had failed on account of the winter, over-stretched resources and the Soviet offensive, which finally petered out in March 1942. Hitler still believed, however, that the Wehrmacht could bring the war on the Eastern Front to a victorious conclusion. But with the summer now approaching, German strategy in the Soviet Union had undergone a complete change: the axis of all German efforts would now be in the South. The new offensives would thrust south-east to the Volga, to Stalingrad and down to the oil-rich foothills of the Caucasus mountains.

The great offensive in the South, with the prime objective being the Caucasus, was planned to develop in four stages.

1. The II Army and IV Panzer Army were to break through to Voronezh on the river Don; VI Army was to break out of the area west of Kharkov and smash the Soviet armies west of the Don in co-operation with IV Panzer Army which would turn southwards along the Don in order to encircle the enemy there.

2. After this move, IV Panzer and VI Army (Army Group B) would co-operate with I Panzer Army and XVII Army (Army Group A) to encircle Stalingrad, on the river Volga.

3. Army Group B was to push down the Don

in a south-easterly direction, while Army Group A thrust eastwards to the river Donets.

4. The fourth phase of the summer offensive was to be the southward push to the Caucasus.

As a preliminary to the plan, it was necessary to cover the southern flank by the German occupation of the Crimea. This task was given to Gen. Erich von Manstein's XI Army. By April 1942, the Germans had occupied the Kerch peninsula, thus effectively isolating the Crimean fortresses, and for the offensive which started on 8 May, Luftflotte 4 mustered some 600 aircraft. Tactical control of air operations in support of XI Army was in the hands of FlKps VIII (von Richthofen) which had been sent to the Crimea from the central front, its place in that sector being taken over by FlKps V – now re-named Luftwaffenkommando Ost. Fliegerkorps IV was still under Luftflotte 4, but was heavily committed against Soviet pressure in the Volchansk and Krasnograd sectors, to the north and south of Kharkov.

The attack on Sebastopol, the key to the Crimea, started on 2 June, with sorties by FlKps VIII averaging 600 per day, and rising to a peak of 700 sorties on 6 June, when the city finally fell. Some 2,500 tons of HE bombs were dropped – some being the heavy SC 1000 type (2,200-lb) – by StG 1, StG 2 and StG 77, by now re-equipped with the improved Junkers Ju 87D. With the fall of Sebastopol, FlKps VIII was rushed to the Kharkov area to support the German offensive aimed at relieving the pressure on Kharkov and encircling

the 6th, 9th and 57th Soviet armies in the Barenkovo salient, and by mid-June, Richthofen's command was in the Kursk sector in preparation for the massive German drive on Voronezh and the Don.

In the Mediterranean, the improved situation in the desert and the ending of FlKps II's second air assault on Malta, enabled the Luftwaffe to redeploy units from this theatre to the Soviet Union, along with refurbished units from Germany. By the start of the German summer offensive there were thus 2,750 combat aircraft on the Russian Front – a situation similar to that at the start of 'Barbarossa'. Of these, 1,500 were in the crucial Don-Caucasus sector of Luftflotte 4, 600 were in the centre under Luftwaffenkommando Ost, 375 under Luftflotte 1 were in the Leningrad sector and 200 under Luftflotte 5 were in the far north. On 20 June 1942, these units were composed of: JG 3, II/JG 5 and 7. and 8./JG 5, JG 51, JG 52, JG 54 and JG 77 with Bf 109F-4 fighters; twin-engined and ground-attack – ZG 1, ZG 2, I and II/Sch.G 1, 13(Zerst)/JG 5; Stukas – StG 1; III/StG 2 and StG 77; Long-range bombers – KG 1, III/LG 1, KG 3, I and II/KG 4, II/KG 26, KG 27, KG 30, KG 51, KG 53, II/KG 54, KG 55, I and III/KG 76, I/KG 77 and KG 100.

That the Wehrmacht would succeed in its second attempt to crush the Soviet Army was uppermost in the minds of German soldiers and commanders alike, but no amount of contingency planning and talk of 'stop-lines' could shroud the fact that this was also to be the last attempt. Another winter on the frozen Russian Steppes was unthinkable. When, on 28 June 1942, Army Groups A and B launched their all-out offensive, the Luftwaffe went over to the attack on the dreaded Blitzkrieg pattern. Supported by the Stukas and ground-attack aircraft of FlKps VIII, General

Hoth's IV Panzer Army fanned out over hundreds of miles of rolling corn towards Voronezh and the Don. Opposition was scant with the Soviet Army trading ground for time.

At first the offensive went brilliantly. In the south, Army Group A crossed the river Donets and then swung south to Rostov, took Proletarskaya on 29 July, Stavropol on 5 August and reached the blazing oilfields at Maikop four days later. Within a week, Kleist's I Panzer Army was in sight of Mount Elburz and was thrusting east towards the Caspian Sea.

In the northern sector the plan also went well. Hoth's IV Panzer and VI Army (Gen. Paulus) followed the line of the Don to the south-east smashing all resistance, but on 23 July the first flaw in the plan appeared. The twin-thrust was split as Hoth was ordered to drive south to assist Army Group A, while Paulus's VI Army swung east to reach Stalingrad on 10 August, where, for the first time, serious Soviet resistance was encountered. Paulus now had to wait another ten days before Hoth would arrive. Meanwhile, it became apparent through the large Soviet reinforcements flooding into the area that the Soviet Army intended to make Stalingrad the crucible of the battle.

The first German attempt to storm Stalingrad, on 19 August, failed, largely due to mishandling by Paulus, and even the massive air support by FlKps VIII, now operating from the Morozovsk airfield complex, failed to alter the situation on the ground. The air attacks of the night of 23/24 August by FlKps I, IV and VIII reduced the city to ruins by high-explosive and incendiary bombing. But the stubbornness of the Soviet defence of Stalingrad baffled the Wehrmacht – and as it became tied down in savage hand-to-hand fighting, it chose to regard it as a battle of attrition in which the Soviet Army would be bled white.

*Above: A Dornier Do 17Z-2 of III Gruppe of Kampfgeschwader 3 being serviced in the open on the Soviet Front in the winter of 1941-2. Note sledge-mounted portable heater*

But it was the Wehrmacht which failed to understand the tactical as well as strategic reality; it was the Wehrmacht which was to become exhausted and be forced to throw in all its reserves, while the Russians built up their strength, committing only enough troops to stop the Germans from breaking through. Stalingrad, and the series of battles that raged around it, became the cemetary of the German VI Army and turning point of the war.

On 23 November, the Soviet armies linked up and completely cut-off the VI Army fighting in Stalingrad. Frantic German counterattacks aimed at its relief failed. On 31 January 1943, Paulus surrendered with the southern group of his beleagured VI Army and, on 2 February, Gen. Schreck capitulated in the northern sector. At the cost of 120,000 men killed or missing and with the capture of 91,000 men, including 24 generals and 2,500 other officers, it was the most catastrophic defeat of German arms in the Second World War.

Throughout the six months of the Stalingrad battles, the Luftwaffe's strength in Russia had remained at the remarkably consistent figure of 2,450–2,500 aircraft. In the north, the Soviet offensives on Lake Ilmen and in the vicinity of Leningrad necessitated combat units being moved from the Stalingrad Front to bolster Luftflotte 1's strength to 550–600 aircraft, but with the worsening situation at Stalingrad in October, some 300 aircraft were hastily transferred back to this front from Luftflotte 1. At this time, Luftflotte 1 was also forced to release FlKps I which was sent south to the

Voronezh area and was re-named Luftwaffen-kommando Don.

Despite the crucial campaign in the Don Basin and the Kuban district of Russia, the Luftwaffe was once more forced to relinquish vital combat units to the Mediterranean. As early as September 1942, I/JG 53 'Pik-As', III/ZG 1 'Wespen' and 6./KG 26 were transferred from the Eastern Front to Luftflotte 2 in Sicily. The Axis reverse at El Alamein, followed on 8 November by the Allied landings in French North Africa, served to accelerate the out-flow from the East. By late December the following units had been posted: Stab, II and III/JG 77 and II/JG 51 'Mölders' with Bf 109s, and III/KG 4, II and III/KG 26, Stab and III/KG 30, II/KG 54 Stab, I, II, III/KG 76 and Stab KG 100 with Ju 88A-4s and He 111H-6s. The Ju 52 transport units, I/KGzbV 1 and KGzbV 102, were also sent, but had returned by early December. The total transfers from the Soviet Union and Northern Norway totalled almost 400 combat aircraft, bringing down the Luftwaffe's strength in Russia to about 2,000 aircraft, reducing the strike forces of FlKps I and VIII in the Don sector to 600–750 aircraft (the normal establishment was over 1,000), and weakening the complement of German single-engined fighters to a mere 375 over the entire Soviet Front.

The Jagdgruppen had received the first Bf 109Gs in August 1942. That superlative fighter, the Focke-Wulf Fw 190A, had first appeared in Soviet skies after I/JG 51's conversion at Jesau in mid-August, and during the autumn both III and IV/JG 51 'Mölders' converted. A fourth Gruppe, I/JG 54 'Grünherz', was operating over the Leningrad front by February 1943. But this injection of Germany's finest fighters to the Soviet Front coincided with the influx of new Soviet aircraft types. The Lavochkin La-5 was powered by the Shevtsov M-82 radial engine developing 1,570bhp at 6,656ft (2050m) and was capable of matching the Bf 109Gs and Fw 190s when flown by a competent pilot. Its introduction in late-1942 was accompanied by the début of the Yak-9. The La-5 and Yak-9 first saw large-scale action against German fighters over Stalingrad in November.

As the situation grew more critical in Stalingrad, the Luftwaffe was forced to divert a considerable portion of its strength to the supply of the VI Army, and also to support the XI Army in the Kuban. At the turn of the year, the Ju 52 units were joined in their task by He 111 bombers of KG 27, KG 55 and I/KG 100; these were augmented in January by He 177s under I(Erganzungsgruppe)/KG 50 and the Fw 200C-4s of 1. and 3./KG 40 – the latter operating under a specially formed unit known as KGzbV 200, first based at Stalino and later Zaporozhe. When the main airfield at Pitomnik was captured by Soviet forces on 16 January, supplies could no longer be landed and had to be dropped by parachute. The entire area was ringed by Soviet AA batteries which caused the Luftwaffe severe losses and, despite the gallantry of the transport pilots, the situation soon became hopeless.

The campaign in the Soviet Union leading to the German defeat at Stalingrad demonstrated that the Luftwaffe still adhered to the battle tactics of Blitzkrieg in close support of ground forces and armour. These tactics, so brilliantly successful in Poland, France and the Balkans, had demonstrably failed to achieve the desired results in the great battles of

attrition in 1942. This was due not only to the immense length of the Soviet Front, which meant that every concentration for an impending offensive left the German flanks exposed, but also to the depth of the battlefield. The Soviet Army exploited these circumstances to the full by withdrawals which extended the German lines of communication until the combat units of the Luftwaffe, drawn far forward away from their supply bases, were weakened and hampered by supply and maintenance difficulties. Thus, the peculiar warfare conditions in the Soviet Union never enabled the carefully-conceived and well-tried Luftwaffe air strategy of combining the heaviest possible close-support with massive bombing attacks on factories and rear supply areas to result in final victory in spite of great initial successes.

# Chapter 7

# The Struggle in the Mediterranean

The operational strength of General Hoffman von Waldau's Fliegerführer Afrika stood at 190 aircraft at the start of the long-awaited British counteroffensive, Operation Crusader, on 18 November 1941. Of these, some 70 were Ju 87B-2/Trop dive-bombers of Stab StG 3, I/StG 1 and II/StG 2, which represented the main striking force pitted against Auchinleck's tank squadrons. The remainder of Fl.Fü. Afrika comprised Stab, I and II/JG 27 with approximately 50 Bf 109E-7 and F-4/Trop fighters, a tactical reconnaissance unit, 2.(H)/14, a Staffel of long-range Bf 110D-3s of 8./ZG 26 and III/LG 1 whose Junkers 88A-4/Trop bombers suffered a high rate of unserviceability on account of the spartan desert conditions. However, von Waldau's small force was bolstered by some 320 aircraft of the Regia Aeronautica, of which half were single-engined Macchi C.200s and C.202s.

On 19 November, the 8th Army, bypassing Sollum and Halfaya Pass, commenced an all-out drive towards Tobruk but was checked by Rommel at Sidi Rezegh and Bir El Gubi. The subsequent tank and artillery battles of Sidi Rezegh were followed, on 7 December, by the relief of the garrison in Tobruk and, by 16 December, Rommel was forced to retire from Gazala to the west. Auchinleck triumphed and followed hard on the heels of the Afrika Korps

and, by 6 January 1942, Rommel had retreated to the El Agheila defensive lines from which he had launched his first attack one year previously.

Throughout the short campaign, the Luftwaffe averaged 100 sorties per day, with peaks of 200, this low-key effort being due primarily to a critical fuel shortage brought about by shipping losses at the hands of the RAF and Royal Navy strike forces based on Malta. In December 1941, Kesselring's Luftflotte 2 arrived in Sicily with Fliegerkorps II from the Central Russian Front, but the addition of some 400 combat aircraft in the Mediterranean theatre could not help Rommel's position in the desert at this time, due to the shortage of airfields in the Gulf of Sirte. The single-engined fighter units in Africa were stiffened by the addition of III/JG 27 (Hptm. Erhard Braune) and III/JG 53 (Hptm. Franz Götz), but the latter returned to Sicily on 26 December.

By January 1942, Luftflotte 2 was fully established at its Headquarters at Taormina, Sicily, with Generalfeldmarschall Albert Kesselring exercising full command over Fliegerkorps II (Sicily), Fliegerkorps X (Greece and Crete) and Fliegerführer Afrika. With almost 650 combat aircraft at his disposal, his task was to finally dispose of Malta and thus secure Axis sea communications in the

Mediterranean as a whole and to North Africa in particular. With the failure to secure a quick victory in the Soviet Union, German attention was now turned to Southern Russia and North Africa from whence final victory could be achieved by the conquest of the Middle East oilfields from the Caucasus in the north and from Suez in the south.

While Kesselring made preparations for the assault on Malta, Rommel's counteroffensive from El Agheila started on 19 January 1942. Once again it was the problem of supply over the long desert routes that accorded either success or failure. The British lines of supply were stretched whereas Rommel had received fuel, men and material with the arrival of a large convoy in Tripoli and by air transport. The forces of Fliegerführer Afrika at the time of Rommel's offensive were: 2.(H)/14, three Gruppen of JG 27 with the Bf 109F-4/Trop, Jabostaffel/JG 53 with Bf 109E-7/Bs, 7./ZG 26 with Bf 110D-3s, Geschwaderstab StG 3 (Major Walter Sigel), I and II/StG 3 and Erg.Staffel StG 1. The serviceability status of these units was consistently low and, on 17 January, JG 27 mustered only 24 aircraft while, out of a strength of 69 Ju 87B-2/Trop dive-bombers, only 54 were fit for action. In the event, this force played little part in Rommel's counter-offensive, save for about 250 sorties on 21 and 22 January. Due to the poor condition of forward airfields, this sortie rate fell to about half during the proceeding weeks, and Rommel's drive to Benghazi and thence Gazala was all the more remarkable in view of the virtual absence of Luftwaffe support. In the ensuing three months, until May 1942, the situation in the desert remained static. Stukageschwader 3 was committed to harassing Tobruk, while JG 27 continued to profit from the superiority of the Bf 109F-4 over the Hurricanes, Kittyhawks and Tomahawks of the Desert Air Force.

In the Mediterranean, all eyes were turned upon Malta. Since April 1941, when the bulk

## The Components of Fliegerkorps II

| Unit | Type | Location | Strength (serviceable) | |
|---|---|---|---|---|
| Stab JG 53 | Bf 109F-4 | Comiso | 6 | (6) |
| I/JG 53 | Bf 109F-4 | Comiso | 34 | (34) |
| II/JG 53 | Bf 109F-4 | Comiso | 37 | (25) |
| I/NJG 2 | Ju 88C-4 | Catania | 12 | (8) |
| 4./NJG 2 | Ju 88C-4 | Catania | 5 | (3) |
| KGr 606 | Ju 88A-4 | Catania | 20 | (10) |
| KGr 806 | Ju 88A-4 | Catania | 17 | (6) One Staffel |
| Stab KG 54 | Ju 88A-4 | Gerbini | 1 | (1) |
| I/KG 54 | Ju 88A-4 | Gerbini | 12 | (7) One Staffel |
| II/KG 77 | Ju 88A-4 | Catania | 20 | (12) |
| III/KG 77 | Ju 88A-4 | Catania | 16 | (12) One Staffel |

## Henschel Hs126
An Henschel Hs 126A-1 of 2.(H)/14, North Africa, July 1941 (see also page 199)

of Fliegerkorps X retired from Sicily, RAF aircraft based on Malta had been able to inflict considerable damage on the ports through which passed the supply of materials for Rommel's Afrika Korps, and Maltese-based reconnaissance aircraft had been able to observe the traffic pattern to North Africa, enabling the RAF and the Royal Navy to reap

valuable rewards from their attacks. To avoid the Malta-based aircraft, Axis convoys had to make large detours almost doubling the sea distance from Messina to Tripoli.

In January 1942, the fighter defence of Malta consisted of three Hurricane squadrons – Nos 126, 185 and 249 – based at Hal Far and Takali, while the Navy provided a flight of Fulmar Is

*Above: Junkers Ju 88A-4s of III Gruppe of Lehrgeschwader 1 operating over the Mediterranean during 1942*

under No 201 Group, Royal Air Force. On 17 January, the forces of Fliegerkorps II earmarked for operations against Malta were composed as the accompanying table shows.

*Above: An Henschel Hs 129B-1 of 8.Staffel of Schlachtgeschwader 2 photographed in the vicinity of Tripoli late 1942*

*Right: Personnel of III Gruppe of Zerstörergeschwader 76 relaxing in front of a Messerschmitt Bf 110C*

The Luftwaffe air offensive on Malta was resumed in mid-January 1942 on a relatively modest scale, with some 65 sorties being flown every day, of which 40–50 sorties were flown by the Ju 88s. The pace continued at this level, amounting to little more than harassing attacks until the middle of March. On 7 March, fifteen Spitfire VCs were flown off HMS *Eagle* and arrived safely due to the efforts of the Hurricanes which successfully engaged a reception committee provided by 44 Messerschmitts of Major Günther Fr. von Maltzahn's JG 53. The Spitfires first saw action on 10 March, but further operations were halted by a period of bad weather.

The Luftwaffe launched a major assault on 21 March, and was to maintain a level of effort for the rest of the month and throughout the following April that was without parallel. At this time Fliegerkorps II was strengthened by 1. and 2.(F)/122 deployed at Gerbini and Trapani, II/JG 3 to San Pietro, III/JG 53 to Gela, 8. and 9./ZG 26 to Trapani, II/LG 1 to Catania and III/Stukageschwader 3 to San Pietro.

On 23 March, a determined effort was made to destroy the Vian convoy from Alexandria. The *Breconshire* was hit by Bf 109F-4/Bs of Jabostaffel/JG 3 at 09.20hrs when she lay off Valetta, the *Clan Campbell* was sunk south of Malta at 10.40hrs, and the remainder of the convoy came under heavy attack. This marked the start of the Luftwaffe's all-out attack on shipping and supplies, and from 24 March to 12 April, Fliegerkorps II flew 2,159 bomber sorties, sinking ships, devastating docks and installations, blocking quays and roadways, and cutting off power, water and communications.

During April 1942, 6,728 tons of bombs were dropped by the Luftwaffe on Malta. Valetta absorbed 3,156 tons, with the remainder aimed at the airfields of Takali, Luqa and Hal Far, the Luftwaffe attacking in force and with

persistant regularity on every day but three when inclement weather prevailed. The crews of the Ju 88s flew three to four sorties a day for four days a week against spirited but totally inadequate RAF opposition. On 20 April, the USS *Wasp* flew off 45 Spitfire VCs manned by pilots of Nos. 601 and 603 Squadrons. As they completed the 600-mile flight to Malta, they were met by a few Hurricanes and Spitfires, but the Bf 109s reported their arrival and

## The Disposition of Luftflotte 2

### 10 May 1942
### LUFTFLOTTE 2
Generalfeldmarschall Albert Kesselring

**Fliegerkorps II**

| Unit | Types | Location | Strength (serviceable) | |
|---|---|---|---|---|
| 1.(F)/122 | Bf 109F-5, Ju 88D-5 | Catania | 14 (8) | |
| 2.(F)/122 | Ju 88D-5 | Trapani | 12 (6) Luftflotte 2 | |
| Stab JG 53 | Bf 109F-4 | Comiso | 5 (3) | |
| II/JG 53 | Bf 109F-4 | Comiso | 42 (27) | |
| III/JG 53 | Bf 109F-4 | Comiso | 39 (25) | |
| I/NJG 2 | Ju 88C-6 | Catania | 12 (8) | |
| Stab III/ZG 26 | Bf 110D-3 | Trapani | 16 (9) with 8./ZG 26 | |
| 10./ZG 26 | Do 17Z-10 | Trapani | 8 (6) | |
| KGr 606 | Ju 88A-4 | Catania | 23 (16) | |
| KGr 806 | Ju 88A-4 | Catania | 28 (10) | |
| Stab KG 54 | Ju 88A-4 | Gerbini | 3 (3) | |
| I/KG 54 | Ju 88A-4 | Comiso | 23 (13) | |
| III/StG 3 | Ju 87D-1 | San Pietro | 23 (10) | |

**Fliegerkorps X**

| Unit | Types | Location | Strength (serviceable) |
|---|---|---|---|
| 2.(F)/123 | Ju 88D-5 | Kastelli | 13 (6) |
| Stab LG 1 | Ju 88A-14 | Eleusis | 1 (1) |
| I/LG 1 | Ju 88A-4 | Heraklion | 29 (16) |
| II/LG 1 | Ju 88A-4 | Eleusis | 31 (15) |
| II/KG 100 | He 111H-16 | Kalamaki | 25 (12) |
| 2./SAGr 125 | Ar 196A-3 | Skaramanka | 8 (4) |
| Gr.Stab 125 | Bv 138C-1 | Skaramanka | 1 (1) |
| 1./SAGr 126 | He 60c, Fokker T.VIII | Skaramanka | 15 (11) |
| 2./SAGr 126 | Ar 196A-3, He 60c | Kavalla | 13 (4) |
| 3./SAGr 126 | Ar 196A-3 | Skaramanka | 16 (10) |

**Fliegerführer Afrika**

| Unit | Types | Location | Strength (serviceable) | |
|---|---|---|---|---|
| 4.(H)/12 | Bf 109, Bf 110, Hs 126 | Martuba | 17 (7) Koluft.Pz.Armee | |
| 1.(F)/121 | Ju 88D-5, Bf 109F-5 | Derna | 10 (9) | |
| Stab JG 27 | Bf 109F-4/Trop | Martuba | 5 (3) | |
| I/JG 27 | Bf 109F-4/Trop | Martuba | 30 (21) | |
| II/JG 27 | Bf 109F-4/Trop | Martuba | 33 (27) | |
| III/JG 27 | Bf 109F-4/Trop | Martuba | 29 (15) | |
| Jabo JG 27 | Bf 109F-4/B | Martuba | 8 (8) | |
| 2./NJG 2 | Ju 88C-6 | Derna | 9 (5) | |
| 7./ZG 26 | Bf 110D-3 | Derna | 12 (5) | |
| 9./ZG 26 | Bf 110D-3 | Maleme | 11 (4) Based in Crete | |
| 12./LG 1 | Ju 88A-4/Trop | Berca | 11 (11) | |
| Stab StG 3 | Ju 87D-1/Trop | Derna-South | 2 (0) | |
| I/StG 3 | Ju 87D-1/Trop | Derna-South | 41 (28) | |

Total: 636 on strength/374 serviceable.

after 325 sorties by Ju 88s and Ju 87s against their bases half of the newly-delivered Spitfires had been destroyed.

As April drew to a close, the situation on Malta grew desperate; the RAF was virtually grounded, while the anti-aircraft batteries were critically short of ammunition. Throughout the month Nos. 126, 185 and 249 squadrons, along with the amalgamated units at Luqa and Takali, claimed over 200 enemy aircraft destroyed, but in relation, their own losses were far more serious: 23 Spitfires and 18 Hurricanes destroyed and 87 more in various states of damage.

The next reinforcement of Malta's beleaguered fighter force came on 9 May, when the USS *Wasp* and HMS *Eagle* flew off 64 more Spitfires which landed at Takali and Luqa at 10.30hrs. The Luftwaffe mounted some nine separate raids during that day in attempts to destroy these aircraft. At 05.25hrs on the following morning, HMS *Welshman* arrived in Grand Harbour, Valetta, with supplies of fuel and ammunition, and when the Luftwaffe struck at 10.20hrs with 20 Ju 87D-1s of III/StG 3 and 10 Ju 88A-4s of KGr 806, it was met by the largest fighter force ever mounted by the RAF over Malta. Thirty-seven Spitfires and 13 Hurricanes were scrambled, and in combats over the harbour these shot down four of III/StG 3's Stukas. In addition to these casualties, Fliegerkorps II lost four Ju 88A-4s and three Bf 109F-4s in the course of the day's fighting.

During May 1942, RAF fighters claimed 122 Axis aircraft destroyed, while the AA shot down a further 15; the cost was 23 Spitfires and two Hurricanes. In mid-May, Luftflotte 2's offensive on Malta was called off due to the now-active campaigns in North Africa, and to the fact that campaigns were to be resumed in the Soviet Union in the near future, the aircraft engaged against Malta now being needed elsewhere. It was becoming increasingly apparent that the Luftwaffe was becoming over-taxed and that major operations in one theatre could now only be mounted at the expense of another. The operations against Malta were not without their effect on the Luftwaffe. Some 300–400 aircraft had been kept heavily engaged from January to May, when they might have been conserved for efforts elsewhere. Moreover, the wastage rate had been high; about 250–300 German aircraft having been lost during April, with some 500 aircraft lost or severely damaged during the entire period.

Malta's ordeal was by no means over, however, and the island was kept in a state of semi-starvation throughout the summer, when desperate attempts were made to send convoys to the island from Gibraltar and Alexandria. The convoys 'Harpoon' and 'Vigorous' suffered near annihilation at the hands of Fliegerkorps II and X and the torpedo-bombers of the Regia Aeronautica's Aerosiluranti on 14 June. The great 'Pedestal' convoy sailed from Gibraltar bound for Malta on 10 August 1942, and on that day, II Fliegerkorps received reinforcements: 20 Ju 88A-4s came in from Fliegerkorps X in Crete, the Torpedo School at Grosseto supplied 10 He 111H-6s and Ju 88A-17s, and a Staffel of StG 3, resting in Sicily, was rapidly made ready. The Luftwaffe and the Regia Aeronautica mustered some 700 aircraft to attack the 'Pedestal' convoy and major actions were subsequently fought between 10–15 August 1942. The losses to both

*Above: A Messerschmitt Bf 110D of 8.Staffel of Zerstörergeschwader 26 flying over the rugged Sicilian terrain in 1942 to rendezvous with a bomber force attacking Malta*

*Above right: A Messerschmitt Bf 109E-4/ Trop fighter of I Gruppe of Jagdgeschwader 27 merging with the North African desert over which it is here seen flying during the summer of 1941*

*A Messerschmitt Bf 110C-4 of the III Gruppe of Zerstörergeschwader 76 taking-off on a mission in the Western Desert during the winter of 1941-42*

sides were appalling, but a few ships, including the vital tanker *Ohio*, managed to reach Malta with enough supplies and fuel to sustain the island until December.

In North Africa, the lull in fighting, which had enabled the British and Rommel's Afrika Korps to renew their resources, came to an end on 26 May 1942. It was Rommel who struck first and opened an offensive from Gazala which was to carry the Afrika Korps into the depths of Egypt – to El Alamein. At first it seemed as if Rommel had miscalculated; that shortages of fuel and water would destroy the Afrika Korps. However, Rommel was saved by his willingness to improvise and by the slow reaction of the British commanders. All German efforts were now concentrated upon the land battle in Libya, with a Blitzkrieg through the Nile Valley and on to Suez. In

*Above: A Focke-Wulf Fw 190F close-support fighter of I Gruppe of Schlachtgeschwader 4 operating in Central Italy in the summer of 1943*

*Left: 'Tante Ju', the ubiquitous Ju 52/3m workhorse of the Luftwaffe's transport component performed yeoman service throughout WW II and is seen here on a Sicilian airfield*

support of Generaloberst Erwin Rommel's Panzerarmee were 312 Luftwaffe and 392 Regia Aeronautica combat aircraft and transports. At the start of the offensive, III/JG 53 and Jabostaffel/JG 53 with 42 Bf 109F-4s joined Neumann's JG 27, while Major Sigel's Stukageschwader 3 was brought to full strength by the arrival of II and III/StG 3. Additional support was provided by the Ju 88s based on Crete and Sicily. The strength of the Desert Air Force opposing the Germans consisted of 320 aircraft, of which about 190 were combat ready.

Such was the diminishing importance of Malta that Kesselring transferred his headquarters to Africa from Taormina at the start of Rommel's offensive. The immediate aim was the seizure of Tobruk by a swift thrust through the Gazala-Bir Hacheim line. In this Rommel failed initially, becoming entangled in the fierce fighting around Bir Hacheim and the 'Knightsbridge' sector. During the first week of the offensive, Luftwaffe air effort was to be the greatest achieved throughout the whole North African campaign – no less than 300–350 sorties per day with the Stukagruppen contributing 100 of these and the fighters flying 150–200 sorties per day, representing 2·5 sorties per serviceable aircraft. Although this effort

fell by about a third during the second week, the third week saw a new peak of intensity led by the assault on Bir Hacheim, which managed to hold out for nine days. With JG 27 and III/JG 53 flying escort, the effort of the Stukagruppen was reinforced by 30–40 daily sorties by the Ju 88s of LG 1 based on Crete. More than 1,400 bomber and dive-bomber sorties were flown against Bir Hacheim until its fall on 11 June.

Ten days later Tobruk fell. This was a terrific blow to Allied morale and as Lt.Gen. Ritchie's 8th Army retired to its defensive positions at El Alamein, for Rommel the road to Egypt and Suez now seemed open. JG 27 and III/JG 53 were constantly in the air, escorting Ju 88s and Ju 87s, and flying Frei Jagd missions over the British lines. Oberleutnant Hans-Joachim Marseille, Staffelkapitän of 3./JG 27, had reached the zenith of a brilliant combat career in North Africa. Since his arrival in Libya, he had scored consistently: his 50th 'kill' had been achieved on 22 February 1942, his 75th on 6 June, and on 18 June, Marseille was awarded the Schwertern (Swords) to the Ritterkreuz for his 101st kill! His rise to fame had been meteoric and he was hailed as 'the unrivalled virtuoso of German fighter pilots'. His greatest achievement came on 1 September when he shot down 17 enemy aircraft in the Imayid sector during Rommel's offensive at Alam Halfa. He received the Brillanten (Diamonds) – as the fourth fighter pilot after Mölders, Galland and Gordon Gollob – on the following day. On 30 September, however, while returning from a Stuka-escort, the engine of his Bf 109G-2 caught fire. Marseille jettisoned the canopy, half-rolled his machine and baled out, but, knocked unconscious by the tailplane, he never pulled the rip-cord of his parachute and was killed. His final score was 158 kills – all but 7 were shot down in

North Africa – in the course of 382 operational flights.

Having failed to make any further progress after the battles of Alam Halfa in September, Rommel was forced hereafter to hold on to his positions west of El Alamein and endeavour to consolidate his forces in the face of growing strangulation imposed by interference with his lines of sea supply. Fuel, little as it was, was passed to the XV and XXI Panzer Divisions at the expense of the Luftwaffe. Thus, although on the eve of the British offensive at El Alamein, the operational strength of the Luftwaffe amounted to only 290 aircraft, it being impossible for logistic reasons to maintain a stronger force in Africa at this crucial time.

When the El Alamein battle started, on 24 October, both I/JG 27 and II/StG 3 had been posted back to Sicily for a renewed bombing assault against Malta. The sole addition to Fliegerführer Afrika prior to El Alamein comprised I/Sch.G 2 (ex-III/ZG 1), based at Bir El Abd with 35 ground-attack Bf 109F-4/Bs.

On the eve of Montgomery's great counter-offensive the strength of the Allied air forces had been boosted to some 750 aircraft, of which 530 were combat ready, and this numerical superiority over the limited and fuel-starved Luftwaffe proved decisive. The constant RAF and US air attacks on the main German airbases at Fuka, Qotaifiya, Daba, Qasaba and Sidi Haneish seriously impaired the effectiveness of the Luftwaffe, and during the first week of the battle combat operations by JG 27 and StG 3 diminished to almost nothing. Following a week of bitter and confused fighting, Rommel's Panzerarmee retired to the Fuka positions on 2 November, and two days later was forced into a fighting retreat along the Via Balbia to the West.

By 15 November, Fliegerführer Afrika was operating from airfields in the Benghazi area, its Stuka strength having fallen to about 30 Ju 87D-3s, while no more than 80–100 Bf 109G-1/Trop and G-2 fighters of Stab, I and III/JG 77 and II/JG 27 remained, and these were further reduced to about 60 with the retreat to Arco and Nofilia, in the Gulf of Sirte. These forces moreover, were in no position to continue operations in the absence of appreciable supplies and ground organisation, and in the prevailing confusion and demoralisation of retreat. Such was the situation of the remnants of Fliegerführer Afrika's forces at the moment when the Allies landed in French North Africa on 8 November 1942.

## The Allied Landings to the German Defeat in Tunisia 8th November–12th May

# 1942–1943

Secure in the knowledge that the Allies would open a second front in the Mediterranean in the Autumn of 1942, German reinforcements started to flow into that theatre as early as October, but there still remained the question of where the Allied landings would be made. Prior to the Allied landings at Oran, Algiers and Casablanca on 8 November, Kesselring's Luftflotte 2 received the following combat units from the Soviet Union, France and the Eastern Mediterranean. From 31 August to 31 October: 11./JG 2, 11./JG 26, II/JG 2, I/JG 53, Stab and III/JG 77, with Fw 190A-4s equipping Hptm. Adolf Dickfeld's II/JG 2 'Richthofen' and the rest with Bf 109Gs; II and III/ZG 1 with Bf 110G-2s and a staffel of Me 210A-1s; and 1. and 2./KG 60, III/KG 30, 9./KG 40, II/KG 54, II/KG 6, II and III/KG 26, III/KG 4 and Stab/KG 100.

During the four weeks following the landings, strong Luftwaffe reinforcements con-

tinued to flow into Luftflotte 2, and by 12 December, the Mediterranean theatre contained a peak strength of 1,220 combat aircraft, of which some 850 were based in Sicily, Sardinia and Tunisia. Of particular importance was the denuding of a large force of Ju 88A-17 and He 111H-6 torpedo-bombers from Luftflotte 5, in Norway, that had been committed against the vital PQ convoys to northern Russia. And the transfer of 120 Ju 88s and He 111s, along with a similar number of Bf 109Gs, from the Southern and Central Fronts in the Soviet Union coincided with the Soviet Army's new offensive on the Don.

Notwithstanding the surprise caused by the landings, German reactions to the threat were prompt. By 9 November, a number of Bf 109G and Stuka units were sent to Bizerta, Tunis-El Aounia and Souk El Arba in Tunisia from Sicily and Sardinia. These moves were accompanied by the air-lifting of supplies by Ju 52s, Me 323s and Go 242s, and by the end of the second week the Luftwaffe had occupied the airfields at Gabes and Dejedeida. A new command, Fliegerführer Tunisien, under Generalmajor Harlinghausen, was formed. On 10 January 1943, this command comprised the following units – 2.(H)/14, II/JG 2, Stab, I and II/JG 53, III/SKG 10 and one staffel of II/StG 3. Due to the shortage of suitable airfields, Luftflotte 2 did not commit any Kampfgruppen to Tunisia, and Harlinghausen's command was destined to be essentially a close-support and tactical organisation. Fliegerführer Tunisien was soon to be in the remarkable position of being able to maintain an equality with numerically superior Allied air forces, owing to the even greater problems of forward supply with which the Allies were faced.

When Montgomery re-opened his offensive against Rommel's defensive position at Beurat, in Tripolitania, on 15 January, the Luftwaffe units in that sector were subordinated to Oberbefehlshaber Süd, and consisted of 4.(H)/12, 1.(F)/121, Major Jochen Müncheberg's JG 77 'Herzas', I Gruppe plus 4./Sch.G 2 and III/StG 3. In addition to the Fl.Fü Tunisien, a Kommando Roth at Gabes consisted of elements of 2.(H)/14, II/JG 51 'Mölders' and a staffel of II/StG 3.

Tripoli fell on 23 January, and the 8th Army pushed forward to Mareth on the Tunisian border, while from the West, the Germans were threatened by the Allied offensive into Tunisia. On 14 February, the Germans launched a counteroffensive against the two Allied thrusts that threatened the armies of Rommel and von Arnim. On this day, the Ju 87s, Hs 129B-2s, Fw 190s and Bf 109Gs of Fliegerführer Tunisien flew 360–375 sorties in support of the successful German thrust to Feriana and Sbeitla, reducing this effort to 250 sorties per day until bad weather intervened. The strength of Fl.Fü Tunisien remained around 300 first-line aircraft throughout this campaign, and this number was maintained during the subsequent offensive by the 8th Army from Mareth on 19 March 1943. The II/JG 2 achieved considerable success in Tunisia; Oblt. Kurt Bühligen claimed 40 'kills' during the campaign, while Oblt. Erich Rudorffer shot down 26 Allied aircraft including eight 'kills' on 9 February and seven on 15 February. However, attrition among experienced fighter pilots was high. For example, Major Joachim Müncheberg of JG 77 was killed on his 500th operational flight in combat with Spitfires of the US 52nd Fighter

*Above: The Messerschmitt Bf 110, a C-4 version of which is seen here during 1941 Mediterranean operations, provided the backbone of the Zerstörergeschwader throughout WW II*

*Above right: An Rb 50/30 camera being carried to a Messerschmitt Bf 110C-5 reconnaissance aircraft in the Western Desert. Note dummy nose guns to mislead intercepting fighters*

*Right: The Messerschmitt Bf 110D with drop tanks beneath the wings was extensively used for shipping escort tasks as well as for long-range fighter-bomber missions*

Group on 23 March, and Hptm. Wolfgang Tonne, Staffelkapitän of 3./JG 53, was killed in an accident on 20 April, his score being 122 victories.

As the German situation in Tunisia deteriorated, so the gradual transfer of Luftwaffe units to Sicily took place. By the beginning of May, only 200 aircraft of Fliegerführer Tunisien remained in Africa, these withdrawing to Sicily in total by 12 May 1943. In the last days of the North African battle, the Luftwaffe in the Mediterranean, although still comprising over 800 aircraft, was an effete force, completely unable to achieve effective intervention. Its influence in the last days of the Tunisian campaign was nil, and Allied aircraft and naval forces were able to counter the frantic German evacuation effort and thus translate defeat in North Africa into a disastrous rout.

# Chapter 8

# The Holding Campaign in the West

## The Night Fighters

# 1940-1943

At the beginning of the war, German defence against nocturnal air attack was almost wholly dependant on flak and searchlights. Indeed, the Flak regiments of the Luftwaffe were considered to be the élite arm, and the efficiency of their weapons, searchlights and prediction equipment was of a very high standard. But the limitations of anti-aircraft artillery were soon to become painfully obvious. On the night of 15/16 May 1940, Royal Air Force Bomber Command was authorised to launch an attack on German industrial targets in the Ruhr for the first time, after months of needless restrictions on its operation. The strategic bombing of Germany had commenced, although it was to be another two years before RAF Bomber Command was in a position to achieve worthwhile results. That night, however, heavy ground haze in the Ruhr robbed the Flak of the possibility of effective action.

Apart from a small number of Staffeln practising a rudimentary form of night fighting with obsolescent Bf 109Ds, no attempt was made to form a realistic nocturnal fighter force until early June 1940, when elements of ZG 1 were sent to Düsseldorf to form the Nacht und Versuchs Staffel (Night and Experimental Unit) under Hptm. Wolfgang Falck. On 17 July 1940, a further development in the creation of a night-fighter force took place when Göring entrusted Josef Kammhuber, ex-Geschwaderkommodore of KG 51, with organisation and formation of Nachtjagd-division 1. Although Kammhuber had no previous experience in night fighting, he applied himself to the task of equipping and expanding his Division with energy and skill.

Promoted to Major, Wolfgang Falck formed his Geschwaderstab NJG 1 at Düsseldorf on 20 July. On that day also, two Gruppen were formed from existing units: I/NJG 1 was formed from two Staffeln of I/ZG 1 and the remnants of IV/JG 2 and equipped with Messerschmitt Bf 110C-2s, and II/NJG 1 was formed from the Zerstörer Staffel/KG 30 with Junkers Ju 88C-2 fighters issued to two

Staffeln, while 4./NJG 1 of the same Gruppe was equipped with the Dornier Do 17Z-10 (Kauz II). Within weeks, III/NJG 1 had been formed from a nucleus of pilots from IV/JG 2. During September, a specialist night intruder Gruppe was also formed. This, the II/NJG 1, had been termed a 'Fernnachtjagd Gruppe' (Long-range night fighter unit), and it was redesignated I/NJG 2 and based at Gilze-Rijn in Holland. To replace the old unit, a new II/NJG 1 was formed from I/ZG 76 and equipped with Bf 110D-1/U1 night-fighters at Deelen-Arnhem. By the Autumn of 1940, the three Gruppen of NJG 1 were operational and based at Venlo, Leeuwarden and St Trond Deelen for specialist night fighter work, while II/NJG 2 embarked on a series of successful night intruder missions across the North Sea against RAF Bomber Command airfields. At this time, NJG 3 was formed on Bf 110s but, by December 1940, the I Gruppe had been posted to FlKps X in Sicily.

Generalmajor Kammhuber had himself no knowledge of radar and his ground organisation, largely drawn from the Flak, had as yet no awareness of its possible application. In Autumn 1940, the Würzburg A, a parabolic reflector ground radar unit, was introduced, but was largely seized upon by the Flak Command as an aid to fire and searchlight prediction. General Martini, the Luftwaffe Signals chief, however, assigned to Kammhuber six trained signals companies equipped with Würzburg A, and, in co-operation with his staff, Kammhuber evolved a night fighting tactical procedure called Helle Nachtjagd (Illuminated Night Fighting). In October 1940, the first Helle Nachtjagd sector was established astride the main RAF Bomber Command route to the Ruhr. This area measured 90km in length and 20km in width, and was split into three sectors. Each sector contained a searchlight battalion, two Würzburg A radar units and attendant night fighters. While one Würzburg radar controlled a master searchlight, the other tracked the movements of the night fighters; the two sources of information were correlated by a ground controller who, in turn, passed R/T instructions to the nightfighter pilots. In good weather conditions the system worked well; the three night fighters in the sector could be vectored simultaneously by the controller, with each pilot attacking his target while it remained in the searchlight.

Kammhuber fully appreciated the limitations imposed on Helle Nachtjagd by bad weather or cloud conditions; even 6/10th cloud cover created considerable difficulties. He therefore concentrated wholly on the perfection of ground control interception based on radar. At this early stage, German night fighters did not carry airborne interception radar, but the new control procedure, known as Himmelbett (Four-poster Bed), enabled a good fighter controller to vector the night fighter to within 400 yards of its quarry. At that stage, the pilot was able to see the bomber's exhaust flashes and carry out a visual attack.

The Himmelbett system relied on two different types of radar equipment, each having advantages over the other. Firstly the Freya radar (manufactured by Gema GmbH and working on 118–130Mcs) offered long-range target location, normally with a maximum of 60–75 miles – the first Freya to be discovered by the British was at Auderville on the Cap de la Hague in February 1941, and by October of that year the RAF had located a line of Freyas stretching from Bödo in Norway to Bordeaux in the Bay of Biscay. Freya could plot range and azimuth but not the altitude of the target. Produced by Telefunken and working on the 545–570Mcs band, the Würzburg Reise was limited to about 30 miles in range but worked to very fine limits and could produce an estimation of target height. In the Himmelbett system two Würzburgs worked in conjunction with a Freya and a number of night-fighters that 'stacked' over a radio beacon. Freya provided the early warning and the Würzburgs plotted the target and the selected night fighter for a ground controlled interception.

What was to be known later as the 'Kammhuber Line' was a series of GCI Himmelbett sectors located at first in the immediate approaches to the Ruhr and then extended, by March 1941, from Antwerp to Sylt, on the Danish border. The Himmelbett system worked well and achieved results, but RAF bombers soon started to fly detours around the searchlight and night fighter zones on their way into Germany, dictating the continual

*Right: An Fw 190A-4 fighter of 8.Staffel of Jagdgeschwader 2 at readiness at an airfield in the vicinity of Brest during the autumn of 1942*

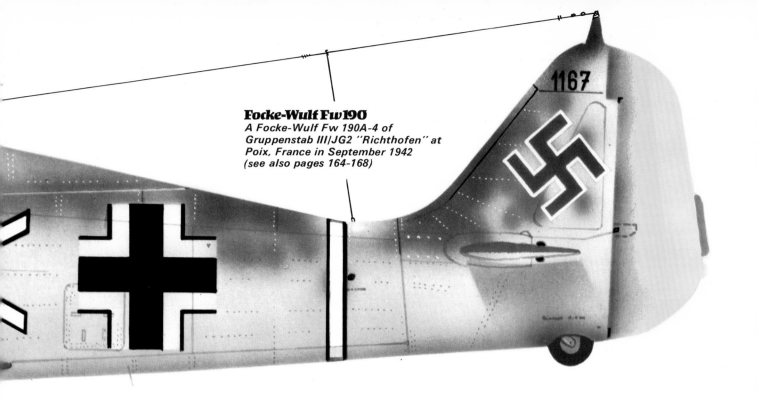

**Focke-Wulf Fw 190**
A Focke-Wulf Fw 190A-4 of Gruppenstab III/JG2 "Richthofen" at Poix, France in September 1942 (see also pages 164-168)

lengthening of the defence line.

Air Marshal Sir Richard Peirse, the AOC Bomber Command, was also encountering problems at this time. Firstly, there was the lack of a clear strategic policy. The original bombing directive called for an offensive against the German synthetic oil industry when weather conditions were suitable, and for raids on large cities (area attacks) for the purpose of 'undermining civilian morale' when bad weather precluded 'precision' attacks. However, RAF Bomber Command was unable to achieve anything approaching a precision night-bombing attack due to the absence of any suitable radio aids to navigation. In March 1941, the Command was forced to concentrate on naval targets due to the escalating losses in British shipping in the Atlantic that were causing great concern. In good weather, coastal targets were easy to locate at night, and Hamburg, Bremen and Kiel were frequently subjected to area attacks. In June and July 1941, the main effort was directed at Brest and the vessels *Scharnhorst,* *Gneisenau* and *Prinz Eugen*. Meanwhile, the oil plan had cooled and, at the end of July, Bomber Command was left without a concrete bombing strategy, switching from attacks on the oil industry to transportation. The bombing directive of 9 July earmarked nine important rail centres, mainly in the Ruhr, for subsequent attack.

In April 1941, Kammhuber's Nachtjagd-division 1, previously subordinated to Luftflotte 2, came under the newly-formed Luftwaffen-befehlshaber Mitte (Air Command Centre),

which controlled all day and night fighter operations over Germany, Denmark and Holland. As of 1 August 1941, Nachtjagddivision 1 became Fliegerkorps XII, with its Headquarters at Zeist, in Holland. The establishment of Stab, I, II and III/NJG 1 and Stab and I/NJG 2 on 31 May was 188 aircraft of which 140 were serviceable.

By late-summer 1941, RAF Bomber Command was beginning to suffer consistent losses to German night fighters and flak, culminating in 37 aircraft being lost on the night of 7 November, which represented 10 per cent of the force despatched. The only way in which Bomber Command could achieve reasonable bombing accuracy was by operation in clear weather and preferably on moonlit nights; such offered ideal opportunities for easy 'kills' by the German night fighters, their crews having every reason to regard the Himmelbett system as sufficient for their task. However, Kammhuber considered airborne radar as an aid to final interception as essential to the efficiency of his command. As early as 1940, Kammhuber had submitted a technical requirement for an airborne radar resulting in the installation, in July 1941, of a pre-production FuG 202 Lichtenstein BC airborne radar set in a Do 215B-5 fighter of 4./NJG 1 based at Leeuwarden. Manufactured by Telefunken GmbH, and working on 490Mcs, Lichtenstein BC offered good azimuth presentation with a minimum range of 200 yards and a maximum of 3,000 yards in expert hands.

Several aces, notably Hptm. Helmut Lent and Oblt. Paul Gildner of NJG 1, would have nothing to do with AI because its cumbersome aerial array caused a reduction in speed of some 15–25mph. This attitude became widespread and prevailed until Oblt. Ludwig Becker of 4./NJG 1 began to achieve positive successes with Lichtenstein BC – his fourth 'kill' using this equipment was picked up at an initial range of 3,060 yards. Although the potential of Lichtenstein BC was now realised and Kammhuber persuaded Hitler to give this apparatus top industrial priority, the loss in aircraft performance that its installation entailed continued to be resisted, and crews often opted to fly aircraft not fitted with radar. By the early months of 1942 FuG 202, was undergoing operational trials in four Bf 110E-1/U1s of I/NJG 2. Despite the high priority, the supply of sets remained slow, and it was not until July 1942 that all II/NJG 1 aircraft were fitted with Lichtenstein, while other units remained partially equipped.

By November 1941, two new Gruppen had been formed – II/NJG 2 and II/NJG 3. During the following month, I/NJG 2 was re-equipped with the Ju 88C-4 fighter and posted to FlKps X in Sicily. The night intruder work of I/NJG 2 had abruptly stopped in October on an express order of Hitler, despite notable successes and enthusiasm of the crews. In March 1942, the first Dornier Do 217J-1s were issued to 4./NJG 1 for combat trials, but the type was considered inferior to the older Do 215B-5.

This period coincided with a time of crisis for RAF Bomber Command in which the lack of a clear-cut bombing policy, the constant diversion of its forces to other tasks and the failure of some of its principal aircraft, had finally come to fruition. The Manchester bomber had been something of a failure owing to the inadequate state of development of its engines, and the Stirling was disappointing primarily as a result of the limitations of the specification to which it had been designed. The bulk of Bomber Command squadrons were equipped with the Wellington, a reliable aircraft but without the range and bomb load to sustain a new offensive. Britain had now entered the phase of the war wherein her fortunes were at their nadir. Something had to be done and the only direct means of attack at her disposal was RAF Bomber Command.

When Air Marshall A. T. Harris assumed command on 22 February 1942, a new directive called for bomber attacks on Germany with the prime objective being the undermining of the morale of the civilian population. Bomber Command was materially assisted at this time by the withdrawal from Brest of the *Scharnhorst* and *Gneisenau*, thus removing an onerous commitment. In addition, the introduction of Gee (TR 1335) in a growing number of bombers enabled a nucleus of the force to locate targets with a modicum of accuracy in all weathers. From this time onwards, all was aimed at trading maximum destructive effort for the minimum of losses. Mass incendiary bombing would achieve the destruction by fire, while the active and passive German defences could be saturated by the concentration of the bomber force over the target in the shortest possible time spread. The navigational aid, Gee, was first used operationally by 22 bombers on 8 March in a raid on Essen. This was followed rapidly by eight other attacks, but despite the assistance given by Gee and the use of marker flares, industrial haze foiled Bomber Command which produced poor results.

Harris next turned to small, easily-identifiable targets to be raided during moonlight periods. These controversial area attacks against mostly civilian targets opened with Lübeck on 28 March, continued with an attack on Rostock a month later and culminated in the first 1,000-bomber raid on 30/31 May 1942 on the city of Cologne and during which 41 RAF bombers were shot down – this representing only 3·8 per cent of the attacking force of 1,046 aircraft. This raid was of propaganda value primarily, and such numbers of aircraft could not be used again until 1944. The political aspect of the Cologne raid was significant and thenceforth RAF Bomber Command underwent expansion and enjoyed high industrial priority. The crisis was over.

To counter this ever-growing threat from RAF Bomber Command, Kammhuber was forced to expand his existing forces. In October 1942, IV/NJG 1 was formed from a nucleus of II/NJG 1, and other Nachtjagdgeschwader underwent expansion. The Messerschmitt Bf 110F was standard equipment for most Gruppen and during the autumn months, the Bf 110G, equipped with either FuG 202 Lichtenstein BC or FuG 212 Lichtenstein C-1, appeared in service. Other types, including the Ju 88C-6b and the Dornier Do 217J-2, were also on strength by the end of the year, when Kammhuber's forces consisted of NJG 1, I/NJG 2, NJG 3, NJG 4 and NJG 5. Together, these had inflicted, in conjunction with Flak, a loss rate of 4·1 per cent of Bomber Command's

sorties – a figure altogether too high if the offensive was to be maintained and increased. The night fighter crews could be satisfied that their efforts were gaining in momentum, but their real test was yet to come.

## Night-Fighters under Luftwaffenbefehlshaber Mitte
### 10 January 1943

| Unit | Types | Strength (serviceable) |
|------|-------|------------------------|
| Stab NJG 1 | Bf 110F-4, Bf 110G-4 | 4 (1) |
| I/NJG 1 | Bf 110F-4, Bf 110G-4 | 31 (24) |
| II/NJG 1 | Bf 110F-4, Do 217J-2 | 29 (24) |
| III/NJG 1 | Bf 110F-4 | 24 (23) |
| IV/NJG 1 | Bf 110F-4 | 27 (21) |
| I/NJG 2 | Ju 88C-6b | 2 (0) |
| Stab NJG 3 | Bf 110G-4 | 2 (0) |
| I/NJG 3 | Bf 110F-4, Do 217J-2 | 27 (17) |
| II/NJG 3 | Bf 110F-4, Do 217J-2 | 27 (16) |
| III/NJG 3 | Bf 110G-4 | 16 (12) |
| IV/NJG 3 | Ju 88C-6b, Do 217J-2 | 21 (11) |
| Stab NJG 4 | Bf 110G-4 | 1 (1) |
| I/NJG 4 | Bf 110F-4, Do 217J-2 | 26 (21) |
| II/NJG 4 | Bf 110F-4, Do 217J-2 | 18 (18) |
| III/NJG 4 | Bf 110F-4, Do 217J-2 | 18 (11) |
| IV/NJG 4 | Bf 110F-4, Do 217J-2 | 18 (14) |
| Stab NJG 5 | Bf 110G-4 | nil |
| I/NJG 5 | Bf 110G-4 | 25 (16) |
| II/NJG 5 | Bf 110G-4 | 22 (11) |
| IV/NJG 5 | Bf 110G-4, Ju 88C-4 | 25 (18) |

## The Day Fighters
# 1941-1943

By November 1940, while the Kampfgruppen of Luftflotte 2 and 3 pounded British cities by night, the Messerschmitt Bf 109Es of the Jagdgruppen were committed to fighter-bomber work and high-altitude Frei Jagd sweeps over the Channel and southern England. Combats with Spitfires and Hurricanes of Fighter Command still raged, although on a much reduced scale than hitherto. The German fighter losses were relatively light, but one of the Luftwaffe's leading 'Experten', Major Helmut Wick, Geschwader Kommodore of JG 2 'Richthofen', was shot down on 28 November by Flt. Lt. J. C. Dundas DFC of No 609 Squadron, in a dogfight off the Isle of Wight.

Rest and re-equipment for the Jagdgruppen

*Below: A Messerschmitt Bf 109F-4 of III Gruppe of Jagdgeschwader 26 at its Channel Coast base early in 1942, this Geschwader, with JG 2, facing the R.A.F. across the channel for two years*

was the order of the day throughout the winter; most units remained at the same airfields from which they had operated during the Battle of Britain under Jafü 2 and Jafü 3. The first unit to be issued with new Messerschmitt Bf 109F-1 was the Geschwaderstab and III/JG 51 at St Omer-Wizernes. Commanded by Major Werner Mölders, the top-scoring German fighter pilot, JG 51 first received the Bf 109F-1 in early February, but its service introduction was marred by structural weaknesses in the tailplane – on 10 February, Lt. Ralf Steckmayer of 11./JG 51 became the first casualty when his Bf 109F-1 crashed under unknown circumstances at Balinghem. After a temporary grounding of all Bf 109F-1s, flying was resumed but resulted in yet another crash. Suspicion turned from the engine to the un-

# Fighters of Hitler's Aces

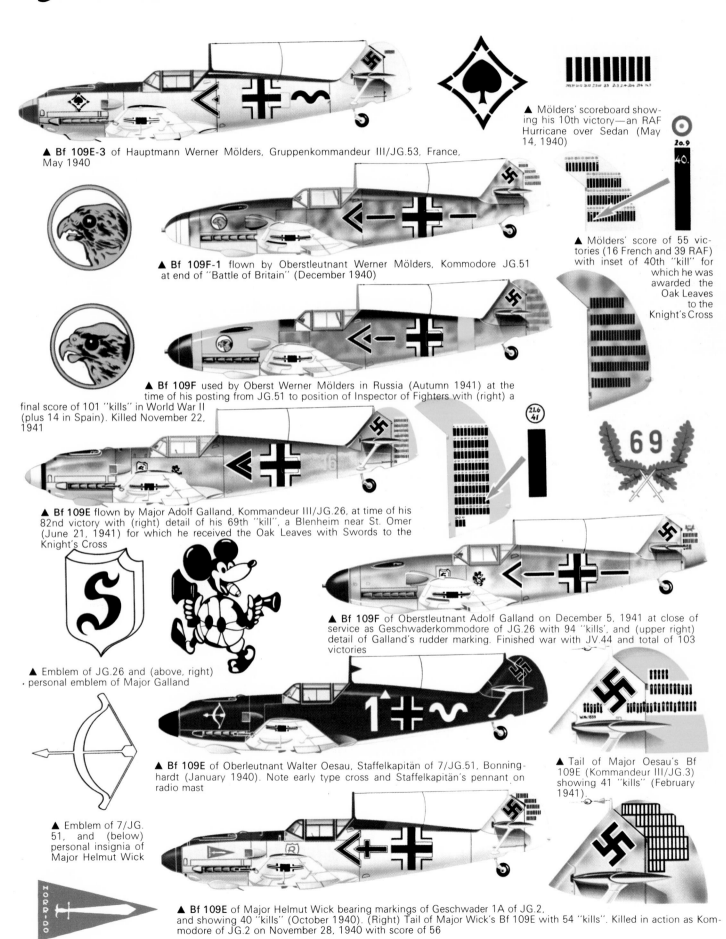

▲ Bf 109E-3 of Hauptmann Werner Mölders, Gruppenkommandeur III/JG.53, France, May 1940

▲ Mölders' scoreboard showing his 10th victory—an RAF Hurricane over Sedan (May 14, 1940)

▲ Bf 109F-1 flown by Oberstleutnant Werner Mölders, Kommodore JG.51 at end of "Battle of Britain" (December 1940)

▲ Mölders' score of 55 victories (16 French and 39 RAF) with inset of 40th "kill" for which he was awarded the Oak Leaves to the Knight's Cross

▲ Bf 109F used by Oberst Werner Mölders in Russia (Autumn 1941) at the time of his posting from JG.51 to position of Inspector of Fighters with (right) a final score of 101 "kills" in World War II (plus 14 in Spain). Killed November 22, 1941

▲ Bf 109E flown by Major Adolf Galland, Kommandeur III/JG.26, at time of his 82nd victory with (right) detail of his 69th "kill", a Blenheim near St. Omer (June 21, 1941) for which he received the Oak Leaves with Swords to the Knight's Cross

▲ Bf 109F of Oberstleutnant Adolf Galland on December 5, 1941 at close of service as Geschwaderkommodore of JG.26 with 94 "kills", and (upper right) detail of Galland's rudder marking. Finished war with JV.44 and total of 103 victories

▲ Emblem of JG.26 and (above, right) personal emblem of Major Galland

▲ Bf 109E of Oberleutnant Walter Oesau, Staffelkapitän of 7/JG.51, Bonninghardt (January 1940). Note early type cross and Staffelkapitän's pennant on radio mast

▲ Tail of Major Oesau's Bf 109E (Kommandeur III/JG.3) showing 41 "kills" (February 1941)

▲ Emblem of 7/JG. 51, and (below) personal insignia of Major Helmut Wick

▲ Bf 109E of Major Helmut Wick bearing markings of Geschwader 1A of JG.2, and showing 40 "kills" (October 1940). (Right) Tail of Major Wick's Bf 109E with 54 "kills". Killed in action as Kommodore of JG.2 on November 28, 1940 with score of 56

Joachim Müncheberg) and III/JG 26 (Hptm. Josef Priller), based at Abbeville-Drucat and Coquelles respectively. At the close of day, when the ships were off the Dutch coast, support was to be provided by I/JG 1. The operation was carried out with brilliant results. A number of Bf 109F-4s of JG 2 were damaged as a result of bad weather landings in Holland, while JG 26 suffered 4 pilots killed – 35 RAF aircraft and six Swordfish of No 825 FAA Squadron were shot down by flak and fighters.

In April 1942, Major Walter Oesau's JG 2 received its first Fw 190A-2s while at the same time Hptm. Johannes Seifert's I/JG 26 underwent conversion at St Omer-Arques. On 18 April 1942, the order of battle of Sperrle's Luftflotte 3 was made up of fighters, reconnaissance units, bombers and coastal aircraft. Their dispositions are shown in the accompanying table.

The Jabostaffeln of JG 2 and JG 26 were formed on 10 March 1942, with the Bf 109F-4/B fitted with bomb-racks capable of carrying an SC 250 (550lb) bomb. Operations started in April, and the RAF could offer no positive defence against these fast, low-flying fighter-bombers which achieved an effect out of all proportion to the effort they represented. The Chain-Home and CHL radar stations situated in Britain were unable to plot the movements of the Jabos on account of their low altitude and Fighter Command was forced to mount standing patrols in order to counter the threat. Most targets were situated along the southern coast of England and only on rare occasions did the Jabos penetrate inland. Canterbury suffered a heavy attack by 10.(Jabo)/JG 2 and JG 26 on 31 October 1942, and this was followed by a maximum effort by the Jabos on London on 20 January and 12 March 1943. By this time, a specialist fighter-bomber unit – SKG 10 – had been formed and, in April 1943, JG 2 and JG 26 transferred their Jabostaffeln to IV/SKG 10.

The Jagdgruppen based in northern France continued to inflict prohibitive casualties on Fighter Command's incursions throughout the summer and, despite the slow introduction of the Spitfire IX, the ascendancy of the Fw 190 remained unchallenged. In July 1942, two high-altitude units (Höhenstaffeln) were operational on Bf 109G-1s, these being 11./JG 2 at Ligescourt and 11./JG 26 at Norrent-Fontes. 'Gustav' preferred little performance gain by comparison with the Bf 109F-4 that it succeeded, and 11./JG 2 suffered a setback when its Staffelkapitän, Oblt. Rudolf Pflanz, was killed over Berck-sur-Mer on 31 July 1942.

Fighter Command received an added commitment on 17 August 1942, when the 8th USAAF flew its B-17E Fortresses on an operational mission to Rouen for the first time. At first targets for the USAAF bombers lay within the combat radius of the Spitfire, but by late October, the B-17s and the B-24s that had followed them to the UK were venturing outside this radius to St Nazaire, Lorient and La Pallice. These attacks were usually inter-

*Above: Adapted from the Dornier Do 217M bomber, the Do 217N-1 night fighter, seen during pre-delivery trials, began to reach the Nachtjagdgruppen during 1942-3*

braced cantilever tail unit which was found to suffer a sympathetic vibration leading eventually to structural failure. Within weeks, all F-1s had been modified, and the problem solved. The introduction of the Bf 109F-2 followed during March and April. This type was on initial issue to JG 51 and II and III/JG 53, but JG 2, JG 3 and JG 26 were partially equipped with it during May.

Royal Air Force fighter pilots first met the Bf 109F in combat during March, but it was not until 8 May, when a Bf 109F-2 flown by Lt. Günther Peopel of 1./JG 3 crashed in Kent, that the RAF could confirm the existence of the new Messerschmitt model. With the rapid withdrawal of Luftflotte 2 from France in June 1941, only JG 2, JG 26 and II/JG 52 remained on the Channel Front; in Norway, two Staffeln of I/JG 77 remained, while elements of JG 1 were stationed in Denmark, Germany and Holland. This last mentioned unit consisted of only one Gruppe and was largely occupied on convoy escorts and training duties.

The restoration of RAF Fighter Command's strength during the winter enabled it to pursue a limited offensive against the forces of Jafü 2 and 3 during the Spring. With the opening of the German offensive in the Soviet Union in June, RAF Fighter Command, under Air Marshal William Sholto-Douglas, and No 2 Group Bomber Command opened a limited campaign against the Luftwaffe in northern France with the object of tying down as many fighter units in that theatre at the expense of the Russian Front. For the next two years, JG 2 and JG 26 fought a lone and bitter battle against the RAF over the Channel and northern France. Pitted against Nos 10, 11 and 12 Groups, Fighter Command, these Geschwader inflicted a 2 to 1 ratio of casualties against the RAF despite their numerical inferiority. The operational strength of JG 2 and JG 26 seldom exceeded 240 aircraft, but they were well led, were always equipped with the latest Bf 109s and Fw 190s and fought with all the advantages that had hitherto been the prerogative of RAF Fighter Command during the Battle of Britain.

Initially the RAF fighter tactics were encompassed within an operation known as the 'Circus'. This was a shallow penetration raid accompanied by a mass of escorting fighters, the object being to bring the Luftwaffe to battle and inflict casualties. The 'Circus' was later modified to include fighter-sweeps (Rodeos) acting in conjunction with the main force, or as a diversion. By late-1941, however, German radar coverage of northern France was efficient, the performance of the latest Bf 109F-4 was superior to the Spitfire VB in all but tight turns, and it was the Luftwaffe that

began to inflict a prohibitive loss rate upon Fighter Command. During August 1941, JG 2 and JG 26 shot down 98 Spitfires and 10 Hurricanes for the loss of eighteen fighter pilots killed in action.

By November 1941, Fighter Command called a halt to offensive operations and embarked on a winter of conservation. The plan for the new offensive called for nothing new, although the faster Boston III in place of the Blenheim IV promised to make the job of the fighter escorts a little easier. All hopes of an effective and less costly offensive due to the widespread re-equipment with the Spitfire VB were dashed with the entry into combat of the Focke-Wulf Fw 190A fighter. The service introduction of the Fw 190A with II/JG 26 in July 1941 had been marred by numerous teething troubles, mainly associated with the new BMW 801 engine. The RAF encountered the Fw 190s during late-summer and autumn, but the new German fighter was unable to display its full potential until 1942.

Both JG 2 and JG 26 were heavily engaged on 12 February 1942 while providing fighter protection for the *Scharnhorst, Gneisenau* and *Prinz Eugen* during Operation Cerberus-Donnerkeil – the daring Channel passage from Brest to Kiel. Operation Donnerkeil (Thunderbolt) was the task of Oberst Adolf Galland, the General der Jagdflieger, and consisted of the air-phase of the operation. The forces under his control consisted of one Gruppe of ZG 26 with Bf 110D-3s, JG 2 with Bf 109F-2s and F-4s, and Major Gerd Schöpfel's JG 26 with Bf 109F-4s Fw 190A-1s and A-2s. The Fw 190 component consisted of II/JG 26 (Hptm.

## The Order of Battle of Luftflotte 3

| Unit | Types | Location | Strength (serviceable) |
|---|---|---|---|
| 3.(F)/122 | Ju 88D-5, Bf 109F-5 | Bernay, Toussus | 13 (9) |
| 3.(F)/123 | Ju 88D-5, Bf 109F-5 | Lannion | |
| Stab JG 2 | Bf 109F-4 | Beaumont-le-Roger | 7 (6) |
| I/JG 2 | Fw 190A-2 | Le Havre:Octeville | 36 (28) |
| 6./JG 2 | Fw 190A-2 | Beaumont-le-Roger | 11 (9) |
| III/JG 2 | Fw 190A-2 | Maupertus | 38 (26) |
| 10.(Jabo)/JG 2 | Bf 109F-4/B | Caen-Carpiquet | 22 (15) |
| Stab JG 26 | Fw 190A-2 | Audembert | 5 (3) |
| I/JG 26 | Fw 190A-2 | St Omer-Arques | 29 (13) |
| II/JG 26 | Fw 190A-2 | Abbeville-Drucat | 31 (19) |
| III/JG 26 | Fw 190A-2 | Wevelghem | 30 (15) |
| 10.(Jabo)/JG 26 | Bf 109F-4/B | St Omer-Wizernes | 12 (10) |
| II/KG 2 | Do 217E-4 | Eindhoven | 20 (19) |
| III/KG 2 | Do 217E-4 | Schiphol | 18 (9) |
| Ku.Fl.Gr 106 | Ju 88A-4 | Dinard | 26 (15) |
| Ku.Fl.Gr 506 | Ju 88A-4 | Lannion | 25 (8) |
| II/KG 40 | Do 217E-4 | Soesterberb | 17 (10) |
| 7. and 8./KG 40 | Fw 200C-4, He 111H-6 | Bordeaux | 25 (10) |

cepted by Hptm. Egon Mayer's III/JG 2 based at Vannes. The Gruppe was faced with numerous combat problems in their attacks on the high-flying, well armed and closely-knit formations of bombers. The head-on attacks, first attempted on 23 November 1942 over St Nazaire, solved some of these difficulties, but they lacked cohesion and results were limited.

Luftflotte 3 was forced to relinquish a number of fighter and fighter-bomber units to other theatres during November, and II/JG 2, 11./JG 2 and 11./JG 26 were posted to Luftflotte 2 in the Mediterranean. The Jabostaffeln and I/JG 2 were sent to the South of France in December, while I/JG 26 was transferred to the Soviet Union during the following month.

# Fighters of Hitler's Aces

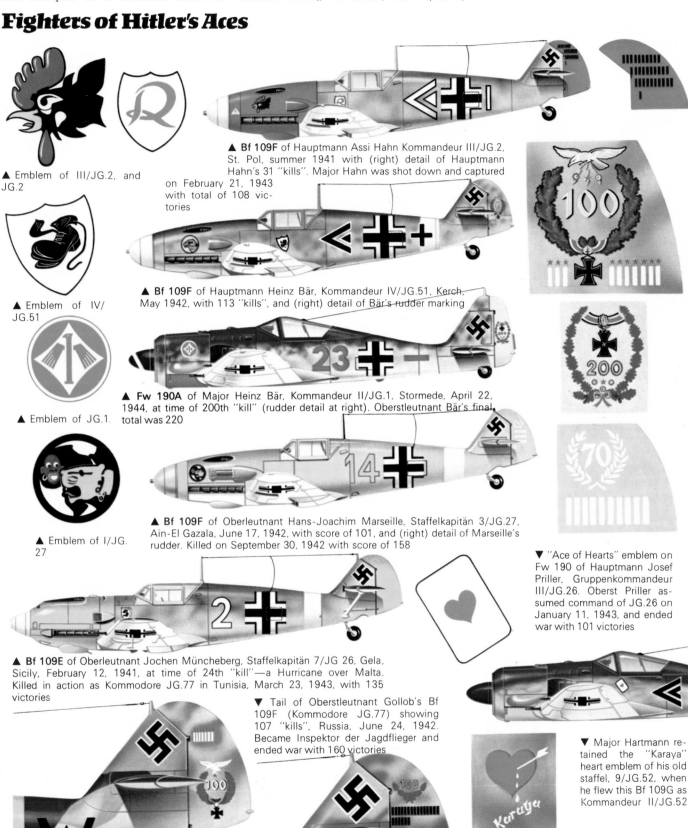

▲ Emblem of III/JG.2, and JG.2

▲ Bf 109F of Hauptmann Assi Hahn Kommandeur III/JG.2, St. Pol, summer 1941 with (right) detail of Hauptmann Hahn's 31 "kills". Major Hahn was shot down and captured on February 21, 1943 with total of 108 victories

▲ Emblem of IV/JG.51

▲ Bf 109F of Hauptmann Heinz Bär, Kommandeur IV/JG.51, Kerch, May 1942, with 113 "kills", and (right) detail of Bär's rudder marking

▲ Emblem of JG.1

▲ Fw 190A of Major Heinz Bär, Kommandeur II/JG.1, Stormede, April 22, 1944, at time of 200th "kill" (rudder detail at right). Oberstleutnant Bär's final total was 220

▲ Emblem of I/JG. 27

▲ Bf 109F of Oberleutnant Hans-Joachim Marseille, Staffelkapitän 3/JG.27, Ain-El Gazala, June 17, 1942, with score of 101, and (right) detail of Marseille's rudder. Killed on September 30, 1942 with score of 158

▼ "Ace of Hearts" emblem on Fw 190 of Hauptmann Josef Priller, Gruppenkommandeur III/JG.26. Oberst Priller assumed command of JG.26 on January 11, 1943, and ended war with 101 victories

▲ Bf 109E of Oberleutnant Jochen Müncheberg, Staffelkapitän 7/JG 26, Gela, Sicily, February 12, 1941, at time of 24th "kill"—a Hurricane over Malta. Killed in action as Kommodore JG.77 in Tunisia, March 23, 1943, with 135 victories

▼ Tail of Oberstleutnant Gollob's Bf 109F (Kommodore JG.77) showing 107 "kills", Russia, June 24, 1942. Became Inspektor der Jagdflieger and ended war with 160 victories

▼ Major Hartmann retained the "Karaya" heart emblem of his old staffel, 9/JG.52, when he flew this Bf 109G as Kommandeur II/JG.52

▲ Tail of Oberleutnant Erich Hartmann's Bf 109F (9/JG. 52) showing 121 "kills". Major Erich Hartmann ended war as Gruppenkommandeur II/JG.52 and Luftwaffe's top-scoring ace with 352 victories

# Chapter 9
# Maritime Operations of the Luftwaffe 1939-1945

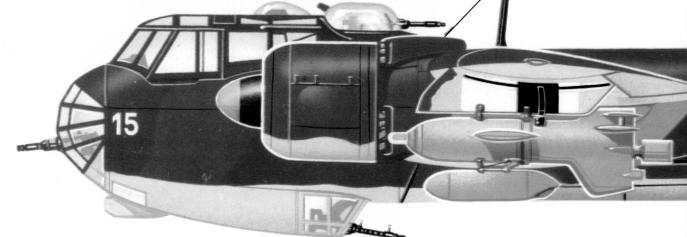

Prior to 1939, so powerful was the concept of a Continental strategic war, with emphasis on land operations supported by strong air forces, that little thought had been given to the possibility and potentiality of maritime operations by the Luftwaffe against enemy shipping. This was a naval affair and, in 1939 the few maritime units whose task was mainly reconnaissance were under the command of a Führer der Seeluftstreitkräfte, himself subordinate to the General der Luftwaffe beim Oberkommando der Kreigsmarine (Ob.d.M). The Seeluftstreitkräfte, or Fleet Air Arm, bore no resemblance to the carrier-borne forces of either the Royal Navy or the US Navy and consisted in the main of maritime reconnaissance types such as the Heinkel He 59B, the Heinkel He 115A and the Dornier Do 18D seaplanes and flying boats. Concentrated within a number of Küstenfliegergruppen, these aircraft were stationed at coastal bases in the Baltic and North Sea, and whereas their prime rôle was that of the 'eyes of the Fleet', offensive capability was restricted to mine-laying and torpedo operations on an experimental scale.

Late in the summer of 1939, the Luftwaffengeneralstab became convinced of the necessity of providing a force of modern bombers for offensive operations against enemy naval forces which might attempt to enter German waters. In addition, it was propounded, these could also attack the bases of the Royal Navy. The use of Seeluftstreitkräfte forces for this purpose was out of the question due to inter-service prejudices and the obsolescence of the naval aircraft, with the result that the Luftwaffe went ahead with the formation of a specialised anti-shipping force on its own initiative. Already in April 1939, General Hans Geisler had been appointed as General zur besonderer Verwendung (Gen. z.b.V) and charged with the task of forming the nucleus of an anti-shipping strike force. He and his staff were stationed at Kiel-Holtenau, under control of Luftflotte 2.

With the outbreak of war in September 1939, Geisler's command was up-graded to Fliegerdivision 10, with Major Martin Harlinghausen as Ia Offizier responsible for operations. Harlinghausen's anti-shipping experience dated back to the Spanish Civil War, and the development of the Luftwaffe anti-shipping arm was to owe much to this ex-naval martinet in the ensuing years. At first, the strike force of Fl.Div 10 consisted of elements of two Kampfgeschwader that were built up to full

strength over the next six months. These were I and II/KG 26 'Löwengeschwader' and I/KG 30 'Adlergeschwader' equipped with He 111P-2 and Junkers Ju 88A-1 bombers respectively, the latter being activated at Jever on 22 September. These bomber units acted in close co-operation with the reconnaissance units of Ob.d.M, and in the opening weeks of the war made their presence felt over the North Sea and in attacks on RN bases at Scapa Flow and in the Firth of Forth. Operations of a more limited nature were also carried out by Do 18s of 2.Staffeln of Kü.Fl.Gr. 106, 406, 506, 806 and 906, while staffeln of these same units used He 115s.

The crews of KG 26 and KG 30 had little or no previous experience of attacking warships, but a select band of officer pilots, one of whom was Major Werner Baumbach of I/KG 30, evolved and perfected their own methods in operations over Scapa and the North Sea. Much German publicity was given to the alleged sinking of the carrier HMS *Ark Royal* on 26 September by I/KG 30, but in fact the vessel was only lightly damaged. Two Ju 88s, including that flown by the Gruppenkommandeur, Hptm. Pöhle, were shot down by Nos. 602 and 603 Squadrons when I/KG 30 attacked the anchorage at Scapa Flow on 16 October, and during which attack the cruiser HMS *Southampton* was hit by a bomb which failed to explode while damage was suffered by HMS *Edinburgh* and HMS *Mohawk*.

On 1 December, II/KG 30 was activated at Barth, followed one month later by the formation of III/KG 30. In February 1940, Fliegerdivision 10 was again up-graded to the status of Fliegerkorps X, and with the anti-shipping operational experience gained by this command it became the natural choice for Weserübung – the closely co-ordinated land–sea operation for the invasion of Denmark and Norway. Both KG 26 and KG 30 were selected to play a leading part in this operation in which a powerful enemy naval reaction was anticipated, and their operations were to be in conjunction with the mine-laying forces of Ob.d.M.

While the parallel development of maritime bombers was in hand, a small number of enthusiastic officers of the Seeluftstreitkräfte had been successful in evolving tactics for aerial sea mining. General Joachim Coeler became the Führer der Seeluftstreitkräft in April 1939, and as soon as his appointment had been confirmed, he set about the task of forming units as specialists in the work of sea mining. At first he met with considerable opposition from

the Kriegsmarine and it was only through continual agitation that he finally gained authority from Ob.d.M to proceed with operations on a limited scale. The early sorties to the Thames Estuary and the coastal regions off Sheerness each had to carry the explicit permission of the Kriegsmarine, but, in time, Coeler was granted clearance to operate independently; the obsolete He 59s were replaced by Do 17Z-2 and He 111P-4 aircraft, and the selected Küstenfliegergruppen ranged to coastal waters off the Clyde, the Firth of Forth, Plymouth, Liverpool, and the Thames Estuary. Standard parachute sea mines of this period were the LMA (1,102-lb) and the LMB III (2,028-lb).

Growing losses on mining operations attracted the attention of Herman Göring, and Coeler was called to give an explanation. This he did with such emphasis on the successes of sea mining operations as opposed to the losses that Göring was convinced of the efficacy of mine-laying and undertook to create a special Luftwaffe command for mine-laying forces; in February 1940, this command was formed and named Fliegerdivision 9. On the formation of this command, the minelaying unit which had been responsible for the development of aircraft and tactics was withdrawn from the influence of the Seeluftstreitkräfte and the Ob.d.M. This move marked the beginning of a disintegration of the Seeluftstreitkräfte, a tendency which became more pronounced as units were seconded to the Luftwaffe proper and then absorbed. In July 1942, the Seeluftstreitkräfte was dissolved.

During the initial phases of Weserübung, KG 26 was deployed at Lübeck-Blankensee and Marx, in Germany, but by 10 April, 1. and 7. Staffeln were installed at Stavanger-Sola and Fornebu. KG 30, at Sylt-Westerland, mustered 84 Ju 88A-1 bombers of which 47 were combat ready on 9 April, the launching day of Weserübung. Elements of this Geschwader were later deployed to Stavanger, Fornebu and Trondheim-Vaernes. The Junkers 88s were heavily committed against the Royal Navy on the first day of Weserübung, flying 47 sorties against British warships. KG 26 also put up 41 sorties, the joint action resulting in damage to the cruisers *Devonshire, Southampton* and *Glasgow,* and the sinking of the destroyer *Gurkha.*

***Right: A Blohm und Voss BV 138C of See Aufklärungsgruppe 130 during a rendezvous with a U-boat along the Arctic Convoy Route during the winter of 1943-44***

**Dornier Do 217**
*A Dornier Do 217E-5 of 6./KG100 based at Marseilles-Istres (see also pages 149-151)*

Prior to Weserübung, extensive sea reconnaissance work was carried out by He 115s of Kü.Fl.Gr. 506 and Major Edgar Petersen's Fernaufklärungsstaffel equipped with Fw 200C-0 Condors, which reconnoitred the sea approaches to Norway up to Lat 63° North. Foreseeing the need for very long range maritime reconnaissance aircraft, Petersen, a navigation specialist on the staff of Fliegerkorps X, had recommended the use of the Fw 200 transport as the only type suitable for adaptation for this work. His efforts resulted in the formation of the Fernaufklärungsstaffel in November 1939, which took on hand six of the ten Fw 200C-0s being built and became operational immediately. On 17 April 1940, this staffel was redesignated 1./KG 40, sent to Aalborg, and then to Copenhagen-Kastrup on 26 April for anti-shipping and supply duties in the Narvik theatre. By late June 1940, the unit had been increased to Gruppe-strength as I/KG 40, and was operational with Fw 200C-1 Condors from Brest and, while administratively it was under Luftflotte 2, it operated under the direct control of the naval command at Lorient, known as Marine Gruppe West.

During the campaigns in the Low Countries and France the aircraft of Fliegerkorps X continued their attacks on naval and merchant shipping, and improved their tactics in the bombing of coastal convoys in British waters. The FlKps X was now stationed at bases in Norway and Denmark under Luftflotte 5 and, in addition to reconnaissance units, consisted of KG 26, KG 30 and Kü.Fl.Gr. 506; all other units had been withdrawn to take part in the

operations in Holland, Belgium and France. Fliegerdivision 9, on the other hand, was able to increase its minelaying forces after the fall of France by a whole Geschwader of some 100 aircraft. This was KG 4 with I and II Gruppe equipped with He 111Hs and the III Gruppe working up on Ju 88A-1s. The remainder of Fliegerdivision 9's forces consisted of KGr. 126 and Kü.Fl.Gr. 106, the former with He 111s and the latter with He 115B-2 seaplanes. On 16 October 1940, Fliegerdivision 9 was renamed Fliegerkorps IX and, at this time, controlled Stab, I, II and III/KG 4, Geschwaderstab KG 40 which was operational on Ju 88s, Stab, II and III/KG 30, KGr. 126 and Kü.Fl.Gr. 106. The only bomber unit remaining in Fliegerkorps X was II/KG 26, the other Gruppen serving with FlKps I as normal bomber units engaged in operations against England.

With the failure to force a decision against Great Britain during the summer, the task of bringing an eventual surrender was entrusted to the Kreigsmarine. The spearhead of these forces was the U-boat arm commanded by Grossadmiral Karl Dönitz, the Oberbefehlshaber der U-Boote, whose bases were now situated along the western coast of France at Brest, Lorient, La Pallice, St. Nazaire and

Bordeaux. The smaller Type IIA U-boat of 303 tons had been supplanted by the 871-ton Type VIIC with ocean-going capability, and its crews ranged far and wide across the North Atlantic, attacking the vital supply convoys from Canada and the United States of America. The amount of shipping sunk by U-boats during the summer of 1940 rose to staggering proportions: in June fifty-eight ships of 284,000 tons, in July thirty-eight ships of 196,000 tons, in August fifty-six ships of 268,000 tons, in September fifty-nine ships of 295,000 tons and in October a peak of 63 ships of 352,000 tons, all with the loss of only six U-boats. Small wonder that the achievements of June to October 1940 were dubbed the 'happy time' by the U-boat commanders and crews.

Allied convoys lacked adequate escort and the merchant vessels, themselves, were pitifully lacking in armament, and these factors were largely instrumental in bringing success to the Condor crews of I/KG 40, by now based at Bordeaux-Mérignac. Throughout August and September 1940, I/KG 40 claimed the destruction of 90,000 BRT, and during the autumn and winter the Condor menace became a baleful factor in the Battle of the Atlantic. To the crews, however, the Condor, despite its 14-

hours' endurance, displayed some notable deficiencies due largely to its airliner pedigree. Its relatively light construction was inadequate for the long periods of low level flight over the sea in which turbulence continually put stress on the airframe; evasive manoeuvres had to be performed delicately, while the bomb load with normal fuel amounted to only four SC 250 (550-lb) bombs – less than that of the very much smaller but purpose-designed Junkers 88. Accordingly, the serviceability of the Fw 200 was to remain low throughout its operational career. Despite this, its early operation against Allied shipping was attended with conspicuous success.

Deliveries of the Fw 200C-1 Condor to I/KG 40 were slow, and for this reason, when III/KG 40 was formed in January 1941, it was equipped with He 111H-6 bombers, with the intention of re-equipping with Fw 200s when these became available. The successes against Allied shipping continued with 63,000 BRT claimed in January, and rising to 22 ships of 84,500 BRT claimed during the following month. One notable individual achievement during this period took place on 16 January 1941, when Hptm. Verlohr, the Staffelkapitän of 1./KG 40, sank two ships totalling 10,857 tons. Several

Condor sorties at the behest of Marine Gruppe West consisted of a three-day detachment to Trondheim-Vaernes, a patrol being flown from Mérignac to reconnoitre the seas off Ireland and the Fw 200 then making its way to either Trondheim or Stavanger in Norway.

The anti-shipping command, FlKps X, had been transferred in December 1940 to the Mediterranean theatre for operations against Malta and the British convoys sailing between Gibraltar and Egypt. It had now become apparent to the Führungsstab (Operations Staff) of OKL that if a blockade of Britain was to be carried out a more formalised structure of anti-shipping commands would have to be set up as soon as possible, while forces were still available and before the impending commitments in the Balkans and the Soviet Union complicated the situation.

In March 1941, a re-grouping of commands took place whereby the whole European coastline facing Great Britain and the Atlantic was covered by anti-shipping forces. In practice, this reorganisation did little more than take over existing anti-shipping forces, but their strength immediately began to increase, particularly in the area facing the Atlantic and Western Approaches. After the withdrawal of

FlKps X from Norway, Luftflotte 5 (Stumpff) created two new subordinate commands. These were Fliegerführer Nord (later split up into Nord and Nord-Ost), and Fliegerführer Lofoten; their duties were anti-shipping operations and reconnaissance for the U-boats and other naval forces to the North of Lat 58°N. The North Sea area from Lat 52°N to 58°N still remained the responsibility, as far as reconnaissance was concerned, of the Führer der Seeluftstreitkräfte, whose Gruppen were based along the western coast of Jutland. Fliegerkorps IX, based in Holland, retained the responsibility for minelaying around the British coasts. To cover the Western Approaches and Atlantic, and South-West coasts of England, the regrouping was completed by the formation of Fliegerführer Atlantik, under Obstlt. Harlinghausen, with Headquarters subordinated to Luftflotte 3 (Sperrle) at Lorient.

The main focus of U-boat and anti-shipping operations by Fl.Fü. Atlantik throughout 1941 was on the Allied convoys to Britain from Gibraltar, the South Atlantic and the United States. The two primary tasks of Harlinghausen's command were therefore divided as follows:

1. Reconnaissance reports to Fliegerführer

Atlantik and the Befehlshaber der U-Boote by Fw 200s of KG 40 concerning the position and movements of shipping for subsequent attack by U-boats. In this capacity the Condors acted as Fühlungshalter (shadowing aircraft) for the U-boats by keeping in visual contact with the convoys and enabling German D/F to fix the position by continual radio (W/T) transmissions. This task was in addition to normal bombing attacks on shipping when the opportunity arose.

2. Attacks of coastal shipping around the eastern, southern and western coastlines of Britain by Ju 88s and He 115 torpedo bombers.

At its inception Fl.Fü. Atlantik's complement of aircraft amounted to 44, but, by April 1941, its establishment consisted of 21 Fw 200C-2 Condors (of which 6–8 were stationed at Trondheim, in Norway) of Obstlt. Petersen's Geschwaderstab and I/KG 40, 26 He 111H-6

*Below: Referred to as the "Scourge of the Atlantic", the Focke-Wulf Fw 200C-3 Condor is seen here serving with the I Gruppe of Kampfgeschwader 40 at Mérignac*

nel in October 1941, his post was filled by a deputy only. The officer appointed as Fliegerführer Atlantik early in 1942 was General-major Kessler, one who hitherto had held obscure posts in the Luftwaffe. Battle returns of 1 January 1942 showed Fliegerführer Atlantik's forces as being I/KG 40 with a strength of 18 Fw 200s, 8. and 9./KG 40 with 18 He 111H-6s (7.Staffel was re-equipping with Fw 200s), Kü.Fl.Gr. 106 with 20 Ju 88A-4s, Kü.Fl.Gr. 506 with 23 Ju 88A-4s, and 2./Kü.Fl.Gr.906 with He 115C-1 torpedo-bombers.

*Above: Focke-Wulf Fw 200C-3/U1 Condors awaiting delivery from Bremen to Kampfgeschwader 40, the principal unit to operate this maritime patrol and anti-shipping aircraft.*

*Left: Arado Ar 196A-3s of 2.Staffel of See-Aufklärungsgruppe 128 which operated from Brest in June 1943 and later from bases in the South of France*

bombers of III/KG 40, 24 He 115B-2 torpedo-bombers of Kü.Fl.Gr. 906 and the reconnaissance 3.(F)/123 with 12 Bf 110s and Ju 88D-2s. The serviceability of I/KG 40 was rarely more than 6 to 8 aircraft out of an operational strength of 25 to 30; a frequent cause of unserviceability were failure of the rear spar and breaking of the fuselage just aft of the wing trailing edge. This parlous situation was reduced slightly by the introduction of the strengthened Fw 200C-3 version that came on strength during the summer. The 'happy time' for the Condor crews, if not entirely for the U-boats, was already over and losses suffered during lone shipping attacks grew alarmingly. Allied merchant vessels now carried machine-guns and 20-mm Oerlikon cannon, and could put up a spirited fight, making the low and slow pass of the Condor a hazardous affair. By November 1941, the classic Condor tactics of a mast-height approach from astern or abeam had been rendered virtually impossible due to its inability to take punishment from even relatively small calibre defensive fire.

After the withdrawal of Luftflotte 2 from France to the Soviet Union at the beginning of June 1941, Fliegerführer Atlantik became the primary anti-shipping strike force based in the West; Fliegerkorps IX restricted itself to mine-laying and was often used on night bomber operations over England, while Fliegerführer Nord and Fl.Fü. Lofoten were employed on reconnaissance duties. On 16 August 1941, the forces under Fliegerführer Atlantik consisted of I/KG 40 with a strength of 28 Fw 200C-3s, II/KG 40 with 24 Do 217E-2s, III/KG 40 with 20 He 111H-6s, three staffeln of KGr. 606 with 20 Ju 88A-4s, two staffeln of Kü.Fl.Gr. 906 with 9 He 115B-2s, and 5./BFGr. 196 with 26 Ar 196A-2s and He 114A-2s. These anti-shipping and convoy protection forces were also bolstered by Stab, II and III/KG 30 which, with II/KG 2, operated under FlKps IX from bases in Holland and Northern France.

By the end of August, KG 30 had retired to Northern Norway, while Kampfgruppe 606 transferred its Ju 88s from France to the Mediterranean during the early part of autumn, thus seriously depleting the anti-shipping component of Fliegerführer Atlantik. Meanwhile two further Gruppen were formed within KG 40; II/KG 40 was established in August on the Dornier Do 217E-2 and operated from Soesterberg under FlKps IX in the coastal anti-shipping rôle and IV(Erg.)/KG 40 was established at Bordeaux as a training and replacement unit for the Geschwader.

There was now an increasing tendency to employ the anti-shipping forces equipped with Ju 88s and Do 217s in bombing raids at night and in bad weather against targets in England. This was done to assuage German public opinion in the face of mounting attacks by RAF Bomber Command and vehement protests at the misuse of these forces by Sperrle and Harlinghausen fell upon deaf ears. Indeed, it was apparent that the importance of Fliegerführer Atlantik had waned. Firstly, the force was accorded fewer combat units and, secondly, when Harlinghausen was wounded during an operational mission over the Bristol Chan-

## Torpedo Bomber Operations
# 1942

Since 1932 German torpedo development had been in the hands of the Kreigsmarine which had purchased the Horten naval torpedo patents from Norway in 1933 and the Whitehead Fiume patents from Italy in 1938. Development in the direction of air-launched torpedoes was pursued in a leisurely manner by the Seeluftstreitkräfte, and the results of trials and reports of combat operations were jealously guarded by the naval parties responsible. When the Luftwaffe finally took an interest in torpedo work to reduce losses suffered on anti-shipping sorties, it received scant assistance from the Kreigsmarine.

In 1941, the Luftwaffe decided to pursue its own development trials with the intention of setting up a powerful force of torpedo-bombers. The first torpedo development establishment was formed at Grossenbrode, on the Baltic coast. Several aircraft types were exhaustively tested and it was soon apparent that the He 111 and, in particular, the faster Ju 88 were the most suitable. Kampfgeschwader 26 was to play the leading rôle in this new torpedo plan, with Stab, I and III/KG 26 selected as the specialist torpedo unit while II/KG 26 remained in the bomber rôle, operating under FlKps X in the Mediterranean. The detachment of a few of KG 26's He 111s to FlKps X in the autumn of 1941 for torpedo operations was shortlived due to lack of torpedoes, or, in some cases, the delivery of the same without warheads.

In January 1942, the Luftwaffe's demands for the centralisation and control of all German and Italian torpedo development were granted. Oberst Martin Harlinghausen was appointed as the head of all Luftwaffe torpedo development, supply, training and operational organisations, with the Torpedo Training School established at Grosseto, south of Leghorn in Italy. During the early months of 1942, I/KG 26 underwent torpedo conversion courses lasting on average between three and four weeks. The Gruppe's He 111H-6s could carry two torpedoes slung on racks beneath the belly; the standard torpedoes used were the German LT F5 and LT F5W, both of 450-mm calibre, with the latter based on the Italian model made by Silurificio Whitehead di Fiume.

While I/KG 26 underwent conversion at Grosseto, its future and the bases from which it would operate had already been decided. With the failure to crush the Soviet Union before the winter of 1941–42, the Anglo-American supply convoys that were being sent to Russia via the Arctic route began to assume even greater importance to the Germans. The forces under Luftflotte 5 available for the interception of these convoys were normally engaged in such duties as the protection of the Petsamo nickel mines, shipping attacks in the White Sea and the bombing of Soviet ports and communications in the area, as well as Wehrmacht support operations on the Finnish Front. In February 1942, these forces consisted of 1.(F)/120, Stab JG 5, 3. and 7./JG 5, Einsatz-

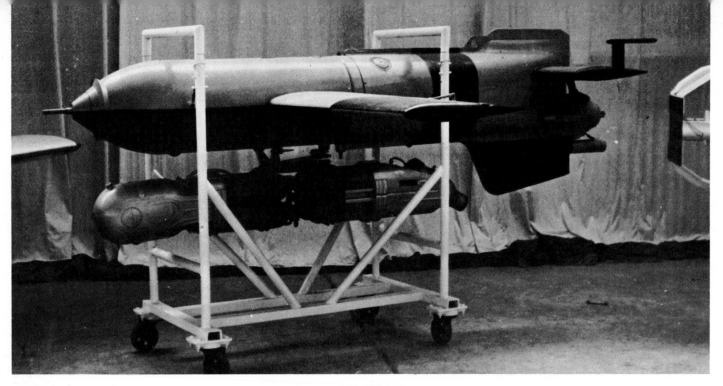

staffel Trondheim, 2./KG 26, 4. Staffel and III/KG 30, and the coastal forces of Kü.Fl.Gr 706 with Ju 88A-4s, 2./Kü.Fl.Gr. 406 with BV 138B-1s, and 1./Kü.Fl.Gr. 906 with He 115C-4s. In addition, I/StG 5, engaged on the Russo-Finnish Front, was available at short notice for short-range anti-shipping strikes over the White Sea.

In March, Göring ordered Luftflotte 5 to collaborate with the Kreigsmarine whenever the Allied supply convoys should pass through the Arctic area. When such convoys were expected, their progress was to be reported by Fw 200s and BV 138s, while all possible striking forces were to be temporarily withdrawn from the Finnish area to the airfields at Banak, Bardufoss and Kirkenes to supplement existing forces and to attack the convoys as soon as they came within range. Long-range reconnaissance was to be undertaken by the Condors of I/KG 40 operating from Trondheim-Vaernes and northern airfields, and was to cover the area of sea between Iceland, Jan Mayen Island, Bear Island and the North Cape, supplemented by the BV 138s of 2./Kü.Fl.Gr. 406. April 1942 saw 2./KG 40 detached to Rechlin and the reconnaissance duties from Vaernes falling upon 1. and 3.Staffeln and III/KG 40, which alternated between Bordeaux and Trondheim. At this time, Petersen had been succeeded by Oberst Pasewaldt as Kommodore. Within I/KG 26, based at Banak and Bardufoss, there were now 12 crews available for torpedo operations with the Heinkel He 111H-6 (Torp).

During March and April, the convoys PQ 13, 14 and 15 sailed for the Soviet ports of Archangel and Murmansk. I/KG 40 located these supply convoys and attacks by I/KG 26 and KG 30 followed in which the collective Allied losses amounted to two cruisers and 15 merchant vessels – seven of the latter being claimed by the Luftwaffe. While convoy PQ 16 set out from Iceland on 21 May 1942, the returning empty convoy, QP 12, left Murmansk on the home run. The escorting ships and the 35 merchantmen of PQ 16 were sighted by KG 40 which sent back position reports to Luftflotte 5's operational headquarters at Banak. The first torpedo attacks by I/KG 26 and high level bombing attacks by the Ju 88A-4s of KG 30 commenced on 25 May, and lasted for five days, with the Stukas of I/StG 5 joining in when the convoy entered the final leg into the White Sea area. Seven vessels were sunk, but the Luftwaffe claimed the destruction of the entire convoy.

After this action the Luftwaffe forces once more retired to their duties on the Finnish

Front. I/KG 26 remained at Banak, however, to await the coming of the next convoy. After the passage of PQ 16, new lessons had been learned which were to form the basis of later tactics when greater torpedo forces were expected to be available. It was found that considerable confusion could be sown among the enemy defensive screens by the use of coordinated torpedo and bomber attacks. The most favourable time was at dusk, with the torpedo-bombers running in from the darker hemisphere aided by the ships pre-occupied in warding off dive-bombing and level-bombing attacks by the Ju 88s of KG 30, thus affording the low-flying Heinkels an element of surprise. The tactic known as 'Golden Zange' (Golden Comb) consisted of a mass torpedo attack by as many as 12 He 111H-6s flying in wide line-abreast, with a simultaneous release of torpedoes to obtain the maximum spread while dividing defensive fire.

The battle returns of Luftflotte 5 of 20 June show the strike force as consisting of Führer Kette KG 26 and I/KG 26 with an establishment of 53 He 111H-6 (Torp) aircraft and III/KG 30 with 35 Ju 88A-4s. The fighters of 2. and 3./JG 5, along with IV/JG 5, were primarily responsible for the defence of Kriegsmarine units based at Trondheim – at this time the battleship *Tirpitz* was stationed near Trondheim along with the cruisers *Hipper* and *Scheer*.

When warnings of the next convoy, PQ 17, were received in early July, the strength of Luftflotte 5 was bolstered by the arrival of the whole of KG 30 and I/StG 5 to 264 combat and reconnaissance aircraft. At this time of year, daylight conditions prevailed throughout the 24-hour cycle and, on 1 July, the convoy was sighted and remained under continual surveillance by Fühlungshalter aircraft. The Heinkel He 115C torpedo bombers of 1./Kü.Fl. Gr. 406 conducted the first aircraft attack on this luckless convoy, when eight intercepted PQ 17 at 18.00hrs on following day. On 4 July, the torpedo bombers of Major Werner Klümper's I/KG 26 and the Ju 88s of KG 30 sank two merchantmen and damaged two others. The likelihood of naval intervention by *Tirpitz* now caused alarm at the British Admiralty, and that evening the order for the convoy to scatter was sent to the incredulous escort commanders. They acted with immediate effect and from here it was a question of *sauve qui pêut*. Throughout the following day, the U-boats and the Luftwaffe fell upon the defenceless and dispersed merchantmen, sinking twelve of their number. Only two vessels

reached Archangel on 10 July, but over the next few days the stragglers came limping in. The final count of this disastrous convoy was 23 ships sunk out of the original total of 33 that sailed from Iceland on 27 June. Luftflotte 5 lost five aircraft during the action and sank thirteen merchantmen and one rescue ship.

By the end of July, III/KG 26, under Hptm. Nocken, had completed the course at Grosseto and had transferred its Ju 88A-4 (Torp) bombers to Rennes-St. Jacques in Brittany. The Gruppe carried out its first torpedo operation against a convoy off the Scillies on 3 August, was transferred to Banak for an impending convoy operation on or about 10 August, but when this did not materialise, was sent back to Rennes. On 1 September 1942, the Gruppe was again sent to Banak. The forces under the control of Luftflotte 5 on 10 September 1942 were as follows: 1.(F)/120 with reconnaissance Ju 88D-5s at Banak and Bardufoss; II/JG 5 with 33 Bf 109G-2s at Alta, Altengaard and Petsamo; IV/JG 5 with 24 Fw 190A-3s at Banak and Bodo; the torpedo-bomber units, I and III/KG 26 with 34 and 24 He 111H-6 and Ju 88A-4 aircraft respectively at Banak; the Geschwaderstab and three Gruppen of KG 30, including the Epr.Staffel KG 30, mustering a strength of 113 Ju 88A-4s, A-6/Us and A-14s, also stationed within the Banak airfield complex, and elements of Kü.Fl.Gr. 406, 706 and 906 forming the seaborne component. A formidable anti-shipping force indeed.

The Convoy PQ 18, which came under attack by German aircraft and U-boats between 11–18 September 1942, differed from previous Arctic convoys in that its anti-aircraft defences, which included an aircraft carrier, were incomparably stronger. Thirteen merchantmen out of a total of 40 were sunk from PQ 18 and three out of 15 were lost on a returning QP convoy that came under attack at the same time, in addition to a tanker, a destroyer, a minesweeper and four aircraft of the Fleet Air Arm. Four U-boats were destroyed and in marked contrast to PQ 17, Luftflotte 5 admitted the loss of no fewer

than 41 of its bombers.

The torpedo attacks by I and III/KG 26 were usually timed to follow immediately after the high-level bombing attacks by KG 30. Owing to bad weather, however, III/KG 26 carried out only four torpedo attacks on PQ 18, and the cloud base (never more than 1,000ft) prevented any attempts at the synchronised torpedo and bombing attacks that had hitherto been so successful. The ring of escorting vessels and the presence of RN Hurricanes and Wildcats rendered the torpedo attacks particularly vulnerable, with I/KG 26's slow Heinkels taking much punishment. Hauptmann Nocken's III/KG 26 attacked PQ 18 off Spitzbergen on the 11th losing two Ju 88s; an attack on the aircraft carrier on the following day cost the Gruppe three or four torpedo-bombers. These were long and strenuous flights, lasting in some cases as long as seven hours. The AA fire was described as horrific; the chances of rescue for a downed crew were nil and, besides, in the freezing waters so far north of the Arctic Circle life was measured in minutes only.

The III/KG 26 employed the 'Golden Zange' tactic during their attacks in which the Ju 88s, flying at sea-level, extended into line abreast when about 20kms from the convoy, a distance of 200–300 metres separating each aircraft. The pilots then approached the convoy from directly abeam and, flying in this fashion, it was relatively easy to slip between the escorting vessels. The formation's spacing prevented individual pilots from selecting the same target, and such was the spread of the convoy that the entire Gruppe flying in line abreast could only 'comb' part of the convoy at a time with its torpedoes. Both LT F5b and Italian LT F5W torpedoes were used; the F5W was preferred as the F 5b's whisker type detonating pistol seldom operated when the target was hit at an acute angle.

The attack itself was launched amidships, with the approaching aircraft at exactly 90° to the course of the ship. The torpedoes were launched at a range of 1,000 metres, and usually from a height of 40 metres (125 feet), the aircraft then pulling up over the nose of the ship. The aircraft had to be flown dead straight and level in order for the weapon to enter the water at the stipulated 12°, and this was considered the time at which the crew was in the greatest danger. Anti-aircraft fire, and in particular 20-mm Oerlikon fire, was considered a greater threat than escorting RN fighters. Owing to the time lag there was seldom any opportunity to observe either the track of the torpedo or the possibility of an eventual strike, and every attempt was made to execute violent evasive action. In the final analysis I/KG 26 claimed ten vessels. KG 30's attempts were recognised as poor and lacking in determination for only 13 per cent of the sinkings were accorded to the Geschwader with the lion's share of 87 per cent being attributed to the torpedo-bombers of KG 26.

The Convoy PQ 18 saw the last of the massed torpedo attacks by the Luftwaffe and never again were the concentration and results achieved in subsequent actions in the Mediterranean and elsewhere. With the Allied landings in North Africa, the Mediterranean became the pivot of anti-shipping operations by the Luftwaffe. During October and November 1942, the Stab, I and III/KG 26 were sent to Grosseto for re-fit, joining II/KG 26. The I and II Gruppen resumed operations from Elmas under FlKps II, while III/KG 26 went to Heraklion under FlKps X. KG 30 was also posted to FlKps II in Sicily, with the exception of the I Gruppe. Subsequent operations saw the anti-shipping forces taking massive casualties in the face of growing Allied air superiority and the negative results achieved were attributed largely to the inexperience of replacement torpedo-bomber crews.

# The Atlantic and the Bay
# 1942-1943

The anti-shipping forces under Fliegerführer Atlantik had been reduced still further by the end of May 1942. They consisted of 3.(F)/123 at Lannion, Stab and III/KG 40 with 19 Fw 200C-4s at Mérignac, Stab KG 6 and Kü.Fl.Gr. 106 with 19 Ju 88A-4s at Dinard and coastal reconnaissance units Stab/Kü.Fl.Gr. 406 and 5./BFGr. 196 at Brest. The Dornier Do 217E-4 bombers were concentrated under FlKps IX, with KG 2 and II/KG 40 based in Holland.

Kampfgeschwader 40 had been relegated to reconnaissance duties for the Befehlshaber der U-boote, while forced at the same time to detach its units to Luftflotte 5; the 1.Staffel was undergoing He 177 conversion at Fassberg, in Germany. The Condors now carried the Rostock ASV radar for shipping search, and the later FuG Hohentwiel radar was also appearing as standard equipment. The III/KG 40's normal patrols at this time were termed the grosse and kleine Aufklärung; the patrols were divided by Lat 45°N with the westerly limit extending to Long 19°W, or on occasions to 25°W. On grosse Aufklärung the northerly limit was Lat 50°N, beyond which there was a grave risk of interception by RAF Beaufighters and Mosquitoes. The Facher (Fan) method of search was a form of 'creeping line-ahead' in which the Condor started from 15°W, for example, flew West for 3 degrees of longitude, turned South for 30 miles and then turned East for another 3 degrees.

The axis of U-boat operations was now centred in mid-Atlantic, with a growing tendency by U-boat commanders to venture far south into the Caribbean and the Gulf of

*Right: The He 115 multi-role seaplane was an impressive machine, used for a variety of tasks ranging from reconnaissance to torpedo bombing*

Mexico. Through the Bay of Biscay there passed, on numerous occasions, damaged U-boats returning from their patrols, and these were frequently subjected to attack from RAF Coastal Command. At the time U-boat sinkings in these circumstances were not serious, but there now arose the need for some form of long-range fighter cover to reduce the threat of attack. In July 1942, III/KG 40 took charge of a small number of Ju 88C-6 fighters for duties over the Bay of Biscay; by September, with the activation of V/KG 40,*the Ju 88s were concentrated in the 13.Staffel with the Gruppe made up to the full strength of four staffeln by December. The formation and conversion took place at Mérignac and when operational the staffeln were sent to Kerlin-Bastard, near Lorient.

It was not until the spring of 1943 that operations for V/KG 40 took on a more serious nature. Five out of every six U-boats made passage through the Bay of Biscay for operations in the Atlantic and the Caribbean, and this small area of sea, only 300 miles in length and 120 miles in width, became the chosen killing ground. Hitherto, Air Vice Marshal G. R. Bromet's 19 Group, RAF Coastal Command, had reaped little success in this area for which it was responsible – seven U-boats had been sunk in the Bay in 1942, with two more added by February 1943. The introduction in March of ASV Mk. III and the American ASV Mk. IV radars, both working on the 10-centimetre band, radically altered the situation. The U-boats carried a radar location aid called Metox 600 which gave range (up to 40 miles) and bearing of the ASV Mk. II (1½-metre band) radar, carried as standard on Coastal Command's patrol aircraft, and this allowed the commander to submerge in good time. With ASV Mk. III, however, there was no such aid to location, and losses in the Bay started to mount. To counter this, the U-boats were fitted with Flakvierling 20-mm and Flak 18 37-mm guns and their crews were encouraged to fight it out on the surface.

In May 1943, V/KG 40's strength averaged some 45 Ju 88C-6s. The Gruppe's HQ was at Kerlin-Bastard, but staffeln were always detached to Mérignac and Cognac. Reinforcement crews were trained in the 10.Staffel of IV/KG 40 at Chateaudun, where new Ju 88C-6s and R-1s were received for allocation. The normal duties of V/KG 40 consisted of U-boat escort and sweeps over the Bay to counter RAF Coastal Command anti-submarine aircraft. Normal patrols, when engaged on counter sweeps, extended to Lat 8–10°W with a northern boundary fixed at Lat 45°N, but on occasions patrols went as far as 15°W. At first, the Ju 88s operated in Schwarme (four aircraft) but in face of increasing Beaufighter opposition, it was common procedure to operate at least eight, or even 16 aircraft in one formation; normal formation was an extended echelon port or starboard. Of all the Allied aircraft frequently encountered over the Bay, the Sunderland was considered the most difficult to shoot down. One example of this occurred on 2 June when a Sunderland of No. 461 RAAF Squadron fought a running battle with V/KG 40s Ju 88s in which the Gruppe lost three without being able to destroy the flying boat. The Ju 88 crews preferred to attack Sunder-

*Formed from elements of KG6.

*Above: Four stages in the destruction of a Junkers Ju 52/3m (MS) minesweeping aircraft, shot down by two RAF Typhoons of the Southern Rhodesia Squadron near the Atlantic*

*U-Boat base at Lorient. The large dural hoop, braced beneath wings and fuselage, was energised by an auxiliary motor supplying a constant 300 amperes*

lands either from head-on or directly abeam in order to avoid the potent rear armament.

At one time, during the summer of 1943, Coastal Command was losing one aircraft per day to V/KG 40 in battles over the Bay of Biscay. The courier service between Portugal and Britain also suffered from the attentions of the Gruppe. The 14.Staffel was on patrol between 12° and 13° West on 2 June 1943 when it intercepted the DC-3 transport carrying

Leslie Howard, a well known British actor who lost his life when the aircraft was shot into the sea. However, the losses of V/KG 40 were consistently high, one crew captured by the British in July 1943 estimated that some 37 crews had been lost since it had joined the Gruppe in November 1942.

Such was the high level of RAF activity in the Bay during the late summer that additional Luftwaffe fighter units were drafted at the

urgent request of Dönitz. The II/ZG 1, under Hptm. Karl-Heinz Matern, was transferred with its Bf 110G-2 fighters from Pratica de Mare to Kerlin-Bastard on 5 August, and a week later the Gruppe was operating patrols from Lanvéoc-Poulmic, near Brest. The forces under Fl.Fü. Atlantik on 30 September 1943 consisted of the fighters of Jagd Kommando Brest with five Fw 190A-4s, 1./SAGr. 128 with 17 Fw 190s and Ar 196s, and 2./SAGr. 128 with six Ar 196A-3s. The V/KG 40 had 44 Ju 88C-6s and II/ZG 1 had 39 Bf 110G-2s on strength. The 2./KG 40 had nine He 177A-5 bombers while 7. and 9.Staffel of KG 40 operated the Condor with the former at Cognac and the latter at Mérignac.

## New Weapons and New Tactics
# 1943-1944

By the late summer of 1943, two of Germany's air-launched guided weapons were ready for action in the anti-shipping rôle. The first was the Ruhrstahl FX 1400 (Fritz-X) stand-off bomb. Carrying a 3,300-lb warhead, Fritz-X was released by its parent aircraft from 16,000–20,000 feet and fell at a terminal velocity approaching the speed of sound. It carried no propulsive motor, but was guided by a bomb aimer in the parent aircraft who was aided by a bright flare mounted in the tail of the bomb. The first unit to use Fritz-X was III/KG 100, formed from Lehr und Erprobungskommando 21, with Do 217K-2s which each carried two such bombs on ETC 2000/XII racks, The second new weapon was the Henschel Hs 293 glider-bomb which carried a 1,100-lb warhead. A small rocket motor accelerated the glider-bomb to 370mph, cutting out after a period of 12 seconds and allowing the weapon to coast in a shallow glide. Once again a flare mounted on the fuselage assisted the bomb aimer in its guidance, flight being controlled by use of a small joystick. This weapon was first issued to II/KG 100 equipped with Do 217E-5s which could carry two Hs 293s under the wings outboard of each engine.

Both units were under the overall command of Major Bernhard Jope, and commenced operations from Marseilles-Istres under Fliegerdivision 2 in late August 1943. The first missions of these Gruppen were attended with some success; a notable achievement occurred on 9 September when III/KG 100 sank the *Roma* and severely damaged the *Italia* battleships. During the following months both II and III/KG 100 were in actions against Allied supply convoys in the Mediterranean and flew missions during the Salerno and Anzio landings. The torpedo bomber units, I and III/KG 26, also operated from bases in Southern France under Fl.Div 2 with tangible results achieved on all their missions, but at an appreciable cost which rose, on one occasion, to 20 per cent of the force involved. Rest and replacement took place of necessity, and after four further missions, in October and November, the anti-shipping units in the Mediterranean remained inactive until 10 January 1944, when an Allied convoy was attacked off Oran.

During the autumn, III/KG 40 started receiving Hs 293 glider-bombs which were fitted to Fw 200s which each carried two of the new weapons and desultory operations with these were commenced on 28 December. The Heinkel He 177, upon which so much reliance had been placed, was also now finally reaching operational units, both as a bomber and an anti-shipping aircraft. The dismal story of its development and operational début are beyond the bounds of this chapter, but, during

*Above: The Fw 200C-3/U2 version of the Condor maritime reconnaissance and anti-shipping aircraft introduced the Lotfe 7D sight which improved bombing accuracy*

late 1943, two Gruppen of KG 40 were undergoing conversion to the He 177A-5. The 1./KG 40 was sent from Fassberg to Chateaudun along with half of 2.Staffel on 19 December, and here joined I/KG 100, also equipped with the He 177. These units were not connected with anti-shipping operations and were earmarked for Operation Steinbock, the retaliatory attacks against Britain, under Fliegerkorps IX. The II/KG 40, however, was intended as an anti-shipping force from the outset. Formed from I/KG 50 (the original Dornier 217-equipped II/KG 40 was redesignated V/KG 2), II/KG 40 was transferred to Bordeaux-Mérignac and flew its first operation on 21 November, when its He 177A-5s attacked a convoy. Twenty Heinkels, each carrying two Hs 293s, were despatched to intercept Convoy SL139/MKS 230, outbound from Britain to ports in North Africa and Sierra Leone. Despite bad weather, Fliegerführer Atlantik insisted on the attack which resulted in one straggler being disabled for the loss of three of II/KG 40's bombers. A disastrous mission was flown against a convoy off Bougie on 26 November, four He 177A-5s being shot down, three crashing in France and casualties included the Gruppenkommandeur, Major Mons. This operation and that preceding it left II/KG 40 with only seven serviceable aircraft. The Gruppe now turned to night operations in which a Kette would drop flares while another launched its Hs 293s from a range of 6–9 miles; this had the salutory effect of reducing losses to a bearable level.

By December 1943, long-range reconnaissance work was conducted by FAGr. 5 which maintained a small force of Ju 290A-5s at Mont de Marsan, in Southern France. The heavy fighter unit, V/KG 40, was incorporated into Stab, I and III/ZG 1 which operated

Ju 88C-6s from Kerlin-Bastard and Vannes. In March 1944, Fliegerführer Atlantik was disbanded and all anti-shipping forces came under the command of FlKps X with Fl.Div 2 subordinated. Grandiose plans calling for an anti-shipping force of major proportions with which to oppose the long-awaited Allied invasion of France all came to nought as units were diverted from their intended tasks and relegated to bombing attacks under the auspices of Operation 'Steinbock'.

Immediately prior to the invasion of Normandy, in June 1944, the anti-shipping forces of Fliegerkorps X consisted of Stab, II and III/KG 40, and III/KG 100 with the torpedo-bomber units of Stab, II and III/KG 26 and Geschwaderstab KG 30 making up the components of Fliegerdivision 2. In all, these amounted to some 200 aircraft, a potentially formidable force, but suffering from a deep-seated weakness in that it contained a high proportion of inexperienced crews. From 6 June until 1 July 1944, the anti-shipping elements of Luftflotte 3 were active over the beachheads during the hours of darkness. In mining operations, 1,906 mines of the BM 1000 and LMB types were laid from the mouth of the River Orne to Courseulles. Within Fliegerdivision 2, the torpedo-bombers flew a total of 384 sorties, with I and III/KG 26 claiming 60,000 BRT sunk for the loss of no aircraft. Weather minima for torpedo operations required a cloud base of 600–900 feet and a visibility of 10–15 miles during the approach flight, which was increased to a base of 900–1,200 feet and a visibility of 15–20 miles in the attack area itself; cloud cover needed was at least 5/10ths. In view of overwhelming Allied air superiority, torpedo attacks were made by night only with – on average – one major operation being flown per week. Loaded with

two LT F5b torpedoes, the Ju 88s made an intermediate stop at Dijon or Chalon-sur-Saone before flying on to the combat area. After the attack a direct flight was made back to bases in Southern France.

Despite the mass of Allied shipping traversing the Channel and lying off the Normandy coast, only five ships were sunk by air attack during the first ten days of the invasion. Mining achieved better results in the sinking of nine warships and 17 auxiliary vessels and merchantmen. By mid-July, the growing losses coupled with the start of the fuel famine enforced termination of large-scale attempts at anti-shipping attack, and the remnants of Fliegerkorps X and Fl.Div 2 retired to bases in Norway and Germany. The eclipse of the once-powerful anti-shipping forces of the Luftwaffe was now complete, and only in Norway was a powerful force maintained in the form of KG 26 with Ju 88A-4 and A-17 torpedo-bombers, which were supplemented later by the new Ju 188E-2. This force, numbering about 110 aircraft, remained dormant until 6 February 1945, when a major attack was made on a convoy bound for the Soviet Union. In the next four days, over 200 torpedo missions were flown, but the attacks proved totally unsuccessful. Further operations were undertaken between 18–23 February, during which some 60 aircraft of KG 26 engaged a returning convoy wherein one vessel was sunk. Thereafter KG 26 relapsed into inactivity from which it was for the final time to emerge only in the last days of the war.

# Chapter 10

# The Prospect of a Long War

The reverses suffered by the Wehrmacht at Stalingrad and El Alamein finally disposed of any German illusions of a swift victory. Some considered the war already lost when the Soviet Union was invaded, and some could see the final outcome with the entry of the United States of America. But, for the majority of Germans, the defeats in the winter of 1942–43 indicated not so much that the war would one day be lost; rather the inescapable fact that Ende Siege would take not months but possibly years to achieve. The Luftwaffe had prepared itself for a short war. And with the Soviet Army on the offensive when, to all intents and purposes, its recent losses should have ensured its virtual defeat; with Germany facing two closing battlefronts in Tunisia and with the day and night bombing of Germany becoming an increasingly significant factor, it was not surprising to find the Luftwaffe in a state of crisis.

The barometer of battle capability of any military force is its morale coupled with its numerical strength. While there was no cause for concern for the fighting spirit of the Luftwaffe's airmen, there most certainly was for the service's diminishing strength, both in manpower and material. From July to December 1942, the Luftwaffe's first-line strength fell from 4,000 to 3,850 aircraft, the lowest since August 1939, due to wastage in the Soviet Union and the Mediterranean theatre. In manpower, the Luftwaffe had grown from 600,000 at the beginning of the war to 1,100,000 men by late 1942, but now the diversion of manpower to the Felddivisionen for ground fighting had started to erode this figure; while recruitment was later to restore strength, the strength reduction was serious at this critical time of change in Germany's fortunes.

Coupled with this manpower drain was the special problem of aircrew training. Like aircraft production, this had been organised upon the assumption of a short war. The Luftwaffe started the war with a large body of fully-trained aircrew, but the first year of the Soviet campaign ate deeply into this force which had already sustained the losses of the Battle of Britain. In the Jagdgruppen, in particular, the reservoir of older experienced pilots was all but exhausted, and the flow from the Jagdschulen was no longer sufficient to replace losses. The result, already evident by the summer of 1942, was contraction and, in consequence, standard deterioration in the training of pilots and crews. At about this time, the IV Gruppe, or Ergänzungsgruppe, of each Geschwader, which hitherto had provided valuable *ab initio* operational experience for freshmen crews, was largely disbanded, its place being taken by Fighter Pools situated at Mannheim, Krakow and Cazaux. This situation applied also to the bomber and close-support arms. It was inevitable, therefore, that crews now suffered some loss of pre-operational experience before reaching the frontline.

The expectation of a short war had manifested itself in Germany's policies in aircraft production and aircraft development. In the first two years of the war, no less than sixteen different aircraft production programmes were started: none lasted longer than six to eight weeks before being shelved or amalgamated to form yet another programme. Under Generalluftzeugmeister Ernst Udet, German aircraft production rose only by 5–10 per cent, despite the pressures and wastage of two years' of continuous air fighting. But so long as a strong reserve could be maintained, the pinch was not felt. However, the battles of attrition in the East now coupled with the entry into the war of the USA, the most highly

Above: Ernst Udet (right), seen here with Hermann Göring, proved a failure as Generalluftzeugmeister and after his suicide his place was taken by the efficient Erhard Milch

industrialised nation in the world, had changed the situation dramatically. If Schmid's 1C Intelligence Staff was to be believed, the combined Anglo-American air forces were estimated to be capable of fielding 10–20,000 bombers by the end of 1943! To this threat Udet had no answer.

After his decease, Udet's place was taken by Erhard Milch, who thus regained the position he had lost in 1938. This remarkable man was aware of the need for a thorough overhaul of the whole production situation in order to counter the growing strength of the RAF and the manufacturing potential of the Soviet and American aircraft industries. Milch's first production programme, authorised in March 1942, was only a modest instalment towards fulfilling the requirements of the Luftwaffe and was deliberately scaled down in order to forestall the objections of Hitler and the Generalstabes of OKW.

Under Milch's direction, German aircraft production rose from just under 1,000 aircraft per month at the end of 1941 to 1,650 per month by the end of 1942; these aircraft included 500 Fw 190s and Bf 109s, 500 He 111s, Ju 88s and Do 217s, 100 Ju 87Ds and 150 Bf 110s. With Germany now on the defensive, fighters assumed highest priority for Milch, and despite much opposition, he managed to boost the output of fighters to over 1,000 per month by June 1943 – 800 of these being Bf 109Gs and Fw 190As. By this time, Allied bombing had underlined the need for priority in fighter production, but much effort was still diverted to the production of bombers and Stukas, and it was not to be until July 1944, when the Luftwaffe's situation was beyond recovery, that all emphasis was laid on the production of fighters. That the Luftwaffe was able to defend Germany with such resilience during 1943 and 1944 was totally due to Milch's first programme, which laid the foundations for a second calling for 2,000 fighters per month by January 1944 and up to 3,000 fighters monthly by July 1944!

At first, the massive scale of the impending Allied bombing offensive was not foreseen. Part of Milch's re-organisation called for the centralisation of aircraft factories to boost production. Thus, for example, production of the Bf 109G was centred at Erla-Leipzig, Regensburg and Wiener Neustadt, the Ju 88 at Bernberg, Oschersleben and Halberstadt, and

the Bf 110G at Brunswick. This was to prove a costly mistake and, when these centres were virtually wiped-out by bombing, it was only the most energetic programme of de-centralisation that was to prevent production grinding to a standstill.

If quantitative production could be maintained, there still remained the problem of quality. German aeronautical research had been, and still was, capable of indisputable brilliance in the design of airframes and engines, but the few aircraft earmarked for the re-equipment of the Luftwaffe in place of older types had failed to come up to standard. Notably these were the Me 210, the He 177, the Hs 129 and the Ju 288, which had either failed to meet operational requirements or, in the case of the last-mentioned type, had never left the research establishments. No priority whatsoever was assigned to the turbine-engined Me 262 and He 280 and, while these

remarkably innovatory fighters were allowed to remain the playthings of the aircraft industry and test centres, the Luftwaffe was forced to soldier on with the established types. Of these, 80 per cent consisted of Bf 109Gs, Fw 190As, Ju 88s, He 111s, Bf 110s and Ju 87Ds, the last three being obsolescent by then current standards. In mitigation, however, the fighter types – the Bf 109G-6, the Fw 190A-6 and the Ju 88C-6 of 1943 – were efficient, high-performance aircraft each possessing formidable capabilities.

The early months of 1943, therefore, were a period of crisis in Luftwaffe dispositions, resources and manpower. In the Soviet Union, the last great Wehrmacht offensives in the Ukraine and the Caucasus had foundered at Stalingrad, and now the Russians were gathering their strength for the summer campaigns. In the Mediterranean, where even the transfer of over 400 combat aircraft from

*Above: A carefully posed publicity photo, an armourer of a Stukagruppe in front of a Ju 87B dive-bomber on the Eastern Front in the summer of 1941*

the Soviet Union had failed to restore the balance, the situation was one of impending defeat in North Africa. And now there was added a third commitment: that of defending Germany and the occupied territories in the West against Anglo-American bombing by day and night.

For the Luftwaffe, the first priority lay in the stabilisation of the situation in the Soviet Union and the Mediterranean. From the point of view of Hitler and the OKW, the first necessity was to bring the Russian advance to a halt, and by reason of this the Soviet Union had the first claim on the Luftwaffe in the Spring of 1943.

# Chapter 11

# Russia 1943-1944

The opening of year 1943 saw the Red Army taking advantage of the massive Wehrmacht concentration in the Stalingrad sector, and going over to the offensive along the entire Eastern Front. The siege of Leningrad was raised on 18 January 1943; in the centre the Soviet armies on the Moscow Front recaptured Rzhev and Vyasma before the completion of their winter campaign, while further south, on the Upper Don, Voronezh was recaptured on 26 January.

It was in the south that the progress of the Soviet Army was most rapid. Bypassing Stalingrad, the southern Soviet thrust reached the Donetz river, taking Rostov, Voroshilovgrad and Kharkov by mid-February, at the same time covering the northern flank by recapturing Kursk on 8 February. Meanwhile, the Wehrmacht was forced to make a precipitate retreat from the Caucasus. Mozdok, three-quarters of the way between the Caspian and the Sea of Azov, was retaken by the Russians at the beginning of January and only five weeks later Krasnodar changed hands, leaving the Germans to defend the narrow bridgehead in the Kuban peninsula.

Throughout this period the Luftwaffe concentrated on Stalingrad, continuously transferring units to that sector at the expense of others, so that by January 1943, out of a total front-line strength of 1,715 aircraft, 900 were concentrated in the Don sector under Luftflotte 4 (FlKps VIII) and Luftwaffenkommando Don (FlKps I); 240 were under Fliegerkorps IV in the Crimea and Caucasus; 380 were on the Moscow Front under Luftwaffenkommando Ost (FlKps V) and 195 were on the Leningrad Front under Luftflotte 1.

These forces consisted of the following units as of 20 February 1943: Single-engined fighters (Fw 190A-4 and Bf 109G-4): II and III/JG 3, Stab, II and III/JG 5, I/JG 26, Stab, I, III and 15.(Span)/JG 51, Stab, I and II/JG 52, Stab, I and II/JG 54; ground-attack (Fw 190A-4, Bf 110G-2, Hs 129B-1): II/ZG 1, 13.(Zerst)/JG 5, Pz. Jäger Staffel JG 51, I and II/SchG 1; dive-bombers (Ju 87D-3): Stab, I and III/StG 1, Stab, I, II and III/StG 2, I/StG 5, Stab and I/StG 77; long-range bombers (He 111H-16 and

Ju 88A-4): Stab, I and III/KG 1, Stab, I and III/KG 3, Stab, II and III/KG 4, I and III/KG 27, I/KG 30, Stab, I and III/KG 51, Stab, II, III and 15./KG 53, and Stab, I and III/KG 55.

The preponderance of Soviet tank and troop concentrations called for an increase in the number of specialised close-support and ground-attack aircraft, and by way of expedience, the Luftwaffe formed Störkampfstaffeln (Harassing bomber units) and Nachtschlachtgruppen (Night ground-attack units) in the spring of 1943, equipped with obsolescent He 46C, He 45C and Ar 66 aircraft. The anti-tank element was now under a Führer der Panzerjäger, who conducted combat operations for I and II/SchG 1 (Bf 109, Hs 123 and Hs 129), Pz.Jäger St./JG 51, Pz.Jäger St. Ju 87, I/ZG 1 (Bf 110) and later Staffel 92 equipped with the Ju 88P-1. With the exception of the Ju 88P-1, which carried a 75-mm cannon, the heaviest tank-busting weapon was the Rheinmetall Flak 18 (BK 3·7) 37-mm cannon installed in the Ju 87G-1 and the Hs 129B-2/R3. While incapable of piercing the armour of the T-34 and KV-1 tanks, the 37mm weapon was capable of immobilising the T-34 by blowing off a track. A further expedient taken at this time was the formation of specialised train-busting units equipped with Ju 88C-6 heavy fighters, and these consisted initially of 9./KG 3, 14./KG 27, 9./KG 55 and 4./KG 76.

None of these measures, however, could do

anything to stem the tide of the Soviet advance which had been carried across the Donetz by mid-February. But by now the momentum of the Soviet Army's offensive had slowed in order to consolidate its position; lines of supply and communication were fully stretched and a number of Soviet Air Force units were grounded due to lack of fuel. It was in these circumstances that the Wehrmacht was able to launch a counteroffensive, on 20 February, that culminated in Manstein's capture of Kharkov and Belgorod between 15–18 March 1943. The offensive saw the reappearance of the classical Blitzkrieg advance, with the armoured spearheads of 2nd SS 'Das Reich' Panzer Division advancing under overwhelming air support from von Richthofen's Luftflotte 4. Fliegerkorps IV bore the main weight of the assault in support of I and IV Panzer Armies in the drive to the Donetz and onwards to the south and south-eastern sectors of Kharkov.

*Right: A Focke-Wulf Fw 189A tactical reconnaissance and army co-operation aircraft of one of the Nahaufklärungs-gruppen operating in support of ground forces on the Finnish Front*

*Below: Henschel Hs 129B-2/R2 anti-tank aircraft of Schlachtgeschwader 9*

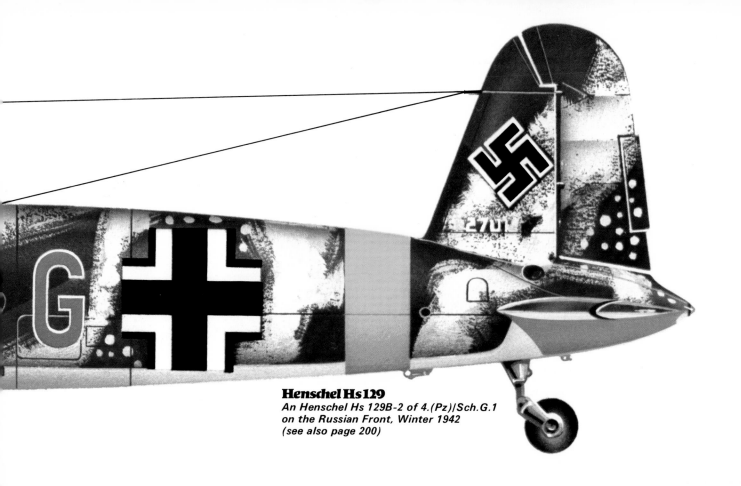

**Henschel Hs 129**
*An Henschel Hs 129B-2 of 4.(Pz)/Sch.G.1
on the Russian Front, Winter 1942
(see also page 200)*

At the same time, Fliegerkorps I supported the assault on the north and north-western sectors, while Fliegerdivision Donetz was assigned a defensive battle on the eastern flank of I Panzer Army, where it was essential to hold the Russians back while the Kharkov attack was in progress. As soon as its task was completed Fl.Div. Donetz took its powerful ground-attack forces away from the Stalino area to support Fliegerkorps IV.

Combat sorties by Richthofen's pilots averaged 1,000 per day, rising to a crescendo, on 23 February, with 1,250 and maintaining the pace until the capture of Belgorod, which effectively re-established the German hold on the Donetz line. By the end of March, the Spring thaw slowed the advance and saw a slackening in Luftwaffe activity, but the limited aims of Manstein's offensive had been achieved. This remarkable recovery undoubtedly saved the Wehrmacht from being overwhelmed after the Stalingrad disaster, and now the dominant feature on the Soviet Front was the huge Orel-Kursk salient that was destined to be the graveyard for either the Wehrmacht or the Soviet Army in the summer of 1943.

When, at the beginning of April 1943, weather conditions made a continuation of intensive operations on the Donetz front impossible, renewed Soviet pressure in the Kuban, to the East of the Crimea, compelled the Luftwaffe to redispose its forces in this new theatre. Some 550–600 strike aircraft, under FlKps VIII, were sent to bases in the Crimea and commenced intensive operations from 17 April onwards. The Russians did not allow the Luftwaffe to relax its effort, and a daily rate of 400 sorties was per force, maintained at the very time that rest and re-equipment was required. This concentration was reduced, however, at the beginning of May, and redistributed fairly evenly over all sectors from Smolensk southwards. By June, the preparations for the Kursk offensive were in progress, and Fliegerkorps VIII was posted to the Kharkov-Belgorod sector facing the southern Kursk salient, while a new command, Luftflotte 6, formed from Luftwaffenkommando Ost, took up position in the Smolensk-Orel sector in the north. This command was led by Generaloberst Robert Ritter von Greim.

Another important change, which met with violent opposition from von Manstein, the Army commander, was the transfer of Wolfram von Richthofen from Luftflotte 4 to officer-commanding Luftflotte 2 in the Mediterranean. After the disaster at Tunis, there had been an increasing tendency to reinforce the Mediterranean at the expense of the Soviet Front. General Dessloch succeeded Richthofen as commander of Luftflotte 4.

Luftwaffe first-line strength in the Soviet Union rose from 2,100 aircraft after the abortive Kuban offensive to approximately 2,500 in June 1943; this figure was achieved by bringing back units from rest and re-equipment. The Luftwaffe's ability to mount a force of this size for the third consecutive summer's operations in the Soviet Union, despite its increased commitments in the Mediterranean and over the Reich, was possible as a result of the remarkable recovery in total first-line strength which took place in the first six months of 1943. At the end of 1942, the total Luftwaffe strength hovered below 4,000, but by June 1943 this figure had increased to almost exactly 6,000 aircraft – a total never again to be achieved throughout the remainder of the war.

## Operation Zitadelle—the Battle for Kursk

# 1943

Aimed at wresting the strategic initiative from the Russians and ultimately turning the course of the war, the planning and preparation of Operation Zitadelle were carried out with unparalleled thoroughness by the Germans. The offensive called for two simultaneous assaults on the northern and southern sectors of the Kursk salient to destroy the Soviet armies, straighten the frontline and, in the event of success, exploit the situation by a plunging advance to the Don river. No effort was to be spared, and among the 2,700 German tanks assembled for the offensive were the latest PzKw V Panthers and PzKw VI Tigers which were to spearhead the assault. The Soviet Army had, however, had adequate time in which to prepare its defences and build up its resources. Anti-tank ditches had been dug along the entire perimeter of the salient and in depth, while 1,300,000 troops supported by 3,600 tanks and 2,400 aircraft, including the latest La-5 and Yak-9 fighters, were deployed to counter the German attacks.

The Luftwaffe fielded at least 1,000 aircraft in direct support of Zitadelle, representing 50 per cent of the total forces available for the whole Soviet Front, from Murmansk to the Sea of Azov. While including several Kampfgruppen with He 111s and Ju 88s, these forces comprised primarily II and III/JG 3, I, III and IV/JG 51, I and III/JG 52 and II/JG 54 with Fw 190A-5 and Bf 109G-6 fighters; the ground-attack units were Stab, I and II/SchG 1 and 4./SchG 2, Stab and I/ZG 1. and Pz.Jäg/JG 51, and the Stukagruppen available were I, II and

*Above: Junkers Ju 87D-8s, believed operated by Stukageschwader 77, taking-off on a close-support sortie in the winter of 1943-44*

III/StG 1, I, II and III/StG 2, III/StG 3, and I, II and III/StG 77 equipped with Ju 87D-5s.

At 04.30hrs on 5 July 1943, after a preliminary bombardment, III Panzer Corps and IV Panzer Army of Manstein's Army Group South struck northwards from Belgorod, while IX Army and II Panzer Army under Mödel's Army Group Centre attacked the northern flank of the Kursk salient from Orel. Both assaults quickly became bogged down in bitter fire-fights with dug-in Soviet troops and armour. Such was the strength of Soviet resistance that Mödel had committed all his reserves to the battle by 9 July, but to no avail. The greatest tank battle in history took place on 12 July, when IV Pz. Army, III Pz. Corps and Einsatzgruppe Kempff lost 350 tanks in combat around Prokhorovka, some 25 miles north of Belgorod. On this day, while the Soviet Army fought the Wehrmacht to a standstill in the Kursk salient, the Russians opened an offensive in the north, threatening the German rear at Orel. Other Soviet counteroffensives followed, and by 23 July both Army Group South and Army Group Centre had been pushed back to their starting lines, thus committing Zitadelle to crushing defeat.

During the opening phases of Zitadelle, the Luftwaffe flew over 3,000 sorties a day, with each serviceable Ju 87D flying up to 5–6 missions per day. This effort decreased to around 1,500 sorties per day after the first week, and then averaged 1,000 per day for the remainder of July. The Jagdgruppen claimed 432 'kills' on the first day, of which II/JG 3 claimed 77 'kills', including 62 bombers, and III/JG 52 shot down 38 Soviet aircraft. German losses on the first day of Zitadelle amounted to only 26 aircraft. In total, the Luftwaffe flew 37,421 sorties throughout the battle, destroying 1,735 enemy aircraft for the loss of 64. Twenty thousand tons of bombs were dropped and Fliegerkorps I alone claimed 1,100 tanks and 1,300 vehicles.

While these impressive figures applied to the battles in the Kursk salient, elsewhere the situation gave cause for concern. German aircraft losses, which in June had totalled 487, rose to 911 in July, and in August were 785 over the entire Eastern Front. By 5 August, the Soviet Army had captured Orel and Belgorod, opening the way for the great autumn offensive, while the entire German position in the south was put at risk by the Soviet re-capture of Kharkov on 23 August.

**Above: The Messerschmitt Gigant heavy transport (the Me 323E version)**

For the Luftwaffe, the failure of Operation Zitadelle was to have widespread repercussions. Generaloberst Hans Jeschonnek, the Chief of Air Staff, had been the apostle of tactical air power in support of the Army, and had staked his reputation on a decisive and quick victory in the Soviet Union. The failure at Kursk, allied with the inability of the Luftwaffe to alter the disastrous situation first in North Africa and now in Sicily, rendered his policies bankrupt. He committed suicide. The Soviet Front, the cornerstone of his policies, was no longer afforded top priority by the Luftwaffe.

## The Russians Assume the Offensive August—May

# 1943-1944

Generaloberst Korten, the ex-commander of Luftflotte 1, was Jeschonnek's successor as Chief of the Air Staff. His views differed radically from those of his predecessor in that he favoured increased emphasis on fighter defence of the homeland, and on the belated constitution of a strategic bomber force. In compliance with these objectives, the Luftwaffe, in his opinion, was henceforth to accord

only the minimum amount of tactical support to the Army. His views, allied with the growing weight of the Allied bombing offensive against Germany, were to result in a marked reduction in German fighter units on the Soviet Front and the withdrawal, in December 1943, of the whole of Fliegerkorps IV from its tactical support duties and its redeployment for strategic bombing.

As early as June 1943, Major Johannes Seifert's I/JG 26, which had exchanged duties with III/JG 54, returned to Northern France; the 7./JG 26, also based in the Soviet Union, returned to the West in mid-July. This month also saw the transfer of Geschwaderstab and I/JG 3 'Udet' from Luftflotte 4, and I/JG 5

'Eismeer' from Luftflotte 5 to the defence of the Reich, while the II and III/JG 3 were both installed at bases in Holland by the end of September. Significantly, no Jagdgruppen were returned from other fronts to Russia to fill this vacuum.

However, the transfer of bomber and single-engined fighter units was balanced, in part, by the strengthening of the ground-attack forces now controlled by the General der Schlachtflieger, Oberst Hubertus Hitschold. The appellation Stukageschwader (StG) was dropped and became Schlachtgeschwader (SG); the old SchG 1, SchG 2 and SKG 10 being re-organised into the new SG 4, SG 9 and SG 10, and the five anti-tank Hs 129 staffeln became IV(Panzer)/SG 9. In addition, the Gruppen of Ju 87Ds were converted on to Fw 190Fs and Gs at the rate of two Gruppen every six weeks.

When the Soviet offensive to liberate the Eastern Ukraine and establish bridgeheads on the Dneiper river opened on 26 August, Fliegerkorps I in the Stalino-Taganrog area and Fliegerkorps VIII in the Poltava-Kharkov area could only muster some 900 first-line aircraft. They were unable to stem the tide of Soviet advance which, by 23 December, had isolated the XVII German Army in the Crimea, had retaken Smolensk, Bryansk, Gomel and Chernikov in the northern sector, and had taken Kiev, Kremenchug and Zaporozhe, pushing the entire German line to the east of the Dneiper.

This time there was to be no German counter-offensive, and such was the numerical strength of the Soviet Army and air forces that, without their pausing for breath, the entire Soviet Front erupted in December 1943, when the Soviet winter offensive got underway. In

comparison with a total strength of 2,500 aircraft in July, the Luftwaffe's resources amounted to 1,710 combat aircraft on 1 January 1944. The bulk of these were concentrated in the South, resulting in only minimal opposition from the Luftwaffe on the Leningrad Front. In the Ukraine, the Soviet Army drove full tilt for the Dneister river, the Carpathians and to the borders of Rumania, beyond which lay the vital oilfields of Ploesti.

In the face of this advance, Fliegerkorps I and VIII managed to fly only 300–350 sorties per day, due to appalling weather, bad airfield conditions, and low serviceability. On 29 February 1944, of the 377 German fighters on the Eastern Front, only 265 were serviceable. These consisted of Bf 109G-6s of Stab, I and III/JG 5, Stab, I, III, IV and 15.(Span)/JG 51, Stab, I, II, III and 15.(Kroat)/JG 52 and I/JG 302, with the Fw 190A-5 units being Stab, I, II and IV /JG 54. The close-support elements consisted of 653 aircraft of which 483 were serviceable for combat. These were Stab, I, II and III/SG 1, Stab and I/SG 2, 10.(Pz)/SG 1, 10.(Pz)/SG 2, Stab, I, II and III/SG 3, 1. and 4./SG 5, Stab, I and III/SG 77 with Ju 87D-5 and Ju 87G-1 types, and II and III/SG 2, Stab, I and II/SG 10, and II/SG 77 with Fw 190Fs and Gs. The Henschel 129 unit was the IV(Pz)/SG 9 with 62 aircraft. This was the strike force, extending from Finland to Nikolaev on the Black Sea, in addition to a force of reconnaissance, night-harassing, and long-range bomber units that made up Luftflotten 1, 4 and 6.

By mid-April 1944, the frontline stretched in the south from Kovel (50 miles SE of Brest-Litovsk), across the Dneister to the Carpathians, and down to Jassy on the Rumanian border. In May 1944, Fliegerkorps VIII and

*Above: A Junkers Ju 87G-1 37-mm cannon-armed anti-tank aircraft of a Panzerjäger-Staffel flying over the Eastern Front in the summer of 1943*

*Right: Refuelling of a Junkers Ju 52/3m transport operating on the Soviet Front being undertaken by an aircrew member. Rapidity of turnround was vital on resupply missions*

Fliegerkorps I had 750 aircraft (40 per cent of the strength on the Soviet Front) stationed in Rumania and Bessarabia in anticipation of the next Soviet offensive that threatened the Rumanian oilfields and the resources of the Balkans. On 9 May, the XVII Army capitulated in the Crimea, but for a while the situation remained static as the Russians brought up their reserves, giving the Germans two months in which to consolidate their defences before the next Soviet offensive.

The history of the Soviet campaigns of 1943 and 1943–44 was the clearest tribute to the tactical skill with which the Soviet Air Forces exploited their numerical air superiority, extending the weakened Luftwaffe opposed to it by constant and ever-shifting pressure up and down the front. But without the pressure exerted in the West by the RAF and USAAF, and in the Mediterranean, the balance in the East would perforce have been radically different, just as the Wehrmacht's opposition in Sicily and Italy would have been radically different if the bulk of its division had not been tied down by the struggle in the Soviet Union.

# Chapter 12

# The Mediterranean 1943-1944

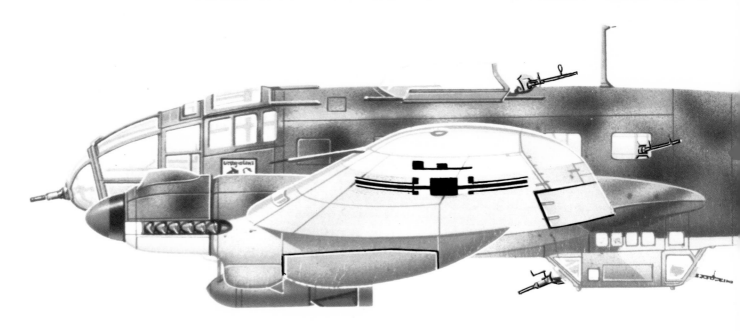

## The Invasion of Sicily

# 1943

The collapse of Axis resistance in Tunisia, on 13 May 1943, left the Luftwaffe faced with a multiplicity of problems which absorbed its attention, to the detriment of other commitments, throughout May and June. First in importance was the rest and refit of the shattered units withdrawn from North Africa, and next was the need to reinforce the Mediterranean theatre, in view of the proved inadequacy of the forces allocated in the early months of the year. In addition, there was the strategic problem of deploying forces to meet the multiple threats of Allied landings. Allied security had been extremely good and the Germans had no means of knowing where the next blow would fall: Sicily, Greece, Crete, Sardinia, and possibly the Italian mainland were all feasible possibilities.

To meet the new situation, a reorganisation and strengthening of the Luftwaffe operational commands was put into effect without delay. The operational area of Luftflotte 2, hitherto encompassing the whole of the Mediterranean, was restricted to Sicily, Sardinia and Italy, while a new command called Luftwaffenkommando Süd-Ost, with Luftflotte status, was established in the Balkans, Greece and Crete. Generalfeldmarschall Albert Kesselring became the supremo of all military forces in the Mediterranean, and his successor as OC Luftflotte 2 was Generaloberst Wolfram von Richthofen. Further changes brought about by the lamentable inefficiency of the Headquarters staff of Luftflotte 2 included the posting in of Gen.Lt. Alfred Bülowius as the commander of Fliegerkorps II and Gen.Lt. Mahncke as chief of tactical operations. Apart from these and other staff officers from the Soviet Union, Gen.Maj. Harlinghausen was relieved of command of the Mediterranean bomber units and replaced by Oberst Pelz,

previously of I/KG 60. At the same time, Gen.Maj. Adolf Galland, the General der Jagdflieger, was despatched on an extended tour of duty in the Mediterranean with the task of restoring morale and efficiency.

At the end of the Tunisian campaign, the total strength of Luftflotte 2 was 880 aircraft of all categories, based in the Central and Eastern Mediterranean. In one and a half months this figure rose to 1,280 (as of 3 July 1943) and of these 440 additional aircraft, 260 were Bf 109G-4 and G-6 fighters – an indication of German concern at growing Allied air superiority. On 10 July 1943, the day of the Allied invasion of Sicily, the overall strength had dropped to 1,150 aircraft, of which 885 were under Luftflotte 2 and 265 were under Luftwaffenkommando Süd-Ost, and of these a mere 175 were stationed in Sicily, indicating the total ignorance of where the actual landings would occur. On the day of the Allied invasion the dispositions and locations of Luftflotte 2 were as shown in the accompanying table.

The units based in Sardinia consisted of 4.(H)/12 with Bf 109F-5 reconnaissance fighters at Decimommanu; and II/JG 51 and III/JG 77 with Bf 109G-6 fighters at Casa Zeppara and Chilivani respectively. On the Italian mainland, IV/JG 3 at Lecce, II/JG 27 and I/JG 53 at Vibo Valentia equipped with Bf 109G-6s were within close proximity to battle area. Elements of II and III/SKG 10 with Fw 190 fighter-bombers were stationed at Montecorvino, which also housed II/ZG 1 with Bf 110G-2 fighters. Twin-engined fighter units consisted of Stab ZG 26 at Naples-Camoldoli, III/ZG 26 at Rome-Ciampino and Pisa, and 10./ZG 26 with Ju 88C-6s at Pratica de Mare.

Widespread Allied bombing of airfields in Sardinia, Sicily and Southern Italy had forced Luftflotte 2 to withdraw its Kampfgruppen to the Foggia area, although a number of units were further north at Piacenza, Viterbo and Airasca. This force consisted of I/LG 1, Stab, I and III/KG 1, Stab, I and III/KG 6, III/KG 30, III/KG 54, Stab, I and II/KG 76 and III/KG 77, and the Geschwaderstab KG 100, equipped with Ju 88A-4, A-14 and A-17 bombers, Stab, I

*Left: A Junkers Ju 88A-14 of 1.Staffel of Kampfgeschwader 77 which flew anti-shipping sorties over the Mediterranean from its Sicilian base. Note gondola-mounted cannon*

**Heinkel He 111**
*An Heinkel He 111H-6 of 2.Staffel,
Kampfgeschwader 26, Ottana, Sardinia,
August 1943 (see also pages 180-185)*

and III/KG 26 at Grosseto with He 111H-6 torpedo-bombers, and II and III/KG 100 at Foggia-Morin with Do 217E-5 and K-2 bombers and in process of working up to operational standard with the Hs 293 glider-bomb and the FX 1400 (Fritz X) stand-off bomb.

In the early hours of 10 July, the 7th US Army under Patton and the 8th British Army under Montgomery landed on the Sicilian coast in the Liccata-Gela and Avola-Pachino sectors. The resistance from Italian defences was stiff at first, but by the end of the first day the Allies had managed to secure their respective beachheads. For a week prior to the invasion, the Allied air forces had pursued an all-out bombing offensive against Axis airfields in Sardinia, Sicily and on the mainland, and this was largely instrumental in reducing the Luftwaffe's scale of effort to 275–300 sorties between 10–12 July, with 50 per cent of these operations being flown at night. In the face of overwhelming Allied air superiority, even this mediocre reaction was not maintained and, thereafter, the average effort fell to about 150 sorties per day, including fighters and fighter-bombers based in Sardinia and southern Italy which moved forward daily to landing grounds in Sicily. By 19 July, Allied bombing had effectively reduced the serviceability of Luftwaffe units to about 35 per cent of actual strength, leaving only 25 aircraft capable of operations based in Sicily.

Combat operations by German fighter and fighter-bomber units continued with negligible effect from bases in Calabria, but the dogged rearguard actions by XV Panzer and Hermann Göring Panzer Divisions were notable for their total lack of air support from the Luftwaffe. The most demonstrable failure of the Luftwaffe was the level of impotence to which the Kampfgruppen had been reduced. At no time did the number of Ju 88s, He 111s and Do 217s fall below 250–300, but this considerable force was hamstrung by low serviceability and a chronic shortage of fully-trained crews, the latter factor now being endemic within the Luftwaffe as a whole. The Kampfgruppen failed to intervene during the Allied build-up for the invasion and their scale of effort during and after the landings was negligible.

The fighting in Sicily finally ceased when Patton's troops entered Messina on 17 August. For four days prior to this event the Jagdgruppen raised their total effort from 60 to 150 sorties per day while covering the evacuation of the remnants of the German forces from Sicily. With the Luftwaffe's defeat over Sicily, out of 1,250 combat aircraft available in July, only approximately 625 remained, covering the whole of the central and western Mediterranean areas, including southern France, Sardinia, Corsica and Italy. This decline marked the end of the Luftwaffe's attempt to contest Allied air superiority in the Mediterranean, but a second factor had by now come into play. During August 1943, 210 aircraft were withdrawn from the Mediterranean, and all but one unit were transferred to the Western Front. The fighter units included II/JG 51, II/JG 27, I/ZG 1 and III/ZG 26 for daylight interception duties over the Reich.

The defeat of the Luftwaffe over Sicily had been total. After the decisive German defeat at Kursk in July, the priority had passed to the Mediterranean, but within two months this pre-eminence had been finally and irrevocably lost.

## The Allied Invasion of Italy

# 1943

At 04.30hrs on 3 September 1943, the first echelons of the British 8th Army waded ashore from their landing craft onto beaches north of Reggio. The landings were virtually unopposed with the XXVI Pz. and XXIX Pz. Grenadier Division electing to pull back when it became apparent that the difficult terrain was enough to slow the British advance.

The Germans realised that this landing was a diversionary feint to be followed by another, more significant Allied invasion. Opinions differed as to where the next blow would fall. Hitler expected an assault in Yugoslavia, Kesselring anticipated a decisive fight near Rome and Vietinghoff, the commander of X Army, expected a landing in the Gulf of Salerno. The Gulf of Salerno proved correct, but, in the meantime, Badoglio's interim government, that had followed the fall of Mussolini, surrendered to the Allies. While militarily this was not too important, the political implications caused grave concern to the Germans, for the surrender put the entire German southern flank in the Central and Eastern Mediterranean at risk. On learning of the Italian surrender, Kesselring stated: 'If we retain our fighting spirit and remain calm, I am confident that we will continue to perform the tasks entrusted to us by the Führer.' The German naval command in Italy was more blunt: 'Italian armistice does not apply to us. The fight continues.'

The Wehrmacht stationed in Southern Italy, composed of crack divisions, immediately

## The Dispositions of Luftflotte 2 in Sicily

| Unit | Types | Location |
|---|---|---|
| Reconnaissance | | |
| 2.(F)/122 | Ju 88D-5, Me 410A-3 | Trapani |
| Fighters | | |
| Stab JG 53 | Bf 109G-6/Trop | Comiso |
| II/JG 53 | Bf 109G-6/Trop | Gerbini |
| III/JG 53 | Bf 109G-6/Trop | Catania |
| Stab JG 77 | Bf 109G-6/Trop | Trapani |
| I/JG 77 | Bf 109G-6/Trop | Trapani and Sciacca |
| Fighter-bombers | | |
| Stab SKG 10 | Fw 190A-5/U3 | Gerbini |
| Part II/SKG 10 | Fw 190A-5/U3 | Gerbini |
| Part III/SKG 10 | Fw 190A-5/U3 | San Pietro |
| IV/SKG 10 | Fw 190A-5/U3 | Gerbini |
| Night-fighters | | |
| II/NJG 2 | Ju 88C-6 | Comiso |
| Ground-attack | | |
| Stab Sch.G 2 | Fw 190F-2 | Castelvetrano |
| I/Sch.G2 (less 4.St) | Fw 190F-2 | (Transferring from Milis to |
| II/Sch.G2 (less 8.St) | Fw 190F-2 | Castelvetrano |

disarmed the Italians and took over the defences. Militarily their dispositions consisted of the XXVI and XXIX Pz. Divisions, under 76 Pz. Corps, in the toe of Italy, the Hermann Göring Pz. and XV Pz. Divisions in the Gaeta-Salerno sector under XIV Pz. Corps, the I Fallschirm Division at Foggia under Vietinghoff's control, and II Pz. Grenadier and II Fallschirm Division in the Rome area under Kesselring's direct control.

On 9 September 1943, the day of the Allied invasion in the Gulf of Salerno, the Luftwaffe's forces consisted of the following: IV/JG 3 at Foggia, I, II and III/JG 53 'Pik-As' at Grazzanise and Cancello-Arnone, and Stab and I/JG 77 'Herzas' at Crotone. The III/JG 77 was at Chilivani in Sardinia and the entire force, equipped with Bf 109G-5 and G-6 fighters, numbered 51 serviceable aircraft out of a strength of 96. The ground-attack and fighter-bomber element, which played an important part in opposing the Salerno landings, comprised II and III/SKG 10 with 68 (41) Fw 190A-5/U3s at Crotone and Montecorvino, and two staffeln of II/SchG 2 with 28 (10) Fw 190F-2s at Ottana.

There is no doubt that the Luftwaffe made an all-out effort to liquidate the Allied bridgehead at Salerno, and Allied forces were not afforded adequate fighter protection. The airfields in Sicily were in a deplorable state and the Allied fighter squadrons based there found their 'loiter' time over Salerno severely limited due to the distance involved. For the first ten days, the Luftwaffe close-support forces maintained the high average of two sorties per serviceable aircraft, beginning with some 170 sorties on 8 September, and rising to a peak effort on 13 September when the German

counterattack threatened to drive the Allies back into the sea. The Fw 190 fighter-bombers, which operated effectively against shipping and landing craft, were supported by IV/JG 3's Bf 109G-5/R2 fighters using the Wfr.Gr 21 rocket mortars, while top-cover was flown by Major Johannes Steinhoff's JG 77 and Obstlt. Günther Maltzahn's JG 53.

Most significant of all, however, was the revival of the long-range bomber force. On the night of 8–9 September, approximately 155 sorties were flown, and further effort of 100 sorties was attained on the night of 10–11 September, the strongest reaction since the Malta battles of March 1942. Conventional bombing sorties were carried out by II/LG 1, I and II/KG 1, Stab and III/KG 54, Stab, I and II/KG 76 and II/KG 77, operating from Foggia, Piacenza, Airasca and Viterbo. Three Gruppen of KG 30, based at Grosseto, carried out torpedo attacks with Ju 88A-17s, in co-operation with I and II/KG 26 from Marseilles-Istres. Of particular interest was the use, on an intensive scale for the first time, of the Hs 293 glider-bomb and the FX 1400 'Fritz' stand-off bomb, used by II and III/KG 100 from bases in Southern France. The Luftwaffe achieved 85 bomb strikes on Allied vessels lying in the Gulf of Salerno, sinking four transports, a heavy cruiser and seven LSTs.

After 15 September, the Allied foothold at Salerno became less critical, and three days later the Germans carried out a strategic withdrawal to their prepared defensive positions on the Volturno river, named the Gustav Line. Naples was captured on 1 October, and on this day the important airfields at Foggia fell into Allied hands, wherein the southern flank of the Reich, the Balkans and northern Italy

*Above: A Junkers Ju 88A-4 with its crew at readiness. This aircraft, belonging to Kampfgeschwader 54, was operating from Bergamo, Italy, in 1943. Note "skull and crossbones" emblem*

came within easy range of Allied bombers. After Salerno, the Luftwaffe in Italy was reduced to a shadow of its former self, the defensive campaigns in this theatre, in themselves ideally suited to the ragged mountainous terrain, were placed firmly into the hands of Kesselring's experienced ground forces. But while the situation remained static in Italy, a new threat had to be faced in the Aegean.

## Operations in the Eastern Mediterranean

# 1943

The large-scale defection by the Italian garrisons in the Eastern Mediterranean compromised the entire German position in the Balkans, Greece and the Aegean, putting the southern flank at risk. However, the German reaction to this threat was systematic, vigorous and effective. Between the Italian capitulation, on 8 September, and 3 October, Luftwaffenkommando Süd-Ost was reinforced by 110 combat aircraft raising its strength to 345 assorted types. Primarily, these included III and IV/JG 27 with Bf 109G-5s, and I and II/StG 3 with Ju 87D-3 dive-bombers, and 11./ZG 26 with Ju 88C-6 heavy-fighters to bolster the elements of LG 1 and SAGr 126 in

Crete.

The first objective was the capture of Cephallonia island, covering the entrance to the Gulf of Corinth, which was attacked on 21 September. The Germans then switched to Corfu, the main fortress on the eastern side of the Strait of Otranto, which fell on 24 September, followed by the capture of Split island on the following day. Air operations proceeded unhindered by Allied intervention due to their tardy exploitation of airbases in Apulia, and the Stuka dive-bombers, which played a leading rôle, suffered minimal losses.

Having secured their supply routes through the Adriatic to their bases in Greece and the Aegean, and having forstalled any likelihood of an Allied invasion of the Balkans via the Strait of Otranto, the Germans now turned their attention to the Dodecanese islands in the eastern Aegean.

Here the British had failed to profit from the capitulation of Italian garrisons in the Dodecanese, wherein lay a number of good airfields, and their intervention was inefficient and piecemeal. While they gained Kos, Samos and Leros, they failed lamentably to secure Rhodes, with its airfields at Maritsa and Calato. The island was secured by a small German force on 12 September, and with the conclusion of operations in the Adriatic on 27 September, III/JG 27 and StG 3 were flown in. Other units, including IV/JG 27, were transferred to bases in Crete and southern Greece for support operations.

The Luftwaffe took advantage of the low Allied priority accorded to this theatre, and subsequent operations in securing the southern flank in the Eastern Mediterranean were to prove a model of efficient and resolute action

by a small compact force against an undetermined enemy.

As dawn broke on 3 October, some 1,200 German troops under Gen.Lt Müller landed on Kos, supported by Stukas and Bf 109Gs flying top-cover. In the two days that were all that were required to eliminate British resistance, StG 3 put up 140–150 sorties in addition to about 65–70 by III and IV/JG 27. The Luftwaffe, using up to 300 aircraft based in the theatre, started the process of softening up Leros which continued throughout October, with an average of 60 sorties by Ju 87s and Ju 88s per day. At first light on 12 November, 90–95 Ju 52/3m transports dropped 675–700 paratroops on the narrow stretch of land between Gurna and Alinda Bay. During the five days' fighting which culminated in the German capture of Leros, the Luftwaffe flew between 675–700 sorties, and at no time was its air supremacy challenged with any lasting effect. The capture of Leros was followed closely by the British evacuation without a fight of Syros and Samos. The Germans had the encouragement which victory affords, and Turkey, who had been quite clearly shown who was still master in the Aegean, refused to join the Allies and remained neutral until the end of the war.

## The Italian Front

# 1943-1944

By December, the Allied 5th and 8th Armies had been halted on the Gustav Line which stretched across the Apennines from Gaeta,

*Above: The Focke-Wulf Fw 58 Weihe was widely used by the Luftwaffe for communications and liaison tasks on all fronts on which the service operated*

through Cassino, to Ortona on the eastern coast. Throughout the following weeks, successive Allied attacks failed to dislodge the 76th and XIV Pz. Corps of Vietinghoff's X Army. In order to counter this enforced stalemate on the Italian Front, the Allies decided to launch a large-scale amphibious landing at Anzio, a distance of 50 miles behind the prepared defences of the Gustav Line.

Such an operation was inconceivable to the Germans, considering it was mid-winter, and the lethargic reconnaissance work carried out by NAGr 11, 2.(F)/122 and 1.(F)/123 failed to note Allied sea and land movements that would have indicated an impending landing. Thus, when Gen. Lucas' 6th US Corps landed astride Anzio and Nettuno on 22 January 1944, the Germans were taken completely by surprise. However, the surprise was not exploited, the Wehrmacht was permitted to recover and the ambitious plan degenerated into a bloody battle of attrition with heavy cost to the Allies.

As always, the German reaction to a major strategic threat was prompt and energetic. By 1 January, the total Luftwaffe strength in the Mediterranean had sunk to 575 aircraft, 307 being under Luftflotte 2 in the Italian theatre, but despite the priority afforded the renewed bombing offensive against the United Kingdom, several bomber units were sent to Italy from France. From 23 January to 3 February, the solitary Geschwaderstab KG 76

in Italy was joined by I and III/LG 1 from the Balkans, I and III/KG 26, part of I and II/KG 30, and I/KG 76 from Luftflotte 3 in France, while Stab KG 100, with He 177A-5 bombers, and II/KG 100 which were transferred to Marseilles-Istres.

The Jagdgruppen under Luftflotte 2 (as of 31 January) consisted of I/JG 4, II/JG 51, I and III/JG 53, and Stab, I and II/JG 77, equipped with Bf 109G-6 fighters. The close-support element consisted of Stab, I and II/SG 4 equipped with Fw 190F-8s, and I/NSGr 9 equipped with Caproni 314s for night ground-attack work. A further 50 single-engined fighters were transferred from Northern Italy to the Anzio area by 23 February, in addition to the crack I/JG 2 'Richthofen', equipped with Fw 190A-6s, under Major Erich Hohagen, which was installed at Canino by the end of the month. Overall the reinforcements to Luftflotte 2 amounted to a rise of 35 per cent, reaching a peak in March 1944 of 600 aircraft, of which 475 were engaged in operations against the Anzio-Nettuno beachhead.

Despite their precarious position at Anzio, the Allies had virtually complete control of the skies, forcing the anti-shipping and bomber units to operate at night. This factor rendered the operations of II and III/KG 100, using the Hs 293 and FX 1400, less effective than they had been at Salerno. By day, the inclement weather curtailed combat operations by the Luftwaffe during the initial phases of the Anzio battle, but in support of the second German counterattack on 16 and 17 February, Fw 190 fighter-bombers flew 160–170 sorties and the Bf 109Gs some 300–350 sorties on each day. This was the peak, however, and such an effort was not again to be mounted for the re-mainder of the Anzio embroglio.

German fighter pilots were engaged in combat by Spitfires, P-51s, P-47s and P-38s whenever they chose to leave the ground. A Messerschmitt pilot of II/JG 77 'Herzas', who was shot down over Cassino on 27 March, told his captors that the Gruppen strength was never above 20 aircraft, of which an average of 12–15 were serviceable, and 15 pilots had been lost during the previous two months. The normal pilot strength of the Gruppe was 50, but II/JG 77 possessed 20–25, of which only a small proportion had any real combat experience. Thus it was that several Gruppen in Italy had been reduced to Staffel strength.

With deadlock at Anzio, the Allies turned once again to exerting pressure on the Gustav Line at Cassino at the beginning of March. The Germans were, therefore, able to return to the purely defensive policy of the previous winter, radically curtailing the scale of air support and again withdrawing surplus Luftwaffe elements for operations elsewhere.

Of the Luftwaffe's offensive force, almost all bomber and torpedo-bomber units were transferred to the Western Front, leaving I and II/SG 4 to carry out desultory fighter-bomber operations. The strength of the Jagdgruppen was further weakened by the transfer of I/JG 4 to Rumania to join III/JG 77, while I/JG 2 returned to France in April 1944. When the Allies opened their offensive across the Garigliano and Rapido rivers on 11 May, they did so in the total absence of the Luftwaffe and, by 4 June, they had taken Rome. The insignificance to which the priority of the Mediterranean theatre had fallen had already been indicated by the transfer, as early as February 1944, of Fliegerkorps II to Northern France,

*Above: During the 8th Army's crossing of the Sangro River, this Me 410A-3 recce aircraft of 2.(F)/122 was brought down by R.A.F. fighters, crashing on the river bank*

*Above right: The Junkers Ju 52/3m transport, seen here flying over the Mediterranean, played a vital role in the resupply of Rommel's Afrika Corps but attrition was high*

*Right: The Messerschmitt Me 410A-3 photo-reconnaisance aircraft operated from Trapani with 2.(F)/122 when the Allies invaded Sicily, a captured example of one of this unit's aircraft being seen here*

followed by Fliegerkorps X to SW France as an anti-shipping command. Operations in Italy were reduced to the status of a Jagdfliegerführer within Luftflotte 2, and by July 1944, the total first-line strength in the Mediterranean had sunk to only 300 aircraft.

The Mediterranean campaigns of 1943–44 were a drain on the resources of the Luftwaffe which interfered with its efforts at expansion and recovery, and therefore vitally affected its capacity to counter the RAF/USAAF bombing offensive against Germany, and ultimately to oppose and withstand the Allied invasion of Normandy. It was not only at Stalingrad but in the Mediterranean that the cream of the Luftwaffe's bomber arm perished, and it was the relentless drain on crews and aircraft which, long after Stalingrad, reduced German offensive air power to a nullity.

# Chapter 13

# The Defence of the Reich

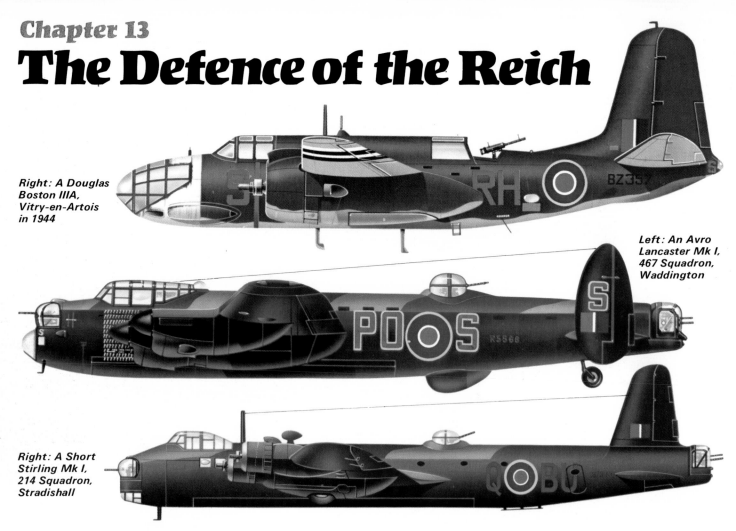

*Right: A Douglas Boston IIIA, Vitry-en-Artois in 1944*

*Left: An Avro Lancaster Mk I, 467 Squadron, Waddington*

*Right: A Short Stirling Mk I, 214 Squadron, Stradishall*

## The Allied Bombing Offensive against Germany

# 1943-1944

Before covering the tactical and operational aspects of the Luftwaffe's counteroffensive against the weight of RAF and USAAF bombing throughout 1943 and 1944, it is necessary to outline the general bombing policies carried out by the Allies, and study the changes, successes and failures experienced by these policies, and their ultimate effect on the Luftwaffe's capacity to fight. From July 1943 until the end of the war, the joint RAF and USAAF bombing offensive against Germany was to be the dominating factor in the air.

The Allied conference at Casablanca, in January 1943, met in a spirit of renewed and justified optimism because, for the first time in the course of the war, the tide of Axis victory had been stemmed at Stalingrad, El Alamein and Guadalcanal. Among the revisions of global strategy discussed at Casablanca came the call for the heaviest possible Allied bombing offensive against the German industrial and economic capacity to wage war. RAF Bomber Command, under Air Chief Marshall A. T. Harris, received the following directive: 'Your primary objective will be the progressive destruction and dislocation of the German military, industrial and economic system, and the undermining of the morale of the German people to the point where their capacity for armed resistance is fatally weakened.' The Casablanca directive gave renewed impetus to the Allied air commanders and, from January 1943 onwards, Germany was to suffer raids by RAF bombers by night and by bombers of the 8th USAAF, later joined by the 15th USAAF, by day on an ever increasing scale.

In the final analysis the subsequent Allied strategic bombing offensive failed either to dislocate German war production or to undermine civilian morale. The production of weaponry increased due to energetic dispersal to less threatened areas, the resolve of the German people, if anything, was sharpened to see the war through to the bitter end, and the entire offensive suffered from disagreements in high quarters and a dispersal of bombing effort until the final year of the war. It was only after May 1944, that the USAAF, belatedly joined by RAF Bomber Command, turned its full effort to the destruction of the oil industry – the life blood of Germany's capacity to wage war.

At the beginning of 1943, the main effort of the Luftwaffe's home defence was directed against the night bomber raids of RAF Bomber Command's Lancasters, Halifaxes, Stirlings and Wellingtons, but a new threat appeared on the scene when the 8th USAAF's Boeing B-17 Fortress bombers commenced operations against targets in Germany on 27 January 1943. Their crews had had five months' of operations against targets in France and the Low Countries, and although their combat missions were still largely experimental in nature, their close, mutually-protected formations had offered reasonable protection against marauding German fighters. In clear weather and by using the Norden bomb-sight, they were able to bomb with relative accuracy. However, their bombs – 500-lb and 1,000-lb GP high-explosive – were not heavy enough to make any impression on the U-boat pens which had constituted their primary target since November 1942.

After Casablanca, the U-boat bases, repair and construction yards remained the top priority of the 8th USAAF and, between January and April 1943, 63 per cent of its attacks were directed at U-boat targets at Emden, Wilhelmshaven, Kiel, Hamburg, Flensburg, Lubeck and Bremerhaven, in addition to the Kriegsmarine's operational bases at La Pallice, St Nazaire and Brest. Throughout this period, RAF Bomber Command devoted 30 per cent of its attacks to the U-boat priority, while committing its major effort against German industry located in large conurbations. In March 1943, Harris' bombers were engaged in an intensive spate of night operations against targets in the Ruhr, attacking Essen, Duisburg, Wuppertal and other towns situated in this great industrial heartland. By now bombing accuracy by night was being assisted by radio navigational aids, although the RAF found it impossible to bomb nocturnally with the same precision as achieved by the 8th USAAF diurnally.

During RAF Bomber Command's campaign, known as the Battle of the Ruhr, the flak defences and in particular Kammhuber's night fighters imparted an average casualty rate of 3·6 per cent on Harris' squadrons, revised bomber tactics having brought the overall rate of 1942 (4·1 per cent) down to a level that was still prohibitive if a long-term offensive was to be followed. Meanwhile, the losses suffered by the 8th USAAF were even higher, and it soon became clear that a change of target priorities was needed. If a bomber offensive was to succeed, it was concluded, then first the enemy air force must cease to give effective opposition.

The Joint Planning Team, responsible for overall policy and set up in April 1943, was soon urging that the Allied bombing effort be diverted from the U-boat priority to that of the destruction of the German aircraft industry; the airframe, engine and ancillary plants that were now producing the Bf 109Gs, Fw 190As, Bf 110Gs and Ju 88Cs in alarmingly high quantities. In order of their priorities the new list of bomber targets, as suggested by the Team, was as follows: aircraft industry, ball-bearing industry, synthetic aviation fuel, machine-tool grinding and sharpening plants, non-ferrous industries, synthetic rubber, U-boat production and maintenance, the motor

industry and transportation.

On 10 June 1943, the 'Pointblank' directive was issued to the Allied bomber chiefs charging them with the following objectives according to the specialised rôles:

* The 8th USAAF's primary objective was to be the destruction of the Luftwaffe Fighter Arm, and the industries that equipped it, supported it, and enabled it to fly.

* RAF Bomber Command was to be employed in accordance with its main aim in the general destruction and disorganisation of German industry, its operations being designed as far as practicable to be complementary to those of the USAAF.

The directive also charged the bomber chiefs to co-operate and co-ordinate their actions in pursuance of the aims, and to assist them a Joint Operational Planning Committee was constituted. It was now that the first serious disagreement arose between the respective commanders. The 8th USAAF was understandably insistent that all efforts were now diverted to the task of neutralising fighter opposition. Harris thought otherwise. His interpretation of the 'Pointblank' directive was that while the 8th concentrated on the German aircraft industry and its ancillaries, RAF Bomber Command would be sent 'against those industrial towns in which there was the largest number of aircraft component factories.' And to this interpretation Harris adhered.

July 1943 was a milestone in the history of the Allied bombing offensive, in which the 8th USAAF turned from U-boat objectives to those within the 'Pointblank' directive and Bomber Command waged the Battle of Hamburg. It was to be a month of major significance for the Luftwaffe as well. Hitherto the B-17s and B-24s of the 8th USAAF, usually 80–100 strong, had flown unescorted raids against coastal targets but, with the start of 'Blitz Week' in July, forces of 250–300 made for targets deep inside Germany, still without escort, and, moreover, these attacks proved

extremely damaging. At the same time, RAF Bomber Command completely neutralised the radar defences of the Kammhuber Line by the first use of 'chaff' – strips of metal foil which obliterated the radar returns of the bombers. The use of 'Window', as this jamming was called, caused considerable scientific and technical problems for the Germans, and Bomber Command's raids were countered only by the reversion to visual night-fighting aided by flares and searchlights. At Hamburg,

*Above upper: Although one wing of this Boeing B-17 Fortress has been hit, the pilot keeps it in formation while the bomb-aimer releases his missiles*

*Above lower: Four B-24 Liberators of the US 8th AF drop their bombs over Tours in France. Smoke markers can be seen and a bridge has been hit*

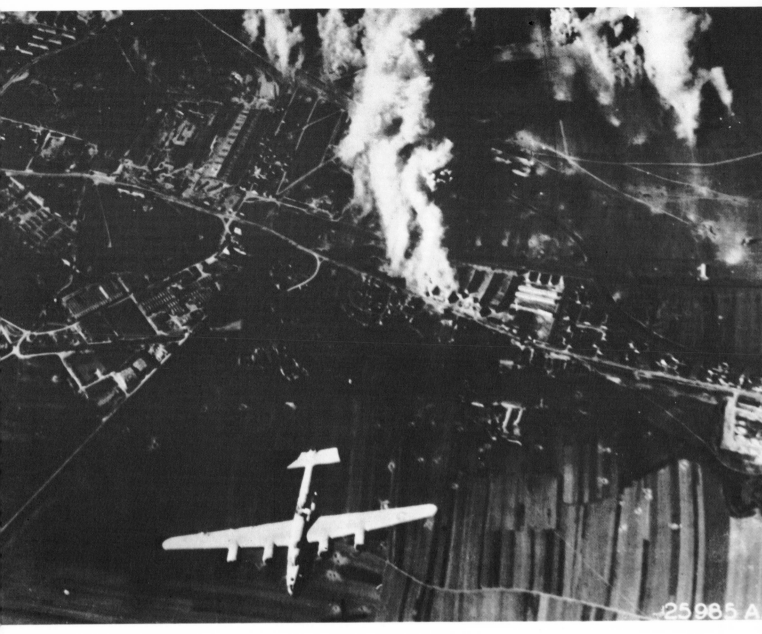

Harris' bombers carried out the first really devastating area attack, causing damage on an unprecedented scale. Thus, the threat posed by the RAF and USAAF assumed new proportions with the ending of July.

These missions of intent coincided with German crises on other battlefronts far removed from the skies over Germany. With the German defeat at Kursk and the decimation of the Luftwaffe over Sicily, the priorities accorded by the Luftwaffe to first the Eastern Front and then the Mediterranean passed finally and irrevocably to the air defence of Germany. From July until October 1943, Luftwaffenbefehlshaber Mitte, the command responsible for the defence of the Reich, turned its full attention to countering the 8th USAAF by strengthening existing Jagdgruppen, calling in others from the respective battlefronts, and concentrating its forces in Germany and Holland. Its first offensive was to culminate in the Schweinfurt massacre on 14 October, forcing the USAAF to cease deep penetration unescorted attacks and to reduce its offensive, within the terms of 'Pointblank', to the point of crisis. As such it was a victory for the Luftwaffe's day fighter forces.

The 'Pointblank' offensive, pursued with such determination by the 8th USAAF had ostensibly failed; there were more German

*Above: A B-24 Liberator in November, 1943 has been hit by heavy flak during a raid carried out by the 98th Bomb Group, 415th Squadron, US 15th AF on the Weiner-Neustadt aircraft plant*

*Below: A Boeing B-17G-25 Fortress (96th BG, US 8th AF, Snetterton Heath). The G version was the final production bomber model of the Fortress and a total of 8,680 G models was built*

fighters in the air than ever before and their attacks had caused a casualty rate that was totally unacceptable. In the altercations that followed between the Allied air chiefs, numerous new proposals were made. The Americans, while maintaining that the prime target remained the German aircraft industry and the defeat of the Luftwaffe, called for greater co-operation between RAF Bomber Command, the 8th USAAF and now the 15th USAAF, which started operations against Southern Germany and Austria from the Foggia bases in October. They also called for a new list of target priorities. To Harris, the reason for the apparent failure of 'Pointblank' was the insufficiency of the forces allocated and the dispersal of effort. Regarding the latter, he indicated the 'abortive' Ploesti raid, in August 1943, when the whole B-24 force had been diverted from the 8th USAAF to bases in North Africa for this purpose. In the end, the Americans decided to proceed with 'Pointblank' but with the proviso that all raids be escorted by long-range fighters and to this they devoted all the resources at their disposal.

In November 1943, RAF Bomber Command turned to a new offensive against industrial areas in Germany that was to last until the end of March 1944. Known as the Battle of Berlin on account of the preponderance of raids against the capital of the Third Reich, this offensive was to culminate in the disastrous Nuremburg raid of 30 March 1944, presenting Harris with a similar crisis to that besetting

General Carl Spaatz, the commander of the 8th USAAF, after Schweinfurt. From 10 June 1943 to 25 March 1944, RAF Bomber Command launched 58 major* raids against Germany. With the exceptions of Berlin and Nuremburg, all the targets lay in the western districts of Germany within range of the 'Oboe' navigational aid. Unable to bomb with the same accuracy as the Americans, Harris stuck to his policy of attacking industry that lay within an agglomeration of large towns and cities wherein the 'undermining of German morale' was a consideration. Few targets, with the exception of Kassel, wherein lay the Betthausen Fw 190 plant, came within the terms of the 'Pointblank' directive, although several of the concerns attacked made essential parts of some nature.

In the battle against the Allied bombing offensive, the Luftwaffe had reasonable grounds for optimism by the winter of 1943–44. The success of the day fighter force in the Autumn had forced the USAAF to revert to shallow penetration targets and now, having recovered from the effect of 'Window' jamming through the use of new equipment and tactics, the night-fighters were inflicting heavy casualties on RAF Bomber Command. However, these results had been achieved only by the concentration of fighters in the West at the expense of other war fronts. Of the total fighter strength of the Luftwaffe, 68 per cent was concentrated in the West, along with 70

*400 or more aircraft.

*Above: A formation of B-17Gs of the 381st BG of the US 8th AF escorted by a P-51 Mustang equipped with drop tanks which enabled it to fly all-the-way with the bombers during day attacks*

per cent of the Flak personnel in the autumn of 1943. On 1 January 1944, 1,650 single- and twin-engined fighters were based in Germany, France, Southern Norway and the Low Countries, in comparison to 365 in the Mediterranean and the Balkans, and 425 on the Soviet Front. At the beginning of 1944, 75 per cent of the fighters based in the West were concentrated within Germany, leaving only a small force in France to counter the activities of RAF No 2 Group and the 9th USAAF.

Under Milch's programme fighter production had soared to a monthly peak of 1,050 aircraft (725 Bf 109Gs and 325 Fw 190s) in July 1943. The 8th USAAF's raids on Augsburg, Regensburg, Marienburg and Wiener Neustadt had been effective only in so far as they reduced this figure to around 1,000 fighters per month for the remainder of 1943. But energetic dispersal and sub-contracting programmes had restored the production rate, although not to the July record.

The fuel situation was in excellent condition, with the synthetic plants reaching peak production. The crisis in aircrew training had been overcome under the influence of General-leutnant Werner Kreipe, and pilots and aircrew were being processed from the schools at a high rate, although their flying standards hardly approached those of the US and RAF aircrews.

In terms of equipment, the Fw 190 was steadily replacing the Bf 109G in several Jagdgruppen and replacing the Ju 87D in the ranks of the Schlachtgruppen; production of the promising He 219 and Ju 188 was proceeding apace, while the deficiencies in the Me 410 and He 177 were ameliorated, and at last the radical Me 262 jet fighter had been earmarked for mass production in the Spring. But it was at this juncture, in February 1944, that the whole situation violently changed; the 8th USAAF renewed its offensive against the German aircraft industry, but the bombers were now escorted by P-51s, P-38s and P-47s, these providing target cover, approach and withdrawal support throughout. The long-range escort fighter at a stroke capsized German defensive strategy, for the Luftwaffe Planning Staff had been lulled into a false sense of security during the winter of 1943–44, on the assurance of the Research and Development Branch that such an aircraft was, in the short term, a technical impossibility.

By April 1944, the 8th USAAF had gained a measure of air superiority over Germany that enabled it to strike targets without incurring the prohibitive losses of the previous Autumn. For the Luftwaffe, the attrition in aircraft and experienced pilots was appallingly high, and the successes against US bombers correspondingly low, despite the use of Sturmgruppen (Assault Groups) with heavily armed Fw 190s. The main source of US bomber casualties now became Flak.

The heavy attacks carried out in February 1944, which saw the culmination of the 'Pointblank' offensive, devastated three engine plants and 23 airframe factories which threatened to bring German aircraft production to a halt. The situation called for desperate remedy. The entire industry was placed under Albert Speer, the Minister for Armament and War Production and controlled through the Jägerstab (Fighter Staff) under Otto Saur. Full priority was accorded to the production of fighters, principally Bf 109Gs and Fw 190s, while the production of other aircraft types was drastically pruned. However, it was not until July 1944 that Saur was at last able to obtain Hitler's consent to a reduction in bomber output in favour of an all-out drive for fighter production.

The subsequent success of the Jägerstab was staggering and neutralised any further attempts by the Allies to forestall aircraft production, albeit of almost totally fighter types, by bombing. The acceptance of fighters in March 1944 exceeded the figure of 1,300 in January, and by April had increased by another 25 per cent. Thereafter, output continued to mount rapidly until a peak of 2,995 (1,605 Bf 109s and 1,390 Fw 190s) was achieved in September, and, although a decline set in, the level remained at 2,300–2,700 per month until the end of the year.

Despite the undoubted success of Jägerstab in reinforcing the Luftwaffe's fighter arm during the Summer of 1944, its efforts were completely nullified by the belated Allied bombing offensive against German oil targets. On 5 April, the Foggia-based 15th USAAF attacked the Ploesti oilfields, already under threat from the Russians in the north. The 8th raided oil objectives for the first time on 12 May, and again on 28 and 29 May 1944. But before any major oil offensive could get under-way both the 8th USAAF and RAF Bomber Command were diverted to transportation and communications targets prior to OVERLORD, the invasion of Normandy on 6 June 1944.

Since its defeat at the hands of the German night fighter force during the Battle of Berlin phase, RAF Bomber Command had switched

to shallow penetration targets and had embarked on the dislocation of the German transportation system with considerable effect. Its Mosquito bombers were, however, in a position to mount an intensive offensive against sundry targets in Germany itself. But it was not until October 1944 that the Lancasters and Halifaxes sought out the oil targets within Germany, being enabled to do so because of the complete dislocation of the German early-warning radar system effected by the Allied advance to the borders of Holland.

After D-Day, the 8th USAAF embarked on the oil offensive proper, attacking the synthetic oil plants at Leuna, Politz, Böhlen, Lutzkendorf, Magdeburg, Zeitz and Ruhland wherein some 40 per cent of German oil needs were provided. German fuel stocks amounted, in September 1943, to 280,000 tons and, by conservation (the Führer Reserve, for example) and added production, this amount had risen to a peak of 574,000 tons in April 1944 – when the Allied oil offensive began the reserves were higher than any time since 1940. While the reserves enabled the Luftwaffe to operate at maximum effort throughout the Normandy battles, the first critical shortage occurred at the end of August 1944. Oil production, which had been 195,000 tons in May, slumped to 52,000 tons in June, to 35,000 tons in July, to 16,000 tons in August and was down to a mere 7,000 tons in September 1944. As the result of the crucial fuel shortage that ensued, the Luftwaffe was in no position to use its vastly increased first-line fighter strength after September. August 1944 also saw a renewal of effort by the 15th USAAF against Ploesti, Brux and other oil plants in the southern sector, and by the end of the month the Russians had overrun the Rumanian oilfields. The crippling of the Luftwaffe had finally been achieved, but on the ground rather than in the air.

Apart from its direct effects on the German

*Above: A formation of Lancasters— this aircraft was the backbone of the RAF bombing effort and featured notably in the sinking of the Tirpitz and the Dams Raid*

war industry, the Anglo-American air offensive in the West, in 1943 and 1944, had the following results applicable to the Luftwaffe's conduct of operations:

*A reduction in the Luftwaffe's strength in the Mediterranean (1,280 aircraft in July 1943 reduced to 475 in July 1944) to a size at which its influence over the course of events was negligible.

*The transfer of first-line fighters from the Soviet Union to Germany at the very moment when the growing numerical superiority of the Soviet Air Forces required strengthening of German fighter opposition.

*The concentration of productive capacity on fighter types brought about the weakening and eventual eclipse of the long-range bomber force. In particular, expansion of the night-fighter arm could only take place at the expense of the bomber arm.

*The exertion of every effort in defence of war industry inflicted a rate of wastage which limited numerical expansion and resulted in a rapid decline in performance and quality: Performance due to the reliance on contemporary aircraft types, at the expense of the development and production of the Focke-Wulf Ta 152, Dornier Do 335 and others, and quality due to the casualties in fighter leaders and experienced pilots.

*The concentration of fighter units in the Reich permitted the Allies to bomb the V-1 launching sites in Northern France with virtual impunity and ultimately facilitated the immediate establishment of Allied air superiority over the beachheads in Normandy at the time of the invasion in June 1944.

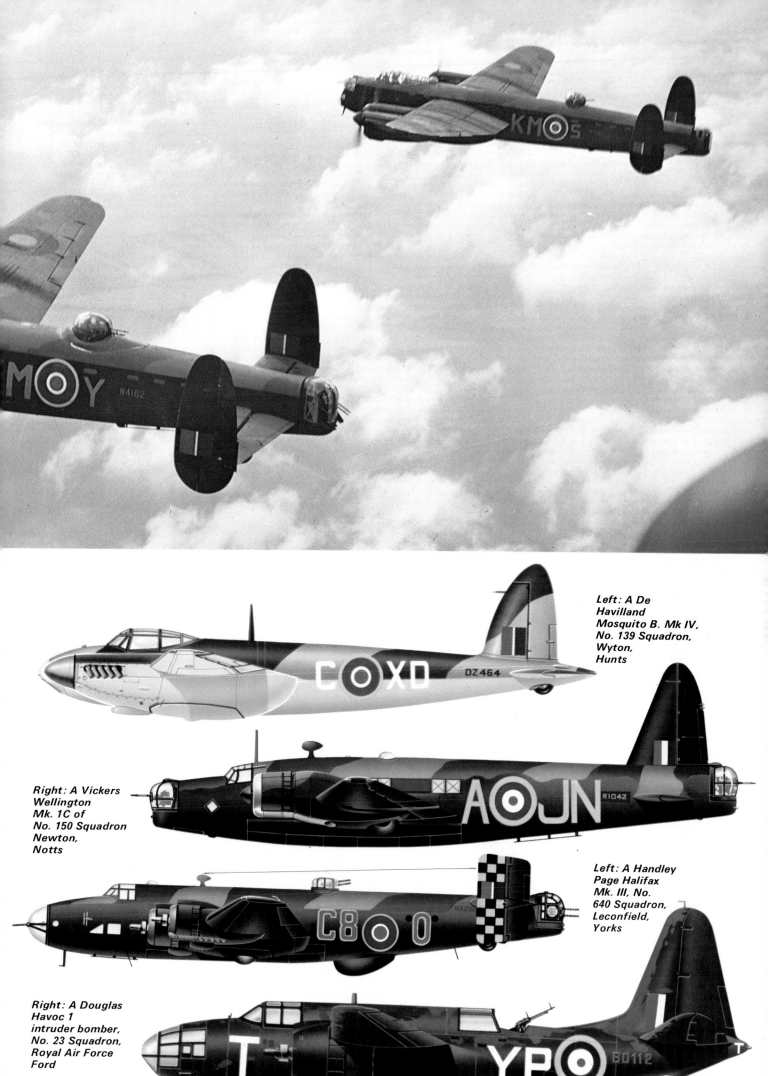

*Left: A De Havilland Mosquito B. Mk IV, No. 139 Squadron, Wyton, Hunts*

*Right: A Vickers Wellington Mk. 1C of No. 150 Squadron Newton, Notts*

*Left: A Handley Page Halifax Mk. III, No. 640 Squadron, Leconfield, Yorks*

*Right: A Douglas Havoc 1 intruder bomber, No. 23 Squadron, Royal Air Force Ford*

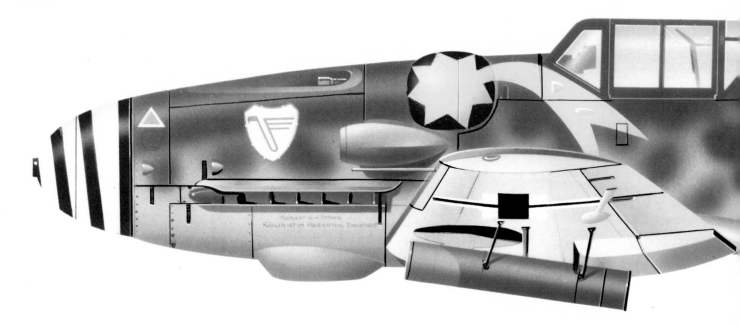

## The Defence of Germany by Day

# 1943-1944

On 1 January 1943, the total strength of the Jagdgruppen in the West was 635 Bf 109Gs and Fw 190s, stationed at airfields that stretched from Banak, in Northern Norway, to Brest-Guipavas on the Atlantic coast in Brittany.

The Geschwaderstab of JG 26, under Major Josef Priller, was at Lille-Vendeville in Northern France, with I/JG 26 at St Omer-Fort Rouge, II/JG 26 at Vitry-en-Artois and III/JG 26 at Wevelghem. Operating under Jafü 2, within Luftflotte 3, the Geschwader was equipped with Fw 190A-4s, with the exception of III/JG 26 and 5./JG 26 which were equipped with Bf 109G-3 and G-4 fighters. By the end of the month, both I/JG 26 and 7.Staffel were in the Soviet Union. In exchange for these units, III/JG 54, under Major Reinhard Seiler, was posted to Vendeville from the Soviet Union for operations in France. By 27 March, however, this Gruppe had been redeployed to Oldenburg, in Germany, under Luftwaffenbefehlshaber Mitte.

The 'Richthofen' Jagdgeschwader (JG 2), based west of the Seine, had been weakened by the transfer of II/JG 2 to Tunisia, but by January, I/JG 27 was working up to operational readiness at Evreux-Fauville after its withdrawal from North Africa. The I/JG 2 was scattered, with individual Staffeln at Triqueville, Beaumont-le-Roger and Evreux wherein the Stab and 12./JG 2 were located. Hauptmann Egon Mayer's III/JG 2, the most experienced unit in combatting the 8th USAAF's B-17s, was based at Vannes-Meuçon, with Staffeln at Brest-Guipavas and Cherbourg. Both Jafü 2 and Jafü 3's fighter forces, therefore, were now up to strength; much of this strength, however, was to be diverted from operations against US bombers to daily combat with RAF Fighter Command and RAF No 2 Group during the Spring, when the 8th USAAF turned to targets in Germany.

The first US raid over German soil, to Wilhelmshaven on 27 January, was inter-

cepted by elements of Obstlt.Dr Erich Mix's JG 1, and the loss of seven of its fighters in return for one B-17 and two B-24s clearly indicated this unit's inexperience in comparison with the battle-hardened pilots of JG 2 and JG 26, that had hitherto opposed the 8th USAAF. Under Luftwaffenbefehlshaber Mitte, the four Gruppen of JG 1 were stationed over a wide area; the Geschwaderstab and II/JG 1 were at Jever, I/JG 1 at Schiphol, Katwijk and Bergen, in Holland, along with elements of IV/JG 1, while the III Gruppe was scattered at airfields from Husum to Aalborg. The remaining Jagdgeschwader in the West and one that was to play little part in the defence of Germany was JG 5. Commanded by Major Günther Scholz, I/JG 5 and elements of IV/JG 5 protected important naval bases in Norway from Banak and Bardufoss.

Between January and the end of March 1943, the activities of JG 1 were limited to the rare occasions when the 8th USAAF raided targets in Germany and Holland – in February, only Emden and Wilhelmshaven were attacked, and in March only Bremen-Vegesack, Wilhelmshaven and Rotterdam. The bulk of 8th USAAF's attacks were on Brest, Lorient, St Nazaire, Amiens, Rennes, Rouen and other targets which lay within range of RAF Fighter Command's Spitfire IXs which could keep JG 2 and JG 26 at bay over most of the bombers' route.

In April, the improvement in weather saw an upsurge in the 8th's activity over Germany. On 17 April, during a raid on Bremen, German fighters from I and III/JG 1 and flak brought down 16 B-17s and caused damage to 48 more. The month saw a strengthening of Luftwaffenbefehlshaber Mitte's fighter units: III/JG 54 and 2./JG 27 were installed at Oldenburg and Schiphol respectively, while JG 1 was reinforced and elements diverted to constitute a new unit, JG 11. The command of JG 1 passed to Major Hans Philipp, an ex-JG 54 'experte' with the Schwertern to the Ritterkreuz, while the Kommodore of JG 11 was Major Anton Mader, who had led II/JG 11 in Tunisia. On 10 May 1943, fighters engaged in the defence of the Reich, with Jagddivisionen 1, 2 and 3, consisted of Stab, I and II/JG 1, 2./JG 27, Stab, I and II/JG 11, Jagdstaffel Helgoland and III/JG 54. In France, under Luftflotte 3, were Stab JG 2, I/JG 2 including 11.Staffel, II/JG 2 consisting of 12.Staffel only and III/JG 2; Stab, II and III/JG 26, 1. and

3./JG 27 and 4./JG 54, the total first-line strength being 354 fighters based on the Western Front.

The major problem faced by the Jagdflieger was the breaking up of the tightly packed formations of B-17s and B-24s, each heavily armed with Colt M-2 0·5-inch machine guns. With or without the attendant Spitfires – and the 8th's incursions over Germany were completely devoid of escort – the problem of attacking B-17s and B-24s was great. The immediate step was to increase the armament of the standard Bf 109G and the Fw 190A. Earlier, the Bf 109F-4/R1 had carried two Mauser MG 151/20s in gondolas under the wings in addition to the normal weaponry. In the Bf 109G this modification was standardised as 'Rustsatz 6'. Thus, the Bf 109G-6/R6 carried three MG 151s in addition to the twin fuselage-mounted MG 131 13-mm machine-guns, although much to the detriment of its performance. It was normal, therefore, to equip only a proportion of a Gruppe's 109s with the additional cannon while the remainder were used for fighter-versus-fighter combat. The Fw 190's normal armament for combat in France consisted of twin MG 17s and two MG 151s, but for anti-bomber work the Rheinmetall MG FF-M 20-mm cannon was re-installed in the outer wing bay, outboard of each undercarriage bay.

Late in July 1943, the Fw 190A-6 became operational with the Jagdgruppen, this aircraft having increased firepower by the deletion of the MG FFs and substitution of the more efficient MG 151 20-mm cannon. In an attempt to break up formations of US bombers, aerial bombing had been tried as early as 22 March, when Lt. Heinz Knoke of 5./JG 1 dropped a 250kg bomb, bringing down three B-17s near Wilhelmshaven. The technique was tried by other units, including 10./JG 26, but effective evasive action by wary US crews was to lead to its eventual discontinuation.

As early as June 1942, the Y-Gerät apparatus, which had proved its efficiency during the Blitz against Britain in the winter of 1940–41 as a blind-bombing aid, was used experimentally to guide day fighters to their targets over great distances. The standard Lorenz VHF transmitter/receiver set (FuG 16) could be fitted with blind-homing apparatus (Zielanflug) with a fixed D/F loop, and this equipment was in widespread use in day and night fighters by

*Tallyho! R/T call indicating visual contact with the enemy.

96

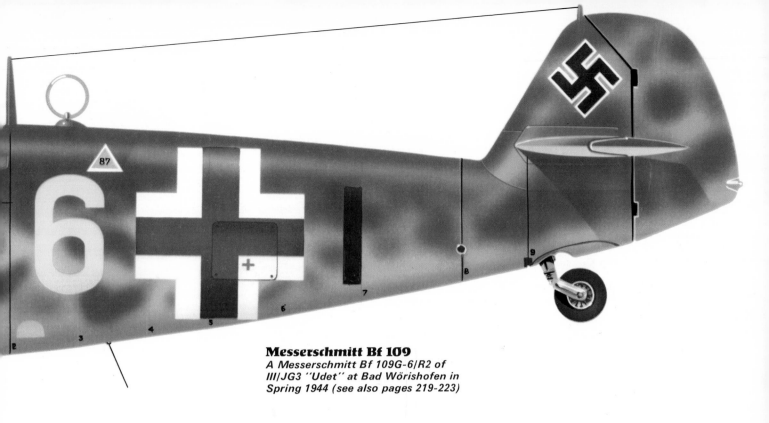

## Messerschmitt Bf 109

*A Messerschmitt Bf 109G-6/R2 of III/JG3 ''Udet'' at Bad Wörishofen in Spring 1944 (see also pages 219-223)*

the summer of 1943. When fitted with a transmitter/receiver that picked up signals from the Y-Gerät ground station and sent modulated carrier wave (MCW) signals back in return, the equipment, now modified to FuG 16zY, enabled the ground station to plot the fighter's range and bearing. Operating on the 38.4-42.4 M/cs frequencies, FuG 16zY was normally installed in one aircraft in a large formation of fighters, nominated the 'Y' aircraft, and this aircraft enabled the ground controller to plot the position of the entire formation between 100km and 200kms with an accuracy of 0·5 per cent.

The 'Y' system thus enabled the controller to vector his formation of fighters to within visual range of the bomber stream in areas that were devoid of radar coverage. His instructions to the 'Y' aircraft were given over the Divisional Commentary (Gemeinschafts Welle), to which wavelength all aircraft of the fighter force were tuned, and could thus be heard by the formation leader and all the fighter pilots, but the 'Y' aircraft's commentary was on a re-transmitted frequency and could only be heard by ground control. Radio silence was observed on pain of subsequent disciplinary action and, in case of the Divisional Commentary being inaudible on account of jamming or because the fighters were out of range, pilots could switch over to the Reichsjägerwelle (Reich Fighter Wave) which broadcast commentaries for the benefit of all fighters operating over Germany – this

recourse was seldom used. This was the primary control system used by Reichsverteidigung forces throughout 1943 and 1944.

In June, III/JG 26 was transferred from Wevelghem to Nordholz, near Cuxhaven on the North German coast, to bolster JG 1 and JG 11. On 13 June, during an attack on Kiel and Bremen by the 8th, III/JG 26's Kommandeur, Hptm. Kurt Ruppert, lost his life when his 'chute folded after baling out at excessive speed. It was a bad day for the 4th Bomb Wing of the 8th as well, for the Wing lost 22 B-17Fs

*Below: Focke-Wulf Fw 190A-4 fighters at readiness at an airfield in France in 1943—the mottle camouflage was unusual for Fw 190s at this period*

out of 26 brought down by flak and fighters. The day was to also see the Thunderbolt cut its teeth, when the 56th Fighter Group bounced 10./JG 26 over Dixmuide shooting down three Fw 190A-4s during a support sweep to Lille. Like the Spitfire, the P-47C was hamstrung by range, and it was not until September 1943 that it was able to furnish continuous escort for the B-17s as far as Emden by using 75 and 108-gallon drop tanks.

On 24 July, the 8th USAAF attacked the nitrate plant at Heroya, in Norway, starting a spate of intensive summer operations within the terms of the 'Pointblank' directive. In what was to be known as 'Blitz Week', Warnemünde, Hamburg, Kiel, Wustrow, Hannover, Kassel and Oschersleben were attacked, while No 2 Group and RAF Fighter Command flew 'Ramrods' to the Luftwaffe airfields at Schiphol, Woensdrecht, Wevelghem, Merville, Triqueville and Abbeville. This immediately prompted the Luftwaffe to increase defences. The Stab and III/JG 26 were sent to Schiphol, I/JG 26 – fresh from Russia – was installed at Grimberghen, while II/JG 26 spent two weeks at Deelen-Arnhem and Volkel before returning to Beauvais on 15 August. By the end of August 1943, JG 3 'Udet', commanded by Obstlt. Wolf-Dietrich Wilcke, was installed at Schiphol, Deelen and Munster-Handorf with three Gruppen of Bf 109G-6s; I/JG 5 had been posted to Germany from Norway at end of July; II/JG 51 (Hptm. Karl Rammelt) arrived at Neubiburg from Sardinia; II/JG 27 (Hptm. Werner Schroer) arrived at Wiesbaden-Erbenheim on 6 August, and while JG 1 and JG 11 were brought up to full Geschwader strength, JGr 25 (Major Herbert Ihlefeld) and JGr 50 (Major Herman Graf) were formed at Neubiburg and Wiesbaden respectively, to combat the fast Mosquitoes which had become a serious menace. Equipped with specially-boosted Bf 109G-6s, the short operational careers of JGr 25 and JGr 50 were to be conspicuous primarily for their lack of success.

The 8th raided Gelsenkirchen on 12 August, losing 25 B-17s despite the efforts of the Thunderbolts which staggered under the load of their long-range tanks. The withdrawal support provided by the Thunderbolts during these missions was growing in efficiency, however. On 17th August, the 8th launched a major attack on the Messerschmitt concern at Regensburg and the VKW ball-bearing works at Schweinfurt. In the first shuttle mission of the war, 147 B-17s made for Regensburg and started suffering fighter attacks at 10.21hrs, after the P-47s departed over Eupen. After bombing Regensburg the force made for bases in North-Africa. Flying their second mission of the day, the 56th Fighter Group was over Eupen at 16.20hrs to meet the returning Schweinfurt force. At the time, the B-17s were under attack from 50–60 German fighters – mostly Bf 109Gs and Fw 190s, with some Bf 110s of ZG 26. In the ensuing engagement the 56th FG claimed 17 German fighters. Of these 6 were Fw 190s claimed by Lt. McCauley, Capt. W. Mahurin and Lt. Schultz: one of these was flown by Major Wilhelm-Ferdinand Galland, Kommandeur of II/JG 26, who was killed when his Fw 190A-6 crashed at Hees-Vlytinghen, west of Maastricht.

Sixty B-17s were lost during Mission 84 to Schweinfurt and Regensburg, but the apparently unfavourable results of the bombing did not discourage the US air chiefs. Among the attacking fighters, several were observed carrying rocket-mortars which were fired, albeit with poor accuracy, well outside the range of the US gunners. This weapon, the Wfr.Gr 21, had been fitted experimentally on the previous day to the Bf 109G-6s of 5./JG 11, and was to be liberally used in subsequent battles of the summer and autumn on the Bf 109 G-6/R2 and Fw 190A-4/R2 (carrying two) and the Bf 110G-2/R3 (carrying four).

Until their eventual decimation at the hands of 8th's fighters, the Zerstörergruppen, and to some extent the Nachtjagdgruppen, were to play an important part in breaking up US bomber formations so that the Bf 109s and Fw 190s could attack stragglers and individual formations. On 30 September 1943, the Zerstörer element consisted of Stab and III/ZG 26 and I/ZG 1 with 97 Bf 110G-2s on strength, and III/ZG 1 and I(Jagd)/KG 51 with 58 Me 410A-1 and B-1 heavy fighters.

By October 1943, the combat radius of the P-47D had been markedly increased by the 108-gallon tank, enabling the Thunderbolts to accept combat as far inland as Duren during a mission to Frankfurt on 4 October. But outside the P-47's radius of action, the German fighters reigned supreme. On 8 October, Bremen and Vegesack were the targets and, once again, as soon as the P-47s had departed, the first concentrated attacks by German fighters, began. Thirty B-17s succumbed to flak and fighters, but the 8th won a victory when Thunderbolts tangled with Geschwaderstab JG 1 over Nordhorn killing Obstlt. Philipp.

Mission 115 to the VKW plants at Schweinfurt, on 14 October, resulted in the loss of 60 B-17s over enemy territory, 5 crashed in England, 12 were Cat.3 write-offs, and a further 121 returned with degrees of battle damage that ranged from severe to superficial: 600 crew-men were missing in action, five were dead on arrival at their bases and 43 were wounded. After the P-47 escort had left the force near Aachen, the US bombers came under continuous attack by relays of Bf 109s and Fw 190s, white-painted Ju 88Cs and Bf 110s of the Nachtjagdgruppen and the Zerstörergruppen's Bf 110G-2s and Me 410s which fired Wfr.Gr 21 rockets, and 30-mm and 37-mm cannon. Fog and other complications prevented the withdrawal cover, by Spitfires and P-47s, from being as efficient as had by now come to be expected, and the US bombers continued to take losses well out over the sea during the return. Luftwaffe losses were approximately 35 out of the 300 day fighters and 40 Zerstörer which took part in the battle. The losses suffered by 8th Bomber Command to flak and fighters was 20·6 per cent of the force, a prohibitive casualty rate.

Schweinfurt was the final proof of the Luftwaffe's ability to inflict consistently high losses on unescorted US bombers, but for the Jagdgruppen revelling in the luxury of unhindered interception, time was running out. The 8th was hard at work, improving the combat radius of the P-47D. The 75- and 108-gallon tanks increased radius to 340 and 375 miles respectively, while new tactics wherein fighters flew to appointed escort areas, throttled back for endurance and held on to their drop tanks until the last minute, allowed this combat radius to be increased. Already moves were afoot to fit a larger drop tank to the P-47. In October, the 55th FG became operational on the Lockheed P-38H Lightning, while the 20th FG was busily working up on the same type. This aircraft had a combat radius of 400 miles, including 15 minutes at emergency boost for dog-fighting in the target area. The North American P-51B was first issued to the 9th USAAF in December 1943, and it was inexplicable that this first-rate long-range fighter went to this tactical command instead of the 8th US Fighter Command. By February 1944, however, the 4th FG within the 8th USAAF became fully operational on the Mustang with other Groups following suit shortly after.

In late-December 1943, all units operating in the defence of Germany were put under a new command, Luftflotte Reich, led by Generaloberst Hans-Jürgen Stumpff. By March 1944, Jagdkorps I, with Jagddivisionen 1, 2, 3 and 7 subordinated, was responsible for all fighter operations within Germany and the Low Countries, while those in France were controlled by Jagdkorps II with Jagddivisionen 4 and 5 and Jafü Brittany subordinated. On 20 February 1944, the day-fighter units under Luftflotte Reich consisted of the following: Stab, I II and III/JG 1, Stab, I, II, III and IV(Sturm)/JG 3, I/JG 5, Stab, I, II, III, 10 and 11./JG 11, Einsatzstaffel Erla, Epr.Kdo 25, I and II/JG 27, II/JG 53, III/JG 54, Sturmstaffel 1, Stab, I, II and III/JG 300, Stab, I, II and III/JG 301 (less 10./JG 301) and Stab, I and II/JG 302 (less 1./JG 302). These units were equipped with Bf 109G-6 and Fw 190A-6 and A-7 fighters. The Zerstörer units were: II/ZG 1, Stab, I, II and III/ZG 26, and Stab, I, II and III/ZG 76, equipped with Bf 110Gs and Me 410s. The total strength of Luftflotte Reich's fighters on this day was 863, of which 517 were combat ready. To this was added six Gruppen of JG 2 and JG 26 under Jafü 4 and 5 within Jagdkorps II in France, along with I and III/ZG 1 based in Brittany.

German aircraft production ensured a steady supply of fighters to these units, while they were backed by an excellent ground control system. There was no shortage of aviation fuel. The performance of the ageing Bf 109G-6 was improved by fitting high-altitude DB 605AS, ASCM and D motors, to which GM 1 and MW 50 power-boosting could be fitted. Firepower was increased by the widespread use of the Rheinmetall MK 108 30-mm cannon – the 'pneumatic hammer', as it was called. Its muzzle velocity was only 500m/sec and the rate of fire 600 rounds per minute, but the effect was devastating, with one strike capable of bringing down a fighter and three sufficient to shoot down a B-17 or B-24. The incendiary qualities of 20-mm ammunition were enhanced by the introduction of the Hexogen A-1 round with high phosphorous content.

It was against strong, well-equipped and resolute forces of Luftflotte Reich, that the 8th and 15th USAAFs resumed deep penetration raids in January 1944 – this time with fighter escort. The casualties to 8th bombers remained high, however, sixty bombers were lost on 11 January against Oschersleben and Wallam, largely due to poorly co-ordinated fighter escort, and this once again emphasised the perils of long-range penetration. During 'Big Week' (19–25 February 1944), which saw the ending of the 'Pointblank' offensive, 21 US bombers were lost on 20 February (Leipzig), 41 on the 22nd (Brunswick), 49 on the 24th (Schweinfurt) and 31 on the 25th (Augsburg, Regensburg and Stuttgart).

The 8th USAAF's offensive against Berlin in conjunction with RAF Bomber Command opened in March 1944 with very heavy losses. On 6 March, 68 B-17s and B-24s and 11 US fighters failed to return, and 37 bombers were lost on the 8th, although on the following day only nine failed to return. But in the great aerial battles of attrition throughout March and April, it was the Luftwaffe that was ultimately the loser. Whether taking-off, assembling, intercepting, recovering and landing, the Jagdgruppen suffered great losses at the hands of the aggressive P-51s, P-47s and P-38s. Fighter aircraft could be replaced, pilots could be replaced, albeit by hastily-trained youngsters with as few as 80 hours' flying time, but not the Kommodoren, Gruppenkommandeure or Staffelkapitäne with their years of experience. Killed in the battles of 1943 were Hptm. Heinrich Setz, Hptm. Fritz Geisshardt, Oblt. Horst Hannig, Obstlt. Johannes Seifert, Major Erwin Clausen, Major Kurt Brandle and

*Right: Luftwaffe fighter pilots at an airfield on the channel coast relax between interception missions during the summer of 1941*

Hptm. Wilhelm Lemke. Now in the Spring of 1944, JG 2 lost two Kommodoren within weeks – on 2 March. Obstlt. Egon Mayer fell over Montmedy in a dogfight with Colonel H. Coen's 365th Fighter Group and on 27 April, Major Kurt Ubben was shot down by P-47s over Château Thierry. Oberst. Wolf-Dietrich Wilcke was killed over Schoppenstadt on 23 March, and on 11 May, Oberst Walter Oesau, Kommodore JG 1, was shot down by P-38s over St Vith, in the Ardennes. These men were irreplaceable and their loss was to be felt keenly in the battles over Normandy in the months to come.

In April, the General der Jagdflieger, Adolf Galland, reported: 'The ratio in which we fight today is about 1 to 7. The standard of the Americans is extraordinarily high. The day fighters have lost more than 1,000 fighters during the last four months, among them our best officers. These gaps cannot be filled. During each enemy raid we lose about 50 fighters. Things have gone so far that the danger of a collapse of our Fighter Arm exists.'

As a desperate remedy Sturmstaffeln were formed, manned by picked crews inculcated with a spirit of determination and recklessness, and encouraged to ram Allied bombers rather than return to base without a 'kill'. The inception of the scheme dated back to the winter of 1943-44, with the formation of Sturmstaffel 1, and by April 1944, IV(Sturm)/JG 3 'Udet', under Major Wilhelm Moritz, was carrying out 'Company Front' assaults on US bombers. The Sturmstaffeln flew the Fw

*Above: Oberstleutnant Josef "Pips" Priller, helped from his Fw 190A-6*

*Below: Bf 109G-6/R2 fighters each equipped with a pair of Wfr.Gr.21 mortars*

190A-8/R7. This aircraft was specially armoured, had the twin MG 131 machine guns removed and carried two MG 151 and two MK 108 cannon. Laden with a 66-gallon Zusatztank, it was heavy and unwieldy in flight. The IV/JG 3 was joined in the summer of 1944 by II(Sturm)/JG 300 and finally by II(Sturm)/JG 4.

The Sturmgruppen, covered usually by two Gruppen of Bf 109G-10s flying up-sun, attacked the bombers from astern in line-abreast in three waves. The pilots usually opened fire with the MG 151s at about 400 yards, bringing the MK 108s into play at 200 yards. At first, short bursts were directed at the tail gunner, then transferred to either of the inboard engines, with break-off following at point-blank range. The results gained by the Sturmgruppen were good, but US fighters continued to shoot down the heavy Fw 190s.

In accordance with orders from Göring, the weight of German fighter attack was concentrated on the destruction of bombers throughout March and April 1944, and, partly to conserve forces, German fighters were ordered to avoid combat with US fighters at all costs. The result was, as the Kommodore of JG 6 pungently remarked, that 'the safest flying that was ever possible was that of an American fighter over Germany.' In no way did this denigrate the performance of US fighter pilots, but it imbued them with a spirit of superiority, the German fighter pilot finding himself restricted and acquiring, as a result, a corresponding sense of inferiority.

In May 1944, the 8th USAAF's bombers sought out transportation targets in the campaign of dislocation prior to the D-Day invasion of Normandy, while flying numerous missions over Germany itself. By this time the P-51 had assumed almost total superiority over the Luftwaffe, ranging as far as Berlin, Dresden and Frankfurt.

# Defence of the Reich

## 3 June 1944 Day Fighters

| Unit | Types | Location | Strength (serviceable) | |
|---|---|---|---|---|
| Stab JG 1 | Fw 190A-8 | Lippspringe | 2 (1) | |
| I/JG 1 | Fw 190A-8 | Lippspringe | 46 (34) | |
| II/JG 1 | Fw 190A-8 | Störmede | 39 (26) | |
| III/JG 1* | Bf 109G-10 | Paderborn | 37 (16) | |
| Stab JG 3 | Bf 109G-10 | Salzwedel | 8 (1) | |
| I/JG 3* | Bf 109G-6/AS | Burg | 28 (17) | |
| II/JG 3 | Bf 109G-6 | Sachau | 50 (25) | |
| III/JG 3 | Bf 109G-6 | Ansbach | 67 (16) | |
| IV(Sturm)/JG 3 | Fw 190A-8 | Salzwedel | 51 (27) | |
| I/JG 5* | Bf 109G-10 | Herzogenaurach | 33 (16) | |
| II/JG 5 | Bf 109G-10 | Gardelegen | 41 (18) | |
| Stab JG 11 | Fw 190, Bf 109G | Rothenburg | 1 (0) | |
| I/JG 11 | Fw 190A-8 | Rothenburg | 17 (17) | |
| II/JG 11* | Bf 109G-6/AS | Hustedt | 36 (21) | |
| III/JG 11 | Fw 190A-8 | Rheinsehlen | 23 (16) | |
| 10./JG 11 | Fw 190, Bf 109G | Aalborg | 9 (7) | |
| JGr.zbV | Bf 109G-14 | Ansbach | 5 (0) | |
| Stab JG 27 | Bf 109G-10 | Seyring | 5 (2) | Defence |
| I/JG 27 | Bf 109G-6 | Fels am Wagram | 44 (31) | of |
| III/JG 27 | Bf 109G-6 | Götzendorf | 23 (19) | Austria |
| IV/JG 27 | Bf 109G-6 | Szombathely (Ungarn) | 21 (17) | |
| II/JG 53 | Bf 109G-6 | Öttingen | 65 (25) | |
| III/JG 54 | Fw 190A-8 | Oldenburg | 21 (11) | |
| Einsatz JGr 104 | Bf 109G-5 | Fürth | 4 (4) | |
| Einsatz JGr 106 | Bf 109G-5 | Lachen-Speyersdorf | 5 (3) | |
| Einsatz JGr 108 | Bf 109G-5 | Voslau (Vienna) | 12 (6) | |
| Stab JG 2 | Bf 109G-10 | Creil | 3 (2) Lft. 3 | |
| I/JG 2 | Bf 109G-10 | Cormeilles-en-Vexin | 23 (15) Lft. 3 | |
| Stab JG 26 | Fw 190A-8 | Lille-Nord | 2 (2) Lft. 3 | |
| I/JG 26 | Fw 190A-8 | Lille-Vendeville | 31 (20) Lft. 3 | |
| III/JG 26 | Bf 109G-10 | Nancy-Essay | 37 (22) Lft. 3 | |
| II/ZG 1 | Bf 110G-4 | Wels (Austria) | 31 (15) | |
| Stab ZG 26 | Me 410B-2 | Königsburg-Neumark | 5 (1) | |
| I/ZG 26 | Me 410B-2 | Königsburg-Neumark | 17 (0) | |
| II/ZG 26 | Me 410B-2 | Königsburg-Neumark | 53 (34) | |
| 7./ZG 26 | Bf 110G-2 | Fels am Wagram | 10 (3) | |

### Day and Night-fighters

| Unit | Types | Location | Strength (serviceable) | |
|---|---|---|---|---|
| Stab JG 300 | Fw 190A-6 | Bonn-Hangelar | 2 (1) | |
| I/JG 300 | Bf 109G-6 | Bonn-Hangelar | 42 (14) | |
| II/JG 300 | Bf 109G-6 | Dortmund | 25 (13) | |
| III/JG 300 | Bf 109G-6 | Wiesbaden-Erbenheim | 46 (25) | |
| I/JG 301 | Bf 109G-6 | Hölzkirchen | 39 (29) | |
| I/JG 302 | Bf 109G-6 | Fels am Wagram | 39 (16) | |

*Denote high-altitude units for combating US fighters.

# Chapter 15

# Pauke! Pauke!*

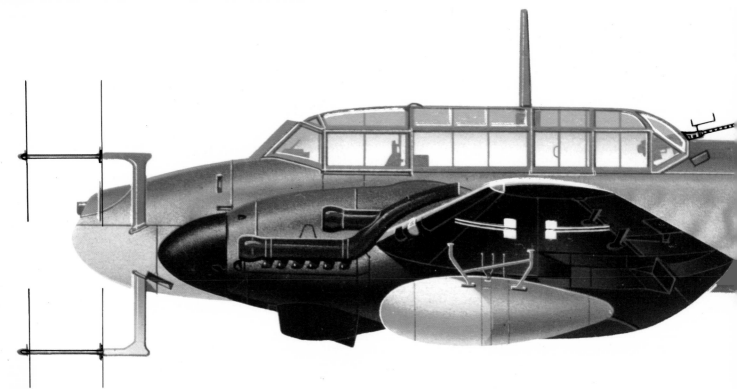

## The Night-Fighter's War

# 1943-1945

'Did they realise how small were their chances if once seen by a fighter? I guess that none knew that the exhausts of their Lancasters could be spotted from a mile-and-a-half, and they could be seen as silhouettes against the stars from nearly a mile away, while the fighter could be seen against the ground at only about a hundred yards.' So wrote an experienced RAF night fighter pilot. Indeed, by 1943, through the efforts of science, the night sky offered but a tattered cloak to hide the nocturnal bomber.

By the beginning of 1943, the Kammhuber Line – the areas covered by Himmelbett fighter-control sectors – stretched from Troyes, 80 miles SE of Paris, to the northern tip of Denmark, extending in depth from the coast to 100–150 miles inland, covering the Low Countries, the Ruhr, Westphalia, the Hannover-Hamburg area, and the whole of Denmark. Only by flying several hundreds of miles were RAF bombers able to avoid this defensive area via the Skaggerak or far to the south of Paris. Almost 95 per cent of the five Nachtjagdgeschwader, operating Bf 110F-4, Ju 88C-6 and Do 217N-2 types, were using the Lichtenstein BC or C-1 radar. The German night-fighter crews were now skilled in its use, eager to fly in all weathers and ruthless in their determination to inflict casualties on RAF Bomber Command. Their leading 'experte', Major Helmut Lent of IV/NJG 1, had claimed his 50th 'kill' on 8 January 1943, and others such as Streib, Gildner, Knacke, Becker and Meurer were adding to their growing list of nocturnal victories.

Against this formidable opposition, RAF Bomber Command was also growing more cunning and determined. In March 1943, when Harris committed his forces to the Battle of the Ruhr, Bomber Command consisted of eighteen

squadrons of Lancaster Mk Is, fourteen squadrons of Halifaxes (mostly Mk II Series IIA), seven squadrons of Stirling I bombers and several units with the Wellington III, IV and X. These bomber units were allocated to Nos 1, 3, 4, 5 and 6 Groups, Bomber Command, while No 8 Group (Pathfinder Force), commanded by Gp.Capt. D. C. T. Bennett, consisted of Nos 7, 35, 83, 109 and 156 Squadrons. The function of this élite force was to locate and mark the target with 250-lb Target Indicator bombs for the following bombers. While 'Gee' (TR 1335) was of little use because of enemy jamming, other aids to navigation had taken its place: 'Oboe' blind-bombing system had first been employed by a No 109 Sqdn Mosquito on Lutterade on 20 December 1942, and H2S radar had first been used to good effect against Hamburg by Nos 7 and 35 Squadrons (No 8 Group PFF) on 30 January 1943. The equipment was sound and other squadrons were receiving it.

All effort was now made to reduce the amount of time over the target, and gone were the great streams of bombers that enabled the Himmelbett operators to direct the night fighters to attack with leisure. Instead of a question of hours, it now took a narrow, compact bomber stream between 30 and 40 minutes to cross the Kammhuber Line. The narrower the width of the stream passing diagonally through the GCI area, the fewer the number of controls that could have bomber aircraft within their range; the shorter the period in which the bombers passed through each GCI area, the fewer the number of possible interceptions which could be effected.

To counter these new tactics, the Himmelbett stations were widened and deepened, and the control system was developed so that two or more night fighters could be brought into action simultaneously in any one Himmelbett sector. Even so, the Himmelbett GCI system was particularly susceptible to saturation tactics and was very uneconomical since it necessitated the wide dispersal of fighters over the whole defensive belt, of which only a few could be brought into action against any one threat. Hence, already by the early summer of 1943, two measures had been adopted which

fell outside the scope of the classic system. These revised night fighting tactics were:

*ZAHME SAU (Tame Sow). This operation, unfettered by the Himmelbett GCI stations, enabled night fighter crews to be directed en masse to the bomber stream by R/T running commentaries from the respective Jagddivision. Once the night fighters had reached the stream, the crews endeavoured to make AI contact with individual targets. Thus, a sortie could start over the North Sea, follow the bomber stream to Mannheim, for example, return with the stream on the out-bound leg and finally land at an airfield far removed from the parent base. In Zahme Sau, the five hours' endurance of the Ju 88C-6b and Ju 88R-1, despite their inferior handling qualities, offered an immediate advantage over the more nimble Bf 110G-4a fighter that became standard equipment for many Nachtjagdgruppen in the late-summer of 1943. Apart from the FuG 212 Lichtenstein C-1 radar, the night-fighter crew was soon able to obtain 'homing' on RAF bombers by additional equipment. Thus, Flensburg (FuG 227/1) could home on the 'Monica' tail-warning device fitted in RAF bombers, while the radar transmissions from H2S could be homed on to by Naxos Z (FuG 350) from a maximum range of 30 miles.

*WILDE SAU (Wild Sow). This was the freelance visual night fighting that dated from before the introduction of Himmelbett, wherein the pilot relied on searchlights and visual contact to make an interception. Wilde Sau fighters operated over the target area, above a flak-free zone, and were aided by searchlights, flares and pyrotechnics. Normally the Flak fire was limited to a certain altitude, say 15,000 feet, above which the Wilde Sau fighters operated. The flares were dropped by special Beleuchter (Illuminator) staffeln, usually Ju 88s.

The reintroduction of visual night fighting was due to the energetic efforts of Obstlt. Hajo Hermann who gained Göring's authority on 27 June 1943 for the formation of a Kommando equipped with twelve Fw 190A-4 fighters fitted with 300 litre (66-gal) drop tanks. The Kommando quickly proved its worth by shooting down 12 RAF bombers over Cologne on the

*Lit 'Kettledrums, Kettledrums' . . . 'I am in visual range of my target' (R/T call).

102

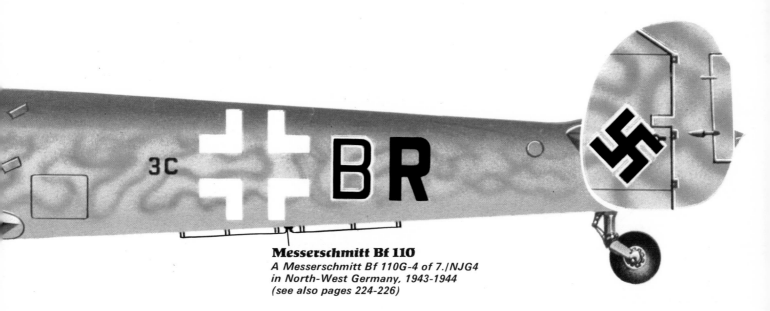

## Messerschmitt Bf 110
**A Messerschmitt Bf 110G-4 of 7./NJG4
in North-West Germany, 1943-1944
(see also pages 224-226)**

night of 3 July, and, as a result, Göring gave his approval for the formation of further Wilde Sau units. Over the summer months, after the formation of JG 300 (Major Kurt Kettner) at Bonn-Hangelar, both JG 301 (Maj. Helmut Weinreich) and JG 302 (Maj. Manfred Mössinger) were formed at Neubiberg and Döberitz. Only one Gruppe of each Geschwader possessed its own aircraft, the other Gruppen sharing their fighters with a Jagdgruppe based on the same airfield, much to the detriment of serviceability. Later on, the Fw 190A-5/U2N and Bf 109G-6/U4N, equipped with the Naxos Z homer, were added to the inventory of the Wilde Sau units. With the onset of winter, losses rose alarmingly and, although some Wilde Sau elements of JG 300 and JG 301 continued night operations, most were retrained for combat operations against day bombers of the 8th USAAF.

The formation of JG 300 proved fortuitous for the Luftwaffe when, in late-July 1943, RAF

Bomber Command commenced the Battle of Hamburg, the second largest city in the Reich. Situated on the coast, Hamburg was an easy target to identify on H2S and, on the night of 24 July, 740 bombers out of a total of 791 despatched dropped 2,396 tons of HE and incendiary on the districts of Barmbeck, Alster, Höheluft and Altona. The raid was completed in two-and-a-half hours, 74 bombers carrying H2S and 'Window' jamming being used for the first time. 'Window' consisted of tinfoil strips cut to a length equivalent to half the wavelength of the Würzburg and Lichtenstein radars, a bundle of 'Window' dropped from an aircraft gave an immediate radar return on the enemy operator's screen. The effect was a catastrophe for the entire Himmelbett GCI control system and for the nightfighters which relied on FuG 202 and FuG 212, with a simultaneous effect on radar searchlights and flak prediction. General Martini, the chief of the Luftwaffe Signals Command,

had for long known about the possible use of metallic strips with their jamming potential, but his warnings had fallen upon deaf ears. Characteristically, it was he who had to take the full blame for the 'surprise' of Window!

A total of 3,095 sorties were despatched by RAF Bomber Command and the 8th USAAF against Hamburg between 24 July and 2 August, 2,630 of these dropping 8,621 tons, including 4,309 tons of incendiaries, on this ancient Hanseatic city. Eighty-seven bombers were lost, but the devastation and fire storms killed 41,800 people and injured 37,439 while thousands were missing presumed killed.

While Kammhuber's Fliegerkorps XII recovered from the effects of 'Window', the

*Below: The final G-series night-fighter production model of the Messerschmitt Bf 110 was the G-4d/R3 with low-drag Lichtenstein SN-2 array seen here with a home-based Nachtjagdgruppe*

*Above: A veritable forest of radar antennae resulted on the nose of the Junkers Ju 88C-6c night fighter when both Lichtenstein BC and SN-2 were employed as seen here*

*Left: 'Did they realise how small were their chances if once seen by a fighter?'... This unusual night photograph shows a Lancaster clearly silhouetted above columns of smoke*

Wilde Sau units came into their own during the long summer nights. When Bomber Command returned to Berlin, JG 300 claimed 56 RAF bombers on the night of 24 August, operating in good visibility above a flak-free zone designated at 4,500m; 47 were claimed on the night of 1 September and a further 26 on the night of 4 September. The first large-scale Zahme Sau operation was flown on the night of 17 August; 40 Lancasters out of a despatched force of 597 were shot down by flak and night fighters using brilliant moonlight. The pace continued throughout the autumn as RAF Bomber Command sought targets at Mannheim, Hannover and Kassel.

Collisions, bad weather, and return fire were constant threats to the German night fighter pilots. NJG 1 lost Hptm. Reinhold Knacke, Oblt. Paul Gildner and Hptm. Ludwig Becker in February 1943, and on 27 September, Maj. Hans-Dieter Frank, the Kommandeur I/NJG 1 with 55 'kills', was lost in a mid-air collision. Hptm. August Geiger of 7./NJG 1, with 53 'kills', was lost on 29 September. Concerning the tactics and organisation of night fighter units, the evidence given by a crew shot down off Texel on 25 July 1943 during the 8th USAAF raid on Hamburg is of interest. Flying a Bf 110G-4a, this crew belonged to 12.

Staffel of IV/NJG 1 based at Leeuwarden. Gruppenstab IV/NJG 1 consisted of three crews, that of the Kommandeur, the Adjutant and the Technical Officer, and the three Staffeln of the Gruppe averaged about ten crews apiece. The Leeuwarden area had been relatively quiet to that time, and this crew had flown only 75 operational flights in 21 months. Losses had been low. The whole of NJG 1 was equipped with the Bf 110G. The aircraft was in plentiful supply and there always were more aircraft than crews. Replacements were drawn from Werl and Schöneberg-Diepensee, where calibration of the Lichtenstein BC was carried out. The operational sector of IV/NJG 1 was based on Leeuwarden with the following fighter-control 'boxes': 'Schleier' at Schiermonnikoog, 'Tiger' at Terschelling, 'Lowe' SW of Leeuwarden, 'Hering' at Medemblik, 'Bisbari' on the east side of the Zuider Zee and 'Salzherring' on the North Sea coast, opposite Medemblik. These were M/F radio beacons over which the fighters orbited prior to instructions from the controller.

The pilot expressed a decided preference for attacking four-engined bombers: there was a considerable danger in over-shooting when approaching a slow bomber, such as the Wellington, whereas it was easier to synchronise speeds when dealing with Lancasters and Halifaxes. With the latter it was seldom necessary to lower flap to reduce speed. One form of attack was to approach from astern to within 30–50 yards and silence the rear gunner with the first burst, after which the bomber could be dealt with at leisure. Another form of attack, which the crews of IV/NJG 1 regarded as their speciality, was to make a slow approach until the fighter was about 150 feet vertically below the bomber and then fly along at synchronised speeds until ready to attack. From this position the night fighter was

immune from the bomber's lookout and from its MG fire. The actual attack was made by pulling up almost vertically and firing when the bomber's nose met the top of the Revi C.12/D gunsight. Operating within the Himmelbett area, normal interceptions lasted between five and seven minutes from the first vector to the kill.

The introduction of 'Window' failed to reduce RAF bomber losses due to night fighters to any marked extent, although those sustained from flak did decrease. If anything, the Wilde Sau and Zahme Sau tactics more than compensated for the set-back in efficient radar control. In September 1943, a new AI radar set, FuG 220 Lichtenstein SN-2, was introduced and units were rapidly re-equipped. SN-2 worked within 73 and 91 M/cs, was unaffected by 'Window' jamming and had a maximum range of 4 miles and a minimum of 400 yards. Its minimum range, therefore, was not as low as FuG 212 Lichtenstein C-1 and for this reason the latter was often retained to enable the crews to get within 200 yards. This led to a veritable forest of aerials on the noses of the night-fighters, reducing their speed advantage even more. But, by early 1944, SN-2 had been perfected and was giving ranges down to 200 yards. Armament was also increased; the Bf 110G-4b/R3 carrying two Mk 108 30-mm cannon and two MG 151/20s. The so-called 'schräge Musik' (Jazz Music) installation of Bf 110s, Ju 88s and Do 217s enabled crews to attack a bomber from directly below, without having recourse to the hair-raising maneouvre described earlier by the pilot of IV/NJG 1. Two MG FFs or MG 151/20s were mounted in the cabin or fuselage at between 70–80° from the vertical, and were aimed by a second Revi C.12/D or 16B gunsight mounted on the canopy roof. The so-called 'schräge Musik' was highly effective and some experienced pilots could stay directly below a cork-screwing bomber while remaining imune from its return fire.

The night war over Germany was becoming increasingly one of radio measure and counter-measure, with each opponent seeking a technological loophole through which to gain an advantage over the other. In November, greater bombing accuracy was attained by the introduction of Gee-H, while the specialist No 100 Group, RAF Bomber Command, was formed under Air Cdr. E. B. Addison. Its rôle was bomber support, and through radio countermeasures (RCM) and the introduction first of Beaufighter VIs and later Mosquitoes for intruder work within the bomber streams and over German night fighter bases, No 100 Group was to provide a valuable service. Bomber Command's first reaction to Wilde Sau was to shorten its attacks to 15–20 minutes' duration, and this was quickly followed by the development of feint or 'spoof' routes and attacks to despatch the German night fighters to the wrong area. The task of the defenders was to be rendered the more difficult by R/T jamming by 'Mandrel' and 'Airborne Cigar', while 'Corona' consisted of further confusion by the broadcast of spurious information.

However, when Harris turned to the Battle of Berlin in November 1943, these measures were in their infancy. This was to be Harris' attempt to end the war by strategic bombing, and it was to end in failure despite the gallantry and determination of his crews. Primarily directed at Berlin, from 18 November 1943 until 31 March 1944, Bomber Command's intensive attacks resulted in the loss of 1,047 bombers with a further 1,682 damaged through enemy action. The offensive was carried out usually in unfavourable weather, with No 8 Group PFF having to sky-mark the target with flares and 'Window' being used extensively.

But the Nachtjagdgruppen had solved the 'Window' problem to a large extent by the introduction of SN-2, while Flensburg and

Naxos allowed them to operate with considerable freedom. The situation on the ground was also improving, with the older Freya and Würzburg radars being replaced by Wasserman and Mammuth radars that were unaffected by the then current wave-length jamming. On 31 December 1943, out of a strength of 517 nightfighters, 334 were combat ready. Allotted to the defence of the Reich were Stab, I, II, III and IV/NJG 1, Stab, I, II and III/NJG 2, Stab, I, II, III and IV/NJG 3, Stab, I, II, III and IV/NJG 5 and Stab, I and II/NJG 6, while Stab, I, II and III/NJG 4 were subordinated to Luftflotte 3 in France. Fliegerkorps XII was now disbanded, Kammhuber was replaced by Generalleutnant Josef Schmid in September 1943, and the latter now took over Jagdkorps I under Luftflotte Reich.

The majority of Nachtjagdgruppen was equipped with the Bf 110G-4b/R3, but the Ju 88C-6b was growing in preponderance, while a small number of units used the Dornier 217N-2. Some Gruppen had a few Fw 190A-5/U2Ns on strength. The I/NJG 1, under Hptm. Manfred Meurer, had several Heinkel 219A-2/R1s along with Bf 110Gs and Ju 88Cs. This excellent fighter was destined to see only limited service, despite its fine performance that enabled it to intercept the Mosquito. Meurer was killed on 2 January in a collision. This was followed on 21 January by the loss of Maj. Heinrich Prinz zu Sayn Wittgenstein, the Kommodore NJG 4, who was shot down by return fire during a raid on Magdeburg. Despite the losses, the Luftwaffe's night fighters reaped a grim harvest, as indicated by the growing losses of Bomber Command: 55 bombers failed to return from Magdeburg on 21 January and 43 were lost out of a force of 683 to Berlin on 28 January. Bomber Command's heaviest raid on Berlin (1,066 despatched) saw the loss of 42 on 15 February, and, on 19 February, 78 were lost out of 823 sent. The Kommandeur of IV/NJG 1, Hptm. Heinz-Wolfgang Schnauffer, destined to become the greatest of all night fighter pilots, claimed his 50th 'kill' on 24 March 1944. On this night, 72 RAF bombers were lost out of 811 sent to Berlin. The climax came on the Nuremburg raid on 30 March, when 94 bombers were either lost or damaged beyond repair.

On this night, 795 bombers were despatched to Nuremburg. The weather over the North Sea precluded any attempt at 'spoof' raids. Thickening cloud over Belgium was followed by a brilliant half-moon which made for almost daylight conditions over Germany. The Nachtjagdgruppen were despatched to the Frankfurt and Bonn sectors on Zahme Sau missions. Before the first RAF bombers had reached the coast, the direction of their course was already plotted from their H2S emissions, enabling Jagddivision 3's fighters to position themselves

in the path. In brilliant moonlight, with several of the Lancasters and Halifaxes leaving long condensation trails, a running battle commenced over Aachen to the target. Over 200 German night fighters were committed to the battle that was to continue well out over the North Sea, amongst the hail and thunderclouds.

The loss of 11·3 per cent of the force committed was prohibitive and the victory accorded to Schmid's night-fighters was instrumental in the decision to curtail deep-penetration night attacks. The Mosquitoes of RAF Bomber Command, to be joined in the summer by the MK XVI capable of carrying a 4,000-lb bomb, continued their sorties deep into Germany, however, and the heavy bomber element was now turned to transportation and communication targets prior to OVERLORD. Even these raids did not go unscathed – the attack on Mailly-le-Camp, in France, which was the depot for the 21st Pz. Division, resulted in NJG 4 and III/NJG 5 shooting down a considerable number of RAF heavies.

The finest night fighter of the Luftwaffe, the Ju 88G-1, was issued to several Gruppen in early June 1944, and the Allies reaped a windfall when one landed in error at Woodbridge, in Suffolk, at 04.25hrs on 13 July. Carrying the very latest in German avionics this aircraft allowed scientists to modify 'Window' to jam the Lichtenstein SN-2 and, for the first time,

*Above: The Heinkel He 219A-5/R1 nightfighter having both SN-2 and C-1 Lichtenstein radar*

*Right: The final version of the Junkers Ju 88 night-fighter to attain production was the Ju 88G-7, the G-7a subtype seen here having Lichtenstein SN-2 for both forward search and tail warning*

*Below right: A Messerschmitt Bf 110G G-4c/R3 with FuG 220b Lichtenstein SN-2 radar and 20-mm and 30-mm cannon*

gave positive evidence of German capability to home on to Monica. In addition to FuG 220, FuG 227 and FuG 16zY, the Junkers carried Peilgerät 6 automatic D/F, FuG 10P short-range R/T and long-range W/T, and FuB1 2F blind-approach.

After the German rout of August and September 1944, the Nachtjagdgruppen suffered a catastrophic set-back when the early-warning radar network was overrun by the Allies. This enabled Bomber Command to execute numerous, and extremely intricate operations, backed up by RAF Mosquito night fighters and copious RCM jamming, against the vital oil and transportation targets deep within Germany. Although the German night fighter force continued to operate efficiently, its back was finally broken by fuel shortage.

## Defence of the Reich

### 3 June 1944 Night-fighters

| Unit | Types | Location | Strength (serviceable) |
|---|---|---|---|
| Stab NJG 1 | He 219A-5, Bf 110G-4 | Deelen-Arnhem | 3 (1) |
| I/NJG 1 | He 219A-2, Bf 110G-4 | Venlo | 34 (14) |
| II/NJG 1 | Bf 110G-4 | Deelen-Arnhem | 21 (11) |
| III/NJG 1 | Bf 110G-4 | Leeuwarden | 21 (17) |
| IV/NJG 1 | Bf 110G-4, Ju 88G-1 | St Trond | 24 (16) |
| Stab NJG 2 | Ju 88G-1 | Deelen-Arnhem | 6 (1) |
| I/NJG 2 | Ju 88G-1 | Rhein-Main | 34 (26) |
| II/NJG 2 | Ju 88G-1 | Butzweilerhof | 33 (18) |
| III/NJG 2 | Ju 88G-1 | Langendiebach | 28 (18) |
| Stab NJG 3 | Ju 88G-1, Bf 110G-4 | Stade | 5 (1) |
| I/NJG 3 | Ju 88C-6, Bf 110G-4 | Vechta | 28 (22) |
| II/NJG 3 | Ju 88C-6 | Plantlünne | 36 (17) |
| III/NJG 3 | Bf 110G-4 | Stade | 28 (22) |
| IV/NJG 3 | Ju 88C-6 | Westerland-Grove | 34 (16) |
| Stab NJG 4* | Ju 88G-1 | Chenay | 2 (1) |
| I/NJG 4* | Ju 88C-6, Bf 110G-4 | Florennes | 19 (12) |
| II/NJG 4* | Do 217N-2, Bf 110G-4 | Coulommiers | 19 (10) |
| III/NJG 4* | Do 217N-2, Bf 110G-4 | Chenay | 20 (8) |
| Stab NJG 5 | Bf 110G-4 | Deelen-Arnhem | 2 (1) |
| I/NJG 5* | Bf 110G-4 | St Dizier | 17 (11) |
| II/NJG 5 | Bf 110G-4 | Gütersloh | 15 (9) |
| III/NJG 5* | Bf 110G-4 | Leon-Athies | 16 (8) |
| IV/NJG 5 | Bf 110G-4 | Erfurt-Bindersleben | 17 (13) |
| Stab NJG 6 | Bf 110G-4 | Schleissheim | 2 (1) |
| I/NJG 6 | Bf 110G-4 | Kitzingen | 23 (17) |
| III/NJG 6 | Bf 110G-4 | Szömbathely (Ungarn) | 6 (3) |
| NJGr 10 | He 219A-5, Bf 110G-4 Bf 109G-6/U4N | Berlin-Werneuchen | 22 (11) |
| I(Beleuchter)/NJG 7 | Ju 88G-1 | Munster-Handorf | 23 (1) |

*Assigned to Jagdkorps II (Luftflotte 3).

# Chapter 16

# The Last Battles

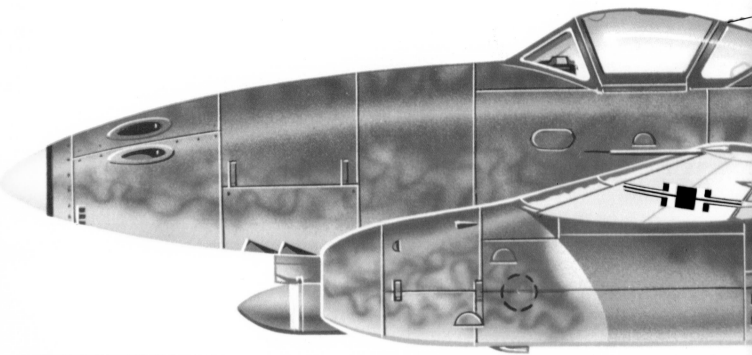

## From D-Day to the Final Defeat of Germany

# 1944-1945

On 1 April 1944, out of a total Luftwaffe strength of 1,675 Bf 109Gs and Fw 190As, 850 were committed to the defence of the Reich against the depredations of the 8th and 15th US Air Forces. Only 135 were stationed in Northern France and Belgium facing the might of the 9th USAAF, the 2nd Tactical Air Force, and RAF Fighter Command. In Norway there remained only 40 Fw 190s of IV/JG 5, while in Italy there were 145 Bf 109Gs of JG 53 and JG 77. In the East, on a front of 1,500 miles from the Baltic to the Caspian, only 515 German fighters faced the overwhelming numbers of the Soviet Air Forces now equipped with Yak-9s and the latest La-7 fighters.

An uneasy lull reigned in the East. The Crimea had been lost, the Northern and Central Fronts had stabilised while the Russians consolidated, while in the South the last offensive of spring had brought the Soviet Army to the borders of Rumania. Such were the resources of the Soviet Army that there could be little delay before the summer offensive. In mid-May, the Allies renewed their offensive in Italy to which the Luftwaffe's opposition was negligible. The next Allied blow would fall in the West, at some point along the coast of Northern France, but when the invasion would come was open to conjecture and all the Wehrmacht could do was to wait and strengthen its defences along the Atlantic Wall.

For the Luftwaffe, the preparation for an Allied invasion of France had started early in 1944, with a re-organisation of command and strengthening of bomber and anti-shipping forces. In August 1943, Gen. Maj. Dietrich Pelz had taken over Fliegerkorps IX in France and the Low Countries, and this command had been steadily reinforced by Kampfgruppen drawn from Italy. In February 1944, Gen.Lt.

Alfred Bülowius' Fliegerkorps II arrived in Northern France in name only, with the task of building up the ground-attack and close-support forces. The maritime command, Fliegerführer Atlantik, was absorbed into Fliegerkorps X (Gen.Lt. Holle) with Fliegerdivision 2 subordinated. Based in the extreme south and south-west of France, both organisations consisted of long-range reconnaissance and anti-shipping units. Jagdkorps II, under Gen. Maj. Werner Junck, was responsible for fighter defence over Northern France and Belgium, with Jafü 4 and 5 subordinated. In May, only two Jagdgeschwader were operational under Jagdkorps II, but it was proposed to rush fighter reinforcements in as soon as the Allies invaded.

It was the bomber and anti-shipping forces that were to be the spearhead of the Luftwaffe's offensive operations against the Allied landings, but by the eve of D-Day, Fliegerkorps IX, which had 550 bombers on strength in December 1943, had been reduced to some 170 by April 1944. This was due to Pelz' bomber campaign, the so-called 'Little Blitz', which had opened on 21 January 1944. To meet the invasion it was hoped that Fliegerkorps X would have five Gruppen of torpedo-bombers and a similar number of Gruppen using Fritz X (FX 1400) and the Hs 293 glider-bomb, but owing to the priority afforded fighter production, the force rose to only some 200–250 aircraft, and even this strength could not be maintained, for by early June 1944 it had dwindled to about 190 aircraft and there was a critical shortage of trained crews. On the day prior to D-Day (Operation OVERLORD), Luftflotte 3 (Sperrle) consisted of 815 combat aircraft. These included 170 single-engined fighters based over the entirety of France, 130 bombers of FlKps IX and 200 anti-shipping aircraft of FlKps X and Fliegerdivision 2.

On 31 May, 1944 the forces under Jagdkorps II consisted of Stab and II/JG 2 at Creil with 21 (15) Bf 109G-6s and Fw 190A-8s, and I and III/JG 2 at Cormeilles-en-Vexin with 48 (33) Fw 190A-8s. Geschwaderstab JG 26 was at Lille-Nord, I/JG 26 at Lille-Vendeville and

Denain, and III/JG 26 at Nancy-Essay; the total strength of the Geschwader amounting to 75 fighters of which 47 were serviceable. The II/JG 26 was resting at Mont-de-Marsan, south of Bordeaux. Bülowius' FlKps II consisted of III/SG 4 and I/SKG 10 with 73 fighter-bombers; Fliegerkorps IX comprised Stab, I, II and III/KG 2, Stab, I and III/KG 6, 1. and 2./KG 66, II/KG 51, Stab, I and III/KG 54, 6./KG 76 and Stab I and III/KG 77, and under Fliegerführer West were Stab, I and III/ZG 1 with Bf 110G-2 fighters, while the forces of Holle's FlKps X consisted of 1.(F)/SAGr 129, III/KG 26, Stab, KG 30, I/KG 40 and Stab and III/KG 100. The reconnaissance forces subordinated to Luftflotte 3 were FAGr 5, 1.(F)/33, Sonder St.Ob.d.L, 7.(F)/121, Aufkl.Gr 123 and 3.(F)/122.

## The Invasion of Normandy and the Retreat to the German Border

# 1944

On the first day of the invasion, some indication of the disparity between the Luftwaffe and the Allied air forces can be gauged from the fact that by comparison with the 100 fighter and 175 bomber sorties mounted by the Luftwaffe on 6 June no fewer than 14,674 were flown by the Allies. Over the beachheads themselves, the Luftwaffe was noteworthy for its virtual absence. During the day, the RAF flew 5,656 sorties in the face of minimal air op-all were shot down by flak. Nevertheless, there was a stiffening of Luftwaffe opposition during the following week. In the 36 hours following the invasion 200 Bf 109Gs and Fw 190s arrived from the Reich, 45 torpedo-bombers were sent to FlKps X from Germany and 90 Ju 88s, Ju 188s and Me 410s reinforced FlKps IX from Germany and Italy. By 13 June, over a thousand aircraft had been rushed to counter the new threat in the West. By 10 June 1944, the following fighter units were based in France

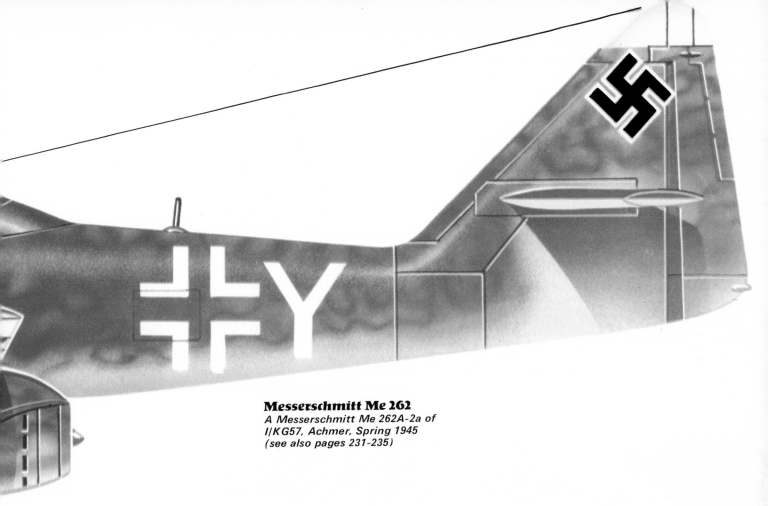

## Messerschmitt Me 262
*A Messerschmitt Me 262A-2a of*
*I/KG57, Achmer, Spring 1945*
*(see also pages 231-235)*

and engaged in combat operations against the Allies: Stab, I, II and III/JG 1, II, III and IV(Sturm)/JG 3, I/JG 5, I, II and 10./JG 11, Stab, I, III and IV/JG 27, II/JG 53 and III/JG 54. There was also an autonomous JGr 200, made up of Jagdschule aircraft, based at Avignon, which took no part in the Normandy operations.

By the end of June 1944, Allied air superiority was such that most Luftwaffe units were suffering from depleted strength and low serviceability. Great difficulty was experienced in getting new aircraft to the Jagdgruppen for, with the bombing of Le Bourget and Toul, spare aircraft had to be ferried from as far afield as Mannheim, Wiesbaden and Cologne.

Five Jagdgruppen had to be withdrawn to Germany for re-fit after only ten days in

*Below: The He 162A was manufactured during the war's closing months and is seen here under construction in a former salt mine at Tarthun*

Normandy. One example of this was the experience of II/JG 1, under Major Heinz Bär, which operated from a small grass strip near Semalle, 6–7kms north of Alençon. At 13.00hrs on 25 June, II/JG 1's airfield was strafed by 16 P-51 Mustangs. The attack was extremely successful and destroyed 15 out of the Gruppe's 24 Fw 190s, putting II/JG 1 out of action for several days. That night, 20 pilots of the Gruppe flew from Le Mans to Köln-Ostheim by Ju 52 to get replacement aircraft, but it was not until 1 July that these arrived. On 1 July, Bülowius took over Jagdkorps II from Junck, with the staff of Fliegerkorps II withdrawing from Normandy, but this commander could do little to urge his pilots to greater efforts in the face of Allied air superiority. The wastage in machines and pilots was immense; JG 26 alone lost 67 pilots in combat from D-Day to 31 August.

The Allied advance in Normandy had been checked at Caen, but on 1 August, the 3rd US Army attacked the weak front at Avranches and broke out to the West, South and East, encircling the German armies in the Falaise Pocket. In the Mortain-Falaise sector, the Wehrmacht suffered its greatest defeat since Stalingrad, but on the Allied side there was considerable disappointment because more than one-third of the German VII Army had eluded the trap. By 26 August, the British 2nd Army and the 1st Canadian Army had reached the Seine, while the US 1st and 3rd Armies had reached Paris, lunged south and reached Troyes. The air situation in the West by this time could hardly have deteriorated further, and to all purposes the Luftwaffe was a spent and exhausted force with little future prospect of recovery.

After a brief sojourn on the airfields in Belgium, the fighter units that had provided the rearguard for the retreating Wehrmacht, namely, III/JG 1, Stab, I, II and III/JG 2, Stab, II and III/JG 3, II/JG 6, I and II/JG 11, Stab, I, II and III/JG 26, III/JG 27, Stab and II/JG 53, Stab and III/JG 76 and I/JG 302 (Wilde Sau), were withdrawn to bases in Germany for re-fit. Nachtjagdgeschwader 2, 4 and 5 were likewise transferred, while FlKps IX's bomber force, which had shrunk to 175 aircraft, was pulled back and was to remain largely ineffective due to the increasingly difficult fuel situation. Meanwhile events in the East had given cause for further concern.

# The Eastern Front
# 1944

Contrary to German expectations, the Soviet summer offensive broke initially against the weak Finnish Front in Karelia on 10 June 1944, but this was opposed by the Luftwaffe in numbers far exceeding those committed to

countering the Anglo-American invasion in the West. Of the 2,085 combat aircraft based in the East in June 1944, 105 were under Luftflotte 5 in the Gulf of Finland sector, 360 under Luftflotte 1 in the Baltic States and around the Narva area, 775 under Luftflotte 6 in the central sector, covering the Polish approaches where the main Soviet blow was expected to fall, and 845 were under Luftflotte 4 in the Balkans and the Carpathian sector.

When the main Soviet offensive opened on the Central Front, on 23 June, the forces of Luftflotte 6 had already been weakened by the transfer of 50 fighters and close-support aircraft to Finland and a Jagdgruppe to Germany following the large-scale despatch of fighters to the Normandy Front. By 3 July, the Russians had taken Vitebsk, Mogilev and Minsk, and were advancing steadily, forcing the Luftwaffe to throw in every available unit: 40 Bf 109G-6s were brought in from Germany (III/JG 11), III/JG 52 and IV/JG 51 were transferred from

Luftflotte 4 in the South, while the need for ground-attack Fw 190s forced the transfer of I and II/SG 4 from the already denuded battlefront in Italy, followed later by III/SG 4 from Normandy. But the reinforced combat units facing the main Soviet assault failed to stem the rout that followed. In the north, Vilna fell on 13 July, followed by Grodno and Pinsk and, in the centre, the Wehrmacht was forced to abandon first Brest-Litovsk, then Lublin and Lwow, and finally Przemsyl on 28 July. By the end of the month, the Luftwaffe's total strength in the East had fallen to 1,750 aircraft, while the average daily effort of 500–600 sorties was inadequate to relieve the hard-pressed ground forces.

It was at this critical moment in time that the Balkan Front suddenly flared up. In Rumania, the Luftwaffe's weakness had already been shown by the paltry effort against the 15th USAAF. During the heavy B-17 and B-24 raids on Ploesti of 9 and 15 July, only 50

*Above: The Focke-Wulf Ta 152C was one of the final developments of the famous Fw 190, but, in the event, it was too late to see service with the Luftwaffe*

sorties (half of which were by Rumanian units) had been put up in defence of the vital oilfields. The fighter units in this sector were elements of JG 77, I/JG 53, II/JG 301 and the nightfighter IV/NJG 6.

All resistance in Rumania came to a precipitate end with the Rumanian *coup d'état* on 23 August 1944, which, in effect, ceded the country's cause to the Soviet Union. The transfer of I/SG 2 and a Rumanian Ju 87D unit to Zilistea was all that the Luftwaffe could spare in an effort to retrieve the situation, but in the face of the Soviet advance across the Pruth river, all German units were quickly withdrawn to Hungary. By the end of August, Constanza, Ploesti and Bucharest had fallen; Bulgaria turned against Germany on 6 September, and thereafter the situation in the Balkans became untenable, with the Wehrmacht extricating itself to the best of its ability. By October 1944, all Luftwaffe combat operations were drastically curtailed due to the oil shortage. The combat units based in the East, as of 10 October 1944, were as follows:

Reconnaissance: NAGr 2, 4, 5, 8, 10, 2.(H)/12, 1. and 7.(H)/32 and Gruppen (H) 14 and 15; long-range reconnaissance: FAGr 2, Stab FAGr 1, 2.(F)/11, 4.(F)/11, 4.(F)/14, 3.(F)/22, 2.(F)/121, 2.(F)/100, 5.(F)/122 and 1.(F)/124; fighters: Stab, III and IV/JG 5 in Finland, Stab, I, II, III and IV/JG 51, Stab, I, II and III/JG 53, I/JG 53, Stab, I and II/JG 54 and Geschwaderstab JG 76; night-fighters: Stab, I and IV/NJG 5, I and 4./NJG 100, NJG Staffel Finland, Einsatz Staffel NJG 102; Zerstörer: IV/ZG 26 in Finland; Schlachtgeschwader: Stab, I, II, III and 10.(Pz)/SG 1, Stab, I, II, III and 10.(Pz)/SG 2, Stab, II, III and 10.(Pz)/SG 3, Stab, I, II and III/SG 4, IV(Pz)/SG 9, Stab, I and III/SG 10, Stab, I, II and 10.(Pz)/SG 77 and the Kroat Staffel. Bomber and heavy ground-attack units were Stab, II and III/KG 4 and the 14.Staffel of KG 3, KG 27 and KG 55.

By December 1944, Luftflotte 1 was cut-off and isolated in the Courland, Luftflotte 6, under Gen.Oberst Ritter von Greim with FlKps II and VIII subordinated, faced the Soviet armies in Central Poland on the line Königsburg-Warsaw-Krakow, while Luftflotte 4, under Gen.Oberst Dessloch with FlKps I and Fl.Div 17 subordinated, occupied the line Krakow-Budapest-Lake Balaton, the latter now joining forces with Luftwaffenkommando Süd-Ost in the Balkans.

# The Closing Ring
# 1944

By September 1944, the steadily shrinking perimeters of the Third Reich had forced a general re-organisation of the command structure within the Luftwaffe. On 21 September, Luftflotte 3 was degraded to the status of Luftwaffenkommando West – an event already presaged by the replacement of Sperrle by Gen. Oberst Dessloch in August – which became subordinated to Luftflotte Reich. This command was responsible for tactical and close-support operations in conjunction with the air defence of Germany and, under its control were Jagdkorps II and Fliegerdivision 5. The strategic fighter defence of Germany was in the hands of Jagdkorps I, under the overall command of Stumpff's Luftflotte Reich, with HQ at Truenbreitzen. Jagdkorps I controlled Jagddivision 1 (Döberitz), Jagddivision 2 (Stade) with Jagdabschnittführer Denmark subordinated, Jagddivision 3 (Dortmund) with Jagdabschnittführer Mittelrhein, Jagddivision 7 (München) and Jagddivision 8 (Vienna); the Eastern Approaches were covered by Jafü Ost-Preussen and Jafü Ober-Silesien.

At the same time Luftflotte 5, in Norway, was down-graded to Luftwaffenkommando Norwegen and similarly, in Italy, Luftflotte 2 relinquished its functions to Luftwaffengeneral Italien (Gen. Ritter von Pohl). In the Balkans also a general re-shuffle of Commands took place, numerous subsidiary formations being placed under Luftwaffengeneral Nord-Balkan covering Northern Yugoslavia, and Luftwaffengeneral Greichenland, both of them being subordinate to Lw.Kdo Süd-Ost. This extensive regrouping resulted in a great concentration of forces which should, theoretically, have added flexibility and effectiveness to the defence of Germany, but in practice this improvement was offset by the increasingly

desperate fuel shortage, the steady decline in the fighting value of crews and pilots, and congestion and increased vulnerability of airfields.

With the resumption of the Allied bombing offensive against the synthetic oil industry, the decision was taken at the end of September 1944 to leave no more than a small force of some 300 Fw 190s and Bf 109Gs to support the Wehrmacht in the West covering the approaches to the Rhine, while no less than 1,260 single-engined day fighters (including some 25 Me 163B-1s of I/JG 400) were allocated to the defence of the Reich, out of a total day fighter strength of 1,975. To provide this accumulation of strength for the defence of the oil installations, even the fighter force on the Eastern Front had to be reduced to no more than 375 aircraft. On top of this, 900 Ju 88Gs and Bf 110Gs of the Nachtjagdgruppen were available against the RAF's night bombing offensive, and altogether 70 per cent of the total Luftwaffe fighter strength was now earmarked for the defence of the oil industry.

For Allied pilots and aircrews, nurtured by the Press that stated, on every occasion, that the Luftwaffe was a beaten force as demonstrated by its absence over the Normandy battlefields, this resurgence of strength came as a grim reminder of the resilience of the Luftwaffe so often displayed in the past. True, the pilots of 1944 were not of the calibre of the Jagdflieger of 1940, but, to the end, they displayed an enthusiasm for flying, an aggressive spirit and tenacity and determination comparable with that of RAF fighter pilots during the Battle of Britain, or the US Navy pilots at Midway.

Within the average Jagdgruppe, at this time, only a tiny minority had any operational experience of more than six months duration, with the exception of the Gruppenkommandeure and the Staffelkapitäne; a small percentage of personnel had an average of three months active service, while the majority of pilots had seen as little as two or three weeks. The training schools had emphasized the technicalities of flying to the detriment of gunnery and tactics. This was revealed in all the fatal mistakes of the inexperienced pilot in combat – absurdly inadequate air-search and pre-occupation with formation keeping; an inability to fly the aircraft to its limits; a tendency to forget to jettison the drop tank or arm the weapons when joining combat and, finally, an inability to break off combat and escape when warranted by a tactical situation. Equipment was good and the fighters were available in quantity, but their pilots lacked

*Above: The Einsatz-Staffel of IV Gruppe of Kampfgeschwader 101 flew its first operation with the Mistel 1 on 24 June 1944, the pilot of the Bf 109F fighter aiming the Ju 88A 'missile'*

the vital element of quality.

The day fighter units under Jagdkorps I and II, on 10 October 1944, were: Stab, I, II and III/JG 2, Stab, I, II and III/JG 26, III/JG 27, Stab, II, III and IV/JG 53 under Luftwaffenkommando West; Stab, I, II and IV(Sturm)/JG 3, Stab, I, II(Sturm), III and IV/JG 4, I, II and IV/JG 27, IV/JG 54, Stab, I II(Sturm), III and IV/JG 300, I/JG 400 and Jagdgruppe 10. Jagdgeschwader 1, 6 and 11 were either in process of re-equipping or formation.

In terms of aircraft performance, the pace was being maintained with that of the Allies. The Bf 109G-14 and K-4 were in widespread use, both having first class high-altitude combat performance, while the Fw 190A-8 and A-9, although much heavier, still displayed the original fighter's formidable qualities in the hands of a good pilot. Hauptmann Robert Weiss's III/JG 54 was the first unit to receive the Fw 190D-9 fighter that restored the performance balance vis-a-vis the Tempest V, the Spitfire XIV and the P-51D Mustang, and on 12 October 1944, 9. and 10./JG 54 were sent to Achmer and Hesepe to provide airfield cover for the Kommando Nowotny. Formed from Epr.Kdo 262 and led by Major Walter Nowotny (ex-Kdr. I/JG 54), this Kommando was the first Me 262 jet fighter interception unit. Its establishment was nominally forty Me 262A-1a fighters, but the strength never exceeded 30 and, during the subsequent operations from Achmer and Hesepe, this strength fell rapidly to no more than three, these losses being compounded by the death of Nowotny on 8 November 1944. The Kommando was subsequently disbanded and provided the nucleus of the similarly equipped III/JG 7 in December.

Fighter operations against the 8th USAAF continued to take a high toll of inexperienced pilots. Seventy pilots were killed and 28 wounded during the Leuna raid on 2 November. The Sturmgruppen, IV/JG 3 and II/JG 300 claimed 30 B-17s, but most of the 500 sorties put up were intercepted by P-51s, with JG 27 alone losing 25 pilots killed in return for seven Mustangs destroyed. Other maximum-effort interceptions on 21 and 26 November resulted in similar losses, but, thereafter, the diversion of fighters to support von Runstedt's Ardennes offensive prevented further mass interception operations.

Towards the end of October 1944, the

operational commands of the Luftwaffe first received warning of a large-scale project in which they were scheduled to play a prominent part. Under a tight cloak of security combat units were concentrated in the Vechta-Twente-Wesel sector during the closing weeks of November for tactical operations in support of the last Wehrmacht offensive in the West. The aim of the offensive was to destroy the Allied forces North of the line Antwerp-Brussels-Luxemburg. The 6th SS Panzer and V Panzer Armies, supported by the VII and XV Armies, were to break through the weak US lines in the Ardennes to the River Meuse

under cover of bad weather, and then exploit their position by thrusting north-west to Antwerp and the Scheldt Estuary to cut off all the British forces and the northern flank of the 1st US Army from their sources of supply and destroy them. It was believed that for all practical purposes the British would drop out of the war as military opponents if this ambitious plan succeeded.

The plan was primarily that of Hitler and his subordinate commanders, von Rundstedt and Manteuffel, considered it impossible of fulfilment, accordingly setting themselves the more limited task of reaching the Meuse and

*Above top: The Messerschmitt Me 262A-1 Schwalbe, the first turbojet-driven fighter to attain operational status; below: the first prototype of the remarkable Dornier Do 335*

wiping out the Aachen salient. The offensive in the Ardennes broke at dawn on 16 December 1944, in weather conditions that kept the opposing air forces grounded. To provide the necessary air support, some 1,200 single-engined fighters had been transferred to Luftwaffenkommando West from units engaged in the defence of the Reich, while about

100 Fw 190 ground attack aircraft were moved in to the area from Luftflotte 6, in the Soviet Union. The total strength of Lw.Kdo West, on 20 December, amounted to 2,360 aircraft, leaving 400 Fw 190s and Bf 109s, and 1,100 night-fighters for the defence of Germany. These units were: Reconnaissance: NAGr 1, NAGr 13, and Einsatz.Kdo Braunegg (Me 262A-1); Fighters: JG 1, JG 2, JG 3, JG 4, JG 6, JG 11, JG 26, JG 27, JG 53, III and IV/JG 54, and JG 77; Ground-attack: Stab, I, II and III/SG 4, and NSGr 1, 2 and 20; Bombers: Stab, I and II/LG 1, I/KG 66, Stab, I, II and III/KG 53 (operating under 'Rumpelkammer' and carrying V-1 flying bombs), Stab, I and 6./KG 51 with 42 Me 262A-2 bombers and 7./KG 76 with 10 Arado Ar 234B-1 bombers. The fighter force kept for defensive purposes were JG 300, JG 301 and I/JG 400, with the Nachtjagdgeschwader 1, 2, 3, 4, 5, 6, NJGr 10, I and II/NJG 11 and II/NJG 100. One Kampfgruppe, II/KG 100 with 44 He 177A-5s, was on the strength of Luftflotte Reich in addition to the above.

The force of 1,770 Bf 109s and Fw 190s now under Lw.Kdo West and 400 reserved for strategic defence contrasted sharply with the strength of 300 and 1,300 respectively on 1 October 1944, but, at the same time, indicated the expansion that had taken place in the Luftwaffe's fighter arm.

Prior to the Ardennes offensive Jagdkorps II was taken over by Gen.Maj. Dietrich Pelz, posted from the now moribund bomber forces of Fliegerkorps IX. The thick fog, which had aided the initial phases of the German offensive, lifted only slightly during the next week, in consequence of which both Allied and German air operations were very badly hampered. During 17 December, the Schlachtgruppen flew 600 sorties, whilst during the following night 250–300 sorties were flown against Allied lines of communication. On the ground, the Panzer spearheads by-passed Bastogne and, by 24 December, were in sight of the Meuse at Dinant. But now the PzKw V Panthers and PzKw VI Royal Tigers of II Panzer Division were at the limit of the German advance, awaiting fuel. The fuel was never to arrive. Then the weather improved, enabling the Allied air forces to operate over the battlefront and, during the four days that preceded another deterioration in the weather, the RAF 2nd Tactical Air Force and the 9th USAAF were able to wrest the initiative away from the Luftwaffe.

Some 600 sorties per day were flown by the Luftwaffe during this critical period, and night-fighters (equipped with bomb racks), night ground attack aircraft and bombers contributed another 200–250 per night. The Me 262 bombers of KG 51 operated in insufficient numbers to achieve any real effect and their contribution consisted of tip-and-run raids on Liege and forward Allied airfields. The 'Mistel' Ju 88/Bf 109 composites also proved to be a dismal failure. The bad weather which set in again on 28 December gave both the Luftwaffe and the Wehrmacht a badly needed respite, but the damage was done. Bastogne was relieved on 26 December, Rochefort was re-captured on 31 December and the US forces went over to the offensive.

Before day-break on 1 January 1945, some 900 aircraft, mostly Fw 190s and Bf 109s, were being readied by their groundcrews on more than a score of airfields in Western Germany in preparation for the Luftwaffe's final, desperate gamble – Unternehmen Bodenplatte (Operation Baseplate). This was to be a low-level, surprise attack on the Allied airfields in Belgium and Holland; the targets chosen were Eindhoven, St Denis-Westrem, Volkel, Evere, Grimberghen, Melsbroek, Antwerp-Duerne, St Trond, Le Culot, Asch and Metz-Frascaty. The fighter units involved were JG 1, JG 3, JG 6, JG 26 with III/JG 54, JG 27

with IV/JG 54 and JG 77 from Jagddivision 3; JG 2, JG 4, JG 11 and JG 53 from Jagdabschnitt Mittelrhein, supported by JG 104, SG 4, NSGr 20 and I/KG 51. The fighters were led by Ju 88 night fighters from 5, 7, and 9./NJG 1, 4, 9, and 10./NJG 3, and 11./NJG 101 which were to provide navigational assistance to the frontline, and then depart. The time over target was to be 09.20 hours.

The attack achieved almost complete surprise, but whereas results were good at Eindhoven, Evere and Melsbroek, some airfields, such as Volkel which housed the crack No 122

Wing of the 2nd TAF, escaped damage entirely while the attacks on other airfields were not pressed home to advantage. A high proportion of the German fighter losses were inflicted by their own flak. The total casualties of all German units taking part in Bodenplatte amounted to 170 killed or missing in action, 67 taken prisoner, and 18 wounded, as against 144 RAF and 134 USAAF aircraft destroyed and 84 and 62 damaged respectively.

Whatever the motivations behind the Bodenplatte attack, the Luftwaffe was given no respite in the weeks that followed, and in early

January 1945, the renewal of Russian pressure in Prussia, Poland and Hungary brought about the transfer of combat units from Lw.Kdo West. By 15 January, 300 aircraft had been sent to the Eastern Front to bolster the 1,875 aircraft already there and, by 22 January, another 500 were about to be transferred or already on their way. These units were JG 1, JG 3, JG 4, JG 11, JG 77 and SG 4, consisting of about 650 fighters and 100 ground-attack Fw 190s. Accordingly, the total fighter and close-support strength available for operations in the East rose to 850–900 and 700 respectively.

At this time another re-shuffle of Commands took place. On the Western Front, Jagdkorps II, the tactical fighter command engaged in the northern sector, was disbanded and its place taken by Fliegerdivisionen 14 and 15. At the same time, Jagddivision 5, operating in the southern sector, was renamed Fl.Div 16, all three being subordinated to Luftwaffen-kommando West. The strategic air defences of Germany were similarly reorganised, Jagd-korps I being disbanded and its functions taken over by Fliegerkorps IX(Jagd) com-manded by Pelz.

*Above: Late in July 1944, the III Gruppe of Kampfgeschwader 3 became operational with He 111H-22 for launching Fi 103 pilotless missiles as one of the last attempts by the Luftwaffe to attack the UK*

The fighter units remaining in the West were held at maximum strength while a strict policy of conservation was inaugurated. Measures were taken whereby only 50 per cent of the Jagdgruppen remaining was to be employed on operations, the remainder having to rest to conserve fuel. These units were forbidden to operate beyond the frontline; combat, even against heavy bombers, was to be avoided except in the most favourable circumstances. When operations were carried out, formations were to be used in maximum possible strength. Defence of the supply lines was now the first consideration.

By the beginning of February 1945, the Russians had reached the Oder and were advancing northwards into Pomerania while, in the southern sector, were debouching into Silesia, by-passing Breslau. The major Wehrmacht counteroffensive at this time took place in Hungary, when Wöhler's Army Group South made a surprise assault and established a bridgehead across the Hron river. On 6 March 1945, the 6th SS Pz., II Pz., VI and III (Hungarian) Armies launched a major offensive to relieve Budapest, but the part played by the Luftwaffe in support of the drive to the Danube was to be relatively minor. The Soviet counterattack of 16 March put the grandiose aspirations of Operation Frühlingserwachen (Spring Awakening) to rout; by 28 March the Soviet Army had reached the Austrian border in the Köszeg-Szombathely sector and, on 13 April, took Vienna. This was followed by the Soviet breakthrough on the Oder-Neisse line between 16–19 April, and the advance and encirclement of Berlin by the end of the month.

Excluding the reconnaissance units, the Luftwaffe combat units stationed on the Eastern Front on 1 April 1945 were as follows:
*Luftflotte* 1 (Prussia): Stab, I and III/JG 51 "Molders", and I/SG 3. Isolated in Courland (Latvia): Stab, I and II/JG 54 "Grünherz", III/ SG 3 and NSGr 3.
*Luftflotte* 4 (FlKps I and Fl.Div 17): Stab JG 76, II/JG 52, I/SG 2, 14.(Pz)/SG 9, Stab, I, II and III/SG 10, NSGr 5, NSGr 7, Stab and 1./NSGr 10.
*Luftflotte* 6 (FlKps II and VIII): Stab, II and III/ JG 1, Stab, II, III and IV/JG 3, Stab, I, II, III and IV/JG 4, Stab, I, II and III/JG 6, Stab, I, II and III/JG 11, Stab, I and III/JG 52, III/JG 54, Stab, I, II and III/JG 77, Eins.Kdo II and V/EJG 1 Stab, I, II and III/SG 1 (less 8.Staffel), Stab, II, III and 10.(Pz)/SG 2, Stab and II/SG 3, Stab, I, II and III/SG 4, 1, 2 and 10.(Pz)/SG 9, Stab, I, II, III and 10.(Pz)/SG 77 and 13./SG 151; II/LG 1, Stab, I and 8./KG 4, and 7./KG 53.

The extensive withdrawals to the Soviet Front had, by the middle of March 1945, reduced the strength of the Luftwaffe in the West to some 1,000–1,100 aircraft, of which 80 were Me 262A-2 fighter-bombers and Ar 234 reconnaissance-bombers. A further 1,000 aircraft were available for the strategic defence of NW Germany, divided roughly equally between day fighters and twin-engined night fighters, with some 50 Me 262A-1s operating in the interceptor capacity.

The Allied advance to the Rhine, culminating in the establishment of the Remagen bridgehead, and the piecemeal destruction of the Ruhr airfields, had led to some local redisposition of Luftwaffe forces to bases further removed from the frontline. Some 400 tactical sorties per day were flown by Me 262 and Ar 234 bombers, and Fw 190s against the 1st US Army's forces at Remagen, and these were joined by Ju 87Ds and Fw 190s of NSGr 20 during periods of bad weather and at night. On 23 March, the British 2nd Army crossed the Rhine at Wesel, followed two days later by the 3rd US Army's crossing at Mainz and Oppenheim. No attempt was made to reinforce the West at the expense of the 2,200 combat aircraft now engaged on the Eastern Front, and, in consequence, Luftwaffe opposition to the Rhine crossings amounted to only 200 fighter sorties flown against the British at Wesel, and 350–400 against the 3rd US Army in the Oppenheim area. Luftwaffe reaction against the latter collapsed after 25 March with the capture of the jet bomber airfields in the Darmstadt and Frankfurt areas.

The fuel situation was as critical as ever and

the major Allied air assault on German airfields, that started on 21 March, reduced the Luftwaffe's capacity for operations still further. The major Luftwaffe effort was now committed to the East but, although it was no longer possible to differentiate between airfields holding units engaged on the Soviet Front and those employed as bases against the Western Allies, the Luftwaffe made no effort to use the seasoned ground-attack units facing the Russians in attacks on British and American armour which roamed Germany more or less at will.

The Luftwaffe units based in the West on 12 April 1945 were as follows:
*Fliegerkorps IX(J):* Stab, II and III/JG 4, Stab, I and III/JG 7 with 71 Me 262A-1s, I/KG(J) 54 with 25 Me 262A-2s, JGr 10, Stab, I and II/ JG 301, I/JG 400, Stab, 1, 4, 7 and 10./NJG 1, Stab, I and III/NJG 2, Stab, I, 7 and 10./NJG 3, Stab, I, 4 and 7./NJG 4, Stab, I, 4, 7 and 10./ NJG 5, 4, 7 and 10./NJG 11, 1./NJG 100 and Kommando Bonow with Ar 234B-1s. The forces under Fliegerdivision 14 consisted of: 2./NAGr 6, 1.(F)/33, 1.(F)/123, Stab, I, II and IV/JG 26, Stab, 6. and III/KG 76 with Ar 234B-1s, NSGr 20 and III/KG 200. The forces under Fliegerdivision 15 were: NAGr 1, Stab, I, II and III/JG 2 and Stab, I, II and III/JG 27.

The third week in April showed a continuing general reduction in strength, though the scale of operations rose to a token 200 sorties per day against the Allied bridgeheads over the Elbe and the US advance on Nuremburg. Effective opposition had by now ceased in the West, while the Luftwaffe effort against the Russian assault against Berlin, which had risen to a peak of 1,100 sorties per day during mid-April, waned as each successive airfield was overrun. Berlin fell on 2 May, and on 8 May 1945, Germany surrendered to the Allies.

*Right: The extraordinary little Heinkel He 162A, the so-called "People's Fighter", was declared operational during the last weeks of the war in Europe, that illustrated belonging to Jagdgeschwader 1*

*Below: The most startling interceptor fighter of WW II was the Messerschmitt Me 163B Komet, this rocket-propelled warplane appearing in action in the summer of 1944*

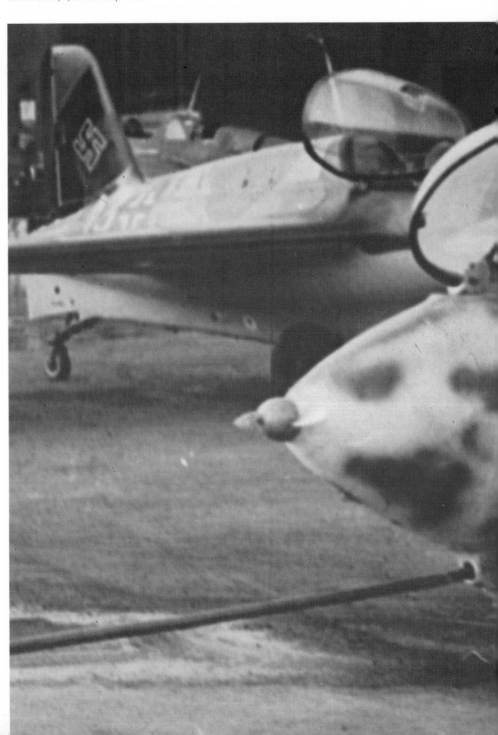

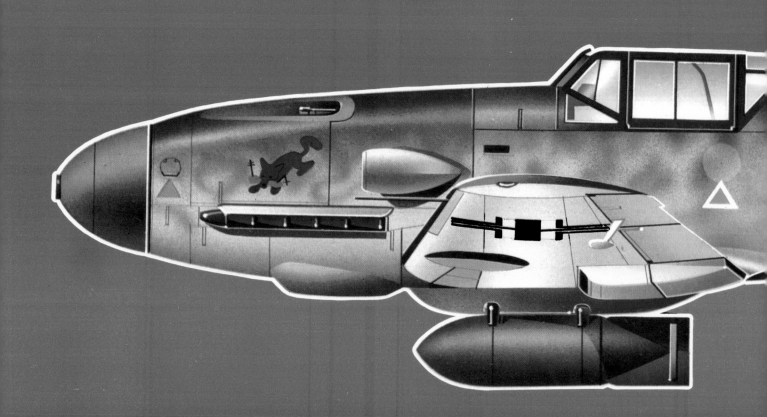

# Aircraft of Hitler's
# Luftwaffe

### A directory of German military aircraft 1930-1945

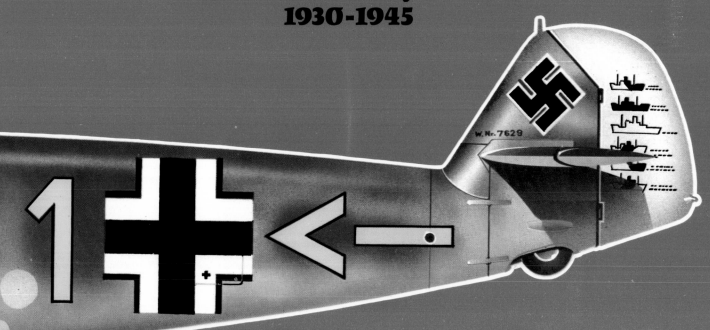

# Contents

| | |
|---|---|
| Arado Ar 65 | 121 |
| Arado Ar 66 | 121 |
| Arado Ar 68 | 122 |
| Arado Ar 67 | 123 |
| Arado Ar 76 | 123 |
| Arado Ar 80 | 123 |
| Arado Ar 81 | 123 |
| Arado Ar 95 | 124 |
| Arado Ar 96 and Ar 396 | 124 |
| Arado Ar 195 | 125 |
| Arado Ar 196 | 126 |
| Arado Ar 197 | 127 |
| Arado Ar 198 | 127 |
| Arado Ar 199 | 127 |
| Arado Ar 234 Blitz | 128 |
| Arado Ar 231 | 130 |
| Arado Ar 232 | 130 |
| Arado Ar 240 and Ar 440 | 131 |
| Bachem Ba 349 Natter | 132 |
| Blohm und Voss Ha 137 | 133 |
| Blohm und Voss Ha 139 | 133 |
| Blohm und Voss Ha 140 | 133 |
| Blohm und Voss Bv 138 | 134 |
| Blohm und Voss Bv 141 | 135 |
| Blohm und Voss Bv 142 | 136 |
| Blohm und Voss Bv 144 | 136 |
| Blohm und Voss Bv 155 | 136 |
| Blohm und Voss Bv 222 Wiking | 137 |
| Blohm und Voss Bv 40 | 138 |
| Blohm und Voss Bv 238 | 139 |
| Bücker Bü 131 Jungmann | 139 |
| Bücker Bü 133 Jungmeister | 140 |
| Bücker Bü 181 Bestmann | 140 |
| DFS 230 | 141 |
| DFS 228 | 142 |
| DFS 331 | 142 |
| Dornier Do 11 | 142 |
| Dornier Do 18 | 143 |
| Dornier Do 17 | 144 |
| Dornier Do 17Z and Do 215 | 145 |
| Dornier Do 15 | 146 |
| Dornier Do 19 | 146 |
| Dornier Do 22 | 146 |
| Dornier Do 23 | 147 |
| Dornier Do 24 | 147 |
| Dornier Do 26 | 148 |
| Dornier Do 214 | 148 |
| Dornier Do 317 | 148 |
| Dornier Do 217 | 149 |
| Dornier Do 335 Pfeil and Do 635 | 152 |
| Fieseler Fi 98 | 154 |
| Fieseler Fi 167 | 155 |
| Fieseler Fi 103 | 155 |
| Fieseler Fi 156 Storch and Fi 256 | 156 |
| Flettner Fl 282 Kolibri | 158 |
| Focke-Wulf Fw 56 Stösser | 158 |
| Focke-Wulf Fw 57 | 159 |
| Focke-Wulf Fw 159 | 159 |
| Focke Achgelis Fa 223 Drache | 159 |
| Focke-Wulf Fw 58 Weihe | 160 |
| Focke-Wulf Fw 62 | 160 |
| Focke-Wulf Fw 186 | 160 |
| Focke-Wulf Fw 187 Falke | 161 |
| Focke-Wulf Fw 189 Uhu | 161 |
| Focke-Wulf Fw 190 and Ta 152 | 164 |
| Focke-Wulf Fw 191 | 169 |
| Focke-Wulf Fw 200 Condor | 170 |
| Focke-Wulf Ta 154 Moskito | 172 |
| Gotha Go 145 | 172 |
| Gotha Go 147 | 173 |
| Gotha Go 229 | 173 |
| Gotha Go 345 | 173 |
| Gotha Go 242 and Go 244 | 174 |
| Gotha-Kalkert Ka 430 | 174 |
| Heinkel He 45 | 175 |
| Heinkel He 46 | 175 |
| Heinkel He 50 | 175 |
| Heinkel He 51 | 176 |
| Heinkel He 59 | 176 |
| Heinkel He 70, He 170 and He 270 | 178 |
| Heinkel He 60 | 178 |
| Heinkel He 72 Kadett and 172 | 179 |
| Heinkel He 74 | 180 |
| Heinkel He 111 | 180 |
| Heinkel He 100 | 181 |
| Heinkel He 112 | 185 |
| Heinkel He 114 | 185 |
| Heinkel He 115 | 186 |
| Heinkel He 116 | 186 |
| Heinkel He 118 | 187 |
| Heinkel He 119 | 187 |
| Heinkel He 176 | 187 |
| Heinkel He 177 Greif | 188 |
| Heinkel He 219 | 190 |
| Heinkel He 178 | 192 |
| Heinkel He 274 | 192 |
| Heinkel He 277 | 193 |
| Heinkel He 280 | 193 |
| Heinkel He 162 Salamander | 194 |
| Henschel Hs 121 | 196 |
| Henschel Hs 122 | 196 |
| Henschel Hs 124 | 196 |
| Henschel Hs 123 | 197 |
| Henschel Hs 125 | 198 |
| Henschel Hs 127 | 198 |
| Henschel Hs 132 | 198 |
| Henschel Hs 126 | 199 |
| Henschel Hs 129 | 200 |
| Henschel Hs 130 | 201 |
| Junkers Ju 52/3m | 202 |
| Junkers Ju 86 | 204 |
| Junkers Ju 87 | 205 |
| Junkers Ju 88 | 208 |
| Junkers W 34 | 212 |
| Junkers Ju 89 | 212 |
| Junkers EF 61 | 212 |
| Junkers Ju 188 | 213 |
| Junkers Ju 252 | 214 |
| Junkers Ju 287 | 214 |
| Junkers Ju 288 | 215 |
| Junkers Ju 290 | 216 |
| Junkers Ju 322 Mammut | 217 |
| Junkers Ju 352 Herkules | 217 |
| Junkers Ju 388 | 218 |
| Junkers Ju 390 | 218 |
| Junkers Ju 488 | 218 |
| Messerschmitt Bf 108 Taifun | 219 |
| Messerschmitt Bf 109 | 219 |
| Messerschmitt Bf 110 | 224 |
| Messerschmitt Me 209-II | 227 |
| Messerschmitt Me 163 Komet | 227 |
| Messerschmitt Me 210 and Me 410 Hornisse | 230 |
| Messerschmitt Me 262 | 231 |
| Messerschmitt Bf 161-162 | 236 |
| Messerschmitt Me 261 | 236 |
| Messerschmitt Me 263 | 236 |
| Messerschmitt Me 264 | 237 |
| Messerschmitt Me 309 | 237 |
| Messerschmitt Me 328 | 237 |
| Messerschmitt Me 321 and Me 323 Gigant | 238 |
| Messerschmitt P.1101 | 238 |
| Siebel Si 201 | 240 |
| Siebel Si Si 204 | 240 |
| Mistel Composite Aircraft | 241 |

# Arado Ar 65

**Ar 65 prototypes, 65E and F**
**Origin:** Arado Handelsgesellschaft, Warnedmünde.
**Type:** Single-seat day fighter.
**Engine:** 750hp BMW VI 7·3 vee-12 water-cooled.
**Dimensions:** Span 36ft 9in (11·20m); length 27ft 6⅝in (8·40m); height 11ft 2⅝in (3·42m).
**Weights:** Empty 3,329lb (1510kg); maximum 4,255lb (1930kg).
**Performance:** Maximum speed 186mph (300km/h); initial climb 2,086ft (635m)/min; service ceiling 24,935ft (7600m).
**Armament:** Two fixed synchronized 7·92mm MG 17.
**History:** First flight (65a) 1931; service delivery (65E) late 1933.

**Development:** It is appropriate that the first aircraft in the technical section of this book should also be the type best fitted to be described as "the first warplane of the Luftwaffe". Designed in contravention of the Versailles Treaty by the Arado Handelsgesellschaft, under chief engineer Walter Rethel, the Ar 65 was a pedestrian but thoroughly workmanlike machine which rested on experience gained with a succession of earlier biplanes (which could hardly have been anything but unarmed "fighters") of the 1920s. The Ar 65 had the typical mixed construction of the early 1930s, with steel-tube/sheet/fabric fuselage and wood/ply/fabric wings. After flying four prototypes, the growing Arado company built the Ar 65E in series for the first para-military air unit in Germany since World War I: the Reklame-

*An Ar 65F in pre-war civil markings, as used at Fliegerschulen*

Staffel (Publicity Squadron). This formed at Berlin-Staaken in 1933, moved to Döberitz in 1934 and on 14 March 1935 openly emerged as the first staffel of the first wing (Jagdgeschwader) of the reborn Luftwaffe, JG 132 (later renumbered JG 2). Most production aircraft were of the more fully equipped Ar 65F type, serving as fighters and then advanced trainers alongside the He 51 until 1940.

# Arado Ar 66

**Ar 66a, b and c, Ar 66B and C**
**Origin:** Arado Handelsgesellschaft, Warnemünde.
**Type:** Primary trainer; later night ground attack.
**Engine:** 240hp Argus As 10C inverted-vee-8 aircooled.
**Dimensions:** Span 32ft 9¾in (10·0m); length 27ft 2¾in (8·30m); height 9ft 7½in (2·93m).
**Weights:** (typical C) Empty 1,997lb (905kg); loaded 2,934lb (1330kg).
**Performance:** Maximum speed 130mph (210km/h); typical range 445 miles (716km).
**History:** First flight 1932; service delivery (66C) late 1933.

**Development:** Helping to sustain the company's flow of unsuccessful Luftwaffe combat types, the Ar 66 was a staple product for ten years, and the total number built was not far short of 10,000. It was the chief design for Arado by Ing Walter Rethel, and was a typical mixed wood/metal biplane with fabric covering, an unusual feature being that there was no fixed fin, except in the Ar 66b second prototype which was a seaplane and needed a ventral fin. The first ten production aircraft, designated 66B, did not see service, but the 66C was built in extremely large numbers, possibly exceeding the total of any other single Luftwaffe sub-type of identical aircraft. As well as the pilot schools the Ar 66C equipped about half the night ground attack (NSGr) groups on the Eastern front, involving about 2,000 aircraft. The Ar 66C equipped units in NSGr 2, 3 and 5 in the Soviet Union, 8 in Finland and 12 in Latvia. The NSGr machines operated on dark nights at treetop height dropping booby traps, 4½ and 9lb (2 and 4kg) anti-personnel bombs and other harassment weapons. Many had their wheels replaced by skis.

*Below: A pupil about to go solo on an Ar 66C in Luftwaffe markings. The forward-mounted tailplane is braced, and the horn-balanced elevator is up, giving an odd appearance*

# Arado Ar 68

**Ar 68G**
**Origin:** Arado Handelsgesellschaft, Warnemünde.
**Type:** Single-seat fighter.
**Engine:** 750hp BMW VI 12-cylinder vee liquid-cooled.
**Dimensions:** Span 36ft 0in (11m); length 31ft 2in (9·5m); height 10ft 10in (3·3m).
**Weights:** Empty 3,307lb (1500kg); loaded 4,410lb (2000kg).
**Performance:** Maximum speed 192mph (310km/h) at 13,125ft (4000m); service ceiling 24,280ft (7400m); range with service load 342 miles (550km).
**Armament:** Two 7·92mm MG 17 machine guns above engine: racks for six 110lb (50kg) bombs.
**History:** First flight November 1933; (Ar 68G) December 1935; termination of production, probably 1937.

**Development:** Forbidden to have a warlike air force by the Versailles Treaty, Germany produced no combat aircraft in the 1920s and early 1930s, though German design teams did produce important prototypes in Spain, Sweden and Switzerland. By the time the Nazi party seized power in 1933 there was a useful nucleus of talent and industrial strength and the Arado firm was, with Heinkel, charged with urgently building a first-line fighter for the new Luftwaffe. The result was the Ar 68V1 prototype, powered by the trusty BMW VI engine, rated at 660hp and constructed of welded steel tube and wood, with fabric covering except over the forward and upper fuselage. Like all Arado aircraft of the period it had a tailplane well behind the fin and rudder, and the single-strut cantilever landing gear was distinctive. Two prototypes flew in 1934 with the 610hp Jumo 210 engine and this was selected for the production Ar 68E which entered service with the newly formed Luftwaffe in 1935. But the Ar 68F reverted to the BMW engine, uprated to 675hp, and the main production centred on the still more powerful Ar 68G. Despite good engines the Ar 68 was never an outstanding

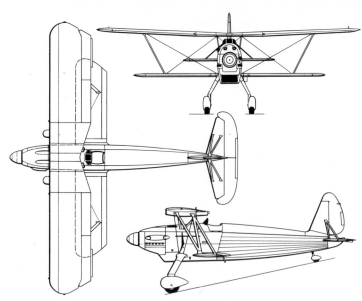

*Above: Three-view of the Ar 68E with Jumo 210Da engine*

machine. It ran second in timing and performance to its great rival the He 51 and, apart from a few used as night fighters, had been relegated to training before World War II. One example of the Ar 68H, with BMW 132Dc radial and enclosed cockpit, was flown and a development, the Ar 197, would have been used aboard the carrier *Graf Zeppelin* had the vessel been commissioned.

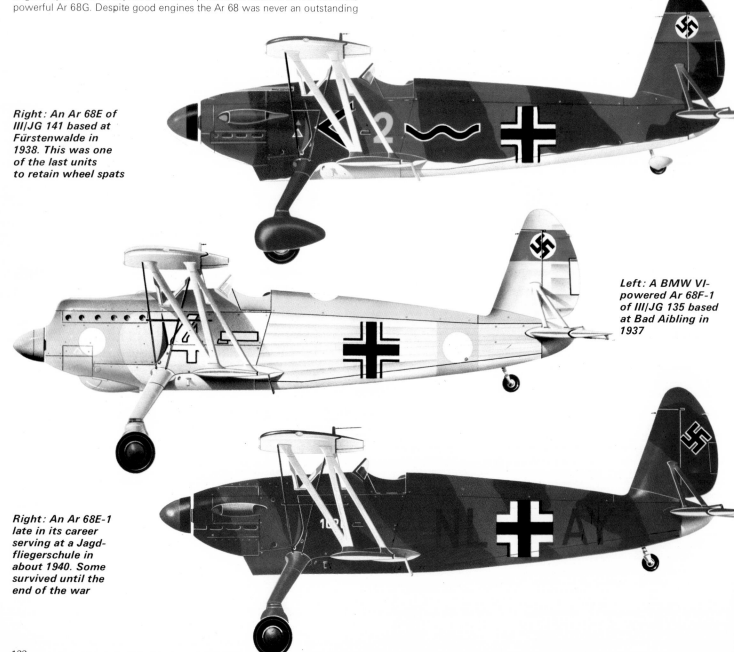

*Right: An Ar 68E of III/JG 141 based at Fürstenwalde in 1938. This was one of the last units to retain wheel spats*

*Left: A BMW VI-powered Ar 68F-1 of III/JG 135 based at Bad Aibling in 1937*

*Right: An Ar 68E-1 late in its career serving at a Jagd-fliegerschule in about 1940. Some survived until the end of the war*

# Arado Ar 67

### Ar 67a

**Origin:** Arado Handelsgesellschaft, Warnemünde.
**Type:** Single-seat fighter prototype.
**Engine:** 525hp Rolls-Royce Kestrel VI, vee-12 water-cooled.
**Dimensions:** Span 31ft 9in (9·68m); length 25ft 11in (7·87m); height 10ft 2in (3·10m).
**Weights:** Empty (no guns) 2,799lb (1270kg); loaded 3,660lb (1660kg).
**Performance:** Maximum speed 211mph (340km/h); service ceiling 30,510ft (9300m).
**Armament:** Two synchronized 7·92mm MG 17 (proposed).
**History:** First flight, late autumn (fall) 1933.

**Development:** Significantly smaller than the Ar 65, the Ar 67a prototype had a much better performance. It confirmed Walter Blume as an excellent designer of combat aircraft, but offered little advance over other types at low altitudes and had an imported engine (the fully supercharged Kestrel was superior at altitude). Only the prototype was built, production orders going to the later Ar 68.

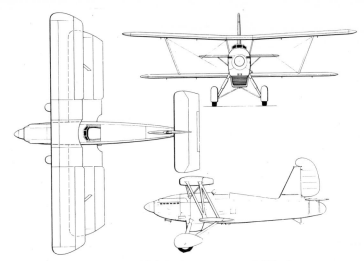
*The Ar 67a prototype, which had no armament fitted*

# Arado Ar 76

### Ar 76 prototypes and 76A

**Origin:** Arado Handelsgesellschaft, Warnemünde.
**Type:** Light fighter and advanced trainer.
**Engine:** 240hp Argus As 10C inverted-vee-8 aircooled.
**Dimensions:** Span 31ft 2in (9·50m); length 23ft 7½in (7·20m); height 8ft 4¼in (2·54m).
**Weights:** Empty 1,653lb (750kg); loaded 2,359lb (1070kg).
**Performance:** Maximum speed 166mph (267km/h); range 292 miles (470km); service ceiling 21,000ft (6400m).

**Development:** One of the first specifications issued by the clandestine Luftwaffe C-Amt (technical procurement section) called for a light home-defence fighter capable of serving as an advanced trainer. The result might have been expected to be a poor fighter and expensive trainer, but four companies were asked to submit designs. The fighter was to have two 7·92mm MG 17 machine guns, and carry light bombs, while the trainer was to carry a single MG 17. The eventual winner was the Fw 56 Stösser, but the various Ar 76 prototypes (first flight, late 1934) were so close that a small batch of Ar 76A was ordered for the new Jagdfliegerschulen (fighter pilot schools) and put into service in 1936.

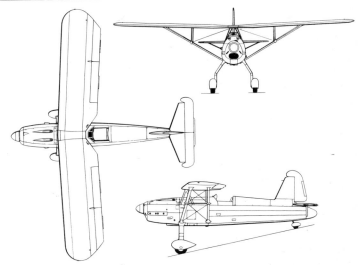
*The Ar 76A-0, of which a small series saw active service*

# Arado Ar 80

### Ar 80 V1, 2 and 3

**Origin:** Arado Handelsgesellschaft, Warnemünde.
**Type:** Single-seat fighter.
**Engine:** (V1) same engine as Ar 67a, (V2) 695hp R-R Kestrel V, (V3) 640hp Junkers Jumo 210C inverted-vee-12 water-cooled.
**Dimensions:** Span 35ft 8½in (10·88m); length 33ft 9½in (10·30m); height 8ft 8¼in (2·65m).
**Weights:** Empty (no guns) 3,620lb (1642 kg); loaded 4,684lb (2125kg).
**Performance:** Maximum speed 217mph (349km/h); range 497 miles (800km); service ceiling 32,800ft (10,000m).

**Development:** In response to the important C-Amt specification for an all-metal monoplane fighter, issued in early 1934, Blume's team created an extremely graceful aircraft with inverted-gull wing and fuselage almost as long as the span. The company had no prior experience of stressed-skin construction, nor of retractable landing gear (so they used spats). Proposed armament was two synchronized 7·92mm MG 17. Unfortunately for Arado the structure weight and drag were both higher than prediction and only three were built in 1935–36. In 1938 the V3 was given a second (tandem) seat to serve as a testbed for advanced high-lift flaps.

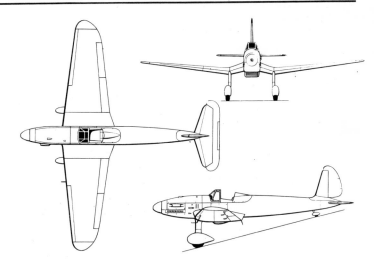
*The Ar 80 V2 (second prototype), re-engined with Jumo 210C*

# Arado Ar 81

### Ar 81 V1, 2 and 3

**Origin:** Arado Handelsgesellschaft, Warnemünde.
**Type:** Dive bomber.
**Engine:** 640hp Junkers Jumo 210Ca inverted-vee-12 water-cooled.
**Dimensions:** Span 36ft 0¾in (11·00m); length 37ft 8¾in (11·50m); height 11ft 10in (3·61m).
**Weights:** Empty 4,244lb (1925kg); loaded 6,768lb (3070kg).
**Performance:** Maximum speed 214mph (344km/h); range 430 miles (692km).
**Armament:** Proposed, one 7·92mm manually aimed MG 15 in rear cockpit, one 7·92mm synchronized MG 17, one 551lb (250kg) bomb.

**Development:** It was on a visit to the United States that Ernst Udet, the World War I ace who headed the C-Amt, first witnessed dive bombing by Curtiss Helldivers. He was fired with enthusiasm and in 1933 started the important Sturzkampfflugzeug programme that was to lead to the immortal Stuka. Arado surprisingly built the Ar 81 as a very long biplane, which despite having twin fins showed instability in flight. With the V3 the Arado team made the rear fuselage deeper and fitted a large single fin. From its first flight in the spring of 1936 it was clear the V3 was better than the Ju 87 in almost all respects, but the monoplane was chosen — mainly because it was a monoplane.

*The Ar 81 V3, with single fin and less-slender rear fuselage*

# Arado Ar 95

**Ar 95 prototypes and A-1**
**Origin:** Arado Handelsgesellschaft, Warnemünde.
**Type:** Torpedo/reconnaissance seaplane (later landplane).
**Engine:** (Most) 880hp BMW 132Dc nine-cylinder radial.
**Dimensions:** Span 41ft (12·50m); length 36ft 5in (11·10m); height (seaplane) 17ft 0¾in (5·20m).
**Weights:** Empty (seaplane) 5,588lb (2535kg); loaded 7,843lb (3558kg).
**Performance:** (Seaplane) maximum speed 187mph (300km/h); range 680 miles (1094km).
**Armament:** (Ar 95A-1) one 7·92mm manually aimed MG 15 in rear cockpit, one synchronized 7·92mm MG 17, one 1,540lb (700kg) torpedo or various loads of bombs/mines/depth charges.

**Development:** This aircraft was designed for use aboard the aircraft carrier *Graf Zeppelin*, using either twin floats or fixed trousered landing gear. Five prototypes had disappointing performance, and in 1937 a new specification was issued (it led to the Fieseler Fi 167). Arado built six Ar 95A-0 seaplanes for the Legion Kondor in Majorca (three were later transferred to Nationalist Spain), and six (three land, three sea) for Chile. In 1939 about a

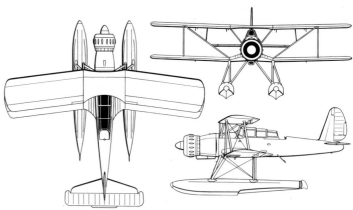

*Above: Three-view of the Ar 95A-1 twin-float seaplane*

dozen Ar 95A-1 seaplanes were delivered to the Luftwaffe, equipping 3/SAGr 125 in the Baltic and south Finland after the invasion of the Soviet Union.

# Arado Ar 96 and Ar 396

**Ar 96A-1, Ar 96B-2 and Ar 396**
**Origin:** Arado Flugzeugwerke; production almost entirely assigned to Ago Flugzeugwerke and to Avia and Letov in Czechoslovakia.
**Type:** Advanced trainer and multi-role tactical.
**Engine:** (96A) 240hp Argus As 10C inverted vee-8 aircooled; (B) 465hp As 410A-1 inverted vee-12 aircooled.
**Dimensions:** Span 36ft 1in (11·00m); length (A) 27ft 1in (8·26m), (B) 29ft 11¼in (9.13m); height 8ft 6¼in (2·60m).
**Weights:** Empty (A) 2,617lb (1187kg) (B) 2,854lb (1295kg); maximum (A) 3,476lb (1577kg), (B) 3,747lb (1695kg).
**Performance:** Maximum speed (A, B) 205mph (330km/h); range (A) 560 miles (900km), (B) 615 miles (990km).
**Armament:** (A) none; (B) invariably one 7·92mm MG 17 above engine on right, sometimes 7·92mm MG 15 in rear cockpit and/or other guns in wing bulges and/or light bombs.
**History:** First flight 1938, (B) January 1940, final delivery (C.2B) 1948.

**Development:** Designed by Walter Blume, the Ar 96 was a typical Arado product, with distinctive tail and clean stressed-skin structure. It proved an ideal advanced trainer, and the Ar 96A entered Luftwaffe service in 1939. In 1940 much larger orders were placed for the 96B with more fuel and a larger engine, and this remained by far the most important advanced

trainer of the Axis. The two-blade Argus propeller had a distinctive pitch-control windmill on the spinner, and there were five chief B sub-types of which a few could be used for gunnery and bombing training. The 96B towed light gliders, and even served in tactical roles on the Eastern front with various augmented armament. Total production by December 1944 was 11,546, and Letov built the C.2B version until 1948. The planned Ar 296 was developed into the 396, an all-wood replacement with 580hp As 411. Crude but effective, this was assigned to the French SIPA works, which after the liberation made large numbers as the S.11, followed by the metal S.12.

*Below: Developed in France and planned for mass-production there and in Czechoslovakia, no Ar 396 reached the Luftwaffe before the capitulation*

*Right: A pair of Ar 96B (probably B-2) trainers serving with a pilot training school (A/B Schule) in about 1942*

*Right, below: An unusual sub-type, possibly an Ar 96B-6, with spatted tailwheel and equipment for blind-flying training (fitted to several versions). These aircraft served at all 13 fighter training wings (JSG)*

# Arado Ar 195

**Ar 195 V1, 2 and 3**
**Origin:** Arado Handelsgesellschaft, Warnemünde.
**Type:** Carrier-based torpedo/reconnaissance landplane.
**Engine:** 880hp BMW 132M nine-cylinder radial.
**Dimensions:** Span 41ft (12·50m); length 34ft 5¼in (10·50m); height 11ft 9¾in (3·60m).
**Weights:** Empty 4,275lb (1939kg); loaded 8,091lb (3670kg).
**Performance:** Maximum speed 180mph (290km/hr); range 404 miles (650km).
**Armament:** One 7·92mm manually aimed MG 15 in rear cockpit, one synchronized 7·92mm MG 17 and 1,540lb (700kg) torpedo or various bomb loads.

**Development:** First flown in the summer of 1938, the Ar 195 competed against the Fi 167 to equip the *Graf Zeppelin*. It was a light and efficient load-carrier, but excessive drag ruined its performance and put the Fieseler way out in front. It had stressed-skin wings, and in some ways (for example, pilot view) equalled the British Albacore. But the drag problem was insuperable and only three were built.

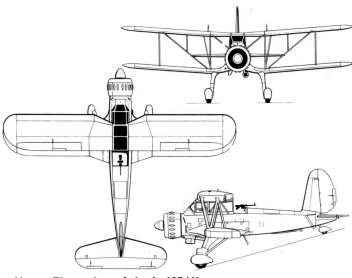

*Above: Three-view of the Ar 195 V1*

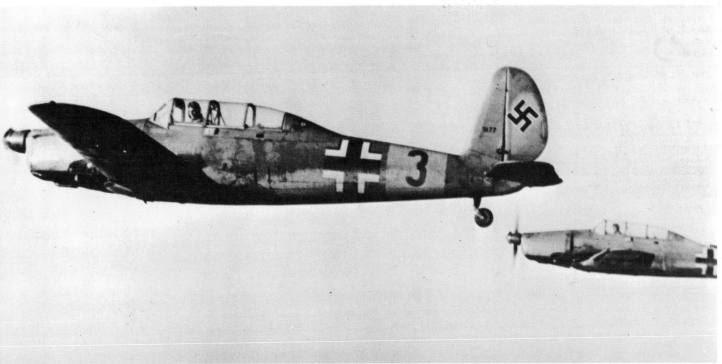

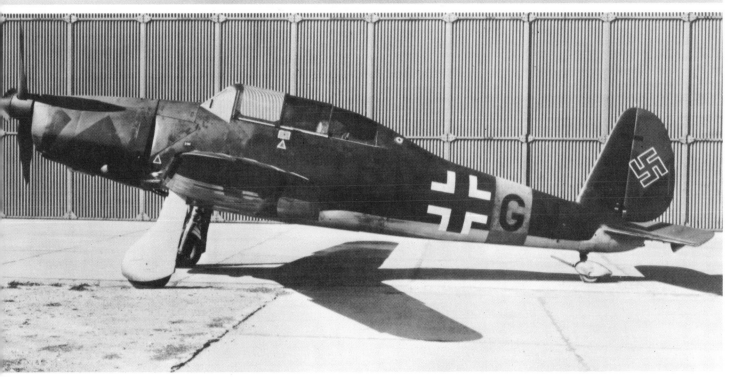

125

# Arado Ar 196

**Ar 196A-1 to A-5 (data for A-3)**
**Origin:** Arado Flugzeugwerke GmbH.
**Type:** Two-seat maritime reconnaissance aircraft.
**Engine:** 960hp BMW 132K nine-cylinder radial.
**Dimensions:-** Span 40ft 8in (12·4m); length 36ft 1in (11m); height 14ft 4½in (4·4m).
**Weights:** Empty 6,580lb (2990kg); loaded 8,223lb (3730kg).
**Performance:** Maximum speed 193mph (310km/h) at 13,120ft (4000m); initial climb 980ft (300m)/min; service ceiling 23,000ft (7020m); range 670 miles (1070km) at 158mph (253km/h).

**Armament:** Two MG FF 20mm cannon in wings outboard of propeller disc, one MG 17 7·92mm in top decking and twin MG 15 on pivoted mounting aimed by observer. Rack under each wing for 110lb (50kg) bomb.
**History:** First flight (196V1) May 1938; first operational service 1 August 1939.

**Development:** One of the very few float seaplanes to be used in World War II outside the Pacific area, the Ar 196 was designed as a replacement for the He 60 biplane on the catapults of all the German Navy's capital ships. Its duties were thus primarily reconnaissance and shadowing of surface vessels, but in comparison with such Allied types as the Curtiss Seagull and Fairey Seafox it had a much higher performance and eventually was given formidable armament. Four prototypes, powered by the 880hp BMW 132Dc engine (derived in Germany from the Pratt & Whitney Hornet), were flown in 1938, two with twin floats and the others with a large central float. The following year, 26 Ar 196A-1s were built, entering service in August aboard the battle cruisers *Gneisenau* and *Scharnhorst*, and at shore bases on the North Sea. In 1940 the Ar 196A-3 entered service, and this type made up

*An Ar 196A-5 of 2/SAGr 126 (lettered DI+FK) operating in the eastern Mediterranean in early 1944. Very few escaped back to Germany*

the bulk of the 401 aircraft built. Though quite outclassed by the best fighters, the A-3 was a versatile multi-role aircraft which actually spent most of the war operating on sea patrols from coastal bases, mainly on the Bay of Biscay and islands in the Mediterranean. Batches were built by Vichy-France at Saint Nazaire and, in a slightly modified A-5 form, by Fokker at Amsterdam in 1943–44. About 50 served with co-belligerent Balkan air forces in the Adriatic and Black Sea. The type was never developed as an effective anti-submarine search and strike machine, despite its obvious potential.

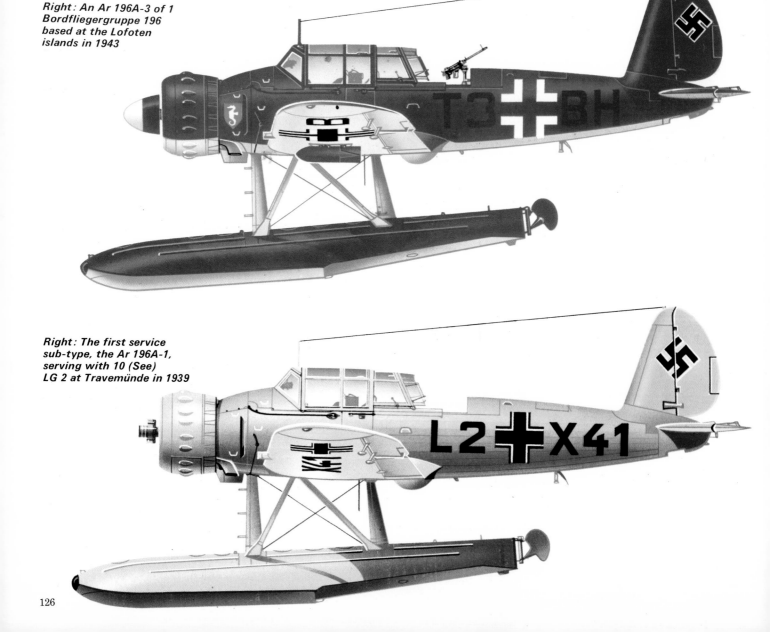

*Right: An Ar 196A-3 of 1 Bordfliegergruppe 196 based at the Lofoten islands in 1943*

*Right: The first service sub-type, the Ar 196A-1, serving with 10 (See) LG 2 at Travemünde in 1939*

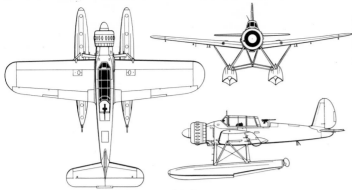

*Above: Three-view of the Ar 196A-3*

*Right: The Ar 196A-4 replaced the A-1 on the catapults of German warships.*

# Arado Ar197

**Ar 197 V1, 2 and 3**
**Origin:** Arado Handelsgesellschaft, Warnemünde.
**Type:** Carrier-based fighter.
**Engine:** (V1) 910hp DB 600 inverted-vee-12, (others) 880hp BMW 132Dc nine-cylinder radial.
**Dimensions:** Span 36ft 1in (11·00m); length (radial) 30ft 2$\frac{1}{4}$in (9·20m); height 11ft 9$\frac{3}{5}$in (3·60m).
**Weights:** Empty (radial) 4,056lb (1840kg); loaded 5,896lb (2674kg).
**Performance:** Maximum speed (radial) 248mph (399km/h); range (drop tank) 1,018 miles (1638km).
**Armament:** Two 20mm MG FF cannon in wings, two synchronized 7·92mm MG 17 in fuselage, four 110lb (50kg) bombs.

**Development:** Last biplane fighter built in Germany, the Ar 197 was another unsuccessful warplane intended for the *Graf Zeppelin* The general structure resembled the Ar 68, but the heavy armament and modest engine power spoilt performance and the continual delay in building the ship meant the aircraft would have been obsolete when it got into service, despite its enclosed cockpit and heavy armament.

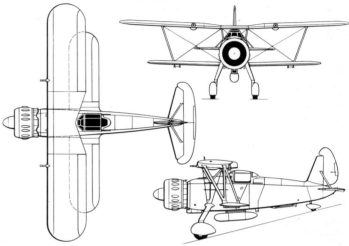

*Above: Three-view of the Ar 197 V3*

# Arado Ar198

**Ar 198 V1**
**Origin:** Arado Handelsgesellschaft, Warnemünde.
**Type:** Tactical recce and army co-operation aircraft.
**Engine:** 900hp BMW-Bramo Fafnir 323A nine-cylinder radial.
**Dimensions:** Span 48ft 10$\frac{1}{2}$in (14·90m); length 38ft 8$\frac{1}{2}$in (11·80m); height 14ft 9$\frac{1}{2}$in (4·50m).
**Weights:** Empty 5,290lb (2400kg); loaded 6,683lb (3031kg).
**Performance:** Maximum speed 223mph (359km/h); range 672 miles (1081km).
**Armament:** Proposed, two 7·92mm manually aimed MG 15 (one upper rear, one lower rear), two synchronized 7·92mm MG 17, four 110lb (50kg) bombs on wing racks.

**Development:** In February 1937 it was clear that the parasol-winged Hs 126 would probably replace the He 46 in tactical recce units, but the Technische Amt in those days looked ahead and ordered a more advanced aircraft with higher performance and all-round defensive firepower. The Fw 189 and Bv 141 were radical answers, but Arado's submission was more conventional and perhaps the least attractive (though it was dubbed *Die Fliegende Aquarium*). Despite clever high-lift flaps its performance was well below prediction, and the V2 and V3 were not even completed.

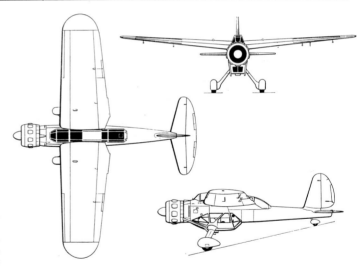

*Above: Three-view of the Ar 198 V1*

# Arado Ar199

**Ar 199 V1 and 2**
**Origin:** Arado Handelsgesellschaft, Warnemünde.
**Type:** Trainer seaplane.
**Engine:** 450hp Argus As 410C inverted-vee-12 aircooled.
**Dimensions:** Span 41ft 8in (12·70m); length 34ft 8$\frac{1}{4}$in (10·57m); height 14ft 4$\frac{1}{4}$in (4·36m).
**Weights:** Empty 3,693lb (1675kg); loaded 4,575lb (2075kg).
**Performance:** Maximum speed 161mph (260km/h); range 460 miles (740km).

**Development:** Unlike most Arado designs of the 1930s this trim seaplane was a technical success, but the Luftwaffe later decided it did not need a trainer seaplane after all. The Ar 199 had a capacious cabin with a rear seat for a trainee nav/radio operator as well as two pilots side-by-side, and the airframe was stressed for catapulting. Despite only two being built, both prototypes went into service as trainers with the Luftwaffe in 1939.

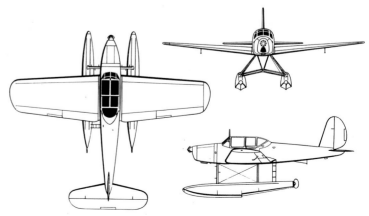

*Above: Three-view of the Ar 199 V2*

# Arado Ar 234 Blitz

**Ar 234B-1 and B-2 Blitz (Lightning)**
**Origin:** Arado Flugzeugwerke GmbH
**Type:** Single-seat reconnaissance bomber.
**Engines:** Two 1,980lb (900kg) thrust Junkers Jumo 004B axial turbojets.
**Dimensions:** Span 46ft 3½in (14·2m); length 41ft 5½in (12·65m); height 14ft 1¼in (4·3m).
**Weights:** Empty 11,464lb (5200kg), loaded 18,541lb (8410kg); maximum with rocket takeoff boost 21,715lb (9850kg).
**Performance:** Maximum speed (clean) 461mph (742km/h); service ceiling 32,800ft (10,000m); range (clean) 1,013 miles (1630km), (with 3,300lb bomb load) 684 miles (1100km).
**Armament:** Two fixed MG 151 20mm cannon in rear fuselage, firing to rear and sighted by periscope, various combinations of bombs slung under fuselage and/or engines to maximum of 3,300lb (1500kg).
**History:** First flight (Ar 234V1) 15 June 1943, (Ar 234V9 with landing gear) March 1944, (Ar 234B-0 pre-production) 8 June 1944; operational delivery September 1944.

**Development:** As the first jet reconnaissance bomber, the Ar 234 Blitz (meaning Lightning) spearheaded Germany's remarkably bold introduction of high-performance turbojet aircraft in 1944, Its design was begun under Walter Blume in 1941, after long studies in 1940 of an official specification for a jet-propelled reconnaissance aircraft with a range of 1,340 miles. The design was neat and simple, with two of the new axial engines slung under a high wing, and the single occupant in a pressurised cockpit forming the entire nose. But to achieve the required fuel capacity no wheels were fitted. When it flew on 15 June 1943 the first 234 took off from a three-wheel trolley and landed on retractable skids. After extensive trials with eight prototypes the ninth flew with conventional landing gear, leading through 20 pre-production models to the operational 234B-1, with ejection seat, autopilot and drop tanks under the engines. Main production centred on the

**continued on page 130 ▶**

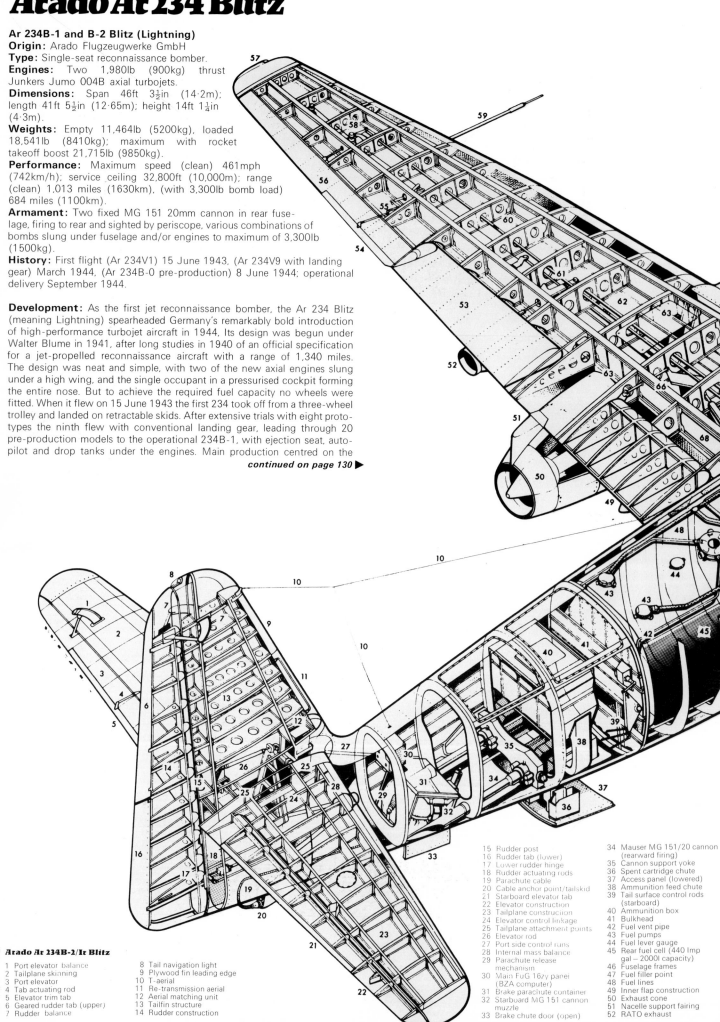

**Arado Ar 234B-2/Ir Blitz**

1  Port elevator balance
2  Tailplane skinning
3  Port elevator
4  Tab actuating rod
5  Elevator trim tab
6  Geared rudder tab (upper)
7  Rudder balance
8  Tail navigation light
9  Plywood fin leading edge
10  T-aerial
11  Re-transmission aerial
12  Aerial matching unit
13  Tailfin structure
14  Rudder construction
15  Rudder post
16  Rudder tab (lower)
17  Lower rudder hinge
18  Rudder actuating rods
19  Parachute cable
20  Cable anchor point/tailskid
21  Starboard elevator tab
22  Elevator construction
23  Tailplane construction
24  Elevator control linkage
25  Tailplane attachment points
26  Elevator rod
27  Port side control runs
28  Internal mass balance
29  Parachute release mechanism
30  Main FuG 16zy panel (BZA computer)
31  Brake parachute container
32  Starboard MG 151 cannon muzzle
33  Brake chute door (open)
34  Mauser MG 151/20 cannon (rearward firing)
35  Cannon support yoke
36  Spent cartridge chute
37  Access panel (lowered)
38  Ammunition feed chute
39  Tail surface control rods (starboard)
40  Ammunition box
41  Bulkhead
42  Fuel vent pipe
43  Fuel pumps
44  Fuel lever gauge
45  Rear fuel cell (440 Imp gal – 2000l capacity)
46  Fuselage frames
47  Fuel filler point
48  Fuel lines
49  Inner flap construction
50  Exhaust cone
51  Nacelle support fairing
52  RATO exhaust

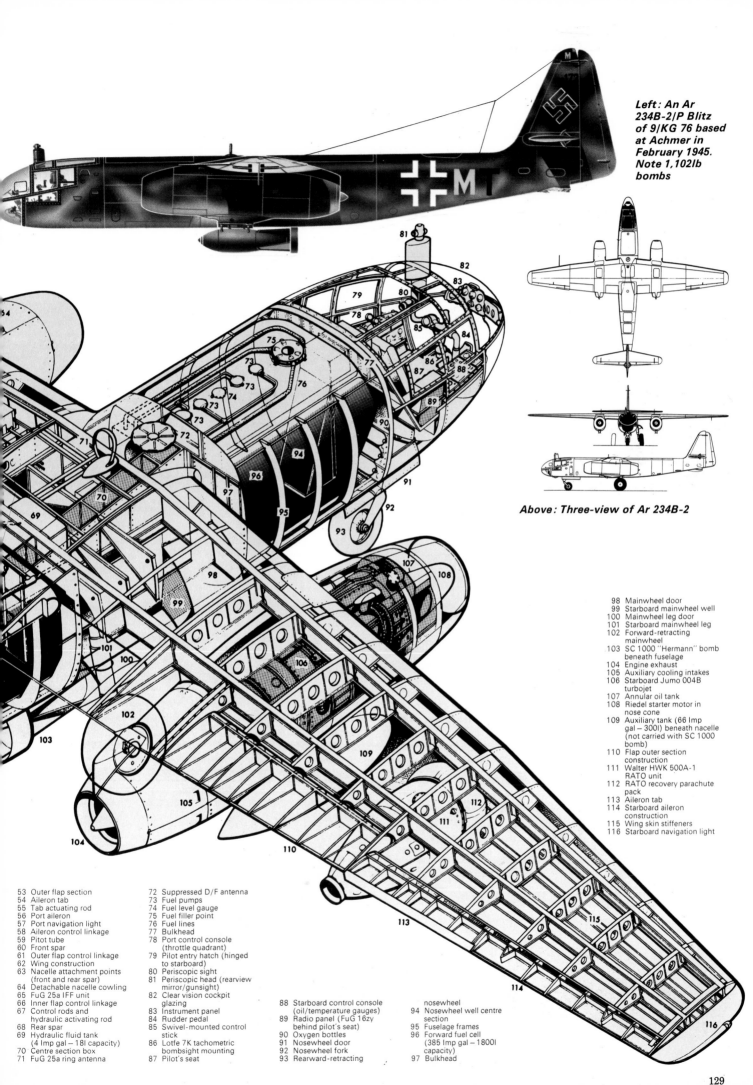

*Left: An Ar 234B-2/P Blitz of 9/KG 76 based at Achmer in February 1945. Note 1,102lb bombs*

**Above: Three-view of Ar 234B-2**

98 Mainwheel door
99 Starboard mainwheel well
100 Mainwheel leg door
101 Starboard mainwheel leg
102 Forward-retracting mainwheel
103 SC 1000 ''Hermann'' bomb beneath fuselage
104 Engine exhaust
105 Auxiliary cooling intakes
106 Starboard Jumo 004B turbojet
107 Annular oil tank
108 Riedel starter motor in nose cone
109 Auxiliary tank (66 Imp gal – 300l) beneath nacelle (not carried with SC 1000 bomb)
110 Flap outer section construction
111 Walter HWK 500A-1 RATO unit
112 RATO recovery parachute pack
113 Aileron tab
114 Starboard aileron construction
115 Wing skin stiffeners
116 Starboard navigation light

53 Outer flap section
54 Aileron tab
55 Tab actuating rod
56 Port aileron
57 Port navigation light
58 Aileron control linkage
59 Pitot tube
60 Front spar
61 Outer flap control linkage
62 Wing construction
63 Nacelle attachment points (front and rear spar)
64 Detachable nacelle cowling
65 FuG 25a IFF unit
66 Inner flap control linkage
67 Control rods and hydraulic activating rod
68 Rear spar
69 Hydraulic fluid tank (4 Imp gal – 18l capacity)
70 Centre section box
71 FuG 25a ring antenna

72 Suppressed D/F antenna
73 Fuel pumps
74 Fuel level gauge
75 Fuel filler point
76 Fuel lines
77 Bulkhead
78 Port control console (throttle quadrant)
79 Pilot entry hatch (hinged to starboard)
80 Periscopic sight
81 Periscopic head (rearview mirror/gunsight)
82 Clear vision cockpit glazing
83 Instrument panel
84 Rudder pedal
85 Swivel-mounted control stick
86 Lotfe 7K tachometric bombsight mounting
87 Pilot's seat

88 Starboard control console (oil/temperature gauges)
89 Radio panel (FuG 16zy behind pilot's seat)
90 Oxygen bottles
91 Nosewheel door
92 Nosewheel fork
93 Rearward-retracting nosewheel
94 Nosewheel well centre section
95 Fuselage frames
96 Forward fuel cell (385 Imp gal – 1800l capacity)
97 Bulkhead

### ▶Arado Ar 234 Blitz

234B-2, made in many sub-variants, most of them able to carry a heavy bomb load. Service over the British Isles with the B-1 began in September 1944, followed by a growing force of B-2s which supported the Battle of the Bulge in the winter 1944–45. In March 1945 B-2s of III/KG76 repeatedly attacked the vital Remagen bridge across the Rhine with 2,205lb (1,000kg) bombs, causing its collapse. Though handicapped by fuel shortage these uninterceptable aircraft played a significant role on all European fronts in the closing months of the war, 210 being handed over excluding the many prototypes and later versions with four engines and an uncompleted example with a crescent-shaped wing.

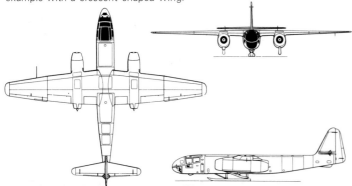

*Above: Three-view of Ar 234 V1 (first prototype)*

*Above: Take-off by the Ar 234 V9, the first of the B-series with conventional landing gear. This aircraft also featured an ejection seat, pressure cabin and drop tanks*

# Arado Ar 231

**Ar 231 V1-V6**
**Origin:** Arado Flugzeugwerke GmbH, Warnemünde.
**Type:** Folding observation aircraft for U-boats.
**Engine:** 160hp Hirth HM 501 inverted six-in-line aircooled.
**Dimensions:** Span 33ft 4½in (10·18m); length 25ft 7½in (7·81m); height 10ft 2¾in (3·12m).
**Weights:** Empty 1,837lb (833kg); loaded 2,315lb (1050kg).
**Performance:** Maximum speed 106mph (170km/h); range 311 miles (500km); endurance 4 hours.

**Development:** Though an attractive little machine (apart from the odd centre section, which had to be slanted so that one wing could fold above the other to fit into the submarine's watertight container) the Ar 231 proved tricky to handle on water or in the air, and was eventually abandoned after a year of testing in 1941–42. The Fa 330 rotor-kite was found more practical.

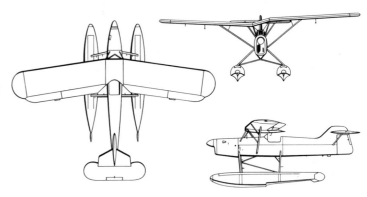

*Above: Three-view of the Ar 231 V1*

# Arado Ar 232

**Ar 232 prototypes, A-series and B-series.**
**Origin:** Arado Flugzeugwerke GmbH.
**Type:** Military transport.
**Engines:** (A) two 1,600hp BMW 801MA 14-cylinder two-row radials; (B) four 1,200hp (water/methanol injection) BMW-Bramo 323R-2 Fafnir nine-cylinder radials.
**Dimensions:** Span (A) 104ft 3½in (31·79m), (B) 109ft 10¾in (33·50m); length 77ft 2in (23·52m); height 18ft 8in (5·69m).
**Weights:** Empty (A) about 26,600lb (12,060kg), (B) typically 28,175lb (12,780kg); max loaded (both) 46,634lb (21,150kg).
**Performance:** Typical cruise (both) 180mph (288km/h); range with max payload of 9,921lb (4500kg) about 660 miles (1050km) (B series range marginally greater); min field length at gross weight, about 3,100ft (945m).
**History:** First flight (V1) about April 1941; (V3) May 1942; service delivery (prototypes) autumn 1942.

**Development:** It was typical of the Luftwaffe that, whereas in 1939 it possessed by far the best-equipped air transport force in the world, by 1945 this had never been re-equipped. Yet there had been some attempt at doing so. In 1939 Arado had competed with Henschel to find the much-needed successor to "Tante Ju", and the Ar 232 was the winner. Both contenders were outstandingly innovative, introducing such features (common in today's transports) as a high wing above an unobstructed cargo hold, tail carried high with full-section rear doors, level floor at truck height, STOL capability and multi-wheel "high flotation" landing gear. Arado's gear was odd, and resulted in the nickname Tausendfüssler (millipede). The 22 small wheels helped in ground operations and could roll across trenches. The twin-BMW 801 aircraft, flown as the Ar 232V1 and V2, was in most ways better than the B-series but had to be dropped to release engines for Fw 190s and Ju 88s. At least 22 aircraft flew, the last 20 being 232B series. Nearly all had MG 131s aimed from nose and rear, a 20mm MG 151 in an EDL 151 dorsal turret and provision for eight infantry MG 34s fired from side windows. Most gained intensive combat experience, and the V2 was the last aircraft out of Stalingrad.

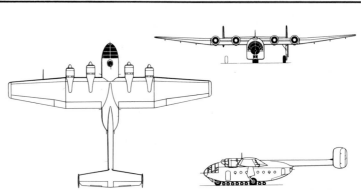

*Above: Three-view of the Ar 232B-0 (four engines)*

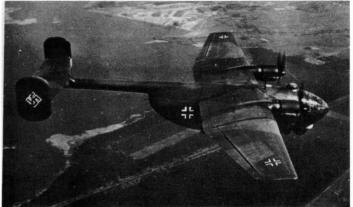

*Above: The Ar 232 V2 served at Stalingrad and later with the Ergänzungs-Transport Gruppe until late 1944. The Ar 232 had a great influence on subsequent military transports*

# Arado Ar 240 and Ar 440

**Ar 240 prototypes, A, B, C series and 440**
**Origin:** Arado Flugzeugwerke GmbH.
**Type:** Zerstörer, heavy fighter, see text.
**Engines:** Two Daimler-Benz inverted-vee-12 liquid-cooled, see text.
**Dimensions:** Span (A-0) 43ft 9in (13·33m), (C-0) 54ft 5in (16·59m); length (A-0) 42ft 0¼in (12·81m); height 12ft 11½in (3·95m).
**Weights:** Empty (A-0) 13,669lb (6200kg), (C-0) 18,650lb (8460kg); maximum (A-0) 22,700lb (10,297kg), (C-0) 25,850lb (11,726kg).
**Performance:** Maximum speed (A-0) 384mph (618km/h), (C-0) 454mph (730km/h) with GM-1 boost at high alt.; max range (A-0) 1,242 miles (2000km).
**Armament:** (A-0) two fixed 7·92mm MG 17 and two remote-control barbettes each with two 7·92mm MG 81; (C-0) four fixed 20mm MG 151 and two barbettes each with two 13mm MG 131, plus external bomb load up to 3,968lb (1800kg).
**History:** First flight (V1) 10 May 1940, (A-0) October 1942, (C-0) March 1943, (440) early summer 1942.

**Development:** In 1938 Arado's technical director, Walter Blume, began studies which were intended to lead to an outstandingly advanced and formidable multi-role combat aircraft, but instead led to years of effort with little reward. Features of the E240 study included tandem seats in a pressurized cockpit, high-lift slats and flaps on a highly loaded wing, a unique dive brake doubling as the tailcone, and upper and lower rear gun barbettes sighted by the observer through an upper/lower magnifying periscope system. But from the start the Ar 240 was dogged by technical misfortune, the enduring problem being unacceptable flying characteristics (the V1 prototype was unstable about all three axes). Later aircraft switched from the 1,075hp DB 601 to the 1,750hp DB 603A and then the 1,475hp DB 605AM or 1,900hp DB 603G with GM-1 power boost; one had BMW 801TJ radials. Small numbers of A-0 series served operationally as reconnaissance aircraft on the Eastern and Italian fronts, but the whole programme was abandoned in 1942. In parallel Arado had developed the totally redesigned 440, which was an excellent machine. Despite enthusiastic reports no production was permitted, though four development 440s flew in late 1942.

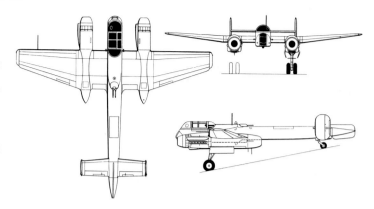

*Above: Three-view of the Ar 240A-01*

*Above: Ar 240A-02 with JG 5 in northern Finland in 1943*

*Below: One of the early prototypes, the Ar 240 V3 which first flew in the spring of 1941*

# Bachem Ba 349 Natter

**Ba 349 V1-V16, A and B series**
**Origin:** Bachem-Werke GmbH, Waldsee.
**Type:** Part-expendable target-defence interceptor.
**Engine:** 4,410lb (2000kg) thrust Walter HWK 109-509C-1 bi-propellant rocket (vertical launch boosted by four 1,102lb (500kg) or two 2,205lb (1000kg) solid motors).
**Dimensions:** Span 11ft 9¾in (3·6m); length (A) 19ft 9in (6·02m); height (flying attitude) 7ft 4½in (2·25m).
**Weights:** Empty 1,940lb (880kg); loaded (with boost rockets) 4,920lb (2232kg).
**Performance:** Maximum speed (sea level) 497mph (800km/h), (at high altitude) 621mph (1000km/h); rate of climb 36,417ft (11,100m)/min; range after climb 20—30 miles (32—48km).
**Armament:** 24 Föhn 73mm spin-stabilized rockets, or 33 R4M 55mm spin-stabilized rockets, or (proposed) two 30mm MK 108 cannon each with 30 rounds.

**Development:** One of the most radical and desperate "fighters" ever built, the Natter (Viper) was born of necessity. In the summer of 1944 the mounting weight of daylight attacks by the US 8th Air Force called for unconventional defences, and the Luftwaffe picked a proposal by Dipl-Ing Erich Bachem for a manned interceptor which could be stationed in the path of hostile heavy bombers. As the American formations passed overhead the interceptor would be blasted vertically off the ground, thereafter climbing almost vertically on an internal rocket. Nearing the bombers, the pilot would sight on one and fire his battery of missiles. He would then use his remaining kinetic energy to climb higher than the bombers and swoop back for a ramming attack. Just before impact he was to trigger a mechanism to separate his seat (or front fuselage) and the rear portion with rocket motor.

Tests showed that no simple ejection system could be incorporated, and the essence of the Natter was simplicity. The structure was wood, apart from the simple metal body with armoured cockpit. Eventually the ramming attack was abandoned, and the only parts saved were the pilot and rocket motor, for hopeful re-use. Following pilotless tests from the near-vertical ramp, and piloted gliding trials towed by an He 111 to about 18,000ft, the first manned shot was attempted on 28 February 1945. At about five seconds from lift-off the canopy came away (apparently hitting Oberleutnant Lothar Siebert) and the Natter curved over and crashed. By April 36 had flown, seven with pilots, but Allied troops overran the factory and launch site before any combat missions could take place.

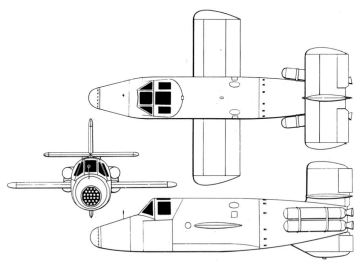

*Above: Three-view of the Ba 349B (production aircraft)*

*Above: One of the Ba 349A Natters, armed with 24 Hs 217 Föhn (Storm) rockets exposed with the streamlined nosecap removed. The interceptor is strapped to its cradle on which it was then to be transported to the launch gantry on a special trailer*

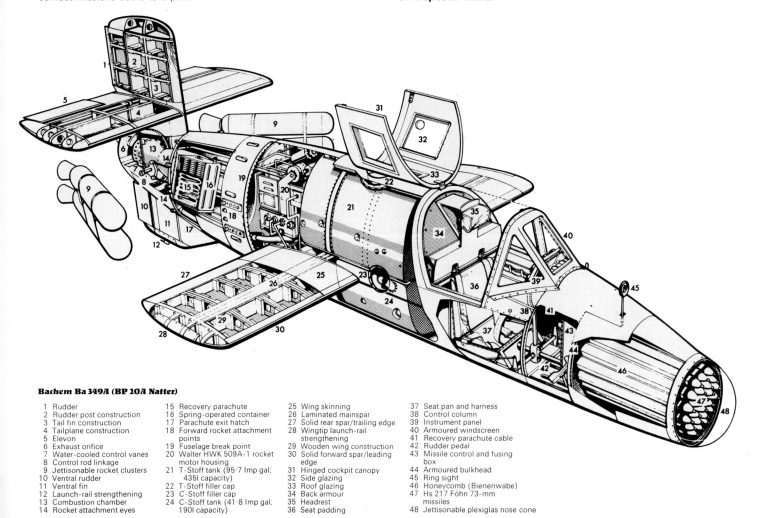

**Bachem Ba 349A (BP 20A Natter)**

1 Rudder
2 Rudder post construction
3 Tail fin construction
4 Tailplane construction
5 Elevon
6 Exhaust orifice
7 Water-cooled control vanes
8 Control rod linkage
9 Jettisonable rocket clusters
10 Ventral rudder
11 Ventral fin
12 Launch-rail strengthening
13 Combustion chamber
14 Rocket attachment eyes
15 Recovery parachute
16 Spring-operated container
17 Parachute exit hatch
18 Forward rocket attachment points
19 Fuselage break point
20 Walter HWK 509A-1 rocket motor housing
21 T-Stoff tank (95·7 Imp gal; 435l capacity)
22 T-Stoff filler cap
23 C-Stoff filler cap
24 C-Stoff tank (41·8 Imp gal; 190l capacity)
25 Wing skinning
26 Laminated mainspar
27 Solid rear spar/trailing edge
28 Wingtip launch-rail strengthening
29 Wooden wing construction
30 Solid forward spar/leading edge
31 Hinged cockpit canopy
32 Side glazing
33 Roof glazing
34 Back armour
35 Headrest
36 Seat padding
37 Seat pan and harness
38 Control column
39 Instrument panel
40 Armoured windscreen
41 Recovery parachute cable
42 Rudder pedal
43 Missile control and fusing box
44 Armoured bulkhead
45 Ring sight
46 Honeycomb (Bienenwabe)
47 Hs 217 Föhn 73-mm missiles
48 Jettisonable plexiglas nose cone

# Blohm und Voss Ha 137

**Ha 137 V1 to V6**
**Origin:** Hamburger Flugzeugbau GmbH.
**Type:** Dive bomber and close-support aircraft.
**Engine:** See text.
**Dimensions:** Span 36ft 7in (11·15m); length 31ft 0¾in (9·46m); height 9ft 2¼in (2·8m).
**Weights:** Empty 4,000lb (1814kg); loaded 5,324lb (2415kg).
**Performance:** Maximum speed (V4) 205mph (330km/h); range 360 miles (580km).
**Armament:** Two 7·92mm MG 17 in fuselage and two more (or 20mm MG FF) in top of landing gear trousers; four 110lb (50kg) bombs on wing racks.

**Development:** Whilst in Japan working for Kawasaki Dipl-Ing Richard Vogt had devised a novel form of wing based on a single strong tubular spar serving as the main fuel tank. He used this for a projected single-seat dive bomber, powered by either a Rolls-Royce Kestrel or Pratt & Whitney (BMW) Hornet, and with the wing having inverted-gull form. After a mock-up review in October 1934 the first prototype (Ha 137 V1) was flown in April 1935 with BMW 132 (Hornet) of 720hp. Though it did not have an observer with rear gun, as specified for the Luftwaffe Sturzbomber requirement (met by the Ju 87), the 137 was so tough and manoeuvrable that three more were bought with 610hp Jumo 210, and one with Kestrel. Ultimately two

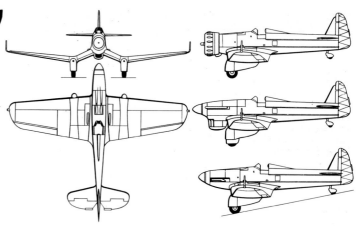

*Three-views of the Ha 137 V5, with V3 (centre) and V1 (top)*

more Jumo-engined examples were flown, but personnel changes (notably Udet's appointment as head of the RLM tech-development staff in 1936) caused it to be dropped, despite its promise as a close-support attack bomber and straffer.

# Blohm und Voss Ha 139

**Ha 139 V1 to V3, V3 rebuilt as B/U and B/MS**
**Origin:** Hamburger Flugzeugbau GmbH.
**Type:** Long-range seaplane, see text.
**Engines:** Four 600hp Junkers Jumo 205C diesels with 12 pistons in six double-ended cylinders.
**Dimensions:** (V3) span 96ft 9½in (29·49m); length 65ft 10¼in (20·06m); height 15ft 9in (4·80m).
**Weights:** Empty (B/U) about 28,660lb (13,000kg); loaded 41,888lb (19,000kg).

**Performance:** (B/U) maximum speed 179mph (288km/h); typical cruise 124mph (200km/h); range 3,075 miles (4948km).

**Development:** Most famous of all Blohm und Voss pre-war aircraft were three fine seaplanes operated on 100 Atlantic crossings (40 North Atlantic, 60 South) by Deutsche Lufthansa. Though they needed major modifications they made Atlantic crossings seem routine, which had never before been done. The third, V3, was bigger than V1 and V2, and was designated Ha 139B. In 1940 it was rebuilt as the 139B/U with long observer nose and many other changes, finally appearing as the 139B/MS minesweeper with large current-carrying degaussing ring for blowing magnetic mines. The first two served as transports in the Norwegian campaign.

*Above: The Blohm und Voss Ha 139B/MS (rebuilt Ha 139 V3) taxying near the company's Hamburg factory in 1942 (note barrage balloon). Subsequent use was limited by lack of spares and it was probably soon scrapped.*

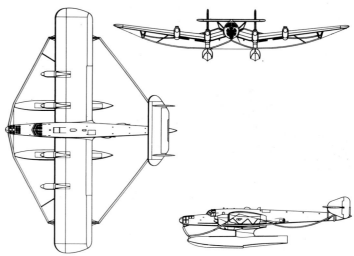

*Above: Three-view of the Ha 139B/MS*

# Blohm und Voss Ha 140

**Ha 140 V1 to V3**
**Origin:** Blohm und Voss, Abt. Flugzeugbau.
**Type:** Recce and torpedo bomber seaplane.
**Engines:** Two 830hp BMW 132K (Hornet) nine-cylinder radials.
**Dimensions:** Span 72ft 2¼in (22·0m); length 54ft 11½in (16·74m); height 10ft 0¼in (3·05m).
**Weights:** Empty 13,889lb (6300kg); max loaded 20,342lb (9227kg).
**Performance:** Maximum speed 207mph (333km/h); max range 1,242 miles (2000km).

**Development:** Originally intended to be powered by two Jumo 210 liquid-cooled engines, this twin-float seaplane grew in size and weight to meet operational requirements and emerged with the licence-built American radial, flying on 30 September 1937. Eventually three were built as back-ups to the He 115 (which was a better aircraft on water and in the air), the V3 having leading-edge slats and being used to test a model Bv 222 vertical tail and the variable-incidence wing proposed for the Bv 144. Most of these important trials were flown in 1940.

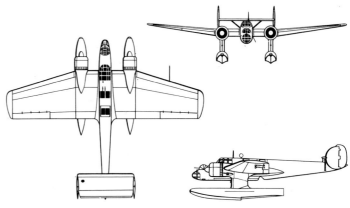

*Above: Three-view of the Ha 140 V1*

# Blohm und Voss BV 138

**Bv 138A-1, B-1 and C-1 (data for C-1)**
**Origin:** Hamburger Flugzeugbau GmbH.
**Type:** Six-crew reconnaissance flying boat.
**Engines:** Three 880hp Junkers Jumo 205D diesels with 12 opposed pistons in six cylinders.
**Dimensions:** Span 88ft 7in (27m); length 65ft 1½in (19·85m); height 19ft 4¼in (5·9m).
**Weights:** Empty 24,250lb .(11,000kg); loaded 34,100lb (15,480kg); (rocket assist) 39,600lb (16,480kg).
**Performance:** Maximum speed 171mph (275km/h); climb to 10,000ft (3050m) in 24min; service ceiling 16,400ft (5000m); maximum range 2,500 miles (4023km).
**Armament:** 20mm MG 151 cannon in front and rear turrets; 13mm MG 131 in cockpit behind centre engine; four 331lb (150kg) depth charges or other stores under inner right wing.
**History:** First flight (Ha· 138V-1) 15 July 1937; first delivery (A-1) January 1940; (C-1) 1941.

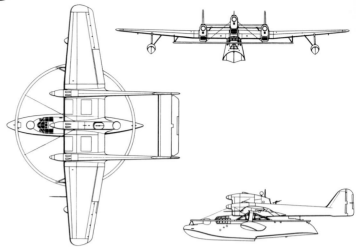

***Three-view of the Bv 138 MS, with degaussing ring***

**Development:** Originally designated Ha 138, reflecting the fact that the aircraft subsidiary of the Blohm und Voss shipyard is (even today) Hamburger Flugzeugbau, the 138 was designed by Richard Vogt and took a long time to reach its final form. Major changes had to be made to the hull, wing, tail and tail booms, though none of the alterations were due to the unusual layout. The first 25 Bv 138A-1 boats were intended to be ocean reconnaissance platforms, but were not a success and ended up as transports in the Norwegian campaign and thereafter. They were underpowered with three 600hp Jumo 205 C diesel engines, the fuel oil being carried inside the tubular main spar of the wing. In late 1940 the Bv 138B-1 entered service,

with 880hp Jumo 205D engines, further modified tail and a 20mm turret at each end of the hull. After building 21, production was switched to the final Bv 138C-1, of which 227 were delivered in 1941—43. This had improved propellers, added a dorsal turret and was greatly improved in equipment. Throughout 1942—45 the 138C gave good front-line service in the Arctic, the Baltic, the North Atlantic and Mediterranean.

*Above: A Bv 138C-1 (letter-code 7R+PL) of 3.(F)/SAGr 125 photographed in 1943 whilst operating over the Black Sea. Based at Constanza, Romania, it reported to the SSM, Seefliegerführer Schwarzes Meer, on shipping-protection patrols*

*Left: Another Bv 138C-1 of the same unit, 3.(F)/SAGr 125, in early 1943*

# Blohm und Voss BV 141

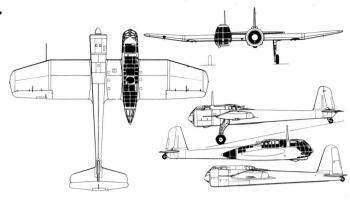

**Bv 141 prototypes, A-series and B-series**
**Origin:** Blohm und Voss, Abt. Flugzeugbau.
**Type:** Tactical recce and army co-operation aircraft.
**Engine:** (Prototypes and A) 960hp BMW 132N nine-cylinder radial, (B) 1,560hp BMW 801A 14-cylinder two-row radial.
**Dimensions:** Span (A) 50ft 8¼in (15·44m), (B) 57ft 3½in (17·46m); length (A) 39ft 10¼in (9·96m), (B) 45ft 9¼in (13·95m); height (A) 13ft 5½in (4·10m), (B) 11ft 9¾in (3·60m).
**Weights:** Empty (A) 6,982lb (3167kg), (B) 10,363lb (4700kg); loaded (A) 8,598lb (3900kg), (B) 12,568lb (5700kg).
**Performance:** Maximum speed (A) 248mph (400km/h), (B) 272mph (438km/h); range (A) 708 miles (1139km), (B) 1,180 miles (1900km).
**Armament:** Two fixed 7·92mm MG 17 firing ahead, one 7·92mm MG 15 manually aimed from dorsal bubble and one MG 15 in rear tailcone; four 110lb (50kg) bombs on wing racks.
**History:** First flight (Ha 141) 25 February 1938; (Bv 141 V1) September 1938; service delivery (A-02) November 1939.

**Development:** Without doubt one of the oddest aircraft ever built, the Bv 141 was in fact a thoroughly pleasant machine in some of its many versions, and its rejection as a regular Luftwaffe type was in large measure due to refusal by the officials to believe that it really made sense. Vogt designed the original Ha 141 to meet the 1937 RLM requirement for a tactical aircraft having a crew of three with excellent all-round vision, able to fly army co-operation, tac-recce, smokescreen, low attack and bomber missions. He rightly judged that the best layout to meet the stated need was a single-engined aircraft with the crew and mission equipment in an all-glazed nacelle mounted beside the engine/tailboom. The original Ha 141 was succeeded by a series of Bv 141 prototypes of the A-series, with streamlined nacelle covered in flat windows. Perhaps surprisingly,

these aircraft were beautiful to handle, their only major fault being troubles with the hydraulic system. The Luftwaffe, however, could not accept the concept of an asymmetric aircraft and rejected the 141 on the ground that it was underpowered. Vogt had already begun the redesigned 141B with BMW 801 engine, but this unfortunately was unpleasant and plagued by troubles. Only five B-series (making 13in all) were built, though Blohm und Voss never lost their enthusiasm for asymmetry and featured it in many jet projects.

*Four views of the Bv 141A-0 with (bottom) the V1 prototype*

*Below: Second of the more powerful and completely redesigned Bv 141B-series, the V10 did not fly until 1 June 1941 because no suitable propeller existed.*

# Blohm und Voss BV 142

**Bv 142 V1 to V4**
**Origin:** Blohm und Voss, Abt. Flugzeugbau.
**Type:** See text.
**Engines:** Four 880hp BMW 132H nine-cylinder radials.
**Dimensions:** Span 96ft 10¾in (29·53m); length (U1) 67ft 1¼in (20·45m); height 14ft 6¾in (4·44m).
**Weights:** (U1) empty 24,427lb (11,080kg); loaded 36,508lb (16,560kg).
**Performance:** Maximum speed 232mph (375km/h) at sea level (possibly faster at height); range (no bombs) 2,423 miles (3900km).

**Development:** Essentially a landplane Ha 139, the four Bv 142 (V1 was strictly Ha 142 because it was built before Hamburger Flugzeugbau was renamed) were built in 1938–39 for Deutsche Lufthansa as transatlantic mailplanes, but did not impress. In 1939 the second was rebuilt for military duties as Bv 142 V2/U1 with long glazed nose, five MG 15 machine guns and four 220lb or eight 110lb (50kg) bombs inside the former mail compartment. V1 was likewise rebuilt, the ventral cupola for guns and bomb-aimer being of He 111H-6 type, but performance was mediocre and V3 and V4 remained transports.

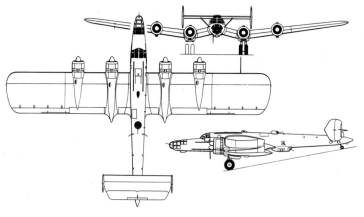

*Three-view of Bv 142 V2/U1*

# Blohm und Voss BV 144

**Bv 144 (V1 only built)**
**Origin:** Blohm und Voss, Abt. Flugzeugbau (programme assigned to Soc. Louis Breguet, Bayonne, France).
**Type:** See text.
**Engines:** Two 1,600hp BMW 801MA 18-cylinder two-row radials.
**Dimensions:** Span 88ft 7in (27·00m); length 71ft 6¼in (21·8m); height 15ft 6¾in (4·75m).
**Weights:** Empty 17,416lb (7900kg); loaded 28,660lb (13,000kg).
**Performance:** Maximum speed (est.) 292mph (470km/h); range 963 miles (1550km).

**Development:** The Bv 144 could have been the world's standard medium-haul airliner, had Germany won the war. It was begun in 1940 to meet future needs of Lufthansa, and its most unusual feature was that Vogt designed the wing with variable incidence, pivoting about the tubular spar. This allowed the fuselage to remain level, leading to a short inwards-retracting landing gear and comfort for the 18 passengers. Breguet was charged with building prototypes, and completed two, the Bv 144 V1 flying by August 1944. The Germans retreated soon after, and eventually the French dropped the Bv 144 despite its advanced design.

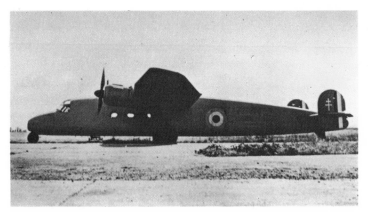

*One of the very few photographs of the Bv 144 V1, this shows it after completion at Bayonne and painted in Free French markings, with Cross of Lorraine on the fin.*

# Blohm und Voss BV 155

**Me 155A and B, Bv 155 V1 to V3**
**Origin:** Messerschmitt AG, later Blohm und Voss, Abt. Flugzeugbau.
**Type:** High-altitude interceptor.
**Engine:** (155B) DB 603A with TKL 15 turbocharger giving 1,450hp at 49,210ft (15,000m).
**Dimensions:** Span (B) 67ft 3in (20·5m); length 39ft 4½in (12·00m); height 9ft 9½in (2·98m).
**Weights:** (B) empty 10,734lb (4870kg); loaded (max armament) 13,263lb (6016kg).
**Performance:** (B) maximum speed 429mph (690km/h) at 52,493ft (16,000m); range at high alt, about 895 miles (1440km).

**Development:** Messerschmitt began the Me 155 as a derivative of the Bf 109 to operate from the resumed carrier *Graf Zeppelin*, but when this unhappy ship again fell from favour the 155 reappeared as a pinpoint bomber with 2,205lb (1000kg) bomb and finally in 1943 as a long-span interceptor to hit high-flying US bombers. In August 1943 work was passed from Messerschmitt (said to be overloaded) to Blohm und Voss, but the two firms disagreed violently on the design. The whole job eventually became the Bv 155, but had to be redesigned. The Bv 155 V1 flew on 1 September 1944 and a further redesign, the V2, in February 1945. With outstanding propulsion and aerodynamic features they would have been unmatched by Allied fighters at heights over 40,000ft, and were intended to have heavy groups of 15, 20 or 30mm cannon. At the final collapse work was well advanced on the V4 (C-series) with fuselage radiators.

*Above: This photograph was taken after the war and shows the still-incomplete Bv 155 V3 at the Royal Aircraft Establishment at Farnborough, England. What appears at first glance to be the rear fuselage is in fact the right-wing radiator. Technical problems were very considerable, and at the collapse in May 1945 a simpler V4 prototype was being built. The V3 later went to the United States*

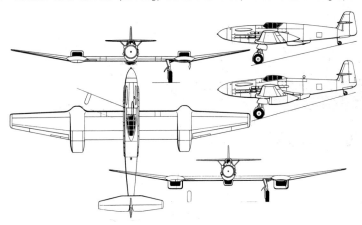

*Three-view of Bv 155 V2 and V3 with (above) two views of V1*

# Blohm und Voss BV 222 Wiking

**Bv 222 prototypes, 222A and 222C**
**Origin:** Hamburger Flugzeugbau GmbH.
**Type:** Strategic transport flying boat; see text.
**Engines:** (Most) six 1,000hp Bramo (BMW) Fafnir 323R nine-cylinder radials, (V7 and 222C) six 980hp Junkers Jumo 207C six-cylinder (12-piston) diesels.
**Dimensions:** Span 150ft 11in (46·00m); length 121ft 4½in (37·00m); height 35ft 9in (10·9m).
**Weights:** Empty (A) about 64,000lb (29,000kg), (C) 67,572lb (30,650kg); maximum (all) 108,030lb (49,000kg).
**Performance:** Maximum speed (all) 242mph (390km/h) without armament, 183mph (295km/h) with; maximum cruise at height 214mph (345km/h), (armed) 156mph (252km/h); maximum range at 152mph (245km/h) 3,790 miles (6100km); endurance 28hr.
**Armament:** Varied greatly from single 7·92mm MG 81 to five/six power turrets; (C) 13mm MG 131 manually aimed in bow, 20mm MG 151 in one or two dorsal turrets and two wing turrets (upper surface behind outer nacelles) plus various MG 131 or MG 81 from side windows.
**History:** First flight 7 September 1940; first service mission 10 July 1941.

**Development:** Deutsche Lufthansa ordered three of the large Bv 222 boats in 1937 for use on the North and South Atlantic. The prototype (222V-1) was civil, but after initial flight trials was modified into a freight transport for the Luftwaffe. There followed nine further aircraft, no two alike, V9 also being the first of four production 222C-0 transports with Jumo engines and improved armament, as well as FuG 200 Hohentwiel radar and FuG 216 rear warning. Only 13 were flown, and decision to drop the diesels led to a switch to the Fafnir, used in the majority of the prototypes, from No 20, which with 14-19 were almost complete. From 1941 the Wikings shuttled from northern Norway to Africa bringing urgent stores.

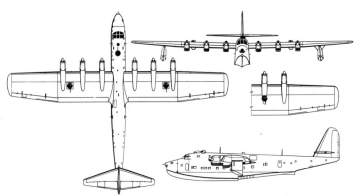

*Three-view of Bv 222C (V9) with inset right wing of V7*

Despite their improving equipment, nearly all were shot down or destroyed at their moorings, but four survived to VE-day, one being scuttled by its crew and the others being flown to Britain and the USA for trials. The Wiking posed many development problems, and always seemed underpowered, but its basic qualities were good.

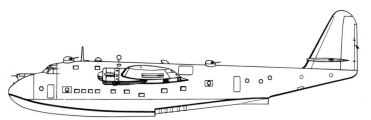

*Above: Bv 222A with initial armament scheme*

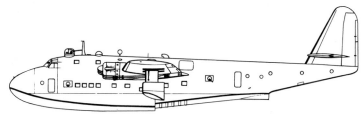

*Above: The Bv 222A (V4) with top of wing turret just visible*

*Shown here on the slipway with all engines operating, the Bv 222 V8 was the last of the radial-engined A-series. It had a brief career with the Luftwaffe, being delivered in the late autumn (probably 26 October) of 1942 and being shot down by RAF fighters before the end of the year whilst serving with LTS See 222 in the Mediterranean.*
*Below, the Jumo-diesel V7, first of the reconnaissance C-series*

# Blohm und Voss BV 40

**BV 40 V1 to V19 and BV 40A**
**Origin:** Blohm und Voss (Abt. Flugzeugbau).
**Type:** Point-defence interceptor glider.
**Dimensions:** Span 25ft 11in (7·90m); length 18ft 8½in (5·70m); height 5ft 4¼in (1·66m).
**Weights:** Empty 1,844lb (836kg); maximum 2,094lb (950kg).
**Performance:** Maximum speed (Bf 109G tug) 344mph (553km/h), (109G towing two BV 40s) 315mph (507km/h); anticipated diving speed in free flight 560mph (900km/h); time to climb to 23,000ft (7000m), (one BV 40) 12 min, (two BV 40s) 16·8min.
**Armament:** Two 30mm MK 108 each with 35 rounds.
**History:** First flight, late May 1944.

**Development:** Desperate situations lead to desperate remedies, and often to genuine technical progress. This was certainly the case in the Luftwaffe's attempts to inflict heavier losses on the US 8th Air Force daylight bomber formations. One answer was the Ba 349, and an even stranger one was a glider, proposed by BV's technical director Richard Vogt. The reasoning was simple: the only way to reduce the chances of fighters being hit by the hail of fire from a B-17 formation was to reduce the frontal area, and the best way to do this was to eliminate the engine. Moreover, most of the BV 40 was planned for simple and cheap production on a vast scale by woodworkers, while the metal cockpit was to be protected by armour and thick glass representing more than one-quarter of the gross weight. Vogt hoped to use one 30mm cannon and trail an explosive charge on a long wire for a second attacking pass, but the best answer was found to be two heavy guns to pump out the maximum firepower in the brief period available in a head-on attack. The whole programme was abandoned in the autumn of 1944 when the flight-test phase had been completed, with six of 19 prototypes, and studies were in hand for heavy bomb loads for release above bomber formations.

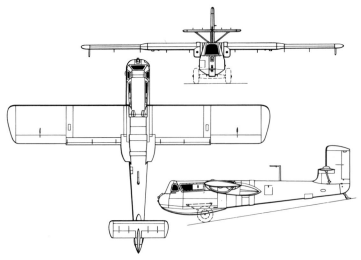

*Above: Three-view of the Bv 40 V1*

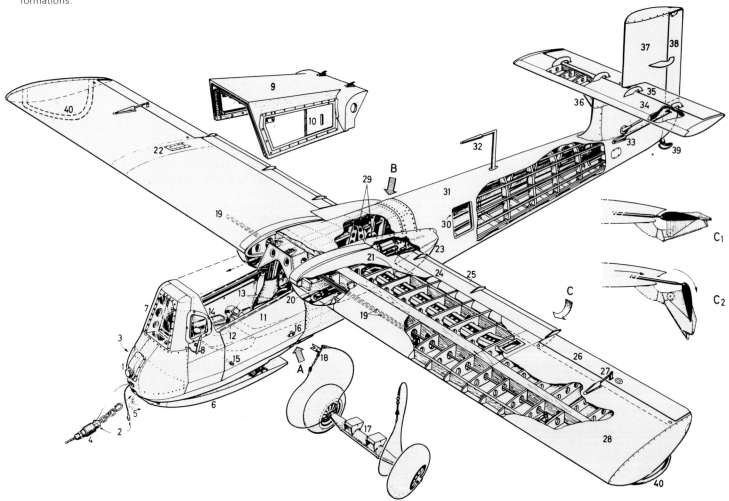

**Blohm und Voss BV 40**

1 Compass housing
2 Plug and socket for intercom
3 Location of forward storage battery.
4 Towing cable head
5 Snap fastener for jacking up
6 Landing skid (extended)
7 Armoured nose and windscreen
8 Hood release lever (in unlocked position)
9 Armoured hood
10 Sliding armour screens
11 Padding for prone pilot
12 Tray for chest parachute (chin rest in front of tray)
13 Pilot safety harness
14 Padded arm rest
15 Locking bolt for trolley
16 Rear trolley-cable fitting
17 Trolley (detached)
18 Mounting and turnbuckle
19 Control rods for flaps (below) and ailerons (above)
20 Port 30-mm MK 108 cannon
21 Port ammunition conveyor
22 Starboard hatch for mounting
23 Gun tray
24 Flap
25 Auxiliary tab
26 Aileron
27 Actuating rod for aileron
28 Wing skinning (4-mm plywood)
29 Adjustable rudder pedals
30 Access hatch to rear storage ammunition conveyor
31 Wooden aft fuselage
32 Pitot head
33 Control cable exit to rudder
34 Tailplane
35 Elevator
36 Tailplane bracing
37 Vertical tail fin
38 Rudder
battery and compressed air bottles
39 Elastic tail skid
40 Wingtip bumper
A Nose break point
B Centre/aft fuselage attachment point
C1 Landing flap in flight position
C2 Landing flap fully lowered (80°).

# Blohm und Voss BV 238

**Bv 238 V1 (others incomplete)**
**Origin:** Blohm und Voss, Abt. Flugzeugbau.
**Type:** Transport (later patrol bomber) flying boat.
**Engines:** Six 1,900hp Daimler-Benz DB 603G inverted-vee-12.
**Dimensions:** Span 197ft 4¾in (60·17m); length (V1) 142ft 8½in (43·50m); height 43ft 11½in (13·13m).
**Weights:** (V1) empty 111,987lb (50,800kg); loaded 176,370lb (80,000kg), (V6, max) 220,462lb (100,000kg).
**Performance:** Maximum speed (V1) 264mph (425km/h); range (V1) 3,790 miles (6100km), (V6) 4,880 miles (7850km).

**Development:** Many thought the Bv 222 big, but it was dwarfed by its monster brother. Planned in late 1940 as a giant oversea transport and patrol boat with slim hull and four very powerful diesels, it was recast as a six-engined machine with extremely high wing loading and design more advanced than the contemporary Martin XPB2M Mars. The Czechs delayed the programme by taking three years to build the FGP 227 flying scale model, which French prisoners then damaged in transit. The FGP 227 eventually flew in September 1944, when the Bv 238 had been designed, built and flown. The V1, an unarmed transport, flew from Lake Schaal in April 1944, becoming the heaviest aircraft at that time. Trials were encouraging, and the V2 was almost complete, and others including the heavily armed V4 and Bv 250 landplane were being built. But straffing P-51s sank the V1 and the whole project was scrapped in late summer 1944.

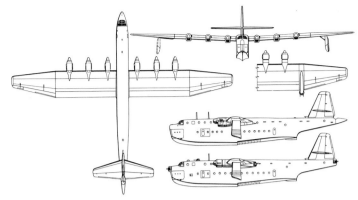

*Above: Three-view of Bv 238 V1 with (inset and bottom) the V4*

*Below: Bv 238 V1 pictured on Lake Schaal in the taxi-trials period preceding first flight in April 1944. Though exceeded in wing span by the Soviet ANT.20 and American Douglas B-19, the Bv 238 was much heavier and more powerful than any previous aircraft. The V4 was being built with two 20mm and 20 13mm guns plus heavy loads of bombs or missiles*

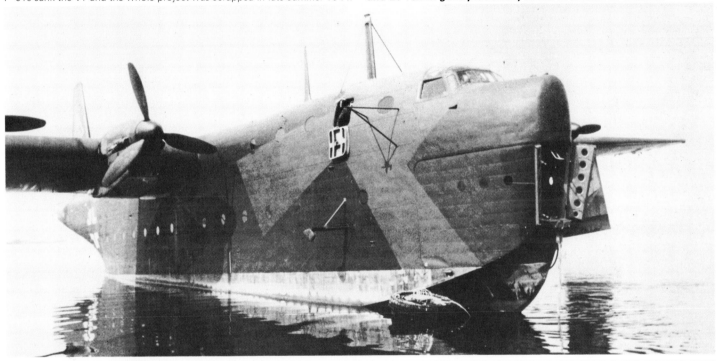

# Bücker Bü 131 Jungmann

**Bü 131A, B and export versions**
**Origin:** Bücker Flugzeugbau GmbH.
**Type:** Primary trainer; later, night ground attack.
**Engine:** (A) 80hp Hirth HM 60R inverted four-in-line; (B) 105hp HM 504A-2.
**Dimensions:** Span 24ft 3½in (7·40m); length (B) 21ft 8½in (6·62m); height 7ft 4½in (2·25m).
**Weights:** Empty 860lb (390kg); maximum 1,499lb (680kg).
**Performance:** Maximum speed (B) 114mph (183km/h); landing speed 51mph (82km/h); range 404 miles (650km).
**History:** First flight (prototype) 27 April 1934; first delivery (Luftsportverband) late 1934, (Luftwaffe) 1935.

**Development:** Carl Clemens Bücker was a seaplane pilot with the German Navy in World War I. In 1919 he went to Sweden as a freelance test pilot, founded the great Saab aircraft company in 1921 and in 1932 returned to his native land to set up his own company at Johannisthal, near Berlin. He brought with him Swedish designer Anders J. Andersson, who succeeded right from the first in injecting a flair for superlative aerobatic handling that made all the Bücker trainers great successes. The first became the Jungmann, one of the two most important primary (*ab initio*) trainers of the reborn Luftwaffe, the other being the He 72. Large numbers continued in production well into World War II, most being of the more powerful B subtype. Many European countries bought Jungmanns, Czechoslovakia built it as the C-104 and it was a standard trainer of the Japanese Army (Kokusai

*Above: This ski-mounted Bü 131 may be serving with an NSGr (night ground-attack) unit on the Eastern Front*

Ki-86) and Navy (Watanabe K9W). In 1942 NSGr (night ground-attack) units of the Luftwaffe on the Eastern front began to use large numbers of these handy machines for night harassment.

# Bücker Bü 133 Jungmeister

**Bü 133B and C**
**Origin:** Bücker Flugzeugbau GmbH.
**Type:** Advanced aerobatic trainer.
**Engine:** (B) 160hp Hirth HM 506 inverted six-in-line, (C) 160hp Siemens Sh 14A-4 seven-cylinder radial.
**Dimensions:** Span 21ft 7¾in (6·60m); length (C) 19ft 9in (6·02m); height 7ft 2½in (2·20m).
**Weights:** (C) Empty 937lb (425kg); maximum 1,290lb (585kg); non-aerobatic category, heavier.
**Performance:** Maximum speed (C) 137mph (220km/h); landing speed 56mph (90km/h); range 311 miles (500km).
**History:** First flight 1935; service delivery (Luftsportverband and Luftwaffe) 1936.

**Development:** Since its appearance the Jungmeister (Young Master, its stable-mate being a mere Young Man) has been probably the most famed aerobatic aircraft in the world. A single-seater, it is more powerful than the Jungmann, and with four ailerons and beautiful handling is a sheer delight to any competent pilot. It was largely the swelling demand for the new machine that spurred the company to move from Johannisthal to a new and much larger factory at Rangsdorf, another Berlin suburb. The works was occupied at the end of 1935, and production of the 133 began at once, a slightly different model going into production by Dornier in Switzerland. All German Jungmeisters were of the C sub-type, and the Luftwaffe used

*Post-war picture of one of today's rebuilt and refined Jungmeisters used for competition aerobatics*

several hundred. Some had skis, but so far as is known none carried armament nor did operational flying as did the 131. CASA in Spain built the 131B. Many Jungmeisters are flying today.

# Bücker Bü 181 Bestmann

**Bü 181A and D** (and see text)
**Origin:** Bücker Flugzeugbau GmbH; licence-built, see text.
**Type:** Multi-role trainer, liaison, transport and glider tug.
**Engine:** 105hp Hirth HM 504 inverted four-in-line.
**Dimensions:** Span 34ft 9in (10·6m); length 25ft 9in (7·85m); height 6ft 9in (2·06m).
**Weights:** Empty (A) 1,056lb (480kg); maximum 1,650lb (750kg).
**Performance:** Maximum speed 133mph (215km/h); cruise 121mph (195km/h); range (typical) 497 miles (800km).
**History:** First flight (prototype) February 1939; service delivery (Luftwaffe) late 1940; final delivery (Germany) 1945, (Sweden) 1946, (Czechoslovakia) 1951, (Egypt) after 1960.

**Development:** Though it was designed as a sports and touring machine, the Bü 181 Bestmann swiftly became the leading wartime primary trainer of the Luftwaffe and was built in large numbers and used for many utility purposes. Moreover, as the sub-heading "History" above shows, it had a remarkably long active life in several countries long after World War II. Unlike earlier Bücker products it was a cabin monoplane, with comfortable side-by-side seating which in Luftwaffe examples was of the bucket type designed for a seat-type parachute. Most of the slender wing was ply-covered; the forward fuselage was of steel tube with detachable metal panels back to the trailing edge, while the rear fuselage was a wooden monocoque. Rangsdorf built at least 5,900 Bestmanns during World War II, and a further 708 (including the slightly altered 181D) were built in 1942–45 by Fokker at Amsterdam. Hagglund in Sweden built 125 as the Sk 25 for the Swedish Air Force, and in Czechoslovakia the Zlin factory began production just as the Germans left and built the Zlin 281 and 381 after the war. The Egyptian Heliopolis works then built a modified version named Gomhouria after studying all available trainers in the late 1950s.

*Below: A captured Bü 181 Bestmann on display in the United States, still in Luftwaffe markings. Just behind is an Ar 234B Blitz jet reconnaissance bomber*

# DFS 230

**DFS 230A-1, B-1, C-1, F-1**

**Origin:** Deutsches Forschungsinstitut für Segelflugzeug; production by Gothaer Waggonfabrik and others.

**Type:** Assault glider.

**Dimensions:** Span (nearly all) 68ft 5½in (20·87m); length (A, B, C) 36ft 10½in (11·24m); height 8ft 11¾in (2·74m).

**Weights:** Empty (B-1) 1,896lb (860kg); maximum (A-1) 4,608lb (2090 kg), (B-1) 4,630lb (2100kg).

**Performance:** Normal towing speed 130mph (210km/h); dive limit speed 180mph (290km/h).

**History:** First flight, early 1937; service delivery (A-0) 1938, (A-1) 1939.

**Development:** Apparently no serious thought had been given to the use of gliders in war until Ernst Udet, later head of the Luftwaffe technical procurement department, visited DFS in 1933. He later placed an order for a military transport glider, the DFS 230, which was flown with conspicuous success by Hanna Reitsch in 1937. After demonstrations before senior officers the DFS 230 became the basis around which the new technique of glider-borne assault was developed. On 10 May 1940 it was put into effect with total success by 45 gliders, towed by Ju 52s to carefully planned pinpoint operations on bridges and forts in the Low Countries. The classic assault was on Fort Eben Emael, in Belgium, on the Albert Canal. The vast modern fortress was knocked out and held by 72 men who arrived silently within the outer walls at dawn. They held until the German Army arrived more than 24hr later, suffering total casualties of six men killed and 20 wounded. In Crete large forces of DFS 230 and other gliders suffered heavily, but took the island. Hundreds of 230s were used in North Africa and Italy, with progressively less effect, but went out in a blaze of glory when Otto Skorzeny's handpicked force stormed the mountain-top hotel where Mussolini was being held under armed guard and flew him out in a Storch. Most 230s were of the B-1 type with braking parachute; the C-1 had three solid fuel rockets in the nose to stop it in 30 metres, and the F-1 was an enlarged model seating 15. Nearly all were delivered before 1941, output being 1,022.

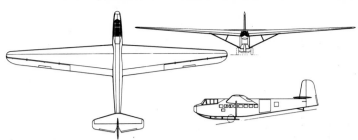

*Above: Three-view of the DFS 230A-1*

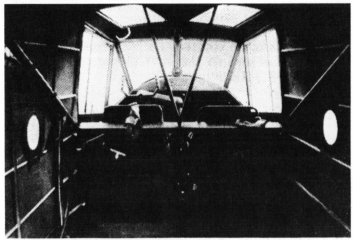

*Above: Interior of the DFS 230 V7*

*Below: Three photographs showing various DFS 230 sub-types in operational service. Left, upper, a 230A-1 on tow; right, upper, an early-production A-1 in all-grey colour scheme; bottom, a 230B-1 (LH+1·8) at Comiso, Italy, in 1942*

# DFS 228

### DFS 228 V1, V2 and A-series
**Origin:** Deutsches Forschungsinstitut für Segelflug, Griesheim.
**Type:** High-altitude reconnaissance aircraft.
**Engine:** Walter 109-509 rocket engine rated at 3,630lb (1650kg) at high altitude.
**Dimensions:** Span 57ft 7¼in (17·56m); length 34ft 8½in (10·58m); height, not stated.
**Weights:** Empty 3,650lb (1642kg); loaded 9,280lb (4210kg).
**Performance:** Maximum speed at high altitude 559mph (900km/h); design ceiling 82,021ft (25,000m); maximum range about 652 miles (1050km) made up of gliding and powered spurts.

**Development:** The DFS (German Institute for Sailplane Flight) promised to meet the German General Staff's need for an uninterceptable reconnaissance aircraft with this remarkable rocket-propelled sailplane, which was a true ancestor of the Lockheed U-2. Shelved in 1940–43 by pressure of other work, the 228 was urgently resurrected and the first two prototypes completed in 1943. Almost entirely made of wood, it had a pressurized nose compartment for the pilot which could in emergency be detached and recovered by parachute – another of today's supposed new ideas. The mid-

*Air-to-air photograph of the DFS 228 V1 airborne in 1943 mounted on the Do 217K V3. Both this and the V2 prototype made many flights, but not with rocket in operation*

fuselage housed rocket propellants and two Zeiss infra-red cameras. By the time Allied troops reached Griesheim, many flights had been made, launched from a Do 217, but none under power.

# DFS 331

### DFS 331 V1
**Origin:** DFS, Griesheim; built by Gothaer Waggonfabrik.
**Type:** Transport glider.
**Dimensions:** Span 75ft 5½in (23·00m); length 51ft 10½in (15·81m); height (on wheels) 11ft 7¾in (3·55m).
**Weights:** Empty 5,005lb (2270kg); loaded 10,517lb (4770kg).
**Performance:** Max speed on tow 168mph (270km/h).

**Development:** Germany failed to follow up her initial world lead in assault gliders. Hans Jacobs at DFS designed the DFS 331 as a bigger and more useful carrier than the DFS 230, but only one Gotha-built prototype flew in 1941. The pilot sat high on the left, near the big loading door.

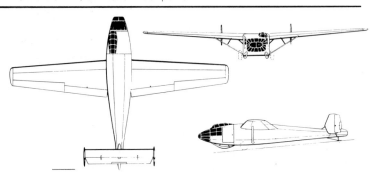

*Above: Three-view of the single DFS 331 prototype*

# Dornier Do 11

### Do F (Do 11a), 11C and D
**Origin:** Dornier Metallbauten, Switzerland; later Dornier-Werke GmbH.
**Type:** Heavy bomber.
**Engines:** (C, D) two 650hp Siemens (Bristol-licence) Sh 22B-2 nine-cylinder radials.
**Dimension:** Span (prior to D) 91ft 10¼in (28·00m), (D) 86ft 3½in (26·29m); length 61ft 8in (18·79m); height 18ft (5·49m).
**Weights:** Empty (D) 13,173lb (5975kg); maximum (D) 18,080lb (8200kg).
**Performance:** Maximum speed (D) 161mph (259km/h); cruise 140mph (225km/h); service ceiling 13,450ft (4100m); max range (bomb load not stated) 596 miles (960km).
**Armament:** Three manually aimed 7·92mm MG 15 in nose, dorsal and ventral positions; internal bomb load of 2,205lb (1000kg).
**History:** First flight (Do F) 7 May 1932, (Do 11C) late 1933.

**Development:** Dornier's Swiss subsidiary at Altenrhein was one of the few German-controlled plants where, in the late 1920s, development of heavy bombers could be contemplated. The first to appear, in 1930, was the Do P, with four Jupiter engines. This was followed by the Do Y, with three, and the Do F, which had only two similar engines but nevertheless promised to be better than its larger ancestors. An innovation was the retractable landing gear, though this gave much trouble and eventually was permanently locked down. Worse, the production Do 11 flew poorly, and after many delays – partly owing to Siemens' late delivery of engines – small numbers entered

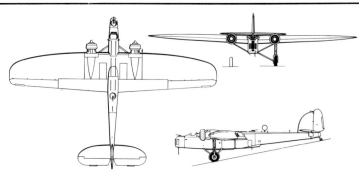

*Above: Three-view of the Do 11D with reduced span*

service as freighters with the German State Railways (a cover for the first Luftwaffe bombing units). By the end of 1934 the short-span Do 11D was well established, with 77 operating in by-now overt Fliegergruppen and the Kampffliegerschulen (war flying schools). But accidents were frequent, and the unpopular Do 11 was never the important bomber it had been planned to be. The improved Do 13 was not much better, but it eventually emerged as the Do 23.

*Below: This Do 11C was probably serving with the Behelfskampfgeschwader (auxiliary bomber group) in 1934. Later it was modified to Do 11D standard*

# Dornier Do 18

**Do 18D, G, H, N**
**Origin:** Dornier-Werke GmbH.
**Type:** D, G, reconnaissance and air/sea rescue; H, trainer, N, rescue.
**Engines:** (D) tandem push/pull Junkers Jumo 205C diesels, each rated at 600hp; (G, H, N) 700hp Jumo 205D.
**Dimensions:** Span 77ft 9in (23·7m); length 63ft 2in (19·25m); height 17ft 9in (5·45m).
**Weights:** (G-1) empty 12,900lb (5850kg); maximum 22,046lb (10,000 kg).
**Performance:** (G-1) Maximum speed at sea level 162mph (260km/h); typical cruise 106mph (170km/h); range 2,175 miles (3500km).
**Armament:** (D-1) typically one 7·92mm MG 15 manually aimed from bow and rear cockpits, with underwing racks for 1,102lb (500kg) load of weapons or stores on each side; (G-1) 13mm MG 131 in bow cockpit, 20mm MG 151 in power dorsal turret, same wing capacity; (H, N) none.
**History:** First flight (civil) 15 March 1935; (D) early 1938; final delivery, late 1939.

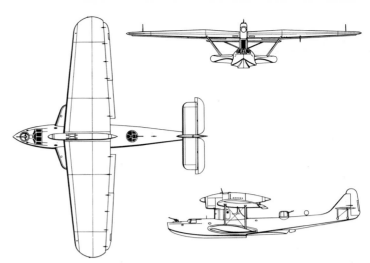

*Above: Three view of Do 18G-1*

**Development:** The Do 18, a pleasant and relatively harmless machine, was the first Luftwaffe type shot down by British aircraft in World War II; a flight of Skuas from *Ark Royal* caught three of the boats shadowing British warships on 26 September 1939 (and it is a fair reflection on the Skua's capabilities as a fighter that two of the boats escaped). Only about 100 were delivered altogether, most being of the more powerful and better armed G version. Nearly all were confined to northern Europe and the Baltic/Atlantic areas. The N used to appear painted white, with prominent red crosses, though post-war evidence confirmed the belief that these sometimes were engaged in Elint (electronic intelligence) missions.

*Above: Head-on view of a Do 18D on beaching chassis*

*Right: Flight deck of a typical Do 18D; German cockpits in 1939 were the best in Europe. Not visible is the bow gun*

*Below: a Do 18D-1 on operational patrol after the outbreak of war. It probably served with KüFlGr 106 over the N Sea*

# Dornier Do 17

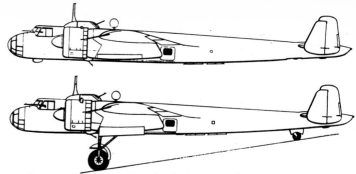

**Do 17E, F, K and P**
**Origin:** Dornier-Werke GmbH.
**Type:** Three-seat medium bomber (17F, reconnaissance).
**Engines:** Two 750hp BMW VI 7·3 12-cylinder vee liquid-cooled; 17P, two 1,000hp BMW 132N nine-cylinder radials.
**Dimensions:** Span 59ft 0½in (18m); length (17E, F) 53ft 3¾in (16·25m); (17P) 52ft 9¾in (16·1m); height (17E, F) 14ft 2in (4·3m); (17P) 14ft 11in (4·57m).
**Weights:** Empty (17E, F) 9,921lb (4500kg); (17P) 10,140lb (4600kg); loaded (17E) 15,520lb (7050kg); (17F) 15,430lb (7000kg); (17P) 16,887lb (7660kg).
**Performance:** Maximum speed (17E, F) 220mph (355km/h); (17P) 249mph (400km/h); service ceiling (17E) 16,730ft (5100m); (17F) 19,685ft (6000m), (17P) 20,340ft (6200m); typical range (17E) 620 miles (1000km); (17F) 994 miles (1600km); (17P) 745 miles (1200km).
**Armament:** (17E) one 7·92mm MG 15 manually aimed from rear ventral hatch and one manually aimed to rear from dorsal position, with internal bomb load of 1,650lb (750kg); (17P) three MG 15s, one (normally fixed to fire ahead) in right windscreen, one in ventral hatch and one in dorsal position, with internal bomb load of 2,205lb (1000kg).
**History:** First flight (single-fin V1 prototype) autumn 1934; (Do 17E) 7 November 1936; (Do 17F) 10 November 1936; (Do 17P) late 1937.

**Development:** Popularly dubbed "the flying pencil" in both Germany and Britain, the Do 17 was not planned as a bomber and secretly tested as a civil transport; its history was the other way round. Deutsche Lufthansa decided its slender body left much too little room for the six passengers, but the Reischsluftfahrtministerium eventually decided the Do 17 was worth developing as a bomber. Numerous prototypes were built with different noses and engines and eventually the Do 17E-1 and the F-1 reconnaissance machine went into large-scale, and widely subcontracted, production for the embryo Luftwaffe. As early as March 1937 both were in combat service, with one Staffel of 17Fs being in Spain with the Legion Kondor (there to prove virtually immune to interception by the Republican forces). In the spring of 1937 a Do 17M prototype with powerful DB 600 engines walked away from all the fighter aircraft at the International Military Aircraft Competition at Zurich. This caused a great sensation and the first nation to buy the new bomber was Jugoslavia, receiving 20 from Germany plus a construction licence. The Jugoslav Do 17Kb-1 had a very early nose profile (the same, in fact, as the Zurich demonstrator) and Gnome-Rhône 14N radial engines. They had a 20mm Hispano cannon and three 7·92mm Brownings. About 70 were on strength when the Germans invaded Jugoslavia in April 1941, two escaping to Greece with cargoes of gold bullion. The several hundred E and F models formed the biggest portion of the Luftwaffe bomber and reconnaissance force up to 1939, but by the end of that year had been relegated to operational training. The later Do 17M (Bramo Fafnir radials of 1,000hp) and Do 17P succeeded the E and F in production during 1937 and saw combat during World War II. They were the final types to retain the slender "flying pencil" shape and hemispherical nose-cap.

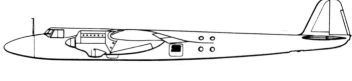

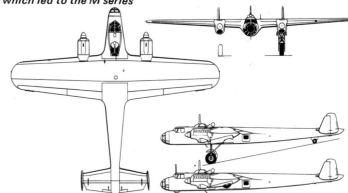

*From the top: Do 17M-1 (bomber), Do 17P-1 (reconnaissance)*

*Above: Do 17a, single-fin first prototype, and the V8 (lower) which led to the M series*

*Above: Three-view of Do 17F-1 (reconnaissance) with side-view (bottom) of E-1 bomber*

*Below: An immaculate Do 17E-1 bomber in 1937 camouflage immediately before delivery from the factory. Similar aircraft saw extensive service in the Spanish civil war and subsequently with the Spanish air force*

# Dornier Do 17Z and Do 215

**Do 17Z-1 and -2 and Do 215A-1, B-1 and B-5**

**Origin:** Dornier-Werke GmbH.

**Type:** Four-seat medium bomber and reconnaissance.

**Engines:** (Do 17Z-2) two 1,000hp Bramo Fafnir 323P nine-cylinder radials: (Do 215B-1) two 1,075hp Daimler-Benz DB 601A 12-cylinder inverted-vee liquid-cooled.

**Dimensions:** (Both) span 59ft 0½in (18m); length 51ft 9½in (15·79m); height 14ft 11½in (4·56m).

**Weights:** Empty (Do 17Z-2) 11,484lb (5210kg); (Do 215B-1) 12,730lb (5775kg); loaded (both) 19,841lb (9000kg).

**Performance:** Maximum speed (Do 17Z-2) 263mph (425km/h); (Do 215B-1) 280mph (450km/h); service ceiling (Do 17Z-2) 26,740ft (8150m); (Do 215B-1) 31,170ft (9500m); range with half bomb load (Do 17Z-2) 721 miles (1160km); (Do 215B-1) 932 miles (1500km).

**Armament:** Normally six 7·92mm Rheinmetall MG 15 machine guns, one fixed in nose, remainder on manually aimed mounts in front windscreen, two beam windows, and above and below at rear; internal bomb load up to 2,205lb (1000kg).

**History:** First flight (Do 17S prototype) early 1938; (Do 17Z-2) early 1939; (Do 215V1 prototype) late 1938; first delivery (Do 17Z-1) January 1939, (Do 215A-1) December 1939; termination of production (Do 17Z series) July 1940, (Do 215 series) January 1941.

**Development:** Whereas the slenderness of the first families of Do 17 bombers had earned them the nickname of "Flying Pencil", the Do 17S introduced a completely new front end with much deeper cabin and extensive window area all round. Such a change had been obvious from the inadequate defensive armament of the earlier models, revealed in the Spanish Civil War, and the penalty of increased weight and drag was to some degree countered by a search for more powerful engines. The S prototype had DB 600 liquid-cooled engines, as did the Do 17U five-seat pathfinder, of which 12 were delivered to the nine Bomber Groups already using earlier Do 17s. The Do 17Z, powered by the Bramo radial engine, was at first underpowered and full bomb load had to await the more powerful Fafnir 323P of the 17Z-2. Between late 1939 and the summer of 1940 about 535 Do 17Z series bomber and reconnaissance machines were delivered and, though they suffered high attrition over Britain, they did much effective work and were the most popular and reliable of all Luftwaffe bombers of the early Blitzkrieg period. The Do 215 was the Do 17Z renumbered as an export version, with the more powerful DB 601 engine. The Do 215A-1 for Sweden became the Do 215B-0 and B-1 for the Luftwaffe and altogether 101 were put into service for bomber and reconnaissance roles; 12 were converted as Do 215B-5 night intruders, with a "solid" nose carrying two cannon and four machine guns, and operated by night over Britain before transfer to Sicily in October 1941.

*Above: One of the small group of Do 215B-1 reconnaissance aircraft put into service with the Luftwaffe in 1939-40 after an embargo had been placed on their export to Sweden*

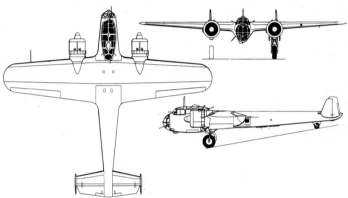

*Above: Three-view of the Do 17Z-2*

*Below: Do 17Z-2 of 15 (Kroat)/KG 53, lettered Al+EZ, over the Eastern Front central sector in autumn 1942. This unit was one of the Croatian volunteer squadrons*

# Dornier Do 15

**Do 15 (Militär Wal 33)**
**Origin:** Dornier Metallbauten GmbH, Friedrichshafen.
**Type:** Reconnaissance flying boat.
**Engines:** Two 750hp BMW VI 7·3 vee-12 water-cooled.
**Dimensions:** Span 76ft 1½in (23·19m); length 59ft 8½in (18·19m); height 18ft 0½in (5·50m).
**Weights:** Empty 11,872lb (5385kg); loaded 17,637lb (8000kg).
**Performance:** Maximum speed 137mph (220km/h); range 1,367 miles (2200km).

**Development:** The push/pull Dornier Wal (whale) was one of the best and most famous flying boats of the period between the great wars. Greatly improved in the ten years from 1923, it was adopted in 1933 as a standard multi-role machine by the Kommando der Fliegerschulen (See), some 30 being delivered for Luftwaffe use by 1935. Most had bow and dorsal MG 15s and four 110lb (50kg) bombs could be carried on wing racks. Survivors were replaced in first-line service by the Do 18 in 1938, thereafter serving as trainer and trials machines.

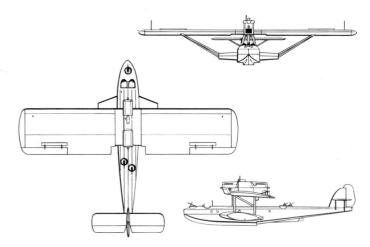

*Three-view of the Do 15 Militär-Wal*

# Dornier Do 19

**Do 19 V1 and V2**
**Origin:** Dornier-Werke GmbH.
**Type:** Strategic bomber.
**Engines:** Four 715hp Bramo (Siemens) 323H-2 Fafnir nine-cylinder radials.
**Dimensions:** Span 114ft 9¾in (35·00m); length 83ft 5¾in (25·4m); height 18ft 11½in (5·77m).
**Weights:** Empty 26,158lb (11,865kg); loaded 40,785lb (18,500kg).
**Performance:** Maximum speed 196mph (315km/h); max range 994 miles (1600km).

**Development:** Popularly called the Ural-bomber, the Do 19 was, with the Ju 89, the first long-range strategic bomber planned for the Luftwaffe. The V1, flown on 28 October 1936, was an efficient but rather severe machine, followed by the more powerful V2 (810hp BMW 132F radials) with two MG 15 machine guns, two cumbersome turrets with 20mm cannon and

*Upper: Air-to-air of the Do 19 V1, the sole prototype flown*

*Immediately above: The Do 19 V1 in civil trim, Dornier's contribution to the "Ural Bomber" test programme*

16 bombs of 220lb (100kg). But Gen Walther Wever, the strategic-minded Chief of Staff, was killed in April 1936, and his successor, Kesselring, thought the great effort needed for heavy bombers could be better put into tactical machines for Blitzkrieg wars. The programme was cancelled on 29 April 1937, against a background of heated argument.

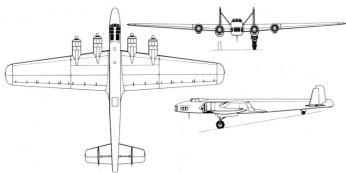

*Above: Three-view of the Do 19 V1, which had no armament*

# Dornier Do 22

**Do 22K and L**
**Origin:** AG für Dornier-Flugzeug, Altenrhein (Switzerland).
**Type:** Torpedo-bomber and recce seaplane (L, landplane).
**Engine:** 860hp Hispano-Suiza 12 Ybrs vee-12.
**Dimensions:** Span 53ft 1¾in (16·20m); length (K) 43ft 0½in (13·12m); height (K) 15ft 11in (4·85m).
**Weights:** (K) empty 5,733lb (2600kg); loaded 8,818lb (4000kg).
**Performance:** Maximum speed (K) 217mph (350km/h); max range (K) 1,429 miles (2300km).

*Above: Shown in German civil markings, this aircraft was the first Do 22L originally built against a Latvian contract*

**Development:** Though actually a substantial warplane of outstanding performance, the Do 22 was built in both German and Swiss factories of the Dornier company entirely for export to foreign customers. The Do 22Kg was sold to Greece, the Kj to Yugoslavia and the Kl to Latvia, most having three to five machine guns and a torpedo or heavy bomb load. The prototype flew in 1935, and deliveries were complete by 1939. A landplane prototype (22L) flew in March 1939.

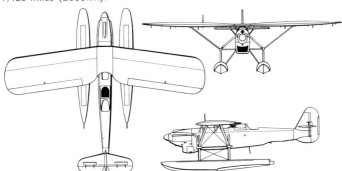

*Three-view of Do 22 as used by Finland and Yugoslavia*

# Dornier Do 23

**Do 13, 23F and G**
**Origin:** Dornier-Werke GmbH.
**Type:** Heavy bomber.
**Engines:** Two 750hp BMW VId vee-12 water-cooled, (G) 750hp BMW VIU liquid-cooled (ethylene glycol).
**Dimensions:** Span 83ft 8in (25·50m); length 61ft 8¼in (18·80m); height 17ft 8½in (5·40m).
**Weights:** Empty (G) 12,346lb (5600kg); maximum 20,282lb (9200kg).
**Performance:** Maximum speed (G) 161mph (259km/h); maximum range at 116mph (187km/h), 840 miles (1352km).
**Armament:** Three manually aimed 7·92mm MG 15 in nose, dorsal and ventral positions; internal bomb load of 2,205lb (1000kg).
**History:** First flight (13) 13 February 1933, (13e) 1 September 1934; service delivery (23F) May 1935.

**Development:** After the disastrous experience with the Do 11 it was only a slight improvement to fly the Do 13, and this in its turn suffered from unacceptable structural and handling faults. Eventually the restressed Do 13e was flown, with span further reduced, Junkers double-wing flaps/ailerons, BMW engines and all other Do 11/13 modifications that had been found to work. Though still no great bomber, at least the 13e was acceptable, so the 222 production-aircraft contract was transferred a second time. For psychological reasons the designation was changed to Do 23, and in 1935 deliveries began to the new Fliegergruppen. Nearly all the production machines — not 222 but 210 were built — were of the G sub-type with improved engine cooling-systems. Clearly Dornier-Werke, the newly formed German parent company, could deliver the lumbering machines at a high rate, because production was complete before 1936. By this time it was already on the way out of the Luftwaffe's new Kampfgruppen, and relegated to training and various utility tasks.

*By 1936 the Do 23 was serving with most of the new Luftwaffe Fliegergruppen, and these were restyled Kampfgruppen. These Do 23G bombers are serving II/KG 253 at Erfurt*

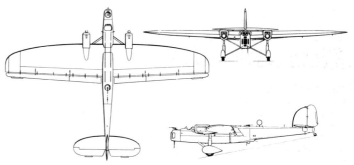

*Above: Three-view of Do 23G*

# Dornier Do 24

**Do 24T**
**Origin:** Dornier-Werke GmbH; production by Weser, Aviolanda and Potez-CAMS (SNCAN); post-war, CASA, Spain.
**Type:** Reconnaissance flying boat (typical crew, six).
**Engines:** Three 1,000hp Bramo Fafnir 323R-2 nine-cylinder radials.
**Dimensions:** Span 88ft 7in (27m); length 72ft 2in (22m): height 17ft 10in (5·45m).
**Weights:** Empty 29,700lb (13,500kg); loaded 40,565lb (18,400kg).
**Performance:** Maximum speed 211mph (340km/h); service ceiling 19,360ft (5900m); maximum range 2,950 miles (4750km).
**Armament:** One 7·92mm MG 15 machine gun in bow turret, one MG 15 in tail turret and one 20mm MG 151/20 or 30mm MK 103 cannon in dorsal turret behind wing; underwing racks for 12 110lb (50kg) bombs or other stores.
**History:** First flight (Do 24V3) 3 July 1937; service delivery (Do 24K) November 1937; withdrawal from service (Spain) 1967.

**Development:** This excellent trimotor flying boat was one of the very few aircraft of the Nazi period to be designed for a foreign government. The customer was the Netherlands and by 1940 a total of 11 had been built by Weserflugzeugbau and flown out to the Dutch East Indies naval air service (MLD). In addition, 26 more had been supplied by the Dutch de Schelde and Aviolanda companies, under a government-purchased licence. After the invasion of the Low Countries production was continued in Holland for the Luftwaffe, with the French Potez-CAMS factory at Sartrouville also assigned to Do 24 production in 1941. Production for the Luftwaffe

*Upper: A Dutch-built Do 24T-1 serving with one of the Seenotstaffeln (unit not identified)*

*Immediately above: Another Dutch-built Do 24T-1, the Luftwaffe receiving 170, plus 48 from France*

amounted to 170 in Holland and 48 in France and the type was met all round the European coasts. One force-landed in Sweden in 1944, was impressed into RSAF service as the Tp 24 and not surrendered to the USSR until 1951. After VE-day the CAMS factory continued in production, making a further 20 aircraft to augment ex-Luftwaffe machines for a force of more than 60 in Aéronavale service until 1955. The remaining aircraft were sold to Spain to augment an original force of 12 purchased from Germany in 1944. Designated HR-5, the Do 24T-3 in Spain and the Spanish Mediterranean and Atlantic islands was the last type of large military flying boat operating in Europe. Since 1969 Dornier has been seeking markets for the proposed Do 24/72 development, powered by three 1,800hp Lycoming turboprops.

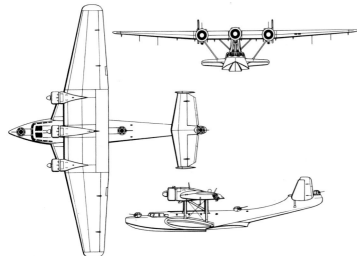

*Above: Three-view of the original Do 24K-2*

# Dornier Do 26

**Do 26 V1 to V6 (26D)**
**Origin:** Dornier-Werke GmbH.
**Type:** Transport/recce flying boat.
**Engine:** Four 880hp Junkers Jumo 205D diesels each with six double-ended cylinders and 12 opposed pistons.
**Dimensions:** Span 98ft 5¼in (30·00m); length 80ft 8½in (24·60m); height 22ft 5¾in (6·85m).
**Weights:** Empty (V6) 24,912lb (11,300kg); max loaded 49,601lb (22,500kg).
**Performance:** Maximum speed 201mph (324km/h); max range 4,412 miles (7100km).

**Development:** Contrasting markedly with previous Dornier boats, the trim and sleek Do 26 had a gull wing, retractable underwing floats, unbraced stressed-skin structure and four diesels in a push/pull arrangement with the rear propeller shafts hinged to raise the blades clear of spray on takeoff or landing. The first two were used by Lufthansa on the North Atlantic in 1938–39, but the last four were converted into military transport/

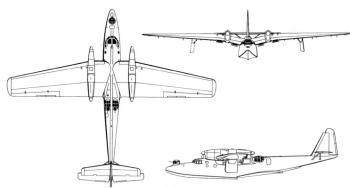

*Above: Three-view of the Do 26D-0*

recce aircraft, called Do 26D, with 20mm MG 151 bow turret and three aft-firing MG 15 machine guns and comprehensive military radio. All five flyable Do 26s participated in the Norwegian campaign, two being shot down by Hurricanes of 46 Sqn on 28 May 1940.

# Dornier Do 214

**Do 214 and 216**
**Origin:** Dornier-Werke GmbH.
**Type:** Do 214, transport flying boat; 216, ocean patrol flying boat.
**Engines:** Eight Daimler-Benz DB 613A double engines (2×DB 603), with total of 32,000hp.
**Dimensions:** Span 196ft 10¼in (60·00m); length (214) 169ft 3in (51·6m).
**Weight:** Loaded (214) 661,390lb (300,000kg).
**Performance:** Maximum speed 280mph (450km/h); max range 6,214 miles (10,000km).

**Development:** Designed in 1941 after tests with the Gö 8 scale model, the Do 214 exemplified the vast scale of German thinking — perhaps way beyond the true state of the aeronautical art. The original purpose was transatlantic passenger and mail service, but by 1942 this had changed to military transport, with a large bow door admitting vehicles and bulky freight to the upper deck. The Do 216 would have been slightly smaller, though with

similar power and gross weight, and would have been armed with 17 MG 151 20mm cannon in eight power turrets (the tail turret having three guns). No Do 214 was completed.

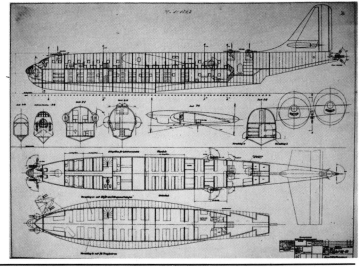

*Right: One of the few Dornier works drawings showing the projected layout of the Do 216, which was not built. Smaller than the immense 214, it would have 17 cannon, four of them in twin turrets in the hinged nose which was intended to admit heavy cargo or weapons*

# Dornier Do 317

**Do 317 V1, V2 and B**
**Origin:** Dornier-Werke GmbH.
**Type:** High-altitude bomber.
**Engines:** (V1, V2) two 1,750hp Daimler-Benz DB 603A inverted-vee-12; (B) two 2,870hp DB 610A/B double engines (2×DB 605).
**Dimensions:** Span (most) 67ft 8¼in (20·65m), (B) 85ft 0in (25·90m); length 55ft 1½in (16·80m); height 17ft 10½in (5·45m).
**Weights:** Empty, not known; loaded (B) 52,910lb (24,000kg).
**Performance:** Maximum speed (V1) 373mph (600km/h), (B) 416mph (670km/h); range (B, without auxiliary bomb-bay tank) 2,237 miles (3600km).

**Development:** This impressive machine was planned in 1939 to meet the Bomber B specification, but in 1940 work was shelved to enable high-altitude effort to be concentrated on the 217P. In 1941 the 317 was resurrected and offered in two versions, the A being a pressurized 217 with new fuselage and internal bomb load of six 1,102lb (500kg) bombs, and the B having long-span wing, more powerful engines, remote-control barbette cannon and very heavy bomb load of up to 12,346lb (5600kg) internal, plus

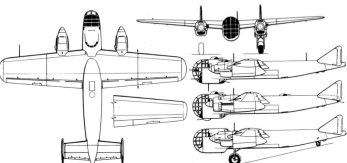

*Above: Three-view of Do 317 V1 with additional side views of Do 317A (top) and 317B (centre)*

two 3,968lb (1800kg) bombs on wing racks. Eventually six prototypes were built, only the first having the pressure cabin; the other five were redesignated Do 217R and sent to III/KG 100 at Orléans-Bricy to launch Hs 293 missiles. The 317 programme was abandoned.

*Below: The Do 317 V1, the first prototype*

# Dornier Do 217

**Do 217E-2, K-2, M-1, J-2/N-2, P-1**

**Origin:** Dornier-Werke GmbH.

**Type:** (E, K, M) four-seat bomber; (J, N) three-seat night fighter; (P) four-seat high-altitude reconnaissance.

**Engines:** (E-2, J-2) two 1,580hp BMW 801A or 801M 18-cylinder two-row radials; (K-2) two 1,700hp BMW 801D; (M-1, N-2) two 1,750hp Daimler-Benz DB 603A 12-cylinder inverted-vee liquid cooled; (P-1) two 1,860hp DB 603B supercharged by DB 605T in the fuselage.

**Dimensions:** Span 62ft 4in (19m); (K-2) 81ft 4½in (24·8m); (P-1) 80ft 4in (24·4m); length 56ft 9¼in (17·3m); (E-2 with early dive brakes) 60ft 10½in (18·5m); (K-2 and M-1) 55ft 9in (17m); (J and N) 58ft 9in (17·9); (P) 58ft 11in (17·95m); height 16ft 5in (5m) (all versions same within 2in).

**Weights:** Empty (E-2) 19,522lb (8850kg); (M-1) 19,985 (9000kg); (K-2, J and N) all about 21,000lb (9450kg); (P) about 23,000lb (10,350kg); loaded (E-2) 33,070lb (15,000kg); (K-2, M-1) 36,817lb (16,570kg); (J and N) 30,203lb (13,590kg); (P) 35,200lb (15,840kg).

**Performance:** Maximum speed (E-2) 320mph (515km/h); (K-2) 333mph (533km/h); (M-1) 348mph (557km/h); (J and N) about 311mph (498km/h); (P) 488mph (781km/h); service ceiling (E-2) 24,610ft (7500m); (K-2) 29,530ft (9000m); (M-1) 24,140ft (7358m); (J and N) 27,560ft (8400m); (P) 53,000ft (16,154m); range with full bomb load, about 1,300 miles (2100km) for all versions.

**Armament:** (E-2) one fixed 15mm MG 151/15 in nose, one 13mm MG 131 in dorsal turret, one MG 131 manually aimed at lower rear, and three 7·92mm MG 15 manually aimed in nose and beam windows; maximum bomb load 8,818lb (4000kg), including 3,307lb (1500kg) external; (K-2) defensive armament similar to E-2, plus battery of four 7·92mm MG 81 fixed rearward-firing in tail and optional pair fixed rearward-firing in

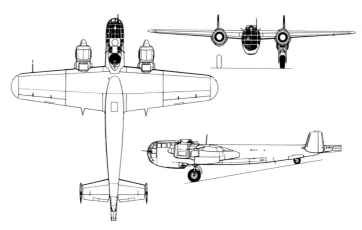

*Above: Three-view of Do 217K-1*

nacelles (all sighted and fired by pilot), and offensive load of two FX 1400 radio controlled glide bombs and/or (K-3 version) two Hs 293 air-to-surface rocket guided missiles; (M-1) as E-2 except MG 15s replaced by larger number of MG 81; (J-2 and N-2) typically four 20mm MG FF cannon and four 7·92mm MG 17 in nose plus MG 131 for lower rear defence (N-2 often had later guns such as MG 151/20 in nose and MG 151/20 or MK 108 30mm in Schräge Musik upward-firing installation) (P) three pairs of MG 81 for defence, and two 1,102lb bombs on underwing racks.

*continued on page 150* ▶

*Below: The long-span sub-type of the redesigned K-series, the Do 217K-2. This carried the FX-1400 guided bomb*

*Left: Do 217E-5 of 6/KG 100 at Istres, with Hs 293 missiles. (See also pages 64-65)*

*Right: Do 217E-2/R19 of 9/KG 2 at Gilze-Rijen in 1941*

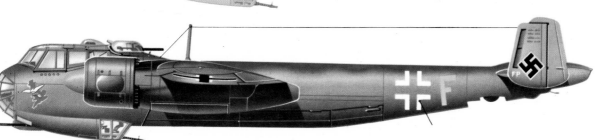

*Left: Do 217E-2 of 6/KG 40 at Merignac in 1942*

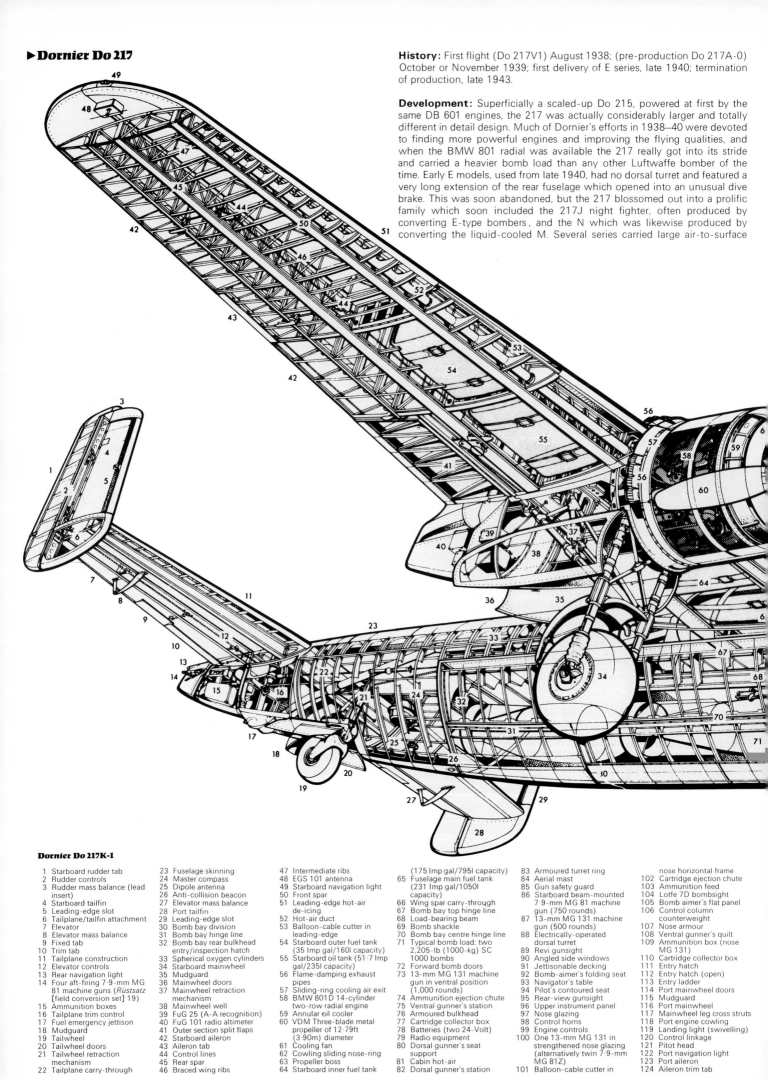

# ▶ Dornier Do 217

**History:** First flight (Do 217V1) August 1938; (pre-production Do 217A-0) October or November 1939; first delivery of E series, late 1940; termination of production, late 1943.

**Development:** Superficially a scaled-up Do 215, powered at first by the same DB 601 engines, the 217 was actually considerably larger and totally different in detail design. Much of Dornier's efforts in 1938–40 were devoted to finding more powerful engines and improving the flying qualities, and when the BMW 801 radial was available the 217 really got into its stride and carried a heavier bomb load than any other Luftwaffe bomber of the time. Early E models, used from late 1940, had no dorsal turret and featured a very long extension of the rear fuselage which opened into an unusual dive brake. This was soon abandoned, but the 217 blossomed out into a prolific family which soon included the 217J night fighter, often produced by converting E-type bombers, and the N which was likewise produced by converting the liquid-cooled M. Several series carried large air-to-surface

## Dornier Do 217K-1

1 Starboard rudder tab
2 Rudder controls
3 Rudder mass balance (lead insert)
4 Starboard tailfin
5 Leading-edge slot
6 Tailplane/tailfin attachment
7 Elevator
8 Elevator mass balance
9 Fixed tab
10 Trim tab
11 Tailplane construction
12 Elevator controls
13 Rear navigation light
14 Four aft-firing 7·9-mm MG 81 machine guns (*Rüstsatz* [field conversion set] 19)
15 Ammunition boxes
16 Tailplane trim control
17 Fuel emergency jettison
18 Mudguard
19 Tailwheel
20 Tailwheel doors
21 Tailwheel retraction mechanism
22 Tailplane carry-through

23 Fuselage skinning
24 Master compass
25 Dipole antenna
26 Anti-collision beacon
27 Elevator mass balance
28 Port tailfin
29 Leading-edge slot
30 Bomb bay division
31 Bomb bay hinge line
32 Bomb bay rear bulkhead entry/inspection hatch
33 Spherical oxygen cylinders
34 Starboard mainwheel
35 Mudguard
36 Mainwheel doors
37 Mainwheel retraction mechanism
38 Mainwheel well
39 FuG 25 (A-A recognition)
40 FuG 101 radio altimeter
41 Outer section split flaps
42 Starboard aileron
43 Aileron tab
44 Control lines
45 Rear spar
46 Braced wing ribs

47 Intermediate ribs
48 EGS 101 antenna
49 Starboard navigation light
50 Front spar
51 Leading-edge hot-air de-icing
52 Hot-air duct
53 Balloon-cable cutter in leading-edge
54 Starboard outer fuel tank (35 Imp gal/160l capacity)
55 Starboard oil tank (51·7 Imp gal/235l capacity)
56 Flame-damping exhaust pipes
57 Sliding-ring cooling air exit
58 BMW 801D 14-cylinder two-row radial engine
59 Annular oil cooler
60 VDM Three-blade metal propeller of 12·79ft (3·90m) diameter
61 Cooling fan
62 Cowling sliding nose-ring
63 Propeller boss
64 Starboard inner fuel tank

(175 Imp gal/795l capacity)
65 Fuselage main fuel tank (231 Imp gal/1050l capacity)
66 Wing spar carry-through
67 Bomb bay top hinge line
68 Load-bearing beam
69 Bomb shackle
70 Bomb bay centre hinge line
71 Typical bomb load: two 2,205-lb (1000-kg) SC 1000 bombs
72 Forward bomb doors
73 13-mm MG 131 machine gun in ventral position (1,000 rounds)
74 Ammunition ejection chute
75 Ventral gunner's station
76 Armoured bulkhead
77 Cartridge collector box
78 Batteries (two 24-Volt)
79 Radio equipment
80 Dorsal gunner's seat support
81 Cabin hot-air
82 Dorsal gunner's station

83 Armoured turret ring
84 Aerial mast
85 Gun safety guard
86 Starboard beam-mounted 7·9-mm MG 81 machine gun (750 rounds)
87 13-mm MG 131 machine gun (500 rounds)
88 Electrically-operated dorsal turret
89 Revi gunsight
90 Angled side windows
91 Jettisonable decking
92 Bomb-aimer's folding seat
93 Navigator's table
94 Pilot's contoured seat
95 Rear-view gunsight
96 Upper instrument panel
97 Nose glazing
98 Control horns
99 Engine controls
100 One 13-mm MG 131 in strengthened nose glazing (alternatively twin 7·9-mm MG 81Z)
101 Balloon-cable cutter in

nose horizontal frame
102 Cartridge ejection chute
103 Ammunition feed
104 Lotfe 7D bombsight
105 Bomb aimer's flat panel
106 Control column counterweight
107 Nose armour
108 Ventral gunner's quilt
109 Ammunition box (nose MG 131)
110 Cartridge collector box
111 Entry hatch
112 Entry hatch (open)
113 Entry ladder
114 Port mainwheel doors
115 Mudguard
116 Port mainwheel
117 Mainwheel leg cross struts
118 Port engine cowling
119 Landing light (swivelling)
120 Control linkage
121 Pitot head
122 Port navigation light
123 Port aileron
124 Aileron trim tab

150

missiles steered by radio command from a special crew station in the bomber. Long-span K-2s of III/KG 100 scored many successes with their formidable missiles in the Mediterranean, their biggest bag being the Italian capital ship *Roma* as she steamed to the Allies after Italy's capitulation. The pressurised high-altitude P series had fantastic performances that would have put them out of reach of any Allied fighters had they been put into service in time. From 1943, Dornier devoted more effort to the technically difficult Do 317, which never went into service.

The bomb bay of bomber Do 217s was 14ft 10in (4·52m) long, and was closed by three sets of doors. With a special extension this bay could even accommodate a torpedo internally (some versions, two), which still remains a rare thing in aviation history. Almost all services were electric, and though this made the aircraft extremely complex the reliability soon reached a satisfactory standard. Local modifications, such as fixed slats along the leading edges of the fins, helped to improve the flight stability, and by the winter 1940–41 the first E-series were entering service with KG 40 as long-range

reconnaissance bombers with a fair measure of enthusiasm. The only lingering problem was that structural strain and even loss of control attended the use of the E-series as a steep dive bomber, using the tail brake, and by autumn 1941 this role had been abandoned. Thereafter most 217 bombers made level deliveries, with guided missiles such as the Hs 293 and FX 1400 becoming ever more prominent.

From early 1941 the Do 217 was developed as both a multi-role bomber and a night fighter and intruder. The first fighters were 217J-1 conversions of E-2 bombers, with a "solid" nose packed with guns and a rear bomb bay carrying light bombs. Later various radar installations were fitted, especially Lichtenstein FuG 202 or 212 with their prominent aerial arrays. It was not an ideal night fighter, being big and heavy and needing a good long runway, and at first the speed and obsolescent MG FF cannon were not inspiring. Later, by 1943 NJG (night-fighter wings) converted to the Do 217N series with liquid-cooled DB 603 engines like the M-series bombers. These had the newer MG 151 cannon, and largely through the missionary work of Experte (ace) Oberleutnant Schönert the 217 was one of the first aircraft to carry the deadly Schräge Musik armament of guns mounted firing diagonally upwards. Many were thus converted into the 217N-2/R22, with four MG 151 firing up at 70°. Most of the 217J-2 aircraft were passed to Italy in 1943.

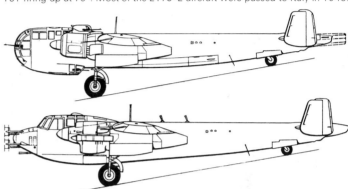

*Above: Side views of Do 217 K-1 and Do 217 N-2*

**Above: The sixth pre-production Do 217E-0, which was retained by Bayerische Motorenwerke for engine-development purposes**

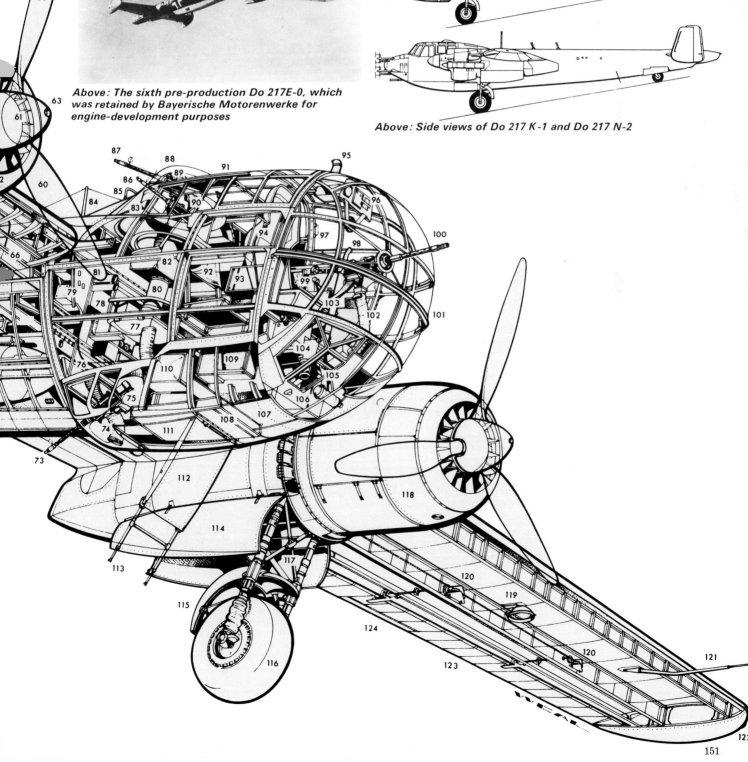

# Dornier Do 335 Pfeil and Do 635

## Do 335A-1 and A-6

**Origin:** Dornier-Werke GmbH.
**Type:** (A-1) single-seat fighter, (A-6) two-seat night fighter.
**Engines:** Two 1,900hp Daimler-Benz DB 603G 12-cylinder inverted-vee liquid-cooled, in push/pull arrangement.
**Dimensions:** Span 45ft 4in (13·8m); length 45ft 6in (13·87m); height 16ft 4in (4m).
**Weights:** Empty (A-1) 16,314lb (7400kg); (A-6) 16,975lb (7700kg); maximum loaded (both) 25,800lb (11,700kg).

**Performance:** Maximum speed (A-1) 413mph (665km/h) sustained, 477mph (765km/h) emergency boost (A-6 about 40mph slower in each case); initial climb (A-1) 4,600ft (1400m)/min; service ceiling (A-1) 37,400ft (11,410m); (A-6) 33,400ft (10,190m); maximum range (both) 1,280 miles (2050km) clean, up to 2,330 miles (3750km) with drop tank.
**Armament:** Typical A-1, one 30mm MK 103 cannon firing through front propeller hub and two 15mm MG 151/15 above nose; underwing racks for light stores and centreline rack for 1,100lb (500kg) bomb; A-6 did not carry bomb and usually had 15mm guns replaced by 20mm MG 151/20s.

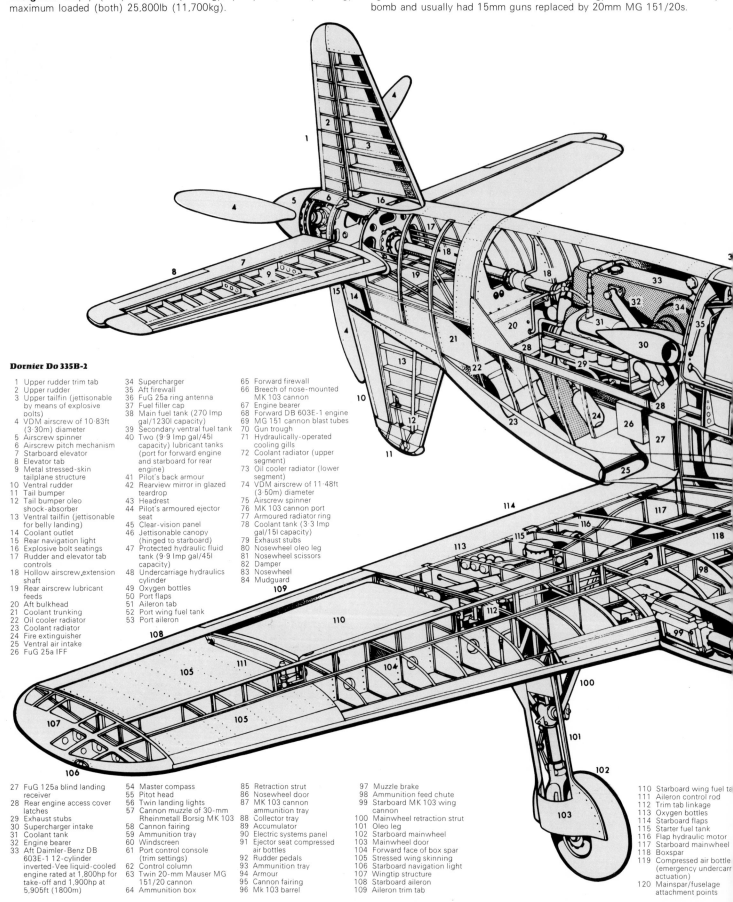

**Dornier Do 335B-2**

1 Upper rudder trim tab
2 Upper rudder
3 Upper tailfin (jettisonable by means of explosive bolts)
4 VDM airscrew of 10·83ft (3·30m) diameter
5 Airscrew spinner
6 Airscrew pitch mechanism
7 Starboard elevator
8 Elevator tab
9 Metal stressed-skin tailplane structure
10 Ventral rudder
11 Tail bumper
12 Tail bumper oleo shock-absorber
13 Ventral tailfin (jettisonable for belly landing)
14 Coolant outlet
15 Rear navigation light
16 Explosive bolt seatings
17 Rudder and elevator tab controls
18 Hollow airscrew extension shaft
19 Rear airscrew lubricant feeds
20 Aft bulkhead
21 Coolant trunking
22 Oil cooler radiator
23 Coolant radiator
24 Fire extinguisher
25 Ventral air intake
26 FuG 25a IFF

27 FuG 125a blind landing receiver
28 Rear engine access cover latches
29 Exhaust stubs
30 Supercharger intake
31 Coolant tank
32 Engine bearer
33 Aft Daimler-Benz DB 603E-1 12-cylinder inverted-Vee liquid-cooled engine rated at 1,800hp for take-off and 1,900hp at 5,905ft (1800m)

34 Supercharger
35 Aft firewall
36 FuG 25a ring antenna
37 Fuel filler cap
38 Main fuel tank (270 Imp gal/1230l capacity)
39 Secondary ventral fuel tank
40 Two (9·9 Imp gal/45l capacity) lubricant tanks (port for forward engine and starboard for rear engine)
41 Pilot's back armour
42 Rearview mirror in glazed teardrop
43 Headrest
44 Pilot's armoured ejector seat
45 Clear-vision panel
46 Jettisonable canopy (hinged to starboard)
47 Protected hydraulic fluid tank (9·9 Imp gal/45l capacity)
48 Undercarriage hydraulics cylinder
49 Oxygen bottles
50 Port flaps
51 Aileron tab
52 Port wing fuel tank
53 Port aileron

54 Master compass
55 Pitot head
56 Twin landing lights
57 Cannon muzzle of 30-mm Rheinmetall Borsig MK 103
58 Cannon fairing
59 Ammunition tray
60 Windscreen
61 Port control console (trim settings)
62 Control column
63 Twin 20-mm Mauser MG 151/20 cannon
64 Ammunition box

65 Forward firewall
66 Breech of nose-mounted MK 103 cannon
67 Engine bearer
68 Forward DB 603E-1 engine
69 MG 151 cannon blast tubes
70 Gun trough
71 Hydraulically-operated cooling gills
72 Coolant radiator (upper segment)
73 Oil cooler radiator (lower segment)
74 VDM airscrew of 11·48ft (3·50m) diameter
75 Airscrew spinner
76 MK 103 cannon port
77 Armoured radiator ring
78 Coolant tank (3·3 Imp gal/15l capacity)
79 Exhaust stubs
80 Nosewheel oleo leg
81 Nosewheel scissors
82 Damper
83 Nosewheel
84 Mudguard

85 Retraction strut
86 Nosewheel door
87 MK 103 cannon ammunition tray
88 Collector tray
89 Accumulator
90 Electric systems panel
91 Ejector seat compressed air bottles
92 Rudder pedals
93 Ammunition tray
94 Armour
95 Cannon fairing
96 Mk 103 barrel

97 Muzzle brake
98 Ammunition feed chute
99 Starboard MK 103 wing cannon
100 Mainwheel retraction strut
101 Oleo leg
102 Starboard mainwheel
103 Mainwheel door
104 Forward face of box spar
105 Stressed wing skinning
106 Starboard navigation light
107 Wingtip structure
108 Starboard aileron
109 Aileron trim tab

110 Starboard wing fuel ta
111 Aileron control rod
112 Trim tab linkage
113 Oxygen bottles
114 Starboard flaps
115 Starter fuel tank
116 Flap hydraulic motor
117 Starboard mainwheel
118 Boxspar
119 Compressed air bottle (emergency undercarr actuation)
120 Mainspar/fuselage attachment points

**History:** First flight (Do 335V1) autumn 1943; (production A-1) late November 1944.

**Development:** Dornier took out a patent in 1937 for an aircraft powered by two engines, one behind the other, in the fuselage, driving tractor and pusher propellers. In 1939–40 Schempp-Hirth built the Gö 9 research aircraft to test the concept of a rear propeller driven by an extension shaft and in 1941 work began on the Do 231 fighter-bomber. This was replaced by the Do 335 and by first flight Dornier had orders for 14 prototypes, ten preproduction A-0s, 11 production A-1s and three dual-control trainer A-10 and A-12 with stepped tandem cockpits. At high speed the 335 was prone to unpleasant porpoising and snaking, but production continued on the A-1, the A-4 reconnaissance batch and the A-6 with FuG 220 radar operated by a rear-seat observer. Though heavy, the 335 was strong and very fast and was notable in having the first production type of ejection seat (for obvious reasons). By VE-day about 90 aircraft had been rolled out, more than 60 flown and about 20 delivered to combat units. Work was also well advanced on a number of versions of the Do 335B heavy fighter, with added 30mm MK 108 cannon in the wings (some having two-stage engines and long-span wings), the Do 435 with various very powerful engines, and the twinned Do 635 with two Do 335 fuselages linked by a new parallel centre-section. The 635, which was being designed and produced by Junkers as the 8-635, would have weighed 72,000lb as a recon-

continued on page 154 ▶

*This shiny but rather "phoney" aircraft is a genuine 335 which, after 25 years in the USA, was restored by Dornier*

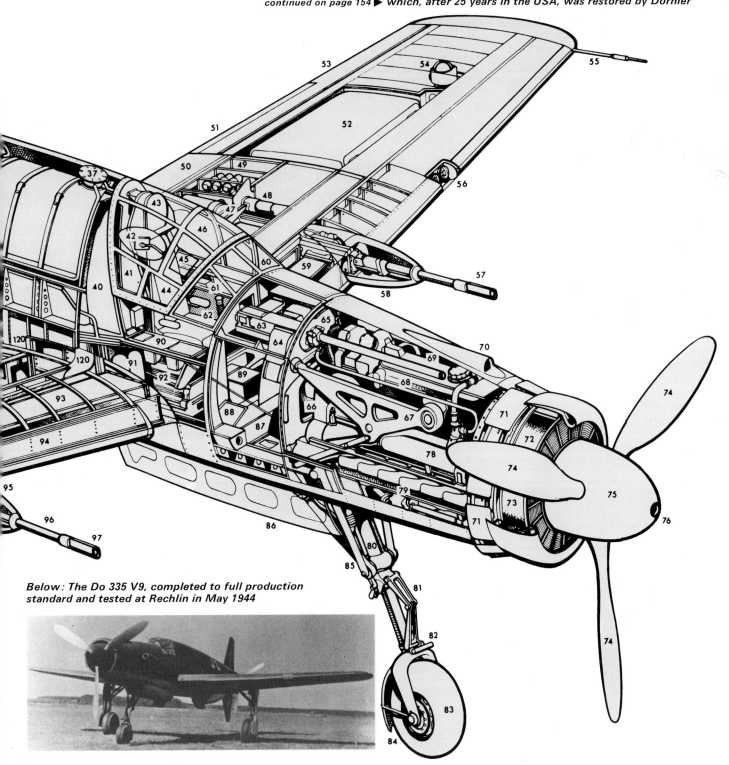

*Below: The Do 335 V9, completed to full production standard and tested at Rechlin in May 1944*

### ▶Dornier Do 335 Pfeil

naissance aircraft, and flown 4,050 miles cruising at 398mph. Pfeil means "arrow".

To create the 335 Dornier had to solve many severe problems, not least of which was the aerodynamic interference from the two propellers, the rear being higher. The tractor propeller had reverse-pitch blades, one of the first ever put into production, and the rear gearbox was coupled to a long extension shaft. Another fairly new feature was the tricycle landing gear, pilots being instructed to land nose-high and slow down before letting the nose gear gently on to the runway. All models had a large ventral fin to protect the pusher propeller, and this scraped on the ground in a normal landing. The main assembly line was at Oberpfaffenhofen, where Dornier today builds the Alpha Jet. Despite crippling shortages of vital items, a large number of different prototypes flew in the final year of the war, most having similar engine installations but with one or two seats, different armament and many having night-fighter radar. By late 1944 effort had transferred from the planned A-series fighter/bomber to the B-series defence interceptor, and many sub-types in this Zerstörer category (a kind of Bf 110 replacement) were soon in the works. Heinkel produced a long-span wing for single- and two-seat B-models to improve high-altitude qualities, but this new wing did not fly.

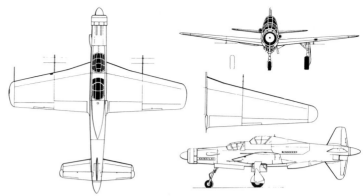

*Above: Three-view of the Do 335A-6 two seat night-fighter, with extended wing of the B-8 (inset)*

*Below: The Do 335 V3, like the second prototype, differed in many respects from the V1 flown in October 1943. Most Do 335s were prototypes*

# Fieseler Fi 98

### Fi 98a

**Origin:** Gerhard Fieseler Werke GmbH.
**Type:** Dive bomber.
**Engine:** 650hp BMW 132A-3 nine-cylinder radial.
**Dimensions:** Span 37ft 8¾in (11·50m); length 24ft 3½in (7·40m); height 9ft 10in (3·00m).
**Weights:** Empty 3,197lb (1450kg); loaded 4,762lb (2160kg).
**Performance:** Maximum speed 183mph (295km/h); range 292 miles (470km).

**Development:** This trim two-bay biplane was Fieseler's attempt to win the Sofort stage of the RLM dive-bomber programme. Planned in 1933, this stage called for a state-of-the-art biplane as a stop-gap until a really formidable forward-thinking dive bomber could be created. From the start the Hs 123 was favoured, only two Fi 98 prototypes were ordered as a back-up and the second was never completed. Planned armament was two synchronized MG 17, and four 110lb (50kg) bombs could be carried under the lower wing.

*The Fi 98a was the unsuccessful competitor to the Hs 123 in the 1935 search for a "Sofort" interim dive-bomber for the new Luftwaffe. Later the Ju 87 became predominant.*

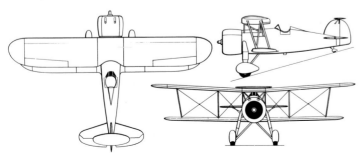

*Three-view of the single Fi 98a*

# Fieseler Fi 167

**Fi 167 V1 and A-0 series**
**Origin:** Gerhard Fieseler Werke GmbH.
**Type:** Carrier-based torpedo and recce aircraft.
**Engine:** 1,100hp Daimler-Benz DB 601B inverted-vee-12.
**Dimensions:** Span 44ft 3½in (13·50m); length 37ft 4¾in (11·40m); height 15ft 9in (4·80m).
**Weights:** Empty 6,173lb (2800kg); loaded 10,690lb (4850kg).
**Performance:** Maximum speed 202mph (325km/h); range with drop tank 808 miles (1300km).

**Development:** Designed as the standard aircraft in its class for the carrier *Graf Zeppelin,* the Fi 167 was as outstanding as its rival, the Ar 195, was not. It surpassed the requirement in every respect, carrying double the specified offensive load at higher speed. Low-speed performance was breathtaking: on one occasion Fieseler himself sank from 9,800ft to 100ft whilst remaining

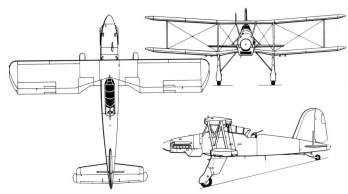

*Three-view of Fi 167A-0*

exactly over the same spot, under full control. Eventually 12 A-0 series aircraft followed the prototype but with no carrier they did coastal work in the Netherlands in 1940—43 and finally served as hacks or were sold to Romania. The 167 was a large dragonfly-like aircraft, which could have been an extremely valuable tactical machine.

*Below: A pleasing study of an Fi 167A-0, probably whilst serving with Erprobungsstaffel 167*

# Fieseler Fi 103

**Fi 103 in four Reichenberg series**
**Origin:** Gerhard Fieseler Werke GmbH, with DFS for piloted programme.
**Type:** Manned air/surface missile or conversion trainer.
**Engine:** Powered models, 660lb (300kg) thrust Argus 109-014 pulsejet impulse duct.
**Dimensions:** Span 18ft 9in (5·715m); length 26ft 3in (8·00m); body diameter 33·0in (838mm).
**Weights:** R.IV, loaded, 4,960lb (2250kg).
**Performance:** Maximum speed (typical) 400mph (645km/h); target approach, about 497mph (800km/h); range from launch at 8,200ft (2500m) about 205 miles (330km).

**Development:** It was in 1943 that a growing clique, led by the famed Flugkapitän Hanna Reitsch (the slim girl who did many of the trickiest test-flying programmes) and SS-Hauptsturmführer Otto Skorzeny (who led the small band that rescued Mussolini from his mountain-top prison), suggested there should be a piloted version of the Fi 103, better known around the world as the V-1 or the Doodlebug. At first such a desperate weapon was deemed unacceptable on political grounds, but in June 1944 the situation itself had become desperate. Within 14 days of go-ahead being sanctioned the DFS at Ainring had completed training and operational variants and testing was in progress. Piloted trials began in September, a disastrous start being rectified when Fraulein Reitsch took a hand, though even she had one major crash and several near misses. Reichenberg I was an unpowered single-seater with landing skid and flaps. Reichenberg II was a trainer with instructor in place of the warhead. R.III was a powered single-seat trainer, and R.IV the operational weapon with engine, warhead, nose fuze and no landing skid. Launched from an He 111, the R.IV was intended to be aimed at its target by the pilot who would bail out in the final seconds, but his chances were slim indeed. The user was to be 5/KG 200, but with 175 missiles on hand none was fired in anger.

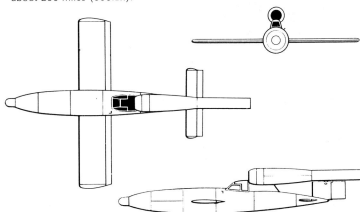

*Three-view of Fi 103 Reichenberg IV (operational type)*

*A Reichenberg IV missile before fitment of the nose fuze*

# Fieseler Fi 156 Storch and Fi 256

**Fi 156A, C, D, E, Fi 256**
**Origin:** Gerhard Fieseler Werke GmbH, Kassel; production almost entirely by Morane-Saulnier, Puteaux, and Benes-Mraz, Czechoslovakia.
**Type:** STOL multi-role, see text.
**Engine:** (Almost all) 240hp Argus As 10C inverted-vee-8 aircooled; certain sub-types used other As 10 models of 260 or 270hp.
**Dimensions:** Span 46ft 9in (14·25m); length 32ft 5¾in (9·90m); height 9ft 10in (3·00m).

**Weights:** (Typical C) empty 2,050lb (930kg); maximum 2,910lb (1320kg).
**Performance:** Maximum speed 109mph (175km/h); minimum speed 32mph (51km/h); ground run (takeoff) 213ft (65m), (landing) 61ft (20m); range (max payload) 236 miles (380km), (max fuel) 600 miles at 60mph (966km at 97mph).
**History:** First flight May 1936; service delivery, about May 1937; final delivery (France) 1949.

**Development:** Though only about 2,700 Storch (Stork) were built for the Axis, 2,549 of them during the war, it was used on every European front and for a vast range of duties. It beat two aeroplanes and a helicopter in a 1935 RLM competition for a STOL army co-op, casevac and liaison machine. It was the first machine of its type in the world, with substantial size, more power than in most lightplanes, and fantastic STOL capabilities. In 1936 Udet hovered the prototype motionless in a light breeze. By 1939

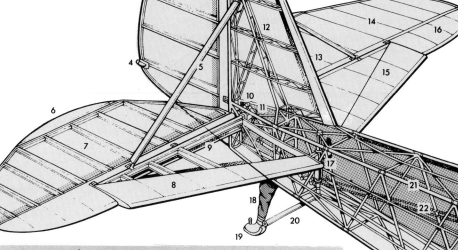

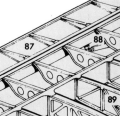

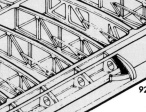

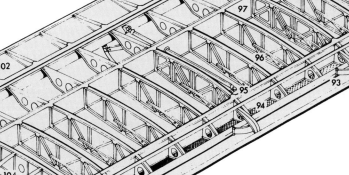

*An early production Fi 156C-1. Nearly all subsequent aircraft of this class were similar*

75

the main version, the 156C, was appearing in several forms, the C-1 being the standard staff aircraft flown by, or for, all leading staff officers. This was also the usual model issued to combat geschwader and other military formations, and it could mount a 7·92mm MG 15 at the upper rear of the

large cabin. There was room for three (six in emergency), but most had only two seats. The side windows were wider than the rest of the fuselage, so that a small lower row could give vertical downwards vision. Another important series were the D sub-types with large side doors for a stretcher. Morane-Saulnier developed the wide five-seat Fi 256, but flew only two before the Germans departed. In 1944 Morane continued production, the post-war MS.500 Criquet having a Salmson radial. Mraz likewise kept building a version called K-65 Cap.

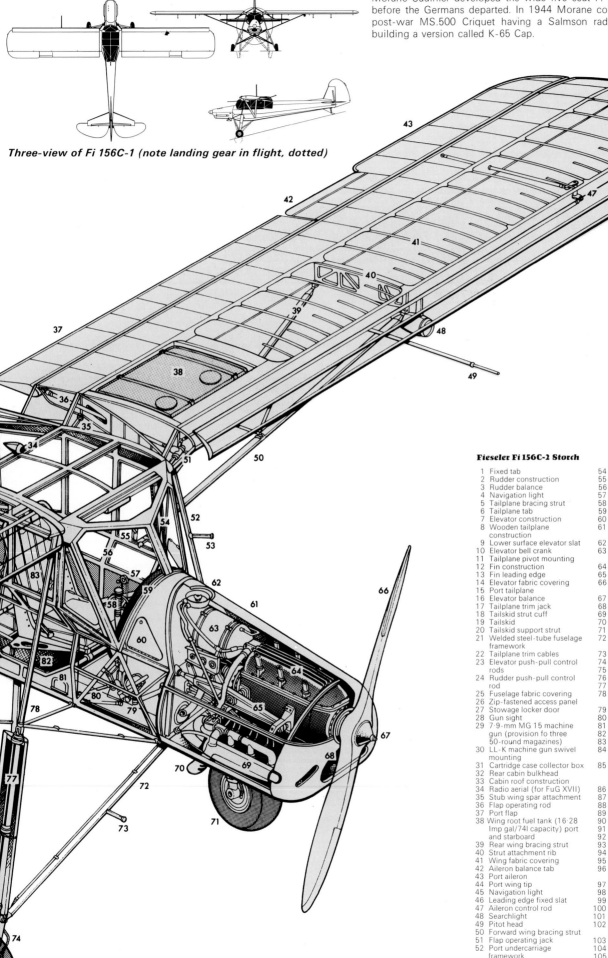

**Three-view of Fi 156C-1 (note landing gear in flight, dotted)**

### Fieseler Fi 156C-2 Storch

1 Fixed tab
2 Rudder construction
3 Rudder balance
4 Navigation light
5 Tailplane bracing strut
6 Tailplane tab
7 Elevator construction
8 Wooden tailplane construction
9 Lower surface elevator slat
10 Elevator bell crank
11 Tailplane pivot mounting
12 Fin construction
13 Fin leading edge
14 Elevator fabric covering
15 Port tailplane
16 Elevator balance
17 Tailplane trim jack
18 Tailskid strut cuff
19 Tailskid
20 Tailskid support strut
21 Welded steel-tube fuselage framework
22 Tailplane trim cables
23 Elevator push-pull control rods
24 Rudder push-pull control rod
25 Fuselage fabric covering
26 Zip-fastened access panel
27 Stowage locker door
28 Gun sight
29 7·9-mm MG 15 machine gun (provision fo three 50-round magazines)
30 LL-K machine gun swivel mounting
31 Cartridge case collector box
32 Rear cabin bulkhead
33 Cabin roof construction
34 Radio aerial (for FuG XVII)
35 Stub wing spar attachment
36 Flap operating rod
37 Port flap
38 Wing root fuel tank (16·28 Imp gal/74l capacity) port and starboard
39 Rear wing bracing strut
40 Strut attachment rib
41 Wing fabric covering
42 Aileron balance tab
43 Port aileron
44 Port wing tip
45 Navigation light
46 Leading edge fixed slat
47 Aileron control rod
48 Searchlight
49 Pitot head
50 Forward wing bracing strut
51 Flap operating jack
52 Port undercarriage framework
53 Access step
54 Windscreen
55 Compass
56 Downward vision windows
57 Trim control
58 Control column
59 Instrument panel shroud
60 Instrument access panel
61 Engine cowlings, detachable
62 Oil tank filler
63 Engine oil tank (2·42 Imp gal/11l capacity)
64 Argus As 10C-3 engine
65 Engine mounting beam
66 Schwarz two-blade fixed-pitch wooden propeller
67 Propeller boss
68 Air intake
69 Exhaust pipe fairing duct
70 Starboard exhaust pipe
71 Port mainwheel
72 Main undercarriage side stay
73 Access step
74 Brake pipe
75 Starboard mainwheel
76 Main undercarriage leg
77 Shock absorber strut
78 Undercarriage mounting framework
79 Rudder pedal
80 Control rod linkage
81 Entry step
82 Cabin door
83 Pilot's seat
84 Observer's/gunner's seat
85 Ammunition magazines (two of 50-round capacity)
86 Starboard flap
87 Plywood flap construction
88 Flap hinge
89 Lattice ribs
90 Wing bracing Vee struts
91 Strut supporting framework
92 Leading edge fixed slat
93 Slat attachment
94 Leading edge construction
95 Aileron control rod linkage
96 Fabric bracing strips between ribs
97 Wooden main spar
98 Aileron hinge
99 Aileron balance weight
100 Balance tab
101 Starboard aileron
102 Plywood aileron construction
103 Aileron outer hinge
104 Wing tip construction
105 Navigation light

# Flettner Fl 282 Kolibri

**Fl 282 prototypes and 282A**
**Origin:** Anton Flettner GmbH.
**Type:** Observation helicopter.
**Engine:** 160hp BMW-Bramo Sh 14A seven-cylinder radial.
**Dimensions:** Diameter of each two-blade main rotor 39ft 2¾in (11·96m); fuselage length 21ft 6¼in (6·56m); height 7ft 2½in (2·20m).
**Weights:** Empty (B) 1,675lb (760kg); loaded 2,205lb (1000kg).
**Performance:** Maximum speed 93mph (150km/h); range (pilot only) 186 miles (300km).

**Development:** First helicopter in mass production in the world, the Kolibri (humming-bird) was an excellent intermeshing-rotor machine used from surface ships and for various land-based programmes. Derived from the Fl 265 (which in 1941 avoided a Bf 109 and Fw 190 in mock combat) the 282 was in service from 1942.

*Above: An Fl 282B Kolibri (aircraft V21) as deployed aboard Kriegsmarine ships*

*Right: Production Fl 282B Kolibris awaiting collection from one of the Flettner factories (Johannisthal or Bad Tölz). The only helicopter in the world to have played a significant role in World War II, the Kolibri served mainly with transport and liaison staffeln, especially Luft-Transportstaffel 40.*

# Focke-Wulf Fw 56 Stösser

**Fw 56 prototypes and A-1**
**Origin:** Focke-Wulf Flugzeugbau GmbH, Bremen.
**Type:** Light fighter and advanced trainer.
**Engine:** 240hp Argus As 10C inverted-vee-8 aircooled.
**Dimensions:** Span 34ft 5½in (10·50m); length 25ft 1¼in (7·55m); height 8ft 4¼in (2·54m).
**Weights:** Empty 1,477lb (670kg); loaded 2,171lb (985kg).
**Performance:** Maximum speed 168mph (270km/h); range 230 miles (370km).

**Development:** The first aircraft masterminded by engineer Kurt Tank, the Stösser (bird of prey) was flown in November 1933 as a small home-defence fighter, emergency fighter and 'practice aircraft'. But its main role was to be that of advanced fighter-trainer. Production of the Fw 56A-1 began in 1936, in which year Udet became interested in the type's good diving qualities and flew extensive dive-bombing trials (mainly for fun). Normal armament was one/two synchronized MG 17 and three 22lb (10kg) practice bombs. About 1,000 had been delivered by 1940, many being used as trials machines, tugs, pick-a-back directors and with the air forces and paramilitary groups in Austria and Hungary.

*Three-view of the Fw 56A-1; side views of V1 (top) and V2 (middle)*

*An Fw 56A-1 Stösser serving with one of the Luftwaffe's Jagdfliegerschulen (fighter-pilot training schools). The Stösser was highly aerobatic and unbreakable in the air.*

# Focke-Wulf Fw 57

**Fw 57 V1 to V3**
**Origin:** Focke-Wulf Flugzeugbau GmbH.
**Type:** Kampfzerstörer fighter/bomber.
**Engines:** Two 910hp Daimler-Benz DB 600A inverted-vee-12.
**Dimensions:** Span 82ft 0in (25·00m); length 53ft 9½in (16·40m); height 13ft 5¼in (4·08m).
**Weights:** Empty (V1) 14,991lb (6800kg); loaded 18,298lb (8300kg).
**Performance:** Maximum speed 251mph (404km/h); ceiling 29,855ft (9100m).

**Development:** This was one of the chief contenders for the 1934 requirement for a Kampfzerstörer, a kind of multi-role tactical fighter/bomber.

*Above: The Fw 57 V2, which differed from the first prototype in many details*

Much larger than its main rivals (Bf 110 and Hs 124), it was intended to carry two 20mm MG FF cannon on manually aimed nose mounts and a third in a Mauser electric dorsal turret, plus six 220lb (100kg) bombs internally. Unfortunately it was grossly overweight, and handling was poor. The V1 flew in 1936, followed by the other two by the end of the year, but by this time the failure of the Fw 57 did not matter because the basic concept had been overtaken by the lighter Bf 110.

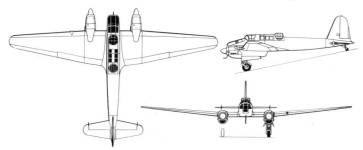

*Above: Three-view of the Fw 57 V1.*

# Focke-Wulf Fw 159

**Fw 159 V1, 2 and 3**
**Origin:** Focke-Wulf Flugzeugbau GmbH.
**Type:** Single-seat fighter.
**Engine:** (V1) 610hp Junkers Jumo 610A inverted-vee-12, (V2, V3) 680hp Jumo 210Da or 730hp 210G.
**Dimensions:** Span 40ft 8in (12·40m); length 32ft 9½in (9·77m); height 12ft 3½in (3·75m).
**Weights:** Empty (V2) 4,134lb (1875kg); loaded 4,960lb (2250kg).
**Performance:** Maximum speed (V2) 239mph (385km/h), (V3, 210G) 252mph (405km/h); range 404 miles (650km).

**Development:** This unique aircraft was a "belt and braces" programme to see if there was an alternative to low-wing monoplane fighters. The Fw 56 was so good that the C-Amt staff suggested to Dipl-Ing Tank that Focke-Wulf should build a parasol-winged fighter. Thus, it could be evaluated against the more likely low-wing Bf 109 and He 112; a few officials thought it might even turn out superior. Tank did a good job in making the Fw 159 sleek and attractive, and the fuselage was covered in easy-access maintenance panels. Unfortunately the basic layout could not compete with the lighter and cleaner low-wing machines, and the final damning feature was persistent failure of the clever but complex landing gear. The V1 was written off for this reason after its first flight in about May 1935, and the second and third (with two synchronized 7·92mm MG 17) were continually being repaired.

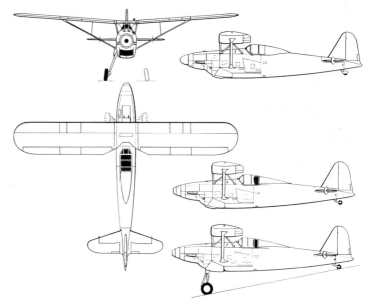

*Three-view of the Fw 159 V3 (landing gear down) with side views of the V1 (top) and V2*

# Focke Achgelis Fa 223 Drache

**Fa 266 and Fa 223E**
**Origin:** Focke Achgelis Flugzeugbau GmbH, Hoykenkamp, Delmenhorst.
**Type:** Transport helicopter.
**Engine:** 1,000hp BMW 301R (previously designated 323Q3 Fafnir) nine-cylinder radial.
**Dimensions:** Diameter of each three-blade main rotor 39ft 4½in (12·00m); distance between rotor centres 41ft 0¼in (12·50m); span (rotors turning) 80ft 4¾in (24·50m); fuselage length 40ft 2¼in (12·25m).
**Weights:** Empty (E) 7,000lb (3175kg); loaded 9,500lb (4309kg); (limit in tests, 11,020lb, 5000kg).
**Performance:** Maximum speed 109mph (175km/h); limit in normal use (also cruising speed) 75mph (121km/h); range with auxiliary tank 435 miles (700 km).

**Development:** The Focke Achgelis Fa 61 of 1936 was one of the first practical helicopters, and certainly the first to make long cross-country flights. The same configuration of left and right rotors geared to the same engine was scaled up to produce the Fa 266, flown tethered in late 1939 and free in August 1940. Easily the most powerful helicopter then built, it was developed as a transport for the Luftwaffe, and – perhaps against all odds – the work bore fruit. The steel tube/fabric fuselage comprised a glazed nose, load compartment, fuel tanks, engine bay and conventional tail. The rotors and main gears were on large outriggers. By late 1940 the 266 Hornisse had become the 223 Drache (Kite), and despite severe delays caused by bombing the operational-test stage was reached in early 1942. Mass-production plans (400 per month) were disrupted, but small numbers reached combat units, especially Luft-Transportstaffel 40, which made many notable missions. The twelfth Drache was lost in a daring rescue on Mont Blanc. Many carried an MG 15 aimed by hand from the nose, and there was much special mission (eg, ASW) equipment. Maximum cargo load was 2,820lb (1280kg). Development continued after 1945 in France (as SE.3000) and Czechoslovakia.

*A production Fa 223E on top of the Dresdener Hutte. This was the most capable type of helicopter of its day*

# Focke-Wulf Fw 58 Weihe

**Fw 58 prototypes, 58B and 58C**
**Origin:** Focke-Wulf Flugzeugbau GmbH.
**Type:** Multi-role crew trainer, transport, ambulance and special duties.
**Engines:** Two 240hp Argus As 10C inverted-vee-8 aircooled.
**Dimensions:** Span 68ft 10¾in (21·00m); length (typical) 45ft 11¼in (14·00m); height (landplane) 13ft 10in (4·21m).
**Weights:** Empty (typical C) 5,291lb (2400kg); loaded 7,937lb (3600kg).
**Performance:** Maximum speed 174mph (280km/h); typical range 497 miles (800km).

**Development:** The Weihe (Kite, a bird also called Drache) was one of the most important utility aircraft of the Luftwaffe, in the class of the Anson or Oxford. First flown as a six-seat civil transport in 1935, it blossomed forth in many military versions with up to three MG 15 or other guns, wing and fuselage bomb racks and wheel/ski/float landing gear. About 4,500 Fw 58C were delivered to the Luftwaffe in 1937–42, called Leukoplast-bomber (sticking-plaster bomber) in the ambulance role. A typical duty was spraying Russian areas with germicides.

*Above: This Fw 58C Weihe is a Sanitätsflugzeug (ambulance), and may be one of the Fw 58S versions specially built for this role. About 2,000 were used for ambulance and casevac duties, but most Weihes were crew-trainers, often with a bombardier nose, or used for communications and light transport*

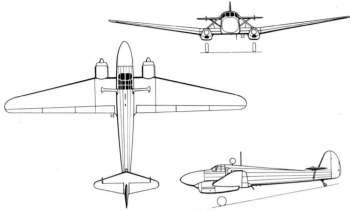

*Above: Three-view of typical Fw 58C*

# Focke-Wulf Fw 62

**Fw 61 V1 and V2**
**Origin:** Focke-Wulf Flugzeugbau GmbH.
**Type:** Shipboard recce seaplane.
**Engine:** 880hp BMW 132Dc nine-cylinder radial.
**Dimensions:** Span 40ft 6¼in (12·35m); length (V1) 36ft 7in (20·0m); height 14ft 1¼in (4·30m).
**Weights:** Empty (V1) 5,070lb (2300kg); loaded 6,283lb (2850kg).
**Performance:** Maximum speed (V1) 174mph (280km/h); service ceiling 19,360ft (5900m).

**Development:** In the autumn of 1936 the RLM issued a specification for a new float-seaplane to operate from surface warships of the Kriegsmarine in succession to the He 60 (the He 114 by this time looking unpromising). The winner was the Ar 196, but the Fw 62 was rated runner-up, and two rather different prototypes of this design were ordered as a back-up. Both flew in the spring of 1937, the first having twin floats and the second a central float, an unusual feature being the use of sprung float struts to

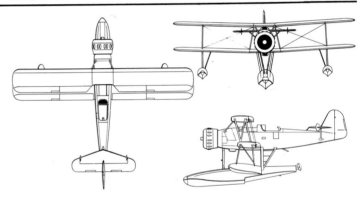

*Three-view of the Fw 62 V2 with central float*

cushion impact in rough-sea landings. The Fw 62 was quite satisfactory, but simply less promising than the Arado monoplane.

# Focke-Wulf Fw 186

**Fw 186 V1**
**Origin:** Focke-Wulf Flugzeugbau GmbH.
**Type:** Observation and army co-operation autogiro.
**Engine:** 240hp Argus As 10C inverted-vee-8 aircooled.
**Dimensions:** Not available.
**Weights:** Not available.
**Performance:** Maximum speed 112mph (180km/h); other data not available.

**Development:** In 1933 Focke-Wulf purchased licence rights to Cierva autogiros, including the "jump-start" technology then under development in which, by spinning up the rotor with a temporary drive from the engine, vertical takeoff was possible. In 1935 Professor Heinrich Focke entered an autogiro design to try to meet the RLM requirement for a STOL observation and army co-operation aircraft (subsequently won by the Fi 156). The Technische Amt soon eliminated the proposed design, not believing a rotary-wing aircraft could be reliable and competitive, but Focke went ahead anyway and the company built two Fw 186 prototypes in 1937–38. In 1937 Focke left Focke-Wulf to establish Focke-Achgelis and concentrate on helicopters. Focke-Wulf did not pursue the Fw 186 after his departure.

*Right: The Focke-Wulf Fw 186 was the last rotary-winged aircraft produced by the Focke-Wulf company (if one discounts the radical Triebflügel jet-propelled VTOL fighter project of 1944). The Fw 186 had the same engine as the Fi 156 Storch but a considerably shorter range. The Luftwaffe finally selected the Storch as its STOL observation type*

# Focke-Wulf Fw 187 Falke

## Fw 187 V1 to V6 and A-0

**Origin:** Focke-Wulf Flugzeugbau GmbH.
**Type:** Zerstörer, heavy fighter.
**Engines:** Two Junkers Jumo 210 inverted-vee-12 liquid-cooled, (V1) 680hp 210Da, (most) 730hp 210Ga, (V6) 1,000hp DB 600A.
**Dimensions:** Span 50ft 2½in (15·30m); length 36ft 5½in (11·01m); height 12ft 7in (3·85m).
**Weights:** Empty (A-0) 8,157lb (3700kg); maximum 11,023lb (5000kg).
**Performance:** (A-0) Maximum speed 326mph (525km/h); initial climb, 3,445ft (1050m)/min; service ceiling 32,800ft (10,000m).
**Armament:** Four 7·92mm MG 17 and two 20mm MG FF.
**History:** First flight, early May 1937, (A-0) about February 1939.

**Development:** Though for various reasons it never went into production, Focke-Wulf's Fw 187 Falke (Falcon) was an extremely fine basis for development and, according to all accounts, could have led to an outstanding family of multi-role aircraft. The cramped single-seat V1 prototype was 50mph (80km/h) faster than the contemporary Bf 109B with two similar engines, despite the fact it weighed more than twice as much and had roughly double the range. The V3 was the first with a more spacious tandem-seat cockpit, alongside which were the four MG 17s, the cannon being under the floor. The V6 reached 392mph (631km/h) on two DB 600A engines, faster than any other fighter in January 1939. Official interest in this promising fighter was slight, and only three A-0 pre-production Falkes were built, being used in combat by an Industrie-Schutzstaffel defending the company works at Bremen (Dipl-Ing Mehlhorn allegedly scored several kills). In the winter 1940–41 the trio were loaned to a Jagdstaffel in Norway, where they were said to be much preferred to the Bf 110; but when the RLM heard about it they were immediately recalled.

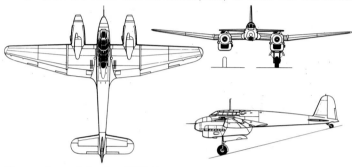

*Three-view of the Fw 187A-0*

*This photograph of the three Fw 187A-0 "pre-production" aircraft was issued for propaganda purposes in the winter of 1940-41. They were then serving with the company's own Schutzstaffel, but loaned to a Luftwaffe unit in Norway*

# Focke-Wulf Fw 189 Uhu

## Fw 189 A-1, -2 and -3

**Origin:** Focke-Wulf Flugzeugbau GmbH; built under Focke-Wulf control by SNCASO, with outer wings from Breguet.
**Type:** Three-seat reconnaissance and close support.
**Engines:** Two 465hp Argus As 410A-1 12 cylinder inverted-vee air-cooled.
**Dimensions:** Span 60ft 4½in (18·4m); length 39ft 4½in (12m); height 10ft 2in (3·1m).
**Weights:** Empty 5,930lb (2690kg); loaded 8,708lb (3950kg).
**Performance:** Maximum speed 217mph (350km/h); climb to 13,120ft (4000m) in 8 min 20sec; service ceiling 23,950ft (7300m); range 416 miles (670km).
**Armament:** (A-2) one 7·92mm MG 17 machine gun in each wing root, twin 7·92mm MG 81 manually aimed in dorsal position and (usually) twin MG 81 in rear cone with limited field of fire; underwing racks for four 110lb (50kg) bombs.
**History:** First flight (Fw 189V1) July 1938; first delivery (pre-production Fw 189A-0) September 1940; final delivery August 1944.

**Development:** Today the diversity of aircraft layout makes us forget how odd this aircraft seemed. It looked strange to the customer also, but after outstandingly successful flight trials the 189 Uhu (Owl) was grudgingly bought in quantity as a standard reconnaissance aircraft. Though it flew in numbers well before the war – no two prototypes being alike – it was unknown by the Allies until it was disclosed in 1941 as "the Flying Eye" of the German armies. On the Eastern front it performed beyond all expectation, for it retained its superb handling (which made it far from a sitting duck to fighters) and also showed great toughness of structure and more than once returned to base with one tail shot off or removed by Soviet ramming attack. Attempts to produce special attack versions with small heavily armoured nacelles were not so successful, but 10 Fw 189B trainers were built with a conventional nacelle having side-by-side dual controls in a normal cockpit, with an observer above the trailing edge. The Fw 189A-3 was another dual-control version having the normal "glasshouse". Eventually the sole source became French factories with assembly at Bordeaux-Mérignac (today the Dassault Mirage plant), which halted as Allied armies approached. There were many different versions and several developments with more powerful engines, but the basic A-1, A-2 (better armament) and A-3 were the only types built in numbers, the total of these versions being 846.

Despite the variety of other sub-types and planned models, only the Fw 189 A-series saw substantial production. This had an airframe basically similar to that of the fourth prototype, with all-metal stressed-skin construction and a capacious glazed nacelle housing the pilot, the overworked nav/radio/bombardier/dorsal gunner, and the flight mechanic/rear gunner. The Fw 189 A-series proved to possess just the right attributes of performance, ability to use short unpaved airstrips, outstanding manoeuvrability, toughness, ability to carry useful armament and operational equipment, and basic simplicity to fit it for sustained operations in the harsh environment it was to encounter on the Eastern front after June 1941. By the summer of 1942 it was the most important tactical reconnaissance aircraft in the Soviet campaign, and examples were also encountered in North Africa.

*continued on page 162* ▶

*Three-view of the Fw 189A-2, with side view (lower) of B-0*

*A standard Fw 189A-2 of an unidentified Luftwaffe Nahaufklärungsgruppe. These excellent aircraft served with the Slovakian, Hungarian and Romanian air forces*

# Focke-Wulf Fw 189 Uhu

*Right: An Fw 189A-1 of 1.(H)/32 at Petsamo (north Finland) in December 1942*

## Focke-Wulf Fw 189A-2

1  Starboard navigation light
2  Aileron control linkage (outer and inner)
3  Starboard aileron
4  Aileron tab
5  Starboard outer flap control linkage
6  Pitot tube
7  ETC 50/VIIId underwing rack fairings

8  Two 110-lb (50-kg) SC 50 bombs
9  Papier-mache "screamers" attached to bomb fins
10  Wing centre/outer section join
11  Starboard engine nacelle
12  Air intake
13  Argus two-bladed controllable-pitch propeller

14  Pitch control vanes
15  Oil cooler intake
16  Engine air intake
17  FuG 212 Lichtenstein C-1 radar array (fitted to night fighter adaptation)
18  Starboard mainwheel
19  Ventral radio mast
20  Optically flat nose panels
21  Rudder pedals
22  GV 219d bomb sight
23  Control column
24  Bomb switch panel
25  Pilot's ring-and-bead sight (for fixed wing-root machine guns)
26  Padded overhead instrument panel

27  Navigator's swivel seat
28  Throttle levers
29  Pilot's seat
30  Mainspar carry-through
31  Centre-hinged two-piece canopy hatch
32  Turnover bar with attached plasticized anti-glare curtain
33  Radio equipment
34  Shell collector box
35  Centre-section camera well (one RB 20/30, RB 50/30, RB 21/18 or RB 15/18 camera)
36  Canvas shell collection chute
37  Dorsal turret
38  MG 81Z twin 7·9-mm

machine gun
39  MG 151 (15-mm) fixed cannon in "schräge Musik" installation (fitted to night fighter adaptation)
40  Starboard tailboom
41  Rudder and elevator control cables
42  Ammunition stowage (dorsal position)
43  Entry handholds
44  Centre-section flap below crew nacelle
45  Wing-root gun access panel (raised)
46  Rear turret-cone drive motor
47  Rear gunner's two-piece quilted pad

48  Ammunition stowage (rear position)
49  Rear canopy opening
50  MG 81Z twin 7·9-mm machine guns (trunnion mounted)
51  Revolving Ikaria powered cone turret
52  Field-of-fire cut-out
53  Aft glazing
54  Tailboom mid-section strengthening frame
55  Starboard tailfin
56  Starboard rudder
57  Rudder tab
58  Elevator construction
59  Tailplane forward spar
60  Elevator tab
61  Tailplane construction

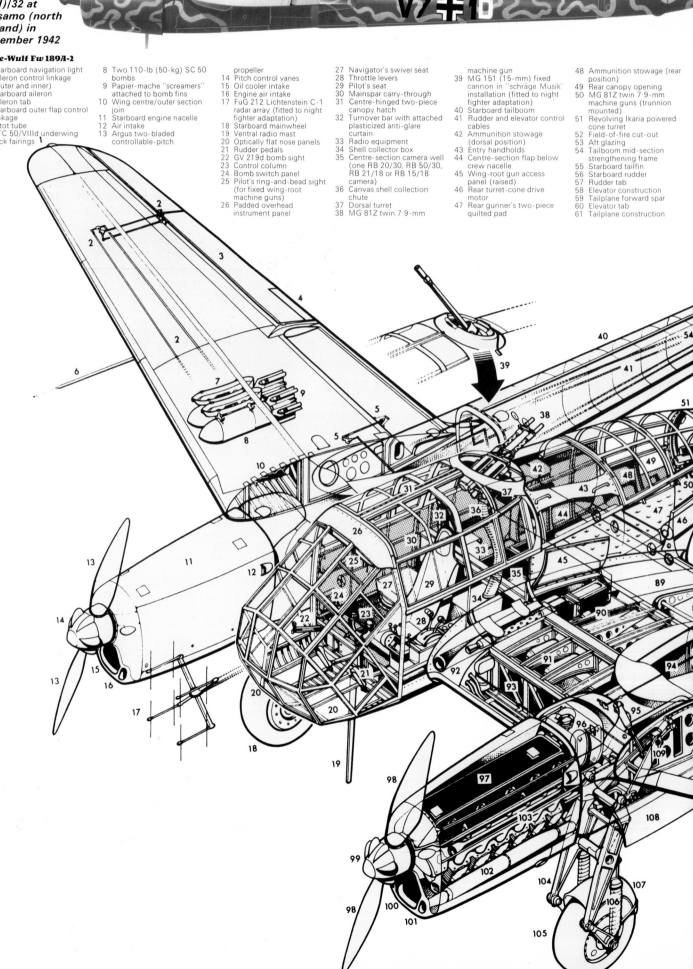

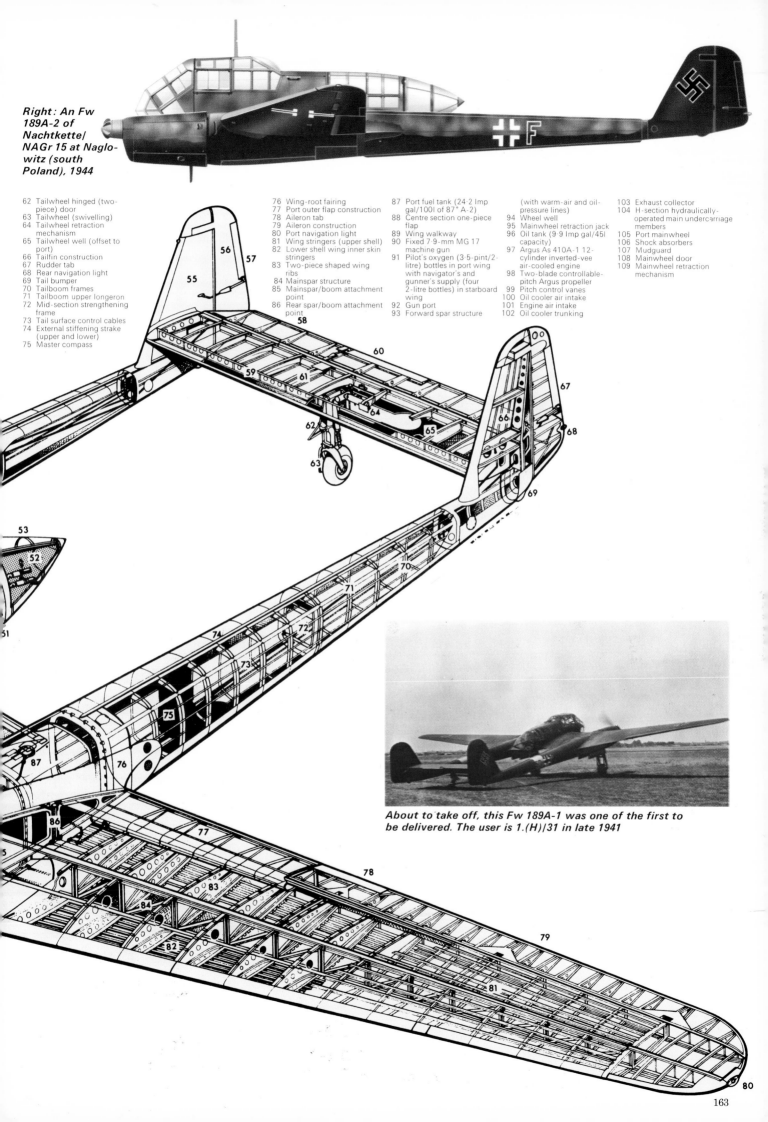

*Right: An Fw 189A-2 of Nachtkette/NAGr 15 at Naglo-witz (south Poland), 1944*

62 Tailwheel hinged (two-piece) door
63 Tailwheel (swivelling)
64 Tailwheel retraction mechanism
65 Tailwheel well (offset to port)
66 Tailfin construction
67 Rudder tab
68 Rear navigation light
69 Tail bumper
70 Tailboom frames
71 Tailboom upper longeron
72 Mid-section strengthening frame
73 Tail surface control cables
74 External stiffening strake (upper and lower)
75 Master compass

76 Wing-root fairing
77 Port outer flap construction
78 Aileron tab
79 Aileron construction
80 Port navigation light
81 Wing stringers (upper shell)
82 Lower shell wing inner skin stringers
83 Two-piece shaped wing ribs
84 Mainspar structure
85 Mainspar/boom attachment point
86 Rear spar/boom attachment point

87 Port fuel tank (24·2 Imp gal/100l of 87° A-2)
88 Centre section one-piece flap
89 Wing walkway
90 Fixed 7·9-mm MG 17 machine gun
91 Pilot's oxygen (3·5-pint/2-litre) bottles in port wing with navigator's and gunner's supply (four 2-litre bottles) in starboard wing
92 Gun port
93 Forward spar structure

(with warm-air and oil-pressure lines)
94 Wheel well
95 Mainwheel retraction jack
96 Oil tank (9·9 Imp gal/45l capacity)
97 Argus As 410A-1 12-cylinder inverted-vee air-cooled engine
98 Two-blade controllable-pitch Argus propeller
99 Pitch control vanes
100 Oil cooler air intake
101 Engine air intake
102 Oil cooler trunking

103 Exhaust collector
104 H-section hydraulically-operated main undercarriage members
105 Port mainwheel
106 Shock absorbers
107 Mudguard
108 Mainwheel door
109 Mainwheel retraction mechanism

*About to take off, this Fw 189A-1 was one of the first to be delivered. The user is 1.(H)/31 in late 1941*

# Focke-Wulf Fw 190

### Fw 190A series, D series, F series and Ta 152H

**Origin:** Focke-Wulf Flugzeugbau GmbH; extremely dispersed manufacture and assembly, and part-subcontracted to Brandt (SNCA du Centre), France; also built in France post-war.

**Type:** Single-seat fighter bomber.

**Engine:** (A-8, F-8) one 1,700hp (2,100hp emergency boost) BMW 801Dg 18-cylinder two-row radial; (D-9) one 1,776hp (2240hp emergency boost) Junkers Jumo 213A-1 12-cylinder inverted-vee liquid-cooled; (Ta 152H-1) one 1,880hp (2,250hp) Jumo 213E-1.

**Dimensions:** Span 34ft 5½in (10·49m); (Ta 152H-1) 47ft 6¾in (14·5m); length (A-8, F-8) 29ft 0in (8·84m); (D-9) 33ft 5¼in (10·2m); (Ta 152H-1) 35ft 5½in (10·8m); height 13ft 0in (3·96m); (D-9) 11ft 0¼in (3·35m); (Ta 152H-1) 11ft 8in (3·55m).

**Weights:** Empty (A-8, F-8) 7,055lb (3200kg); (D-9) 7,720lb (3500kg); (Ta 152H-1) 7,940lb (3600kg); loaded (A-8, F-8) 10,800lb (4900kg); (D-9) 10,670lb (4840kg); (Ta 152H-1) 12,125lb (5500kg).

**Performance:** Maximum speed (with boost) (A-8, F-8) 408mph (653km/h); (D-9) 440mph (704km/h); (Ta 152H-1) 472mph (755km/h); initial climb (A-8, F-8) 2,350ft (720m)/min; (D-9, Ta 152) about 3,300ft (1000m)/min; service ceiling (A-8, F-8) 37,400ft (11,410m); (D-9) 32,810ft (10,000m); (Ta 152H-1) 49,215ft (15,000m); range on internal fuel (A-8, F-8 and D-9) about 560 miles (900km); (Ta 152H-1), 745 miles (1200km).

**Armament:** (A-8, F-8) two 13mm MG 131 above engine, two 20mm MG 151/20 in wing roots and two MG 151/20 or 30mm MK 108 in outer wings; (D-9) as above, or without outer MG 151/20s, with provision for 30mm MK 108 firing through propeller hub; (Ta 152H-1) one 30mm MK 108 and two inboard MG 151/20 (sometimes outboard MG 151/20s as well); bomb load (A-8, D-9) one 1,100lb (500kg) on centreline; (F-8) one 3,968lb (1800kg) on centreline; (Ta 152H-1) one 30mm MK 108 and two 20mm MG 151 (some reconnaissance H-models unarmed).

**History:** First flight (Fw 190V1) June 1, 1939, (production Fw 190A-1) September 1940, (Fw 190D) late 1942.

**Development:** Though flown well before World War II this trim little

### Focke-Wulf Fw 190A-8

1 Pitot head
2 Starboard navigation light
3 Detachable wingtip
4 Pitot tube heater cable
5 Wing lower shell 'floating rib'
6 Aileron hinge
7 Wing lower shell stringers
8 Leading-edge ribs
9 Front spar
10 Outboard 'solid rib'
11 Wing upper shell stringers
12 Aileron trim tab
13 Aileron structure
14 Aileron control linkage
15 Ammunition box (125 rounds)
16 Starboard 20mm Mauser MG 151/20E cannon (sideways mounted)
17 Ammunition box rear suspension arm
18 Flap structure
19 Wing flap upper skinning
20 Flap setting indicator peep-hole
21 Rear spar
22 Inboard wing construction
23 Undercarriage indicator
24 Wing rib strengthening
25 Ammunition feed chute
26 Static and dynamic air pressure lines
27 Cannon barrel
28 Launch tube bracing struts
29 Launch tube carrier strut
30 Mortar launch tube (auxiliary underwing armament)
31 Launch tube internal guide rails
32 21cm (WfrGr.21) spin-stabilized Type 42 mortar shell
33 VDM three-blade constant-speed propeller
34 Propeller boss
35 Propeller hub
36 Starboard undercarriage fairing
37 Starboard mainwheel
38 Oil warming chamber
39 Thermostat
40 Cooler armoured ring (6·5mm)
41 Oil tank drain valve
42 Annular oil tank (12·1 gal/55 litres)
43 Oil cooler
44 Twelve-blade engine cooling fan; 3·17 times propeller speed
45 Hydraulic-electric pitch control unit
46 Primer fuel line
47 Bosch magneto
48 Oil tank armour (5·5mm)
49 Supercharger air pressure pipes
50 BMW 801D-2 fourteen-cylinder radial engine
51 Cowling support ring
52 Cowling quick-release fasteners
53 Oil pump
54 Fuel pump (engine rear face)
55 Oil filter (starboard)
56 Wing root cannon synchronization gear
57 Gun troughs/cowling upper panel attachment
58 Engine mounting ring
59 Cockpit heating pipe
60 Exhaust pipes (cylinders 11–14)
61 MG 131 link and case chute
62 Engine bearer assembly
63 MG 131 ammunition boxes (400 rpg)
64 Fuel filter recess housing
65 MG 131 ammunition cooling pipes
66 MG 131 synchronization gear
67 Ammunition feed chute
68 Twin fuselage 13mm Rheinmetall MG 131 guns
69 Windscreen mounting frame
70 Emergency power fuse and distributor box
71 Rear-hinged gun access panel
72 Engine bearer/bulkhead attachment
73 Control column
74 Transformer
75 Aileron control torsion bar
76 Rubber pedals (EC pedal unit with hydraulic wheel-brake operation)
77 Fuselage/wing spar attachment
78 Adjustable rudder push rod
79 Fuel filler head
80 Cockpit floor support frame
81 Throttle lever
82 Pilot's seat back plate armour (8mm)
83 Seat guide rails
84 Side-section back armour (5mm)
85 Shoulder armour (5mm)
86 Oxygen supply valve
87 Steel frame turnover pylon
88 Windscreen spray pipes
89 Instrument panel shroud
90 30mm armoured glass quarterlights
91 50mm armoured glass windscreen
92 Revi 16B reflector gunsight
93 Canopy
94 Aerial attachment
95 Headrest
96 Head armour (12mm)
97 Head armour support strut
98 Explosive-charge canopy emergency jettison unit
99 Canopy channel slide
100 Auxiliary tank: fuel (25·3 gal/115 litres) or GM-1 (18·7 gal/85 litres)
101 FuG 16ZY radio transmitter-receiver
102 Handhold cover
103 Primer fuel filler cap
104 Autopilot steering unit (PKS 12)
105 FuG 16ZY power transformer
106 Entry step cover plate
107 Two tri-spherical oxygen bottles (starboard fuselage wall)
108 Auxiliary fuel tank filler point
109 FuG 25a transponder unit
110 Autopilot position integration unit
111 FuG 16ZY homer bearing converter
112 Elevator control cables
113 Rudder control DUZ-flexible rods
114 Fabric panel (Bulkhead 12)
115 Rudder differential unit
116 Aerial lead-in
117 Rear fuselage lift tube
118 Triangular stress frame
119 Tailplane trim unit
120 Tailplane attachment fitting
121 Tailwheel retraction guide tube
122 Retraction cable lower pulley
123 Starboard tailplane
124 Aerial
125 Starboard elevator
126 Elevator trim tab
127 Tailwheel shock strut guide
128 Fin construction
129 Retraction cable upper pulley
130 Aerial attachment stub
131 Rudder upper hinge
132 Rudder structure
133 Rudder trim tab
134 Tailwheel retraction mechanism access panel
135 Rudder attachment/actuation fittings
136 Rear navigation light
137 Extension spring
138 Elevator trim tab
139 Port elevator structure
140 Tailplane construction
141 Semi-retracting tailwheel
142 Forked wheel housing
143 Drag yoke
144 Tailwheel shock strut
145 Tailwheel locking linkage
146 Elevator actuation lever linkage
147 Angled frame spar
148 Elevator differential bellcrank
149 FuG 25a ventral aerial
150 Master compass sensing unit
151 FuG 16ZY fixed loop homing aerial
152 Radio compartment access hatch
153 Single tri-spherical oxygen bottle (port fuselage wall)
154 Retractable entry step
155 Wing-root fairing
156 Fuselage rear fuel tank (64·5 gal/293 litres)
157 Fuselage/rear spar attachment
158 Fuselage forward fuel tank (51 gal/232 litres)
159 Port wing root cannon ammunition box (250 rounds)
160 Ammunition feed chute
161 Wing root MG 151/20E cannon
162 Link and case chute
163 Cannon rear mount support bracket
164 Upper and lower wing shell stringers
165 Rear spar
166 Spar construction
167 Flap position indicator scale
168 Flap actuating electric motor
169 MG 151/20E cannon (sideways mounted)
170 Aileron transverse linkage
171 Ammunition box (125 rounds)
172 Ammunition box rear suspension arm
173 Aileron control linkage
174 Aileron control unit
175 Aileron trim tab
176 Port aileron structure

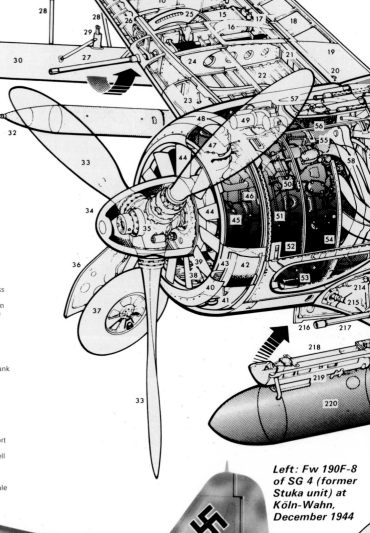

*Left: Fw 190F-8 of SG 4 (former Stuka unit) at Köln-Wahn, December 1944*

fighter was unknown to the Allies and caused a nasty surprise when first met over France in early 1941. Indeed, it was so far superior to the bigger and more sluggish Spitfire V that for the first time the RAF felt not only out-numbered but beaten technically. In June 1942 an Fw 190A-3 landed by mistake in England, and the Focke-Wulf was discovered to be even better than expected. It was faster than any Allied fighter in service, had far heavier armament (at that time the standard was two 7·92mm MG 17s over the engine, two of the previously unknown Mauser cannon inboard and two 20mm MG FF outboard), was immensely strong, had excellent power of manoeuvre and good pilot view. It was also an extremely small target, much lighter than any Allied fighter and had a stable widetrack landing gear (unlike the Bf 109). Altogether it gave Allied pilots and designers an inferiority complex. Though it never supplanted the 109, it was subse-quently made in a profusion of different versions by many factories.

The A series included many fighter and fighter bomber versions, some having not only the increasingly heavy internal armament but also two or four 20mm cannon or two 30mm in underwing fairings. Most had an emergency power boost system, using MW 50 (methanol/water) or GM-1 (nitrous oxide) injection, or both. Some carried torpedoes, others

were two-seaters, and a few had autopilots for bad weather and night interceptions. The F series were close-support attack aircraft, some having the Panzerblitz array of R4M rockets for tank-busting (also lethal against heavy bombers). There were over 40 other special armaments, and some versions had armoured leading edges for ramming Allied bombers. The G was another important series of fighter/dive bombers, which actually preceded the F. The G-0 carried the SC 1000 bomb of 2,200lb (1000kg), but the G-1 introduced a strengthened landing gear and other structural changes which permitted the carriage of the Luftwaffe's largest bomb, the SC 1800 weigh-ing 3,968lb (1800kg). This formidable weapon had to have its lower fins cropped to give adequate ground clearance, and it was an impressive tech-nical achievement to clear for routine operational use such a heavy store on a small fighter (one of the smallest in World War II) based on unpaved forward airstrips. Many other G sub-types carried very heavy weapon loads, some having a lengthened tailwheel yoke to hold the fuselage more level to provide clearance for a 198 Imp gal torpedo-shaped drop tank; this worked perfectly, whereas Messerschmitt and Skoda wasted much time with strange long rear wheels under the mid-fuselage before accepting the same

*continued on page 166* ▶

177 Port navigation light
178 Outboard wing stringers
179 Detachable wingtip
180 A-8/R1 variant underwing gun pack (in place of out-board wing cannon)
181 Link and case chute
182 Twin unsynchronized MG 151/20E cannon
183 Light metal fairing (gondola)
184 Ammunition feed chutes
185 Ammunition boxes

(125 rpg)
186 Carrier frame restraining cord
187 Ammunition box rear suspension arms
188 Leading-edge skinning
189 Ammunition feed chute
190 Ammunition warming pipe
191 Aileron bellcrank
192 Mainwheel strut mounting assembly
193 EC-oleo shock strut
194 Mainwheel leg fairing

195 Scissors unit
196 Mainwheel fairing
197 Axle housing
198 Port mainwheel
199 Brake lines
200 Cannon barrel
201 FuG 16ZY Morane aerial
202 Radius rods
203 Rotating drive unit
204 Mainwheel retraction electric motor housing
205 Undercarriage indicator
206 Sealed air-jack

207 BSK 16 gun-camera
208 Retraction locking hooks
209 Undercarriage locking unit
210 Armament collimation tube
211 Camera wiring conduits
212 Wheel well

213 Cannon barrel blast tube
214 Wheel cover actuation strut
215 Ammunition hot air
216 Port inboard wheel cover
217 Wing root cannon barrel
218 ETC 501 carrier unit

219 ETC 501 bomb rack
220 SC 500 bomb (500 kg, 1,102 lb)

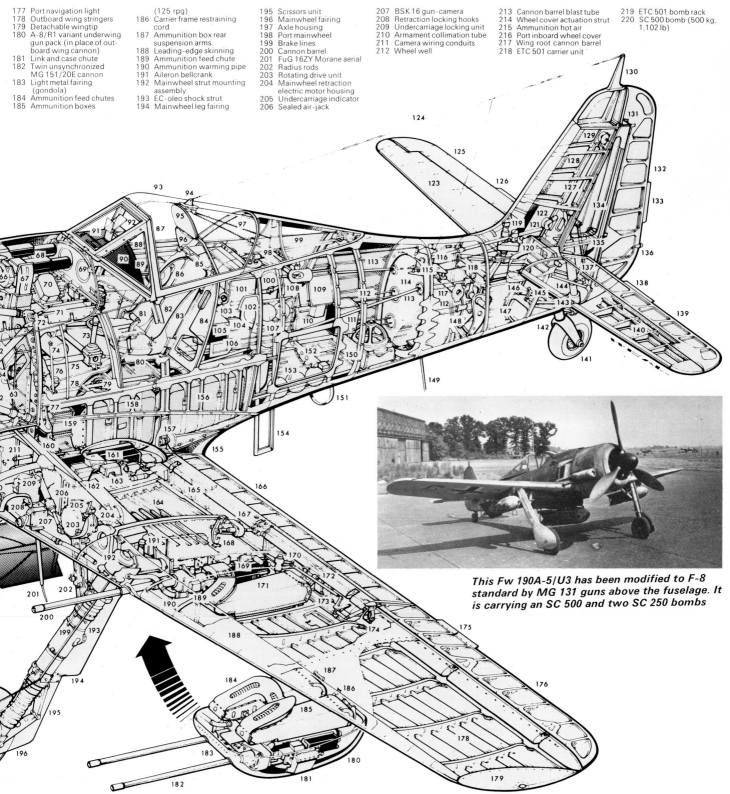

*This Fw 190A-5/U3 has been modified to F-8 standard by MG 131 guns above the fuselage. It is carrying an SC 500 and two SC 250 bombs*

## Focke-Wulf Fw 190/Focke-Wulf Ta 152

simple solution. The Fw 190F incorporated all the structural strengthening of the G, as well as (usually) a new bulged canopy giving a better view in attacks on surface targets. In this case the extra disposable load was partly used up in providing much-enhanced armour protection for survivability in the close-support role, which on the Eastern Front had become by far the main task of the 190 by 1943. Conversely, by 1943 the 190, designed as a fighter, had replaced virtually all Ju 87s as close-support bombers and was by a wide margin the most important tactical attack aircraft of the Luftwaffe in all theatres.

Nevertheless by this time developments were afoot that were also to restore the 190 as a leading dogfighter. By the middle of 1943 the main effort was devoted to what the RAF called the "long-nosed 190", the 190D. This went into production in the autumn of 1944, after much development, as the Fw 190D-9 ("Dora 9"). This was once more the fastest fighter

in the sky and the later D-models were redesignated Ta 152 in honour of the director of Focke-Wulf's design team, Dipl-Ing Kurt Tank. The early 152C series were outstandingly formidable, but the long-span H sacrificed guns for speed and height. Tank himself easily outpaced a flight of P-51D Mustangs which surprised him on a test flight; but only ten of the H sub-type had flown when the war ended. Altogether 20,051 Fw 190s were delivered, plus a small number of Ta 152s (67, excluding development aircraft). It is curious that the Bf 109, a much older and less attractive design with many shortcomings, should have been made in greater quantity and flown by nearly all the Luftwaffe's aces.

In 1945 the Fw 190A-5 was put into production at an underground plant in France managed by SNCASO. By 1946 a total of 64 had been delivered, some later being shipped to Argentina. These aircraft were designated N 900.

continued on page 168 ▶

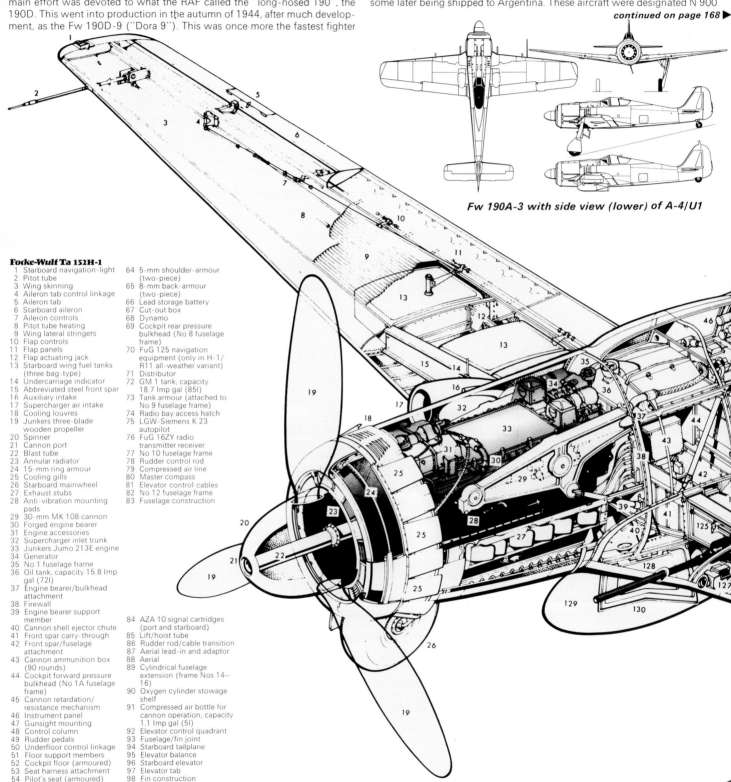

**Fw 190A-3 with side view (lower) of A-4/U1**

### Focke-Wulf Ta 152H-1

1 Starboard navigation-light
2 Pitot tube
3 Wing skinning
4 Aileron tab control linkage
5 Aileron tab
6 Starboard aileron
7 Aileron controls
8 Pitot tube heating
9 Wing lateral stringers
10 Flap controls
11 Flap panels
12 Flap actuating jack
13 Starboard wing fuel tanks (three bag-type)
14 Undercarriage indicator
15 Abbreviated steel front spar
16 Auxiliary intake
17 Supercharger air intake
18 Cooling louvres
19 Junkers three-blade wooden propeller
20 Spinner
21 Cannon port
22 Blast tube
23 Annular radiator
24 15-mm ring armour
25 Cooling gills
26 Starboard mainwheel
27 Exhaust stubs
28 Anti-vibration mounting pads
29 30-mm MK 108 cannon
30 Forged engine bearer
31 Engine accessories
32 Supercharger inlet trunk
33 Junkers Jumo 213E engine
34 Generator
35 No 1 fuselage frame
36 Oil tank, capacity 15.8 Imp gal (72l)
37 Engine bearer/bulkhead attachment
38 Firewall
39 Engine bearer support member
40 Cannon shell ejector chute
41 Front spar carry-through
42 Front spar/fuselage attachment
43 Cannon ammunition box (90 rounds)
44 Cockpit forward pressure bulkhead (No 1A fuselage frame)
45 Cannon retardation/resistance mechanism
46 Instrument panel
47 Gunsight mounting
48 Control column
49 Rudder pedals
50 Underfloor control linkage
51 Floor support members
52 Cockpit floor (armoured)
53 Seat harness attachment
54 Pilot's seat (armoured)
55 Instrument panel shroud
56 Revi 16B gunsight
57 Armoured-glass windscreen
58 Starboard instrument console
59 Canopy rubber-tube pressurization
60 Rearward-sliding cockpit canopy
61 Headrest
62 20-mm head-armour
63 Turn-over bar and shroud
64 5-mm shoulder-armour (two-piece)
65 8-mm back-armour (two-piece)
66 Lead storage battery
67 Cut-out box
68 Dynamo
69 Cockpit rear pressure bulkhead (No 8 fuselage frame)
70 FuG 125 navigation equipment (only in H-1/R11 all-weather variant)
71 Distributor
72 GM 1 tank, capacity 18.7 Imp gal (85l)
73 Tank armour (attached to No 9 fuselage frame)
74 Radio bay access hatch
75 LGW-Siemens K 23 autopilot
76 FuG 16ZY radio transmitter receiver
77 No 10 fuselage frame
78 Rudder control rod
79 Compressed air line
80 Master compass
81 Elevator control cables
82 No 12 fuselage frame
83 Fuselage construction
84 AZA 10 signal cartridges (port and starboard)
85 Lift/hoist tube
86 Rudder rod/cable transition
87 Aerial lead-in and adaptor
88 Aerial
89 Cylindrical fuselage extension (frame Nos 14–16)
90 Oxygen cylinder stowage shelf
91 Compressed air bottle for cannon operation, capacity 1.1 Imp gal (5l)
92 Elevator control quadrant
93 Fuselage/fin joint
94 Starboard tailplane
95 Elevator balance
96 Starboard elevator
97 Elevator tab
98 Fin construction
99 Tailwheel retraction cable
100 Rudder upper hinge
101 Rudder construction
102 Tailwheel leg retraction guide
103 Rudder hinge control
104 Rudder tab
105 Rear navigation light
106 Electric lead
107 Tailwheel torque tube
108 Tailwheel shock-absorber
109 Elevator tab
110 Elevator balance
111 Elevator construction
112 Semi-retractable tailwheel (380 x 150-mm)
113 Fin spar attachment
114 Antenna
115 D F loop
116 Retractable entry step
117 Spring-loaded hand/foothold
118 Rear fuselage fuel tank (protected), capacity 80 Imp gal (362l)
119 Rear spar/fuselage attachment
120 Forward fuselage fuel tank (protected), capacity 51 Imp gal (233l)
121 Wing gun breech fairing
122 Port MG 151/20 wing gun
123 Shell ejector chute
124 Port ammunition box (175 rounds)
125 Undercarriage retraction guide track
126 Wing gun forward mounting
127 BSK 16 camera gun

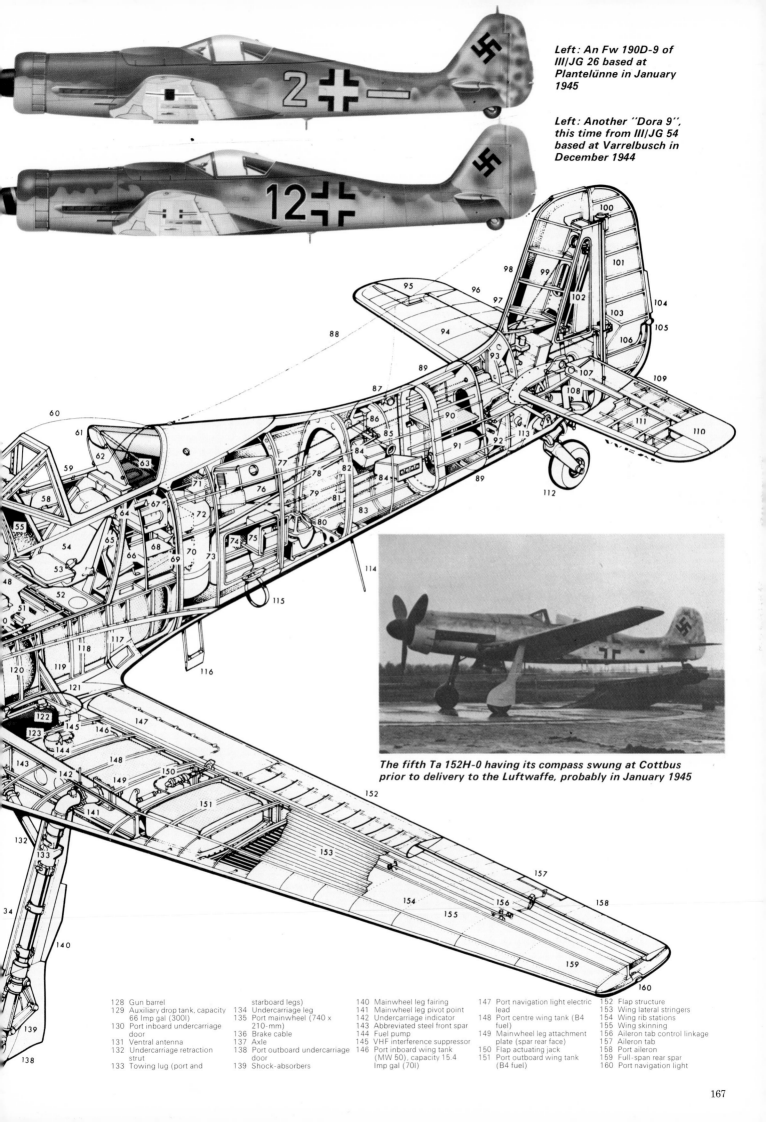

*Left: An Fw 190D-9 of III/JG 26 based at Plantelünne in January 1945*

*Left: Another "Dora 9", this time from III/JG 54 based at Varrelbusch in December 1944*

**The fifth Ta 152H-0 having its compass swung at Cottbus prior to delivery to the Luftwaffe, probably in January 1945**

128 Gun barrel
129 Auxiliary drop tank, capacity 66 Imp gal (300l)
130 Port inboard undercarriage door
131 Ventral antenna
132 Undercarriage retraction strut
133 Towing lug (port and starboard legs)
134 Undercarriage leg
135 Port mainwheel (740 x 210-mm)
136 Brake cable
137 Axle
138 Port outboard undercarriage door
139 Shock-absorbers
140 Mainwheel leg fairing
141 Mainwheel leg pivot point
142 Undercarriage indicator
143 Abbreviated steel front spar
144 Fuel pump
145 VHF interference suppressor
146 Port inboard wing tank (MW 50), capacity 15.4 Imp gal (70l)
147 Port navigation light electric lead
148 Port centre wing tank (B4 fuel)
149 Mainwheel leg attachment plate (spar rear face)
150 Flap actuating jack
151 Port outboard wing tank (B4 fuel)
152 Flap structure
153 Wing lateral stringers
154 Wing rib stations
155 Wing skinning
156 Aileron tab control linkage
157 Aileron tab
158 Port aileron
159 Full-span rear spar
160 Port navigation light

*A pair of Fw 190G-3 extended-range fighter/bombers are pictured flying over Romania in early 1944 (II/SG 10?)*
*Above, right: Ta 152C V7 (Ta 152C-0/R11), flown in December 1944 and equipped with the bad-weather "Rüstsatz" package*

*Right: Fw 190A-4 of 2/JG 2 based at Abbeville in May 1943*

*Left: Fw 190A-2 of II/JG 26 based at Abbeville in summer 1942*

*Right: Fw 190A-2 of 1/JG 26 based at Omer-Arques, summer of 1942*

*Left: Fw 190A-3 of IV/JG 26 based at Abbeville-Drucat, summer 1942*

*Right: Fw 190A-8 of II/JG 11 based at Darmstadt in early 1945*

*Left: Fw 190A-4 of 10 (Jabo)/JG 26 based at St Omer-Wizernes, autumn 1942*

*See also profile on pages 58-59*

# Focke-Wulf Fw 191

**Fw 191 V1 to V6, 191A, B and C**
**Origin:** Focke-Wulf Flugzeugbau GmbH.
**Type:** Advanced medium bomber.
**Engines:** See text.
**Dimensions:** Span 85ft 3½in (26·00m); length 64ft 4¾in (19·63m); height 18ft 4½in (5·60m).
**Weights:** (191B) Empty 35,940lb (16,300kg); maximum 56,445lb (25,600kg).
**Performance:** Maximum speed (B) 393mph (632km/h); service ceiling 27,887ft (8500m); maximum range (reduced speed, presumably no bombs) 2,394 miles (3850km); range with max weapon load, about 870 miles (1400km).
**Armament:** See text.
**History:** First flight (V1) early 1942.

**Development:** In July 1939 the RLM issued a specification that became called the Bomber B, a wide-ranging and technically difficult requirement that was intended to lead to a bomber of advanced design but which caused millions of marks and man-hours to be wasted. Features were to include two of the extremely powerful new engines (2,500hp class) then on the testbed, remotely sighted defensive cannon barbettes, a pressure cabin, and the ability to make dive-bombing attacks. The Ar 340 and Do 317 were rejected or shelved and the Fw 191 and Ju 288 ordered as prototypes. Focke-Wulf's design team under E. Kösel chose the six-bank Jumo 222 engine, but accepted the lower-powered BMW 801 radial to get the first V1 prototype into the air. A source of trouble was soon identified in the Multhopp wing flaps which also served as dive brakes; they fluttered severely. Another was the extremely complicated all-electric nature of the Fw 191, and a third was the fact that with the 801 engines it was dangerously under-powered. The planned armament comprised dorsal and ventral barbettes

each with a 20mm MG 151 flanked by two 7·92mm MG 81, two twin MG 81 barbettes in the tail of the engine nacelles, and a chin barbette with another pair of MG 81. Bomb load comprised up to 6,614lb (3000kg) internally (two torpedoes could be carried) plus an overload of the same weight externally (not allowed for in the maximum weight given above, and certainly never attained in practice). Eventually the 191B switched to the DB 610 double engine, of 2,870hp, and a heavier armament of six MG 151 and four 13mm MG 131 in four fuselage barbettes, but lack of suitable engines was one of the reasons for dropping the whole programme in 1943. This was despite the fact that Kösel had a 191C on the drawing board with four separate engines (DB 601, 605, 628 or Jumo 211).

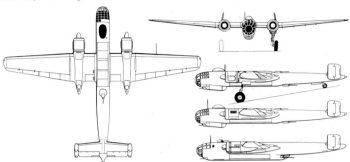

*Above: Three-views of the Fw 191 V1 with side views of Fw 191 V6 (centre) and proposed Fw 191C (bottom)*
*Below: Two photographs of the Fw 191 V1, first flown in early 1942. Though judged one of the two winners in the preliminary "Bomber B" selection process (the other was the Ju 288), the complex and all-electric Fw 191 gave almost as much trouble as the He 177 and never did lead to production*

# Focke-Wulf Fw 200 Condor

## Fw 200C-0 to C-8

**Origin:** Focke-Wulf Flugzeugbau GmbH, in partnership with Hamburger Flugzeugbau (Blohm und Voss).

**Type:** Maritime reconnaissance bomber and (C-6 to -8) missile launcher, many used as transports.

**Engines:** Usually four 1,200hp BMW-Bramo Fafnir 323R-2 nine-cylinder radials.

**Dimensions:** Span 107ft 9½in (30·855m); length 76ft 11½in (23·46m); height 20ft 8in (6·3m).

**Weights:** (C-3/U-4) empty 28,550lb (12,951kg); loaded 50,045lb (22,700kg).

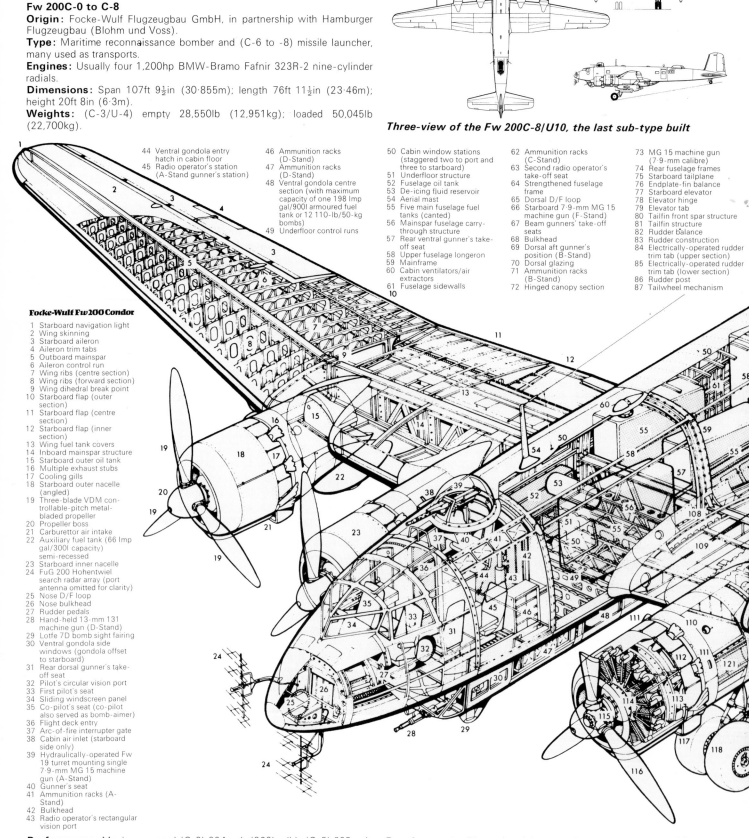

*Three-view of the Fw 200C-8/U10, the last sub-type built*

### Focke-Wulf Fw 200 Condor

1 Starboard navigation light
2 Wing skinning
3 Starboard aileron
4 Aileron trim tabs
5 Outboard mainspar
6 Aileron control run
7 Wing ribs (centre section)
8 Wing ribs (forward section)
9 Wing dihedral break point
10 Starboard flap (outer section)
11 Starboard flap (centre section)
12 Starboard flap (inner section)
13 Wing fuel tank covers
14 Inboard mainspar structure
15 Starboard outer oil tank
16 Multiple exhaust stubs
17 Cooling gills
18 Starboard outer nacelle (angled)
19 Three-blade VDM controllable-pitch metal-bladed propeller
20 Propeller boss
21 Carburettor air intake
22 Auxiliary fuel tank (66 Imp gal/300l capacity) semi-recessed
23 Starboard inner nacelle
24 FuG 200 Hohentwiel search radar array (port antenna omitted for clarity)
25 Nose D/F loop
26 Nose bulkhead
27 Rudder pedals
28 Hand-held 13-mm 131 machine gun (D-Stand)
29 Lotfe 7D bomb sight fairing
30 Ventral gondola side windows (gondola offset to starboard)
31 Rear dorsal gunner's take-off seat
32 Pilot's circular vision port
33 First pilot's seat
34 Sliding windscreen panel
35 Co-pilot's seat (co-pilot also served as bomb-aimer)
36 Flight deck entry
37 Arc-of-fire interrupter gate
38 Cabin air inlet (starboard side only)
39 Hydraulically-operated Fw 19 turret mounting single 7·9-mm MG 15 machine gun (A-Stand)
40 Gunner's seat
41 Ammunition racks (A-Stand)
42 Bulkhead
43 Radio operator's rectangular vision port
44 Ventral gondola entry hatch in cabin floor
45 Radio operator's station (A-Stand gunner's station)
46 Ammunition racks (D-Stand)
47 Ammunition racks (D-Stand)
48 Ventral gondola centre section (with maximum capacity of one 198 Imp gal/900l armoured fuel tank or 12 110-lb/50-kg bombs)
49 Underfloor control runs
50 Cabin window stations (staggered two to port and three to starboard)
51 Underfloor structure
52 Fuselage oil tank
53 De-icing fluid reservoir
54 Aerial mast
55 Five main fuselage fuel tanks (canted)
56 Mainspar fuselage carry-through structure
57 Rear ventral gunner's take-off seat
58 Upper fuselage longeron
59 Mainframe
60 Cabin ventilators/air extractors
61 Fuselage sidewalls
62 Ammunition racks (C-Stand)
63 Second radio operator's take-off seat
64 Strengthened fuselage frame
65 Dorsal D/F loop
66 Starboard 7·9-mm MG 15 machine gun (F-Stand)
67 Beam gunners' take-off seats
68 Bulkhead
69 Dorsal aft gunner's position (B-Stand)
70 Dorsal glazing
71 Ammunition racks (B-Stand)
72 Hinged canopy section
73 MG 15 machine gun (7·9-mm calibre)
74 Rear fuselage frames
75 Starboard tailplane
76 Endplate-fin balance
77 Starboard elevator
78 Elevator hinge
79 Elevator tab
80 Tailfin front spar structure
81 Tailfin structure
82 Rudder balance
83 Rudder construction
84 Electrically-operated rudder trim tab (upper section)
85 Electrically-operated rudder trim tab (lower section)
86 Rudder post
87 Tailwheel mechanism

**Performance:** Maximum speed (C-3) 224mph (360km/h); (C-8) 205mph (330km/h); initial climb, about 656ft (200m)/min; service ceiling 19,030ft (5800m); range with standard fuel, 2,206 miles (3550km).

**Armament:** Typical C-3/C-8, one forward dorsal turret with one 15mm MG 151/15 (or 20mm MG 151/20 or one 7·92mm MG 15), one 20mm MG 151/20 manually aimed at front of ventral gondola, three 7·92mm MG 15 manually aimed at rear of ventral gondola and two beam windows (beam guns sometimes being 13mm MG 131) and one 13mm MG 131 in aft dorsal position; maximum bomb load of 4,626lb (2100kg) carried in gondola and beneath outer wings (C-6, C-8, two Hs 293 guided missiles carried under outboard nacelles).

**History:** First flight (civil prototype) 27 July 1937; (Fw 200C-0) January 1940; final delivery (C-8) February 1944.

**Development:** Planned solely as a long-range commercial transport for the German airline Deutsche Lufthansa, the prewar Fw 200 prototypes set up impressive record flights to New York and Tokyo and attracted export orders from Denmark, Brazil, Finland and Japan. Transport prototype and production versions were also used by Hitler and Himmler as VIP executive machines and several later variants were also converted as special transports. In 1938 the Japanese asked for one Condor converted for use as a long-range ocean reconnaissance machine. The resulting Fw 200V-10 prototype introduced a ventral gondola and led to the Fw 200C-0 as the prototype of a Luftwaffe aircraft which had never been requested or planned and yet which was to prove a most powerful instrument of war. Distinguished by long-chord cowlings, twin-wheel main gears (because of the increased gross weight) and a completely new arma-

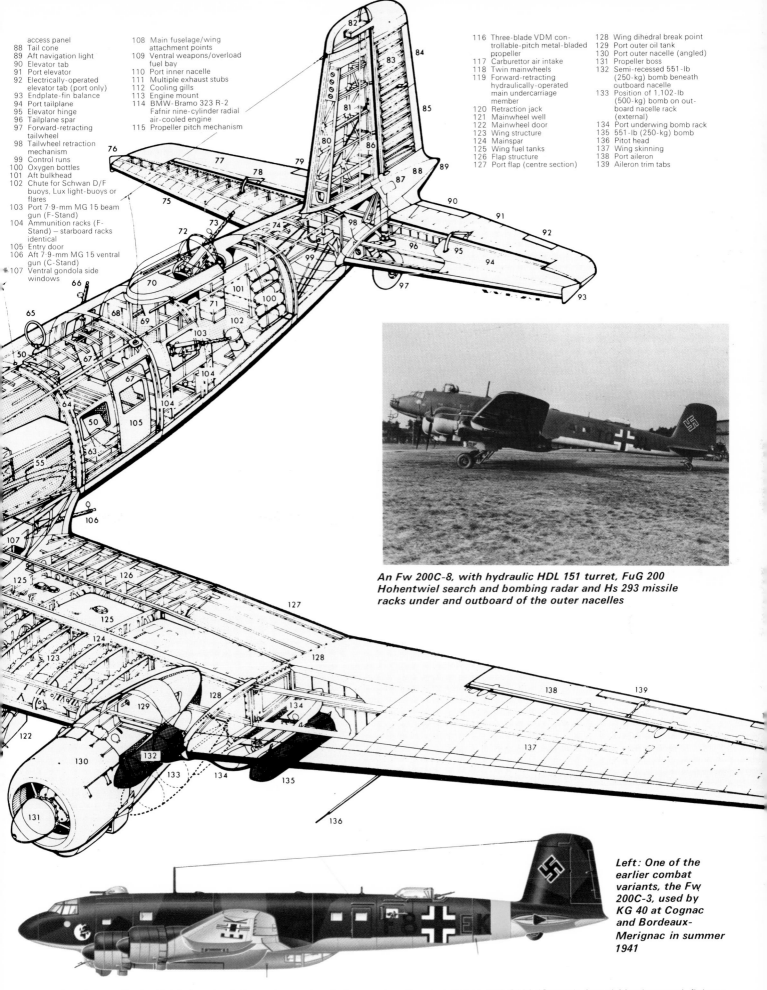

access panel
88 Tail cone
89 Aft navigation light
90 Elevator tab
91 Port elevator
92 Electrically-operated elevator tab (port only)
93 Endplate-fin balance
94 Port tailplane
95 Elevator hinge
96 Tailplane spar
97 Forward-retracting tailwheel
98 Tailwheel retraction mechanism
99 Control runs
100 Oxygen bottles
101 Aft bulkhead
102 Chute for Schwan D/F buoys, Lux light-buoys or flares
103 Port 7·9-mm MG 15 beam gun (F-Stand)
104 Ammunition racks (F-Stand) — starboard racks identical
105 Entry door
106 Aft 7·9-mm MG 15 ventral gun (C-Stand)
107 Ventral gondola side windows

108 Main fuselage/wing attachment points
109 Ventral weapons/overload fuel bay
110 Port inner nacelle
111 Multiple exhaust stubs
112 Cooling gills
113 Engine mount
114 BMW-Bramo 323 R-2 Fafnir nine-cylinder radial air-cooled engine
115 Propeller pitch mechanism

116 Three-blade VDM controllable-pitch metal-bladed propeller
117 Carburettor air intake
118 Twin mainwheels
119 Forward-retracting hydraulically-operated main undercarriage member
120 Retraction jack
121 Mainwheel well
122 Mainwheel door
123 Wing structure
124 Mainspar
125 Wing fuel tanks
126 Flap structure
127 Port flap (centre section)

128 Wing dihedral break point
129 Port outer oil tank
130 Port outer nacelle (angled)
131 Propeller boss
132 Semi-recessed 551-lb (250-kg) bomb beneath outboard nacelle
133 Position of 1,102-lb (500-kg) bomb on outboard nacelle rack (external)
134 Port underwing bomb rack
135 551-lb (250-kg) bomb
136 Pitot head
137 Wing skinning
138 Port aileron
139 Aileron trim tabs

*An Fw 200C-8, with hydraulic HDL 151 turret, FuG 200 Hohentwiel search and bombing radar and Hs 293 missile racks under and outboard of the outer nacelles*

*Left: One of the earlier combat variants, the Fw 200C-3, used by KG 40 at Cognac and Bordeaux-Merignac in summer 1941*

ment and equipment fit, the C-0 led to the C-1, used operationally from June 1940 by KG 40 at Bordeaux-Merignac. By September 1940 this unit alone had sunk over 90,000 tons of Allied shipping and for the next three years the C-series Condors were in Churchill's words, "the scourge of the Atlantic". But, though the Fw 200 family continued to grow in equipment and lethality, the Allies fought back with long-range Coastal Command aircraft, escort carriers and CAM (Catapult-Armed Merchantman) fighters and by mid-1944 surviving Condors were being forced into transport roles on other fronts. Total production was 276 and one of the fundamental failings of the Condor was structural weakness, catastrophic wing and fuselage failures occurring not only in the air but even on the ground, on take-off or landing.

# Focke-Wulf Ta 154 Moskito

**Ta 154 V1 to V15, A and C series**
**Origin:** Focke-Wulf Flugzeugbau GmbH, prototypes to V7 at Hanover–Langenhagen, V8–V15 (A-0 series) at Erfurt, production A-1 at Posen, Poland.
**Type:** Night and all-weather fighter.
**Engines:** Two Junkers Jumo inverted-vee-12 liquid-cooled, (V1, 2) 1,520hp 211N, (V3-V15, A-1) 1,750hp 213E, (C) 1,776hp 213A.
**Dimensions:** Span 52ft 6in (16·00m); length (with SN-2) 41ft 2⅜in (12·56m); height (most) 11ft 9¾in (3·60m).
**Weights:** (A-1) Empty 14,122lb (6405kg); max loaded 21,050lb (9548kg).
**Performance:** Maximum speed (A-1) 404mph (650km/h); service ceiling 35,760ft (10,900m); range (two drop tanks) 1,156 miles (1850km).
**Armament:** (A-0, A-1) two 30mm MK 108 and two 20mm MG 151 in sides of fuselage.

**Development:** Hailed by the propaganda machine as "Germany's Mosquito", the wooden Ta 154 had an excellent performance and came near to being a major combat type. The Luftwaffe never considered defensive aircraft at all until 1941; then, for obvious reasons, in September 1942 the RLM issued a specification for a fighter to shoot down RAF heavy bombers at night. Tank had the Ta 154 V1 flying by 7 July 1943, and development generally went well, though the whole project posed inherently high risk in the use of wood for the structure of so advanced an aircraft. It was only the need to conserve light alloy, and the great success of the British Mosquito, that drove this policy relentlessly forward. By the summer of 1944 all 15 development aircraft had flown, most with C-1 or later SN-2 Lichtenstein radar, and A-1 production machines were coming off the line in Poland. The 154C was to follow, with two ejection seats under a sliding bubble canopy and Schräge Musik 30mm cannon, while the Ta 254 was a still later family. But on 28 June 1944 the second A-1 broke up in flight. It was found that, whereas the Tego-Film bonding used in earlier aircraft was satisfactory, the cold glue hastily brought in as adhesive after destruction by the RAF of the Tego-Film plant contained excess acid which ate away the wood. The 154 thus never got into service — not even six Pulk-Zerstörer conversions packed with explosives intended to break up US bomber formations.

*Above: Ta 154 V3 (Ta 154A-03/U1), the first with Jumo 213 engines, full armament and FuG 212 Lichtenstein C-1 radar*

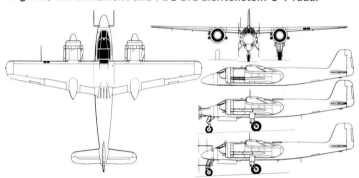

*Ta 154 V15, with side views of the V1 (top) and the V3 (centre)*

# Gotha Go 145

**Go 145A, B and C**
**Origin:** Gothaer Waggonfabrik AG, Gotha; production subcontracted to Ago, BFW (Messerschmitt) and Focke-Wulf; built under licence by CASA, Spain, and Demag, Turkey.
**Type:** Primary trainer, but see text.
**Engine:** 240hp Argus As 10C inverted-vee-8 aircooled.
**Dimensions:** Span 29ft 6¼in (9·00m); length 28ft 6½in (8·70m); height 9ft 6¼in (2·90m).
**Weights:** Empty (A) 1,940lb (880kg); maximum 3,043lb (1380kg).
**Performance:** Maximum speed 132mph (212km/h); typical range 404 miles (650km).
**History:** First flight February 1934; service delivery 1935; final delivery (Germany) not before 1943, (Spain) about 1945.

**Development:** The Go 145 is another of the many types of aircraft which made a giant contribution to World War II yet today are almost forgotten.

This biplane trainer was not only manufactured in enormous numbers — at least 9,965 in Germany, plus more than 1,000 in Spain and Turkey — but it also became a combat type and stayed in the very forefront of battle from 1942 until the final collapse in 1945. The basic machine was wooden, with fabric covering, but it was so tractable and strong that, as well as equipping roughly half the elementary flying training schools for the Luftwaffe from 1936 onwards, the Go 145 was chosen to equip the night harassment squadrons on the Eastern Front (triggered by the maddening pinpricks of the Soviet Po-2). At first called Störkampfstaffeln, they were progressively expanded and upgraded, and Go 145 output was expanded to meet the demand. In October 1943, after ten months, they were reclassified NSGr, the same as other night attack units, and many hundreds of 145s equipped six whole geschwader, plus the Ost-Flieger Gruppe. They carried various guns, light bombs, loudspeakers and even rockets. The only other sub-type in Luftwaffe use was the 145C gunnery trainer.

*Below: A standard Go 145A, one of the most numerous types of the entire Luftwaffe. This example was still being used in the pilot-training role.*

# Gotha Go 147

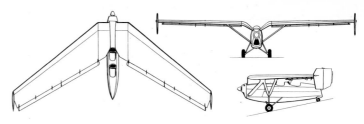

*Above: Three-view of Go 147b*

**Go 147a and 147b**
**Origin:** Gothaer Waggonfabrik AG.
**Type:** STOL observation aircraft.
**Engine:** (a) 140hp Siemens Sh 14A radial; (b) 240hp Argus As 10 inverted-vee-8.
**Dimensions:** (b) Span 40ft 1½in (12·22m); length 19ft 2⅝in (5·86m); height 9ft 6in (2·93m).
**Weights:** Empty (b) 2,083lb (945kg); loaded 2,524lb (1145kg).
**Performance:** (b) Maximum speed 137mph (220km/h).

**Development:** These two research aircraft were tailless machines to the general design of Dr A. Kupper, with gull wing swept at 38° and fitted with tip fins and rudders. Tested in 1936–39, these machines were intended to carry a synchronized MG 17 and manually aimed MG 15 fired by the observer in the rear cockpit. Unfortunately flight characteristics did not prove satisfactory.

*Right: The Go 147b is one of the least-known German aircraft of the Nazi period, and few photographs of it have been published. First flown in 1936, it proved a disappointing machine and was abandoned before the war.*

# Gotha Go 229

**Horten research aircraft and Ho IX V1 to V3 (Go 229 A-0)**
**Origin:** Gothaer Waggonfabrik AG, to Horten design.
**Type:** Single-seat fighter/bomber.
**Engines:** (229) two 1,980lb (900kg) thrust Junkers Jumo 004B turbojets.
**Dimensions:** Span 54ft 11¾in (16·75m); length 24ft 6¼in (7·47m); height 9ft 2¼in (2·80m).
**Weights:** Empty 10,140lb (4600kg); max loaded 19,840lb (9000kg).
**Performance:** Maximum speed 607mph (977km/h); abs ceiling 52,500ft (16,000m); range at 393mph (635km/h) with two drop tanks 1,970 miles (3170km).

**Development:** Walter and Reimar Horten were pioneers of the tailless all-wing aircraft, and though both brothers were Luftwaffe officers they contrived to have built a succession of beautifully graceful sailplanes with outstanding performance in 1936–40, followed by examples with two 80hp Hirth and then two 240hp Argus pusher engines. In 1942 the Hortens were released from uniform and headed Sonderkommando 9 to build the Ho IX jet fighter. This eventually materialised as the Go 229 (Ho IX V2), flown in January 1945 with outstandingly good results. Planned armament was four

30mm MK 103 or 108 cannon plus two 2,205lb (1000kg) bombs. The programme was halted by arrival at Friedrichsroda of US troops, the various Go 229 sub-types remaining active projects to the last.

*Above: The Ho IX V2 at Oranienburg where flight testing began in January 1945. Handling was outstanding.*

# Gotha Go 345

**Go 345A and B**
**Origin:** Gothaer Waggonfabrik AG.
**Type:** Assault glider.
**Dimensions:** Span 68ft 10½in (21·00m); length 42ft 7½in (13·00m); height 13ft 9¼in (4·20m).
**Weights:** Empty 5,445lb (2470kg); loaded (no pulse-ducts) 9,040lb (4100kg).
**Performance:** Maximum speed (free glide) 230mph (370km/h), (on level, with Argus ducts) 193mph (310km/h).

**Development:** Though there was no RLM requirement, Gotha persisted in work on a new transport glider, and after design by Avions Gourdou in France the Go 345 emerged in 1944 as the 345A with eight troops and side doors and the 345B carrying freight loaded through the stubby hinged nose. A prototype 345B was tested in 1944, but no example was flown of the A or of the Argus-duct powered version which could have flown (slowly and noisily) for considerable distances after release from its tug.

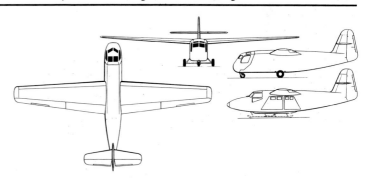

*Above: Three-view of the Go 345B with additional side view of Go 345A (lower)*

*Below: A heavily retouched photograph of the prototype Go 345B flown in the summer of 1944. This was the only Go 345 to fly, and illustrations are hard to find*

# Gotha Go 242 and Go 244

**Go 242A, B and C, Go 244B and Ka 430**
**Origin:** Gothaer Waggonfabrik AG, Kassel; production subcontracted.
**Type:** Transport glider (244, transport aeroplane).
**Engines:** (244) two 700hp Gnome-Rhône 14M4/5 14-cylinder radials.
**Dimensions:** Span 80ft 4½in (24·50m); length 51ft 10in (15·81m); height (242) 14ft 4¼in (4·40m), (244) 15ft 5in (14·70m).
**Weights:** Empty (242A-2) 7,056lb (3200kg), (244B-2) 11,245lb (5100kg); maximum (242A-2) 15,655lb (7100kg), (244B-2) 17,198lb (7800kg).
**Performance:** Maximum speed (242 on tow) 149mph (240km/h), (244) 180mph (290km/h); maximum range at sea level (244) 373 miles (600km).
**History:** First flight (242) early 1941, (244) late 1941, (430) 1944.

**Development:** This family of tactical transports was the only Gotha of World War II (other than the Go 145 designed much earlier). The 242 was a simple machine with nacelle of steel tube and fabric lifted and controlled by wooden wings and tail. It could carry 21 troops or light vehicles and stores loaded through the hinged rear fairing, took off on jettisonable wheels and landed on skids. The tug was usually the He 111, but the Bf 110 could cope on a good airfield; sometimes the He 111Z was used, and experiments were made with solid rocket ATO motors. Air bottles worked lift spoilers and flaps. Variants were A-1 (freight only), A-2 (troops), B-1 (nosewheel), B-2 (oleo landing gear), B-3 and -4 (paratroop), B-5 (dual trainer) and C-1 (flying boat). The number built was 1,528, in 1941–43, of which 133 were fitted with engines (almost always the French GR 14M, but sometimes the BMW 132Z or Russian M-25A) to become the Go 244. The 244B-1 to B-5 were conversions of the same 242 models, but they proved vulnerable in the Soviet Union and North Africa and were soon scrapped. The Ka 430, named for Gotha's lead designer Albert Kalkert, was a refined development with single tailboom. Experiments with the prototype included rocket braking.

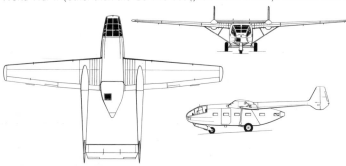

*Above: Three-view of Go 242B-1*

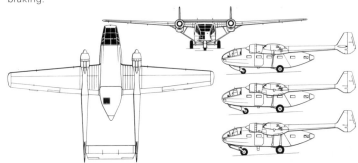

*Above: Go 244B-1 (middle), with Go 244 V1 (upper) and B-2 (lower)*

*Above: One of the Go 242A-0 pre-production gliders with slim tailbooms mounted above the wing.*

*Above: A standard Go 244B-1, probably originally built as a 242B-1. It had inadequate engine power*

# Gotha-Kalkert Ka 430

**Ka 430A-0**
**Origin:** Gothaer Waggonfabrik AG to Kalkert design.
**Type:** Assault glider.
**Dimensions:** Span 63ft 11¾in (19·50m); length 43ft 4½in (13·22m); height 13ft 8in (4·16m).
**Weights:** Empty 3,990lb (1810kg); loaded 10,140lb (4600kg).
**Performance:** Max speed on tow 186mph (300km/h); limit in free flight 199mph (320km/h).

**Development:** After he left Gotha in October 1940 Dipl-Ing Kalkert continued the design of improved assault gliders in collaboration with his former company, and in 1943 completed the Ka 430 design, with exceptionally good characteristics. Ratio of empty to gross weight was good, the single tail boom still allowed a full-section rear door, and it was planned to carry crew armour and a 13mm MG 131 dorsal turret. Loads could include 12 equipped troops or 3,080lb (1400kg) freight. Kalkert's company,

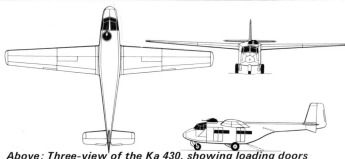

*Above: Three-view of the Ka 430, showing loading doors*

Mitteldeutsche Metallwerke, received an order for 30 pre-production Ka 430A-0 gliders, but only 12 were completed in 1944 before the programme had to be abandoned.

*Below: Artist's impression of Ka 430A-0*

# Heinkel He 45

## He 45a, b, c, d and C
**Origin:** Ernst Heinkel AG, Rostock-Marienehe; production, see text.
**Type:** Reconnaissance-bomber and advanced trainer.
**Engine:** (usually) 750hp BMW VI 7·3 vee-12 water-cooled.
**Dimensions:** Span 37ft 8¾in (11·50m); length (most) 34ft 9¼in (10·59m); height 11ft 9¾in (3·60m).
**Weights:** (C) empty 4,641lb (2105kg); loaded 6,052lb (2745kg).
**Performance:** Max speed 180mph (290km/h); range 746 miles (1200km).

**Development:** A sturdy and reliable machine, the He 45 was designed in 1931, and was possibly the first aircraft designed as a front-line type for the future Luftwaffe. The He 45a flew in the spring of 1932, the wooden wings and steel-tube fuselage having fabric covering and provision being made for a hand-aimed MG 15 in the rear cockpit. The He 45b added a synchronized MG 17 and a bomb load up to 440lb (200kg). In 1934 the He 45 was the leading aircraft in Erhard Milch's new production programme, and by 1936 no fewer than 512 had been delivered. Heinkel built 69 (including some for China, called He 61), BFW built 156, Gothaer Wagonfabrik 68 and Focke-Wulf 219, with various sub-type letters though all were virtually identical. At least 40 served with Nationalist Spain and six He 45C with the Legion Kondor. By 1939 most He 45C were serving in schools, but in autumn 1942 most survivors were transferred to Störkampfstaffeln (night harassment squadrons) on the Eastern front.

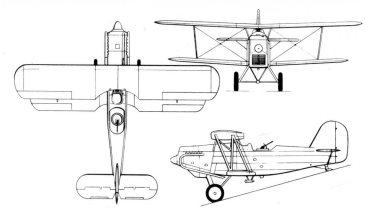

*Above: Three-view of He 45C*

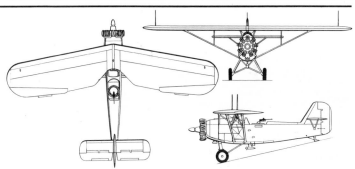

*Right: Early production He 45c, later re-styled He 45C, in pre-Nazi German livery in 1934*

# Heinkel He 46

## He 46a to f plus licensed variants
**Origin:** Ernst Heinkel AG; production, see text.
**Type:** Reconnaissance and army co-operation.
**Engine:** (most) 650hp Bramo SAM 22B (322B) nine-cylinder radial.
**Dimensions:** Span 45ft 11¼in (14·00m); length 31ft 2in (9·50m); height 11ft 1¾in (3·40m).
**Weights:** (C) empty 3,892lb (1765kg); max loaded 5,071lb (2300kg).
**Performance:** Max speed 161mph (260km/h); range 621 miles (1000km).

**Development:** Flown even earlier than the He 45, in 1931, the He 46a was an unusual biplane, with swept upper wing and unswept lower wing mounted well aft (giving the pilot a good view but the observer a poor one). Powered by a Siemens-built Bristol Jupiter, it was otherwise a pleasant aircraft, and the He 46b with lower wing removed and upper enlarged was very good. But the more powerful production engine, developed by Siemens (Bramo), vibrated excessively and caused such continual trouble the cowling was invariably left off permanently — though they stayed on the AS Panther-powered He 46Bu for Bulgaria and GR 14K-powered He 46Un for Hungary. By 1936 the Luftwaffe had received 481 of the standard He 46c (later called 46C) model, of which Heinkel built 200, Siebel 159, Fieseler 12, Gothaer Waggonfabrik 24 and MIAG 83. They had a 7·92mm MG 15 in the observer's cockpit, and provision for 20 bombs of 22lb (10kg). In 1937 this lumbering machine equipped 18 of the 24 Nahaufklärungsstaffeln (recce squadrons) and was also serving with Nationalist Spain. By 1939 most were used as trainers and hacks, but in spring 1943 this elderly machine blossomed out as a major Störkampfstaffeln (night harassment squadron) type, remaining in that role until in mid-1944 few were left.

*Above: Three-view of He 46C*

*Right: An He 46C in World War II but not yet in night-attack colour scheme*

# Heinkel He 50

## He 50 aW, aL, b, L (later redesignated 50A), aCh and bCh (B).
**Origin:** Ernst Heinkel AG; production, see text.
**Type:** Reconnaissance and dive bomber.
**Engine:** (most) 650hp Bramo SAM 22B (322B) nine-cylinder radial.
**Dimensions:** Span 37ft 8¾in (11·50m); length (most) 31ft 6in (9·60m); height 14ft 5¼in (4·40m).
**Weights:** (A) empty 3,528lb (1600kg); loaded 5,777lb (2620kg).
**Performance:** Maximum speed 146mph (235km/h); range at altitude at 110mph (177km/h) 373 miles (600km).

**Development:** This quite small but very capable aircraft was one of the first dive bombers built outside the USA, and it was designed to meet a 1931 order from the Japanese Navy. The He 50aW was a 390hp seaplane flown in mid-1931 (and underpowered) while the landplane He 50aL had a 490hp Siemens Jupiter and was better. The aL dropped 1,102lb (500kg) concrete blocks in dive-bombing demonstrations against targets floating in the Breitling near the Warnemünde factory. By 1933 Heinkel was delivering the He 50L, later designated 50A, with SAM 22B engine and flown in the dive-bombing role as a single-seater. A 1,102lb bomb load could be

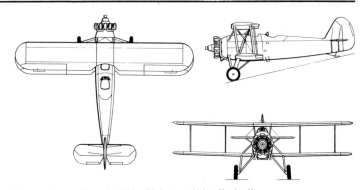

*Three-view of typical He 50A as originally built*

carried, with forward-firing MG 17, and if an observer was carried (with 551lb, 250kg, bomb load) he had an MG 15. Heinkel built 25 and BFW 35, and the Luftwaffe also took the second Chinese batch of He 50bCH, redesignating them 50B. In spring 1943 these old biplanes found front-line employment, manned mainly by Estonians, in NSGr 11 on the Eastern front.

# Heinkel He 51

### He 51A-1, B-2 and C-1

**Origin:** Ernst Heinkel AG; production see text.

**Type:** (A-1) Single-seat fighter (B-2) reconnaissance seaplane; (C-1) land ground attack.

**Engine:** One 750hp BMW VI 7·3Z vee-12 water-cooled.

**Dimensions:** Span 36ft 1in (11m); length 27ft 6¾in (8·4m); (B-2) about 31ft (9·45m); height 10ft 6in (3·2m); (B-2) about 11ft (3·35m).

**Weights:** (A-1), empty 3,223lb (1462kg); loaded 4,189lb (1900kg).

**Performance:** Maximum speed (A-1) 205mph (330km/h); initial climb 1,969ft (600m)/min; service ceiling 24,610ft (7500m); range 242 miles (390km).

**Armament:** Standard, two 7·92mm Rheinmetall MG 17 synchronized above fuselage; (B-2) same plus underwing racks for up to six 22lb (10kg) bombs; (C-1) same plus underwing racks for four 110lb (50kg) bombs.

**History:** First flight (He 49a) November 1932; (He 49b) February 1933; (He 51A-0) May 1933; service delivery of A-1, July 1934.

**Development:** Gradually, as the likelihood of Allied legal action receded, Heinkel dared to build aircraft that openly contravened the Versailles Treaty. The most startling was the He 37, obviously a prototype fighter, which in 1928 achieved 194mph, or 20mph faster than the RAF Bulldog which was still a year away from service. Land and seaplane versions led to a succession of He 49 fighter prototypes in the 1930s and these in turn provided the basis for the refined and formidable He 51. This was the first fighter ordered into production by the Reichsluftfahrtministerium for the reborn Luftwaffe.

Though the initial order for He 51A-1s was only 75, Heinkel was unused to such an order and many were built under licence by Ago, Erla, Arado and Fieseler – which were also fast tooling for their own designs. In March 1935 the Luftwaffe was publicly announced, and JG1 "Richthofen" fighter squadron was combat-ready at Döberitz with its new Heinkels. In November 1936, 36 He 51A-1s went to Spain with the Legion Kondor, giving a sufficiently good showing for the Nationalists to buy at least 30 from Heinkel. There followed a total of 50 of various He 51B seaplane versions, the 38 B-2s being for service aboard cruisers. The final batch comprised 79 C-1 ground attack fighters, of which 28 served in Spain. The He 51 was still in active service in September 1939, operating in the close-support role in Poland, and remained as an advanced trainer until 1943.

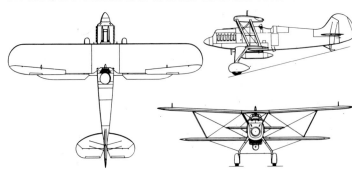

*Above: Three-view of He 51C-1*

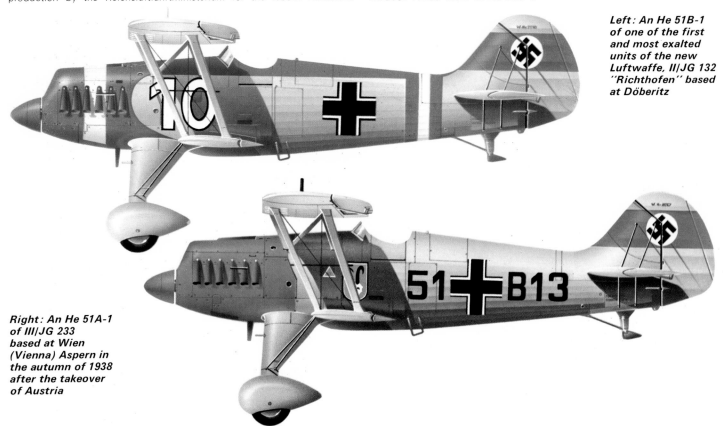

*Left: An He 51B-1 of one of the first and most exalted units of the new Luftwaffe, II/JG 132 "Richthofen" based at Döberitz*

*Right: An He 51A-1 of III/JG 233 based at Wien (Vienna) Aspern in the autumn of 1938 after the takeover of Austria*

# Heinkel He 59

### He 59B, C, D, E and N

**Origin:** Ernst Heinkel AG, Marienehe; production subcontracted to Walter Bachmann AG, Ribnitz; also some built under licence (about 1935) by Arado Flugzeugwerke.

**Type:** See text.

**Engines:** Two 660hp BMW VI vee-12 water-cooled.

**Dimensions:** Span 77ft 9½in (23·70m); length (most) 57ft 1¾in (17·40m); height 23ft 3¾in (7·10m).

**Weights:** (C-2) empty 13,702lb (6215kg); maximum 19,842lb (9000kg).

**Performance:** Maximum speed (typical) 134mph (215km/h); extreme range with max fuel 1,087 miles (1750km).

**Armament:** Three or four 7·92mm MG 15 (later, MG 81) manually aimed from bow, dorsal and ventral positions; many sub-types carried at least one 20mm MG FF, and most B-2 having provision for 2,205lb (1000kg) of mines, bombs or other ordnance.

**History:** First flight (landplane second prototype) September 1931; service delivery (He 59A-0) August 1932; final delivery from new, probably 1936.

**Development:** One of the first military aircraft built in Germany after the Versailles Treaty (which it openly contravened), the He 59 was destined to serve in an extraordinary variety of roles long after its antiquated appearance might have suggested it was obsolescent. In fact like many Axis warplanes it proved to be more and more useful, and though few were left by 1943 there were in that year at least 18 units operating different He 59 sub-types in mining, ground attack, rescue, transport, electronic warfare and psy-war missions. It was planned as a land or seaplane torpedo bomber, but in 1932 entered service mainly in the reconnaissance role. In the Kondor Legion in Spain it made heavy bombing attacks on Republican ports (often after a quiet gliding run-in at night), and in 1940 more than 180 were intensively used for all manner of missions – the most daring of which was the flying-in of ten He 59C-2 rescue transports to the Waal at Rotterdam to disgorge 60 troops who captured the city's main bridge. Most mining missions in 1939–43 were flown by B-2 or B-3 versions, but many were rebuilt as He 59N radio/radar trainers.

*Right: More than half of the surviving He 59s were rebuilt from 1942 as He 59N navigation trainers. Most carried full armament (though this one does not) and some were used to instruct aircrew on the Hohentwiel and other radars*

*Above: Last duty for many He 51s was advanced training at Jagdfliegerschulen (note tailwheel). Behind, an He 46C*

*Above: This He 51B-1 was photographed at an A/B Schule in about 1941. Armament was usually retained*

*Left: During World War II most He 51s were assigned to Jagdfliegerschulen (fighter-pilot schools) or to A/B pilot schools. This He 51B was at A/B 123 at Agram (Zagreb) in spring 1942*

*Right: Even in the training role the He 51 continued to be emblazoned with colourful badges and emblems. This He 51B wears a winged shield on which is a gryphon rising from the sea, the badge of A/B 71 at Prossnitz, 1942*

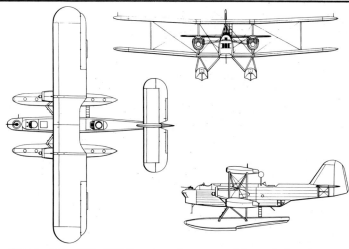

*Three-view of He 59B-2 reconnaissance and torpedo bomber*

# Heinkel He 70, He 170 and He 270

**He 70 (many versions), He 170 and 270**
**Origin:** Ernst Heinkel AG; (170) Manfred Weiss Flugzeug und Motorenfabrik, Budapest.
**Type:** (Most) three-seat reconnaissance bomber.
**Engine:** (70F) 750hp BMW VI 7·3 vee-12 water-cooled; (170) 910hp WM-K-14 (licenced GR 14K Mistral Major 14-cyl radial); (270) 1,175hp DB 601Aa inverted-vee-12.
**Dimensions:** Span 48ft 6¾in (14·80m); length 39ft 4½in (12·00m); height 10ft 2in (3·10m).
**Weights:** (F-2) empty 5,203lb (2360kg); loaded (recce) 7,465lb (3386kg), (bomber) 7,630lb (3460kg).
**Performance:** Maximum speed 224mph (360km/h); range on internal fuel 559 miles (900km).
**Armament:** (F-2) 7·92mm MG 15 manually aimed from rear cockpit, six 110lb (50kg) or 24 bombs of 22lb (10kg) internally.
**History:** First flight 1 December 1932; service delivery (DLH) March 1933, (Luftwaffe E-1) late autumn 1934, (170) September 1937; last delivery (170) February 1938.

**Development:** Possibly the most streamlined aircraft created in the inter-war years, the He 70 gained great prestige for the reborn German industry, and especially for Heinkel and the Günter brothers who designed it. Early versions were four-passenger high-speed transports for Deutsche Lufthansa, but after many development models the He 70E-1 went into production in 1934 as a recce-bomber. Crews apparently disliked it because they were unfamiliar with modern high-performance aircraft, but staffel A/88 did well with the Legion Kondor and the aircraft later transferred to the Spanish Nationalist air force and served until about 1945. Altogether about 280 military He 70s were built for the Luftwaffe, the standard He 70F-1 and F-2 serving during World War II. The He 170 was built in Hungary and used briefly on the Eastern front. Only one prototype was built of the He 270, in 1938, because despite an excellent performance it was by then outclassed.

*Below: One of the first radial-engined members of this graceful family was the He 170A-01, which led to a version produced in, and used by, Hungary in World War II.*

# Heinkel He 60

**He 60a and b, A, B, C, D and E**
**Origin:** Ernst Heinkel AG; production, see text.
**Type:** Reconnaissance seaplane.
**Engine:** (Most) 660hp BMW VI 6·0 vee-12 water-cooled.
**Dimensions:** Span 44ft 3¾in (13·50m); length 37ft 8¾in (11·50m); height 17ft 4¾in (5·30m).
**Weights:** (C) empty 6,019lb (2730kg); max loaded 7,840lb (3556kg).
**Performance:** Maximum speed 149mph (240km/h); range (typical) 513 miles (825km).

**Development:** Designed to meet an early requirement for a shipboard reconnaissance aircraft, the He 60a flew in early 1933. Its behaviour was excellent, though it was judged heavy and to have little margin of power for later development. After various modifications with prototypes the He 60A went into production in late 1933, being succeeded by the He 60B in mid-1934 and generally similar He 60C in the autumn. By 1935 this was being built by Heinkel and by Arado and Weser. By 1936 this tough two-seat seaplane was standard with the Küstenfliegergruppen, with MG 15 aimed by the observer. Weser built the He 60D with forward-firing MG 17, and Heinkel delivered six He 60E to Nationalist Spain. Arado and Weser built a total of 100 each, and survivors served with Kü.Fl.Gr. and SAGr. units until late 1943.

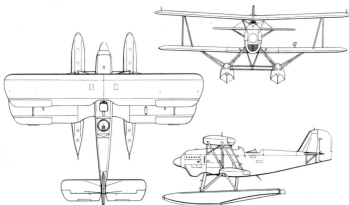

*Three-view of He 60C (D-series similar).*

*Above: Large numbers of He 60D-1 seaplanes were used from 1936 until 1943, chiefly in the Baltic and Gulf of Finland*

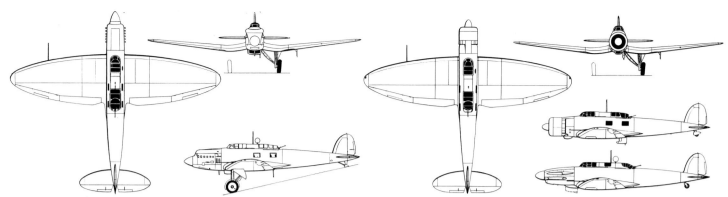

Above: Three-view of He 70F-2 reconnaissance bomber

Above: Three-view of He 170A, plus He 270 V1 (lower right)

Right: This He 70F-series reconnaissance-bomber served for many years in its original 1937 Aufkl. livery

Left: One of the first production model, the He 70E-1, in the markings of A/B 116 pilot school at Göppingen in 1940-41

Right: Many He 70s were painted in the Heinkel company scheme of silver and black. This one was assigned to 3 Aufkl. Gr (F)/123 at Grossenhain in 1936.

# Heinkel He 72 Kadett and 172

He 72A, 72B and 172
**Origin:** Ernst Heinkel AG.
**Type:** Primary trainer.
**Engine:** (A) 140hp Argus As 8B inverted in-line aircooled; (B) 160hp Siemens Sh 14A seven-cylinder radial.
**Dimensions:** Span 29ft 6¼in (9·00m); length (B) 24ft 7¼in (7·50m); height 8ft 10¼in (2·70m).
**Weights:** (B) empty 1,191lb (540kg); loaded 1,907lb (865kg).
**Performance:** (B) maximum speed 115mph (185km/h); typical range 510 miles (820km).

**Development:** The trim Kadett (cadet) was one of the chief primary trainers of the Luftwaffe, the others being the Fw 44, Ar 66 and Go 145. Lower-powered than most, it was in the class of the contemporary Tiger Moth, and was delightful to fly. The Argus-engined prototype flew in 1933, and by the end of the following year more than 100 He 72A production machines had been delivered, most to NSFK units, flying clubs and export customers. By early 1934 the main model, the more powerful He 72B-1, was being produced at the rate of about 100 per month, a much higher output than Heinkel had previously been able to achieve. Total production was several thousand, continuing until after 1936. Small numbers were built of derived versions including the 72BW seaplane, 72B-3 Edelkadett (leading cadet) and He 172 with engine in a slim NACA cowl (many Kadetts had a Townend-ring cowl). In 1936 a standard 72B-1 became the first aircraft to fly with liquid-rocket thrust when trials began with a 298lb (135kg) thrust Walter research engine. The 72B-1 was a standard *ab initio* type until proper training collapsed in late 1944.

Above: An early He 72B Kadett pictured in pre-war civil markings. Wartime Kadetts were usually grey or olive

Right: Despite this scene, the He 72A was not mass-produced.

# Heinkel He 74

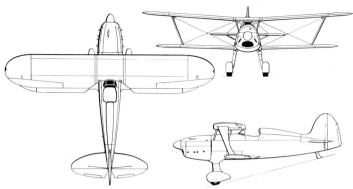

**He 74a, b and B**
**Origin:** Ernst Heinkel AG.
**Type:** Advanced trainer and light home-defence fighter.
**Engine:** 240hp Argus As 10C inverted-vee-8 aircooled.
**Dimensions:** Span 26ft 8¾in (8·15m); length 21ft 2in (6·45m); height 7ft 2½in (2·20m).
**Weights:** (B) empty 1,697lb (770kg); loaded 2,242lb (1017kg).
**Performance:** (B) maximum speed 174mph (280km/h); range 230 miles (370km).

**Development:** Though designed to meet the RLM Heimatschutzjäger (Home-defence Fighter) requirement of 1933, Heinkel's He 74 was a neat biplane, instead of the specified parasol or high-wing monoplane. It thus stood little chance (the winner was the Fw 56), but the Günter brothers' choice of two wings was vindicated by the little Heinkel's outstanding performance and manoeuvrability. Only three were built, the planned armament of an MG 17 never being flown.

*Above: Three-view of the He 74b*

*Below: The second (74b) prototype was an outstanding machine, but lost to the Fw 56 purely on aesthetic grounds*

# Heinkel He 111

**He 111 B series, E series, H series and P series**
**Origin:** Ernst Heinkel AG; also built in France on German account by SNCASO; built under licence by Fabrica de Avione SET, Romania, and CASA, Spain.
**Type:** Four-seat or five-seat medium bomber (later, torpedo bomber, glider tug and missile launcher).
**Engines:** (He 111H-3) two 1,200hp Junkers Jumo 211D-2 12-cylinder inverted-vee liquid-cooled; (He 111P-2) two 1,100hp Daimler-Benz DB 601A-1 12-cylinder inverted-vee liquid-cooled.
**Dimensions:** Span 74ft 1¾in (22·6m); length 53ft 9½in (16·4m); height 13ft 1½in (4m).
**Weights:** Empty (H-3) 17,000lb (7720kg); (P-2) 17,640lb (8000kg); maximum loaded (H-3) 30,865lb (14,000kg); (P-2) 29,762lb (13,500kg).
**Performance:** Maximum speed (H-3) 258mph (415km/h); (P-2) 242mph (390km/h) at 16,400ft (5000m), at maximum weight, neither version could exceed 205mph (330km/h); climb to 14,765ft (4500m) 30–35min at normal gross weight, 50min at maximum; service ceiling (both) around 25,590ft (7800m) at normal gross weight, under 16,400ft (5000m) at maximum; range with maximum bomb load (both) about 745 miles (1200km).
**Armament:** (P-2) 7·92mm Rheinmetall MG 15 machine gun on manual mountings in nosecap, open dorsal position and ventral gondola; (H-3) same, plus fixed forward-firing MG 15 or 17, two MG 15s in waist windows and (usually) 20mm MG FF cannon in front of ventral gondola and (sometimes) fixed rear-firing MG 17 in extreme tail; internal bomb load up to 4,410lb (2000kg) in vertical cells, stored nose-up; external bomb load (at expense of internal) one 4,410lb (2000kg) on H-3, one or two 1,102lb (500kg) on others; later marks carried one or two 1,686lb (765kg) torpedoes, Bv 246 glide missiles, Hs 293 rocket missiles, Fritz X radio-controlled glide bombs or one FZG-76 ("V-1") cruise missile.
**History:** First flight (He 111V1 prototype) 24 February 1935; (pre-

production He 111B-0) August 1936; (production He 111B-1) 30 October 1936; (first He 111E series) January 1938; (first production He 111P-1) December 1938; (He 111H-1) January or February 1939; final delivery (He 111H-23) October 1944; (Spanish C.2111) late 1956.

**Development:** A natural twin-engined outgrowth of the He 70, the first He 111 was a graceful machine with elliptical wings and tail, secretly flown as a bomber but revealed to the world a year later as a civil airliner. Powered by 660hp BMW VI engines, it had typical armament of three manually

*The first sub-type to feature the short asymmetric nose was the He 111P-0, one of which is seen here after roll-out from the enormous new Oranienburg factory in late 1938*

# Heinkel He 100

**He 100 V1 to V8 and 100D-1**
**Origin:** Ernst Heinkel AG.
**Type:** Single-seat fighter.
**Engine:** 1,175hp Daimler-Benz DB 601 Aa inverted-vee-12 liquid-cooled.
**Dimensions:** Span 30ft 10¾in (9·41m); length 26ft 10¾in (8·195m); height 11ft 9¾in (3·60m).

**Weights:** (D-1) empty 3,990lb (1810kg); max loaded 5,512lb (2500kg).
**Performance:** (D-1) maximum speed 416mph (670km/h); service ceiling 36,090ft (11,000m); range 559 miles (900km).

**Development:** Undaunted by loss of the Luftwaffe's fighter orders to BFW with the 109, Heinkel proposed a much faster fighter, with structure completely different from the rather unimpressive He 112 to make it more efficient and much quicker and cheaper to build. The resulting Projekt 1035 was completed on 25 May 1937 and at the end of that year the now-informed RLM sanctioned a prototype and ten pre-production machines. Heinkel managed to secure the number "100" though this had been previously alotted to Fieseler. The first prototype flew on 22 January 1938, and was clearly outstandingly fast, being small and having a surface-evaporation cooling system instead of a draggy radiator. Though there were many problems, and Luftwaffe test pilots disliked the high wing loading, Udet himself flew the V2 to a new world 100km circuit record at 394·6mph (634·73km/h). On 30 March 1939 Hans Dieterle, flying the clipped-wing V3, took the world speed record at 463·92mph (746·6km/h). But the RLM saw no reason for mass production, and six prototypes were sold to the Soviet Union and three He 100D-0 to Japan, with armament of two MG 17 and a 20mm MG/FF. The remaining 12 He 100D-1 fighters formed a Heinkel-Rostock defence unit, but in 1940 were publicised by Goebbels' propaganda machine in such a way as to convince Britain there was a fighter in large-scale service called the "He 113".

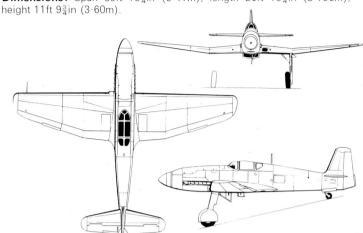

*Above: Three-view of He 100D-1*

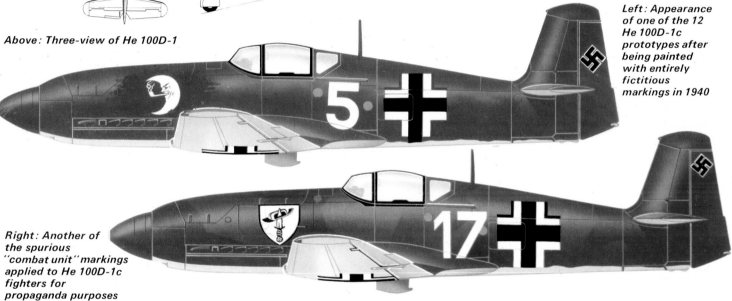

*Left: Appearance of one of the 12 He 100D-1c prototypes after being painted with entirely fictitious markings in 1940*

*Right: Another of the spurious "combat unit" markings applied to He 100D-1c fighters for propaganda purposes*

aimed machine guns but the useful bomb load of 2,200lb (1000kg) stowed nose-up in eight cells in the centre fuselage. In 1937 a number of generally similar machines secretly flew photo-reconnaissance missions over Britain, France and the Soviet Union, in the guise of airliners of Deutsche Lufthansa. In the same year the He 111B-1 came into Luftwaffe service, with two 880hp Daimler-Benz DB 600C engines, while a vast new factory was built at Oranienburg solely to make later versions. In February 1937 operations began with the Legion Kondor in Spain, with considerable success, flight performance being improved in the B-2 by 950hp DB 600CG engines which were retained in the C series. The D was faster, with the 1,000hp Jumo 211A-1, also used in the He 111 F in which a new straight-edged wing was introduced. To a considerable degree the success of the early elliptical-winged He 111 bombers in Spain misled the Luftwaffe into considering that nothing could withstand the onslaught of their huge fleets of medium

bombers. These aircraft – the trim Do 17, the broad-winged He 111 and the high-performance Ju 88 – were all extremely advanced by the standards of the mid-1930s when they were designed. They were faster than the single-seat fighters of that era and, so the argument went, therefore did not need much defensive armament. So the three machine guns carried by the first He 111 bombers in 1936 stayed unchanged until, in the Battle of Britain, the He 111 was hacked down with ease, its only defence being its toughness and ability to come back after being shot to pieces. The inevitable result was that more and more defensive guns were added, needing a fifth or even a sixth crew-member. Coupled with incessant growth in equipment and armour the result was deteriorating performance, so that the record-breaker of 1936–38 became the lumbering sitting duck of 1942–45. Yet the He 111 was built in ever-greater numbers, virtually all the later sub-types being

*continued on page 182* ▶

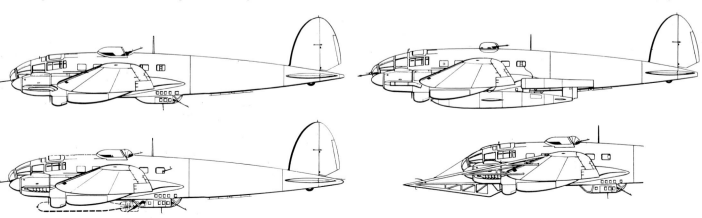

*Top: He 111H-1; above: He 111H-6 (with torpedo)*

*Top: Penultimate sub-type, H-22; above: H-8 with cable fender*

## ▶Heinkel He 111

members of the prolific H-series. Variations were legion, including versions with large barrage-balloon deflectors, several kinds of missiles (including a V-1 tucked under the 'left wing root), while a few were completed as saboteur transports. The most numerous version was the H-6, and the extraordinary He 111Z (Zwilling) glider tug of 1942 consisted of two H-6s joined by a common centre wing carrying a fifth engine. Right to the end of the war the RLM and German industry failed to find a replacement for the old "Spaten" (spade). and the total produced in Germany and Romania was at least 6,086 and possibly more than 7,000. Merlin-engined C.2111 versions continued in production in Spain until 1956.

*continued on page 184* ▶

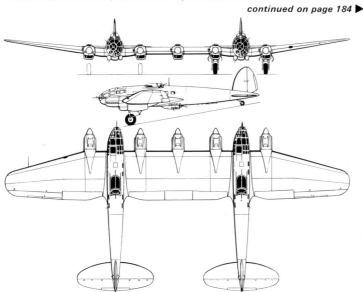

*Above: Brain-child of Gen Ernst Udet, the He 111Z (Z for zwilling or twin) was a five-engined tug for the Me 321 glider.*

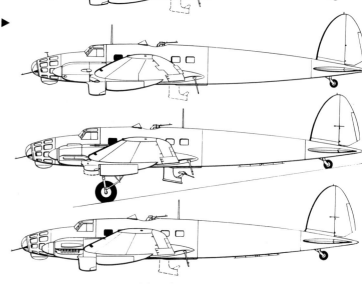

*Above: reading down: He 111A-0, B-2 and D-1, all with elliptical wings, and the straight-tapered F-4 and J-1*

### Heinkel He 111H-3

1 Starboard navigation light
2 Starboard aileron
3 Lattice ribs
4 Front spar
5 Rear spar
6 Aileron tab
7 Starboard flap
8 Outboard fuel tank (220 gal/1,000 litres capacity)
9 Wing centre section/outer panel break line
10 Inboard fuel tank (154 gal/700 litres capacity) inboard of nacelle
11 Oil tank cooling louvres
12 Oil cooler air intake
13 Supercharger air intake
14 Three-blade VDM propeller
15 Airscrew pitch-change mechanism
16 Junkers Jumo 211D-1 12-cylinder inverted-vee liquid-cooled engine
17 Exhaust manifold
18 Nose-mounted 7·92mm MG 15 machine gun
19 Ikaria ball-and-socket gun mounting (offset to starboard)
20 Bomb sight housing (offset to starboard)
21 Starboard mainwheel
22 Rudder pedals
23 Bomb aimer's prone pad
24 Additional 7·92mm MG 15 machine gun (fitted by forward maintenance units)
25 Repeater compass
26 Bomb aimer's folding seat
27 Control wheel
28 Throttles
29 Pilot's seat
30 Retractable auxiliary windscreen (for use when pilot's seat in elevated position)
31 Sliding roof hatch
32 Forward fuselage bulkhead
33 Double-frame station
34 Port ESAC bomb bay (vertical stowage)
35 Fuselage windows (blanked)
36 Central gangway between bomb bays
37 Double-frame station
38 Direction finder
39 Dorsal gunner's (forward) sliding canopy
40 Dorsal 7·92mm MG 15 machine gun
41 Dorsal gunner's cradle seat
42 FuG 10 radio equipment
43 Fuselage window

44 Armoured bulkhead (8mm)
45 Aerial mast
46 Bomb flares
47 Unarmoured bulkhead
48 Rear fuselage access cut-out
49 Port 7·92mm beam MG 15 machine gun
50 Dinghy stowage
51 Fuselage frames
52 Stringers
53 Starboard tailplane
54 Aerial
55 Starboard elevator
56 Fin front spar
57 Fin structure
58 Rudder balance
59 Fin rear spar/rudder post
60 Rudder construction
61 Rudder tab
62 Tab actuator

63 Remotely-controlled 7·92 mm MG 17 machine gun in tailcone (fitted to some aircraft only)
64 Rear navigation light
65 Elevator tab
66 Elevator structure
67 Tailplane main spar
68 Tailplane front spar
69 Semi-retractable tailwheel

70 Tailwheel shock-absorber
71 Rudder control linkage
72 Fuselage/tail frame
73 Rudder control cables
74 Elevator push-pull control rods
75 Master compass
76 Observation window fairing
77 Glazed observation window in floor

The chief bomber at the start of World War II was the He 111P family, with DB 601A engines. This formation, photographed in the spring of 1939, is of P-1 bombers of III/KG 255, which on 1 May of that year was redesignated III/KG 51. This wing was extremely active during most of the war, and was among the leaders of those which operated against Britain from bases in northern France

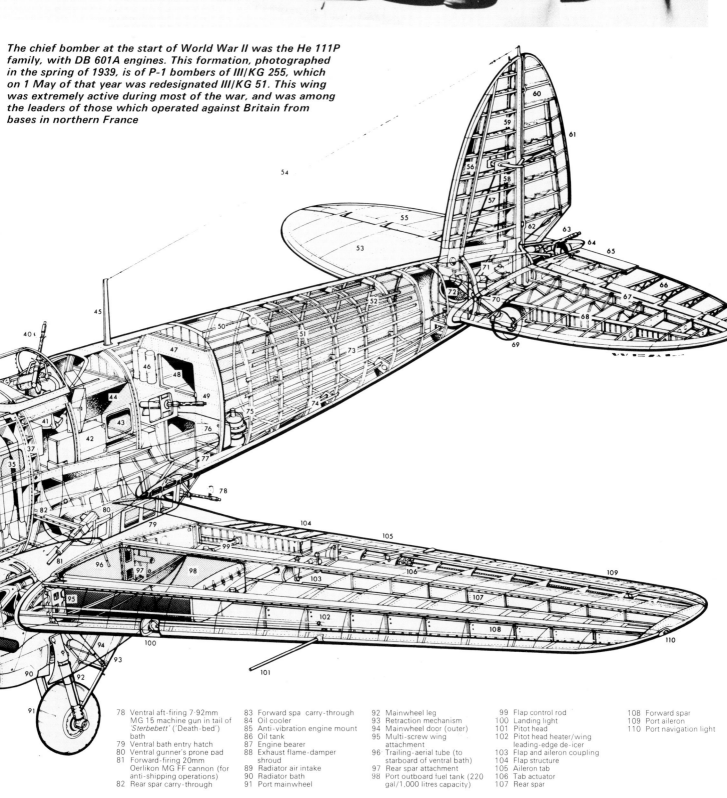

| | | |
|---|---|---|
| 78 Ventral aft-firing 7·92mm MG 15 machine gun in tail of 'Sterbebett' ('Death-bed') bath | 83 Forward spa carry-through | 92 Mainwheel leg |
| | 84 Oil cooler | 93 Retraction mechanism |
| | 85 Anti-vibration engine mount | 94 Mainwheel door (outer) |
| | 86 Oil tank | 95 Multi-screw wing |
| 79 Ventral bath entry hatch | 87 Engine bearer | attachment |
| 80 Ventral gunner's prone pad | 88 Exhaust flame-damper | 96 Trailing-aerial tube (to |
| 81 Forward-firing 20mm | shroud | starboard of ventral bath) |
| Oerlikon MG FF cannon (for | 89 Radiator air intake | 97 Rear spar attachment |
| anti-shipping operations) | 90 Radiator bath | 98 Port outboard fuel tank (220 |
| 82 Rear spar carry-through | 91 Port mainwheel | gal/1,000 litres capacity) |

| | |
|---|---|
| 99 Flap control rod | 108 Forward spar |
| 100 Landing light | 109 Port aileron |
| 101 Pitot head | 110 Port navigation light |
| 102 Pitot head heater/wing leading-edge de-icer | |
| 103 Flap and aileron coupling | |
| 104 Flap structure | |
| 105 Aileron tab | |
| 106 Tab actuator | |
| 107 Rear spar | |

# ►Heinkel He 111

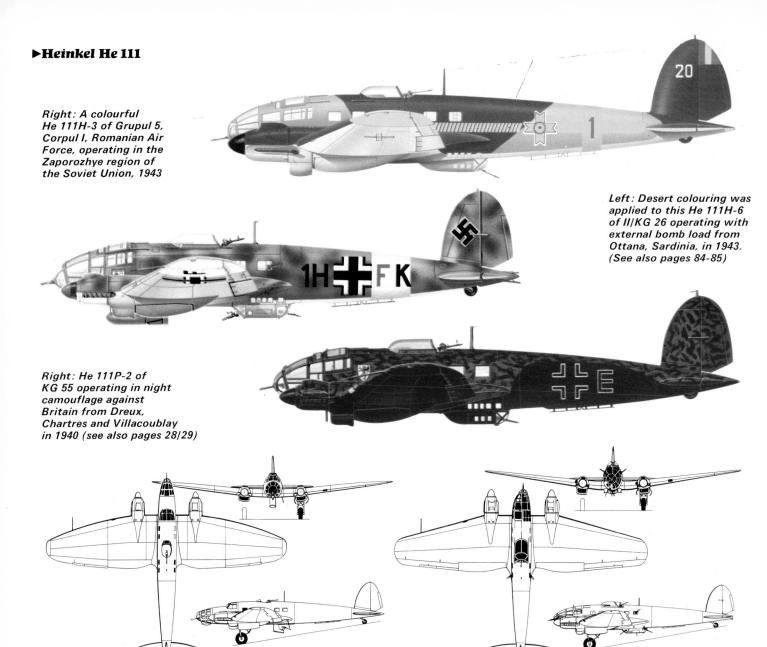

*Right: A colourful He 111H-3 of Grupul 5, Corpul I, Romanian Air Force, operating in the Zaporozhye region of the Soviet Union, 1943*

*Left: Desert colouring was applied to this He 111H-6 of II/KG 26 operating with external bomb load from Ottana, Sardinia, in 1943. (See also pages 84-85)*

*Right: He 111P-2 of KG 55 operating in night camouflage against Britain from Dreux, Chartres and Villacoublay in 1940 (see also pages 28/29)*

*Above: Three-view of the He 111E-3, showing landing gear and ventral "dustbin" extended. Powered by 1,010hp Jumo 211 engines, this was the most important elliptical-winged version, and it saw much active service in Spain*

*Above: Three-view of the He 111H-16*

*Below: An early He 111H-1 modified with additional radio equipment for anti-shipping use (pioneered by KG 26)*

# Heinkel He 112

**He 112B-0 and B-1**
**Origin:** Ernst Heinkel AG.
**Type:** Single-seat fighter and light ground attack.
**Engine:** One 680hp Junkers Jumo 210Ea inverted-vee-12 liquid-cooled.
**Dimensions:** (He 112) span 29ft 10¼in (9·1m); length 30ft 6in (9·3m); height 12ft 7½in (3·85m).
**Weights:** Empty 3,571lb (1620kg); loaded 4,960lb (2250kg).
**Performance:** Maximum speed 317mph (510km/h); initial climb 2,300ft (700m)/min; service ceiling 27,890ft (8500m); range 684 miles (1100km).
**Armament:** Two 20mm Oerlikon MG FF cannon in outer wings and two 7·92mm Rheinmetall MG 17 machine guns in sides of fuselage; underwing racks for six 22lb (10kg) fragmentation bombs.
**History:** First flight (He 112V-1) September 1935; (B-series production prototype) May 1937; final delivery (Romania) September 1939.

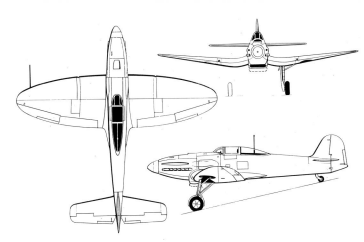

*Above: Three-view of the He 112B-1 (700hp Jumo 210G)*

**Development:** One of the first requirements issued by the rapidly expanded RLM under the Nazis was a specification for a completely new monoplane fighter to replace the Ar 68 and He 51. Heinkel's team under the Gunthers used He 70 experience to create the shapely He 112, which was much smaller and of wholly light-alloy stressed skin construction. Powered by a British Kestrel, it was matched at Travemünde against the similarly powered Bf 109 prototype, as well as the "also rans", the Ar 80 and Fw 159. Though Heinkel's fighter was marginally slower, it had better field performance, much better pilot view (especially on the ground), a wide-track landing gear and considerably better manoeuvrability. Many, especially Heinkel, were amazed when the Messerschmitt design was chosen for the Luftwaffe, though the He 112 was continued as an insurance. Nothing Heinkel could do with improved versions could shake the RLM's rejection, despite the delight of the RLM test pilots in flying them. Thirty He 112B-0 fighters were supplied to the Luftwaffe for evaluation, but 17 were promptly shipped to Spain (not as part of the Legion Kondor but flown by volunteer civilians). There they were judged superior to the Bf 109C, and 15 continued in Spanish service until after World War II. All but one of the other Luftwaffe machines were sold to the Japanese Navy, which disliked them intensely because of their high wing loading. Romania bought 13 B-0 and 11 B-1 fighters in 1939 and used them in the 1941 invasion of the Soviet Union.

*Above: Six of the 30 B-0 fighters supplied to augment the Luftwaffe during the 1938 Munich talks, later exported*

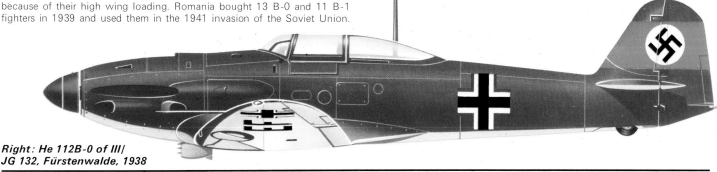

*Right: He 112B-0 of III/ JG 132, Fürstenwalde, 1938*

# Heinkel He 114

**He 114 V1 to V9, A, B and C series**
**Origin:** Ernst Heinkel AG.
**Type:** Reconnaissance seaplane.
**Engine:** (A-2) 970hp BMW 132K nine-cylinder radial.
**Dimensions:** Span 44ft 7½in (13·60m); length 38ft 2½in (11·64m) height 16ft 10¾in (5·15m).
**Weights:** (A-2) empty 5,104lb (2315kg); max loaded 8,090lb (3670kg).
**Performance:** (A-2) maximum speed 208mph (335km/h); range 571 miles (920km).

**Development:** Designed to succeed the He 60, the He 114 V1 flew in the spring of 1936 (DB 600A engine) but nine prototypes were needed to try to rectify the many water and air faults. Small numbers of several versions served briefly with the Luftwaffe, Romania, Spain and Sweden, with rear-cockpit MG 15 and two 110lb (50kg) bombs.

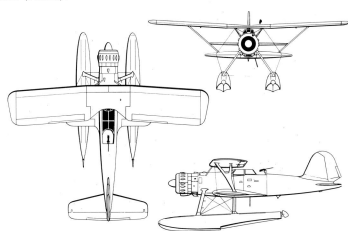

*Three-view of He 114A-2*

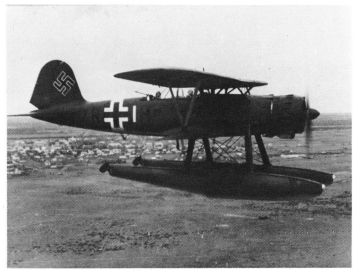

*This He 114C-1 was photographed in 1941 whilst serving with I/SAGr 125 in the Baltic and off the coasts of Latvia and Estonia and into the Gulf of Finland. These aircraft were later transferred to Romania*

# Heinkel He 115

**He 115A, B, C, D and E**
**Origin:** Ernst Heinkel AG, Marienehe.
**Type:** Multi-role seaplane, see text.
**Engines:** Two BMW 132 nine-cylinder radials, (B-1) usually 865hp 132N, (C-1) usually 970hp 132K.
**Dimensions:** Span 73ft 1in (22·275m); length (typical) 56ft 9½in (17·30 m); height (typical) 21ft 7¾in (6·60m).
**Weights:** Empty (B-1) 14,748lb (6690kg); maximum 22,928lb (10,400kg).
**Performance:** Maximum speed (B, C, typical) 203mph (327km/h); maximum range (full weapons) 1,300 miles (2090km), (max fuel) 2,050 miles (3300km).
**Armament:** See text.
**History:** First flight (prototype) about October 1936; service delivery (115A-0) July 1937; final delivery about July 1944.

**Development:** A wholly outstanding machine in all respects, the 115 was tough, beautiful to fly at speeds down to 75 knots, and carried a substantial load at relatively high speeds. In 1938 the prototype was specially stream-lined to set class records, and the first Luftwaffe operational version, the A-1, was sold to Norway and Sweden with small changes. Most A-models carried one LTF 5 or 6b torpedo or up to 2,205lb (1000kg) of mines of other stores, and the nose and rear cockpits each had a 7·92mm or 0·303in gun. By 1939 long-range B models were in production, which could carry the new 2,028lb (920kg) magnetic mine in addition to a 1,102lb (500kg) bomb load at a cruising speed of some 150mph. The B-2 had floats streng-thened for ice or snow. In April 1940 the Norwegian aircraft were engaged in fierce combat and made many bombing missions on German forces before the four survivors set out for Scotland. One of these was fitted with eight wing machine guns and used by the RAF on secret agent-dropping between Malta and North Africa. Another Norse escapee was used in Finland. In 1940 production centred on the C series, with many variants and often an MG 151 cannon in the nose. The single D had 1,600hp BMW 801 engines, and after being out of production 18 months a further 141 E-models were built in 1944 to bring the total past the 400 mark. Like the earlier versions the E-series were used for armed reconnaissance, minelaying, utility transport and casevac and even shallow dive bombing and torpedo bombing.

*Above: The He 115 was an outstandingly tough and tractable aircraft, even in its first production form, the Weser-built He 115B-0 of 1939*

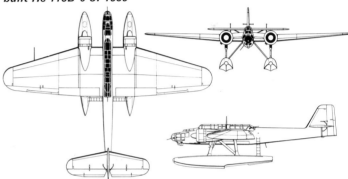

*Above: Three-view of He 115B-1; later types had nose cannon*

*Below: Winching up a practice torpedo into the internal weapon bay of an He 115B-1 in early 1940*

# Heinkel He 116

**He 116 V1 to V8, A, B and R**
**Origin:** Ernst Heinkel AG.
**Type:** Transport, later reconnaissance.
**Engines:** Four 240hp Hirth HM 508H inverted-vee-8 aircooled.
**Dimensions:** Span 72ft 2in (22·00m); length (B-0) 46ft 11in (14·295m); height 10ft 10in (3·30m).
**Weights:** (B-0) empty 8,862lb (4020kg); loaded 15,533lb (7046kg).
**Performance:** (B-0) maximum speed 202mph (325km/h); range 2,120 miles (3410km).

**Development:** Designed in 1936 to fly Lufthansa routes over distant mountains, the He 116 did not receive the expected high-altitude Hirth engines and the V1 prototype flew in spring 1937 on lower-rated units. Eight A-series mail carriers were built, followed by the He 116R with rocket takeoff boost (on 30 June 1938 this flew 6,214 miles, 10,000km, non-stop)

and finally six He 116B-0 were delivered to the Luftwaffe in 1938 as long-range photographic aircraft. Having neither pressurization nor armament they never crossed an enemy frontier, but did useful photographic work in Germany.

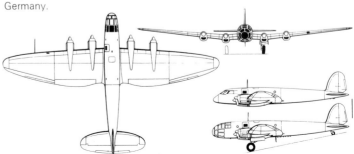

*Three-view of He 116B-0, with side view (upper) of A-series*

# Heinkel He 118

**He 118 V1 to V5 and A-0**
**Origin:** Ernst Heinkel AG.
**Type:** Dive bomber.
**Engine:** (V1) Rolls-Royce Buzzard, (others) 910hp Daimler-Benz DB 600C inverted-vee-12 liquid-cooled.
**Dimensions:** Span 49ft 6½in (15.09m); length 38ft 8¾in (11.80m); height 13ft 8¾in (4.18m).
**Weights:** (A-0) empty 5,952lb (2700kg); loaded 9,082lb (4120kg).
**Performance:** Max speed 245mph (395km/h); range 652 miles (1050km).

**Development:** Designed as a competitor in the second phase of the Sturzbomber programme for a definitive dive bomber, this beautiful machine was certainly the most advanced contender. The V1 flew in late 1935 on a British engine of 955hp, and two much-modified DB-powered aircraft followed in early 1936. But despite its fine qualities its timid performance in the fly-off at Rechlin in early June 1936 gave the great Stuka programme to Junkers. Later in that month Udet himself forgot to set coarse pitch in a vertical dive and had to bail out of a disintegrating third prototype. V4 and V5 went to the Japanese Navy and Army, respectively. Ten A-0 pre-produc-

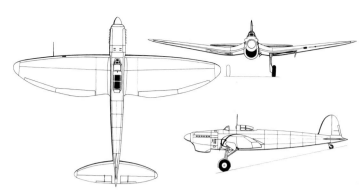

*Three-view of He 118 V1 (Rolls-Royce Buzzard)*

tion machines had provision for two MG 17 in the wings, an MG 15 in the rear cockpit and internal bomb load of 551lb (250kg) or 1,102lb (500kg) when flown solo. The He 118's only claim to fame is that it was the first aircraft to fly with a turbojet, an HeS 3A being air-tested under the fuselage of V2 in early 1939.

# Heinkel He 119

**He 119 V1 to V8**
**Origin:** Ernst Heinkel AG.
**Type:** High-speed reconnaissance bomber.
**Engine:** 2,350hp Daimler-Benz DB 606, comprising a coupled pair of inverted-vee-12 liquid-cooled.
**Dimensions:** Span 52ft 2in (15.89m); length (most) 48ft 6½in (14.79m); height 17ft 8½in (5.40m).
**Weights:** (V6) empty 11,464lb (5200kg); loaded 16,678lb (7565kg).
**Performance:** Maximum speed (V6) 367mph (590km/h); range 1,940 miles (3120km).

**Development:** A private venture by Heinkel to test radical ideas by the Günter brothers, the 119 was one of the most advanced aircraft to fly prior to World War II. The main unusual feature was that two of the most powerful engines were buried in the slim fuselage, coupled to a common gearbox driving a tractor propeller via a long shaft. On each side of this shaft sat the two pilots, in a unique transparent nose. There was no conventional radiator, the two engines being cooled by an evaporative system which condensed the steam between double wing skins. Like the later Moskito the 119 was thought to have such a high performance it could not be intercepted, and it had no armament. The V1 flew in mid-1937, reaching 351mph. Subsequently its speed was cut by fitting upper and lower MG 15s, at the insistence of the RLM, while the V2 had a prominent lash-up radiator. V3 was

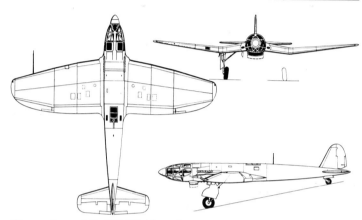

*Three-view of He 119 V6 (A-series recce prototype)*

a seaplane (it still reached 354mph), while V4 was a very fast aircraft which unfortunately made a forced landing after the 370mph outward leg of what was to have been a record flight. V5 to V8 were production prototypes for recce and bomber versions never put into production, the bomber having an internal bay for up to 2,205lb (1000kg). V7 and 8 went to Japan, while others became testbeds for the troublesome DB 606 and 610 engines.

# Heinkel He 176

**He 176 V1**
**Origin:** Ernst Heinkel AG.
**Type:** Experimental.
**Engine:** 1,323lb (600kg) thrust Walter HWK R1-203 liquid-propellant rocket.
**Dimensions:** Span (first wing) 13ft 1½in (4.00m), (second wing) 16ft 5in (5.00m); length 17ft 1in (5.20m); height 4ft 11in (1.50m).
**Weights:** (First wing) empty 3,462lb (1570kg); loaded 4,409lb (2000kg).
**Performance:** Maximum speed (theoretical, if sufficient fuel) 466mph (750km/h).

**Development:** First aircraft ever designed for rocket propulsion, the futuristic He 176 was ready for testing in the summer of 1938. Tiny and almost perfectly streamlined, it was towed behind a 7.6-litre Mercedes along the beach at Usedom (near Peenemünde) but refused to lift. Subsequent trials under power were a fiasco; it would not fly. Not until March 1939, with a bigger wing, could it just make a hop. On 20 June 1939 it flew for 50 seconds, and despite Udet's strong disapproval flew again on 3 July before Hitler. In fact the aircraft was so limited that propellants ("cold" mix of HTP and calcium permanganate) ran out before speed exceeded 215mph, though with more tankage 466mph might have been attainable.

*Below: One of the few illustrations believed to show the true shape of the He 176. Most published to date are misleading*

# Heinkel He 177 Greif

## He 177A-0 to A-5

**Origin:** Ernst Heinkel AG; also built by Arado Flugzeugwerke.

**Type:** He 177, six-seat heavy bomber and missile carrier.

**Engines:** Two 2,950hp Daimler-Benz DB 610A-1/B-1, each comprising two inverted-vee-12 liquid-cooled engines geared to one propeller.

**Dimensions:** Span 103ft 1¼in (31.44m); length 72ft 2in (22m); height 21ft (6.4m).

**Weights:** Empty 37,038lb (16,800kg); loaded (A-5) 68,343lb (31,000kg).

**Performance:** Maximum speed (at 41,000lb 18,615kg) 295mph (472 km/h); initial climb 853ft (260m)/min; service ceiling 26,500ft (7080m); range with FX or Hs 293 missiles (no bombs) about 3,107 miles (5000km).

**Armament:** (A-5/R2) one 7·92mm MG 81J manually aimed in nose, one 20mm MG 151 manually aimed at front of ventral gondola, one or two 13mm MG 131 in forward dorsal turret, one MG 131 in rear dorsal turret, one MG 151 manually aimed in tail and two MG 81 or one MG 131 manually aimed at rear of gondola; maximum internal bomb load 13,200lb (6000kg), seldom carried; external load, two Hs 293 guided missiles, FX 1400 guided bombs, mines or torpedoes (more if internal bay blanked off and racks added below it).

**History:** First flight (He 177V-1) 19 November 1939; (pre-production He 177A-0) November 1941; service delivery (A-1) March 1942; (A-5) February 1943.

**Development:** The Heinkel 177, Germany's biggest bomber programme in World War II, is remembered as possibly the most troublesome and unsatisfactory aircraft in military history, and it was only through dogged courage and persistence that large numbers were put into service. Much of the fault lay in the stupid 1938 requirement that the proposed heavy bomber and anti-ship aircraft should be capable of dive bombing. Certainly the wish to reduce drag by using coupled pairs of engines was mistaken, because no engines in bomber history have caught fire so often in normal cruising flight. Six of the eight prototypes crashed and many of the 35 pre-production A-0s (built mainly by Arado) were written off in take-off swings or in-flight fires. Arado built 130 A-1s, followed by 170 Heinkel-built A-3s and 826 A-5s with repositioned engines and longer fuselages. About 700 served on the Eastern Front, many having 50mm and 75mm guns for tank-busting; a few nervously bombed Britain in 400mph shallow dives, without any proper aiming of their bombs. So bothersome were these beasts that Goering forbade Heinkel to pester him any more with plans to use four separate engines, but Heinkel secretly flew the He 277, with four 1,750hp DB 603A, at Vienna, as the first of a major programme (*see* page 193).

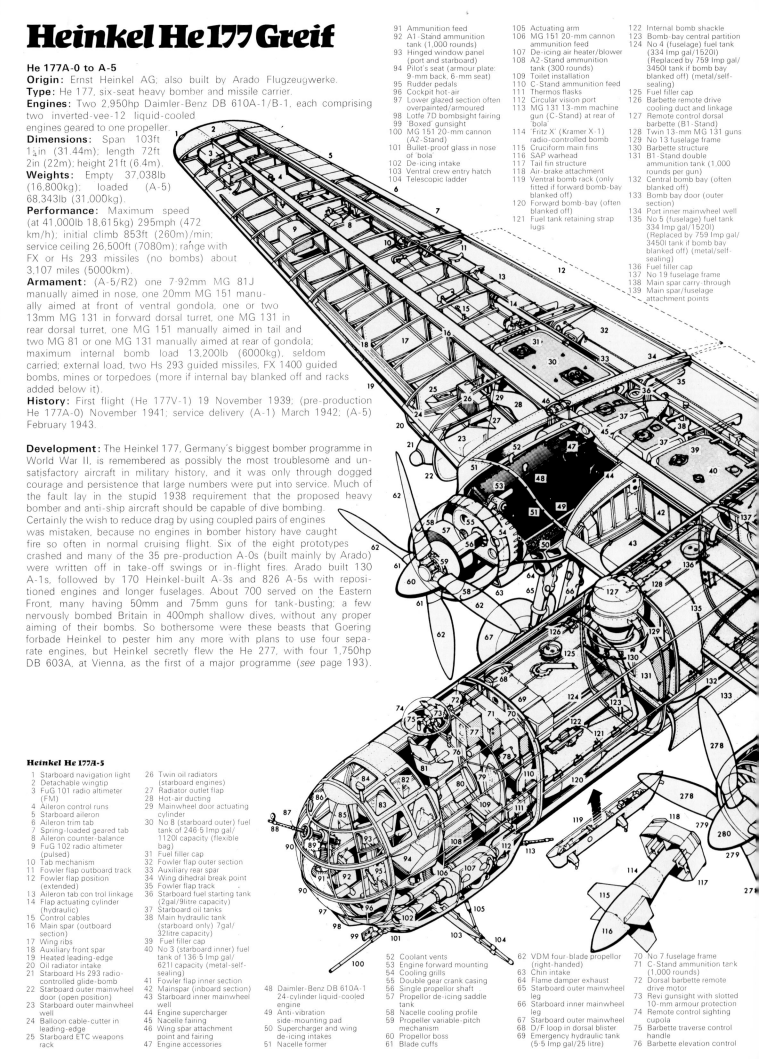

### Heinkel He 177A-5

1. Starboard navigation light
2. Detachable wingtip
3. FuG 101 radio altimeter (FM)
4. Aileron control runs
5. Starboard aileron
6. Aileron trim tab
7. Spring-loaded geared tab
8. Aileron counter-balance
9. FuG 102 radio altimeter (pulsed)
10. Tab mechanism
11. Fowler flap outboard track
12. Fowler flap position (extended)
13. Aileron tab control linkage
14. Flap actuating cylinder (hydraulic)
15. Control cables
16. Main spar (outboard section)
17. Wing ribs
18. Auxiliary front spar
19. Heated leading-edge
20. Oil radiator intake
21. Starboard Hs 293 radio-controlled glide-bomb
22. Starboard outer mainwheel door (open position)
23. Starboard outer mainwheel well
24. Balloon cable-cutter in leading-edge
25. Starboard ETC weapons rack
26. Twin oil radiators (starboard engines)
27. Radiator outlet flap
28. Hot-air ducting
29. Mainwheel door actuating cylinder
30. No 8 (starboard outer) fuel tank of 246·5 Imp gal/1120l capacity (flexible bag)
31. Fuel filler cap
32. Fowler flap outer section
33. Auxiliary rear spar
34. Wing dihedral break point
35. Fowler flap track
36. Starboard fuel starting tank (2gal/9litre capacity)
37. Starboard oil tanks
38. Main hydraulic tank (starboard only) 7gal/32litre capacity)
39. Fuel filler cap
40. No 3 (starboard inner) fuel tank of 136·5 Imp gal/621l capacity (metal-self-sealing)
41. Fowler flap inner section
42. Mainspar (inboard section)
43. Starboard inner mainwheel well
44. Engine supercharger
45. Nacelle fairing
46. Wing spar attachment point and fairing
47. Engine accessories
48. Daimler-Benz DB 610A-1 24-cylinder liquid-cooled engine
49. Anti-vibration side-mounting pad
50. Supercharger and wing de-icing intakes
51. Nacelle former

52. Coolant vents
53. Engine forward mounting
54. Cooling grills
55. Double gear crank casing
56. Single propeller shaft
57. Propeller de-icing saddle tank
58. Nacelle cooling profile
59. Propeller variable-pitch mechanism
60. Propellor boss
61. Blade cuffs

62. VDM four-blade propeller (right-handed)
63. Chin intake
64. Flame damper exhaust
65. Starboard outer mainwheel leg
66. Starboard inner mainwheel leg
67. Starboard outer mainwheel
68. D/F loop in dorsal blister
69. Emergency hydraulic tank (5·5 Imp gal/25 litre)

70. No 7 fuselage frame
71. C-Stand ammunition tank (1,000 rounds)
72. Dorsal barbette remote drive motor
73. Revi gunsight with slotted 10-mm armour protection
74. Remote control sighting cupola
75. Barbette traverse control handle
76. Barbette elevation control

91. Ammunition feed
92. A1-Stand ammunition tank (1,000 rounds)
93. Hinged window panel (port and starboard)
94. Pilot's seat (armour plate: 9-mm back, 6-mm seat)
95. Rudder pedals
96. Cockpit hot-air
97. Lower glazed section often overpainted/armoured
98. Lotfe 7D bombsight fairing
99. 'Boxed' gunsight
100. MG 151 20-mm cannon (A2-Stand)
101. Bullet-proof glass in nose of 'bola'
102. De-icing intake
103. Ventral crew entry hatch
104. Telescopic ladder

105. Actuating arm
106. MG 151 20-mm cannon ammunition feed
107. De-icing air heater/blower
108. A2-Stand ammunition tank (300 rounds)
109. Toilet installation
110. C-Stand ammunition feed
111. Thermos flasks
112. Circular vision port
113. MG 131 13-mm machine gun (C-Stand) at rear of 'bola'
114. 'Fritz X' (Kramer X-1) radio-controlled bomb
115. Cruciform main fins
116. SAP warhead
117. Tail fin structure
118. Air-brake attachment
119. Ventral bomb rack (only fitted if forward bomb-bay blanked off)
120. Forward bomb-bay (often blanked off)
121. Fuel tank retaining strap lugs

122. Internal bomb shackle
123. Bomb-bay central partition
124. No 4 (fuselage) fuel tank (334 Imp gal/1520l) (Replaced by 759 Imp gal/3450l tank if bomb bay blanked off) (metal/self-sealing)
125. Fuel filler cap
126. Barbette remote drive cooling duct and linkage
127. Remote control dorsal barbette (B1-Stand)
128. Twin 13-mm MG 131 guns
129. No 13 fuselage frame
130. Barbette structure
131. B1-Stand double ammunition tank (1,000 rounds per gun)
132. Central bomb bay (often blanked off)
133. Bomb bay door (outer section)
134. Port inner mainwheel well
135. No 5 (fuselage) fuel tank 334 Imp gal/1520l) (Replaced by 759 Imp gal/3450l tank if bomb bay blanked off) (metal/self-sealing)
136. Fuel filler cap
137. No 19 fuselage frame
138. Main spar carry-through
139. Main spar/fuselage attachment points

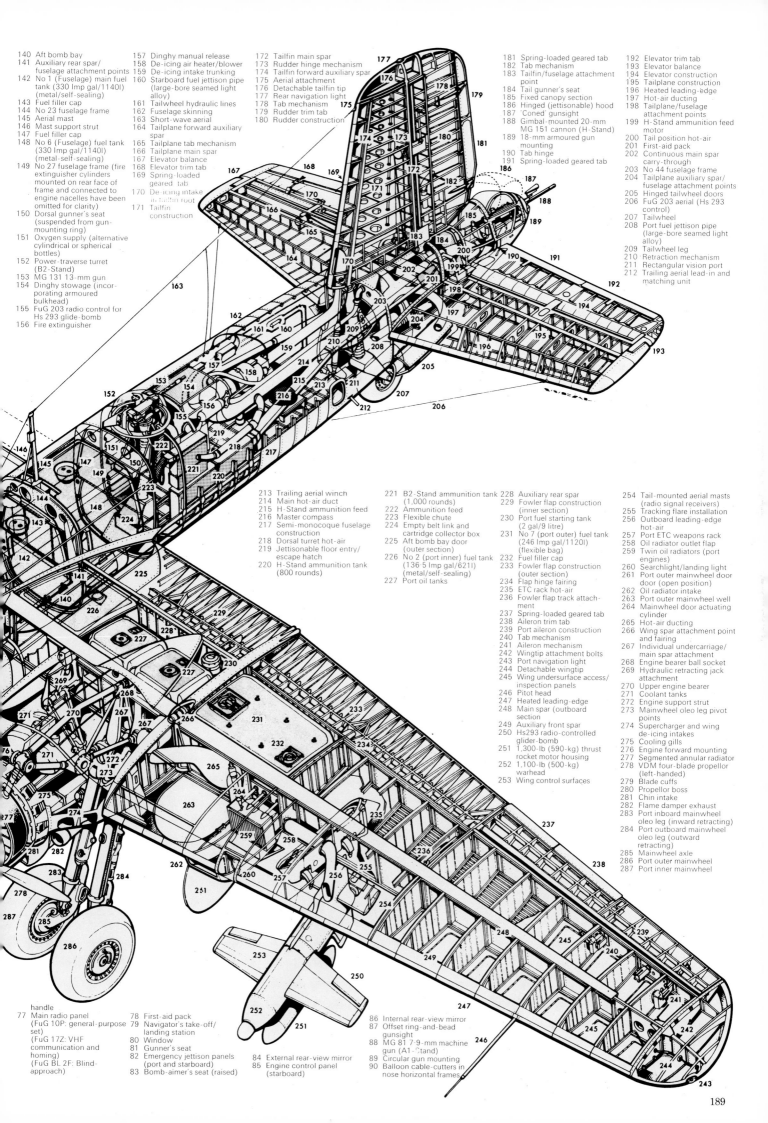

140 Aft bomb bay
141 Auxiliary rear spar/ fuselage attachment points
142 No 1 (Fuselage) main fuel tank (330 Imp gal/1140l) (metal/self-sealing)
143 Fuel filler cap
144 No 23 fuselage frame
145 Aerial mast
146 Mast support strut
147 Fuel filler cap
148 No 6 (Fuselage) fuel tank (330 Imp gal/1140l) (metal/self-sealing)
149 No 27 fuselage frame (fire extinguisher cylinders mounted on rear face of frame and connected to engine nacelles have been omitted for clarity)
150 Dorsal gunner's seat (suspended from gun-mounting ring)
151 Oxygen supply (alternative cylindrical or spherical bottles)
152 Power-traverse turret (B2-Stand)
153 MG 131 13-mm gun
154 Dinghy stowage (incorporating armoured bulkhead)
155 FuG 203 radio control for Hs 293 glide-bomb
156 Fire extinguisher

157 Dinghy manual release
158 De-icing air heater/blower
159 De-icing intake trunking
160 Starboard fuel jettison pipe (large-bore seamed light alloy)
161 Tailwheel hydraulic lines
162 Fuselage skinning
163 Short-wave aerial
164 Tailplane forward auxiliary spar
165 Tailplane tab mechanism
166 Tailplane main spar
167 Elevator balance
168 Elevator trim tab
169 Spring-loaded geared tab
170 De-icing intake trunking in tailfin root
171 Tailfin construction

172 Tailfin main spar
173 Rudder hinge mechanism
174 Tailfin forward auxiliary spar
175 Aerial attachment
176 Detachable tailfin tip
177 Rear navigation light
178 Tab mechanism
179 Rudder trim tab
180 Rudder construction

181 Spring-loaded geared tab
182 Tab mechanism
183 Tailfin/fuselage attachment point
184 Tail gunner's seat
185 Fixed canopy section
186 Hinged (jettisonable) hood
187 'Coned' gunsight
188 Gimbal-mounted 20-mm MG 151 cannon (H-Stand)
189 18-mm armoured gun mounting
190 Tab hinge
191 Spring-loaded geared tab

192 Elevator trim tab
193 Elevator balance
194 Elevator construction
195 Tailplane construction
196 Heated leading-edge
197 Hot-air ducting
198 Tailplane/fuselage attachment points
199 H-Stand ammunition feed motor
200 Tail position hot-air
201 First-aid pack
202 Continuous main spar carry-through
203 No 44 fuselage frame
204 Tailplane auxiliary spar/ fuselage attachment points
205 Hinged tailwheel doors
206 FuG 203 aerial (Hs 293 control)
207 Tailwheel
208 Port fuel jettison pipe (large-bore seamed light alloy)
209 Tailwheel leg
210 Retraction mechanism
211 Rectangular vision port
212 Trailing aerial lead-in and matching unit

213 Trailing aerial winch
214 Main hot-air duct
215 H-Stand ammunition feed
216 Master compass
217 Semi-monocoque fuselage construction
218 Dorsal turret hot-air
219 Jettisonable floor entry/ escape hatch
220 H-Stand ammunition tank (800 rounds)

221 B2-Stand ammunition tank (1,000 rounds)
222 Ammunition feed
223 Flexible chute
224 Empty belt link and cartridge collector box
225 Aft bomb bay door (outer section)
226 No 2 (port inner) fuel tank (136·5 Imp gal/621l) (metal/self-sealing)
227 Port oil tanks

228 Auxiliary rear spar
229 Fowler flap construction (inner section)
230 Port fuel starting tank (2 gal/9 litre)
231 No 7 (port outer) fuel tank (246 Imp gal/1120l) (flexible bag)
232 Fuel filler cap
233 Fowler flap construction (outer section)
234 Flap hinge fairing
235 ETC rack hot-air
236 Fowler flap track attachment
237 Spring-loaded geared tab
238 Aileron trim tab
239 Port aileron construction
240 Tab mechanism
241 Aileron mechanism
242 Wingtip attachment bolts
243 Port navigation light
244 Detachable wingtip
245 Wing undersurface access/ inspection panels
246 Pitot head
247 Heated leading-edge
248 Main spar (outboard section)
249 Auxiliary front spar
250 Hs293 radio-controlled glider-bomb
251 1,300-lb (590-kg) thrust rocket motor housing
252 1,100-lb (500-kg) warhead
253 Wing control surfaces

254 Tail-mounted aerial masts (radio signal receivers)
255 Tracking flare installation
256 Outboard leading-edge hot-air
257 Port ETC weapons rack
258 Oil radiator outlet flap
259 Twin oil radiators (port engines)
260 Searchlight/landing light
261 Port outer mainwheel door door (open position)
262 Oil radiator intake
263 Port outer mainwheel well
264 Mainwheel door actuating cylinder
265 Hot-air ducting
266 Wing spar attachment point and fairing
267 Individual undercarriage/ main spar attachment
268 Engine bearer ball socket
269 Hydraulic retracting jack attachment
270 Upper engine bearer
271 Coolant tanks
272 Engine support strut
273 Mainwheel oleo leg pivot points
274 Supercharger and wing de-icing intakes
275 Cooling gills
276 Engine forward mounting
277 Segmented annular radiator
278 VDM four-blade propellor (left-handed)
279 Blade cuffs
280 Propellor boss
281 Chin intake
282 Flame damper exhaust
283 Port inboard mainwheel oleo leg (inward retracting)
284 Port outboard mainwheel oleo leg (outward retracting)
285 Mainwheel axle
286 Port outer mainwheel
287 Port inner mainwheel

handle
77 Main radio panel (FuG 10P: general-purpose set) (FuG 17Z: VHF communication and homing) (FuG BL 2F: Blind-approach)

78 First-aid pack
79 Navigator's take-off/ landing station
80 Window
81 Gunner's seat
82 Emergency jettison panels (port and starboard)
83 Bomb-aimer's seat (raised)

84 External rear-view mirror
85 Engine control panel (starboard)

86 Internal rear-view mirror
87 Offset ring-and-bead gunsight
88 MG 81 7·9-mm machine gun (A1-Stand)
89 Circular gun mounting
90 Balloon cable-cutters in nose horizontal frames

189

# Heinkel He 219

### He 219A-0 to A-7, B and C series

**Origin:** Ernst Heinkel AG.

**Type:** A-series, two-seat night fighter.

**Engines:** Usually two 1,900hp Daimler-Benz DB 603G inverted-vee-12 liquid-cooled; other engines, see text.

**Dimensions:** (A-series) span 60ft 2in or 60ft 8in (18·5m); length (with aerials) 50ft 11¾in (15·54m); height 13ft 5½in (4·1m).

**Weights:** (A-7) empty 24,692lb (11,200kg); loaded 33,730lb (15,200kg).

**Performance:** (A-7) maximum speed 416mph (670km/h); initial climb 1,804ft (550m)/min; service ceiling 41,660ft (12,700m); range 1,243 miles (2000km).

**Armament:** Varied, see text.

**History:** First flight (219V-1) 15 November 1942; service delivery (prototypes) May 1943; (production 219A-1) November 1943.

**Development:** Ernst Heinkel was the pioneer of gas-turbine jet aircraft, flying the He 178 on 27 August 1939 and the He 280 twin-jet fighter as a glider on 22 September 1940 and with its engines on 2 April 1941 (before the purely experimental Gloster E.28/39). But Heinkel was unable to build the extremely promising He 280 in quantity, which was fortunate for the Allies. He had no spare capacity for the He 219 either, which had excited little official interest when submitted as the P.1060 project in August 1940 as a high-speed fighter, bomber and torpedo carrier. It was only when RAF night attacks began to hurt, at the end of 1941, that he was asked to produce the 219 as a night fighter (Uhu meaning Owl). The He 219V-1, with 1,750hp DB 603AS and two MG 151/20 cannon, plus an MG 131 in the rear cockpit, was fast and extremely manoeuvrable and the test pilots at Rechlin were thrilled by it. Successive prototypes had much heavier armament and radar and 100 were ordered from five factories in Germany, Poland and Austria. The order was soon trebled and Luftwaffe enthusiasm was such that even the early prototypes were sent to Venlo, Holland, to form a special trials unit. The first six night sorties resulted in the claimed destruction of 20 RAF bombers, six of them the previously almost immune Mosquitoes! More than 15 different versions of the 219 then appeared, immediately proving outstandingly formidable. The A-2/R1 had 603As, two MG 151/20 in the wing roots and two or four in a belly tray and two 30mm MK 108 firing upward at 65° in a Schräge Musik (Jazz Music) installation for destroying

*continued on page 192* ▶

**Above:** *This He 219A-5/R2 is pictured shortly after capture in 1945. Possessed of tremendous firepower and excellent performance, it was a most formidable aircraft*

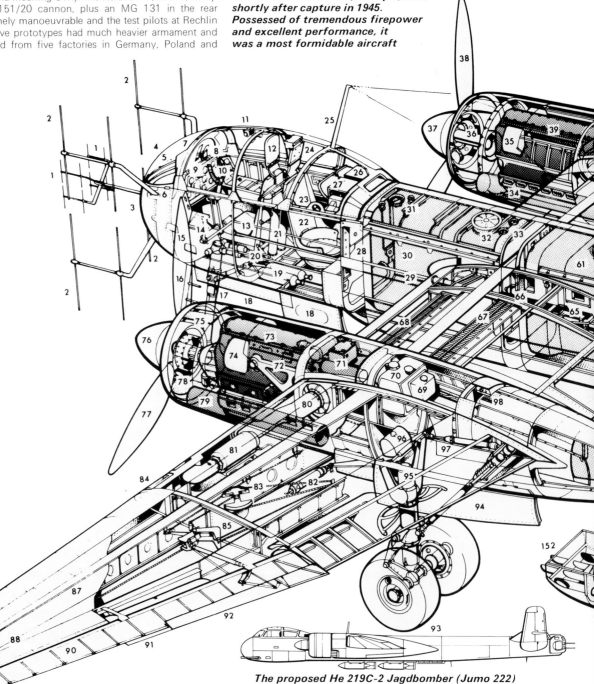

*The proposed He 219C-2 Jagdbomber (Jumo 222)*

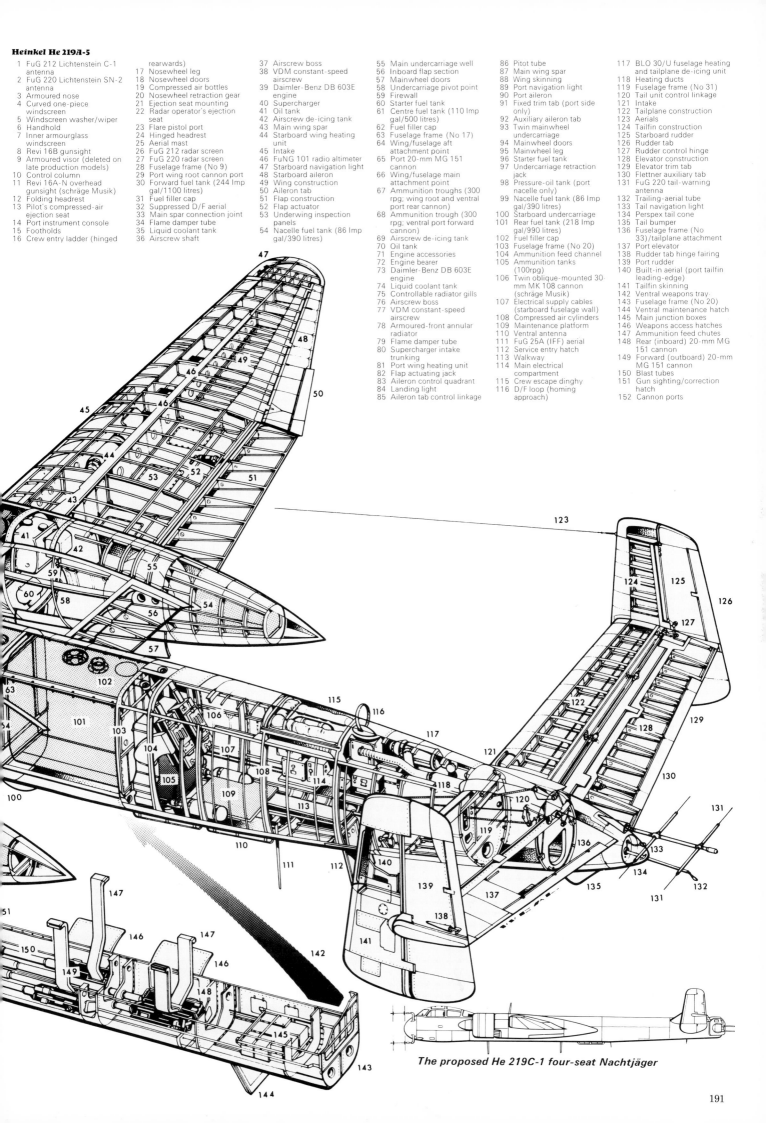

# Heinkel He 219A-5

1. FuG 212 Lichtenstein C-1 antenna
2. FuG 220 Lichtenstein SN-2 antenna
3. Armoured nose
4. Curved one-piece windscreen
5. Windscreen washer/wiper
6. Handhold
7. Inner armourglass windscreen
8. Revi 16B gunsight
9. Armoured visor (deleted on late production models)
10. Control column
11. Revi 16A-N overhead gunsight (schräge Musik)
12. Folding headrest
13. Pilot's compressed-air ejection seat
14. Port instrument console
15. Footholds
16. Crew entry ladder (hinged rearwards)
17. Nosewheel leg
18. Nosewheel doors
19. Compressed air bottles
20. Nosewheel retraction gear
21. Ejection seat mounting
22. Radar operator's ejection seat
23. Flare pistol port
24. Hinged headrest
25. Aerial mast
26. FuG 212 radar screen
27. FuG 220 radar screen
28. Fuselage frame (No 9)
29. Port wing root cannon port
30. Forward fuel tank (244 Imp gal/1100 litres)
31. Fuel filler cap
32. Suppressed D/F aerial
33. Main spar connection joint
34. Flame damper tube
35. Liquid coolant tank
36. Airscrew shaft
37. Airscrew boss
38. VDM constant-speed airscrew
39. Daimler-Benz DB 603E engine
40. Supercharger
41. Oil tank
42. Airscrew de-icing tank
43. Main wing spar
44. Starboard wing heating unit
45. Intake
46. FuNG 101 radio altimeter
47. Starboard navigation light
48. Starboard aileron
49. Wing construction
50. Aileron tab
51. Flap construction
52. Flap actuator
53. Underwing inspection panels
54. Nacelle fuel tank (86 Imp gal/390 litres)
55. Main undercarriage well
56. Inboard flap section
57. Mainwheel doors
58. Undercarriage pivot point
59. Firewall
60. Starter fuel tank
61. Centre fuel tank (110 Imp gal/500 litres)
62. Fuel filler cap
63. Fuselage frame (No 17)
64. Wing/fuselage aft attachment point
65. Port 20-mm MG 151 cannon
66. Wing/fuselage main attachment point
67. Ammunition troughs (300 rpg; wing root and ventral port rear cannon)
68. Ammunition trough (300 rpg; ventral port forward cannon)
69. Airscrew de-icing tank
70. Oil tank
71. Engine accessories
72. Engine bearer
73. Daimler-Benz DB 603E engine
74. Liquid coolant tank
75. Controllable radiator gills
76. Airscrew boss
77. VDM constant-speed airscrew
78. Armoured-front annular radiator
79. Flame damper tube
80. Supercharger intake trunking
81. Port wing heating unit
82. Flap actuating jack
83. Aileron control quadrant
84. Landing light
85. Aileron tab control linkage
86. Pitot tube
87. Main wing spar
88. Wing skinning
89. Port navigation light
90. Port aileron
91. Fixed trim tab (port side only)
92. Auxiliary aileron tab
93. Twin mainwheel undercarriage
94. Mainwheel doors
95. Mainwheel leg
96. Starter fuel tank
97. Undercarriage retraction jack
98. Pressure-oil tank (port nacelle only)
99. Nacelle fuel tank (86 Imp gal/390 litres)
100. Starboard undercarriage
101. Rear fuel tank (218 Imp gal/990 litres)
102. Fuel filler cap
103. Fuselage frame (No 20)
104. Ammunition feed channel
105. Ammunition tanks (100rpg)
106. Twin oblique-mounted 30-mm MK 108 cannon (schräge Musik)
107. Electrical supply cables (starboard fuselage wall)
108. Compressed air cylinders
109. Maintenance platform
110. Ventral antenna
111. FuG 25A (IFF) aerial
112. Service entry hatch
113. Walkway
114. Main electrical compartment
115. Crew escape dinghy
116. D/F loop (homing approach)
117. BLO 30/U fuselage heating and tailplane de-icing unit
118. Heating ducts
119. Fuselage frame (No 31)
120. Tail unit control linkage
121. Intake
122. Tailplane construction
123. Aerials
124. Tailfin construction
125. Starboard rudder
126. Rudder tab
127. Rudder control hinge
128. Elevator construction
129. Elevator trim tab
130. Flettner auxiliary tab
131. FuG 220 tail-warning antenna
132. Trailing-aerial tube
133. Tail navigation light
134. Perspex tail cone
135. Tail bumper
136. Fuselage frame (No 33)/tailplane attachment
137. Port elevator
138. Rudder tab hinge fairing
139. Port rudder
140. Built-in aerial (port tailfin leading-edge)
141. Tailfin skinning
142. Ventral weapons tray
143. Fuselage frame (No 20)
144. Ventral maintenance hatch
145. Main junction boxes
146. Weapons access hatches
147. Ammunition feed chutes
148. Rear (inboard) 20-mm MG 151 cannon
149. Forward (outboard) 20-mm MG 151 cannon
150. Blast tubes
151. Gun sighting/correction hatch
152. Cannon ports

*The proposed He 219C-1 four-seat Nachtjäger*

bombers by formating below them. The A-7/R1 had MK 108s in the wing roots and two of these big guns and two MG 151/20 in the tray, plus the Schräge Musik with 100 rounds per gun (the most lethal of all). Some versions had three seats, long-span wing and DB 603L turbocharged engines, or Jumo 213s or even the 2,500hp Jumo 222 with six banks of four cylinders. The B and C families would have been enlarged multi-role versions with rear turrets. Total A-type production was only 268, the officials at one time ignoring Luftwaffe enthusiasm by ordering production to be stopped!

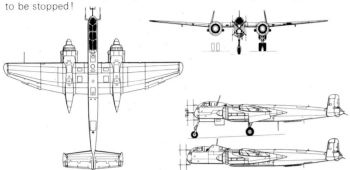

He 219A-5/R1; (lower) A-5/R4 with MG 131 in rear cockpit for defence

*The He 219A-7/R4 was one of the most important operational versions, with high-altitude equipment but armament reduced to only four MG 151, two in the wing roots and two in the ventral tray. It had ejection seats as standard*

# Heinkel He 178

**He 178 V1 and V2**
**Origin:** Ernst Heinkel AG.
**Type:** Experimental.
**Engine:** 992lb (450kg) thrust, later 1,102lb (500kg), Heinkel HeS 3B turbojet.
**Dimensions:** Span 23ft 3½in (7·20m); length 24ft 6½in (7·48m); height 6ft 10½in (2·10m).
**Weights:** Empty 3,572lb (1620kg); loaded 4,405lb (1998kg).
**Performance:** Maximum speed (sea level, est.) 435mph (700km/h).

**Development:** Though it had a rather brief and not very useful life, the He 178 is one of the great aircraft of history because it was the first jet. Hans-Joachim Pabst von Ohain was the moving spirit behind the engine, which was built as a private venture by Heinkel, as was the aircraft. A very small and limited machine, the 178 had a dural fuselage and wooden wing, and initially burned gasoline (petrol) but later switched to diesel J2. A brief hop was made on 24 August 1939, and a longer flight followed on 27 August, though even this was little more than a circuit (the landing gear was not retracted and a bird ingested on takeoff caused loss of thrust). The RLM was then told about the project, and showed little interest, though Udet and Milch

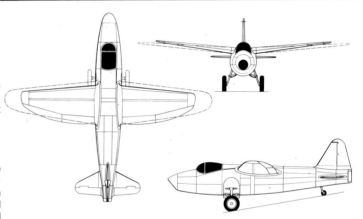

*Three-view of He 178 V1; the V2 (larger wings) never flew*

watched the V1 on 1 November 1939 at its base at Marienehe. The V1 hardly flew again, and was destroyed in the Berlin Air Museum by bombs in 1943. The V2 never flew.

# Heinkel He 274

**He 274 V1 and V2**
**Origin:** Ernst Heinkel AG; programme assigned to SAUF, Suresnes, France.
**Type:** Heavy bomber.
**Engines:** Four 1,850hp Daimler-Benz DB 603A-2 inverted-vee-12 with turbochargers.
**Dimensions:** Span 145ft 0¼in (44·20m); length 78ft 1¼in (23·80m); height 18ft 0½in (5·50m).
**Weights:** Empty 46,964lb (21,300kg); max loaded 83,786lb (38,000kg).
**Performance:** Maximum speed (sea level) 267mph, (36,090ft, 11,000m) 360mph (580km/h); ceiling 46,915ft (14,300m); range 2,640 miles (4250km).

**Development:** Probably the most formidable bomber built in Europe in World War II, the He 274 could have been started at the same time as the

He 177—and it is fortunate for Britain that it was not. While Heinkel strove to make the "bug-ridden" He 177 work, the He 177A-4 was under development at Vienna-Schwechat as a pressurized high-altitude version. But commonality with the 177 was gradually found to be impossible, and in late 1941 the 177A-4 was recast as the He 274 and assigned to SAUF (Farman) at Suresnes, near Paris. Work went amazingly slowly, and the French contrived to miss by a hair's breadth having the 274 V1 ready before the Germans left in July 1944. The two prototypes were impressive aircraft, and first flight finally came with French markings in December 1945, with the designation AAS 01A.

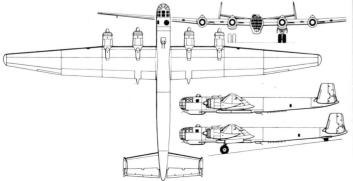

*Three-view of He 274 V1 (upper side view, initial form)*

*Above: French ground crew preparing the AAS 01A (French designation for the He 274 V1) which flew at Orleans-Bricy in December 1945. It would have been an outstanding bomber*

# Heinkel He 277

**He 277 V1 to V3, B-5, B-6 and B-7 series**
**Origin:** Ernst Heinkel AG.
**Type:** Heavy bomber, recce and anti-shipping aircraft.
**Engines:** (B-5) four 1,850hp Daimler-Benz DB 603A inverted-vee-12; (B-6) 2,060hp Jumo 213F.
**Dimensions:** Span (B-5) 103ft 1¾in (31·44m), (B-6) 131ft 2¾in (40·00m); length 72ft 8in (22·15m), (B-6, various 69ft 11in to 73ft); height 21ft 10½in (6·66m).
**Weights:** (B-5) empty 48,067lb (21,800kg); maximum loaded 98,096lb (44,490kg).
**Performance:** Maximum speed (all) 354mph (570km/h); range (B-5) 3,728 miles (6000km), (B-6) 4,474 miles (7200km).

**Development:** The simplest way of solving the main problem with the He 177 was to use four separate engines, and this would also have made a superior aircraft; but Goering got so fed up with Heinkel's incessant requests to be allowed to build the He 277 that he expressly forbade any further mention of it (this was about November 1941). Heinkel obeyed, but secretly went ahead on his own at Vienna-Schwechat with a bomber he called "He 177B". One day in May 1943 he told Hitler this aircraft could meet all the demands for a new bomber the Führer was making and was promptly

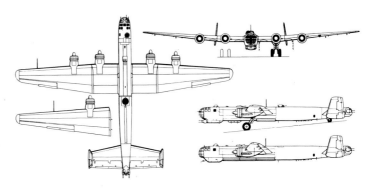

*Three-view of He 277B-5/R2 (inset and lower side view, B-7)*

told to build it, so it became legal as the 277. The V1 flew in late 1943, and a more advanced V2 followed in February 1944. Soon there were several advanced proposed production versions, with a frightening array of cannon turrets and barbettes and heavy loads of bombs and missiles. But on 3 July 1944 the whole programme was stopped, with the order to build nothing but fighters.

# Heinkel He 280

**He 280 V1 to V8**
**Origin:** Ernst Heinkel AG.
**Type:** Single-seat fighter.
**Engines:** (Most) two 1,852lb (840kg) thrust Junkers Jumo 004A turbojets.
**Dimensions:** Span 39ft 4¼in (12·00m); length (most) 33ft 5½in (10·20m); height 10ft 5¾in (3·19m).
**Weights:** (V6) empty 7,386lb (3350kg); loaded 11,465lb (5200kg).
**Performance:** (V6) maximum speed 508mph (817km/h); range at height 382 miles (615km).

**Development:** A truly remarkable achievement, the He 280 was the world's first jet combat aircraft, the first twin-jet and the first jet to be other than a research aircraft. Yet it emerged at a time when the German leaders had a fixation on a brief Blitzkrieg victory, and showed no interest in jets or anything else that could not be used at once. The He 280 V1 was complete in September 1940 and flew as a glider on the 11th of that month behind an He 111. Fritz Schäfer then flew it on two 1,290lb (585kg) thrust HeS 8A centrifugal jets on 2 April 1941. Eventually eight of these attractive twin-finned machines were flown, but they came to nothing—despite Heinkel arranging a mock dogfight with an Fw 190 in early 1942 which the jet won easily. Intended armament was three 20mm MG 151; the proposed He 280B would have had six, plus 1,102lb (500kg) bomb load. Trials completed included twin Argus 014 duct propulsion, glider tests with no engine nacelles, and V-type butterfly tails.

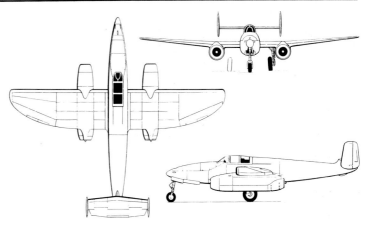

*Above: Three-view of He 280 V2*

*Below: The He 280 V1 landing after its successful maiden flight on 2 April 1941 (the engine cowlings were left off because fuel had been collecting in them, presenting a fire hazard). At full load this aircraft reached 485mph and had excellent manoeuvrability. It was the second jet aircraft in the world, and far ahead of other fighters*

# Heinkel He 162 Salamander

### He 162A-2

**Origin:** Ernst Heinkel AG; first batch Vienna-Schwechat, production totally dispersed with assembly at Mittelwerke Nordhausen (Mittelwerke), Bernberg (Junkers) and Rostock (Heinkel).

**Type:** Single-seat interceptor.

**Engine:** One 1,760lb (800kg) thrust BMW 003E-1 or E-2 Orkan single-shaft turbojet.

**Dimensions:** Span 23ft 7¾in (7·2m); length 29ft 8½in (9m); height 8ft 6½in (2·6m).

**Weights:** Empty 4,796lb (2180kg); loaded 5,940lb (2695kg).

**Performance:** Maximum speed 490mph (784km/h) at sea level, 522mph (835km/h) at 19,700ft (6000m); initial climb 4,200ft (1280m)/min; service ceiling 39,500ft (12,040m); range at full throttle 434 miles (695km) at altitude.

**Armament:** Early versions, two 30mm Rheinmetall MK 108 cannon with 50 rounds each; later production, two 20mm Mauser MG 151/20 with 120 rounds each.

**History:** First flight 6 December 1944; first delivery January 1945.

**Development:** Popularly called "Volksjäger" (People's Fighter), this incredible aircraft left behind so many conflicting impressions it is hard to believe the whole programme was started and finished in little more than six months. To appreciate the almost impossible nature of the programme, Germany was being pounded to rubble by fleets of Allied bombers that darkened the sky, and the aircraft industry and the Luftwaffe's fuel supplies were inexorably running down. Experienced aircrew had nearly all been killed, materials were in critically short supply and time had to be measured not in months but in days. So on 8 September 1944 the RLM issued a specification calling for a 750km/h jet fighter to be regarded as a piece of consumer goods and to be ready by 1 January 1945. Huge numbers of workers were organised to build it even before it was designed and Hitler Youth were hastily trained in primary gliders before being strapped into the new jet. Heinkel, which had built the world's first turbojet aircraft (He 178, flown 27 August 1939) and the first jet fighter (He 280 twin-jet, flown on its jet engines 2 April 1941) won a hasty competition with a tiny wooden machine with its engine perched on top and blasting between twin fins. Drawings were ready on 30 October 1944. The prototype flew in 37 days and plans were made for production to rise rapidly to 4,000 per month. Despite extreme difficulties, 300 of various sub-types had been completed by VE-day, with 800 more on the assembly lines. I/JG1 was operational at Leck, though without fuel. Despite many bad characteristics the 162 was a fighter of a futuristic kind, created in quantity far quicker than modern

43 Exhaust centre body
44 Exhaust outlet
45 Jet efflux fairing
46 Heat-resistant aft dorsal decking
47 Light metal tailplane
48 Starboard fin housing R/T receiver aerial
49 Starboard rudder
50 Rudder tab
51 Elevator
52 Elevator tab
53 Tailcone (movable through +3° to −2°)
54 Port tail...n structure
55 Rudder structure
56 Tailplane/tailfin attachment
57 Port tailfin upper and lower plates (housing R/T transmitter and IFF aerials)
58 Tailskid
59 Dural fuselage skinning
60 Monocoque fuselage construction
61 Control cables
62 Downswept wing root fillet

### Heinkel He 162A-2

1 Pitot tube
2 Moulded plywood nose
3 Nosewheel retraction mechanism
4 Spring-loaded nosewheel extension assembly
5 Shock abosrber scissor
6 Nosewheel
7 Nosewheel fork
8 Nosewheel leg
9 Nosewheel door
10 Gun trough
11 Nosewheel well
12 Rudder pedal
13 Window panel (visual nosewheel retraction check)
14 Wooden instrument panel
15 One-piece moulded windscreen
16 Revi 16G gunsight (interchangeable with the Revi 16B)
17 Jettisonable hinged clearvision canopy
18 Ventilation disc
19 Heinkel cartridge-operated ejection seat
20 Ejection seat handle grip
21 Throttle control quadrant
22 Retractable entry step
23 Gun barrel shroud in cockpit wall
24 Port 20-mm MG 151 cannon
25 Ammunition chute
26 Main oxygen supply bottle (3·5 pint/2 litre capacity)
27 Explosive charge ejector rail
28 Pilot's headrest
29 Canopy hinge
30 Ammunition box behind cockpit (120 rounds per gun)
31 Flexible main tank (153 Imp gal/695l capacity)
32 Fuel lines
33 FuG 25a IFF radio compartment
34 Beech plywood wing skinning
35 Jet intake
36 Riedel two-stroke starter motor bullet
37 Oil tank
38 BMW 003E-1 Sturm axial-flow turbojet
39 Riedel starter fuel tank
40 Seven-stage axial compressor casing
41 FuG 24 R/T homing loop
42 Annular combustion chamber

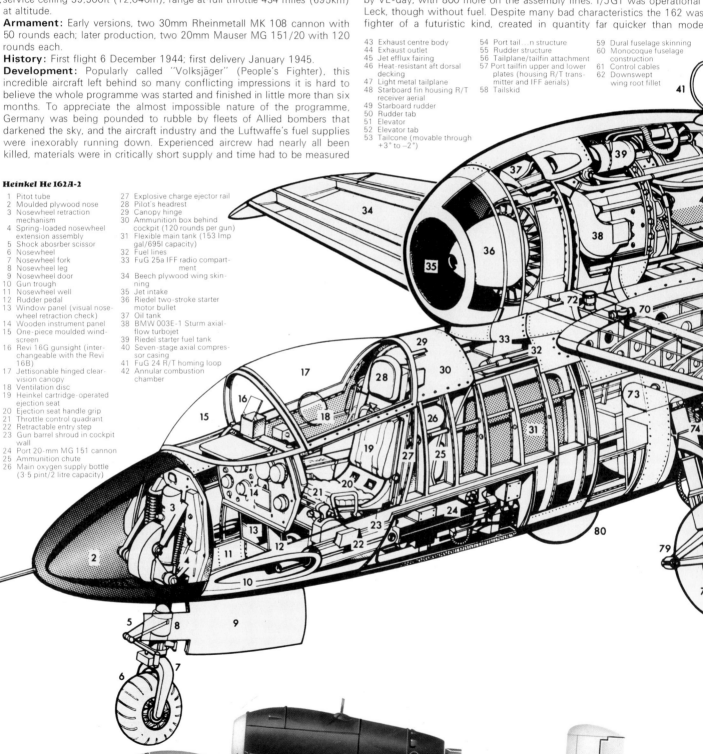

*Left:* He 162A-2 of I/JG 1 at Parchim for pilot conversion in March 1945

120076

194

aircraft are even drawn on paper.

The fuselage was a light metal monocoque, with moulded plywood nose, and the one-piece wing was of wood, with metal tips, held to the upper longerons by four bolts. Likewise the metal tailplane carried wooden fins, and the entire rear fuselage could be adjusted in incidence from +3° to −2°. One concession to complexity was that the BMW 003 did drive an alternator and hydraulic pump, because it was calculated that with such an aircraft the pilot would be unable to pump the flaps and landing gear by a manual

hydraulic system. The simple main gears folded neatly into bays in the fuselage and were extended against the airstream by strong springs. Nearly all the fuel was contained in a single flexible cell under the engine, though in some aircraft there was a sealed centre section serving as a pioneer integral tank. Another pioneer feature was the form of the blown acrylic transparencies that formed the windshield and canopy, the former lacking any strong panel offering protection against birds or bullets. Yet another was the ejection seat; Heinkel reasoned that the pilot would have no chance of escape

continued on page 196 ▶

63 Hydraulically-operated flaps
64 Port aileron
65 Detachable downswept aluminium wingtip
66 Wooden T-section rear spar
67 Wooden wing structure
68 Wooden T-section forward mainspar
69 Impregnated integral wing tank (39·6 Imp gal/180l capacity)
70 Vertical wing/fuselage attachment bolts (four stations)
71 Single rear horizontal engine mounting(attachment bolt
72 Two forward vertical engine

mounting/attachment bolts
73 Pressure-fed oil tank
74 Mainwheel hydraulic retraction jack
75 Mainwheel extension spring
76 Wooden mainwheel door
77 Mainwheel leg
78 Mainwheel tyre (660mm ×190mm)
79 Shock absorber scissor
80 Narrow-track main undercarriage assembly
81 Assisted take-off rocket unit (attached to fuselage immediately aft of mainwheel well)

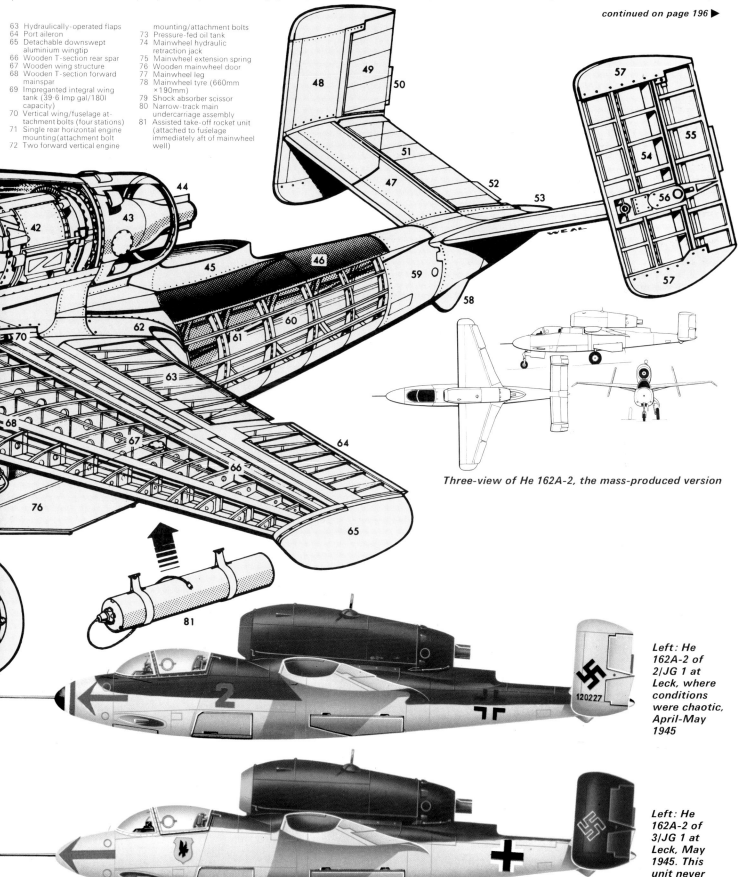

*Three-view of He 162A-2, the mass-produced version*

*Left: He 162A-2 of 2/JG 1 at Leck, where conditions were chaotic, April-May 1945*

*Left: He 162A-2 of 3/JG 1 at Leck, May 1945. This unit never converted*

► **Heinkel He 162 Salamander**

without a seat that could be catapulted out by an explosive cartridge. On its first public showing the pilot, Flugkapitän Peter, had no chance even to use his seat because the wing came apart through defective wood bonding (the same trouble had afflicted the Ta 154 because the Goldschmitt Tego-Film plant had been bombed and a hastily contrived alternative adhesive had to be used). Amazingly, however, a vast production organization was created in woods, caves and salt mines, which was to pour forth a flood of Volksjägers to be flown by Hitler Youth members previously experienced on nothing but a few flights in primary gliders. It reflects the world of fantasy that eventually surrounded the Nazi leaders that such a scheme could seriously have been expected to work.

*Above: An unpainted He 162A-2 captured with shattered canopy*

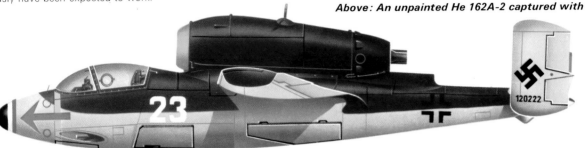

*Left: Another He 162A-2 Salamander from 3/JG 1 based at Leck in the final weeks of World War II*

# Henschel Hs 121

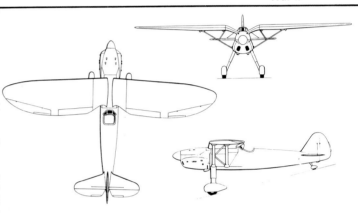

**Hs 121a**
**Origin:** Henschel Flugzeugwerke AG, Johannisthal.
**Type:** Light fighter or advanced trainer.
**Engine:** 240hp Argus As 10C inverted-vee-8 aircooled.
**Dimensions:** Span 32ft 9¾in (10·00m); length 23ft 11¼in (7·30m); height 7ft 6½in (2·30m).
**Weights:** Empty 1,565lb (710kg); loaded 2,116lb (960kg).
**Performance:** Maximum speed 174mph (280km/h); range 311 miles (500km).

**Development:** Another of the light home-defence fighters of 1933, this trim machine was Henschel's first aircraft, and it looked good but flew very badly. First flight was on 4 January 1934. Dipl-Ing Friedrich Nicolaus and his growing design staff refused to give up, and turned the V2 prototype into the Hs 125.

*Three-view of Hs 121a*

# Henschel Hs 122

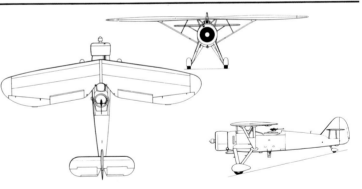

**Hs 122a, b, V3 and B-0**
**Origin:** Henschel Flugzeugwerke AG.
**Type:** Reconnaissance and army co-operation.
**Engine:** (a) Rolls-Royce Kestrel; (others) 660hp Siemens (Bramo) Sh 22B (SAM 22B) nine-cylinder radial.
**Dimensions:** Span 47ft 6¾in (14·50m); length 33ft 7½in (10·24m); height 11ft 1¾in (3·40m).
**Weights:** (B-0) empty 3,638lb (1650kg); loaded 5,566lb (2525kg).
**Performance:** Maximum speed 164mph (265km/h); range 373 miles (600km).

**Development:** With this good-looking parasol monoplane Henschel gained confidence, and were judged to have the best chance of replacing the old He 46. The British-engined prototype flew in early 1935. The Henschel was adequate, but as there was no urgency the RLM told the company to fit a more powerful engine and refine the design further. Seven Hs 122B-0 were

*Three-view of Hs 122B-0*

delivered in 1936 and used for various purposes. It was the fourth of this batch that was rebuilt into the eventual production winner, the Hs 126.

# Henschel Hs 124

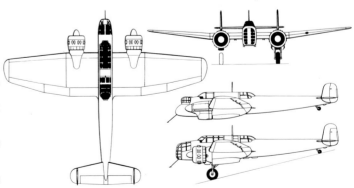

**Hs 124 V1 to V3**
**Origin:** Henschel Flugzeugwerke AG.
**Type:** Heavy fighter-bomber, recce and close support.
**Engines:** (V1) two 640hp Jumo 210C inverted-vee-12; (V2, V3) 880hp BMW 132 Dc nine-cylinder radial.
**Dimensions:** Span 59ft 8½in (18·19m); length (V2) 47ft 6¾in (14·50m); height 12ft 3½in (3·75m).
**Weights:** (V2) empty 9,347lb (4240kg); loaded 15,906lb (7215kg).
**Performance:** Maximum speed (V2) 273mph (440km/h); max range (bomb-bay tank) 2,610 miles (4200km).

**Development:** This rather pedestrian machine was one of the contenders in the 1934 Kampfzerstörer competition for a multi-role combat machine with cannon turrets, bombs and almost everything else. An all-metal stressed-skin machine, the Hs 124 could carry six 220lb (100kg) bombs in its internal bay in lieu of extra fuel. The V1 flew with a dummy nose turret, but the V2 had a blunt glazed nose intended to mount two of the forthcoming MG 151 cannon, aimed by various sights and linkages by the bombardier and fired

*Three-view of Hs 124 V2 (upper side view, V1)*

by the pilot. The radio operator had a dorsal MG 15. At all times 12 bombs of 110lb (50kg) could be hung under the wings. The Kampfzerstörer concept was outmoded before the Hs 124 flew, in spring 1936.

# Henschel Hs 123

## Hs 123A-1

**Origin:** Henschel Flugzeugwerke AG.
**Type:** Single-seat dive bomber and close-support.
**Engine:** One 880hp BMW 132 Dc nine-cylinder radial.
**Dimensions:** Span 34ft 5½in (10·5m); length 27ft 4in (8·3m); height 10ft 6½in (3·2m).
**Weights:** Empty 3,316lb (1504kg); loaded 4,888lb (2217kg).
**Performance:** Maximum speed 214mph (345km/h); initial climb 2,950ft (900m)/min; service ceiling 29,530 ft (9000m); range 530 miles (850km).
**Armament:** Two 7·92mm Rheinmetall MG 17 machine guns ahead of pilot; underwing racks for four 110lb (50kg) bombs, or clusters of anti-personnel bombs or two 20mm MG FF cannon.
**History:** First flight, spring 1935 (public display given 8 May); first delivery (Spain) December 1936; final delivery, October 1938.

**Development:** Though representing a class of aircraft generally considered obsolete by the start of World War II, this trim little biplane was kept hard at work until 1944, achieving results which in retrospect seem almost unbelievable. The prototype needed extensive modification to produce the A-1 production version, which was tested in the Spanish Civil War. Contrary to the staff-college theories then adhered to by the newly formed Luftwaffe, the Henschels were able to give close support to ground troops of a most real and immediate kind, strafing and bombing with great accuracy despite the lack of any radio link or even an established system of operation. Eventually the Luftwaffe realised that the concept of a close-support aircraft was valid, but few Henschels were allowed to operate in this role, and all the effort and money was put into the Ju 87, and the Hs 123 was phased out of production before World War II. Yet in the Polish campaign these aircraft proved unbelievably useful, having the ability to make pinpoint attacks with guns and bombs and, by virtue of careful setting of the propeller speed, to make a demoralising noise. Moreover, it established an extraordinary reputation for returning to base even after direct hits by AA shells. As a result, though the whole force was incessantly threatened with disbandment or replacement by later types, the Hs 123 close-support unit II (Schlacht)/

LG2 was sent intact to the Balkans in April 1941 and thence to the USSR. Here the old biplanes fought around the clock, proving far better adapted to the conditions than more modern types and continuing in front-line operations until, by the end of 1944, there were no more left.

*Above: An Hs 123A-1 in front-line service, possibly with (Schlacht)/LG 2, in the Blitzkrieg through the Low Countries in May 1940. Later the spats were left off*

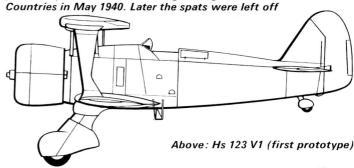

*Above: Hs 123 V1 (first prototype)*

*Above: Hs 123 V6, the first with armour and headrest*

*Above: Three-view of Hs 123A-1*

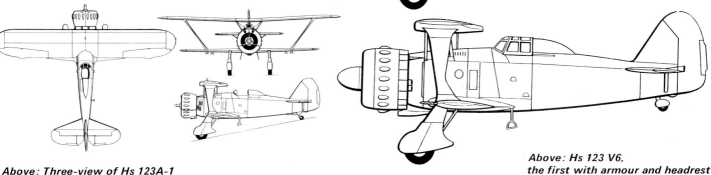

*Left: An Hs 123A of A/B 71 pilot training school at Prossnitz (now Prostejov) in Moravia (Czecho-slovakia) in the summer of 1941*

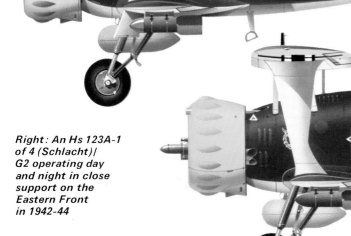

*Right: An Hs 123A-1 of 4 (Schlacht)/ G2 operating day and night in close support on the Eastern Front in 1942-44*

*See also profiles on pages 8-9 and 14-15*

# Henschel Hs 125

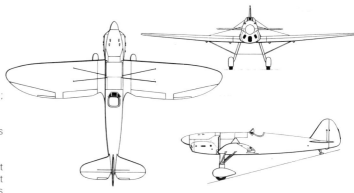

**Hs 125a (V1) and b**
**Origin:** Henschel Flugzeugwerke AG.
**Type:** Light fighter or advanced trainer.
**Engine:** 240hp Argus As 10C inverted-vee-8 aircooled.
**Dimensions:** Span 32ft 9¾in (10·00m); length 23ft 11¼in (7·30m); height 7ft 6½in (2·30m).
**Weights:** Empty 1,529lb (693kg); loaded 2,145lb (973kg).
**Performance:** Maximum speed 174mph (280km/h); range 311 miles (500km).

**Development:** In less than three months in the spring of 1934 this neat little machine was produced from the high-gull-winged Hs 121. When it flew, in the summer, it was apparent it was a much better machine than in its original form, and the two prototypes did much flying of a para-military nature until, in 1935, the Fw 56 was chosen for the Luftwaffe requirement.

*Above: Three-view of Hs 125b*

# Henschel Hs 127

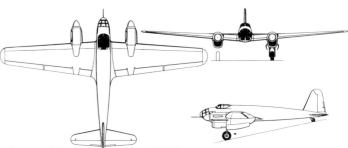

**Hs 127 V1 and V2**
**Origin:** Henschel Flugzeugwerke AG.
**Type:** High-speed bomber.
**Engines:** Two 850hp Daimler-Benz DB 600D inverted-vee-12 liquid-cooled.
**Dimensions:** No data, but span about 59ft (18m) and length about 39ft (12m).
**Weights:** No data, but empty probably about 11,000lb (5000kg) and loaded about 17,600lb (8000kg).
**Performance:** Maximum speed alleged 354mph (570km/h).

**Development:** With the Fw 57 and Bf 162 this aircraft competed unsuccessfully against the Ju 88 in the Schnellbomber competition of 1935. This competition was virtually written around the Junkers design, and before prototypes were ordered Focke-Wulf pulled out. Henschel and BFW had virtually no chance, but the Hs 127 was said to have been a remarkably fine performer. It was certainly faster than its rivals, and carried the exceptional

*Above: Three-view of Hs 127 V1*

weight of 3,307lb (1500kg) of bombs internally (though one wonders how, because the wing spars passed through the only possible place for a fuselage bomb bay). V1 flew in late 1937 and V2 in spring 1938, V3 being left unfinished. The Hs 127 was a stressed-skin three-seater, with no armament in the prototypes.

# Henschel Hs 132

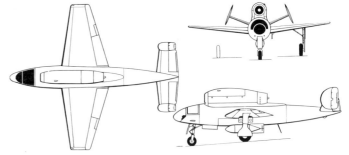

**Hs 132 V1, V2 and A, B and C**
**Origin:** Henschel Flugzeugwerke AG.
**Type:** Dive bomber.
**Engine:** 1,760lb (800kg) thrust BMW 003A-1 turbojet.
**Dimensions:** Span 23ft 7½in (7·20m); length 29ft 2½in (8·90m); height 9ft 10in (3·00m).
**Weights:** Empty, not known; loaded 7,496lb (3400kg).
**Performance:** Maximum speed (with bomb) 435mph (700km/h), (clean) 485mph (780km/h); range (with bomb, at 32,800ft, 10,000m) 696 miles (1120km).
**Development:** In 1937 the DVL research into dive bombing led to the Berlin-Charlottenberg B9 being built to study the advantages of the pilot lying prone, to better resist g forces. Extensive B9 testing throughout World War II showed how great the advantages were, and it was also clear that frontal area could be reduced. This led to the Henschel Hs 132 prone-pilot dive bomber, begun in early 1944. The 132A-series were to be dive bombers with 1,102lb (500kg) bomb but no guns. The 132B, with Jumo 004 engine, was to carry a similar bomb as well as two 20mm MG 151 cannon. It was

*Above: Three-view of Hs 132A*

believed Allied AA gunners would be unable to hit so small an aircraft diving at over 500mph. There were other projected versions, but the Soviet army occupied the factory just as the V1 was about to begin flight testing.

*Below: The only known photograph of the complete Hs 132 V1, which was captured just before first flight*

# Henschel Hs 126

**Hs 126A and B**
**Origin:** Henschel Flugzeugwerke AG, Schönefeld.
**Type:** Army co-operation; later multi-role tactical.
**Engine:** One nine-cylinder radial, (A-0) 830hp Bramo Fafnir 323A, (A-1) 880hp BMW 132Dc, (B) 900hp BMW Bramo Fafnir 323A-2 or Q-2.
**Dimensions:** Span 47ft 6¾in (14·50m); length 35ft 7¾in (10·85m); height 12ft 3¾in (3·75m).
**Weights:** Empty (B-1) 4,480lb (2032kg); maximum 7,209lb (3270kg).
**Performance:** Maximum speed 221mph (355km/h); service ceiling 27,070ft (8250m); maximum range at sea level 360 miles (580km).
**Armament:** One synchronized 7·92mm MG 17 and one manually aimed 7·92mm MG 15; light bombs or 110lb (50kg) bomb or extra tank.
**History:** First flight August 1936; service delivery (A-0) June 1937; final delivery January 1941.

**Development:** Developed in early 1936 from the disappointing Hs 122, the parasol-winged Hs 126 was a thoroughly sound machine very like the British Lysander in character though more conventional. The crew of two sat below and behind the wing in a capacious tandem cockpit, the pilot's portion being enclosed. Typical photographic, radio and light bombing equipment was carried, and the aircraft proved to have excellent STOL capability and ability to absorb much punishment. Altogether about 802 were delivered, maintaining the Aufklärungsstaffeln (recce squadrons) at a front-line strength of around 280 aircraft. By June 1941 virtually all were on the Eastern Front or in the Balkans or North Africa. A few survived until 1944—45 in operations against partisans in the Balkans, but most had been replaced by the Fw 189 and used for towing gliders. The 200-odd combat veterans served in Nachtschlacht (night ground attack) wings, often using a variety of armament schemes.

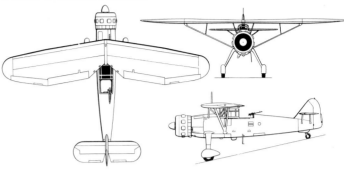

*Above: Three-view of Hs 126A (B-series very similar)*

*Above: An Hs 126B-1 of 2 (H)/14 in North Africa in 1941. This was the only Hs 126 unit in that theatre, the rest having been assigned to the Eastern Front*

*Above: The Hs 126 V1 (first prototype)*

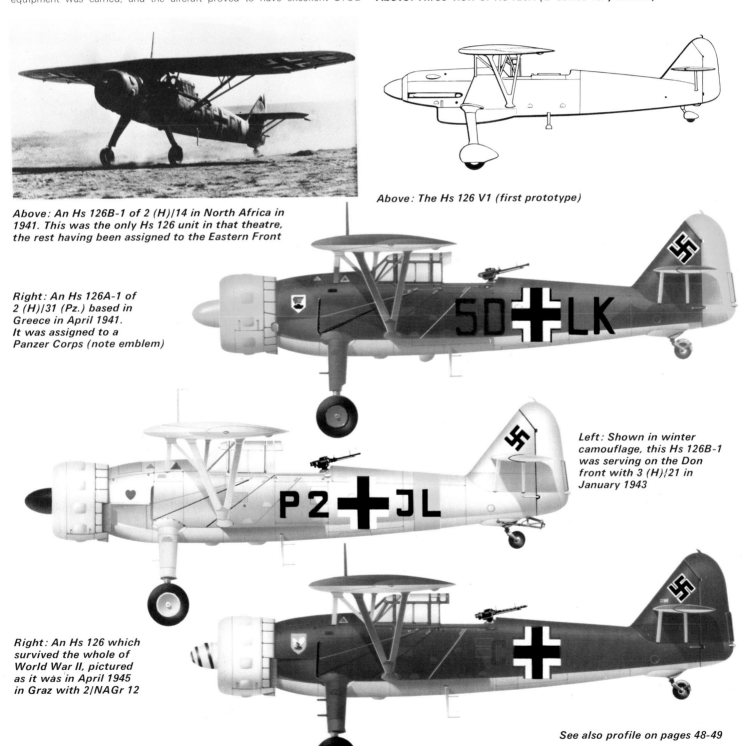

*Right: An Hs 126A-1 of 2 (H)/31 (Pz.) based in Greece in April 1941. It was assigned to a Panzer Corps (note emblem)*

*Left: Shown in winter camouflage, this Hs 126B-1 was serving on the Don front with 3 (H)/21 in January 1943*

*Right: An Hs 126 which survived the whole of World War II, pictured as it was in April 1945 in Graz with 2/NAGr 12*

*See also profile on pages 48-49*

199

# Henschel Hs 129

## Hs 129A and B series

**Origin:** Henschel Flugzeugwerke AG.

**Type:** Single-seat close support and ground attack.

**Engines:** (B-series) two 690hp Gnome-Rhône 14M 04/05 14-cylinder two-row radials.

**Dimensions:** Span 46ft 7in (14·2m); length 31ft 11¾in (9·75m); height 10ft 8in (3·25m).

**Weights:** (Typical B-1) empty 8,940lb (4060kg); loaded 11,265lb (5110kg).

**Performance:** (Typical B-1) maximum speed 253mph (408km/h); initial climb 1,390ft (425m)/min; service ceiling 29,530ft (9000m); range 547 miles (880km).

**Armament:** See text.

**History:** First flight (Hs 129V-1) early 1939; service delivery (129A-0) early 1941; first flight (129B) October 1941; service delivery (129B) late 1942.

**Development:** Though there were numerous types of specialised close support and ground attack aircraft in World War I, this category was virtually ignored until the Spanish Civil War showed, again, that it is one of the most important of all. In 1938 the RLM issued a specification for such an aircraft — the whole purpose of the Luftwaffe being to support the Wehrmacht in Blitzkrieg-type battles — to back up the purpose-designed Ju 87 dive bomber. Henschel's Dipl-Ing F. Nicolaus designed a trim machine somewhat resembling the twin-engined fighters of the period but with more armour and less-powerful engines (two 495hp Argus As 410A-1 air-cooled inverted-vee-12s). The solo pilot sat in the extreme nose behind a windscreen 3in thick, with armour surrounding the cockpit. The triangular-section fuselage housed self-sealing tanks, guns in the sloping sides and a hardpoint for a bomb underneath. Test pilots at Rechlin damned the A-0 pre-production batch as grossly underpowered, but these aircraft were used on the Eastern Front by the Romanian Air Force. The redesigned B-series used the vast numbers of French 14M engines that were available and in production by the Vichy government for the Me 323. Altogether 841 B-series were built,

and used with considerable effect on the Eastern Front but with less success in North Africa. The B-1/R1 had two 7·92mm MG 17 and two 20mm MG 151/20, plus two 110lb or 48 fragmentation bombs. The R2 had a 30mm MK 101 clipped underneath and was the first aircraft ever to use a 30mm gun in action. The R3 had a ventral box of four MG 17. The R4 carried up to 551lb of bombs. The R5 had a camera for vertical photography. The B-2 series changed the inbuilt MG 17s for MG 131s and other subtypes had many kinds of armament including the 37mm BK 3·7 and 75mm BK 7·5 with muzzle about eight feet ahead of the nose. The most novel armament, used against Russian armour with results that were often devastating, was a battery of six smooth-bore 75mm tubes firing recoilless shells down and to the rear with automatic triggering as the aircraft flew over metal objects.

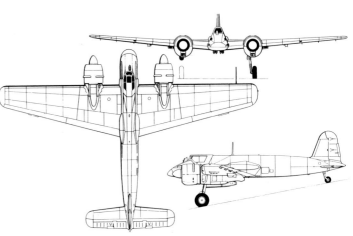

*Above: Three-view of Hs 129B-1/R4*

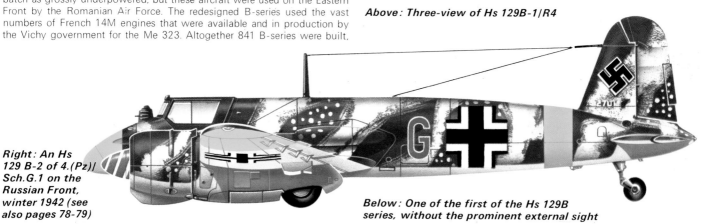

*Right: An Hs 129 B-2 of 4.(Pz)/ Sch.G.1 on the Russian Front, winter 1942 (see also pages 78-79)*

*Below: One of the first of the Hs 129B series, without the prominent external sight*

# Henschel Hs130

**Hs 128 V1 and V2, Hs 130 A-series, B, C-series, D, E-series and F.**
**Origin:** Henschel Flugzeugwerke AG.
**Type:** High-altitude research (128), recce (A, E) or bomber (C).
**Engines:** See text.
**Dimensions:** Span (A-0) 95ft 1¾in (29·00m); (E-0) 108ft 3¼in (33·00m); length (A-0) 49ft 0½in (14·95m), (E-0) 72ft 2in (22·00m); height (A-0) 16ft 1in (4·90m), (E-0) 18ft 4½in (5·60m).
**Weights:** Empty, (A-0) not known, (E-0) 26,900lb (12,200kg); max loaded (A-0) 25,750lb (11,680kg), (E-0) 39,900lb (18,100kg).
**Performance:** Maximum speed (A-0) 292mph (470km/h), (E-0) 379mph (610km/h), max range (A-0) 1,385 miles (2230km), (E-0) 1,860 miles (3000km).

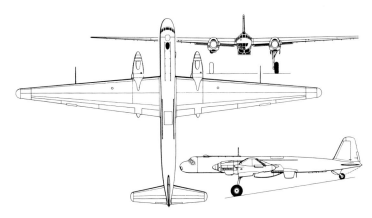

*Above: Three-view of Hs 130E-0*

**Development:** Today few people—even World War II aircraft buffs—are familiar with the Hs 130, yet it was one of the biggest aircraft-development programmes in history. It was not one aircraft but a large series of quite different aircraft, and it all began when, in 1938, Dr Seewald, of the DVL, asked Henschel if they were interested in building a high-altitude research machine to test pressure cabins and DVL engine turbochargers. The result was a major pressure-cabin development programme, which led to the Hs 128 V1 flown at Adlershof in 1939 on two 1,175hp DB 601 engines with DVL turbochargers. The Hs 128 V2 had the same 85ft 4½in wing but Jumo 210 engines with two-stage turbochargers, and was expected to exceed 50,000ft. By November 1940 three prototypes had flown of the Hs 130A recce aircraft with shorter span and remote-control cameras. Various DB 601 or 605 engines were used, and eventually span extended beyond that of the 128 in the 1943 batches of A-0/U6. The 130B bomber was not built, but there were three Hs 130C bombers, in the 1939—42 Bomber B programme, and these were totally new aircraft with 1,850hp DB 603 engines, crew of four, two twin-MG 131 barbettes plus MG 15 in the tail, and bomb load of 8,818lb (4000kg). DB engines for the 130D were not developed, and the final stage accomplished was the Hs 130E series with the HZ-Anlage, comprising two 1,860hp DB 603B supercharged by a DB 605T in the fuselage. The 130E V1 flew in September 1942, and several variants flew later at heights close to 50,000ft. The 130F was to have had four 1,800hp BMW 801TJ.

*Above: A retouched photograph of the first of the totally redesigned Hs 130 E family, first flown in April 1943*

*Below: Retouched photograph of the Hs 130 V2, second prototype of the A-series, with BMW 801A engines (later 801J turbocharged)*

# Junkers Ju 52/3m

**Ju 52/3m in many versions; data for 3m g5e to 3m g14e**

**Origin:** Junkers Flugzeug und Motorenwerke AG; also built in France on German account by a SNCASO/Breguet/Amiot group; built under licence by CASA, Spain.

**Type:** Passenger and freight transport (also bomber, reconnaissance, mine countermeasures, cas-evac and glider tug).

**Engines:** Three (one in Ju 52) of following types: 600hp BMW Hornet, 725hp BMW 132A, 830hp BMW 132T (standard on nearly all wartime versions), 925hp Bristol or PZL Pegasus, 750hp ENMASA Beta E-9C or

loading door and an autopilot, the g8e was built in great numbers with 132Z engines and 13mm MG 131 dorsal gun, the g9e had a glider hook and strengthened landing gear, and the g14e had pilot armour as standard.

Until 1936 at least half the 450 aircraft then built were delivered as bombers, but later nearly all were equipped as magnetic-mine busters, glider tugs, troop transports, freighters and casualty-evacuation ambulances. These were the roles of most military versions, which were by far the most common transports on every front on which Nazi Germany fought. It is typical of the Nazi regime that, despite a wealth of later and more capable aircraft, the old "Auntie Ju" or "Iron Annie" was kept in full production throughout the war. Good STOL performance, with patented "double wing" flaps, robust construction, interchangeable wheel/ski/float landing gear and great reliability were the Ju 52's attributes. Total German output was 4,845. Many were built in France where 400 were completed as AAC.1s in 1947. The final 170 were built in Spain as CASA 352-Ls for the Spanish Air Force, which used them as T.2B multi-role transports until 1975.

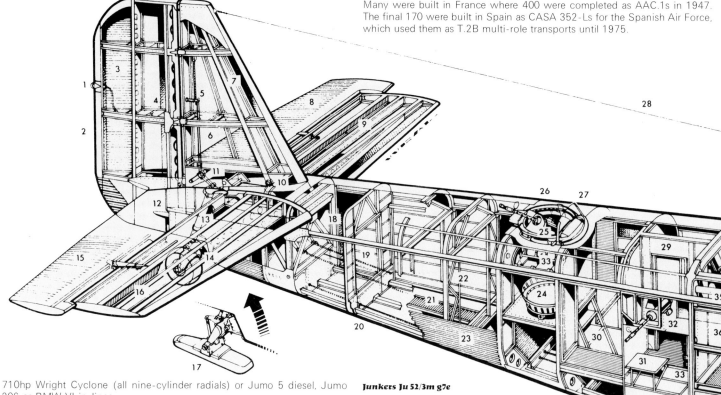

710hp Wright Cyclone (all nine-cylinder radials) or Jumo 5 diesel, Jumo 206 or BMW VI in-lines.

**Dimensions:** Span 95ft 11½in (29·25m); length 62ft (18·9m); height (landplane) 14ft 9in (4·5m).

**Weights:** Empty 12,346lb (5600kg); loaded 24,317lb (11,030kg).

**Performance:** Maximum speed 190mph (305km/h); initial climb 689ft (210m)/min; service ceiling 18,045ft (5500m); range 808 miles (1300km).

**Armament:** Usually none; in combat zones it was usual to mount one 13mm MG 131 manually aimed from open dorsal cockpit and two 7·92mm MG 15s manually aimed from beam windows.

**History:** First flight (Ju 52) 13 October 1930; (Ju 52/3m) May 1932; (Ju 52/3m g3e bomber) October 1934; final delivery (AAC.1) August 1947; (CASA 352-L) 1952.

**Development:** One of the great aircraft of history, the Ju 52/3m was briefly preceded by the single-engined Ju 52 which had no military history. Most early Ju 52/3m versions were 15/17-passenger airliners which sold all over the world and also made up 75 per cent of the giant fleet of Lufthansa (reducing that airline's forced landings per million kilometres from 7 to only 1·5). In 1935 the 3m g3e bomber, with manually aimed MG 15s in a dorsal cockpit and ventral dustbin and bomb load of 3,307lb (1500kg) equipped the first bomber squadrons of the Luftwaffe.

The first version built in substantial numbers was the Ju 52/3m ge, and this was destined to be the backbone of both the Luftwaffe's embryonic bomber force and also its tactical transport force throughout its entire history. Sub-types progressed from ge to g14e, with a wealth of sub-sub-types for particular purposes. The original ge was intended as only an interim bomber pending delivery of the purpose-designed Do 11, but (as related in the description of the Do 11 and 13) the Dornier was a flop and was far outnumbered by the reliable and effective Junkers despite the latter's ungainly form and corrugated duralumin skin. The chief version by 1935 was the Ju 52/3m g3e, which poured from the main Dessau factory and from a second Junkers plant opened at Bernberg, from ATG at Leipzig and from Weser Flugzeugbau. As a bomber the g3e had two vertical bomb bays accommodating a maximum of 3,307lb (1500kg), with a glazed bombing station between them together with a ventral "dustbin" accommodating a gunner with MG 15 machine gun which could be winched up and down by a hand-turned screw linkage. A second MG 15 gunner was accommodated in the rear roof of the fuselage. Large numbers of g3e and g4e (with tailwheel) bombers fought in Spain with the Legion Kondor and Nationalist Air Force. The g5e had fittings for wheels, floats or skis, the g7e had a larger

### Junkers Ju 52/3m g7e

| | |
|---|---|
| 1 Rear navigation light | 42 Fuselage |
| 2 Rudder tab | corrugated skin |
| 3 Corrugated rudder skin | 43 Fuselage frames |
| 4 Rudder post | 44 Rectangular windows |
| 5 Rudder control linkage | 45 Wind-driven generator |
| 6 Fin structure | 46 Radio equipment |
| 7 Fin front spar | 47 Aerial mast |
| 8 Elevator (port) | 48 Twin-loop D/F |
| 9 Multi-spar tailplane | 49 Inner section trailing-edge |
| construction | flap |
| 10 Fin/fuselage attachment | 50 Outer section flap control |
| point | linkage |
| 11 Control linkage | 51 Outer section trailing-edge |
| 12 Rudder lower hinge | flap |
| 13 Tailwheel shock-absorber | 52 Flap hinge fairings |
| 14 Tailwheel | 53 Wing spars |
| 15 Starboard elevator | 54 Port navigation light |
| 16 Tailplane spar | 55 Pitot head |
| 17 Alternative tail-ski | 56 Corrugated wing skin |
| attachment | 57 Underwing inspection |
| 18 Aft fuselage frame | panels |
| 19 Control lines | 58 Port oil filler |
| 20 Fuselage lower longeron | 59 'Condor-Haube' gun |
| 21 Inspection walkway | position |
| 22 Fuselage frame | 60 MG 15 (7·9-mm) machine |
| 23 Fuselage corrugated skin | gun |
| 24 Dorsal gunner's raised | 61 Port engine cowling |
| station | (NACA cowling) |
| 25 Ring-mounted 7·9-mm MG | 62 Pilot's seat |
| 81 (or 13-mm MG 131) | 63 Radio-operator/gunner's |
| 26 Open dorsal gun position | jump-seat |
| 27 Windscreen | 64 Co-pilot's seat |
| 28 Aerial | 65 Raised cockpit floor |
| 29 Toilet | 66 Control column |
| 30 Steps | 67 Rudder pedals |
| 31 Side-gunner's step | 68 Bulkhead |
| 32 Beam-mounted 7·9-mm | 69 Centre-engine |
| MG 15 (starboard station) | oil tank |
| 33 Ammunition magazines | |
| 34 Beam-mounted 7·9-mm | |
| MG 15 (port station) | |
| 35 Cabin hot-air | |
| 36 Cabin rear bulkhead | |
| 37 Port entry door | |
| 38 Enlarged (two-part) cargo- | |
| loading hatch | |
| 39 Underfloor strengthened | |
| structure | |
| 40 Corrugated floor | |
| 41 Canvas seats (stowed) | |

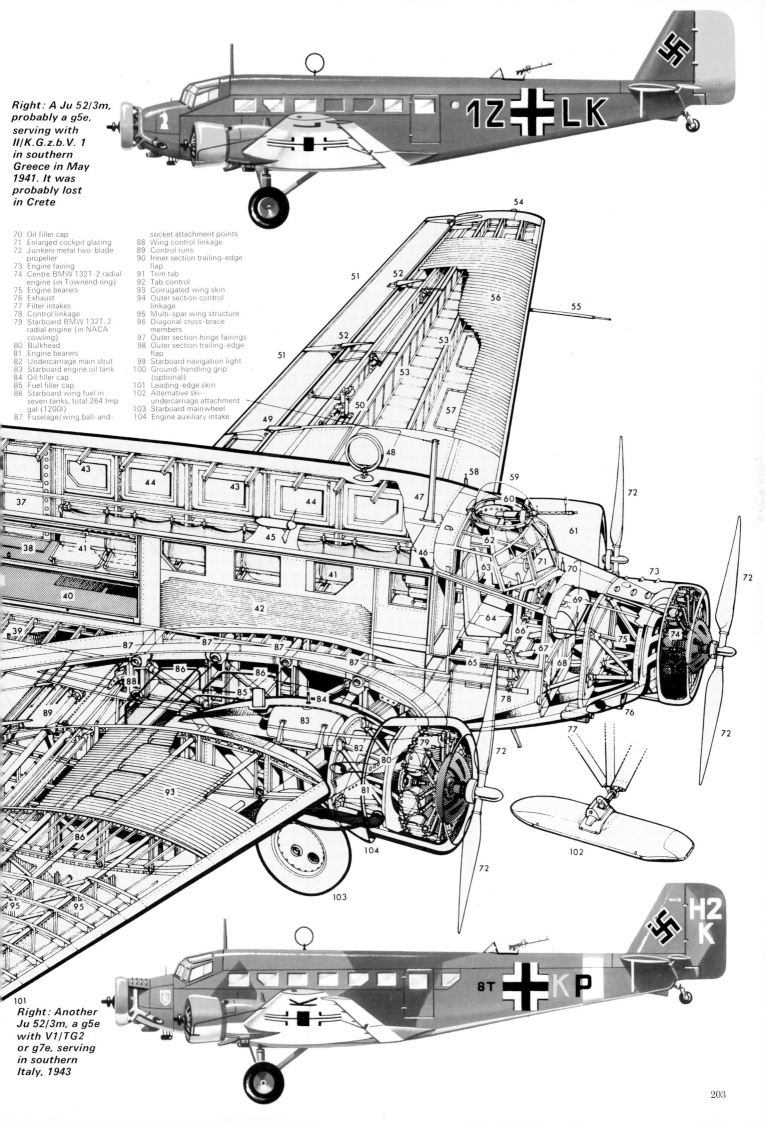

*Right: A Ju 52/3m, probably a g5e, serving with II/K.G.z.b.V. 1 in southern Greece in May 1941. It was probably lost in Crete*

70 Oil filler cap
71 Enlarged cockpit glazing
72 Junkers metal two-blade propeller
73 Engine fairing
74 Centre BMW 132T-2 radial engine (in Townend ring)
75 Engine bearers
76 Exhaust
77 Filter intakes
78 Control linkage
79 Starboard BMW 132T-2 radial engine (in NACA cowling)
80 Bulkhead
81 Engine bearers
82 Undercarriage main strut
83 Starboard engine oil tank
84 Oil filler cap
85 Fuel filler cap
86 Starboard wing fuel in seven tanks, total 264 Imp gal (1200l)
87 Fuselage/wing ball-and-

socket attachment points
88 Wing control linkage
89 Control runs
90 Inner section trailing-edge flap
91 Trim tab
92 Tab control
93 Corrugated wing skin
94 Outer section control linkage
95 Multi-spar wing structure
96 Diagonal cross-brace members
97 Outer section hinge fairings
98 Outer section trailing-edge flap
99 Starboard navigation light
100 Ground-handling grip (optional)
101 Leading-edge skin
102 Alternative ski-undercarriage attachment
103 Starboard mainwheel
104 Engine auxiliary intake

*Right: Another Ju 52/3m, a g5e with V1/TG2 or g7e, serving in southern Italy, 1943*

# Junkers Ju 86

**Ju 86D, E, G, K, P and R**

**Origin:** Junkers Flugzeug und Motorenwerke AG; also built by Henschel, and built under licence by Saab, Sweden.

**Type:** (D, E, G and K) bomber; (P) bomber/reconnaissance; (R) reconnaissance.

**Engines:** (D) two 600hp Junkers Jumo 205C six opposed-piston cylinder diesels; (E, G) two 800 or 880hp BMW 132 nine-cylinder radials; (K) two 905hp Bristol Mercury XIX nine-cylinder radials; (P, R) two 1,000hp Jumo 207A-1 or 207B-3/V turbo-charged opposed-piston diesels.

**Dimensions:** Span 73ft 10in (22·6m); (P) 84ft (25·6m); (R) 105ft (32m); length (typical) 58ft 8½in (17·9m); (G) 56ft 5in (17·2m) (P, R) 54ft (16·46m), height (all) 15ft 5in (4·7m).

**Weights:** Empty (E-1) 11,464lb (5200kg); (R-1) 14,771lb (6700kg); loaded (E-1) 18,080lb (8200kg); (R-1) 25,420lb (11,530kg).

**Performance:** Maximum speed (E-1) 202mph (325km/h); (R-1) 261mph (420km/h); initial climb (E) 918ft (280m)/min; service ceiling (E-1) 22,310ft (6800m); (R-1) 42,650ft (13,000m); range (E) 746 miles (1200km); (R-1) 980 miles (1577km).

**Armament:** (D, E, G, K) three 7·92mm MG 15 manually aimed from nose, dorsal and retractable ventral positions; internal bomb load of four 551lb (250kg) or 16 110lb (50kg) bombs; (P) single 7·92mm fixed MG 17, same bomb load; (R) usually none.

**History:** First flight (Ju 86V-1) 4 November 1934; (V-5 bomber prototype) January 1936; (production D-1) late 1936; (P-series prototype) February 1940.

**Development:** Planned like the He 111 as both a civil airliner and a bomber, the Ju 86 was in 1934 one of the most advanced aircraft in Europe. The design team under Dipl-Ing Zindel finally abandoned corrugated skin and created a smooth and efficient machine with prominent double-wing flaps and outward-retracting main gears. The diesel-engined D-1 was quickly put into Luftwaffe service to replace the Do 23 and Ju 52 as the standard heavy bomber, but in Spain the various D-versions proved vulnerable even to biplane fighters. The E-series bombers, with the powerful BMW radial, were faster and the fastest of all were the Swedish Bristol-engined Ks, of which 40 were built by Junkers (first delivery 18 December 1936) and 16 by Saab (last delivery 3 January 1941). Many D and E bombers were used against Poland, but that was their swan-song. By 1939 Junkers was working on a high-altitude version with turbocharged engines and a pressure cabin and this emerged as the P-1 bomber and P-2 bomber/reconnaissance which was operational over the Soviet Union gathering pictures before the German invasion of June 1941. The R series had a span increased even beyond that of the P and frequently operated over southern England in 1941–2 until — with extreme difficulty — solitary Spitfires managed to reach their altitude and effect an interception. Total military Ju 86 production was between 810 and 1,000. Junkers schemed many developed versions, some having four or six engines.

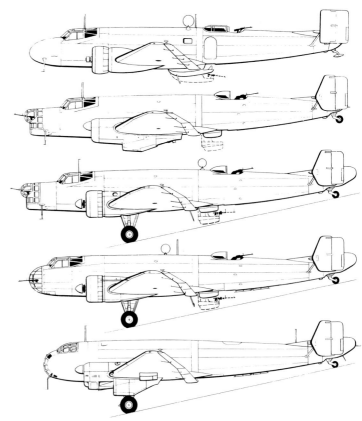

*Above, from the top:* Ju 86 ab I (V1), Ju 86A-1, Ju 86E-2 (D-1 has same tail-end), Ju 86G-1 and Ju 86P-1

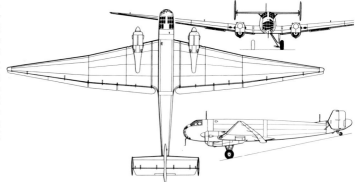

*Above: Three-view of Ju 86R-1*

*Below: Bombers of KG 253 on manoeuvres in the winter 1936-37. The aircraft in the foreground is a Ju 86A-1, while that just behind is a D-1 (see drawings above)*

# Junkers Ju 87

## Ju 87A, B and D series

**Origin:** Junkers Flugzeug und Motorenwerke AG; also built by Weser Flugzeugbau and components from SNCASO, France.

**Type:** Two-seat dive bomber and ground attack.

**Engine:** (Ju 87B-1) one 1,100hp Junkers Jumo 211Da 12-cylinder inverted-vee liquid-cooled; (Ju 87D-1, D-5) 1,300hp Jumo 211J.

**Dimensions:** Span (Ju 87B-1, D-1) 45ft 3¼in (13·8m); (D-5) 50ft 0½in (15·25m); length 36ft 5in (11·1m); height 12ft 9in (3·9m).

**Weights:** Empty (B-1, D-1) about 6,080lb (2750kg); loaded (B-1) 9,371lb (4250kg); (D-1) 12,600lb (5720kg); (D-5) 14,500lb (6585kg).

**Performance:** Maximum speed (B-1) 242mph (390km/h); (D-1) 255mph (408km/h); (D-5) 250mph (402km/h); service ceiling (B-1) 26,250ft (8000m); (D-1, D-5) 24,000ft (7320m); range with maximum bomb load (B-1) 373 miles (600km); (D-1, D-5) 620 miles (1000km).

**Armament:** (Ju 87B-1) two 7·92mm Rheinmetall MG 17 machine guns in wings, one 7·92mm MG 15 manually aimed in rear cockpit, one 1,102lb (500kg) bomb on centreline and four 110lb (50kg) on wing racks; (D-1, D-5) two MG 17 in wings, twin 7·92mm MG 81 machine guns manually aimed in rear cockpit, one bomb of 3,968lb (1800kg) on centreline; (D-7) two 20mm MG 151/20 cannon in wings; (Ju 87G-1) two 37mm BK (Flak 18, or Flak 36) cannon in underwing pods; (D-4) two underwing WB81 weapon containers each housing six MG 81 guns.

**History:** First flight (Ju 87V1) late 1935; (pre-production Ju 87A-0) November 1936; (Ju 87B-1) August 1938; (Ju 87D-1) 1940; termination of production 1944.

**Development:** Until at least 1942 the Ju 87 "Stuka" enjoyed a reputation that struck terror into those on the ground beneath it. First flown with a British R-R Kestrel engine and twin fins in 1935, it entered production in 1937 as the Ju 87A with large trousered landing gear and full equipment for dive bombing, including a heavy bomb crutch that swung the missile well clear of the fuselage before release. The spatted Ju 87B was the first aircraft in production with the Jumo 211 engine, almost twice as powerful as the Jumo 210 of the Ju 87A, and it had an automatic device (almost an auto-pilot) to ensure proper pull-out from the steep dive, as well as red lines at 60°, 75° and 80° painted on the pilot's side window. Experience in Spain had shown that pilots could black-out and lose control in the pull-out. Later a whole formation of Ju 87Bs in Spain was late pulling out over misty ground and many hit the ground. In Poland and the Low Countries the Ju 87 was terribly effective and it repeated its success in Greece, Crete and parts of the Russian front. But in the Battle of Britain its casualty rate was such that it was soon withdrawn, thereafter to attack ships and troops in areas where the Axis still enjoyed some air superiority. In 1942–45 its main work was close support on the Eastern front, attacking armour with big guns (Ju

continued on page 206 ▶

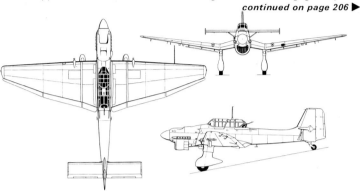

*Above: Three-view of Ju 87B-2*

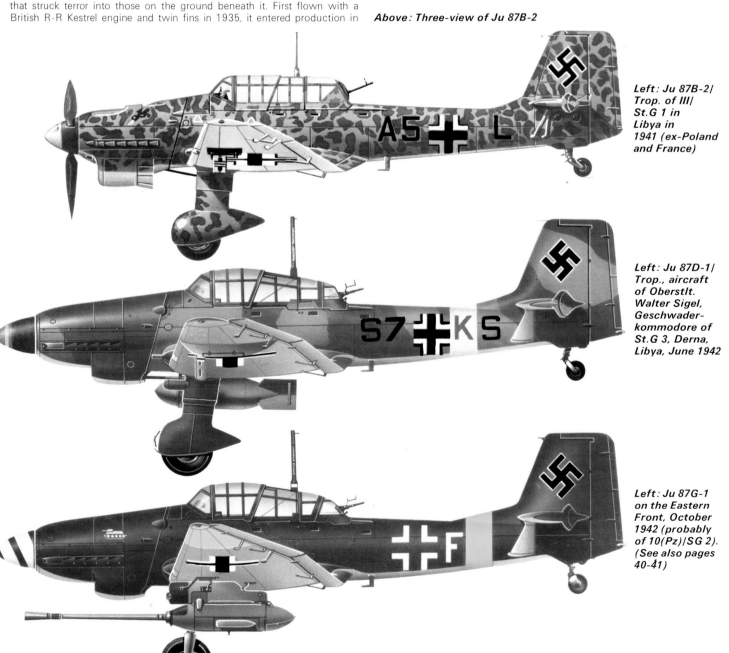

*Left: Ju 87B-2/Trop. of III/St.G 1 in Libya in 1941 (ex-Poland and France)*

*Left: Ju 87D-1/Trop., aircraft of Oberstlt. Walter Sigel, Geschwader-kommodore of St.G 3, Derna, Libya, June 1942*

*Left: Ju 87G-1 on the Eastern Front, October 1942 (probably of 10(Pz)/SG 2). (See also pages 40-41)*

## ▶ Junkers Ju 87

87G-1) and even being used as a transport and glider tug. Total production, all by Junkers, is believed to have been 5,709.

Though substantial numbers were built of the Ju 87A series with Jumo 210 engine, these were replaced in front-line units in 1939 by the more powerful B-series, serving thereafter until early 1943 as dive-bomber trainers. The Ju 87B was the first production application of the Jumo 211 engine, which by mid-1938 was available in improved Jumo 211Da form rated at 1,200hp with direct fuel injection, making the engine insensitive to accelerations and flight attitudes. By the start of World War II all nine Stukagruppen had re-equipped with the Ju 87B-1, which was developed into sub-types with better radio, armour, skis, sand filters and many other improvements. Nevertheless the basic vulnerability of the Ju 87 had by this time resulted in a planned phase-out of production by 1940. Production was tapering off as the war started, but the shattering effect of the aircraft in Poland caused its run-down to be postponed. In the campaign in the West in May 1940 the Stuka did even more to blast a path for the Wehrmacht, and not even its inability to survive over England was enough to stop it coming off the production line. In the spring of 1941 the greatly improved D-series thus entered production, with more power, greatly increased bomb load, extensive armour and many other changes. But the whole programme was totally unplanned. Output was always being tapered off, only to be suddenly boosted to meet urgent demands. Better aircraft kept failing to appear, Junkers themselves failed to produce the planned Ju 187, and output kept rising and falling until it at last ended in September 1944 when more than 5,700 had been delivered. Many of the final sub-types were of the G-series with tank-busting cannon, or dual-control H-series trainers. Most of the Stukas in action on the Eastern front after late 1942 had to be restricted (if possible) to night operations with large flame-damping exhaust pipes. Only a very few, flown by crews either deeply experienced or just joined, survived to VE-day. Various models served with the Slovakian, Romanian and Hungarian air forces and with the Regia Aeronautica (giving rise to the erroneous belief by the Allies it was built in Italy as the "Breda 201"), and among many special versions or modifications were fleet carrier-based models intended for *Graf Zeppelin*, glider tugs, large belly freight pods and passenger pods fitted above the wings.

***Right: A Ju 87B-2 operating in Sicily in 1942. The B-2 introduced ejector exhaust, broader propeller blades and many other changes and could carry a 2,205lb bomb load***

*Above: Three-view of Ju 87G-1*

*Above: Ju 87D-3 with two two-seat passenger pods*

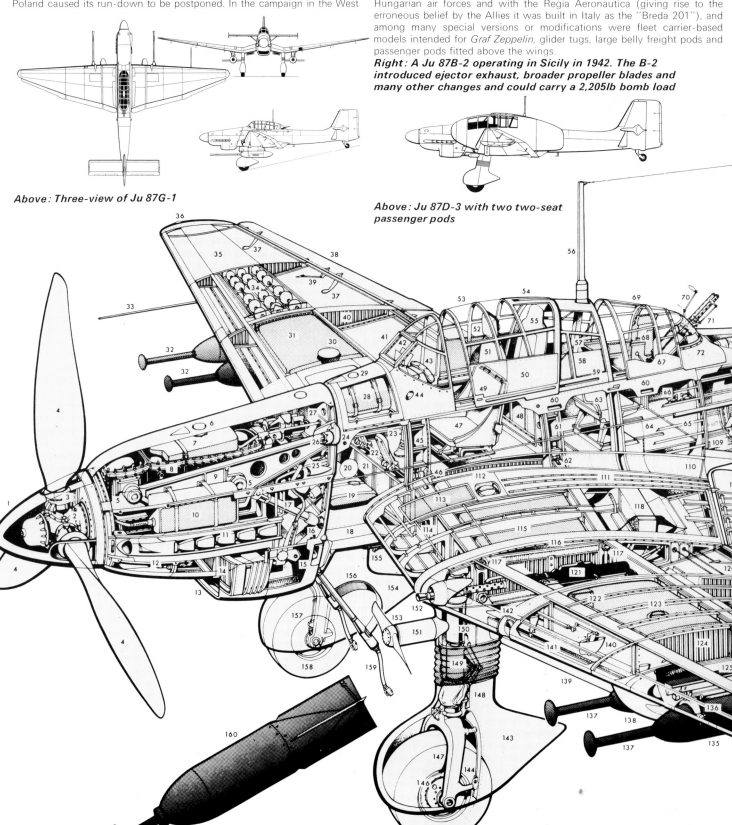

Above: A Ju 87D (probably a D-8) in winter camouflage on the Eastern Front in 1943. At about this time the vulnerability of the Ju 87 caused wholesale replacement by the Fw 190, the Stukas being reassigned to Nachtschlacht (night attack) units

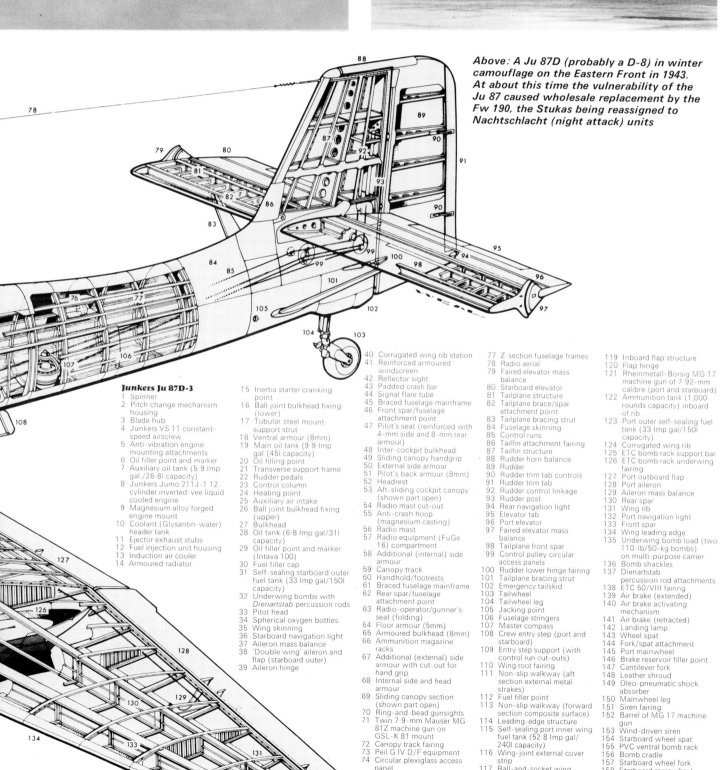

### Junkers Ju 87D-3

1 Spinner
2 Pitch change mechanism housing
3 Blade hub
4 Junkers VS 11 constant-speed airscrew
5 Anti-vibration engine mounting attachments
6 Oil filler point and marker
7 Auxiliary oil tank (5·9 Imp gal./26·8l capacity)
8 Junkers Jumo 211J-1 12-cylinder inverted-vee liquid cooled engine
9 Magnesium alloy forged engine mount
10 Coolant (Glysantin-water) header tank
11 Ejector exhaust stubs
12 Fuel injection unit housing
13 Induction air cooler
14 Armoured radiator
15 Inertia starter cranking point
16 Ball joint bulkhead fixing (lower)
17 Tubular steel mount support strut
18 Ventral armour (8mm)
19 Main oil tank (9·9 Imp gal (45l capacity)
20 Oil filling point
21 Transverse support frame
22 Rudder pedals
23 Control column
24 Heating point
25 Auxiliary air intake
26 Ball joint bulkhead fixing (upper)
27 Bulkhead
28 Oil tank (6·8 Imp gal/31l capacity)
29 Oil filler point and marker (Intava 100)
30 Fuel filler cap
31 Self-sealing starboard outer fuel tank (33 Imp gal/150l capacity)
32 Underwing bombs with Dienartstab percussion rods
33 Pitot head
34 Spherical oxygen bottles
35 Wing skinning
36 Starboard navigation light
37 Aileron mass balance
38 'Double wing' aileron and flap (starboard outer)
39 Aileron hinge
40 Corrugated wing rib station
41 Reinforced armoured windscreen
42 Reflector sight
43 Padded crash bar
44 Signal flare tube
45 Braced fuselage mainframe
46 Front spar/fuselage attachment point
47 Pilot's seat (reinforced with 4-mm side and 8-mm rear armour)
48 Inter-cockpit bulkhead
49 Sliding canopy handgrip
50 External side armour
51 Pilot's back armour (8mm)
52 Headrest
53 Aft-sliding cockpit canopy (shown part open)
54 Radio mast cut-out
55 Anti-crash hoop (magnesium casting)
56 Radio mast
57 Radio equipment (FuGe 16) compartment
58 Additional (internal) side armour
59 Canopy track
60 Handhold/footrests
61 Braced fuselage mainframe
62 Rear spar/fuselage attachment point
63 Radio-operator/gunner's seat (folding)
64 Floor armour (5mm)
65 Armoured bulkhead (8mm)
66 Ammunition magazine racks
67 Additional (external) side armour with cut-out for hand grip
68 Internal side and head armour
69 Sliding canopy section (shown part open)
70 Ring-and-bead gunsights
71 Twin 7·9-mm Mauser MG 81Z machine gun on GSL-K 81 mount
72 Canopy track fairing
73 Peil G IV D/F equipment
74 Circular plexiglass access panel
75 Back-to-back L-section stringers (fuselage horizontal break)
76 First-aid stowage
77 Z-section fuselage frames
78 Radio aerial
79 Faired elevator mass balance
80 Starboard elevator
81 Tailplane structure
82 Tailplane brace/spar attachment point
83 Tailplane bracing strut
84 Fuselage skinning
85 Control runs
86 Tailfin attachment fairing
87 Tailfin structure
88 Rudder horn balance
89 Rudder
90 Rudder trim tab controls
91 Rudder trim tab
92 Rudder control linkage
93 Rudder post
94 Rear navigation light
95 Elevator tab
96 Port elevator
97 Faired elevator mass balance
98 Tailplane front spar
99 Control pulley circular access panels
100 Rudder lower hinge fairing
101 Tailplane bracing strut
102 Emergency tailskid
103 Tailwheel
104 Tailwheel leg
105 Jacking point
106 Fuselage stringers
107 Master compass
108 Crew entry step (port and starboard)
109 Entry step support (with control run cut-offs)
110 Wing root fairing
111 Non-slip walkway (aft section external metal strakes)
112 Fuel filler point
113 Non-slip walkway (forward section composite surface)
114 Leading-edge structure
115 Self-sealing port inner wing fuel tank (52·8 Imp gal/240l capacity)
116 Wing-joint external cover strip
117 Ball-and-socket wing attachment points
118 Armoured coolant radiator (port and starboard)
119 Inboard flap structure
120 Flap hinge
121 Rheinmetall-Borsig MG 17 machine gun of 7·92-mm calibre (port and starboard)
122 Ammunition tank (1,000 rounds capacity) inboard of rib
123 Port outer self-sealing fuel tank (33 Imp gal/150l capacity)
124 Corrugated wing rib
125 ETC bomb rack support bar
126 ETC bomb rack underwing fairing
127 Port outboard flap
128 Port aileron
129 Aileron mass balance
130 Rear spar
131 Wing rib
132 Port navigation light
133 Front spar
134 Wing leading edge
135 Underwing bomb load (two 110-lb/50-kg bombs) on multi-purpose carrier
136 Bomb shackles
137 Dienartstab percussion rod attachments
138 ETC 50/VIII fairing
139 Air brake (extended)
140 Air brake activating mechanism
141 Air brake (retracted)
142 Landing lamp
143 Wheel spat
144 Fork/spat attachment
145 Port mainwheel
146 Brake reservoir filler point
147 Cantilever fork
148 Leather shroud
149 Oleo-pneumatic shock absorber
150 Mainwheel leg
151 Siren fairing
152 Barrel of MG 17 machine gun
153 Wind-driven siren
154 Starboard wheel spat
155 PVC ventral bomb rack
156 Bomb cradle
157 Starboard wheel fork
158 Starboard mainwheel
159 Bomb release trapese
160 551-lb (250-kg) bomb with Dienartstab attachment

# Junkers Ju 88

**Many versions: data for Ju 88A-4, C-6, G-7, S-1**

**Origin:** Junkers Flugzeug und Motorenwerke AG, dispersed among 14 plants with subcontract or assembly by ATG, Opel, Volkswagen and various French groups.

**Type:** Military aircraft designed as dive bomber but developed for level bombing, close support, night fighting, torpedo dropping, reconnaissance and as pilotless missile. Crew: two to six.

**Engines:** (A-4) two 1,340hp Junkers Jumo 211J 12-cylinder inverted-vee liquid-cooled; (C-6) same as A-4; (G-7) two 1,880hp Junkers Jumo 213E 12-cylinder inverted-vee liquid-cooled; (S-1) two 1,700hp BMW 801G 18-cylinder two-row radials.

**Dimensions:** Span 65ft 10½in (20·13m) (early versions 59ft 10¾in); length 47ft 2¼in (14·4m); (G-7, 54ft 1½in); height 15ft 11in (4·85m); (C-6) 16ft 7½in (5m).

**Weights:** Empty (A-4) 17,637lb (8000kg); (C-6b) 19,090lb (8660kg), (G-7b) 20,062lb (9100kg); (S-1) 18,300lb (8300kg); maximum loaded (A-4) 30,865lb (14,000kg); (C-6b) 27,500lb (12,485kg); (G-7b) 32,350lb (14,690kg); 23,100lb (10,490kg).

**Performance:** Maximum speed (A-4) 269mph (433km/h); (C-6b) 300mph (480km/h); (G-7b) (no drop tank or flame-dampers) 402mph (643km/h); (S-1) 373mph (600km/h); initial climb (A-4) 1,312ft (400m)/min; (C-6b) about 985ft (300m)/min; (G-7b) 1,640ft (500m)/min; (S-1) 1,804ft (550m)/min; service ceiling (A-4) 26,900ft (8200m); (C-6b) 32,480ft (9900m); (G-7b) 28,870ft (8800m); (S-1) 36,090ft (11,000m); range (A-4) 1,112 miles (1790km); (C-6b) 1,243 miles (2000km); (G-7b) 1,430 miles (2300km); (S-1) 1,243 miles (2000km).

**Armament:** (A-4) two 7.92mm MG 81 (or one MG 81 and one 13mm MG 131) firing forward, twin MG 81 or one MG 131 upper rear, one or two MG 81 at rear of ventral gondola and (later aircraft) two MG 81 at front of gondola; (C-6b) three 20mm MG FF and three MG 17 in nose and two 20mm MG 151/20 firing obliquely upward in Schräge Musik installation; (G-7b) four MG 151/20 (200 rounds each) firing forward from ventral fairing, two MG 151/20 in Schräge Musik installation (200 rounds each) and defensive MG 131 (500 rounds) swivelling in rear roof; (S-1) one MG 131 (500 rounds) swivelling in rear roof; bomb loads (A-4) 1,100lb

*continued on page 210* ▶

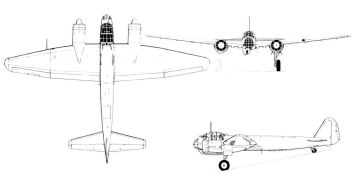

*Above: Three-view of Ju 88A-4 (increased span)*

*Above: Swinging the compass of a Ju 88A-3, one of the original family of short-span (59ft 10¾in or 60ft 3½in) Ju 88s with which the Luftwaffe began World War II. The A-3 was a dual-control conversion trainer*

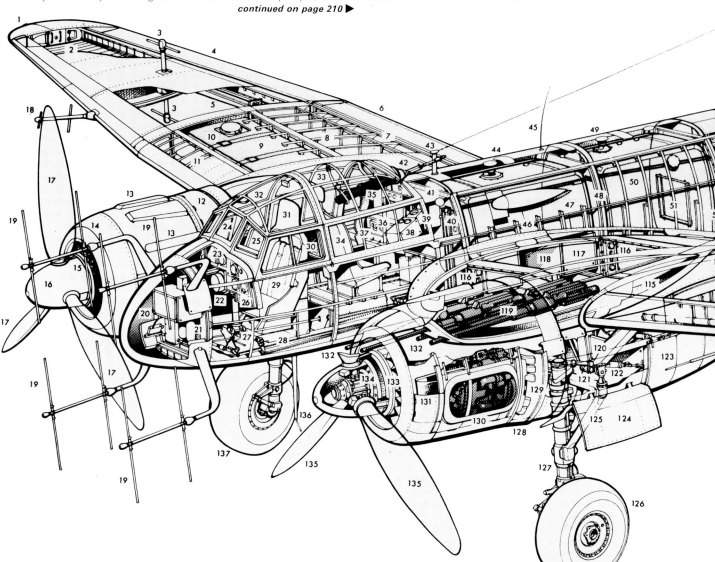

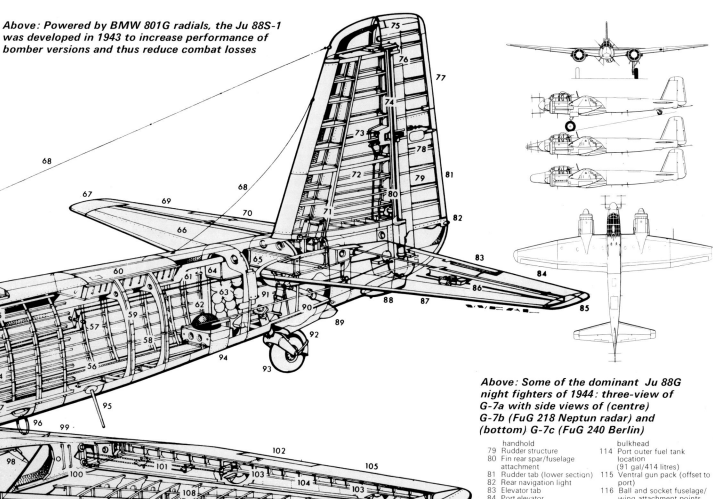

*Above: Powered by BMW 801G radials, the Ju 88S-1 was developed in 1943 to increase performance of bomber versions and thus reduce combat losses*

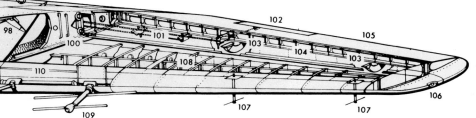

*Above: Some of the dominant Ju 88G night fighters of 1944: three-view of G-7a with side views of (centre) G-7b (FuG 218 Neptun radar) and (bottom) G-7c (FuG 240 Berlin)*

## Junkers Ju 88G-1

| | | |
|---|---|---|
| 1 Starboard navigation light | 40 Control linkage | 79 Rudder structure |
| 2 Wingtip profile | 41 Bulkhead | 80 Fin rear spar/fuselage |
| 3 FuG 227 Flensburg homing receiver aerial | 42 Armoured gun mounting | attachment |
| 4 Starboard aileron | 43 Aerial post/traverse check | 81 Rudder tab (lower section) |
| 5 Aileron control lines | 44 Fuel filler cap | 82 Rear navigation light |
| 6 Starboard flap | 45 Whip aerial | 83 Elevator tab |
| 7 Flap-fairing strip | 46 Forward fuselage fuel tank (105 gal/480 litres) | 84 Port elevator |
| 8 Wing ribs | 47 Fuselage horizontal construction joint | 85 Elevator balance |
| 9 Starboard outer fuel tank (91 gal/414 litres) | 48 Bulkhead | 86 Elevator tab actuator |
| 10 Fuel filler cap | 49 Fuel filler cap | 87 Heated leading-edge |
| 11 Leading-edge structure | 50 Aft fuselage fuel tank (230 gal/1,046 litres) | 88 Tailbumper/fuel vent outlet |
| 12 Annular exhaust slot | 51 Access hatch | 89 Tailwheel doors |
| 13 Cylinder head fairings | 52 Bulkhead | 90 Tailwheel retraction mechanism |
| 14 Adjustable nacelle nose ring | 53 Control linkage access plate | 91 Shock-absorber leg |
| 15 Twelve-blade cooling fan | 54 Fuselage stringers | 92 Mudgard |
| 16 Propeller boss | 55 Upper longeron | 93 Tailwheel |
| 17 Three-blade variable-pitch VS 111 propeller | 56 Maintenance walkway | 94 Access hatch |
| 18 Leading-edge radar array | 57 Control linkage | 95 Fixed antenna |
| 19 Lichtenstein SN-2 radar array | 58 Fuselage horizontal construction joint | 96 D/F loop |
| 20 SN-2 radar | 59 'Z'-section fuselage frames | 97 Lower longeron |
| 21 Bulkhead | 60 Dinghy stowage | 98 Nacelle/flap fairing |
| 22 Gyro compass | 61 Fuel vent pipe | 99 Port flap |
| 23 Instrument panel | 62 Master compass | 100 Wing centre/outer section attachment point |
| 24 Armoured-glass windscreen sections | 63 Spherical oxygen bottles | 101 Aileron controls |
| 25 Folding seat | 64 Accumulator | 102 Aileron tab (port only) |
| 26 Control column | 65 Tailplane centre-section carry-through | 103 Aileron hinges |
| 27 Rudder pedal/brake cylinder | 66 Starboard tailplane | 104 Rear spar |
| 28 Control lines | 67 Elevator balance | 105 Port aileron |
| 29 Pilot's seat | 68 Aerial | 106 Port navigation light |
| 30 Sliding window section | 69 Starboard elevator | 107 FuG 101a radio altimeter aerial |
| 31 Headrest | 70 Elevator tab | 108 Wing structure |
| 32 Jettisonable canopy roof section | 71 Fin front spar/fuselage attachment | 109 Leading-edge radar array |
| 33 Gun restraint | 72 Fin structure | 110 Front spar |
| 34 Radio operator/gunner's seat | 73 Rudder actuator | 111 Pitot head |
| 35 13mm MG 131 gun | 74 Rudder post | 112 Landing lamp |
| 36 Radio equipment | 75 Rudder mass balance | 113 Mainwheel well rear |
| 37 Ammunition box (500 rounds) | 76 Rudder upper hinge | 114 Port outer fuel tank location (91 gal/414 litres) |
| 38 Lichtenstein SN-2 indicator box | 77 Rudder tab (upper section) | 115 Ventral gun pack (offset to port) |
| 39 FuG 227 Flensburg indicator | 78 Inspection/maintenance handhold | 116 Ball and socket fuselage/wing attachment points |
| | | 117 Port inner fuel tank location (93·4 gal/425 litres) |
| | | 118 Ammunition boxes (200 rpg) |
| | | 119 Four Mauser MG 151 20mm cannon |
| | | 120 Mainwheel leg retraction yoke |
| | | 121 Leg pivot member |
| | | 122 Mainwheel door actuating jack |
| | | 123 Mainwheel door (rear section) |
| | | 124 Mainwheel door (front section) |
| | | 125 Leg support strut |
| | | 126 Port mainwheel |
| | | 127 Mainwheel leg |
| | | 128 Annular exhaust slot |
| | | 129 Exhaust stubs (internal) |
| | | 130 BMW 801D engine (part-deleted to show gun pack) |
| | | 131 Annular oil tank |
| | | 132 Cannon muzzles (5 deg. downward angle) |
| | | 133 Twelve-blade cooling fan (3·17 times propeller speed) |
| | | 134 Propeller mechanism |
| | | 135 Three-blade variable-pitch VS 111 propeller |
| | | 136 FuG 16ZY aerial |
| | | 137 Starboard mainwheel |

## ► Junkers Ju 88

(500kg) internal and four external racks rated at 2,200lb (1000kg) (inners) and 1,100lb (500kg) (outers) to maximum total bomb load of 6,614lb (3000kg); (C-6b and G-7b, nil); (S-1) up to 4,410lb (2000kg) on external racks.

**History:** First flight (Ju 88V1) 21 December 1936; (first Ju 88A-1) 7 September 1939; (first fighter, Ju 88C-0) July 1939; (Ju 88C-6) mid-1942; (first G-series) early 1944; (S series) late 1943; final deliveries, only as factories were overrun by Allies.

**Development:** Probably no other aircraft in history has been developed in so many quite different forms for so many purposes — except, perhaps, for the Mosquito. Flown long before World War II as a civil prototype, after a frantic design process led by two temporarily hired Americans well-versed in modern stressed-skin construction, the first 88s were transformed into the heavier, slower and more capacious A-1 bombers which were just entering service as World War II began. The formidable bomb load and generally good performance were offset by inadequate defensive armament, and in the A-4 the span was increased, the bomb load and gun power substantially augmented and a basis laid for diverse further development. Though it would be fair to describe practically all the subsequent versions as a hodge-podge of lash-ups, the Ju 88 was structurally excellent, combined large internal fuel capacity with great load-carrying capability, and yet was never so degraded in performance as to become seriously vulnerable as were the Dornier and Heinkel bombers. Indeed, with the BMW radial and the Jumo 213 engines the later versions were almost as fast as the best contemporary fighters at all altitudes and could be aerobatted violently into the bargain. A basic design feature was that all the crew were huddled together, to improve combat morale; but in the Battle of Britain it was found this merely made it difficult to add proper defensive armament and in the later Ju 188 a much larger crew compartment was provided. Another distinctive feature was the large single struts of the main landing gear, sprung with stacks of chamfered rings of springy steel, and arranged to turn the big, soft-field wheels through 90°

to lie flat in the rear of the nacelles. In 1940 to 1943 about 2,000 Ju 88 bombers were built each year, nearly all A-5 or A-4 versions. After splitting off completely new branches which led to the Ju 188 and 388, bomber development was directed to the streamlined S series of much higher performance, it having become accepted that the traditional Luftwaffe species of bomber was doomed if intercepted, no matter how many extra guns and crew it might carry. Indeed even the bomb and fuel loads were cut in most S sub-types, though the S-2 had fuel in the original bomb bay and large bulged bomb stowage (which defeated the objective of reducing drag). Final bomber versions included the P series of big-gun anti-armour and close-support machines, the Nbwe with flame-throwers and recoilless rocket projectors, and a large family of Mistel composite-aircraft combinations, in which the Ju 88 lower portion was a pilotless missile steered by the fighter originally mounted on top. Altogether bomber, reconnaissance and related 88s totalled 10,774, while frantic construction of night fighter versions in 1944–45 brought the total to at least 14,980.

The Ju 88 night fighters (especially the properly designed G-series) were extremely formidable, bristling with radar and weapons and being responsible for destroying more Allied night bombers than all other fighters combined. The Ju 88 fighter family began in the summer of 1939, when the V7 prototype was authorized for conversion into a Zerstörer with heavy forward-firing armament. Despite its size, the Ju 88 was clearly potentially a better heavy fighter than the Bf 110, having excellent speed, great manoeuvrability and immense structural strength. In the long-range anti-shipping and intruder roles it promised to have few, if any, equals, and the V7 with an MG FF cannon and three MG 17 machine guns firing ahead also demonstrated that the Ju 88 was a superb gun platform. In 1939 there was little apparent need for such a heavy fighter, but Junkers managed to continue fighter development with the BMW-radial-powered C-series. The Ju 88C-2 was for more than a year the only fighter sub-type, used in small numbers for coastal and anti-shipping patrol and then proving ideal for the newly formed night-fighter force in July 1940. The C-2 units made many night intruder missions over Britain, and in December received the C-4, designed

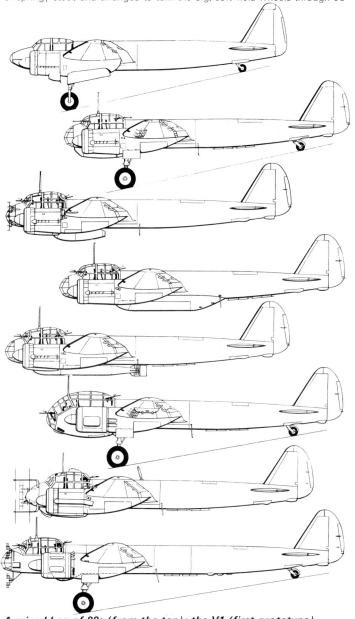

*A mixed bag of 88s (from the top): the V1 (first prototype), A-1, A-6/U, A-15, A-17, B-0, C-6 fighter and long-range H-1*

Left: a Ju 88A-4 of I/KG 54 "Totenkopf" (Death's head) at Gerbini, April 1942

from the start as a fighter, and one wing was transferred to the Mediterranean theatre. The C-4 had two extra 20mm cannon in the offset ventral blister, and could also carry 12 MG 81 machine guns in two pods for ground attack. Via the C-5 came the C-6, built in much greater numbers, with a wide variety of weapons firing in all directions. On the Eastern front some had noses painted to look like the less formidable bomber, presumably to deceive Soviet pilots into getting in front. From the C-6b the night-fighter versions carried radar, either Lichtenstein FuG 202 or 212. A parallel series was the Ju 88R, with BMW radials instead of Jumo 211, an example of which defected to Aberdeen on 9 May 1943 and laid bare most of the previously secret features of what was by now a very formidable and refined aircraft. Many other sub-types followed, some of them having Schräge Musik slanting cannon armament, and leading finally to the superb G-series with Ju 188 tail to restore the lost performance and safe handling which had been degraded by overloading with weapons and radar. Subject of the cutaway, the G also had properly thought-out night-fighter armament, with guns moved from the nose (where they blinded the pilot) to a ventral tray. Lethality of these late-model G-series was greatly augmented by adding FuG 350 Naxos, which homed unerringly on the RAF bomber's $H_2S$ radar, and FuG 227 Flensburg which homed on the bomber's Monica rear-warning radar, which had been added for the bomber's own protection!

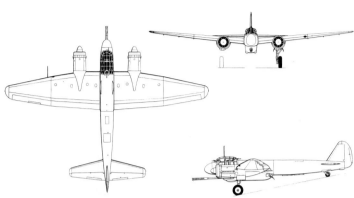

Above: Three-view of anti-tank P-1

Below: One of the "ordinary" Ju 88 bomber versions was the A-14, which could operate conventionally (as here) or with an MG FF forward-firing cannon in the anti-shipping role

# Junkers W34

### W 33 variants and W 34 variants
**Origin:** Junkers Flugzeug und Motorenwerke AG.
**Type:** Transport and utility.
**Engine:** (33) 310hp Junkers L-5 in-line; (34hau) 650hp Bramo SAM 22B (322) nine-cylinder radial; (34hi) 660hp BMW 132, same layout.
**Dimensions:** Span 58ft 2¾in (17·75m); length (34hi landplane) 33ft 8¼in (10·27m); height (land) 11ft 7in (3·53m).
**Weights:** (34hi) empty 3,748lb (1700kg); loaded 7,056lb (3200kg).
**Performance:** (34hi) maximum speed 165mph (265km/h); range (typical) 559 miles (900km).

**Development:** Immediately after World War I Junkers flew the F 13 all-metal cantilever monoplane transport that exerted a giant influence on transport aircraft and sold all over the world. The W 33 and 34 appeared in 1926 and sold in even greater numbers, and the 34 was in service in hundreds with the Luftwaffe right through World War II, though the last was delivered in 1934. Normally seating six, these robust corrugated-skin workhorses were used as crew trainers, liaison aircraft, close-support transports and in many special roles.

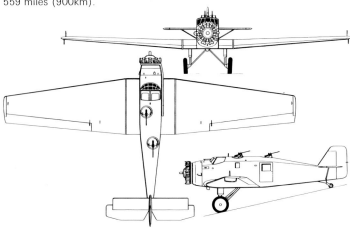

*Above: Junkers K 43 reconnaissance-bomber version*

*Above: The W 34hi was the most common Luftwaffe version, and more than 1,000 of this variant served with 11 training schools and as liaison, ambulance, transport, trials and photographic utility aircraft*

# Junkers Ju 89

### Ju 89 V1 and V2
**Origin:** Junkers Flugzeug und Motorenwerke AG.
**Types:** Heavy bomber.
**Engines:** Four inverted-vee-12, (V1) 1,075hp Jumo 211A, (V2) 960hp DB 600A.
**Dimensions:** Span 115ft 8½in (35·25m); length 86ft 11¼in (26·49m); height 24ft 11¼in (7·60m).
**Weights:** Empty (V2) 37,480lb (17,000kg); loaded 50,266lb (22,800kg).
**Performance:** Maximum speed (V2, no armament) 242mph (390km/h); max range 1,242 miles (2000km).

**Development:** Spurred by far-seeing Generalleutnant Walther Wever, the RLM issued a specification in mid-1935 for a Langstrecken-Grossbomber (long-range heavy bomber), which was popularly called the Ural-bomber, though it had to reach the tip of Scotland as well. The Do 19 and Ju 89 were the main responses, and the Junkers was by far the more capable. The Ju 89 V1 flew in December 1936, followed by V2 in early 1937. Under the leadership of Dipl-Ing Ernst Zindel this very big and impressive machine had taken shape quickly, with smooth dural skin, double-wing flaps, hydraulic landing gear and crew of nine. Intended armament comprised a 20mm cannon in dorsal and ventral turrets and front and rear MG 15 machine guns. Internal bomb load was 16 bombs of 220lb (100kg) or similar combinations. After Wever's death the programme trickled on until termination on 29 April 1937. The two Ju 89s continued intensive flying; V1 gained load/height records in 1938, one being 11,023lb (5000kg) to the excellent height of 30,551ft — well over 10,000ft above the ceiling of a Stirling with a similar load.

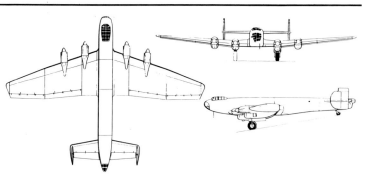

*Above: Three-view of the Ju 89 V1*

*Above: Early flight trials showed that the rudders ought to be enlarged, and V1 is seen after this modification*

# Junkers EF 61

### EF 61 V1 and V2
**Origin:** Junkers Flugzeug und Motorenwerke AG.
**Type:** High-altitude research aircraft.
**Engines:** Two 950hp Daimler-Benz DB 600A inverted-vee-12 liquid-cooled.
**Dimensions:** Span 88ft 7in (27·00m); length 47ft 0¾in (14·34m); height, not known.
**Weights:** Not known.
**Performance:** Maximum speed about 217mph (350km/h); ceiling, designed to exceed 49,200ft (15,000m).

**Development:** Probably Junkers was world leader in high-flying aircraft until the Hs 128/130 programme. The Ju 49 of 1931 was the first aircraft in the world with a pressure cabin, and in the two EF 61 research aircraft of 1936 work went much further. Odd in that much of their outer skin was fabric, these aircraft had a crew of two in a pressure cabin forming the nose. V1 had a large pilot porthole in the nose, a sandwich of special plastics called Reilit. V2 had a raised metal cupola offset to the left, with small ports. At the rear of this cupola was provision for an MG 15, while four 551lb

(250kg) bombs could be carried in an internal bay. Both aircraft crashed, V1 due to control flutter. In December 1937 the official view was that much more research would be needed before bombers could fly high enough to be immune to interception.

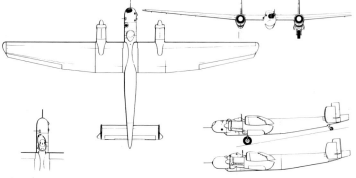

*Above: Three-view of EF 61 V1 with (lower side view and inset) EF 61 V2*

# Junkers Ju 188

### Ju 188A, D and E series

**Origin:** Junkers Flugzeug und Motorenwerke AG; with subcontract manufacture of parts by various French companies.

**Type:** Five-seat bomber (D-2, reconnaissance).

**Engines:** (Ju 188A) two 1,776hp Junkers Jumo 213A 12-cylinder inverted-vee liquid-cooled; (Ju 188D) same as A; (Ju 188E) two 1,700hp BMW 801G-2 18-cylinder two-row radials.

**Dimensions:** Span 72ft 2in (22m); length 49ft 1in (14·96m); height 16ft 1in (4·9m).

**Weights:** Empty (188E-1) 21,825lb (9900kg); loaded (188A and D) 33,730lb (15,300kg); (188E-1) 31,967lb (14,500kg).

**Performance:** Maximum speed (188A) 325mph (420km/h) at 20,500ft (6250m); (188D) 350mph (560km/h) at 27,000ft (8235m); (188E) 315mph (494km/h) at 19,685ft (6000m); service ceiling (188A) 33,000ft (10,060m); (188D) 36,090ft (11,000m); (188E) 31,170ft (9500m); range with 3,300lb (1500kg) bomb load (188A and E) 1,550 miles (2480km).

**Armament:** (A, D-1 and E-1) one 20mm MG 151/20 cannon in nose, one MG 131 in dorsal turret, one 13mm MG 131 manually aimed at rear dorsal position and one MG 131 or twin 7·92mm MG 81 manually aimed at rear ventral position; 6,614lb (3000kg) bombs internally or two 2,200lb (1000kg) torpedoes under inner wings.

**History:** First flight (Ju 88B-0) early 1940; (Ju 88V27) September 1941; (Ju 188V1) December 1941; (Ju 188E-1) March 1942.

**Development:** In 1939 Junkers had the Jumo 213 engine in advanced development and, to go with it, the aircraft side of the company prepared an improved Ju 88 with a larger yet more streamlined crew compartment, more efficient pointed wings and large squarish tail. After protracted development this went into production as the Ju 188E-1, fitted with BMW 801s because the powerful Jumo was still not ready. The plant at Bernburg delivered 120 E-1s and a few radar-equipped turretless E-2s and reconnaissance F versions before, in mid-1943, finally getting into production with the A-1

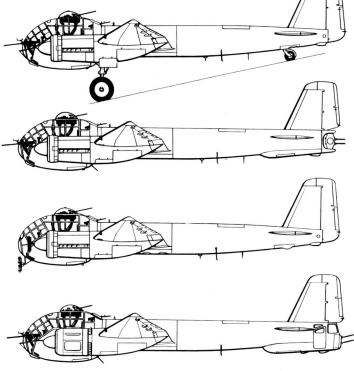

*Above, from the top: Ju 188A-2, Ju 188C, Ju 188D-2 and Ju 188G-0*

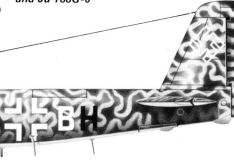

*Left: A Ju 188D-2, with Hohentwiel radar, operated by 1 (F)/124 at Kirkenes in 1944*

version. Leipzig/Mockau built the A-2 with flame-damped exhaust for night operations and the A-3 torpedo bomber. The D was a fast reconnaissance aircraft, and the Ju 188S was a family of high-speed machines, for various duties, capable of up to 435mph (696km/h). Numerous other versions, some with a remotely controlled twin-MG 131 tail turret, led to the even faster and higher-flying Ju 388 family. All these aircraft, and the even greater number of stillborn projects, were evidence of the increasingly urgent need to make up for the absence of properly conceived new designs by wringing the utmost development out of the obsolescent types with which the Luftwaffe had started the war.

In the summer of 1944 the 188R-0 series was tested as a possible future night fighter, but main production in this category continued with the outstanding Ju 88G-series (which in fact were hard to beat). The only area where by 1944 the Ju 188 appeared to have a future was in high-altitude missions, because failure of the Bomber B programme (Ju 288 and Fw 191, especially) had led to something like a procurement crisis in the Luftwaffe which was solved only by eventually abandoning all aircraft programmes except jets and fighters. The high-flying Ju 388J, K and L were paralleled by the Ju 188S and T, in which armament was eliminated in favour of extra speed and height. The streamlined 188S bomber, with very highly rated Jumo 213E-1 engines, reached 426mph (685km/h) at 37,730ft (11,500m), while the 188R reconnaissance aircraft reached 435mph. But by mid-1944 most programmes were in chaos, and after a few S and R had come off the line the rest were turned into low-level 188S-1/U close-support aircraft with 50mm BK-5 cannon. Despite its excellent qualities, and the esteem in which it was held by its crews, the 188 never served in large numbers nor made any impact on the war. In 1945–46 12 were assembled by SNCASE in France, and used with others (mainly E and F models) by the French Aéronavale as hacks and testbeds. The 188 was an outstanding machine, but the Luftwaffe received fewer than 1,100 of them.

*Below: One of the best torpedo bombers of World War II was the Ju 188E-2, capable of carrying FuG 200 Hohentwiel navigation and precision-bombing radar and two LT 1b or LT F5b torpedoes and still prove hard to catch. Some, but not this one, were devoid of the EDL 131 turret*

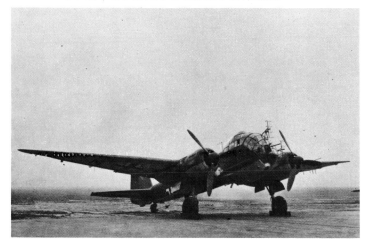

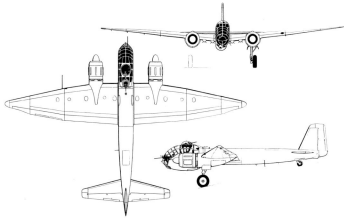

*Three-view of the radial-engined Ju 188E-1 bomber*

# Junkers Ju 252

**Ju 252 V1 to V15 and A-1**
**Origin:** Junkers Flugzeug und Motorenwerke AG.
**Type:** Transport.
**Engines:** (A-1) three 1,350hp Junkers Jumo 211F inverted-vee-12 liquid-cooled.
**Dimensions:** Span 111ft 10¼in (34.09m); length 82ft 4¼in (25.10m); height 18ft 10½in (5.75m).
**Weights:** (A-1) empty 28,884lb (13,100kg); max loaded 52,911lb (24,000kg).
**Performance:** Maximum speed 272mph (439km/h); range with max payload 2,473 miles (3980km).

**Development:** In December 1938 Junkers discussed with Lufthansa the EF 77 study for a Ju 52/3m replacement. After much changing due to the airline making new demands, the Ju 252 V1 flew in October 1941. It was a pressurized 35-passenger airliner of outstanding speed and range, but before first flight the RLM ordered Junkers to produce the 252 as an armed Luftwaffe machine. With much difficulty an EDL 131 (single MG 131) turret was added, plus beam-window MG 15s. It was still a vast improvement over the Ju 52, but Junkers was then told to stop building the Ju 252

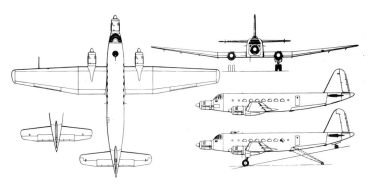

*Three-view of Ju 252A-1 (inset and upper side view, V1)*

except those aircraft for which most parts had already been made (a total of 15, all given Versuchs-numbers). The order went out that the 252 had to be redesigned to use wood, and engines already stockpiled. The result was the 352.

*Below: The seventh production Ju 252A-1 had no EDL 131 turret*

# Junkers Ju 287

**Ju 287 V1 to V3 and A-0**
**Origin:** Junkers Flugzeug und Motorenwerke AG.
**Type:** (V1) testbed, (V3) heavy bomber.
**Engines:** (V1) four 1,980lb (900kg) thrust Jumo 004 turbojets (plus four 2,645lb, 1200kg, thrust Walter 501 takeoff assistance rockets); (V3) six 1,760lb (800kg) thrust BMW 003A turbojets.
**Dimensions:** Span 65ft 11¾in (20.11m); length (V1) 60ft 0½in (18.30m); height, not known.
**Weights:** (V1) empty 27,583lb (12,510kg); loaded 44,092lb (20,000kg).
**Performance:** Maximum speed (V1) 348mph (560km/h), (V3, est) 537mph (865km/h); range with max bomb, V3 est, 985 miles (1585km).

**Development:** This large jet bomber was begun as a totally new project in early 1943, using DVL data on swept wings for high-subsonic performance. Dipl-Ing Wocke boldly decided to sweep the wing not backwards but forwards, accepted aeroelastic hazards (which it was believed could be conquered in the structural design) to gain in the aerodynamics, especially in lateral control at the stall. As the Ju 287 was so radical it was deemed prudent to test the wing in a hastily built low-speed aircraft while the new bomber was being designed. The resulting testbed, designated Ju 287 V1, flew at Brandis on 16 August 1944. It combined the fuselage of an He 177, nosewheels from two B-24 Liberators, mainwheels of Ju 352 type (all fixed and spatted) and tail made of Ju 388 parts. In 17 flights this ungainly harbinger of the future demonstrated excellent characteristics, and there is no doubt that the proposed Ju 287A would have been an outstandingly advanced aircraft that would have posed the Allies severe problems. The 287 V2, with new fuselage housing the retracted landing gears and with six BMW 003 engines on the wings, was almost ready for flight when the airfield was overrun, and it flew in 1947 in the Soviet Union. The production prototype V3, which did not get very far, would have had the pressurized three-man cockpit, bomb bay ahead of the main spar for 8,818lb (4000kg) and remote-control tail barbette with two MG 131.

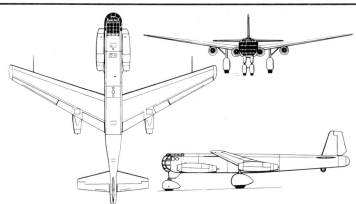

*Above: Three-view of the hasty lash-up Ju 287 V-1*

*When this photograph was taken the V1 was tufted and fitted with a camera ahead of the tail to explore airflow*

# Junkers Ju 288

Ju 288 A-series (V1 to V7), B-series (V9 to V14) and C-series (V101 to V108)

**Origin:** Junkers Flugzeug und Motorenwerke AG.
**Type:** Medium bomber.
**Engines:** See text.
**Dimensions:** Span (A) 60ft 0in (18·29m), (B, C) 74ft 4in (22·65m); length (A) 52ft 2in (15·89m), (B) 58ft 4¾in (17·79m), (C) 59ft 5¾in (18·12m); height (A) 13ft 7in (4·15m), (B, C) 14ft 9in (4·50m).
**Weights:** Empty (A) 26,240lb (11,900kg), (B) not known but about 28,660lb (13,000kg), (C) 29,546lb (13,400kg); max loaded (A) 38,900lb (17,645kg), (B) 46,186lb (20,950kg), (C) 49,493lb (22,450kg).
**Performance:** Maximum speed (A) 416mph (670km/h), (B) 388mph (625km/h), (C) 407mph (655km/h); range with max internal bomb load (A) 2,237 miles (3600km), (B) 1,678 miles (2700km), (C) 1,616 miles (2600km).

**Development:** Though one of the least-known of the world's warplanes the Ju 288 produced three distinct families of bombers that were among the most advanced of their day. It is fortunate for the Allies that the programme could hardly have had less impact on the war, and all the Luftwaffe got for enormous expenditure was a few weeks of desultory and dangerous supposed operational use by a few surviving prototypes. The Luftwaffe's biggest development programme during World War II was Bomber B, and this was originally to a specification written around a proposal by Junkers. The RLM always expected Junkers to win, and construction of the Ju 288 V1 began in February 1940 in advance of a contract. Backed by testing with modified Ju 88s, the V1 flew in January 1941, with 1,600hp BMW 801A radials. The next seven all flew in 1941, V5 having 2,500hp Jumo 222A-1/B-1 multibank engines with ducted spinners. Four 13mm MG 131 were in two remote-control barbettes, and bomb load was 6,614lb (3000kg). By 1942 action had switched to the 288B series, with much longer span, new tail, big four-seat cabin (all 288s were pressurized) and 2,700hp DB 606A-1/B-1 double engines. But by spring 1942 the C-series had taken over with bigger and stronger structure, belly deepened with front and rear twin-MG 131 barbettes, twin MG 131 dorsal and single MG 151 in tail, and bomb load of 6,614lb internal plus 4,409lb (total 11,023lb, 5000kg) on wing racks. In June 1943 the whole Bomber B programme collapsed, because it was consuming too many resources and would interfere with production (of obsolescent aircraft). At least 17 of 22 Ju 288s crashed, but a few were thrown into battle in mid-1944 armed with 5cm BK 5 guns.

*Below: The Ju 288 V14 was the final B-series prototype, and it had Jumo 222 engines, but when it flew (August 1942) this family had already been superseded by the C-series*

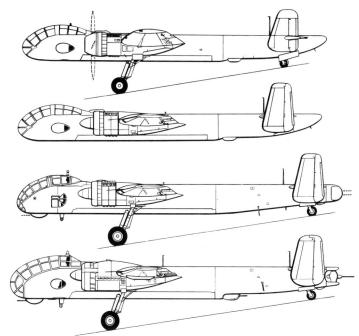

*Above (from top): Ju 288A (V5), Ju 288A (V8), Ju 288B (V14) and Ju 288C (V103)*

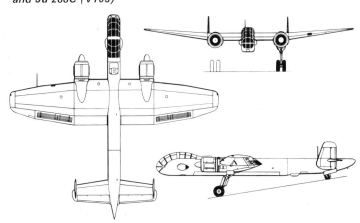

*Above: Three-view of Ju 288A (V1), first short-span model*

# Junkers Ju 290

### Ju 290 A-1 to A-8 and B-1, B-2 and C

**Origin:** Junkers Flugzeug und Motorenwerke; design and development at Prague-Letnany, prototypes at Dessau and production at Bernburg.

**Type:** Long-range transport and reconnaissance bomber.

**Engines:** Four BMW 801 14-cylinder radials, (A) usually 1,700hp 801D, (B) 1,970hp 801E.

**Dimensions:** Span 137ft 9½in (42·00m); length 92ft 1in to 97ft 9in (A-5, 93ft 11½in, 28·64m); height 22ft 4¾in (6·83m).

**Weights:** Empty, not known (published figures cannot be correct); maximum (A-5) 99,141lb (44,970kg), (A-7) 101,413lb (45,400kg), (B-2) 111,332lb (50,500kg).

**Performance:** Maximum speed (all, without missiles) about 273mph (440km/h); maximum range (typical) 3,700 miles (5950km), (B-2) 4,970 miles (8000km).

**Armament:** See text.

**History:** First flight (rebuilt Ju 90V5) early 1939, (production 290A-0) October 1942; programme termination October 1944.

**Development:** In 1936 Junkers considered the possibility of turning the Ju 89 strategic bomber into the Ju 90 airliner. With the death of Gen Wever the Ju 89 was cancelled and the Ju 90 became the pride of Deutsche Lufthansa. By 1937 the civil Ju 90S (Schwer = heavy) was in final design, with the powerful BMW 139 engine. By 1939 this had flown, with a new wing and BMW 801 engines, and via a string of development prototypes led to the Ju 290A-0 and A-1 transports first used at Stalingrad. The A-2 was an Atlantic patrol machine, with typical armament of five 20mm MG 151 (including two power turrets) and six 13mm MG 131. There were many other versions, and the A-7 introduced a bulbous glazed nose; armament of the A-8 series was ten MG 151 and one (or three) MG 131, the most powerful carried by any bomber of World War II. The B carried more fuel and pressurized crew compartments, and like some A versions had radar and could launch Hs 293 and other air/surface missiles. In 1944 three A-5 made round trips to Manchuria.

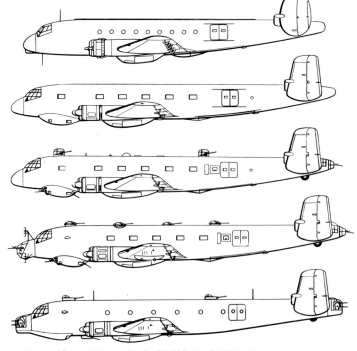

*Above (from the top): Ju 90 V4, Ju 90 V11 (Ju 290 V1), Ju 290A-2, Ju 290A-8, and Ju 290B-1*

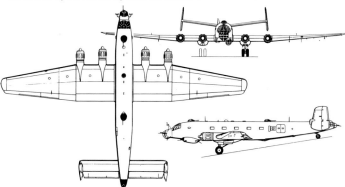

*Above: Three-view of Ju 290A-7*

*Above: The first of the 11 Ju 290A-5 maritime reconnaissance aircraft, most of which served with FAGr 5. Features included FuG 200 Hohentwiel radar, additional firepower, better armour protection and facilities for fuel jettison*

*Below: The first of five Ju 290A-3 reconnaissance aircraft, which served with FAGr 5 at Mont de Marsan. The A-3 had a Focke-Wulf low-drag rear dorsal turret and better tail turret*

*Above: The first of 25 A-7 series at Bernburg; none reached service*

# Junkers Ju 322 Mammut

**Ju 322 V1 and V2**
**Origin:** Junkers Flugzeug und Motorenwerke AG.
**Type:** Giant assault glider.
**Dimensions:** Span 203ft 5in (62·00m); length 99ft 3in (30·25m); height 32ft 9in (10·00m).
**Weights:** Empty (with take-off trolley) 52,900lb (26,000kg); loaded 79,366lb (36,000kg).
**Performance:** Design gliding angle 1:50 (if correctly reported, ridiculously optimistic); no other data.

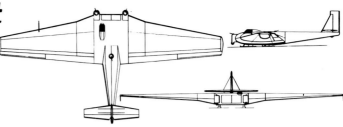

*Above: Three-view of Ju 322 Mammut*

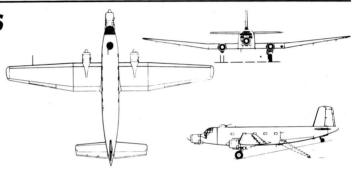

*Above: The only known Ju 322 photograph, taken after its landing*

**Development:** Had Junkers, and Hitler, been cleverer the British might have found their island swamped by masses of the biggest and most awesome gliders the world had ever seen. The vital need to fly in really heavy equipment with the leading assault troops called for a Grossraumlastensegler — a monster glider carrying a PzKW IV tank, Flak 88 and half-track crew/ammo tug or an SP gun and all crew, ammo and fuel. On 12 October 1940 Messerschmitt (code name Warschau-Süd) was to complete design of a glider in steel tube and fabric, while Junkers did one in wood (Warschau-Ost), 14 days being allowed. By this time plans and materials had to be ready for mass-production, the first batch being 100. Both companies worked frantically, but Junkers ran into every kind of trouble. Their vast flying-wing Mammut was delayed months by snags with the giant take-off trolley, and then a tank crashed through V1's floor. Finally, in April 1941 a Ju 90 just managed to get V1 off the long Merseburg runway, but the glider was uncontrollable and cast loose just before the Ju 90 would have crashed. It landed in open country, but the two complete Mammuts and 98 more-or-less finished examples were sawn up for fuel.

# Junkers Ju 352 Herkules

**Ju 352 V1 to V12 and A-series**
**Origin:** Junkers Flugzeug und Motorenwerke AG.
**Type:** Transport.
**Engines:** Three 1,000hp (1,200 with 96-octane fuel) BMW-Bramo 323R-2 nine-cylinder radials.
**Dimensions:** Span 112ft 2¾in (34·20m); length 80ft 8½in (24·60m); height 18ft 10¼in (5·74m).
**Weights:** Empty (A-1, typical from lightened 26th aircraft) 27,561lb (12,500kg); loaded 43,216lb (19,600kg).
**Performance:** Maximum speed 230mph (370km/h); cruising speed 149mph (240km/h); range with max useful load (in early aircraft about 8,000lb, 3630kg) 1,120 miles (1800km).

*Above: Three-view of Ju 352A-1 Herkules*

**Development:** In 1942 the Dessau project staff had to redesign the Ju 252 to make use of non-strategic materials and stockpiled engines. The resulting Ju 352 was naturally inferior, despite its popular name of Herkules. The wing was wood and nearly all the fuselage was steel-tube and fabric. The low-powered radial engines drove reverse-pitch propellers and the hydraulic Trapoklappe (rear loading ramp) allowed loading of heavy vehicles or freight whilst holding the fuselage level. Loads were similar to the 252 but fuel capacity was considerably less. Most production machines had an MG 151 turret and two MG 131 mounts in beam windows. Manufacture at Fritzlar was abandoned in September 1944 when two prototypes, ten A-0 and 33 A-1 had been flown.

*Below: The third (V3) Ju 352, otherwise the Ju 352A-03, which first flew in November 1943*

# Junkers Ju 388

**Ju 388L-series, J-series and K-series**
**Origin:** Junkers Flugzeug und Motorenwerke AG.
**Type:** (L) Recce, (J) night fighter, (K) bomber.
**Engines:** (Most) two 1,890hp BMW 801TJ 18-cyl two-row radials, (some) two 1,750hp Junkers Jumo 213E inverted-vee-12 liquid-cooled.
**Dimensions:** Span 72ft 2in (22·00m); length (L-1) 49ft 10½in (15·20m), (J-1) 53ft 5½in (16·29m) (58ft 1in with tail-warning radar); height 14ft 3in (4·35m).
**Weights:** Empty (L-1) 22,810lb (10,345kg), (J-1) 22,928lb (10,400kg); loaded (L-1, J-1) 32,350lb (14,675kg).
**Performance:** Maximum speed at altitude (L-1) 407mph (655km/h), (J-1) 362mph (582km/h); service ceiling (typical) 44,000ft (13,500m); range (L-1, internal fuel only) 1,838 miles (2950km).

**Development:** Originally the Ju 188S and T, these extremely important combat aircraft began as the Hubertus project in September 1943. The only type to reach the Luftwaffe in quantity was the L-1, built by ATG at Merseburg and Weser at Bremen. This was a pressurized three-seater, and like other versions had extremely highly rated turbocharged engines giving almost full power at around 35,000ft. None of the numerous K-series got into service, but the J-1 was so good a night and all-weather fighter it continued after the cancellation of all except "emergency fighter" pro-

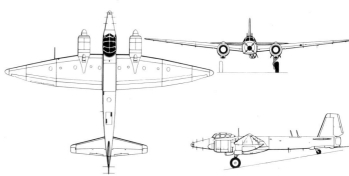

*Above: Three view of the Ju 388J-1 (V-4)*

grammes in July 1944. Most J-series did not have the twin-MG 131 tail barbette, but typical armament included two 30mm and two MG 151 firing ahead and two MG 151 in a Schräge Musik oblique installation in the rear fuselage. Nose radar included the FuG 218 Neptun with Morgenstern (Morning Star) aerial array mostly enclosed in a plywood nosecone.

*Below: The Ju 388 V2, prototype of the 388J Störtebeker (a legendary German pirate) night-fighter with SN-2 radar. Later versions had Morgenstern radar and no tail turret*

# Junkers Ju 390

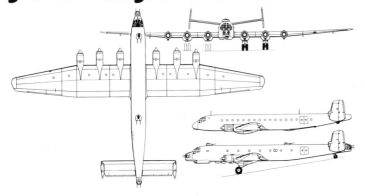

*Three-view of the proposed Ju 390A-1 (upper side view, V1)*

**Ju 390 V1 to V3 and A-1**
**Origin:** Junkers Flugzeug und Motorenwerke AG.
**Type:** Long-range bomber or reconnaissance aircraft.
**Engines:** Six 1,970hp BMW 801E 18-cylinder two-row radials.
**Dimensions:** Span 165ft 1in (50·30m); length (A-1) 112ft 2½in (34·20m); height 22ft 7in (6·89m).
**Weights:** Empty (A-1) 81,350lb (36,900kg); loaded 166,448lb (75,500kg).
**Performance:** Maximum speed (A-1) 314mph clean (505km/h) or 267mph (430km/h) with max external weapons; max range in recce role 6,027 miles (9700km).

**Development:** Early in the Ju 290 programme Dipl-Ing Kraft considered adding extra fuselage and wing panels and two more engines to produce a very capable strategic aircraft with minimal risk or cost. In mid-1942 prototypes V1 to V3 were ordered as a transport, a maritime recce aircraft and a heavy bomber. V1 flew in August 1943, and could carry 22,046lb (10,000kg) cargo 4,971 miles (8000km). V2 flew in October 1943, with FuG 200 Hohentwiel radar, and not only demonstrated a 32-hour endurance but once flew within 12 miles of the US coast near New York. The uncompleted V3 and A-series would have carried four 3,968lb (1800kg) bombs or various missiles, with eight 20mm MG 151 and eight 13mm MG 131.

# Junkers Ju 488

**Ju 488 V401-406**
**Origin:** Junkers Flugzeug und Motorenwerke AG.
**Type:** Heavy bomber.
**Engines:** (V401-402) four 1,890hp BMW 801TJ radials; (rest) four 2,500hp Jumo 222A-3/B-3 multi-bank liquid-cooled.
**Dimensions:** Span 102ft 7⅞in (31·27m); length 76ft 3in (22·23m); height 20ft 0in (6·10m).
**Weights:** Empty (V401) 46,297lb (21,000kg); loaded 79,366lb (36,000kg).
**Performance:** Maximum speed (V401, at altitude) 429mph (690km/h); range with internal fuel and full bomb load 2,113 miles (3400km).

**Development:** The RLM eagerly accepted the Junkers proposal of early 1944 to provide the Luftwaffe with its missing strategic bomber by doing the obvious: put together an assortment of parts of the Ju 88, 188, 288 and 388 to create an impressive four-engined bomber. The first two prototypes, V401 and 402, were to comprise new centre wing and fuselage sections made by Latécoère at Toulouse, France, plus the pressurized forward fuselage and wings of the 388K, the centre and aft fuselage of the 188E, the wooden ventral bomb pannier of the 88A-15 and the tail of the 288C. Latécoère

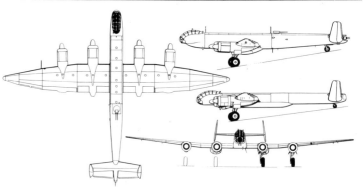

*Three-view of the Ju 488 V401 as it would have looked (upper side view, the proposed V403)*

finished the new bits in mid-July but a team of Maquis saboteurs destroyed them as they were about to be shipped. The redesigned V403 with steel tube/fabric fuselage and much greater bomb/fuel loads was abandoned in November 1944.

# Messerschmitt Bf 108 Taifun

## M-37, Bf 108A and B

**Origin:** Bayerische Flugzeugwerke (BFW), Augsburg Haunstetten.
**Type:** Four-seat communications, liaison, ambulance and utility.
**Engine:** 240hp Argus As 10C inverted-vee-8 aircooled.
**Dimensions:** (B) span 34ft 10in (10·62m); length 27ft 2½in (8·29m); height 7ft 6½in (2·30m).
**Weights:** (B) empty 1,940lb (880kg); loaded 2,981lb (1352kg).
**Performance:** Maximum speed (B) 196mph (315km/h); range with four passengers 870 miles (1400km).

**Development:** Partly because of a bitter 1929 dispute with Erhard Milch, Prof Willi Messerschmitt was extremely unpopular with the Nazis and especially with the RLM. When the BFW company was rebuked in 1933 for building aircraft for export Messerschmitt replied that he had never been allowed to do anything else, and so he was awarded a contract for six examples of a sporting aircraft for the 1934 Challenge de Tourisme Internationale. The result was the Bf 108 Taifun, and though many of Messerschmitt's antagonists criticized it and tried to get it withdrawn the 108's sheer excellence gradually won converts. In fact it was probably the best and most modern four-seater built anywhere in the world before World War II. Large numbers were seen in many countries by 1939, and 885 were built by 1944, the last 359 by Nord in France (which built versions after the war). Most were used by the Luftdienst, which did second-line tasks, but one belonging to the Luftwaffe got lost in April 1940 and crash-landed in

*Above: This Bf 108B Taifun is seen in pre-war civil livery*

Belgium. Until it was returned, most politely, the German high command was somewhat apprehensive because on board was a complete set of plans for the invasion of the western countries on 10 May 1940.

# Messerschmitt Bf 109

## Bf 109B, C, D, E, F, G, H and K series, S-99 and 199, Ha-1109-1112

**Origin:** Bayerische Flugzeugwerke, later (1938) renamed Messerschmitt AG; very widely subcontracted throughout German-controlled territory and built under licence by Dornier-Werke, Switzerland, and Hispano-Aviación, Spain (post-war, Avia, Czechoslovakia).
**Type:** Single-seat fighter (many, fighter bomber).
**Engine:** (B, C) one 635hp Junkers Jumo 210D inverted-vee-12 liquid-cooled; (D) 1,000hp Daimler-Benz DB 600Aa, same layout; (E) 1,100hp DB 601A, 1,200hp DB 601N or 1,300hp DB 601E; (F) DB 601E; (G) 1,475hp DB 605A-1, or other sub-type up to DB 605D rated 1,800hp with MW50 boost; (H-1) DB 601E; (K) usually 1,550hp DB 605ASCM/DCM rated 2,000hp with MW50 boost; (S-199) 1,350hp Jumo 211F; (HA-1109) 1,300hp Hispano-Suiza 12Z-89 upright vee-12 or (M1L) 1,400hp R-R Merlin 500-45.
**Dimensions:** Span (A to E) 32ft 4½in (9·87m); (others) 32ft 6½in (9·92m); length (B, C) 27ft 11in (8·51m); (D, E, typical) 28ft 4in (8·64m); (F) 29ft 0½in (8·85m); (G) 29ft 8in (9·04m); (K) 29ft 4in (8·94m); (HA-1109-M1L) 29ft 11in (9·12m); height (E) 7ft 5½in (2·28m); (others) 8ft 6in (2·59m).
**Weights:** Empty (B-1) 3,483lb (1580kg); (E) 4,189lb (1900kg) to 4,421lb

(2005kg); (F) around 4,330lb (1964kg); (G) 5,880lb (2667kg) to 6,180lb (2800kg); (K, typical) 6,000lb (2722kg); maximum loaded (B-1) 4,850lb (2120kg); (E) 5,523lb (2505kg) to 5,875lb (2665kg); (F-3) 6,054lb (2746kg); (G) usually 7,496lb (3400kg); (K) usually 7,439lb (3375kg).
**Performance:** Maximum speed (B-1) 292mph (470km/h); (D) 323mph (520km/h); (E) 348–354mph (560–570km/h); (F-3) 390mph (628km/h); (G) 353 to 428mph (569–690km/h); (K-4) 452mph (729km/h); initial climb (B-1) 2,200ft (670·5m)/min; (E) 3,100 to 3,280ft (1000m)/min; (G) 2,700 to 4,000ft (1220m)/min; (K-4) 4,823ft (1470m)/min; service ceiling (B-1) 26,575ft (8100m); (E) 34,450ft (10,500m) to 36,090ft (11,000m); (F, G) around 38,000ft (11,600m); (K-4) 41,000ft (12,500m); range on internal fuel (all) 365–460 miles (typically, 700km).
**Armament:** (B) three 7·92mm Rheinmetall-Borsig MG 17 machine guns above engine and firing through propeller hub; (C) four MG 17, two above engine and two in wings, with fifth through propeller hub in C-2; (early E-1) four MG 17, plus four 50kg or one 250kg (551lb) bomb; (later E-1 and most other E) two MG 17 above engine, each with 1,000 rounds (or two MG 17 with 500 rounds, plus 20mm MG FF firing through propeller hub) and two MG FF in wings, each with 60-round drum; (F-1) two MG 17 and

*continued on page 220* ▶

*Left: Bf 109D-1 of 10 (Nacht)/JG 26, at Jever, in autumn 1939*

*Right: A Bf 109D-1 of Jagdflieger-schule 1 at Werneuchen, 1940*

*Left: A Bf 109D-1 of FFS A/B 123 (Kroat) at Agram (Zagreb) in March 1942*

## ▶Messerschmitt Bf 109

one MG FF; (F-2) two 15mm MG 151 and one MG FF; (F-4) two MG 151, one MG FF and one 20mm MG 151 in fairing under each wing; (G-1) two MG 17 or 13mm MG 131 over engine and one MG 151; (G-6) one 30mm MK 108, two MG 131 above engine and two MG 151 under wings; (K-4) two MG 151 above engine and one MK 108 or 103; (K-6) two MG 131 above engine, one MK 103 or 108 and two MK 108 under wings; (S-199) two MG 131 above engine and two MG 151 under wings; (HA-1109 series) two wing machine guns or 20mm Hispano 404. Many German G and K carried two 210mm rocket tubes under wings or various bomb loads.

**History:** First flight (Bf 109 V-1) early September 1935 (date is unrecorded); (production B-1) May 1937; (Bf 109E) January 1939; (Bf 109F prototype) July 1940; replacement in production by Bf 109G, May 1942.

**Development:** During World War II the general public in the Allied nations at first regarded the Messerschmitt as an inferior weapon compared with the Spitfire and other Allied fighters. Only in the fullness of time was it possible to appreciate that the Bf 109 was one of the greatest combat aircraft in history. First flown in 1935, it was a major participant in the Spanish Civil War and a thoroughly proven combat aircraft by the time of Munich (September 1938). Early versions were the Bf 109B, C and D, all of lower power than the definitive 109E. The E was in service in great quantity by the end of August 1939 when the invasion of Poland began. From then

continued on page 222 ▶

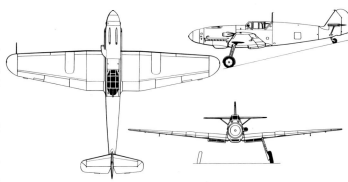

*Above: Three-view of Bf 109H-1 high-altitude variant (1944)*

*The original V1 prototype, with Rolls-Royce Kestrel*

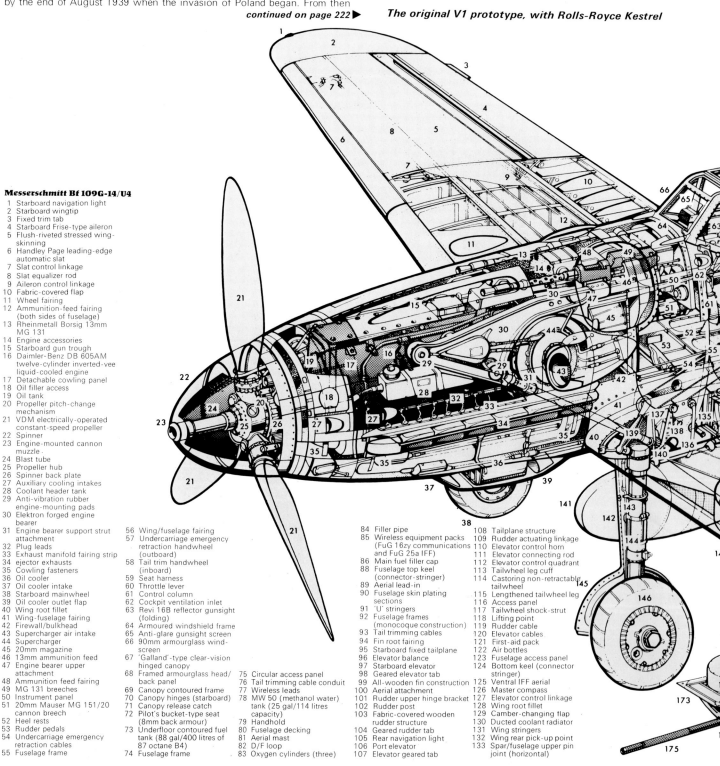

**Messerschmitt Bf 109G-14/U4**

1 Starboard navigation light
2 Starboard wingtip
3 Fixed trim tab
4 Starboard Frise-type aileron
5 Flush-riveted stressed wing-skinning
6 Handley Page leading-edge automatic slat
7 Slat control linkage
8 Slat equalizer rod
9 Aileron control linkage
10 Fabric-covered flap
11 Wheel fairing
12 Ammunition-feed fairing (both sides of fuselage)
13 Rheinmetall Borsig 13mm MG 131
14 Engine accessories
15 Starboard gun trough
16 Daimler-Benz DB 605AM twelve-cylinder inverted-vee liquid-cooled engine
17 Detachable cowling panel
18 Oil filler access
19 Oil tank
20 Propeller pitch-change mechanism
21 VDM electrically-operated constant-speed propeller
22 Spinner
23 Engine-mounted cannon muzzle
24 Blast tube
25 Propeller hub
26 Spinner back plate
27 Auxiliary cooling intakes
28 Coolant header tank
29 Anti-vibration rubber engine-mounting pads
30 Elektron forged engine bearer
31 Engine bearer support strut attachment
32 Plug leads
33 Exhaust manifold fairing strip
34 ejector exhausts
35 Cowling fasteners
36 Oil cooler
37 Oil cooler intake
38 Starboard mainwheel
39 Oil cooler outlet flap
40 Wing root fillet
41 Wing-fuselage fairing
42 Firewall/bulkhead
43 Supercharger air intake
44 Supercharger
45 20mm magazine
46 13mm ammunition feed
47 Engine bearer upper attachment
48 Ammunition feed fairing
49 MG 131 breeches
50 Instrument panel
51 20mm Mauser MG 151/20 cannon breech
52 Heel rests
53 Rudder pedals
54 Undercarriage emergency retraction cables
55 Fuselage frame
56 Wing/fuselage fairing
57 Undercarriage emergency retraction handwheel (outboard)
58 Tail trim handwheel (inboard)
59 Seat harness
60 Throttle lever
61 Control column
62 Cockpit ventilation inlet
63 Revi 16B reflector gunsight (folding)
64 Armoured windshield frame
65 Anti-glare gunsight screen
66 90mm armourglass windscreen
67 'Galland'-type clear-vision hinged canopy
68 Framed armourglass head/back panel
69 Canopy contoured frame
70 Canopy hinges (starboard)
71 Canopy release catch
72 Pilot's bucket-type seat (8mm back armour)
73 Underfloor contoured fuel tank (88 gal/400 litres of 87 octane B4)
74 Fuselage frame
75 Circular access panel
76 Tail trimming cable conduit
77 Wireless leads
78 MW 50 (methanol water) tank (25 gal/114 litres capacity)
79 Handhold
80 Fuselage decking
81 Aerial mast
82 D/F loop
83 Oxygen cylinders (three)
84 Filler pipe
85 Wireless equipment packs (FuG 16zy communications and FuG 25a IFF)
86 Main fuel filler cap
88 Fuselage top keel (connector-stringer)
89 Aerial lead-in
90 Fuselage skin plating sections
91 'U' stringers
92 Fuselage frames (monocoque construction)
93 Tail trimming cables
94 Fin root fairing
95 Starboard fixed tailplane
96 Elevator balance
97 Starboard elevator
98 Geared elevator tab
99 All-wooden fin construction
100 Aerial attachment
101 Rudder upper hinge bracket
102 Rudder post
103 Fabric-covered wooden rudder structure
104 Geared rudder tab
105 Rear navigation light
106 Port elevator
107 Elevator geared tab
108 Tailplane structure
109 Rudder actuating linkage
110 Elevator control horn
111 Elevator connecting rod
112 Elevator control quadrant
113 Tailwheel leg cuff
114 Castoring non-retractable tailwheel
115 Lengthened tailwheel leg
116 Access panel
117 Tailwheel shock-strut
118 Lifting point
119 Rudder cable
120 Elevator cables
121 First-aid pack
122 Air bottles
123 Fuselage access panel
124 Bottom keel (connector stringer)
125 Ventral IFF aerial
126 Master compass
127 Elevator control linkage
128 Wing root fillet
129 Camber-changing flap
130 Ducted coolant radiator
131 Wing stringers
132 Wing rear pick-up point
133 Spar/fuselage upper pin joint (horizontal)

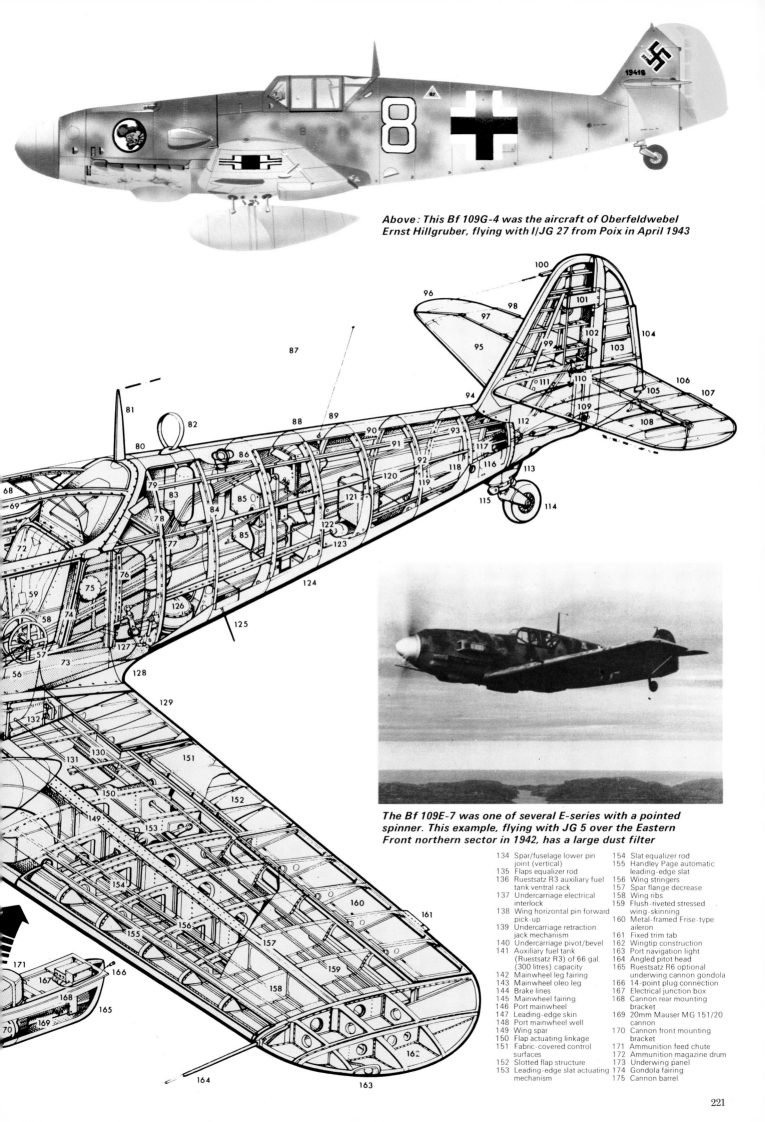

*Above: This Bf 109G-4 was the aircraft of Oberfeldwebel Ernst Hillgruber, flying with I/JG 27 from Poix in April 1943*

*The Bf 109E-7 was one of several E-series with a pointed spinner. This example, flying with JG 5 over the Eastern Front northern sector in 1942, has a large dust filter*

134 Spar/fuselage lower pin joint (vertical)
135 Flaps equalizer rod
136 Ruestsatz R3 auxiliary fuel tank ventral rack
137 Undercarriage electrical interlock
138 Wing horizontal pin forward pick-up
139 Undercarriage retraction jack mechanism
140 Undercarriage pivot/bevel
141 Auxiliary fuel tank (Ruestsatz R3) of 66 gal. (300 litres) capacity
142 Mainwheel leg fairing
143 Mainwheel oleo leg
144 Brake lines
145 Mainwheel fairing
146 Port mainwheel
147 Leading-edge skin
148 Port mainwheel well
149 Wing spar
150 Flap actuating linkage
151 Fabric-covered control surfaces
152 Slotted flap structure
153 Leading-edge slat actuating mechanism

154 Slat equalizer rod
155 Handley Page automatic leading-edge slat
156 Wing stringers
157 Spar flange decrease
158 Wing ribs
159 Flush-riveted stressed wing-skinning
160 Metal-framed Frise-type aileron
161 Fixed trim tab
162 Wingtip construction
163 Port navigation light
164 Angled pitot head
165 Ruestsatz R6 optional underwing cannon gondola
166 14-point plug connection
167 Electrical junction box
168 Cannon rear mounting bracket
169 20mm Mauser MG 151/20 cannon
170 Cannon front mounting bracket
171 Ammunition feed chute
172 Ammunition magazine drum
173 Underwing panel
174 Gondola fairing
175 Cannon barrel

221

### ▶Messerschmitt Bf 109

until 1941 it was by far the most important fighter in the Luftwaffe, and it was also supplied in quantity to numerous other countries. Japan and the Soviet Union. During the first year of World War II the "Emil", as the various E sub-types were called, made mincemeat of the many and varied types of fighter against which it was opposed, with the single exception of the Spitfire (which it greatly outnumbered). Its good points were small size, fast and cheap production, high acceleration, fast climb and dive, and good power of manoeuvre. Nearly all 109Es were also fitted with two or three 20mm cannon, with range and striking power greater than a battery of eight rifle-calibre guns. Drawbacks were the narrow landing gear, severe swing on take-off or landing, extremely poor lateral control at high speeds, and the fact that in combat the slats on the wings often opened in tight turns; while this prevented a stall, it snatched at the ailerons and threw the pilot off his aim. After 1942 the dominant version was the 109G ("Gustav") which made up over 70 per cent of the total received by the Luftwaffe. Though formidably armed and equipped, the vast swarms of "Gustavs"

were nothing like such good machines as the lighter E and F, demanding constant pilot attention, constant high power settings, and having landing characteristics described as "malicious". Only a few of the extended-span

*Above: Bf 109G-5 of 7/JG 27, operating as part of a semi-independent Schwärme in the Mediterranean (photo from He 111)*

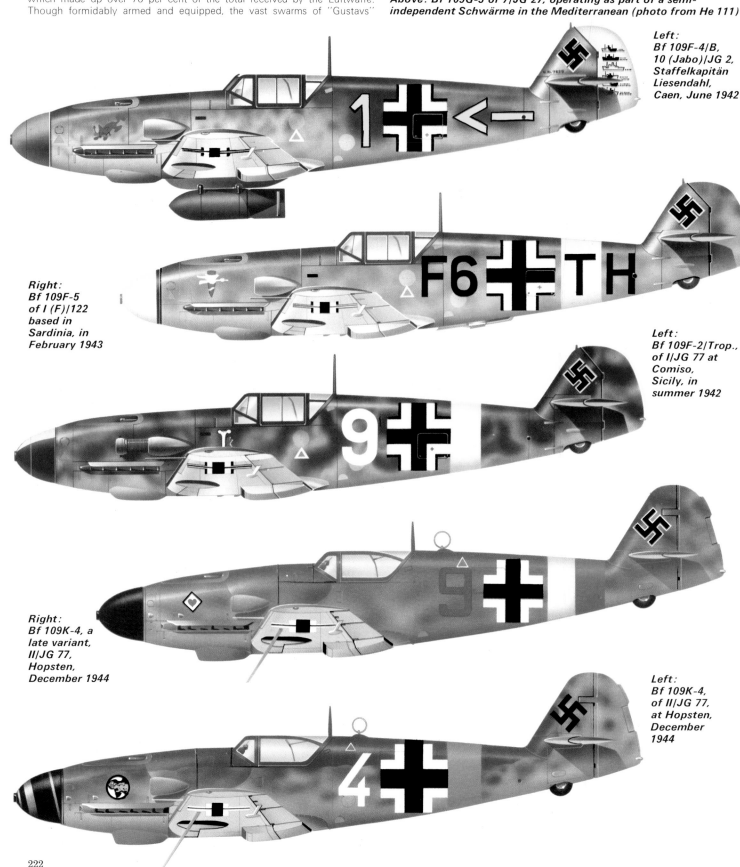

*Left:*
*Bf 109F-4/B,*
*10 (Jabo)/JG 2,*
*Staffelkapitän*
*Liesendahl,*
*Caen, June 1942*

*Right:*
*Bf 109F-5*
*of I (F)/122*
*based in*
*Sardinia, in*
*February 1943*

*Left:*
*Bf 109F-2/Trop.,*
*of I/JG 77 at*
*Comiso,*
*Sicily, in*
*summer 1942*

*Right:*
*Bf 109K-4, a*
*late variant,*
*II/JG 77,*
*Hopsten,*
*December 1944*

*Left:*
*Bf 109K-4,*
*of II/JG 77,*
*at Hopsten,*
*December*
*1944*

high-altitude H-series were built, but from October 1944 the standard production series was the K with clear-view "Galland hood", revised wooden tail and minor structural changes. After World War II the Czech Avia firm found their Bf 109 plant intact and began building the S-99; running out of DB 605 engines they installed the slow-revving Jumo, producing the S-199 with even worse torque and swing than the German versions (pilots called it "Mezak" meaning mule), but in 1948 managed to sell some to Israel. The Spanish Hispano Aviación flew its first licence-built 1109 in March 1945 and in 1953 switched to the Merlin engine to produce the 1109-M1L Buchón (Pigeon). Several Hispano and Merlin versions were built in Spain, some being tandem-seat trainers. When the last HA-1112 flew out of Seville in late 1956 it closed out 21 years of manufacture of this classic fighter, during which total output probably exceeded 35,000.

*Right: A Bf 109F-4 of the "Ungarische Jagdstaffel", in the Stalingrad sector, late 1942. Operating under Luftwaffe control, they painted tails Hungarian (see below)*

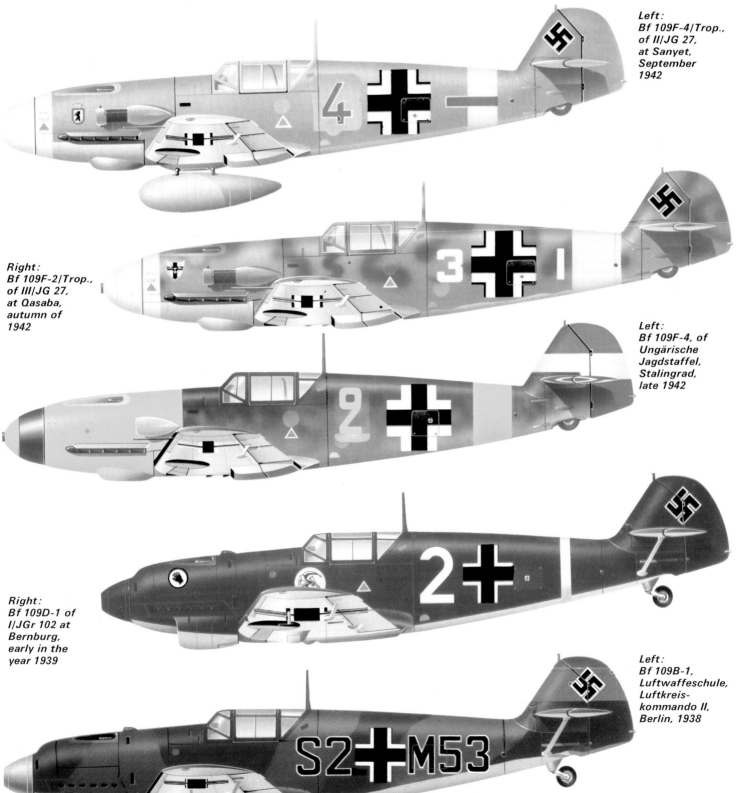

*Left:
Bf 109F-4/Trop.,
of II/JG 27,
at Sanyet,
September
1942*

*Right:
Bf 109F-2/Trop.,
of III/JG 27,
at Qasaba,
autumn of
1942*

*Left:
Bf 109F-4, of
Ungärische
Jagdstaffel,
Stalingrad,
late 1942*

*Right:
Bf 109D-1 of
I/JGr 102 at
Bernburg,
early in the
year 1939*

*Left:
Bf 109B-1,
Luftwaffeschule,
Luftkreis-
kommando II,
Berlin, 1938*

*See also profiles on pages 20/21, 32/33, 96/97*

223

# Messerschmitt Bf 110

### Bf 110B series to H series

**Origin:** Bayerische Flugzeugwerke, after 1938 Messerschmitt AG; widely dispersed manufacture.

**Type:** Two-seat day and night fighter (also used on occasion for ground attack and reconnaissance).

**Engines:** Two, 1,100hp Daimler-Benz DB 601A; (later C-4s) 1,200hp DB 601N 12-cylinder inverted-vee liquid-cooled; (G, H) two 1,475hp DB 605B, same layout.

**Dimensions:** Span 53ft 4¾in (16·25m); length 39ft 8½in (12·1m); height 11ft 6in (3·5m).

**Weights:** Empty 9,920lb (4500kg); loaded 15,430lb (7000kg).

**Performance:** Maximum speed 349mph (562km/h) at 22,966ft (7000m); climb to 18,045ft (5500m), 8 minutes; service ceiling 32,800ft (10,000m); range 528 miles (850km) at 304mph (490km/h) at 16,400ft (5000m).

**Armament:** Two 20mm Oerlikon MG FF cannon and four Rheinmetall 7·92mm MG 17 machine guns fixed firing forward in nose, one 7·92mm MG 15 manually aimed machine gun in rear cockpit; C-4 B also fitted with racks under centre section for four 551lb (250kg) bombs. (G-4 night fighter) two 30mm MK 108 and two 20mm MG 151 firing forward, and two MG 151 in Schräge Musik installation firing obliquely upwards (sometimes two 7·92mm MG 81 in rear cockpit).

**History:** First flight (Bf 110V1 prototype) May 12, 1936; (pre-production Bf 110C-0) February 1939; operational service with Bf 110C-1, April 1939; final run-down of production (Bf 110H-2 and H-4) February 1945.

**Development:** As in five other countries at about the same time, the Reichsluftfahrtministerium decided in 1934 to issue a requirement for a new kind of fighter having two engines and exceptional range. Called a Zerstörer (destroyer), it was to be capable of fighting other aircraft as well as could single-seaters, possibly making up in firepower for any lack in manoeuvrability. Its dominant quality was to be range, to escort bombers on raids

### Messerschmitt Bf 110G-4b/R3

1 The Hirschgeweih (Stag's Antlers) array for the FuG 220b Lichtenstein SN-2 radar
2 Single-pole type antenna for the FuG 212 Lichtenstein C-1 radar
3 Camera gun
4 Cannon muzzles
5 Cannon ports
6 Blast tubes
7 Starboard mainwheel
8 Armour plate (10-mm)
9 Twin 30-mm Rheinmetall Borsig MK 108 (Rüstsatz/ Field Conversion Set 3) with 135 rpg
10 Armoured bulkhead
11 Supercharger intake
12 Position of nacelle-mounted instruments on day fighter model
13 Exhaust flame damper
14 Auxiliary tank
15 Three-blade VDM airscrew
16 Leading-edge automatic slat
17 Pitot tube
18 FuG 227/1 Flensburg homing aerial fitted to some aircraft by forward maintenance units (to home on Monica tail-warning radar emissions)
19 Stressed wing skinning
20 Starboard aileron
21 Trim tab
22 Slotted flap
23 Hinged canopy roof
24 Armoured glass windscreen (60-mm)
25 Instrument panel
26 Cockpit floor armour (4-mm)
27 Twin 20-mm Mauser MG 151 cannon with 300 rounds (port) and 350 rounds (starboard)
28 Pilot's seat
29 Control column
30 Pilot's back and head armour (8-mm)
31 Cannon magazine
32 Centre section carry-through
33 Radar operator's swivel seat
34 D/F loop
35 Aerial mast
36 Upward-firing cannon muzzles
37 Two 30-mm MK 108 cannon in schräge Musik (oblique music) installation firing obliquely upward (optional installation supplied as an Umrüst-Bausatz/Factory Conversion Set)
38 Ammunition drums
39 Aft cockpit bulkhead
40 FuG 10P HF R/T set
41 FuB1 2F airfield blind approach receiver
42 Handhold
43 Oxygen bottles
44 Aerials
45 Master compass
46 Starboard tailfin
47 Rudder balance
48 Rudder
49 Tab
50 Starboard elevator
51 Starboard tailplane
52 Variable-incidence tailplane
53 Elevator tab
54 Centre section fairing
55 Rear navigation light
56 Port elevator
57 Port tailfin
58 Rudder
59 Hinged tab
60 Tailwheel
61 Fuselage frames
62 Control lines
63 Dipole tuner
64 Batteries
65 Transformer
66 Slotted flap
67 Fuel tank of 57·3 Imp gal (260·5l) capacity
68 Oil tank of 7·7 Imp gal (35l) capacity
69 Ventral antenna
70 Coolant radiator
71 Radiator intake
72 Hinged intake fairing
73 Aileron tab
74 Aileron construction
75 Wingtip
76 Flensburg aerial (see 18)
77 Port navigation light
78 Leading-edge automatic slat
79 Wing ribs
80 Mainspar
81 Underwing auxiliary fuel tank (66-Imp gal/300-l capacity)
82 Landing light
83 Undercarriage door
84 Mainwheel well
85 Supercharger intake
86 Undercarriage pivot point
87 Mainwheel leg
88 Mainwheel
89 Oil cooler
90 Oil cooler intake
91 VDM airscrew
92 Pitch-change mechanism
93 Armoured ring (5-mm)
94 Coolant tank
95 Exhaust flame damper

*Left:
Bf 110G-2
of 5/ZG 76,
Grossenhain,
winter
1943-44*

penetrating deep into enemy heartlands. Powered by two of the new DB 600 engines, the prototype reached 316mph, considered an excellent speed, but it was heavy on the controls and umimpressive in power of manoeuvre. Too late to be tested in the Spanish Civil War, the production Bf 110B-1, which was the first to carry the two cannon, was itself supplanted by the C-series with the later DB 601 engine with direct fuel injection and greater

power at all heights. By the start of World War II the Luftwaffe had 195 Bf 110C fighters, and in the Polish campaign these were impressive, operating mainly in the close-support role but demolishing any aerial opposition they encountered. It was the same story in the Blitzkrieg war through the Low Countries and France, when 350 of the big twins were

**continued on page 226 ▶**

96 Anti-vibration engine
   mounting pad
97 Daimler-Benz DB 605B-1
   12-cylinder inverted-Vee
   engine (rated at 1,475hp
   for take-off and 1,355hp

at 18,700ft/5700m)
98 Forged engine bearer
99 Fuel tank (82·5-Imp gal/
   375-l capacity)
100 Fuselage/mainspar
    attachment point

101 Fuselage/forward auxiliary
    spar attachment point
102 Waffenwanne 151Z, a
    ventral tray housing a pair
    of 20-mm MG 151 cannon
    (optional)

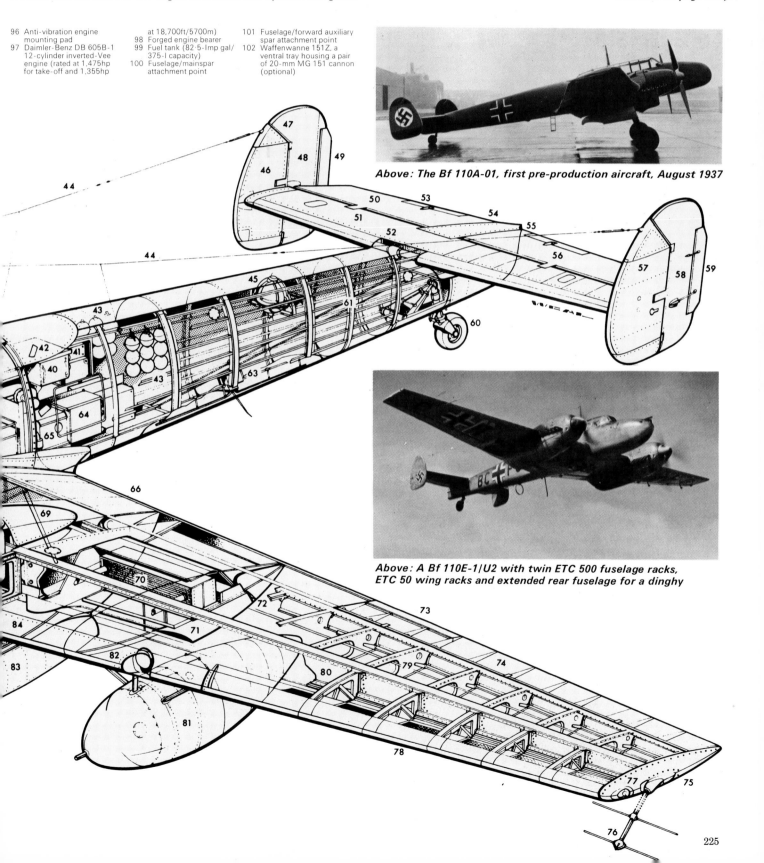

*Above: The Bf 110A-01, first pre-production aircraft, August 1937*

*Above: A Bf 110E-1/U2 with twin ETC 500 fuselage racks, ETC 50 wing racks and extended rear fuselage for a dinghy*

## ▶Messerschmitt Bf 110

used. Only when faced with RAF Fighter Command in the Battle of Britain did the Bf 110 suddenly prove a disaster. It was simply no match for the Spitfire or even the Hurricane, and soon the Bf 109 was having to escort the escort fighters! But production of DB 605-powered versions, packed with radar and night-fighting equipment, was actually trebled in 1943 and sustained in 1944, these G and H models playing a major part in the night battles over the Reich in 1943–45.

From late 1940 it had been planned progressively to run down Bf 110 production as the Me 210 came into full production and service. Despite this basic intention it was only natural that new versions of 110 should appear, and the first significant new family was the D-series Langstrecke (long-range) aircraft which had racks for two drop tanks and two 1,102lb (500kg) bombs – though this enormous load demanded a long runway. The D-3 was a specialized convoy escort, with two large drop tanks, extra oil tank and dinghy. By the late spring of 1941 the E-series had blossomed into a profuse family with DB 601N engines, various new equipment and often a third seat for a control officer (Leitoffizier) in night fighter versions. The F-series brought a much-needed increase in power with the 1,350hp DB 601F, and much improved armour protection including a thick bulletproof windscreen. This was confidently expected to be the final family of this basically obsolescent Zerostörer, though in 1941–42 it gave rise to many new and modified sub-types of which an increasing proportion were night fighters. Among them was the Bf 110F-4/U1 with two 30mm MK 108 cannon in an oblique Schräge Musik installation in the rear fuselage for destroying RAF bombers by night. Equally significant was the Bf 110F-4a with full forward-directed armament, including hard-hitting MG 151 cannon instead of the old MG FFs, and with FuG 202 Lichtenstein radar served by a draggy aerial array called Matratze (mattress).

When it became evident in early 1942 that the Me 210 was unacceptable, full-scale resumption of Bf 110 production was the only alternative. This put

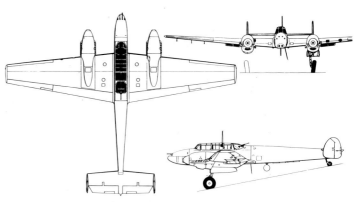

**Three-view of Bf 110C-3 of early 1940**

tremendous urgency behind the development of the G-series, which had been half-heartedly begun in 1941, with the more powerful DB 605 engine. In fact the G was destined to be built in larger numbers than all other versions combined, production being trebled in 1943 and sustained in 1944. Amazingly, this basically outmoded aircraft remained in production until March 1945. There were numerous sub-types of Bf 110G, most having three (a few, even four) seats. Heavily overloaded, they were sluggish even with DB 605 engines, but still effective against RAF night bombers. The best feature of the 110 was its pleasant handling, which even carriage of mighty loads of weapons and night-fighter radar could not impair. Total production was about 6,050.

*Below: A long-range escort Bf 110D, probably a D-3, with extended rear fuselage for dinghy stowage*

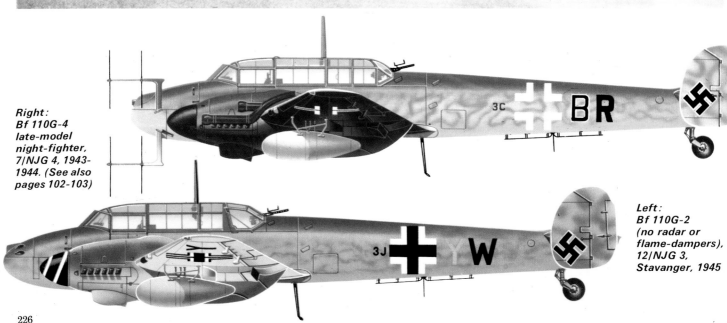

*Right: Bf 110G-4 late-model night-fighter, 7/NJG 4, 1943-1944. (See also pages 102-103)*

*Left: Bf 110G-2 (no radar or flame-dampers), 12/NJG 3, Stavanger, 1945*

# Messerschmitt Me 209-II

**Me 209 V1 to V6 and A-series**
**Origin:** Messerschmitt AG.
**Type:** (V1-V3) Racer, (V4-V6) fighter.
**Engine:** One inverted-vee-12 (see text).
**Dimensions:** Span (V1) 25ft 7in (7·80m), (V4) 32ft 11¼in (10·04m), (A) 35ft 11in (10·95m), (H) 43ft 6in (13·26m); length (V1) 23ft 9½in (7·25m), (V4) 23ft 9in (7·24m), (A) 31ft 6¾in (9·62m), (H) 32ft 5¾in (9·90m); height (most) 13ft 1½in (4·00m), (H) 10ft 10in (3·3m).
**Weights:** Empty (A) 7,360lb upwards (3338kg), (H) 6,636lb (3010kg); loaded (V1) 5,545lb (2515kg), (V4) 6,174lb (2800kg), (A) 9,006lb (4085kg), (H) 9,480lb (4300kg).
**Performance:** Maximum speed (V1) 469mph (755km/h), (V4) 373mph (600km/h), (A) 463mph (745km/h), (H) 460mph (740km/h).

**Development:** On 26 April 1939 Fritz Wendel flew Me 209 V1 to a world absolute speed record at 469·22mph (755·138km/h) that stood for piston aircraft for 30 years. The tiny racer had flown with a normal DB 601 engine on 1 August 1938 but for the record had a 601ARJ with special fuel giving about 2,300hp for 1 minute. It was possibly the most unpleasant and dangerous aircraft of its era. V4 was a supposed fighter, flown on 12 May 1939, but the company much later created a new design with the same designation (sometimes called 209-II), the "V5" flying on 3 November 1943.

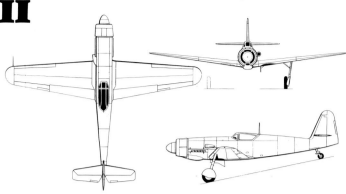

*Three-view of Me 209A-1 (V5)*

Powered by a 1,900hp DB 603G and armed with one 30mm and two 20mm, this 209A-1 was followed by the A-2 with Jumo 213 and numerous variants with much heavier armament. The 209H was a high-altitude fighter with 2,000hp DB 627 which was delayed by bombing and was cancelled when complete in 1944.

# Messerschmitt Me 163 Komet

**Me 163B-1**
**Origin:** Messerschmitt AG.
**Type:** Single-seat interceptor.
**Engine:** One 3,750lb (1700kg) thrust Walter HWK 509A-2 bi-propellant rocket burning concentrated hydrogen peroxide (T-stoff) and hydrazine/methanol (C-stoff).
**Dimensions:** Span 30ft 7in (9·3m); length 18ft 8in (5·69m); height 9ft 0in (2·74m).
**Weights:** Empty 4,191lb (1905kg); loaded 9,042lb (4110kg).
**Performance:** Maximum speed 596mph (960km/h) at 32,800ft (10,000m); initial climb 16,400ft (5000m)/min; service ceiling 54,000ft (16,500m); range depended greatly on flight profile but under 100km (62 miles); endurance 2½min from top of climb or eight min total.
**Armament:** Two 30mm MK 108 cannon in wing roots, each with 60 rounds.
**History:** First flight (Me 163V1) spring 1941 as glider, August 1941 under power; (Me 163B) August 1943; first operational unit (I/JG400) May 1944.

**Development:** Of all aircraft engaged in World War II the Me 163 Komet (Comet) was the most radical and, indeed, futuristic. The concept of the short-endurance local-defence interceptor powered by a rocket engine was certainly valid and might have been more of a thorn in the Allies' side than it was. Even the dramatically unconventional form of the Me 163, with no horizontal tail and an incredibly short fuselage, did not lead to great difficulty; in fact, the production fighter was widely held to have the best and safest characteristics of any aircraft in the Luftwaffe. But the swift strides into uncharted technology were bold in the extreme. It was partly to save weight and drag that the tailless configuration was adopted, and partly because the moving spirit behind the project was at first Dr Alex Lippisch, who liked tailless designs. Choice of two rocket propellants that reacted violently when they came into contact solved the problem of ignition in the combustion chamber but added an extremely large element of danger. Moreover, the 163 had no landing gear, taking off from a jettisoned trolley and landing on a sprung skid, and the landing impact often caused sloshed residual propellants together causing a violent explosion. Many aircraft were lost this way, and the original test pilot, glider champion Heini Dittmar, was badly injured when the skid failed to extend. Nevertheless by 1944 these bat-like specks were swooping on US bomber formations with devastating effect. Numerous improved versions were flying at VE day, but only 370 Komets had seen service and these had suffered high attrition through accidents.

The roots of the project went back to the 1920s, with both Lippisch aerodynamics and the various rocket research projects that led to the Hellmuth Walter development of engines suitable for manned aircraft from 1936. It

*continued on page 228* ▶

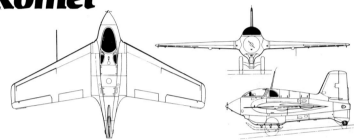

*Three-view of Me 163B-1a (showing trolley and skid)*

*Above: Pre-flight test of the rocket propellant feed system and valves, with water purging the steam generator and C-Stoff being vented in a cloud. The Komet was one of the most dangerous aircraft on the ground, both to its pilots and ground crews, but in the air it was beautiful. The example above is a B-1a, probably of I/JG 400*

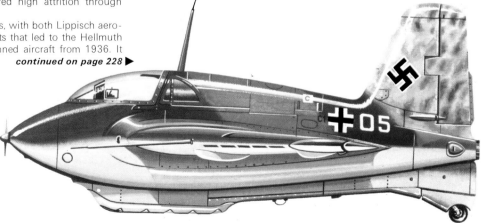

*Right: One of the first production Me 163B-1a Komets, assigned to Erprobungskommando 16 at Zwischenahn in July 1944. Drawn in flight trim*

# ►Messerschmitt Me 163 Komet

is worth emphasizing that nothing remotely like either the airframe or the engine was attempted in Britain, nor in any other country except the Soviet Union. The early aircraft research was centred at the DFS (German sailplane research institute), where the first tailless rocket aircraft was planned as the DFS 194. In March 1938 the design was complete, but in January 1939 it was transferred to Messerschmitt. Shortly after this the Walter R I-203 rocket flew (very badly) in the He 176 research aircraft. Results with this aircraft were poor, but when a similar motor was fitted to the DFS 194 tailless aircraft the speed reached 342mph (550km/h) and climb was fantastic. Swiftly sanction for a rocket fighter was gained, and glidihg trials with the Me 163 V1 began in the spring of 1941. Again the tailless machine floated like a bird (the main snag being that instead of landing where the pilot wanted, it kept floating) and in July–September 1941 Dittmar pushed the speed under

rocket power higher and higher, far beyond the world speed record until, on 2 October 1941, he reached about 1004km/h (623·85mph), a speed measured by theodolites on the ground. At all times the flight characteristics of all 163 versions were exemplary, but there were countless snags and catastrophes due to the dangerous propellants, the failure of hydraulics, the extreme difficulty of taking off exactly into wind on the unsprung dolly, and the equally rigorous constraints upon the pilot in landing. Everything had to be exactly right, because if the aircraft yawed, swung or ran too far on to rough ground, it would turn over and the propellants explode.

The final developments were the Me 163C, with fully retractable tail-wheel, long body of improved form, increased-span centre section and new motor with a small chamber to give 660lb (300kg) for cruising flight, and the derived Me 263.

## Messerschmitt Me 163B-1a

1 Generator drive propeller
2 Generator
3 Compressed air bottle
4 Battery and electronics packs
5 Cockpit ventilation intake
6 Solid armour (15-mm) nose cone
7 Accumulator pressuriser
8 Direct cockpit air intake
9 FuG 25a radio pack
10 Rudder control assembly
11 Hydraulic and compressed air points
12 Elevon control rocker-bar
13 Control relay
14 Flying controls assembly box
15 Plastic rudder pedals
16 Radio tuning controls
17 Torque shaft
18 Port T-stoff cockpit tank

19 Control column
20 Hinged instrument panel
21 Armourglass windscreen brace
22 Revi 16B gunsight
23 Armourglass internal windscreen (90-mm)
24 Armament and radio switches (starboard console)
25 Pilot's seat
26 Back armour (8-mm)
27 Head and shoulder armour (13-mm)
28 Radio frequency selector pack
29 Headrest
30 Mechanically-jettisonable hinged canopy
31 Ventilation panel
32 Fixed leading-edge wing

(13 Imp gal/60l capacity) slot
33 Trim tab
34 Fabric-covered starboard elevon
35 Position of underwing landing flap
36 Inboard trim flap
37 FuG 16zy radio receiving aerial
38 T-Stoff filler cap
39 Main unprotected T-Stoff fuselage tank (229 Imp gal/1040l capacity)
40 Aft cockpit glazing
41 Port cannon ammunition box (60 rounds)
42 Starboard cannon ammunition box (60 rounds)
43 Ammunition feed chute
44 T-Stoff starter tank
45 Rudder control upper bell crank

46 C-Stoff filler cap
47 HWK 509A-1 motor turbine housing
48 Main rocket motor mounting frame
49 Rudder control rod
50 Disconnect point
51 Aerial matching unit
52 Fin front spar/fuselage attachment point
53 Tailfin construction
54 Rudder horn balance
55 Rudder upper hinge
56 Rudder frame
57 Rudder trim tab
58 Rudder control rocker-bar
59 Linkage fairing
60 Fin rear spar/fuselage attachment point
61 Rocket motor combustion chamber
62 Tailpipe

63 Rudder root fairing
64 Rocket thrust orifice
65 Vent pipe outlet
66 Hydraulic cylinder
67 Lifting point
68 Tailwheel fairing
69 Steerable tailwheel
70 Tailwheel axle fork
71 Tailwheel oleo
72 Tailwheel steering linkage
73 Coupling piece/vertical lever
74 Wingroot fillet
75 Combustion chamber support brace
76 Gun-cocking mechanism
77 Trimp flap control angle gear (bulkhead mounted)
78 Worm gear
79 Trim flap mounting
80 Port inboard trim flap
81 Elevon mounting

82 Rocker-bar
83 Elevon actuation push-rod
84 Port elevon
85 Wing rear spar
86 Trim tab
87 Elevon outboard hinge
88 Wingtip bumper
89 Wing construction
90 Fixed leading-edge wing slot
91 Elevon control bell crank
92 Position of port underwing landing flap
93 Push-rod in front spar
94 Front spar
95 FuG 25a aerial
96 Pitot head
97 Wing tank connecting-pipe fairing
98 C-Stoff leading-edge tank (16 Imp gal/73l capacity
99 Gun-cocking compressed air bottle

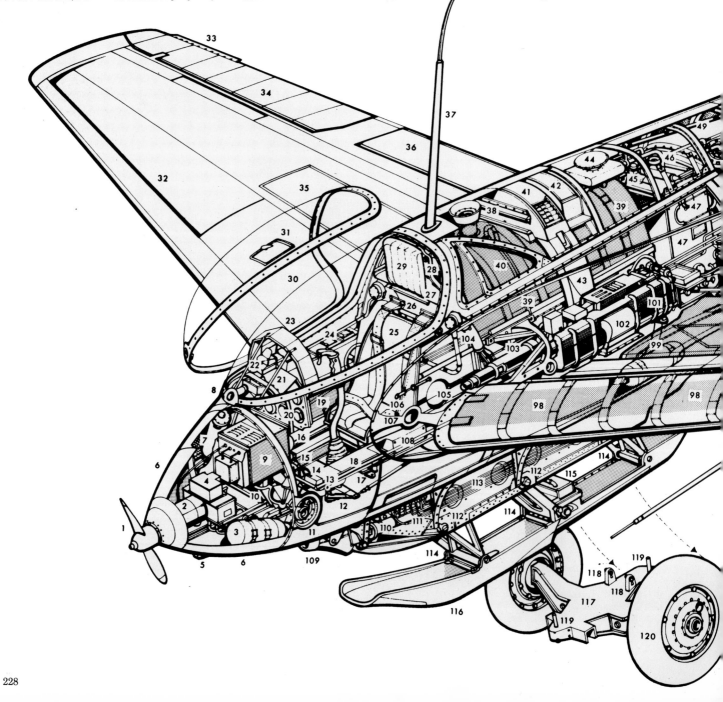

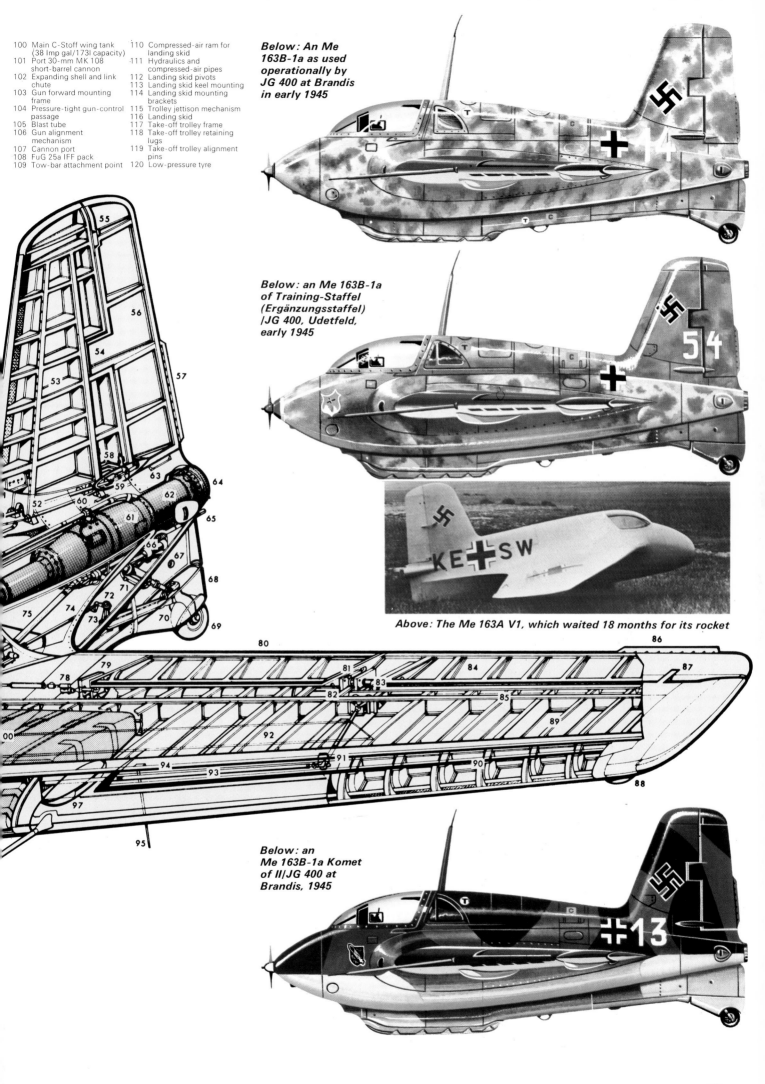

100 Main C-Stoff wing tank (38 Imp gal/173l capacity)
101 Port 30-mm MK 108 short-barrel cannon
102 Expanding shell and link chute
103 Gun forward mounting frame
104 Pressure-tight gun-control passage
105 Blast tube
106 Gun alignment mechanism
107 Cannon port
108 FuG 25a IFF pack
109 Tow-bar attachment point
110 Compressed-air ram for landing skid
111 Hydraulics and compressed-air pipes
112 Landing skid pivots
113 Landing skid keel mounting
114 Landing skid mounting brackets
115 Trolley jettison mechanism
116 Landing skid
117 Take-off trolley frame
118 Take-off trolley retaining lugs
119 Take-off trolley alignment pins
120 Low-pressure tyre

*Below: An Me 163B-1a as used operationally by JG 400 at Brandis in early 1945*

*Below: an Me 163B-1a of Training-Staffel (Ergänzungsstaffel) /JG 400, Udetfeld, early 1945*

*Above: The Me 163A V1, which waited 18 months for its rocket*

*Below: an Me 163B-1a Komet of II/JG 400 at Brandis, 1945*

# Messerschmitt Me 210 and Me 410 Hornisse

**Me 210A, B and C series, Me 410A and B series**
**Origin:** Messerschmitt AG.
**Type:** Two-seat tactical aircraft for fighter, attack and reconnaissance duties with specialised variants.
**Engines:** (Me 210, usual for production versions) two 1,395hp Daimler-Benz DB 601F inverted-vee-12 liquid-cooled; (Me 410A series, usual for production versions) two 1,750hp DB 603A of same layout; (Me 410B series) two 1,900hp DB 603G.
**Dimensions:** Span (210) 53ft 7¼in, later 53ft 7¾in (16·4m); (410) 53ft 7¾in; length (without 50mm gun, radar or other long fitment) (210) 40ft 3in (12·22m); (410) 40ft 10in or 40ft 11½in (12·45m); height (both) 14ft 0½in (4·3m).
**Weights:** Empty (210A) about 12,000lb (5440kg); (410A-1) 13,560lb (6150kg); maximum loaded (210A-1) 17,857lb (8100kg); (410A-1) 23,483lb (10,650kg).
**Performance:** Maximum speed (both, clean) 385mph (620km/h); initial climb (both) 2,133ft (650m)/min; service ceiling (210A-1) 22,967ft (7000m); (410A-1) 32,800ft (10,000m); range with full bomb load (210A-1) 1,491 miles (2400km); (410A-1) 1,447 miles (2330km).
**Armament:** Varied, but basic aircraft invariably defended by two remotely-controlled powered barbettes on sides of fuselage each housing one 13mm MG 131 and, if bomber version, provided with internal weapon bay housing two 1,102lb (500kg) bombs; external racks on nearly all (210 and 410) for two 1,102lb stores (exceptionally, two 2,204lb). Normal fixed forward-firing armament of two 20mm MG 151/20 and two 7·92mm MG 17. Me 410 versions had many kinds of bomber-destroyer armament, as described in the text.
**History:** First flight (Me 210V-1) 2 September 1939; (pre-production 210A-0) April 1941; final delivery (210) April 1942; first flight (310) 11 September 1943; (410V-1) probably December 1942.

**Development:** Planned in 1937 as a valuable and more versatile successor to the Bf 110 twin-engined escort fighter, the Me 210 was little more than a flop and made hardly any contribution to the German war effort. After severe flight instability and landing-gear problems some progress was made in 1941 towards producing an acceptable machine which could be put into production against the order for 1,000 placed "off the drawing board" in June 1939. Accidents were nevertheless frequent and manufacture was terminated at the 352nd aircraft. This major blow to the Luftwaffe and the company, which was reflected in an official demand for Willi Messerschmitt's resignation from the board, was partly salvaged by a further redesign and change to the DB 603 engine. The Me 310 was a high-altitude fighter-bomber with 58ft 9in wing and pressure cabin, but this was abandoned in favour of a less radical change designated 410. As with the 210, the reconnaissance 410s usually had cameras in the bomb bay and no MG 17s, while some attack or destroyer versions had four forward-firing MG 151 cannon, or two MG 151 and a 50mm BK 5 gun with 21 rounds. The Me 410A-2/U-2 was a little-used night fighter with SN-2 Lichtenstein radar and two MG 151 and two 30mm MK 108. Many of the 1,121 Me 410s carried Rüstsatz external packs housing two more MG 151, MK 108 or MK 103, and occasionally experienced pilots fitted as many as eight MG 151 all firing ahead. The 210mm rocket tube was a common fitment by 1944, some aircraft having a pack of six rotating tubes in the bomb bay.

It is doubtful if any aircraft judged a failure has ever been built in so many versions as the Me 210 and 410. There appear to have been over 140 different permutations in armament involving almost every weapon available to the Luftwaffe prior to the end of 1944, though usually very few aircraft were built with any one scheme. The heavy 50mm BK 5 gun was used against tanks and B-17s alike, while the experimental 210mm rotary dispenser (just like a revolver chamber) would have been formidable. Surprisingly, very few of either the 210 or 410 carried night-fighter radar, though FuG 200 Hohentwiel ASV radar (air/surface vessel) was standard on the 410B-6 anti-shipping fighter. Another late sub-type was the B-5 torpedo bomber, with the L 10 Friedensengel gliding torpedo which could be released at a distance from a suitable altitude. The final version, left unfinished, was the 410H with span increased to 75ft 5in (22·97m) to carry greater weapon loads at high altitude. Fortunately Messerschmitt AG had become the largest aircraft organization in Germany, and could survive even the collapse of the supposedly vital Me 210 and 410.

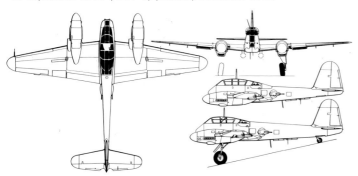

*Above: Three-view of Me 210A-2 (upper side view, A-0)*

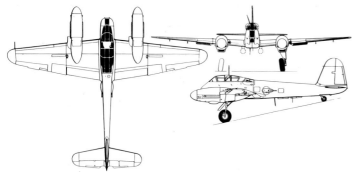

*Above: Three-view of Me 410A-1 Hornisse*

*Above: One of the propaganda photographs issued early in the career of the Me 210 to bolster its reputation*

*Left: To rectify inadequacies in the reconnaissance role the Me 410A-3 had a deep forward fuselage housing two cameras*

# Messerschmitt Me 262

**Me 262A-1a Schwalbe, Me 262A-2 Sturmvogel, Me 262B-1a**

**Origin:** Messerschmitt AG.

**Type:** (A-1a) single-seat fighter, (A-2a) single-seat bomber, (262B-1a) two-seat night fighter.

**Engines:** Two 1,980lb (900kg) thrust Junkers Jumo 004B single-shaft axial turbojets.

**Dimensions:** Span 40ft 11½in (12·5m); length 34ft 9½in (10·6m), (262B-1a, excluding radar aerials) 38ft 9in (11·8m); height 12ft 7in (3·8m).

**Weights:** Empty (A-1a, A-2a) 8,820lb (4000kg); (B-1a) 9,700lb (4400kg); loaded (A-1a, A-2a) 15,500lb (7045kg); (B-1a) 14,110lb (6400kg).

**Performance:** Maximum speed (A-1a) 540mph (870km/h); (A-2a, laden) 470mph (755km/h); (B-1a) 497mph (800km/h); initial climb (all) about 3,940ft (1200m)/min; service ceiling 37,565ft (11,500m); range on internal fuel, at altitude, about 650 miles (1050km).

**Armament:** (A-1a) four 30mm MK 108 cannon in nose, two with 100 rounds each, two with 80; (A-1a/U1) two 30mm MK 103, two MK 108 and two 20mm MG 151/20; (A-1b) as A-1a plus 24 spin-stabilised R4/M 50mm rockets; (B-1a) as A-1a; (B-2a) as A-1a plus two inclined MK 108 behind cockpit in Schräge Musik installation; (D) SG 500 Jagdfaust with 12 rifled mortar barrels inclined in nose; (E) 50mm MK 114 gun or 48 R4/M rockets; bomb load of two 1,100lb (500kg) bombs carried by A-2a.

**History:** First flight (262V1 on Jumo 210 piston engine) 4 April 1941; (262V3 on two Jumo 004-0 turbojets) 18 July 1942; (Me 262A-1a) 7 June 1944; first delivery (A-0 to Rechlin) May 1944; first experimental combat unit (EK 262) 30 June 1944; first regular squadron (8/ZG26) September 1944.

*continued on page 232* ▶

*Below: A standard Me 262A-1a Schwalbe fighter of the Kommando Nowotny in late 1944. Hitler reluctantly allowed one in every 20 to be a fighter (but his decree was ignored)*

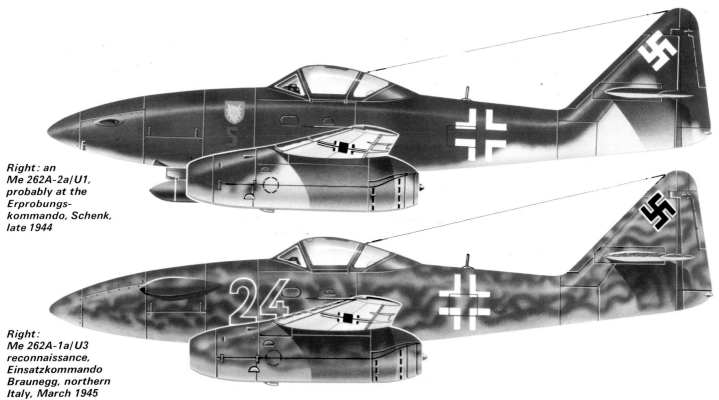

*Right: an Me 262A-2a/U1, probably at the Erprobungs-kommando, Schenk, late 1944*

*Right: Me 262A-1a/U3 reconnaissance, Einsatzkommando Braunegg, northern Italy, March 1945*

# ▶Messerschmitt Me 262

**Development:** In the Me 262 the German aircraft industry created a potentially war-winning aircraft which could have restored to the Luftwaffe command of the skies over Germany. Compared with Allied fighters of its day, including the RAF Meteor I, which entered service at the same time, it was much faster and packed a much heavier punch. Radar-equipped night fighter versions and sub-types designed to stand off from large bomber formations and blast them out of the sky were also developments against which the Allies had no answer. Yet for years the programme was held back by official disinterest, and by the personal insistence of Hitler that the world-beating jet should be used only as a bomber! It was in the autumn of 1938 that Messerschmitt was asked to study the design of a jet fighter, and the resulting Me 262 was remarkably unerring. First flown on a piston engine in the nose, it then flew on its twin turbojets and finally, in July 1943, the fifth development aircraft flew with a nosewheel. Despite numerous snags, production aircraft were being delivered in July 1944 and the rate of

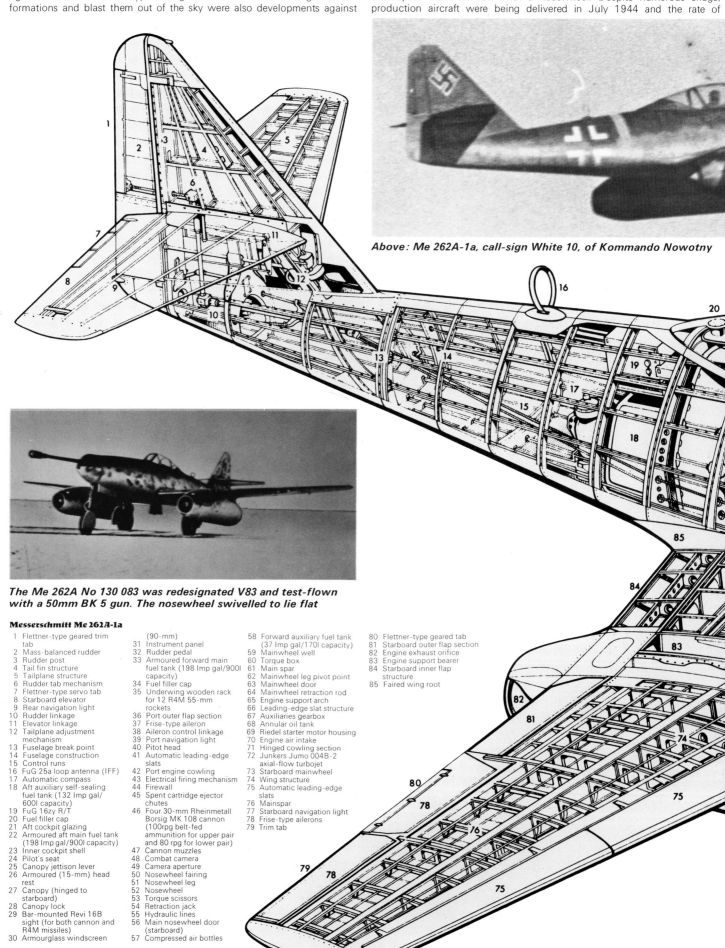

*Above: Me 262A-1a, call-sign White 10, of Kommando Nowotny*

*The Me 262A No 130 083 was redesignated V83 and test-flown with a 50mm BK 5 gun. The nosewheel swivelled to lie flat*

## Messerschmitt Me 262A-1a

1. Flettner-type geared trim tab
2. Mass-balanced rudder
3. Rudder post
4. Tail fin structure
5. Tailplane structure
6. Rudder tab mechanism
7. Flettner-type servo tab
8. Starboard elevator
9. Rear navigation light
10. Rudder linkage
11. Elevator linkage
12. Tailplane adjustment mechanism
13. Fuselage break point
14. Fuselage construction
15. Control runs
16. FuG 25a loop antenna (IFF)
17. Automatic compass
18. Aft auxiliary self-sealing fuel tank (132 Imp gal/600l capacity)
19. FuG 16zy R/T
20. Fuel filler cap
21. Aft cockpit glazing
22. Armoured aft main fuel tank (198 Imp gal/900l capacity)
23. Inner cockpit shell
24. Pilot's seat
25. Canopy jettison lever
26. Armoured (15-mm) head rest
27. Canopy (hinged to starboard)
28. Canopy lock
29. Bar-mounted Revi 16B sight (for both cannon and R4M missiles)
30. Armourglass windscreen
31. Instrument panel
32. Rudder pedal
33. Armoured forward main fuel tank (198 Imp gal/900l capacity)
34. Fuel filler cap
35. Underwing wooden rack for 12 R4M 55-mm rockets
36. Port outer flap section
37. Frise-type aileron
38. Aileron control linkage
39. Port navigation light
40. Pitot head
41. Automatic leading-edge slats
42. Port engine cowling
43. Electrical firing mechanism
44. Firewall
45. Spent cartridge ejector chutes
46. Four 30-mm Rheinmetall Borsig MK 108 cannon (100rpg belt-fed ammunition for upper pair and 80 rpg for lower pair)
47. Cannon muzzles
48. Combat camera
49. Camera aperture
50. Nosewheel fairing
51. Nosewheel leg
52. Nosewheel
53. Torque scissors
54. Retraction jack
55. Hydraulic lines
56. Main nosewheel door (starboard)
57. Compressed air bottles
58. Forward auxiliary fuel tank (37 Imp gal/170l capacity)
59. Mainwheel well
60. Torque box
61. Main spar
62. Mainwheel leg pivot point
63. Mainwheel door
64. Mainwheel retraction rod
65. Engine support arch
66. Leading-edge slat structure
67. Auxiliaries gearbox
68. Annular oil tank
69. Riedel starter motor housing
70. Engine air intake
71. Hinged cowling section
72. Junkers Jumo 004B-2 axial-flow turbojet
73. Starboard mainwheel
74. Wing structure
75. Automatic leading-edge slats
76. Mainspar
77. Starboard navigation light
78. Frise-type ailerons
79. Trim tab
80. Flettner-type geared tab
81. Starboard outer flap section
82. Engine exhaust orifice
83. Engine support bearer
84. Starboard inner flap structure
85. Faired wing root

production was many times that of the British Meteor. On the other hand the German axial engines were unreliable and casualties due to engine failure, fires or break-up were heavy. The MK 108 gun was also prone to jam, and the landing gear to collapse. Yet the 262 was a beautiful machine to handle and, while Allied jets either never reached squadrons or never engaged enemy aircraft, the 100 or so Me 262s that flew on operations and had fuel available destroyed far more than 100 Allied bombers and fighters. Even more remarkable, by VE-day total deliveries of this formidable aircraft reached 1,433.

The two main production versions in 1944 were the A-2a Sturmvogel bomber, with four MK 108 cannon and two 551lb (250kg) bombs, and the A-1a Schwalbe fighter. The A-1a/U1 had the even harder-hitting armament of two of the big MK 103 30mm cannon, two MK 108 and two MG 151, and many prototypes flew with the 50mm BK 5 cannon, the R4M spin-stabilized air/air rocket and several other advanced weapons which had no counter-

**continued on page 234** ▶

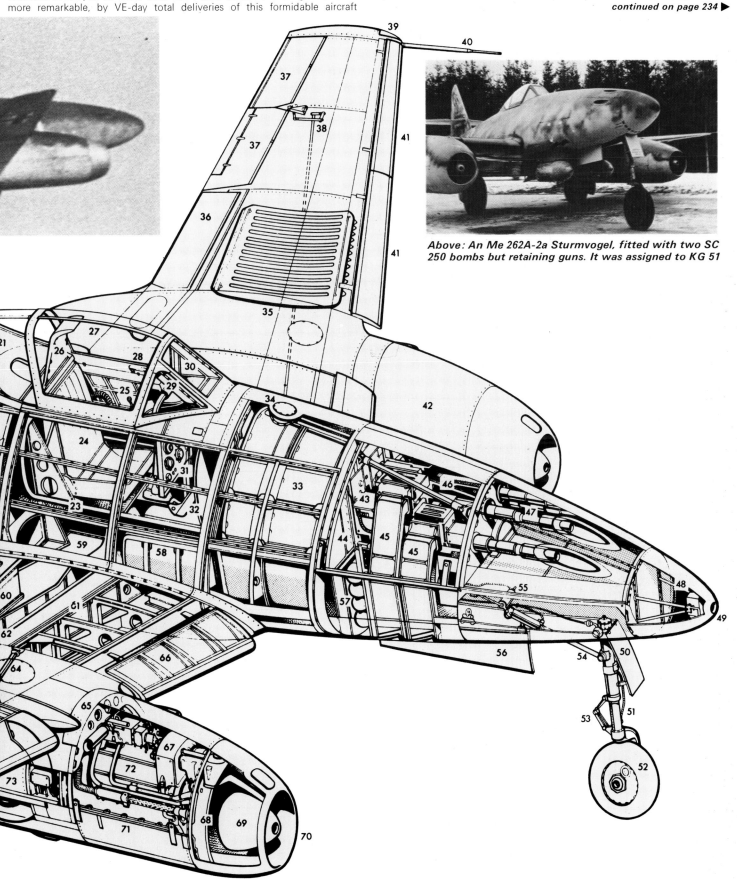

Above: An Me 262A-2a Sturmvogel, fitted with two SC 250 bombs but retaining guns. It was assigned to KG 51

## ▶Messerschmitt Me 262

part in the Allied countries — such as the MK 114 and 214 cannon of 55mm calibre and high rate of fire, and the MG 213 revolver cannon which served as the basis for almost all post-war aircraft guns. Trials did not begin with the Ruhrstahl X-4 wire-guided air/air missile, nor with the SG 500 Jagdfaust with twelve RZ 73 rockets in oblique barrels. One variant which actually saw limited combat use was the A-2a/U2 with prone bombardier in a new wooden nose, the cannon being removed. Many variants had night-fighter radar, the A-1a flying with FuG 220 (SN-2 Lichtenstein) with conventional ''antlers'' aerial array, followed by various kinds of tandem-seat Me 262B-series night fighters including the lash-up B-1a used against RAF Mosquito intruders and the B-2a with extra fuselage sections to restore the original

fuel capacity. The final NF versions would have had the Morgenstern or Berlin aerial systems imposing much less penalty on aircraft performance, as was also the case with the Ju 88G series. Another family built in some numbers was the Me 262C-series home-defence interceptors with rocket boost. Some, such as the C-1a, had a Walter R II-211/3 motor in the rear fuselage; others, such as the C-2b, had the BMW 003R propulsion package on each wing comprising a BMW 003A turbojet coupled with a BMW 718 bi-propellant rocket. Test pilot Karl Baur reported how anxious he was to get the gear and flaps up before they were torn off and then keep the nose high enough to avoid exceeding critical Mach number . . . . ''The fuel burned off at 6000 metres, and I coasted on up to around 8000 metres (26,000ft), the elapsed time from unstick being about 1½ minutes.''

*Above: Another photograph of the Me 262A-2a pictured on the previous page. The first Sturmvogel unit, III/KG 51, became operational at Hopsten, near Rheine, in October 1944. The Luftwaffe was delighted at the results achieved, but the Allies regarded the sporadic attacks as no more than pinpricks*

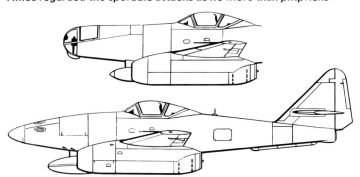

*Top: The Me 262A-2a/U2 two-seat bomber with bombardier replacing guns; immediately above: rocket-boosted Me 262C-1a*

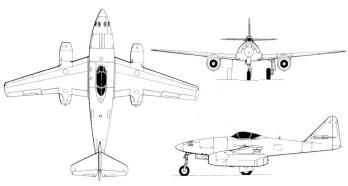

*Above: Three-view of Me 262A-1a*

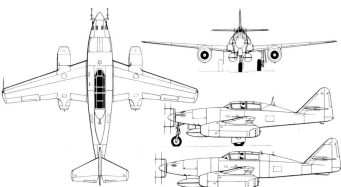

*Three-view of Me 262B-1a night fighter (lower side view, the long-fuselage B-2a optimised to this role)*

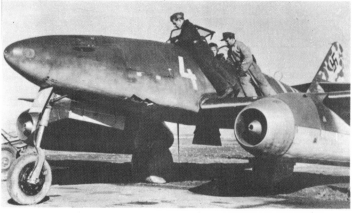

*Above: Starting engines of an Me 262A-1a of the Kommando Nowotny in late October 1944 (probably at Achmer)*

*Right: Take-off of the first Me 262C-1a Heimatschützer (Home protector) with tail rocket, converted from A-1a No 130 186*

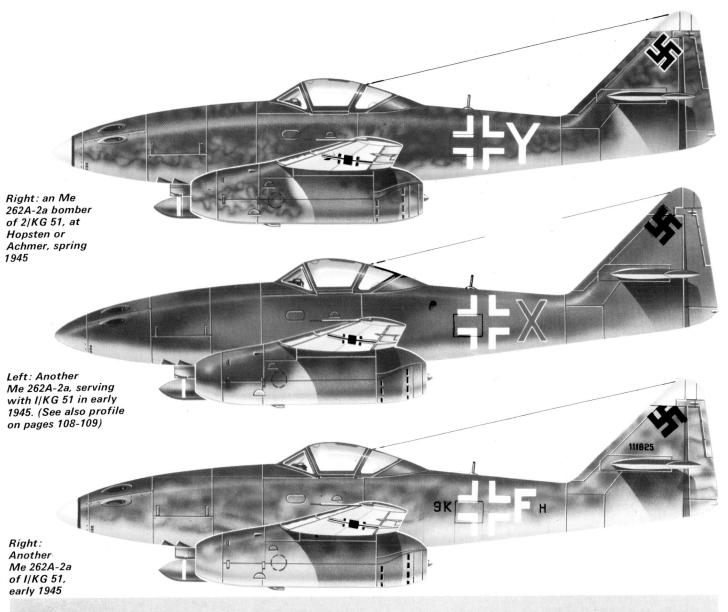

Right: an Me
262A-2a bomber
of 2/KG 51, at
Hopsten or
Achmer, spring
1945

Left: Another
Me 262A-2a, serving
with I/KG 51 in early
1945. (See also profile
on pages 108-109)

Right:
Another
Me 262A-2a
of I/KG 51,
early 1945

# Messerschmitt Bf 161-162

**Bf 161 V1 and V2 and Bf 162 V1 to V3**
**Origin:** Bayerische Flugzeugwerke AG.
**Type:** (161) reconnaissance aircraft, (162) light bomber.
**Engines:** Two 986hp Daimler-Benz DB 600Aa inverted-vee-12 liquid-cooled.
**Dimensions:** Span 56ft 3½in (17·16m); length (162) 41ft 10in (12·75m); height 11ft 9in (3·58m).
**Weights:** Empty (162) 9,700lb (4400kg); loaded 12,787lb (5800kg).
**Performance:** Maximum speed 298mph (480km/h); range (162) 485 miles (780km).

**Development:** These closely related aircraft were derived from the Bf 110 to meet the RLM 1935 need for a Schnellbomber (fast bomber), the 161 being a company proposal for a reconnaissance machine. The Bf 162 V1 flew in spring 1937, and the propaganda machine put out pictures in 1939—40 bearing false service markings and called the Messerschmitt "Jaguar". A three-seater, it carried ten 110lb (50kg) bombs, plus two 551lb (250kg) externally as overload. The two 161 prototypes had different noses, flying (with the third 162) in 1938.

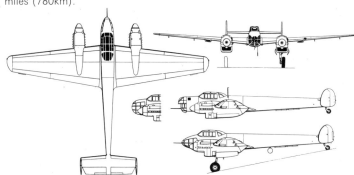

Three-view of Bf 162 V1 (upper side view, 161 V2; inset, 161 V1)

*The Bf 162 V2 carried civil registration, flying in September 1937. It was eventually used for research*

# Messerschmitt Me 261

**Me 261 V1 to V3**
**Origin:** Messerschmitt AG.
**Type:** Long-range aircraft.
**Engines:** (V1, V2) two 2,700hp Daimler-Benz DB 606A/B double engines; (V3) two 2,950hp DB 610A-1/B-1 double engines.
**Dimensions:** Span 88ft 1¾in (26·87m); length 54ft 8¾in (16·675m); height 15ft 5¾in (4·72m).
**Weights:** No data.
**Performance:** (V3) maximum speed 385mph (620km/h); range at 248mph (400km/h) 6,835 miles (11,000km).

**Development:** Called Adolfine in honour of the Führer, this was one of the few German aircraft designed to break records (its original purpose was to fly the Olympic flame from Berlin to Tokyo). The thick wing formed an integral tank, the landing gears turned 90° to lie flat in the rear of the nacelles, and the small fuselage housed a crew of five. The low-priority work was delayed, V1 not flying until 23 December 1940. The seven-crew V3 flew in 1943. Though they carried no armament V3 and possibly the others were used on long-range reconnaissance missions with Auf./Ob.d.L.

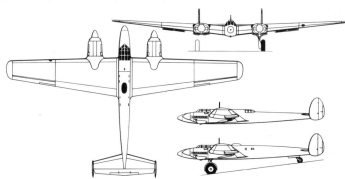

Three-view of Me 261 V2 (upper side view, Me 261 V1)

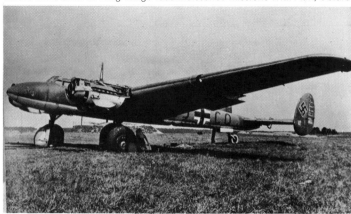

*The Me 261 V2 at Lechfeld in 1944 in a sorry state. It had been caught there by Allied bombers, together with the first prototype, and was never repaired. Designed for ultra-long-range missions, the basic type lacked defensive armament*

# Messerschmitt Me 263

**Me 163D and 263A (Ju 248)**
**Origin:** Messerschmitt AG; transferred to Junkers.
**Type:** Interceptor.
**Engine:** Walter HWK 109-509C-4 rocket with 3,750lb (1700kg) main chamber and 660lb (300kg) cruise chamber.
**Dimensions:** Span 31ft 2in (9·50m); length 25ft 10½in (7·88m); height 8ft 10¼in (2·70m).
**Weights:** Empty 4,640lb (2105kg); loaded 11,354lb (5150kg).
**Performance:** Maximum speed 620mph (1000km/h) at height; time to 49,213ft (15,000m) 3 min; max endurance, about 1hr including 15min under power.

**Development:** In retrospect the Me 163 need not have suffered from its most serious faults, and the 263 emerged on the Lippisch/Messerschmitt drawing boards in winter 1943—44 to rectify them. The new design had a larger and better-shaped body housing more propellants, a new engine with separate low-thrust cruise chamber for long endurance, and a proper landing gear. The 163D V1 was completed in spring 1944 but the RLM transferred the programme to Junkers to ease Messerschmitt's burdens. At Dessau Prof Hertel improved the 263A-1 into the Ju 248, with automatic slats, bubble hood and cut-down rear fuselage, larger flaps and other changes. Two 30mm MK 108 were fitted in the wing roots. The RLM insisted on restoration of the

Me 263A-1 designation, and hastened production, planning for the 5,511lb (2500kg) BMW 708 nitric-acid motor when ready, but in the chaos of late 1944 tooling was never finished, though a single Dessau-built 263A-1 flew as a glider in August 1944. It was briefly developed further by the Russians.

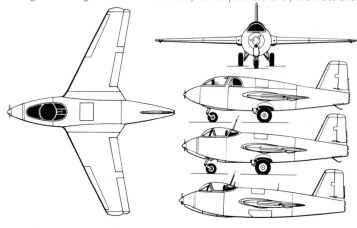

*Three-view of Me 263 V1 (centre side view) with (upper) initial form and (lower) proposed Me 263A*

# Messerschmitt Me 264

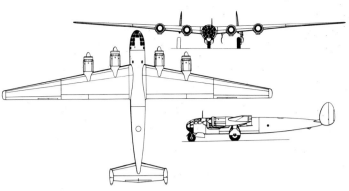

**Three-view of Me 264 V1**

**Me 264 V1 to V3**
**Origin:** Messerschmitt AG.
**Type:** Ultra-long-range bomber.
**Engines:** (V1) four 1,340hp Jumo 211J-1 inverted-vee-12; (V2, V3) four 1,700hp BMW 801D or G 18-cylinder radials.
**Dimensions:** Span (V1) 127ft 7½in (38·90m), (V2, V3) 141ft 1in (43·00m); length 68ft 6¾in (20·90m); height 14ft 1¼in (4·30m).
**Weights:** (V3) empty 46,627lb (21,150kg); max loaded 123,460lb (56,000kg).
**Performance:** (V3 at reduced weight) maximum speed with GM-1 boost at height 351mph (565km/h); max range at 217mph (350km/h) 9,321 miles (15,000km).

**Development:** Ignoring an RLM rule that it should concentrate exclusively on fighters Messerschmitt AG began development of an ultra-long-range machine in 1940, while the High Command (OKL) discussed propaganda and material value of an Amerika-Bomber, either carrying a small load to the US eastern seaboard and returning to its European base or else a heavier load and ditching offshore near a U-boat to bring back the crew. The Me 264 V1 flew in December 1942, but the RLM favoured the Ju 390 for its commonality, and told Messerschmitt to build V2 and V3 as maritime recce-bombers. Neither flew, because of Allied bombing, but V3 would have carried a 4,410lb (2000kg) bomb load and defensive armament of two 20mm and four MG131. Overload takeoffs would have needed jettisonable auxiliary landing gears and six a.t.o. rockets.

**The first prototype pictured at Neu-Offing in late 1942**

# Messerschmitt Me 309

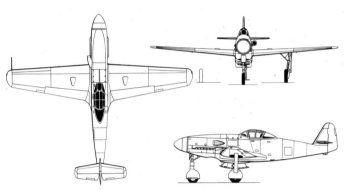

**Three-view of Me 309 V1**

**Me 309 V1 and V2**
**Origin:** Messerschmitt AG.
**Type:** Single-seat fighter.
**Engine:** (V1 early) 1,750hp DB 603A-1, (V1 later and others) 1,475hp DB 605B inverted-vee-12 liquid-cooled.
**Dimensions:** Span 36ft 2¾in (11·04m); length (V1) 31ft 0½in (9·46m); height 11ft 3in (3·45m).
**Weights:** Empty (V1) 7,783lb (3530kg); loaded (V1) 9,371lb (4250kg), (V4) 10,736lb (4870kg).
**Performance:** Maximum speed (V1) 455mph (733km/h), (V4) 360mph (580km/h) at low level (faster at height).

**Development:** With lukewarm support from the RLM, Messerschmitt planned the 309 as the definitive next-generation fighter to succeed the 109. Features included wide-track tricycle landing gear, retractable radiator and a pressure cabin, and numerous 109 testbeds were used in support. Finally the 309 V1 flew in June 1942, and after many modifications was subjected to official tests which showed a Bf 109G could turn better. There were problems with the nosewheel and the Fw 190D was judged superior in any case.

V2 was irreparably damaged on its first landing, V3 flew in March 1943 and V4 in July 1943 carried four 13mm, two 20mm and two 30mm. The B-1 dive bomber would have had two 551lb (250kg) bombs, and the Me 609 was a twinned version.

# Messerschmitt Me 328

**Me 328 V1, A-series and B-series**
**Origin:** Messerschmitt AG; development and prototypes by DFS, and pre-production aircraft by Jacob Schweyer.
**Type:** See text.
**Engines:** See text.
**Dimensions:** Span (small) 20ft 11¾in (6·40m), (large) 27ft 10½in (8·50m); length (most) 22ft 4¾in (6·83m), (fuselage engines) 28ft 2½in (8·63m); height (on skid) (A) 6ft 10½in (2·10m), (B) 8ft 2½in (2·50m).
**Weights:** Empty (B-0, B-1) 3,400lb (1542kg); loaded (A-1) 4,850lb (2200kg), (A-2) 8,378lb (3800kg), (B-1) 5,953lb (2700kg), (B-2) 10,595lb (4730kg).
**Performance:** Maximum speed at low level (A-1) 469mph (755km/h), (A-2) 572mph (920km/h), (B-1) 423mph (680km/h), (B-2) 367mph (590km/h).

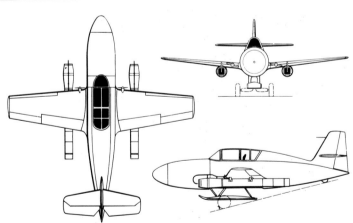

**Three-view of Me 328B-1 fighter-bomber (wing engines)**

**One of the unpowered prototypes built by DFS, pictured balancing on its skid. Many towline flights were made**

**Development:** This programme, extraordinary even for Nazi Germany, began in 1941 as a parasite fighter for launch from a bomber and subsequent retrieval. After widespread research and development the V1 glider began pick-a-back tests with Do 217 as carrier in autumn 1943. Powered tests began with two 660lb (300kg) thrust As 014 pulsejets on the rear fuselage, with severe problems. Then tests were made with two ducts under the wings, some being hung as far aft as possible because the intense noise damaged the wooden airframe. The A-1 fighter had two wing ducts and the A-2 four on the fuselage; respective armament was two MG 151 and two MK 103. The work then switched to assault (some expendable) with bomb loads up to 3,087lb (1400kg), the B-1 having wing engines and the B-2 bigger ducts of 880lb (400kg) each. Takeoff was by rocket trolley, cable winch and other means. Other versions were to be catapulted from U-boats.

# Messerschmitt Me 321 and Me 323 Gigant

**Me 321A and B, Me 323D and E**
**Origin:** Messerschmitt AG.
**Type:** (321) heavy cargo glider; (323) heavy cargo transport.
**Engines:** (321) none; (323 production variants) six 1,140hp Gnome-Rhône 14N 48/49 14-cylinder two-row radials.
**Dimensions:** Span 180ft 5½in (55m); length 92ft 4¼in (28·15m); height (321B-1) 33ft 3½in (10·15m); (323) 31ft 6in (9·6m).
**Weights:** Empty (321B-1) 27,432lb (12,400kg); (323D-6) 60,260lb (27,330kg); (323E-1) 61,700lb (28,010kg); maximum loaded (321B-1) 75,852lb (34,400kg); (323D-6) 94,815lb (43,000kg); (323E-1) 99,208lb (45,000kg).
**Performance:** Maximum speed (321 on tow) 99mph (160km/h); (323D series) 177mph (285km/h); initial climb (321 towed by three Bf 110) 492ft (150m)/min; (323D series) 710ft (216m)/min; service ceiling (323D) about 13,100ft (4000m); range with "normal" payload (presumably not maximum) 684 miles (1100km).
**Armament:** See text.

**History:** First flight (321V-1) 7 March 1941; service delivery (321) about June 1941; final delivery (321) April 1942; first flight (323V-1) some reports claim April 1941 but others, much more plausible, state "autumn 1941"; service delivery (323D-1) May 1942; final delivery March 1944.

**Development:** Following the dramatic vindication of the previously untried Blitzkrieg concept of airborne forces in May 1940 the Reichsluftfahrtministerium (RLM) asked Junkers and Heinkel to design huge transport gliders far bigger than the little DFS 230 used in the invasion of the Benelux countries. Junkers' Ju 322 Mammut was an expensive failure, but the Me 321 Gigant went into production, despite the fact it was extremely tiring to fly on account of the very high control forces needed. Made chiefly of welded steel tube, with plywood or fabric covering, it carried the large

*Below: An Me 321A-1, without a.t.o. rockets, being towed off by an He 111Z. Most Me 321 flying was done earlier, with the dangerous "Troika schlepp" of three Bf 110 tugs.*

# Messerschmitt P.1101

**P.1101 V1**
**Origin:** Messerschmitt AG.
**Type:** Interceptor.
**Engine:** (Initial trials) 1,980lb (900kg) thrust Jumo 004B turbojets, (later) 2,866lb (1300kg) thrust Heinkel-Hirth 109-011 turbojet.
**Dimensions:** Span (40° sweep) 27ft 0½in (8·24m); length 30ft 1in (9·13m); height 9ft 2¼in (2·80m).
**Weights:** Empty 5,724lb (2596kg); loaded 8,950lb (4060kg).
**Performance:** (011 engine) maximum speed 553mph (890km/h) at sea level, 609mph (980km/h) at height.

**Development:** The story of this unique prototype has no parallel in aviation history. It was conceived early in World War II as a research aircraft to investigate the use of sweepback for high-speed flight, as had been suggested by Büsemann in 1935. Two years were wasted after Büsemann's public lecture before Betz at the DVL began research on swept wings (nobody in the future Allied countries made any move to do anything). About four years then elapsed before Voigt at Messerschmitt saw the advantage of swept wings, and in 1942 the P.1101 was started. But two more years were wasted before the RLM asked for a single-jet fighter; then, in September 1944, the work of building the P.1101 began. When US troops entered the Oberammergau research facility six months later they found the aircraft almost complete. In the United States it again languished. Finally, much modified and fitted with a variable-sweep wing by Bell, it at last flew as the Bell X-5 on 20 June 1951.

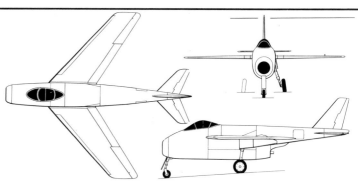

*Three-view of Messerschmitt P.1101 VI*

*Above and right: The P.1101 V1 as it was when captured at the unknown Oberammergau plant, with mock-up engine.*

payload of 48,500lb (22 tonnes), or a company of infantry. The 321A-1 had a single pilot but most of the 175 built were 321B-1 with a pair of crew who served as navigator and radio operator and manned two twin 7·92mm MG 15 machine guns in beam windows. Usual towing scheme was three Bf 110 in formation, but the specially built He 111Z was preferable and many units used various arrangements of take-off boost rockets. Dipl-Ing Degel then studied the powered 321C and D and eventually these became the 323V-1 with four engines (complete nacelles already in production at SNCASO for the Bloch 175) and 323V-2 with six. The six-engined Gigant went into production, the D-1 having three-blade metal propellers and the D-2 two-blade wooden, each having five MG 15 in the nose and mounts for six MG 34 infantry m.g. in beam windows. Most later had five 13mm MG 131 added, but this did not stop Beaufighters shooting 14 into the sea as they ferried petrol to Rommel. Final versions in the run of 210 were the E-series with 1,340hp Jumo 211F, the E-1 having an MG 151 20mm turret above each centre-engine nacelle, and the 323G with 1,320hp Gnome-Rhône 14R.

There were a surprising number of special versions. One of the most remarkable was the Me 323E-2/WT (Waffenträger = weapon carrier), in which no fewer than 11 MG 151 20mm cannon were installed. One was in a power-operated nose turret and four in single EDL 151 electric turrets above the wing. Four 13mm MG 131 (at least) were also carried, as well as several tons of armour and bullet-proof glass, but eventually it was considered that ordinary escort fighters would be better. Perhaps the most fascinating of all the many projects with which these capable monsters were associated was the carriage of a 17·7 ton (18,000kg, 39,690lb) bomb. The project got as far as flight trials, despite the fact that not even a standard He 177 had much chance of delivering such a bomb accurately — or even carrying it. The Me 323, specially modified for the test, was assisted off the ground by an He 111Z tug. Shortly before letting the monster bomb go, the Gigant's rear fuselage began to break. The crew managed to release the bomb; but the giant aircraft went into an uncontrollable dive and crashed. It was subsequently revealed that the structure had been weakened by bullet strikes from US fighters which strafed the test field a few days earlier.

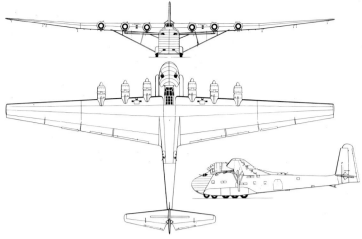

*Above: Three-view of Me 323D-1*

*Below, left: Loading an artillery piece, probably a 7·5cm Pak.40 anti-tank gun, through the open nose of an Me 323D-1*

*Below, upper: An Me 321A-1 of the Grossraumlastenseglergruppe (great glider group) formed in June 1941. Though 200 were built they were handicapped by lack of suitable tugs.*

*Below, lower: An Me 323D-0 (V12, last pre-production model)*

# Siebel Si 201

**Si 201 V1 and V2**
**Origin:** Siebel Flugzeugwerke KG.
**Type:** Observation and army co-op.
**Engine:** 240hp Argus As 10C inverted-vee-8 aircooled.
**Dimensions:** Span 45ft 11¼in (14·00m); length 34ft 1½in (10·40m); height 11ft 1¾in (3·40m).
**Weights:** Empty 2,469lb (1120kg); loaded 3,175lb (1440kg).
**Performance:** Maximum speed 115mph (185km/h); range 280 miles (450km).

**Development:** Similar to Britain's Fane AOP (air observation post), the Si 201 was a STOL pusher with perfect all-round view for the pilot and observer seated in tandem. With the Bf 163 (no relation to the Me 163) the Si 201 was requested by the RLM in 1935 in evaluation against the Fi 156. In the event the Fi 156 was in production before either of the other machines flew (in 1938) and the whole exercise was rather a waste of effort. The Si 201 was in any case not impressive.

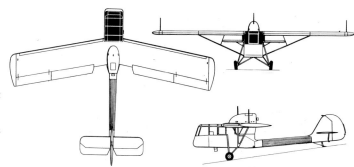

*Above: Three-view of the Si 201 V2 (swept wings)*

*Below: STOL take-off by the Si 201 V2, which had wings with greater sweepback and simplified high-lift flaps and slats. Flight testing revealed various deficiencies, and neither this nor the tractor Bf 163 replaced the Storch*

# Siebel Si 204

**Si 204A-series and D-series**
**Origin:** Siebel Flugzeugwerke KG; production, see text.
**Type:** Crew trainer, transport, ambulance and other roles.
**Engines:** Two 600hp Argus As 411 inverted-vee-12 aircooled.
**Dimensions:** Span 69ft 11¾in (21·33m); length (most) 39ft 2½in (11·95m); height 13ft 11½in (4·25m).
**Weights:** Empty (D-2) 8,709lb (3950kg); loaded 12,347lb (5600kg).
**Performance:** Maximum speed (typical) 226mph (364km/h); range 1,119 miles (1800km).

**Development:** Derived from the smaller Fh 104 Hallore, the leading Luftwaffe light-twin executive and liaison machine, the Si 204A first flew in early 1941. It was considerably larger, and had an all-metal stressed-skin structure and twin fins. The 204A had a stepped airline-type cockpit and 360hp As 410 engines, but the main version was the more powerful 204D of 1942 with all-glazed nose. Production was assigned to SNCAC at Bourges in France (which built 21 in 1942 and 147 in 1943) and to the Czech factories of BMM (which built 492) and Aero (which built 515). Luftwaffe 204D versions were used for every kind of bombing, gunnery, radar, navigation and other aircrew training, as well as eight-passenger transport and various towing and other duties. Production continued after World War II as the Czech C-103 and French NC 701 Martinet.

*Below: The Si 204 V20 (20th prototype), which, as noted on the fin, was the first Si 204D-1. There were many sub-types, some of them carrying a dorsal turret and internal bomb load for bomber crew training*

# Mistel Composite Aircraft

### Mistel composite aircraft
Impracticable to give data in the usual way, since there were so many variations and combinations, many of which are numerically unrecorded.

The concept of launching an aeroplane from above, or below, another goes back to the earliest days of aviation. In the early 1930s the Soviet Union launched pairs of fighters from above the wings of TB-1 bombers as part of a wide programme of new combat-aircraft techniques. In 1941 a different pick-a-back scheme was suggested — reputedly by Siegfried Holzbauer, Junkers test pilot — to the RLM as a way of making further use of operationally "tired" Ju 88 airframes. He believed that they could be converted into pilotless missiles, carrying enormous warheads with multiple fuze systems, which could be flown to their target by the pilot of a fighter riding on top. After release, the fighter pilot could then steer the explosive-packed bomber into its target by the radio command link method such as was then in advanced development for the Hs 293 and Fritz X missiles.

The idea was initially rejected (as indeed any new idea would in the 1941 climate, which had a deep-seated belief the war was already won). In 1942 the DFS tested the practicality of flying a DFS 230 with a powered aircraft (Kl 35 or Fw 56) mounted above it. The bold experiment was then made of using a Bf 109E as upper component, and this made the RLM look at Holzbauer's idea again, and in 1943 an order for a Mistel (Misteltoe) conversion was received. The first conversion, flown in July 1943, comprised a Ju 88A-4 and Bf 109F, the latter having landing gear retracted and being supported on slim struts. The launch procedure was for the pilot of the upper component to release the rear strut, which pivoted back to hit a yoke ahead of the Ju 88 fin. This triggered the electrical release of the main fighter attachments. Demonstration that the scheme worked led to a further 15 conversions as weapons, code-named Beethoven. Tests with hollow-charge warheads of Ju 88 fuselage size against the French battleship *Oran* were encouraging, and in further tests a thickness of 60ft of reinforced concrete was breached.

Junkers, DFS, Patin and Askania together developed a workable Mistel control system. It required substantial system changes and additions to both upper and lower components. On takeoff, and in emergencies (eg, if intercepted by hostile fighters) the fighter pilot could operate the flight controls of his own aircraft and the lower component in unison. Normally he could fly his own aircraft and merely use switches to re-trim the bomber's elevators or combined rudder/ailerons. The Ju 88 also had to have structural changes and a reskinned mid-fuselage. The training versions were the Mistel S1 (Ju 88A-4/Bf 109F), S2 (Ju 88G-1/Fw 190A-8) and S3A (Ju 88A-6/Fw 190A-6). The first operational version was Mistel 1 (rebuilt Ju 88A-4/Bf 109F) with the bomber's crew compartment replaced by a 7,716lb (3500kg) warhead with long contact fuze to give the correct stand-off distance.

Mistel 1 was first used by 2/KG 101, which after studying the possibility of attacks on Gibraltar and Leningrad, moved to Grove in Denmark to blast Scapa Flow. Before its attack it was moved to St Dizier in France and there took off on night attacks on invasion shipping in Seine bay, scoring several hits but failing to sink any ships. But instructions were received urgently to convert 75 Ju 88G night fighters, to add a third Ju 88 wheel to avoid the burst tyres that had caused several takeoff accidents (which at full load exceeded Ju 88 overload limits), and to form II/KG 200 out of the short-lived III/KG 66 as the chief Mistel formation, with 100 composites on strength. This force built up in early 1945, nearly all being Mistel 2, but increasingly receiving the Mistel 3C, a complete change of policy in which the lower component was not a worn-out machine but one straight from the production line. The 3C lower component was the long-fuselage (8ft 11¾in longer, with more fuel) Ju 88G-10 or H-4, the upper component being an Fw 190A-8 with doppelreiter overwing tanks and belly tank. On the outward trip the 190 drew 95-octane fuel from the Mistel, leaving it with its own 87-octane supply and tanks almost dry. Normally there was no radio command guidance, the Mistel merely being set up on line for its target and left to itself.

Over 250 Mistels were built or converted, but the inexorable defeat of Hitler's Third Reich was scarcely affected by them. The planned Eisenhammer (iron hammer) mission, that was really to smash the Allies, never took place. Mistels had to be thrown into the battle in twos and threes, sometimes hitting their targets but with very heavy in-flight losses and invariably used up in trying to hit a tactical target such as a bridge.

In the closing weeks of the war other Mistel combinations included the Ju 88G-7/Ta 152H, Ta 154/Fw 190, Ar 234/Fi 103, Do 217K/DFS 288 and, for research, Si 204/Lippisch DM-1. There were many projects, such as the Ju 287/Me 262 and Ar 234C/Arado E.377 (small pilotless bomber), and the Führungsmaschine (Ju 88H-4/Fw 190A-8) intended as a long-range pathfinder, the lower component having extra fuel, centimetric radar and crew of three. The upper component in this case was purely an escort.

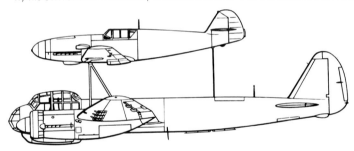

*Mistel S 1, a Ju 88A-4 and Bf 109F*

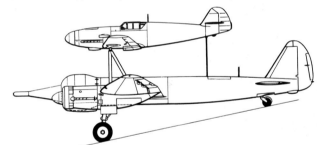

*Mistel 1, rebuilt Ju 88A-4 and Bf 109F*

*Mistel S 2, a Ju 88G-1 and Fw 190A-8*

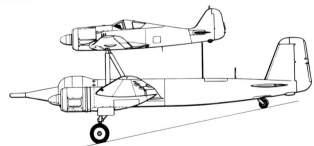

*Mistel 2, rebuilt Ju 88G-1 and Fw 190A-6*

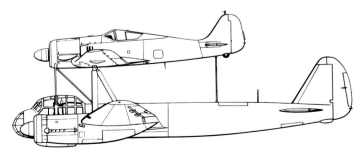

*Mistel S 3A, a Ju 88A-6 and Fw 190A-6. This was a difficult combination, as the upper and lower components used different grades of fuel (see text)*

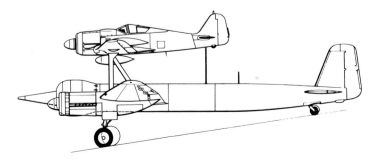

*Mistel 3C, the last type of Mistel combination in production comprising a new Ju 88G-10 or H-4 (long fuselage) rebuilt with an Fw 190A-8 on top with doppelreiter overwing tanks*

# The Luftwaffe Chain of Command

Reichsmarschall Hermann Goering was the Commander-in-Chief (Oberbefehlshaber der Luftwaffe: Ob.d.L) of the German Air Force. Although an independent arm, the Air Force High Command (Oberkommando der Luftwaffe: OKL) was subordinate to German High Command (Oberkommando der Wehrmacht: OKW) which was ultimately responsible to Adolf Hitler for the operational conduct of the Army, Navy and Air Force.

The Luftwaffe Air Ministry (Reichsluftfahrtministerium) was situated at Leipzigerstrasse 7, Berlin W8, headed by Ob.d.L in his additional capacity as Air Minister. The Deputy Air Minister and Generalluftzeugmeister was initially Erhard Milch, then Ernst Udet until November 1941, and then Milch once again who held the post until the end of the war. The Chief of Air Staff was successively Jeschonnek, Korten and Koller. The RLM included some sixteen Inspectorates, each covering a special branch of the service.

## Administrative

The basis of the Administration and Supply organisation of the Luftwaffe was the Luftgau, which was a territorial area command within Germany responsible for training, administration, maintenance, supply and field defence.

## Operational

The Luftflottenkommando or Luftflotte (Air Fleet Command) were established on a territorial basis. The commander of the Luftflotte, normally a Generaloberst or higher, was responsible for the field formations under him regardless of their operational role. The subsidiary formations under the Luftflotte, normally a limited number, were the Fliegerkorps, the Fliegerdivision, the Jagdkorps, the Jagddivision, and the Jagdfliegerführer, in addition, there were localised commands known as Fliegerführer (Air Commander) e.g., Fliegerführer Atlantik, Fliegerführer Afrika, etc. Thus, a fighter unit would be controlled possibly by a Jagdfliegerführer or Jafü (Fighter Commander) for its tactical employment, who was in turn subordinated to a Fliegerkorps or Fliegerdivision under the final control of the Luftflotte.

## Tactical

The basis of all tactical units was the Gruppe (equivalent to the RAF Wing and the US Group). This formation was led by a Gruppenkommandeur or Kommandeur, an executive post held by an aircrew member whose rank could vary considerably – normally it was a Major in the case of bomber units and a Hauptmann in fighter units. He had his own operational and administrative Staff (Stab) or Gruppenstab, and flew combat operations with his Stabsschwarm (Staff Flight) usually of 3 to 4 aircraft. Under his command there were three, or sometimes four, Staffeln (equivalent to RAF and USAAF Squadrons) led by a Staffelkapitän, an executive post that could be held by any aircrew officer from Leutnant to Hauptmann. In the temporary absence of the Staffelkapitän, the unit was led by a Staffelführer. For tactical operations, the Staffel was split into Schwarm (Section of four aircraft) or Rotte (pair of aircraft) in the case of fighters, fighter-bombers or close-support aircraft, or Kette (Flight of three aircraft) in the case of bombers and dive-bombers.

The Staffel normally comprised between 12 and 16 aircraft, with the number of aircrew varying according to the strength; normally there were 20–25 pilots and 150 ground crew in the case of single-engined fighter units and 80 groundcrew in the case of twin-engine fighter units. Thus, a Gruppe consisted of 40–50 aircraft on establishment with around 500 ground personnel. Reconnaissance units were always organised on the basis of the Gruppe, and this applied to other units, the most common of which are shown in the accompanying table.

Invariably, a tighter operational control was needed for the more important frontline units and this led to the subordination of three Gruppen to a Geschwader (equivalent roughly to the USAAF Combat Wing, and the RAF having no direct parallel). The Geschwader bore the prefix that indicated its role in warfare, i.e., Jagdgeschwader (Fighter Geschwader). The Geschwaderkommodore or Kommodore was usually a Major or above in rank and flew operations with his Geschwaderstab. His staff consisted of an Adjutant, a IIa Officer (Adj.'s assistant: commissioned rank), a IIb Officer (Adj.'s assistant: non-commissioned rank), a Staff Major, a Ia Operations Officer, a Ic Intelligence Officer, a Nachtrichten Offizier (Intelligence Officer), a TO (Technical Officer), a Kfz-Offizier (Armaments Officer) and a IVa (Administrative Officer). The control of the entire Geschwader was normally exercised from the Gefechtsstand (Battle HQ) situated on the Geschwaderstab's airfield, but this was not always the case, and it was common for a Geschwader to have its Gruppen scattered over a wide area, even possibly in different theatres of war. The principle types of Geschwader, as indicated by their role, are shown in the appropriate table.

According to type, the Geschwader varied in its operational establishment: the Jagdgeschwader usually had between 120–125 aircraft, whereas the Kampfgeschwader had about 80–90 on strength. The "fourth" Gruppe was normally the operational training unit for the Geschwader, but it could be used for operations if needed, and in 1941, some Jagdgeschwader were already using the fourth Gruppe as a fully fledged combat formation. In October 1943, JG 2 and JG 26 became the first Geschwader to increase the strength of their Gruppen from three to four Staffeln, thus raising the establishment to about 160 aircraft.

The Gruppen number was indicated by the Roman figure, whilst that of the Staffel was the Arabic figure: thus III/JG 27 was the third Gruppe, and 10./JG 11 was the tenth Staffel.

## Principal Types of Gruppe Organisation

| | | |
|---|---|---|
| Aufklärungsgruppe (Fern) | Aufklr.Gr (F) | Reconnaissance Wing (Long-range) |
| Aufklärungsgruppe (Heer) | Aufklr.Gr (H) | Reconnaissance Wing (Army co-op) |
| Nahaufklärungsgruppe | NAGr | Short-range tactical recco |
| Fernaufklärungsgruppe | FAGr | Long-range reconnaissance |
| See-Auflkärungsgruppe | SAGr | Maritime reconnaissance |
| Küstenfliegergruppe | Kü.Fl.Gr | Coastal Flying Wing |
| Nachtschlachtgruppe | NSGr | Night close-support Wing |

## Principal Types of Geschwader

| | | |
|---|---|---|
| Kampfgeschwader | KG | Bomber |
| Lehrgeschwader | LG | Operational training |
| Jagdgeschwader | JG | Day Fighter |
| Nachtjagdgeschwader | NJG | Night Fighter |
| Schlachtgeschwader | Sch.G | Close-Support: became SG after October 1943. |
| Nachtschlachtgeschwader | NSG | Night Close-Support |
| Stukageschwader | StG | Dive-Bomber: became SG after October 1943 |
| Zerstörergeschwader | ZG | Destroyer or heavy-fighter |
| Schnelles Kampfgeschwader | SKG | Fast Bomber |
| Kampfgeschwader zur besonderer Verwendung | KGzbV | Lit: Bomber unit for special purposes: usually transport units |
| Transportgeschwader | TG | Transport (after 1943) |

## Luftwaffe Officer and NCO Ranks and Grades

| | | |
|---|---|---|
| Reichsmarschall | | Marshal of the Royal Air Force |
| Generaloberst | | |
| Generalfeldmarschall | | Air Chief Marshal |
| General | | Air Marshal |
| Generalleutnant | | Air Vice-Marshal |
| Generalmajor | | Air Commodore |
| Oberst | Obst. | Group Captain |
| Oberstleutnant | Obstlt. | Wing Commander |
| Major | Maj. | Squadron Leader |
| Hauptmann | Hptm. | Flight Lieutenant |
| Oberleutnant | Oblt. | Flying Officer |
| Leutnant | Lt. | Pilot Officer |

The ranks and grades of Non-commissioned and cadet personnel are difficult to equate with those of the Royal Air Force, and bear more resemblance to those in the British Army. Therefore the following NCO and cadet ranks have only approximate equivalents.

| | | |
|---|---|---|
| Oberfähnrich | Obfhr. | Senior Officer Cadet |
| Fahnenjunker-Oberfeldwebel | Fhj.-Ofw. | Cadet Warrant Officer |
| Oberfeldwebel | Ofw. | Warrant Officer |
| Fähnrich | Fhr. | Officer Cadet |
| Fahnenjunker-Feldwebel | Fhj.-Fw. | Cadet Sergeant Major |
| Feldwebel | Fw. | Sergeant Major |
| Fahnenjunker-Unteroffizier | Fhj.-Uffz. | Cadet Sergeant |
| Unteroffizier | Uffz. | Sergeant |
| Obergefreiter | Obgefr. | Corporal |
| Gefreiter | Gefr. | Lance Corporal |
| Flieger | Flg. | Airman |

# Glossary

**A/B Schule:** Flying Training School (Single-engined aircraft)

**A.G.:** Aktiengesellschaft (Joint-Stock Company)

**A-Stand:** Forward gunner's position

**Aufklärung:** Reconnaissance

**Aufklärungsstaffel (F):** Long-range Reconnaissance Squadron

**Aufklärungsstaffel (H):** Tactical Reconnaissance Squadron

**AVG:** Aerodynamische Versuchsanstalt Göttingen (Göttingen Aerodynamic Experimental Establishment)

**B-Schule:** Blind-flying School

**B-Stand:** Dorsal gunner's position

**Befehlshaber:** Commander

**Behelfs-:** Auxiliary

**BK:** Bordkanone (Fixed aircraft cannon)

**BMW:** Bayerische Motorenwerke/München (Bavarian Engine Works/Munich)

**Bola:** Bodenlafette (ventral gun mounting)

**Bordfliegerstaffel:** Shipboard squadron

**Bramo:** Brandenburgische Motorenwerke (Brandenburg Engine Works)

**BT:** Bombentorpedo (bomb-torpedo)

**Buna:** Trade name for a synthetic rubber used for tyres, fuel tanks, etc.

**C-Amt:** Technical Department of the Luftfahrtkommissariat (later Technisches Amt of the RLM)

**C-Schule:** Flying Training School (Multi-engined aircraft)

**C-Stand:** Ventral gunner's position

**C-Stoff:** Catalyst (30% hydrazine, hydrate, 57% methanol and 13% water) used by Walter R II-211/HWK 509A rocket motor

**DB:** Daimler-Benz

**Deichselschlepp:** Pole-tow air trailer (see page 58)

**Düppel:** A town near the Danish border where metal foil strips (known as "Window" to the R.A.F.) for radar countermeasures were first found, the name of the town subsequently being applied by the Luftwaffe to this device.

**DFS:** Deutsches Forschungsinstitut für Segelflug (German Research Institute for Gliding Flight)

**DLH:** Deutsche Lufthansa (German State Airline)

**DLV:** Deutscher Luftsportverband (German Aviation Sport Union)

**DSV:** Deutsche Schiffsbau-Versuchsanstalt (German Shipbuilding Experimental Institute)

**DVL:** Deutsche Versuchsanstalt für Luftfahrt (German Aviation Experimental Establishment)

**DVS:** Deutsche Verkehrsfliegerschule (German Commercial Pilot's School)

**EDL:** Elektrische Drehringlafette (electrically-operated swivel mounting)

**Einsatzkommando:** Operational Detachment

**EJG:** Ergänzungs-Jagdgeschwader (Fighter Replacement Training Group)

**EKdo:** Erprobungs-Kommando (Proving or Test Detachment)

**Erprobungs-:** Proving- or Test- (e.g., EGr.210)

**Entwicklungs-:** Development (e.g., EF 61)

**Ergänzungs-:** Replacement (e.g., EJG 3)

**Erprobungsstelle:** Proving (or Test) Centre (Abbrev.: E-Stelle)

**Ersatz:** Replacement or Substitute

**ETC:** Elektrische Trägervorrichtung für Cylinderbomben (Electrically-operated carriers for cylindrical bombs)

**EZ:** Einheitszielvorrichtung (Standard Sighting Device)

**FA:** Ferngesteuerte Anlage (Remotely-controlled installation – e.g., gun barbette)

**FAGr:** Fernaufklärungsgruppe (Long-range Reconnaissance Wing)

**FDL:** Ferngerichtete Drehringlafette (Remotely-sighted swivel mounting)

**FDSL:** Ferngerichtete Drehring-Seitenlafette (Remotely-sighted lateral swivel mounting)

**Feldwebel:** Equivalent to Sergeant (R.A.F.) or Airman 1st Class (U.S.A.F.)

**Fernaufklärung:** Long-range reconnaissance

**Fernnachtjagd:** Long-range night interception or intrusion

**FFS:** Flugzeugführerschule (Pilot's School)

**FHL:** Ferngerichtete Hecklafette (Remotely-sighted tail mounting)

**Flak:** Fliegerabwehrkanone (Anti-aircraft gun)

**Flieger:** Airman or Pilot

**Flugkapitän:** A rank in German civil aviation

**Forschungsanstalt:** Research Establishment

**FuG:** Funkgerät (Radio or radar set)

**Fuhrungsstab:** Operations Staff

**FZG:** Fernzielgerät (Remote aiming device/bomb sight)

**Gefreiter:** Leading Aircraftsman (R.A.F.) or Airman 3rd Class (U.S.A.F.)

**General der Jagdflieger:** General of Fighters

**General der Kampfflieger:** General of Bombers

**General der Nachtjagd:** General of Night Fighting

**Generalfeldmarschall d.Lw.:** Equivalent of Marshal of the R.A.F. or (U.S.A.F) General of the Air Force

**Generalleutnant d.Lw.:** Equivalent of Air Vice Marshal (R.A.F.) or Major General (U.S.A.F.)

**General-Luftzeugmeister:** (Lit) Master-General of Air Material/Equipment (Chief of Aircraft Procurement and Supply)

**General-Luftzeugmeisteramt:** Department of the Chief of Aircraft Procurement and Supply

**Generalmajor d.Lw.:** Equivalent to Air Commodore (R.A.F.) or Brigadier General (U.S.A.F.)

**Generaloberst d.Lw.:** Equivalent to Air Chief Marshal (R.A.F.) or General (U.S.A.F.)

**Geschwader:** Group

**G.m.b.H.:** Gesellschaft mit beschränkter Haftung (Limited-liability Company)

**GM-1:** Nitrous oxide

**GPV:** Gegnerpfeil-Visier (Flight path pointer sight)

**Grossraumlastensegler:** Large-capacity cargo glider

**Gruppe:** Equivalent to Wing (R.A.F.)

**Gruppenkommandeur:** Officer commanding a Gruppe

**Hauptmann:** Equivalent to Flight Lieutenant (R.A.F.) or Captain (U.S.A.F.)

**HDL:** Hydraulische Drehringlafette (Hydraulically-operated swivel mounting)

**Heeres-:** Army (e.g., Heeresaufklärungsstaffel or Army Reconnaissance Squadron)

**Helle Nachtjagd:** (Lit) "Light (or Bright) Night Chase"—night interception over searchlight-illuminated zones

**Himmelbett:** (Lit) "Four-poster Bed"—a Luftwaffe term for ground-controlled night interception over a limited area

**HVA:** Heeresversuchsanstalt (Army Experimental Establishment)

**HWK:** Hellmuth Walter Werke

**Jabo:** Jagdbomber (Fighter-bomber)

**Jabo-Rei:** Jagdbomber mit vergrösserter Reichweite (Extended-range fighter-bomber)

**Jagd-:** Fighter-, chase, pursuit

**JFS:** Jagdfliegerschule (Fighter Training School)

**JG:** Jagdgeschwader (Fighter Group)

**JGr:** Jagdgruppe (Fighter Wing)

**Jumo:** Junkers Motorenbau

**Kampf-:** (Lit) Battle

**Kampfgeschwader:** Bomber Group—(Lit: Battle Group)

**Kampfzerstörer:** Heavy Fighter (Lit: Battle Destroyer)

**Kdo:** Kommando (Detachment)

**Kette:** Element of three aircraft

**KG:** Kampfgeschwader (Bomber Group)

**K.G.:** Kommandit-Gesellschaft (Limited-partnership Company)

**KGzbV:** Kampfgeschwader zur besonderen Verwendung (Battle Group for Special Duties/Transport Group)

**Konstructionsleitung:** Design Direction

**Kriegsmarine:** German Navy (after 1935)

**Kurier-:** Courier or special messenger

**Kübelwagen:** Simplified open-top version of the Volkswagen (Lit: Bucket Car)

**Kü. Fl.:** Küstenflieger (Coastal Aviation)

**KWK:** Kampfwagenkanone (Tank gun, e.g., KWK 39)

**Langstrecken-:** Long range

**Lehr-:** Instruction (e.g., Lehrgeschwader or Instructional Group)

**Lotfe:** Lotfernrohr (Telescopic bomb sight)

**LS:** Lastensegler (cargo glider)

**LT:** Lufttorpedo (aerial torpedo)

**LTS:** Lufttransportstaffel (Air Transport Squadron)

**Luftwaffenführrungsstab:** Luftwaffe Operations Staff

**Luftwaffengeneralstab:** Luftwaffe Air Staff

**Major:** Equivalent to Squadron Leader (R.A.F.) or Major (U.S.A.F.)

**MG:** Maschinengewehr (Machine gun)

**Mistel:** Lit: Mistletoe. Adopted as generic term for the lower component of all pick-a-back aircraft combinations

**MK:** Maschinenkanone (Machine cannon)

**MW 50:** Methanol-Water mixture (50% methanol, 49·5% water and 0·5% anti-corrosion fluid)

**Nahaufklärungs-:** Short-range reconnaissance

**NJG:** Nachtjagdgeschwader (Night Fighter Group)

**NSGr:** Nachtschlachtgruppe (Night Harassment Wing)

**NRb:** Nacht-Reihenbildkamera (Night automatic aerial camera)

**Ob.d.L.:** Oberbefehlshaber der Luftwaffe (Commander-in-Chief of the Luftwaffe)

**Ob.d.M.:** Oberbefehlslhaber der (Kriegs) Marine (Commander-in-Chief of the Kriegsmarine)

**Oberfeldwebel:** Equivalent to Flight Sergeant (R.A.F.) or Master Sergeant (U.S.A.F.)

**Oberingenieur:** Senior Engineer

**Oberleutnant:** Equivalent to Flying Officer (R.A.F.) or First Lieutenant (U.S.A.F.)

**OKH:** Oberkommando des Heeres (Army High Command)

**OKL:** Oberkommando der Luftwaffe (Luftwaffe High Command)

**OKM:** Oberkommando der Marine (Naval High Command)

**Projekt:** Project

**PaK:** Panzerabwehrkanone (Anti-tank canon)

**Panzerstaffel:** Tank (Destroyer) Squadron

**PC:** Panzerbombe, cylindrisch (Cylindrical armour-piercing bomb)

**Peilgerät:** D/F set

**Pulk:** Luftwaffe term for close formation of U.S.A.F. day bombers.

PV: Periskopvisier (Periscopic sight)
Pz: Panzer (Tank or Armour)

Q-Rohr: Screen for IS/Spanner Anlage (infra-red sighting device)

Rüstsatz: Field Conversion Set
R-Gerät: Rauchgerät (Auxiliary Take-off Assistance Rocket)
R-Stoff: Rocket fuel (known as Tonka) consisting of 57% crude oxide monoxylidene and 43% tri-ethylamine)
Rb: Reihenbildkamera (automatic aerial camera)
Reichs: State-
Reklamefliegerabteilung: Publicity Flying Department
Reklamestaffel: Publicity Squadron
Revi: Reflexvisier (reflector sight)
Ritterkreuz: Knights Cross of the Iron Cross. First of five grades of the higest German decoration for bravery, the higher grades being signified by the addition of Oak Leaves, Oak Leaves and Swords, Diamonds, Oak Leaves and Swords, and Golden Oak Leaves, Diamonds and Swords
RLM: Reichsluftfahrtministerium (State Ministry of Aviation)
Rotte: A pair of aircraft (usually fighters) flying in loose formation
RVM: Reichsverkehrsministerium (State Ministry of Transport)
RWM: Reichswehrministerium (State Ministry of Defence)

SAGr: See-Aufklärungsgruppe (Maritime Reconnaissance Wing)
SC: Splitterbombe, Cylindrisch (Cylindrical fragmentation bomb)
Sch.G.: Schlachtgeschwader (Close Support or Assault Group). Abbreviation "SG" later used
Schlacht-: Close support or assault
Schlepp-: Tow or towing
Schwarm: Section of four fighters
Schnellbomber: Fast bomber
"schräge Musik": Lit: Oblique or Jazz music. Luftwaffe term for fixed weapons firing obliquely upward
SD: Splitterbombe, Dickwand (Thick-walled fragmentation bomb)
Sd.Kdo.: Sonderkommando (Special Detachment)
Seenotdienst: Air-sea Rescue Service
Seenotstaffel: Air-sea Rescue Squadron
Seilschlepp: Cable tow
SG: Sondergerät (Special Equipment), also Schlachtgeschwader (Close Support or Assault Group) and Schleppgerät (towing equipment)
SKG: Schnellkampfgeschwader (Lit: High-speed Battle Group)
Sonder-: Special
Spanner-Anlage: Lit: Boot Tree installation. Name applied to early infra-red night interception aid
S-Stoff: Rocket fuel comprising 90–97% nitric acid and 3–10% sulphuric acid
Stab: Staff
Stabsschwarm: Staff section (in a Gruppe)
Staffel: Equivalent to Squadron (R.A.F.)
Staffelkapitän: Squadron commander (regardless of rank)
Starrschlepp: Rigid tow
St.G.: Sturzkampfgeschwader or Stukageschwader (Dive Bomber Group)
Störkampfstaffel: Night Harassment Squadron
Stuka: Abbrev. of Sturzkampfflugzeug (Dive Bomber)
Sturm-: Assault: (e.g., Sturmgruppe—Assault Wing)
Stuvi: Sturz(kampf)visier (Dive-bombing sight)
SV-Stoff: Rocket fuel (known as Salbei) consisting of 85–88% nitric acid and 12–15% sulphuric acid

T-Stoff: Rocket fuel comprising 80% hydrogen peroxide plus oxyquinoline or phosphate as a stabilizer
Technisches Amt: Technical Office of the RLM
TK: Turbo-Kompressor (Turbo-supercharger)

TL-Strahltriebwerk: Turbo-Lader Strahltriebwerk (Lit: Turbo-compressor jet powerplant—turbojet engine)
Troika-Schlepp: Lit: Triple tow (from the Russian three-horse sleigh, or Troika)

Umbau: Lit: Re-build (reconstruction)
Umrüst-Bausatz: Factory Conversion Set

Versuchs: Experimental
Vierling: Quadruple mounting (e.g., FDL 131V)
Verband, Verbände: Formation, formations
VS: Verstell(luft)schraube (Variable-pitch airscrew)

Waffenprüfplatz: Weapons Proving Ground
WB: Waffenbehälter (Weapon container)
Wfr.Gr.: Werfer-Granate (Rocket-propelled shell)
Wilde Sau: Lit: Wild Sow (usually translated as "Wild Boar"). Applied to method of night interception
WT: Waffentropfen ("Weapon Drop"—a detachable drop-shaped weapon container)
Wüstennotstaffel: Desert (or Wilderness) Rescue Squadron

X-Gerät: Lit: X-Apparatus, an early blind-flying and target approach aid

Y-Gerät: Lit: Y-Apparatus, a blind-flying and range-finding aid

Zwilling: Twin or coupled (e.g., He 111Z, MG 81Z)
Zahme Sau: Lit: Tame Sow (usually translated as "Tame Boar"). Applied to method of night interception
ZG: Zerstörergeschwader (Destroyer or Heavy Fighter Group)
ZFR: Zielfernrohr (Telescopic gunsight) e.g., ZFR 4a

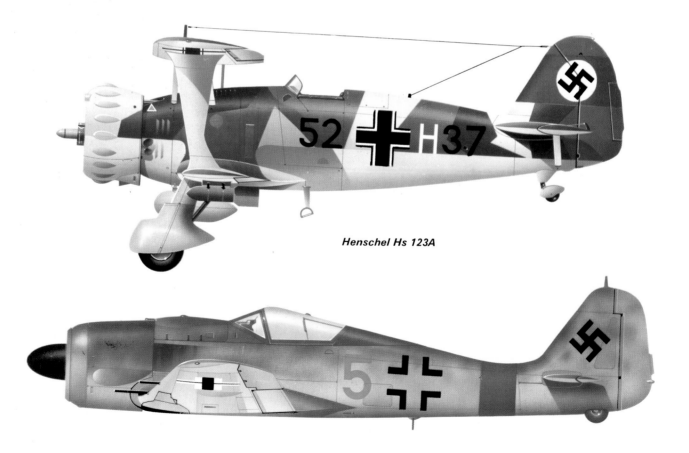

*Henschel Hs 123A*

*Focke-Wulf Fw 190A-8*

# Index

References to pictures are shown in **bold** type.


Adler Tag 21, 22
Aerobatic competitions
rebuilt Bücker Bü 133 *Jungmeister* **140**
Air intelligence
failure before Anzio landings 87; reports on Soviet Air Force 1941 40
Airborne Cigar' RAF R/T jamming 105
Air-borne forces
Fall Gelbe (Plan Yellow) 1940 16, 18; Operation 'Merkur' Crete 1941 36
Air races and competitions
Challenge de Tourisme Internationale 1934 219
Aircraft carriers
convoy defence rôle 70; *Graf Zeppelin* 122, 124, 125, 126, 136, 155, 206; HMS *Ark Royal* 33, 64, 143; HMS *Eagle* 50, 52; HMS *Illustrious* 33; USS *Wasp* 50, 52
Aircraft production
fighter units 1943 93; 1944 98; Milch's reorganization 1941–2 76; shortfall 1941 44
Aircrew training **12**, 76, 93, **123**
Airframe construction
steel tube/sheet/fabric **121**; stressed-skin **123**; Tego-Film wood bonding 172
Ambulance/casevac aircraft
Focke-Wulf Fw 58C *Weihe* **160**
Ammunition
Hexogen A-1 20mm incendiary 98
Anglo-Polish Mutual Assistance Pact 1939 13
Anti-shipping strike forces 30, 64, **84**; *see also* Convoys
Anti-tank armament 78
Arado Ar 65 E & F **9**, **121**
Arado Ar 66 a.b.c., Ar 66 B & C 10, 78, **121**, 179
Arado Ar 67a **123**
Arado Ar 68E **122**
Arado Ar 68G **122**, 185
Arado Ar 76A **123**
Arado Ar 80.V1, 2 & 3 **123**, 185
Arado Ar 81.V1, 2 & 3 **123**
Arado Ar 95 A1 **124**
Arado Ar 96A-1, Ar 96B-2 and Ar 396 **124**
Arado Ar 195.V1, 2 & 3 **125**, 155
Arado Ar 196.A1-A5 **69**, **126**, 160
Arado Ar 197.V1, 2 & 3 **126**
Arado Ar 198.V1 **127**
Arado Ar 199.V1 & 2 **127**
Arado Ar 231.V1–V6 **130**
Arado Ar 232 A & B series **130**
Arado Ar 234 B-1 and B-2 *Blitz* 116, **128–130**, **140**
Arado Ar 240 A, B & C, Ar 440 **131**
Arado Ar 340 169
Ardennes Offensive Dec/44
effect of weather on operations 114
Army co-operation aircraft
Arado Ar 198.V1 **127**; Blohm und Voss Bv 141 A & B series **135**; equipment 1939 13; Fieseler Fi 156 *Storch* **156–7**, 240; Fw 186 autogiro **160**; Heinkel He 46 a to f **175**, 196; Henschel Hs 122 B-0 **196**, 199; Henschel Hs 126 A & B 13, **35**, **41**, **49**, 127, **199**; Siebel Si 201 V1 & 2 **240**
Autogiros
Focke-Wulf Fw 186 **160**
Avro Lancaster Mk 1 **90**, **94** 102

Bachem Ba 349 *Natter* V1 to V16, A and B Ser. **132**
Badges and emblems **177**
Balkans and Greece
Operation 'Marita' 33
Battle of Britain
bomber attacks on cities 24; Luftwaffe bombers vulnerability 22, **26**; preliminary Channel actions 21–22
Battle of the Atlantic
Focke-Wulf Fw 200 *Condor* operations 66
Bell X-5 (Messerschmitt P.1101) 238
Blackburn Skua carrier-borne fighter 143
Blitzkrieg
failure in Russia 1942 46
Blohm und Voss Bv 40.V1–V19, Bv 40A **138**
Blohm und Voss Bv 138 A-1 B-1, C-1 **64**, **134**
Blohm und Voss Bv 141 A & B series 127, **135**
Blohm und Voss Bv 142.V1-V4 **136**
Blohm und Voss Bv 144.V1 133, **136**
Blohm und Voss Bv 155 A & B.V1-V3 **136**
Blohm und Voss Bv 222 *Wiking* 133, **137**
Blohm und Voss Bv 238.V1 **139**
Blohm und Voss Ha 137 V1 to V6 **133**
Blohm und Voss Ha 139 V1-V3 (rebuilt as B/U & B/MS) **133**
Blohm und Voss Ha 140 V1 to V3 **133**
Boeing B-17 Fortress 62, 90, **91**, **92**, **93**
Bomb sights
Lotfe 7D (Fw 200C-3/U2) **75**; Norden (U.S.) 90
Bomber Geschwader (Kampfgeschwader)
KG2.•Do 172 **30**; KG4 mine laying operations 66; KG26 anti-shipping rôle 64; KG26 Y-Gerät, He 111 H-4's 29; KG30 anti-shipping rôle 64, 86; KG100 28, 29, 148; KG152 **11**; KG253 **11**
Bomber groups (Kampfgruppen)
equipment 1939 13; Western dispositions May/41 30
Bombers
Arado Ar 234 B-2 *Blitz* 116, **128–130**; defensive armament of U.S. formations 96; Dornier Do 11a, C and D **142**; Dornier Do 17 E-1 **144**; Dornier Do 17 P-1 13, **18**, **144**; Dornier Do 17Z and Do 215 11, **22**, **30**, **39**, **45**, **145**; Dornier Do 19 11, 146; Dornier Do 23 G **10**, **147**; Dornier Do 217 E, K & M **62**, **65**, 69, 74, **149**, **151**; Dornier Do 317. V1, V2 and B **148**; Focke-Wulf Fw 191 **169**; Heinkel He 45 **175**; Heinkel He 111 10, 11, 12, 13, **21**, **30**, 64, **85**, **115**; A-0, B-2, D-1 **182**; E-3 **184**; F-4 **182**; H-1 **26**, **181**, **184**; H-3 **184**; H-6 (torp) **181**, 184; H-8 181; H-16 **184**; H-22 **115**, **181**; J-1 182; P-0 13, **15**, **180**; P-1 **183**; P-2 64, **184**; Heinkel He 119 V5-8 **187**; Heinkel He 170 A-01 **178**; E-1 **179**; Heinkel He 177 Greif 11, 72, 77, 94, **190**, 192; Heinkel He 270 V1 **179**; Heinkel He 274 **192**; Heinkel He 277.B-5/R2 (B-7) **193**; Henschel Hs 127 **198**; Henschel Hs 130C 201; Junkers Ju 52/3m g3e 10, **11**, 12, **202–203**; Junkers Ju 86 D, E, G & K 10, **18**, **204**; Junkers Ju 88 11, 13, **21**, 26, **49**, 86, 210; Junkers Ju 88 A1, 4 & 5 210; Junkers Ju 89 V1 11, **212**; Junkers Ju 188 94, 210, 218; A-2, C, E-1, G-0 **213**; Junkers Ju 287 **214**; Junkers Ju 288 77; A(V1), (V5), (V8), (V11), (V14) and C (V103) **215**; Junkers Ju 388K 218; Junkers Ju 390.V1-V2 **218**; Junkers Ju 488 V401-406 **218**; Messerschmitt Bf 162 V1-3 **236**; Messerschmitt Me 262A-2a *Sturmvogel* 231, **233**, **234**, 235; A-2a/U2 **233**, **235**; Messerschmitt Me 264 V1 **237**; vulnerability over Dunkirk 18
Bombing
Allied 'Pointblank' objectives 1943 91; B-17E daylight raids 1942 62; 1943/4 96, 98; incendiary attacks by night 29; long-range force, Italy, Sep./44 86; L. bomber arm attrition 1943–4 88; night attacks on Britain 1940- 26; RAF tactics & equipment 1943 102; strategic bomber force 1944 81; U.S. long-range fighter escorts 94, 98
Bombs
SC250 **78**, **165**, **233**; SC500 **78**, **165**
Boulton and Paul Defiant 29
Bristol Beaufighter 29, 72, 73
Bristol Beaufighter V1
night intruder operations 105
Bristol Blenheim IV
'circus' ops. N. France 1941 62
Bücker Bü 131 *Jungmann* **139**
Bücker Bü 133 *Jungmeister* **12**, **140**
Bücker Bü 181 A & D *Bestmann* 140

Cannon
Mauser MG 151/20 96, 105; Rheinmetall MG 151 15mm 40, 100; Rheinmetall MG FF 20mm 13, 96, 105, **211**; Rheinmetall MK 108 30mm 98, 100, 105; Rheinmetall Flak 18 (Bk 3.7) 37mm 78, **82**; Rheinmetall Flak (BK 5) 50mm **232**; Rheinmetall M MG 75mm 78
Caproni 314's for NS Gr 9 88
Carrier-based fighters
Arado Ar 197-V3 **126**
Catapult aircraft 126, **127**, 237
Civil airline companies, training & organization functions 8
Cockpit layout
Dornier Do 18D **143**
Combined operations
Operation Weserübung 1940 16
Communications aircraft
Focke-Wulf Fw 58 Weihe **87**; Messerschmitt Bf 108 *Taifun* **219**
Consolidated B-24 Liberator 62, **91**, **92**, 93
Convoys
attacks on Arctic convoys 70; Axis convoys to N. Africa 1942 49; Malta actions 1942 50, 52; missile attacks 1943 75
'Corona' RAF R/T hoax 105
Crete
Operation 'Merkur' 35
Curtis Tomahawk II 38

Defensively equipped merchant ships (DEMS) 69
De Havilland Mosquito B Mk IV, XVI 72, 94, **95**, 98, 106
Designers
Andersson, Anders J. **139**; Bachem, Erich **132**; Blume, Walter **123**, **124**; Büsemann swept wing research 238; Degl Dipl. Ing. 239; Focke, H Heinrich 160; Gunter, Walter and Siegfried **178**, **180**; Hertel *Prof.* 236; Horten, Walter and Reimar **173**; Jacobs, Hans **142**; Kalkert, Albert **174**; Kösel, E. 169; Kraft Dipl. Ing. 218; Kupper, A. 173; Lippisch, *Dr.* Alexander 227; Nicolaus, Friedrich **196**, 200; Rethel, Walter **121**; Tank, Kurt 158, 159, 166; Vogt, Richard **133**, **134**, **135**, **136**, **138**, 238; Wocke Dipl. Ing. 214; Zindel Dipl. Ing. 204, 212
Deutsche Lufthansa
bomber prototype transports 10; B & V Bv 142 trans-Atlantic mailplane **136**; B & V Bv 144 project **136**; Bv 222 flying boat **137**; Blohm und Voss Ha 139 trans-Atlantic service **133**; Do 17 rejected as transport 144; Focke-Wulf Fw 200 record flights 170; formation & development 1926–9; Heinkel He 116A mail carriers **186**; Junkers Ju 52/3m **202**, 214; Junkers Ju 90.S 216
Deutscher Luftsportverband 10
Deutsches Forschungsinstitut für Segelflugzeug (DFS)
DFS 194 tailless rocket aircraft 228; DFS 228 V1, V2 & A Ser. 331 V1 **140**, **142**; DFS 230 A-1, B-1, C-1, F-1 18, **141**, 238; DFS 331 V1 **142**
Dilley *Oberleutnant* Bruno 14
Dive bombers (Sturzkampfflugzeug)
Arado Ar 81 **123**; Blohm und Voss Ha 137 V1 to V6 **133**; Fieseler Fi 98 **154**; Heinkel He 50 **175**; Heinkel He 118 V1 **187**; Henschel Hs 123 11, 12, 154, **197**; Henschel Hs 132 V1 **198**; Junkers Ju 87 11, **36**, 123, 197, 200; A 12; B-1 13, **16**, **18**, **22**, **77**; B-2 **205**, **206**; -2 trop **205**; D-1 trop **205**; D-3 78, 94, 206; D-8 **80**, **207**; G-1 **18**, **82**, 205, **206**; Junkers Ju 88 V1 **210**; A-1 **210**; A-3 **208**; A-6/U **210**; A-14 211; A-15 & 17 **210**; B-0 210; H-1 **210**; S-1 **209**; Messerschmitt Me 309 B-1 (projected) 237
Dornier *Dr. Ing.* Claudius 8
Dornier Do 11a, C and D **142**
Dornier Do 15 *Wal* 33, **146**
Dornier Do 17 E, F, K & P, 13, **18**, 60, **144**
Dornier Do 17 Z-1 and -2, and Do 215 A-1, B-1 and B-5 11, 12, **22**, **30**, **39**, **45**, 64, **145**
Dornier Do 18 D, G, H, N 64, **143**
Dornier Do 19 V1 and V2 11, **146**, 212
Dornier Do 22 K and L **146**
Dornier Do 23 F & G **10**, **147**
Dornier Do 24 K-2 **147**
Dornier Do 24 T **147**
Dornier Do 26 V1 to V6 (26D) **148**
Dornier Do 214 and 216 **148**
Dornier Do 215 B-5 60
Dornier Do 217 E-2, K-2, M-1, J-2/N-2, P-1 **62**, **65**, 69, 70, 74, 102, **142**, **149**
Dornier Do 231 153
Dornier Do 317 V1, V2 and B **148**, 169
Dornier Do 335 A-1 and A-6 Pfeil and Do 635 94, **113**, **152–3**
Dornier Do 435 153
Douglas Boston 111A 62, **90**
Douglas Havoc 1 **95**

Engines
Argus As Panther 175; Argus As 8-B 140hp 179; Argus As 10C 240hp A-8 air cooled 121, 123, 124, 156–7, 158, 160, 172, 173, 180, 196, 198, 219, 240; Argus As 410 A-1 A-12 air cooled 161, 200, 240; Argus As 410C A-12 air cooled 127; Argus As 411 600hp A-12 air cooled 240; Argus 109–014 pulsejet 155, 173, 193, 237; Bloch 175 for Me 323 V-1 239; BMW 003A-1 turbojet 198, 214, 234; BMW 003E-1 turbojet 194; BMW 003R turbojet 234; BMW V1 660hp V-12 water cooled 176, 178, 202; BMW V1 7.3 750hp V-12 water cooled 121, 122, 144, 146, 147, 175, 178; BMW 132 720hp 9 cylinder radial P & W derivative 132, 202; 132-A3 650hp 154, 202, 212; 132-DC 880hp 122, 124, 160, 196, 197, 199; 132-H 880hp 136, 204; 132-K 960hp 126, 133, 185, 186; 132-M 880hp 125; 132-N 960hp 135, 144, 186; 132-T 830hp 202; BMW 139 216; BMW 301R (prev. 323Q3 Fafrir) 1000hp 159; BMW 718 rocket motor 234; BMW 801-A 1580hp radial 149, 215; -D 1700hp 149, 164, 169, 208, 216, 237; -E 1970hp 216, 218; -G2 1700hp 208, 213, 237; -M1 18 cyl 1580hp 149; -MA 1600hp 14 cyl 130; TJ 1890 218; BMW-Bramo Fafnir 323-A 9 cyl radial 127, 145, 199; R-2 130, 136, 147, 170, 217; BMW-Bramo Sh 14A 160hp radial 158; Bristol 925hp 202; Bristol Mercury XIX 905hp radial 204; Bristol (PZL) Pegasus 202; Daimler-Benz DB 600A 960hp A-12 liquid cooled 212, 225; Aa 1000hp 219, 236; C 910hp 126, 159, 187; D 198; Daimler-Benz 601-A and variants A-12 liquid cooled 40, 131, 145, 155, 169, 178, 180, 181, 201, 219, 224, 230, 237; ARJ 2300hp special 227; Daimler-Benz 603A with TKL turbocharger 136, 148, 149, 190, 192, 193, 201; E-1, 152–3; G 1900hp, 190, 191, 227, 230; Daimler-Benz DB 605 A1-D 1475hp-1800hp 98, 219- B 1475hp 224, 237; T 149, 169, 201; Daimler-Benz DB 606 A/B double engines 187, 236; Daimler-Benz DB 610 A-1/B-1 double engines 148, 169, 187, 188–9, 236; Daimler-Benz DB 613A double engines; Daimler-Benz DB 627 2000hp 227; Daimler-Benz DB 628 169; ENMASA Beta E-9C 750hp 202; Gnome-Rhône 14K 175, 178; M4/5 700hp 14 cyl radial 174, 200; N 48/49 1140hp 238; R 1320hp; Heinkel HeS 8A Centrifugal jet 193; Heinkel HeS 3b turbojet 187, 192; Heinkel-Hirth 109-011 turbojet 238; Hirth HM60R 80hp 139, 173; Hirth HM501 160hp 130; Hirth HM504 A-2 105hp 139, 140; Hirth HM506 160hp 140; Hispano-Suiza 12 Ybrs 860hp V-12 146; Z-89 219; Jumo V diesel 137, 202; Junkers Jumo 004A turbojet 193, 198, 214; Junkers Jumo 004B turbojet 173, 231, 238; Junkers Jumo 204D 240; Junkers Jumo 205C 600hp diesel 133, 143, 204; D 880hp 134, 143, 148; Junkers L-5 310hp 212; Jumo 206 202; Junkers-Jumo 207 A-1 204; B-3V turbo-charged 204; C 980hp 137; Junkers-Jumo 210C A-12 cylinder water-cooled 123, 133, 161, 196, 205; D 635hp 219; Da 680hp 122, 159, 161,

159, 161, 185; two-stage turbocharger 201; Junkers Jumo 211A 1075hp A-12 cylinders liquid cooled 212; D-2 180; Da 205; F 1350hp 214, 219, 239; J1 205, 206, 208, 237; N 169, 172; Junkers Jumo 213 A-1 1776hp A-12 cylinder liquid cooled 164, 172, 213; E 1750hp 218; E-1 1880hp 164, 172, 192, 208, 213, 227; F 193; Junkers Jumo 222 169, 192; A-1/B-1 2500hp 215; A-3/B-3 2500hp 218; Junkers-Jumo 610A 610hp A-12 159; Orkan E-2 single-shaft turbojet 194; power boosting GM1 & MW50 98; TKL 136, 201, 204; Rolls-Royce Buzzard 187; Rolls-Royce Kestrel VI 525hp V-12 water cooled 123, 133, 196, 205; Rolls-Royce Merlin 500-45 1400hp 219; Shevtsov M-82 1570hp radial 46; Siemens (Bramo) 323 H-2 Fafrir 146; Siemens (Bramo) Sh 14A-4 160hp radial 140, 179; Siemens (Bramo) Sh 22B-2 650hp radial 142, 175, 196, 213; Walter HWK 109-509 3630lbs thrust rocket motor 142; A-2 227; C-1 4410lbs thrust 132; C-4 236; Walter HWK R1-203 liquid-propellant rocket 187; Walter HWK R11-211/3 rocket 234; Walter 298lb thrust research motor in He 72 B-1 179; Wright Cyclone 710hp 202
Exports by German aircraft industry 139, 140, 144, 146, 147, 175, 185, 186, 212

Fairey Fulmar fighters RN 33, 49

Fairey Swordfish torpedo/ reconnaissance RN 62
Falck, *Maj.* Wolfgang 58
Fall Gelbe (Plan Yellow) 16
Fieseler Fi 98a **154**
Fieseler Fi 103 in four Reichenberg series **155**
Fieseler Fi 156 A, C, D, E *Storch* and Fi 256 **156–7** 240
Fieseler Fi 167 V1 and A-0 series 124, **155**
Fighter aces ('Experten') 38, 42, 55, 56, 60, 98, **100**, 102, 105
Fighter Geschwader (Jagdgeschwader)
JG2 **12**, 62, **121**; JG 26 operations from France 1941–43 62; JG 27 pilots, N. Afrika/41 38; JG 51 Bf 109 F-1s. Feb/41 61; JG 51 Fw 190A's Leningrad/43 46; JG 132 *see* JG 2; JG 300 night fighting ops. 1943 105
Fighter groups (Jagdgruppen) dispositions in the west 1943 96; equipment 1939 13; 1941–1943 61–63
Fighter pilot schools (Jagdfliegerschulen) **12**, 76, **122**, **123**, **158**
Fighter pilots 76, **98**, **100**, 110
Fighter training wing (JSG) aircraft
Arado Ar 96 B-6 **124**
Fighter/bombers (Zerstörer) 13
Focke-Wulf Fw 57 **159**, 198; Focke-Wulf Fw 190 **55**, **59**, 62, **78**, **164–168**; Görings directive Oct 1940 25; Gotha Go 229 **173**; Henschel Hs 124 V1, V3 159, **196**; Junkers Ju 88 C-6 73; 88V 210; Luftwaffe tactics Oct/40 25; Messerschmitt Bf 109 E & F 25, 62; Messerschmitt Bf 110 D, E 13, **22**, 26, **52**, **56**, **225**, **226**; Messerschmitt Bf 162 198; Messerschmitt Me 310 high altitude 230; Messerschmitt Me 328 V1 ser B **327**; *see also* Ground attack aircraft
Fighter tactics
aerial bombing against U.S. formations 96; Luftwaffe 'Rotte' & 'Schwarm' formations 12, 242; R.A.F. revisions July/40 22; Sturmstaffeln 'Company Front' 100, 101
Fighters
Arado Ar 65 **121**; Arado Ar 67 **123**; Arado Ar 68 E, F-1 **122**, 185; Arado Ar 76 **123**; Arado Ar 80 **123**; Arado Ar 240 and Ar 440 *Zerstörer*; armament 1934 10; 1939 13; 1940 40; 1943 97, 98; 1944 100; Blohm und Voss Bv 155 **136**; Defence of the Reich, dispositions June/44 101; Dornier Do 335 A1 **113**, **152–3**; Focke-Wulf Fw 159 **159**, 185; Focke-Wulf Fw 187 *Falke* **161**; Heinkel He 51 A1, B 10, 12, **176**, 185; Heinkel He 100 D-1 and D-1c **181**; Heinkel He 112 B-0, B-1 159, 181, **185**; Heinkel He 162 A-2 *Salamander* **116**, **194–196**; Heinkel He 280 V1 to V8 77, **193**, 194; Junkers Ju 248 (Me 263A) **236**; Messerschmitt Bf 109 **97**; V-1 proto. 220; B-1 223; D-1 **219**, **223**; E **11**; E-4/B **44**; E-4/Trop **52**; E-7/Trop **39**; F 42; F-2/Trop 109, **222**, **223**; F-4 **60**; F-4/Trop **223**; F-5 **222**; G-2 **42**; G-4 **221**; G-5 **222**; H-1 high alt. **220**; K-4 **222**; Messerschmitt Bf 110 D3 11, 224, **226**; Messerschmitt Me 163 B-1 Komet **116**, **227–229**; D 236; Messerschmitt Me 209-11H high altitude 227; A1-V5 **227**; Messerschmitt Me 210 A-1 77, 226, **230**; Messerschmitt Me 262 A-1a *Schwalbe* 77, **109**, 113, 116, **231–234**; C-1a and 2b rocket boost 94, **234**; Messerschmitt Me 263A **236**; Messerschmitt Me 309 V1 & 2 **237**; Messerschmitt Me 410 A-1 *Hornisse* **230**; Messerschmitt P.1101 V1 **238**; Me 109/Spitfire encounters 18, 112
Fighters (night)
armament 105; Bristol Beaufighter 1F 29; Defence of the Reich, dispositions June/44 106; Dornier Do 172-10 *Kauz II* 58; Dornier Do 215 B-5 60; Dornier Do 217 J.N. 60, **62**, 102, **149**, **151**; Dornier Do 335 A6 **154**; Focke-Wulf Ta 154 *Moskito* **172**, 187; Heinkel He 219 *Uhu* 94; A-5/R1 **106**, **192**; A-5/R2 **190**; A-5/R4 **192**; A-7/R4 **192**; C-1 **191**; C-2 **190**; Junkers Ju 88 C-6, G-7a.b.c. 58, 60, 102, **106**, **208–209**, **210**; Junkers Ju 388 J-1 (V4) **218**; Messerschmitt Bf 110 E, F, G, & H 58, 60, 102, **103**, 105, **224**, **225**, **226**; Messerschmitt Me 262B-1a 231, **234**; Messerschmitt Me 410 A-2/U2 230
FLAK (Fliegerabwehrkanone) 10, 13
scores against U.S. daylight raiders 98
Flettner F1 282 *Kolibri* **158**
Fliegerdivision
position in Luftflotte 242
Fliegerführer (localised command)
position in Luftflotte 242
Fliegerführer Afrika composition and actions 1941 32, 38, 48; composition Jan/42 48
Fliegerführer Atlantik disposition & operations 1941/3 30, 67, 69, 74, 75, 108
Fliegerführer Tunisien composition Nov/42 56
Fliegerkorps
composition Fl.kps II 1942 48; disposition of Fl.kps X Jan/41 33; Flkps VIII ground-attack formation 12; Flkps IX and X antishipping forces 30; Operation 'Merkur' Flkps XI 35; Operation Weserübung 1940 15; operations in the South Flkps VIII 44–46; position in Luftflotte 242
Flying and gliding clubs training function 8
Flying boats
Blohm und Voss Bv 138 **64**; Blohm und Voss Bv 222 *Wiking* **137**; Dornier Do 15 *Wal* **146**; Dornier Do 18 64, **143**; Dornier Do 24 **147**; Dornier Do 26 **148**; Dornier Do 214 **148**
Focke, Heinrich 8
Focke Achgelis Fa 223 *Drache* **159**
Focke Achgelis Fa 266 *Hornisse* 159
Focke-Wulf Fw 44 10, 179
Focke-Wulf Fw 56 A-1 *Stösser* 9, 123, **158**, 180, 198, 241
Focke-Wulf Fw 57 V1 to V3 **159**, 198
Focke-Wulf Fw 58 B and C *Weihe* **87**, **160**
Focke-Wulf Fw 62 V1 and V2 **160**
Focke-Wulf Fw 159 V1, 2 and 3 **159**, 185
Focke-Wulf Fw 186 V1 auto auto giro **160**
Focke-Wulf Fw 187 V1 to V6 and A0 *Falke* **161**
Focke-Wulf Fw 189 A-1, 2 and 3 *Uhu* 127, **161–163**, 199
Focke-Wulf Fw 190 A series, D series, F series and Ta 152H 46, **55**, **58**, 62, **78**, 94, **97**, 108, **164–168**; A-2 **168**, **169**; A-3 **166–169**; A-4 **58**, **97**, **168**, **169**, A-4/U1 **166**; A-5/U3 **78**, **165**; A-8 **168**; D-9 **167**; F-8 **55**, **164**; G-3 **168**; Ta 152H-0 167; C-0/R11 168
Focke-Wulf Fw 191 V1 to V6, 191 A, B and C **169**, 213
Focke-Wulf Fw 200 C-0 to C-8
*Condor* 46, 65, **66–67**, **69**, 74, **75**, **170–171**; C-3 67, 171; C-3U/1 69; C-3U/2 **75**; C-8 **171**; C-8U/10 **170**
Focke-Wulf Ta 152 (redesignated Fw 190 D series) 94, **111**, **166–168**
Focke-Wulf Ta 154 V1 to V15, A and C series *Moskito* **172**, 196

Galland, *Oberst.* Adolf **26**, 62, 84, 100
Geisler *Genlt.* Hans 15, 33 anti-shipping strike force 64; Flkps X Mediterranean area of ops. 33; Flkps X Weserübung operations 15
Geschwader 242
Glider tugs
Bücker Bü 181 *Bestmann* **140**; Heinkel He 111Z *Zwilling* **238**, 239; Junkers Ju 52 18; Junkers Ju 90 217; Messerschmitt Bf 110 239
Gliders
Bv 40.V1 point-defence interceptor **138**; DFS 230 A-1, B-1, C-1, F-1 18, **141**, 238; DFS 231 **142**; Gotha Go 242 **174**; Gotha Go 345 **173**; Gotha-Kalkert Ka 430 **174**; Junkers Ju 322 *Mammut* **217**, 238; Messerschmitt Me 321 A & B **238–239**; operations, Fall Gelbe 1940 16, 18; Operation 'Merkur' Crete 1941 35
Gliding torpedoes
L10 Friedensengel (Me 410 B5) 230
Gloster Gladiator fighter 33
Göring, Hermann 10, 18, 22, 29, 64, 70, 101
'Golden Zange' *see* Torpedo/bombers: convoy attack tactics
Gotha 60 145 A, B and C **172**, 179
Gotha Go 147 a and b **173**
Gotha Go 229 Horten research aircraft and Ho IX VI to V3 (Go 229 A-0) **173**; Ho IX V2 173
Gotha Go 242 A, B and C, Go 244B and Ka 430 **174**; A-0, B-1 **174**
Gotha Go 345 A and B **173**
Gotha-Kalkert Ka 430 A-0 **174**
Greim *Genmaj.* Robert Ritter von
Luftflotte 6 Poland Dec/44 112; Luftwaffenkommando Ost. June/43 80
Ground-attack
Legion Condor experience, Spain 1937 12; Stukageschwader become Schlachtgeschwader 1944 82
Ground attack aircraft
Arado Ar 66 (Störkampfstaffeln) 78, **121**; Blohm und Voss Ha 137 V1 to V6 **133**; Bücker Bü 131 *Jungmann* (Störkampstaffeln) **139**; Gotha Go 145 (Störkampfstaffeln) **172**; Heinkel He 45 (Störkampfstaffeln) 78, **175**; Heinkel He 46 (Störkampfstaffeln) 78, **175**; Heinkel He 50 bCH (Störkampfstaffeln) 175; Heinkel He 51 C1 12, 176; Henschel Hs 123 A-1 154, **197**; Henschel Hs 126 A and B (Nachtschlacht) 199; Henschel Hs 129 B **50**, 77, **78**, **200**; improvisation E. Front Feb/43 78; Junkers Ju 87 12, 78, **82**, 123, 197, 200, **205–207**; Junkers Ju 88 P-1 78, **208**, **211**; Messerschmitt Bf 110 D 224, **226**
Ground Control Interception (GCI)
Luftwaffe organization 1941 58; 1943/4 97; RAF organization 1940 20, 28; *see also* Night fighting systems
Grumman Wildcat, carrier-borne fighter 72
Gruppe
command and tactical status 242
Gun sights
Revi C 12/D, 16B 105
Gun turrets
HDL 151 (Fw 200 C-8) **171**

Handley Page Halifax Mk III 94, **95**, 102
Handley Page Manchester bomber 60
Harlinghausen *Genmaj.* Martin Fliegerführer Atlantik 1941 67; Fliegerführer Tunisien 1943 56; Fliegerkorps X antishipping units 64, 84; Luftwaffe Torpedo Training School, Grosseto 69
Hawker Hurricane
Battle of Britain 20; Battle for France 18; Malta 1941 33, 1942 49; N. Africa 33; RN convoy protection 72
Hawker Tempest V 112
Heavy strategic fighters *see* Fighter/bombers
Heinkel, Ernst 8
Heinkel He 45 a.b.c.d and e 10, 78, **175**
Heinkel He 46 a to f plus licensed variants 10, 78, 127, **175**, 196
Heinkel He 50 aW, aL, bL (later redesignated 50A) aCH and bCH (B) **175**
Heinkel He 51 A-1, B-2 and C-1 **9**, 10, **12**, 121, **176**, 185; A-1 **9**, **176**; B-1 **176**; C-1 **176**
Heinkel He 59 C, D, E and N 64, **176**
Heinkel He 60 a and B, A, B, C, D and E 126, 160, **178**, 185
Heinkel He 70, He 170 and He 270 **178–9**, 180, 185
Heinkel He 72 A and B *Kadett* and 172 **179**
Heinkel He 74 a, b and B **180**
Heinkel He 100 V1 to V8, and 100 D-1 **181**
Heinkel He 111 B series, E series, H series and P series 10, 11, 12, 13, **15**, **16**, **21**, **26**, **28**, **30**, 64, **85**, **115**, **180–184**
Heinkel 111Z *Zwilling* glider tub **182**
Heinkel He 112 B-0 and B-1 159, 181, **185**
Heinkel He 114 V1 to V9, A, B and C series 160, **185**
Heinkel He 115 B, C, D and E 64, 65, **72**, 133, **186**
Heinkel He 116 V1 to V8 A, B and R **186**
Heinkel He 118 V1 to V5 and A0 **187**
Heinkel He 119 V1 to V8 **187**
Heinkel He 162 A-2 *Salamander* **109**, **116**, **194–196**
Heinkel He 176 V1 **187**, 227
Heinkel He 177 *Greif* 11, 72, 74, 77, 94, **188–189**, 192
Heinkel He 178 V1 and V2 190, 192, 194
Heinkel He 219 A-0 to A-7, B and C series 94, **106**, **190–192**
Heinkel He 274 V1 and V2 **192**
Heinkel He 277 V1 to V3, B-5, B-6 and B-7 series **193**
Heinkel He 280 C1 to V8 77, 190, **193**, 194
Helicopters
Flettner F1 282 *Kolibri* **158**; Focke Achgelis Fa 223 *Drache* **159**; Fa 266 *Hornisse* 159
Henschel Hs 121a **196**, 198
Henschel Hs 122 a, b, V3 and B-0 **196**, 199
Henschel Hs 123 A-1 **9**, 11, 12, **14**, 154, **197**
Henschel Hs 124 V1 to V3 159, **196**
Henschel Hs 125a (V1) and b **198**
Henschel Hs 126 A and B 13, **35**, **41**, **49**, 127, **199**
Henschel Hs 127 V1 and V2 **198**
Henschel Hs 128 V1 and V2 201, 212
Henschel Hs 129 A and B series **50**, 77, **78**, **200**
Henschel Hs 130 V1 and V2, Hs 130 A-series, B, C-series, D, E-series and F **201**, 212
Henschel Hs 132 V1, V2 and A, B and C **198**
Hitler, Adolf
Ardennes offensive 1944 113; Chancellor & Supreme Commander 10; Directive No 6 for Fall Gelbe 16; foreign policy 1934 10; long term plans for 'Barbarossa' 40; Operation Seelöwe postponed 25; strategy in Russia, summer/42 44
Hubertus project Sep/43 218

Ilyushin I1 2 bomber 41
'Italluft'
Gen von Pohl's liaison mission Italy/40 32

Jafü (Fighter commander) 242
Jagddivision
position in Luftflotte 242
Jagdfliegerführer
position in Luftflotte 242
Jagdkorps
position in Luftflotte 242
Junkers, *Prof.* Hugo 8
Junkers Ju 49 212
Junkers Ju 52/3m many versions; data for 3mg5e to 3mg14e 10, **11**, 12, 13, **55**, **74**, **82**, **88**, **202–203**
Junkers Ju 86 D, E, G, K, P and R 10; Ju 86 ab1 (V1), A-1, D-1, E-2 **204**; Ju 86 G-1 **18**, **204**; P-1 **204**
Junkers Ju 87A, B and D series 11, 12, 13, **16**, **18**, **22**, **41**, **77**, 78, **80**, **82**, 94, 123, 197, 200, **205–207**
Junkers Ju 88 many versions: data for Ju 88 A-4, C-6, G-7, S-1 11, 13, **21**, 26, **49**, 60, 64, 69, 78, **84**, **86**, 102, 106, **208–211**, 241
Junkers Ju 89 V1 and V2 11, **212**, 216
Junkers Ju 90 airliner **216**
Junkers Ju 187 206
Junkers Ju 188 A, D and E series 75, 94, 210, **213**
Junkers Ju 248 228, **236**
Junkers Ju 252 V1 to V15 and A-1 **214**, 217
Junkers Ju 287 V1 to V3 and A-0 **214**
Junkers Ju 288 A(V1-V7) B (V9-V14) C (V101-V108) 77, 213, **215**
Junkers Ju 290 A1-8, B1, 2 and C 75, **216**
Junkers Ju 322 V1 and V2 *Mammut* glider **217**
Junkers Ju 352 V1-12 & A series *Herkules* 215, **217**
Junkers Ju 388 L, J and K series 210, 213, **218**
Junkers Ju 390 V1 to V3 & A1 **218**
Junkers Ju 488 V401–406 **218**
Junkers Ju EF61 V1 and V2 **212**
Junkers W34 W33 variants and W34 variants **212**

Kammhuber, *General major* Josef 58
Keitel *Gen.* Wilhelm Chief of OKW 10
Keller *Gen maj* Alfred Luftflotte 1 Operation 'Barbarossa' 1941 40
Kesselring *Genfm.* Albert 8; Luftflotte 2 Battle of Britain 20; Operation 'Barbarossa' 1941 40, 42; redepolyment Sicily Dec/41 44, 48; Luftflotte 4 Poland 1939 14; C in C Mediterranean 1943 84
Kette (flight of three aircraft) 75, 242
Klemm K1 35 (*Mistel* project) 241
'Knickebein', radio navigation aid 28
Kommando Nowotry (Me 262) 112, **231**
Küstenfliegergruppen 64, 66

Landing gear
multi-wheel 'high flotation' **130**; retractable **142**, **159**, 204; single Strut cantilever **122**, **123**; ski **139**, **203**; skids **116**, **130**, **227–229**, **237**; tricycle **152–154**
Lavochkin La-5 fighter 46, 80
Lavochkin La-7 fighter 108
Legion Kondor **11**, 12, 124
Lindbergh, Charles **12**
Lockheed P-38 Lightning 88, 94, 98
Long range record designs
Messerschmitt Me 261 *Adolfine* **236**
Löhr, *Gen maj* Alois
Luftflotte 1 Poland 1939 14; Luftflotte 4 Operation 'Barbarossa' 1941 40; Operation 'Marita' Apl/41 33

Lörzer, *Gen.* Bruno 14
Fliegerkorps II Fall Gelbe
1940 16
Luftflotten
Battle of Britain 20;
campaign in the South 1942
44–46; composition
Operation 'Taifun' 1941 42;
definition of Luftflotten 242;
dispositions 1939 14; Fall
Gelbe 1940 16; final phase,
E. Front 111–112, 116;
Göring's plan for attacks on
England 29; losses sustained
July-Oct 1940 26;
Luftflotte 1 Feb/43 78;
Luftflotte 2 May/42 48–52;
Nov/42 55; Sicily/43 85;
Luftflotte 3 Apl/42 62;
June/44 108; Luftflotte 5
diversionary raids Op.
Seelöwe 20, 22; Operation
'Barbarossa' opening phases
40; Operation 'Marita' Apl/
41 33; Operation
'Weserübung' 1940 15;
Luftwaffe Reich day-fighter
units 1944 98, 112
Luftwaffe
aircrew shortage 1943/4 85,
109; anti-shipping units 30,
64–75; Balkans and Greece
Apl/41 30, 33; battle for
France 1940 16–18; chain
of command 242; disposition
Fall Gelbe 1940 16; E. Front
improvisations & transfers
1944 111; effects of allied
bombing 1943–4 94; fighter
tactics & formations 12;
FLAK (Fliegerabwehr-
kanone) arm 10; Flieger-
führer Afrika June/41–
Oct/42 38, 55; fuel stocks
1943–4 94, 106, 110, 112;
Luftwaffenbefchlshaber
Mitte 1943, 60, 92;
manpower 1939 13;
manpower and materials
1942 76; Mediterranean
commitments 1941 32;
modernisation & expansion
1934 10; night bomber
offensive 1940/1 28; night
fighter organization 1941
58–60; Norwegian
campaign 1940 15-16, 64;
Officer and NCO ranks and
grades 242; organization and
strength Aug/39 13; oil
industry fighter defence 112;
Operation 'Barbarossa' 40;
Operation 'Bodenplatte'
Jan/45 114; Operation
'Sealion' objectives 20;
Operation 'Taifun' 42;
Operation 'Zitadelle' 80;
Order of Battle in the West
Aug/40 24–25; organization
and strength 1935 10;
'Ostbauprogramm' 1940 40;
overstretched resources
1942–3 56, 76; Polish
campaign 1939 14, **16**;
post-'Zitadelle' policies 81;
preparations against Allied
invasion 108; reactions to
Normandy landings 109;
serviceability problems 85,
109; Stalingrad and the
South 1942 44–46;
units in the West Apl/45
116; units operating in Italy
Sep/43 86
Luftwaffengeneral Italien 112
Luftwaffengeneral Nord Balkan
112
Luftwaffenkommando
Norwegen 112
Luftwaffenkommando Süd. Ost.
consolidation in E.
Mediterranean 84, 86–87,
112
Luftwaffenkommando West
Sep/44 112, 113, 114

Macchi C200 & C202 Folgore
fighters 48
Machine guns
Colt M-2 0·5in (U.S.) 96;
Rheinmetall MG-17 7·9mm
13, 40, 96; Rheinmetall
Borsig MG 131 13mm **70**,
96, **165**
Malta
Flkps II attacks 1942 48–52;
Flkps X attacks 1941 33
'Mandrel' RAF R/T jamming
105
Manufacturers
Ago Flugzeugwerke 124;
Arado Handelsgesellshaft,
Warnemunde **121** et seq;
ATG 10; Avia (Czecho-
slovakia) 124; Anton
Flettner GmbH **158**;
Bachem-Werke GmbH,
Waldsee 132; Bayerische
Flugzeugwerke 8; Blohm
und Voss Abt. Flugzeugbau
10, **133**, **136**; Breguet, Soc.
Louis, Bayonne, France 136;
Bücker Flugzeugbau GmbH
**139**, **140**; CASA, Spain 147;
Dornier-Werke GmbH **142**;
Ernst Heinkel AG 8, 175ff;
Focke Achgelis Flugzeugbau
GmbH 159; Focke-Wulf
Flugzeugbau GmbH 8, **158**;
Gerhard Fieseler Werke
GmbH 154; Gothaer
Waggonfabrik 10, **141**, **142**,
**172**; Hamburger Flugzeug-
bau GmbH, subsidiary of
Blohm und Voss **133**, 134;
Henschel Flugzeugwerke
AG 10, 196; Jacob
Schweyer 237; Junkers
Flugzeug und Motorenwerke
AG 8, 202; Letov (Czecho-
slovakia) 124; Messer-
schmitt AG 8, 136, **219**;
Mitteldeutsche Metallwerke
174; Potez-CAMS,
Sartrouville **147**
Marseille, *Oberfahnrich* Hans-
Joachim 39, 55
Messerschmitt, *Prof.* Willi 8,
219, 230
Messerschmitt Bf 108 M-37,
Bf 108 A and B *Taifun*
**219**
Messerschmitt Bf 109 ser.
B-K, S-99-199, Ha 1109-
1112 **11**, 13, **39**, 40,
**42**, **44**, **52**, **60**, 62, **97**,
108, 159, 185, **218–223**,
241
Messerschmitt Bf 110 ser. B,
C, F & G (Bf 110 C-4/B)
11, 13, **22**, 26, **35**, **38**,
**52**, **56**, 69, 74, 102, **103**,
159, 161, **224–226**
Messerschmitt Bf 161–162
V1 & V2, V1-3 198, **236**
Messerschmitt Bf 163 240
Messerschmitt *Jaguar* A *see*
Messerschmitt 162 V1
Messerschmitt Me 155 A and
B (Bv 155 V1 to V3) **136**
Messerschmitt Me 163 B-1
*Komet* **116**, **227–229**
Messerschmitt Me 163 D **236**
Messerschmitt Me 209–11
V1–6 & A ser. **227**
Messerschmitt Me 210 ser. A,
B & C 77, 226, **230**
Messerschmitt Me 261 V1-3
**236**
Messerschmitt Me 262 A-1a
*Schwalbe*, A-2 *Sturmvogel*,
B-1a 77, 94, **109**, **113**, 116,
**231–235**
Messerschmitt Me 263 A (Ju
248) 228
Messerschmitt Me 264 V1-3
**237**
Messerschmitt Me 309 V1 &
V2 **237**
Messerschmitt Me 310 high
altitude fighter/bomber
230
Messerschmitt Me 321 & Me
323
*Gigant* **81**, 200, **238**
Messerschmitt Me 328 V1 ser.
A & B **237**
Messerschmitt Me 410 A and B
series *Hornisse* **88**, 94,
230
Messerschmitt Me 609
(projected) 237
Messerschmitt P.1101 V1 **238**
Mikoyan/Gurevich MiG-3
fighter 41
Milch, Erhard 9, 10, 11, 44,
76, 219
Military transport aircraft
Arado Ar 232 **130**
Mine layers
Dornier Do 172-2 64;
Heinkel He 59 B2/3 64,
176; Heinkel He 111 P-4
64; Heinkel He 115 66,
133, **186**
Mine-laying operations
Fliegerdivision 9, 64, 75;
pre-D.Day activities 75
Minesweeping operations
Blohm und Voss Bv 138
MS **134**; B & V Ha 139
B/MS **133**; Junkers Ju
52/3m **74**, **202–203**
Missiles
Fieseler Fi 103 IV manned
air/surface **115**, **155**; FZG 76
Flying bomb 'V1' 94;
Henschel Hs 293 glider-
bomb **70**, 85, 86, 108, 148,
**149**, 151, **171**, 241;
Junkers Ju 88 pilotless
*Mistel* **112**, **208**, 241;
Reichenberg IV *see*
Fieseler F1 103; Ruhrstahl
FX 1400 (Fritz X) 74, 85,
86, 108, 149, 151, 241;
Ruhrstahl X-4 wire-guided
air/air 234
*Mistel* composite aircraft 114;
S1 Ju 88A-4 & Bf 109F; S2
Ju 88 G-1 & Fw 190 A-8;
S3A Ju 88 A-6 & Fw 190
A-6 **241**
Mölders *Maj lt.* Werner
JG 51 receives Bf 109 F-1
Feb/42 61; successes
'Barbarossa' 1941 42

Nachtschlachtgruppen (Night
ground-attack units)
E. Front Feb/43 78, **161**, **163**
Night 'blitz'
Luftwaffe target-finding
techniques 29
Night fighting systems
Helle Nachtjagd (Illuminated
Night Fighting) 58;
Himmelbett 'Kamnihuber
Line' 58, 90, 91, 102; Wilde
Sau (Wild Sow) 102;
Zahme Sau (Tame Sow)
102, 105
Night ground attack groups
(NSGr) 78, **121**, **161**, **163**,
172
Night-fighter groups
(Nachtjagdgruppen)
equipment 1943 106
Night-fighter squadrons
(Nachtjagdgeschwader)
aircraft types 1943 102;
casualties 105
Night fighter tactics 102, 105
Night intruders
units and equipment 1940
58
North American P-51 Mustang
88, **93**, 94, 98, 110, 112

Oberkommando der Luftwaffe
(OKL) 14
Oberkommando der Wehrmacht
(OKW) 10
Operation Adlerangriff 1940 21
Operation 'Bodenplatte' Jan/45
114
Operation 'Donnerkeil' 1942 62
Operation 'Marita' Apl/41
Luftflotte 4 33
Operation 'Merkur'
Fliegerkorps XI para. and
airborne assault 35
Operation 'Seelöwe' (Sealion)
Luftwaffe functions 20
Operation Steinbock 1943 75
Operation 'Taifun'
operating difficulties 42
Operation 'Weserübung' 1940
15, 64
Operation 'Zitadelle' 80

Parachute mines
BM 1000 sea mines 75;
LMA sea mines 64; 75;
LMB V sea mines 29
Paratroops
Fall Gelbe (Plan Yellow)
1940 16, 18; Operation
'Merkur' Crete 1941 35;
Operation 'Weserübung'
1940 16
Paris Air Agreement 1926 8
Petlyakov Pe-2 bomber 41
Photographic survey
Heinkel He 116 B-0 **186**
Pohl, *Gen* Ritter von
'Italluft' liaison mission
June/40 32; Luftwaffen-
general Italien Sep/44 112
Priller *Oberstleutnant* Josef
'Pips' **100**
PZL P7 fighter (Poland) 14
PZL P.11c fighter (Poland) 14

Racing aeroplanes
Messerschmitt Me 209-11,
V1-V3 **227**
Radar
Airborne Interception (AI)
RAF 28, 29; allied 'Window'
jamming 91, 103; ASV Mk
III RAF 73; ASV Mk IV
USAF 73; Freya early
warning 58; He 59N radio/
radar training aircraft 176;
Lichtenstein FuG 20C
Hohentwiel ASV 72, **171**,
218, 230; Lichtenstein FuG
202, 212 60, 102, 103, 105,
151, 172, 211, 226;
Lichtenstein FuG 218
Neptun **209**, 218; Lichten-
stein FuG 220 105, **106**,
153, 172, **218**, 230, 234;
Lichtenstein FuG 227/1
Flensburg 102, 106, 211;
Lichtenstein FuG 240
Berlin **209**; Lichtenstein
FuG 350 Naxos 102, 103,
211; Lichtenstein SN-2 *see*
Radar: Lichtenstein FuG
220; Metox 600 location
aid 73; H2S (RAF) bomber
equipment 102, 211;
Mammuth ground unit 106;
Monica (RAF) tail warning
102, 106; Rostock ASV 72;
Wasserman ground unit 106;
Würzburg A ground unit
58, 106
Radar aerial systems
Berlin **103**, 209, 234; Ju
88C-6c 105; Matratze 60,
**106**, **226**; Morgenstern 218
Radio
Fu B1 2F blind approach
system 106; RAF Knickebein
jamming 29; RAF RCM
jamming 106; RAF R/T
jamming 105
Radio aids to navigation 28,
59, 60; Gee (TR 1335)
RAF 1942 & Gee-H 1943
60, 102, 105; Lorenz
VHF T.R. (FuG 16zY) 97,
106; 'Oboe' RAF 93, 102
Reconnaissance
Anzio build-up unnoticed
87; formation of Fernauf-
klärungsstaffel 1939 65;
Luftwaffe rôle Fall Gelbe
1940 18
Reconnaissance aircraft
Arado Ar 234 B-1 and B-2
Blitz 116, **128–130**; DFS
228 V1, V2 and A series
**142**; Dornier Do 17 F-1
**144**; Dornier Do 17 M-1
**18**, **144**; Dornier Do 215
B-1 **145**; Dornier Do 217 P
**149**; Focke-Wulf Fw 189
*Uhu* **161**; Heinkel He 45 &
46 10; Heinkel He 70 F-2
**179**; Heinkel He 119 V6
(A-series recce prototype)
**187**; Henschel Hs 122 **196**;
Henschel Hs 130 A & E series
**201**; Junkers Hu 52/3m
**202–203**; Junkers Ju 86
P & R **204**; Junkers Ju
188 D2 **213**; Junkers Ju
188 R 213; Junkers Ju
388 L 218; Messerschmitt
Bf 110c **38**; Messerschmitt
Bf 110 D3 69, 224;
Messerschmitt Bf 161 V1 &
2 **236**; Messerschmitt Me
210 **230**; Messerschmitt
Me 262 A-la/U3 **231**;
Messerschmitt Me 410 A-3
**88**, 94, **230**
Reconnaissance (maritime)
aircraft
Arado Ar 196 A1 to A5 **126**;
Arado Ar 231 **130**; Blohm
und Voss Bv 138 C-1 **134**;
Blohm und Voss Bv 222
C-ser. **137**; Dornier Do 15
**146**; Dornier Do 18 64, **143**;
Dornier Do 24 **147**; Dornier
Do 26 **148**; Focke-Wulf Fw
62; Focke-Wulf Fw 200
*Condor* 65, **67**, **69**, **75**,
**170–171**; 'Facher' search
method 72; Heinkel He 51
B2 176; Heinkel He 59B
64; Heinkel He 70 E-1
**178–9**; Heinkel He 114
**185**; Heinkel He 115 64,
65, 67; Heinkel He 277
**193**; Junkers Ju 290 A-3 &
A-5 **216**; Junkers Ju 390
V3 **218**; Messerschmitt Me
264 V2 & 3 237
Reichsverteidigung (Reich
defence)
radio control systems 1943/4
97
Republic P-47 Thunderbolt 88,
94, 98
Research and Development
Branch misjudgement,
long-range fighter escorts
94
Research aircraft
Berlin Charlottenberg B9
(prone pilot) 198; Go 8
scale model Do 214 148;
Gotha Go 147 **173**; Gotha
Go 229 (Ho IX V2) **173**;
He 70 F-1/2 trials aircraft
178; Heinkel He 176
(Walter R1-203 rocket
motor) **187**, 228; Heinkel
He 178 pure jet **192**;
Henschel Hs 128 V1 and
V2 high altitude **201**;
Junkers Ju EF 61 V1 and
V2 high altitude **212**;
Junkers Ju 287 V1 testbed
**214**; Messerschmitt P.1101
**238**; Schempp-Hirth Go 9
153
Richthofen *Gen maj. Freiherr*
Wolfram von
Flkps VIII Fall Gelbe 1940
18; Operation 'Marita' Apl/
41 33; Legion Kondor,
Spain 1937 12; Lfl IV E.
Front 1943 78
Rocket assisted take-off
(RATO) 174, 239; Heinkel
He 116R **186**; Ju 287
Walter 501 2645 lb.
thrust 214; Messerschmitt
Me 264 V2 & 3 237
Rocket engine development
Helmuth, Walter 227
Rocket mortars
Wfr. Gr 21 (Bf 109 G-5/R2)
86, 98, **100**
Rocket projectors
SG 500 Jagdfaust (RZ 73
rockets) 234
Rockets
Hs 217 Föhn **132**; RAM
Panzerblitz **165**
Rotor-kites
Fa 330 130
Rotte (pair of aircraft) 12, 242
Royal Air Force
aircrew losses, Battle of
Britain 24; Battle of Berlin
1943/4 105; Bomber
Command losses 1944 106;
Bomber Command strategy
1941 59; bombing directive
1943 90; Coastal Command
(Bay of Biscay) 1943 73;
Desert Air Force units 1941
38, 48; 1942 55; Fighter
Command resources, Battle
of Britain 20; night fighting
techniques 1940 28, 29;
night intruder ops. 1943
105; Pathfinder Force
techniques 102; radio
counter measures (RCM)
105; 2nd TAF activities 1944
93; 2nd TAF Ardennes
initiative 114
Royal Navy
losses to Luftwaffe, Crete
1941 38; Norway 1940 64
Ruhrstahl X-4 wire-guided
air/air missile 234
'Rüstsatz 6' Bf 109 cannon
gondola 96, **221**

Schmidt, *Gen.* Josef 'Beppo'
Air Intelligence IC. RLM 40
Schräge Musik, night fighter
armament 105, 149, **162**,
172, 190, 208, 218, 226
Schwarm (section of four
aircraft) 12, 242
Seaplanes
Arado Ar 95 A-1 **124**;
Arado Ar 196 **69**, **126**, 160;
Arado Ar 199 V1 and V2
**127**; Arado Ar 231 **130**;
Blohm und Voss Ha 139
**133**; Dornier Do 22 **146**;
Focke-Wulf Fw 62 **160**;
Heinkel He 50A W 175;
Heinkel He 51 B2 176;
Heinkel He 59 D **177**;
Heinkel He 60C, D-1 **178**,
185; Heinkel He 72 BW
179; Heinkel He 114 A-2,
C-1 **185**; Heinkel He 115
B-0, B-1 64, 66, **72**, 133,
**186**; Heinkel He 119 V3
187
Seeckt, *Gen.* Hans von 8
Seefliegerführer Schwarzes
Meer (SSM) 134
Seeluftstreitkräfte (Fleet Air
Arm) 64
Short Sterling Mk 1 60, **90**, 102
Short Sunderland flying boat 73
Siebel Fh 104 *Hallore* 240
Siebel Si 201 V1 & 2 **240**
Siebel Si 204 A & D ser. **240**
Soviet Air Force (V-VS)
losses, 'Barbarossa' 1941 41
Soviet Union
Air Forces (V-VS) equip-
ment & men 1941 40;
Lipetz military flying training

centre 10
Spanish Civil War
  Luftwaffe involvement 11
Speed records
  Heinkel He 100 181
Sperrle, *General major* Hugo 8;
  Legion Kondor, Spain 1936
  12; Lfl III Battle of Britain
  20; Fall Gelbe 1940 16;
  strength June/44 108
Staffeln (squadrons)
  position in Gruppe 242
STOL observation aircraft
  Fieseler Fi 156 *Storch*
  **156–7**; Flettner F1 282
  *Kolibri* **158**; Fw 186 auto
  giro **160**; Gotha Go 147
  **173**; Henschel Hs 126
Störkampfstaffeln (Harassing
  bomber units)
  E. Front Feb/43 78
Strategic bombing
  'Adlerangriff' 1940 21;
  Allies' belated oil target
  effort 90; switch to cities
  Sept '40 24; *see also*
  Bombing
Student *Gen maj.* Kurt
  Flkps XI Operation
  'Merkur' May/41 35
Stuka (Sturzkampflugzeug)
  *see* Junkers Ju 87
Stumpff *Gen maj.* Hans-
  Jurgen 8, 16; Luftflotte 5
  Norwegian operations 1940
  16; Operation 'Barbarossa'
  1941 40; Luftflotte Reich

Dec/43 98; Sept/44 112
Sturmstaffeln ramming tactics
  100
Supermarine Spitfire Mk 1 13
Supermarine Spitfire V-B, C &
  Mk IX 50, 62, 96, 112
Swept wing research 238

Target-defence interceptors
  Bachem Ba 349 *Natter* **132**;
  Blohm und Voss Bv 40
  glider **138**
Technical procurement section
  (Luftwaffe C-Amt) **123**
Technisches Amt (Technical
  Office)
  Udet abandons strategic
  bomber designs 11
Tego-Film bonding 172
Test centres (Erprobungsstelle)
  Rechlin 11
Testing units (Lehr und
  Erprobungskommando) 74
Test pilots
  Baur, Karl 234; Dieterle,
  Hans 181; Dittmar, Heini
  227; Holzbauer, Siegfried
  241; Reitsch, Hann 140,
  155; Schafer, Fritz 193;
  Siebert, *Oberleutnant*
  Lothar 132; Wendel, Fritz
  227
Test-bed aircraft
  Blohm und Voss Ha 140
  V3 133; Junkers Ju 287
  V1 **214**
Torpedo/bombers
  convoy attack tactics 70;

Heinkel He 111 H-6 **181**,
  **184**; Heinkel He 115  64,
  65, 67, 69, 70, 133, **186**;
  Junkers Ju 88 A-4 (Torp)
  70, 75, 86, **208**, **211**;
  Junkers Ju 188 E-2 75,
  **213**; Messerschmitt Me 410
  B5 230
Torpedo/reconnaissance
  aircraft Arado Ar 95 **124**;
  Arado Ar 195 V1 **125**;
  Blohm und Voss Ha 140
  V1 to V3 **133**; Dornier Do 22
  **146**; Fieseler Fi 167 **155**;
  Heinkel He 59 B-2 **177**;
  Junkers Ju 88 **208**
Torpedo/reconnaissance
  Gruppe (SAGr)
  3/SAGr 125 Baltic & S.
  Finland operations 124
Torpedoes
  Grossenbrode development
  centre 69; LT F 5 & 5W
  airlaunched 69, 72, 75
Training aircraft
  Arado Ar 65 F **121**; Arado
  Ar 66C 10, **121**, 179; Arado
  Ar 68 E-1 **122**; Arado Ar 76
  **123**; Arado Ar 96 **124**;
  Arado Ar 199 V seaplane
  **127**; Bücker Bü 131
  *Jungmann* **139**; Bücker Bü
  133 *Jungmeister* **13**, **140**;
  Bücker Bü 181 *Bestmann* **140**;
  Fieseler Fi 103 **155**; Focke-
  Wulf Fw 44 10, 179;
  Focke-Wulf Fw 56 *Stösser*
  **158**, 180, 198; Focke-Wulf

Fw 189 B **161**; Gotha Go
  145 **172**, 179; Heinkel He
  45 **175**; Heinkel He 51 121;
  Heinkel He 72 A and B
  *Kadett &* 172 **179**; Heinkel
  He 74 **180**; Henschel Hs 121
  **196**, 198; Henschel Hs 125
  **198**; Siebel Si 204 ser. A &
  D **240**
Transport aircraft
  Blohm und Voss Bv 222
  *Wiking* **137**; Blohm und
  Voss Bv 238 138; DFS 331
  glider **142**; Dornier Do 26
  **148**; Dornier Do 214 **148**;
  equipment 1939 13; Focke-
  Wulf Fw 200 C-4 46; Gotha
  Go 242 glider **174**; Gotha
  Go 244 **174**; Gotha Go 345
  glider **173**; Heinkel He 59
  C-2 176; Heinkel He 116
  B-0 **186**; Junkers F13 212;
  Junkers Ju 52 3m ge 10,
  13, **55**, **82**, **88**, **202–203**,
  214; 3mg5e **203**; Junkers
  Ju 252 **214**, 217; Junkers
  Ju 290 A.0 and 1 216; A-7,
  A-8, B-1 216; Junkers Ju
  352 **217**; Junkers W 34 hi
  **212**; Messerschmitt Me 323
  *Gigant* 81, 238, **239**;
  *see also* Helicopters

Udet, Ernst 11, 44, **76**, **123**,
  133, 140, 156, 181, 187
Undercarriage *see* Landing gear
United States Army Air Force
  8th USAAF daylight raids

1943/4 62, 90, 94, 96, 98,
  108, 112; 9th USAAF
  activities 1944 93; 9th
  USAAF Ardennes initiative
  114; 15th USAAF daylight
  raids 1943/4 93, 94, 98,
  108, 111
Unternehmen Bodenplatte
  (Operation Baseplate)
  Jan/45 114

Versailles, Treaty: Air Clauses
  8
Vickers Wellington Mk 1C 15,
  16, **95**, 102
*Volksjäger* (People's Fighter)
  *see* Heinkel He 162
  *Salamander*

Waldau *Gen.* Hoffman von
  Fliegerführer Afrika 1941 48
Wever, *Gen.* Walther, Chief of
  Air Staff 8, 10, 146, 212
Window' radar jamming 91,
  103
Wulf, Georg 8

X-Gerät, radio navigation aid
  28

Yakovlev Yak-1 fighter 41
Yakovlev Yak-9 fighter 46, 80,
  108
Y-Gerät, radio navigation aid
  28, 96, 106

'Zahme Sau' night fighting
  operations 102, 105

# Picture Credits

Unless otherwise credited, all photographs in this book were
supplied by Pilot Press Limited. All colour profiles, cutaway
drawings and three-view diagrams were also supplied by Pilot
Press Limited.

**Bapty:** 15, 21
**Bapty-Fliegende Front:** 31, 72
**Blitz:** 21 (middle)
**Dornier-Pressestelle:** 143 (top two), 146 (top), 148, 153 (top)
**Robert Hunt Library, London:** 17
**Image Press:** 13, 74
**Imperial War Museum:** 21 (bottom), 26 (top), 93, 94, 104
**John G. Moore Collection:** 19, 23 (top), 32, 34, 37, 39 (top), 43, 45,
  47 (top), 51, 52, 53, 54, 56, 57, 66, 71, 75, 77, 79, 81, 83, 87, 89, 99
**Messerschmitt Archiv:** 226, 227, 229, 230 (right), 231, 233, 234 (bottom),
  236 (top), 238, 239 (left)
**United States Air Force/John McClancy Collection:** 91, 92

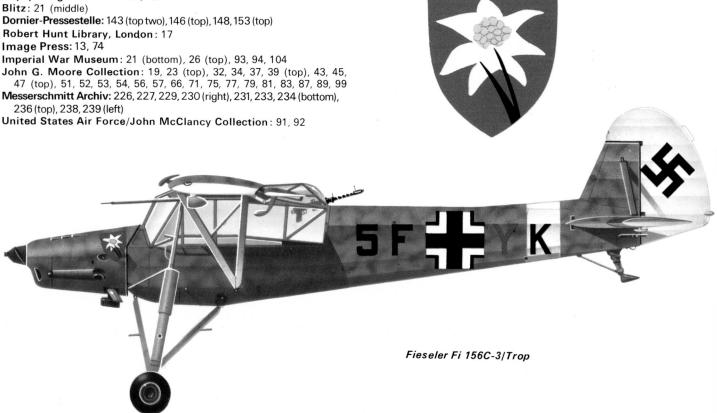

*Fieseler Fi 156C-3/Trop*